THE
ELMO
JENKINS
TRILOGY

McMILLIAN
MOODY

Published by

OBT·Bookz

Cover design by OBT Graphix

**This trilogy includes all three Elmo Jenkins
novels in their unabridged form.**

Ordained Irreverence (released August 2011)
Some Things Never Change (released August 2012)
The Old Man and the Tea (released August 2013)

DEDICATION

To the hundreds-of-thousands of readers who have
downloaded one or more of the Elmo Jenkins novels.
His adventure continues on because of you.

ACKNOWLEDGMENTS

To my gifted wife Diane. Thank you for the
inspiration and the encouragement.

Thanks to Bev Harrison
our wonderful editor.

A special thanks to Glenn Hale
for his help with each novel.

And to the Potter.
Continue to mold and squeeze
and shape and smooth and fashion
this vessel for Your use.

TABLE of CONTENTS

i

Preface

On December 12, 2003 I decided to write a book. Both of my kids were away at college, and my wife Diane and I were settling quietly into the empty nest. Writing a book would be my new hobby. I had no intention of trying to get it published. Why would any sane person put themselves through that humiliating exercise? From the sidelines I'd watched Diane, an uber-gifted author, face crushing rejection time and again as she tried to get published. Noooo, not me, I'm no masochist. This writing project would be purely R&R.

I decided it would be great fun to write a novel loosely based on my own experiences as minister. One summer while in seminary, I'd participated in an internship program at a large downtown church in the Midwest. This would be the framework for my story. Thus, young Elmo Jenkins came to be.

That December evening, a decade ago, I sat at my computer and typed the opening sentence to my new novel:

> "Relentless self-promotion and butt-dumb luck had conspired to provide me the opportunity to live the dream."

Eight years later when I'd finally finished the book, that sentence ended up in the second chapter. After extensive editing it now reads as follows:

> "Relentless self-promotion and uncanny dumb luck along with a dash of divine intervention had conspired to provide me this golden opportunity. It was my time. I was ready to live the dream!"

You might ask why it took me eight years to write a book that only has 253 pages? Well, I'd write three or four chapters and grow weary of the task, then set it aside. A few years later I'd pick it back up and write some more. And so on. Besides it was never going to be published anyway.

But during that eight-year period, the world of publishing went through a seismic shift. Thanks to the Internet and companies like Amazon, authors could sidestep the gatekeepers of old and take their books directly to the readers. Diane, who was experiencing great success as an indie author, encouraged me to finish the novel and publish it.

I did, and have since published two sequels which brings us to this trilogy. All three Elmo books in one volume. Who knew?

I'm often asked if the stories in these novels really happened, and if the characters are based on real people I knew. In some cases, yes. But these books are indeed fiction. Let's just say the anecdotes and the players in them were inspired by the people I worked with and the folks we ministered to.

I sincerely appreciate your interest in the Elmo Jenkins books and hope you find a few laughs along the way.

McMillian Moody

P.S. Never use the term 'butt-dumb' in any way, shape, or form.

BOOK ONE

ORDAINED
IRREVERENCE

McMILLIAN
MOODY

ELMO JENKINS BOOK ONE

PROLOGUE

There are episodes in life that help define who we become. A special relationship, a death in the family, a financial windfall, a battlefield experience, a mission trip, etc. This is a story about one such episode.

Six months that changed my life forever.

— Elmo Jenkins

1

The Epiphany

As one of the 457 ministerial wannabes suffering through the righteous rigors at Harvest Morgan Seminary, I had not distinguished myself as an academician or a theologian. Not even close. There, amongst the budding Billy Grahams, Martin Luthers, and Mother Teresas, I trudged daily, basically void of inspiration. It was all Greek to me. Literally. The tedious, arcane, and often inane required regimen of my religious studies had systematically whittled away the honest desire that had once inspired me to pursue a life of ministry. My fellow seminarians seemed to thrive, either storming the mission fields of the world, bringing down the heavens with their glorious singing voices, or filling the pulpits of churches around the globe with profound, life-changing rhetoric.

Me? I was tone deaf, possessed marginal oratorical skills, and refrained from even *mentioning* the word "missionary" for fear God would make me one. So what was I to do with my burning desire to serve God? Finishing the last semester of my class work, I needed only to complete an internship of some sort to finalize my seminary degree. But then what?

My epiphany happened on a most unusual day. I'd tenaciously pursued one of my female classmates in hopes of getting a date. The evasive Dolly had demurred on numerous occasions, but in a weak moment (no doubt the result of sleep deprivation; it was, after all, finals week), Dolly said yes—but only on *her* terms. Terms which I found constricted at best. Yet by accepting her conditions, I reasoned, I could surely parlay this limited event into a more meaningful opportunity in the future.

Her plan? We would attend her aunt and uncle's annual Spring Open House. The family expected her to bring a date, and as she reminded me, I was available and obviously willing. However, she neglected to share with me two important facts. One, she failed to mention that Aunt Geneva and Uncle Smitty were, in fact, the Fitzsimonses—by far the wealthiest family in this part of the state. Old money. *Real* old money. Second, Dolly also forgot to warn me that this might well be the stuffiest, most excruciating two hours of my young life.

We arrived fashionably late. *Quite a handsome couple*, I thought to myself. Within seconds, I realized we were the youngest attendees by at least thirty years. After introducing me to our hosts, Dolly excused herself—never to return. She had abandoned me! I felt like tearing my jacket and yelling out UNCLEAN! I figured the heartless shrew had arranged to have an escape vehicle warmed up and waiting at the rear door.

Fortunately, all was not lost. Numerous tables of free food were waiting to be plundered. "Which way to the buffet?" I asked a thin waiter with a pencil mustache.

So there I was, pondering my shrunken self-esteem, entombed in a mansion full of crusty old rich people. After pilfering my way through the shrimp tray and mentally comparing the small crustaceans to my measly existence, I noticed another non-geezer in the room. With natural dark hair, he appeared to be in his mid-forties. He looked as out of place as I felt, so I approached him and introduced myself.

"Hello," I said, extending my hand. "It's nice to find someone else at this *shindig* who's not on oxygen or sporting glaucoma glasses. My name is Ellington." I paused then added, "Ellington Jenkins," to keep it formal. Who knew? He might be somebody important.

He shook my hand and studied me for a moment before a broad smile warmed his face. "Yes, this annual get-together tends to skew toward the geriatric. Nice to meet you, Ellington. I'm Tom Applebee."

Turns out Tom was the Associate Pastor at First Church, the largest and most respected church in our entire city. We hit it off immediately. Together, we suffered through Geneva's stuffy reading of an original poem entitled *Ode to a Gilded Debutante*. The torture continued through a painful trilogy of songs by some has-been Irish tenor. When we could endure no more, we escaped outside to the quiet of the poolside cabana where I explained my background and seminary experience at Tom's request.

Later, as Tom and I made a stop at the dessert table, he told me about a six-month internship program at First Church. And then it happened. He casually asked, "Think you'd be interested?"

For the briefest of moments, time stood still. There, flanked by caramel flan and raspberry sorbet, my future illuminated right before my eyes. Like Michelangelo's painting on the ceiling of the Sistine Chapel, God reached down His finger and touched my life. Like Peter on the Mount of Transfiguration, I knew something mighty powerful had just happened, but I was still in a fog.

"Ellington?"

I blinked, jarred back to reality, my divine moment-of-destiny vision receding back into my subconscious. Taking an anxious gulp of sparkling water, I found my voice. "Yes, Mr. Applebee. I would love to apply for your internship."

I survived the party, applied for the First Church internship, and God made good on my epiphany. I got the job! The doorway to all my tomorrows opened wide. At long last, I had found purpose and focus, and my stature at the good ol' seminary soared like an eagle. I was more than ready for this new challenge.

As for Dolly, I'm sure she's still wonderin' who let the air out of her car tires.

My bad.

2

The New Rules

Cue the balloons. My fifteen minutes of fame had arrived. My genesis. My new beginning, if you will. Relentless self-promotion and uncanny dumb luck, along with a dash of divine intervention, had conspired to provide me this golden opportunity. It was my time. I was ready to live the dream!

I lingered in my car, securely parked in the staff lot, staring across the street at my Mecca.

First Church.

Forbidding yet graceful, her Frank Lloyd Wright-inspired facade formed a face that appeared to be smiling down on me.

Not Second Church. Not Main Street Church. Not even the ubiquitous Whispering Creek Community Church. No, this was First Church. The Pope of all churches. I sat there momentarily awestruck, reminding myself to breathe. I felt a bit overwhelmed. In silence, I savored each detail, my mind adrift, remembering just how I had arrived at this life-changing moment.

The mid-morning sun ricocheted off the First Church steeple and darted across my face, awakening me from my musings. I tossed my parking pass on the dash of my modest but efficient Nissan Sentra, and checked to make sure my tie was straight. Grabbing my valise, I headed for the entrance to the church office. While waiting for a chance to cross First Boulevard, I began taking deep breaths in a vain attempt to calm my nerves.

A hearse was parked in front of the church ahead of several long black limousines. No doubt cars queued up for a drive to the cemetery. *Man, I hate funerals.*

Jogging across the street, I spotted Dr. Horace Jorgensen sitting in the front passenger seat of the hearse. The renowned, beloved Senior Pastor of First Church—a living icon, a man known all around the world for his profound and articulate preaching, friend to the presidents and confidant of the high and mighty—sat a mere ten yards away from me.

Suddenly, he pitched forward, his eyes wide, his mouth gaping as if struggling for air. Concerned, I glanced at the driver. He didn't appear alarmed. In fact, he was smirking. For a brief, irrational moment, I panicked. *My God, he's choking!* I quickened my pace toward the vehicle. *I must rescue this great man of the faith! Who knows but that God put me in this moment for such a time as this?*

Fortunately, I paused long enough to come to my senses. I took a second more careful look. Dr. Jorgensen *wasn't* dying. He was laughing. No, scratch that. He was *guffawing,* his signature red hair clearly visible through the tinted windshield. With tears in his eyes, he was enjoying the laugh of a lifetime.

How odd, I thought. He'd obviously just performed some dead soul's funeral service. The corpse in its casket rested less than three feet behind him. Yet there he was, busting a gut laughing? I would later learn that the hearse driver had shared a hilarious story with Dr. Jorgensen, and though it was coarse and very inappropriate, the pastor found it "quite humorous."

At seminary, we were taught that in order to survive on a church staff, you have to develop the ability to separate yourself from the pain and suffering of those you minister to. You must be sympathetic and helpful to your church members during times of sickness or loss, but you must also be able to emotionally disengage when the task was completed.

As I neared the hearse, the passenger window slowly lowered. "Good morning, Mr. Jenkins," he said with an oversized smile as he shook my hand. "I understand this is your first official day with us."

"Dr. Jorgensen." I responded as though startled, pretending I hadn't been staring at him. And since I had yet to be briefed on the proper staff protocol, I simply added, "Good morning to you, sir." I stood there smiling for a long awkward moment, not knowing what to do next. Here was the Grand Poobah of my new vocational life, and I was sinking like the Titanic.

The seasoned veteran took pity and rescued me. "So Jenkins, are you ready for your first day here at Crisis Central?" He smiled again.

Since he'd brought it up twice, I knew I'd better respond to his query. "Well, to be honest, sir, I'm a bit nervous."

"Nervous?" he shot back, a befuddled expression creasing his face.

Damn! First day, first conversation, and I've already screwed up.

"Nervous?" he repeated. "There's no time to be nervous around here. Gird your loins, son, and go get after it." And with a chuckle, he waved goodbye as the hearse pulled away.

The funeral procession sped off leaving me there to ponder my first two lessons.

Rule #1: Avoid total candor when conversing with other
staff members.
Rule #2: Never think or say the word "damn" again.

I gathered myself, took a deep breath and headed for the main entrance. As I approached the steps, I took one more quick glance at the church's magnificent art deco design and promptly missed the first step, slamming my right shin into the concrete edge, and immediately broke new Rule #2.

3

The Closet

Cooling my heels in the guest area of the church office, I daydreamed about my new life on the staff of First Church. Popular folklore at the seminary embraced the notion that staff members at First Church were treated like royalty. Plush offices, personal assistants, and memberships at private country clubs and restaurants around town. I'd always questioned the veracity of those rumors, but the truth would now be found in the tasting.

Steeped in a rich heritage, legendary First Church had played a prominent role in the life of our city for over 150 years. The current building, over 100 years old, had been the tallest structure in town for many of those years with a steeple reaching twelve stories into the sky. Since its beginning, only five senior pastors had filled its pulpit, each lasting at least a quarter of a century. These men not only pastored First Church, they also sat on the boards of numerous local banks and foundations. They also contributed regularly to the daily newspapers, and socialized with the wealthy and powerful members of the community. These interactions brought many of the same rich and famous people through the doors of First Church—politicians, professional athletes, doctors and lawyers. Some even became members of the church.

"Mr. Jenkins."

Jarred from my daydream, I turned my attention back to the receptionist.

"Mr. Jenkins, Pastor Applebee will see you now." According to the nameplate on her desk, her name was Juliann. She was *gorgeous*. Someone must have theorized that a beauty queen at the front desk would create a good first impression. Worked for me.

I got up, collected myself and approached the door to the inner office area. As I reached for the door handle a loud buzzer sounded off. I jumped back, embarrassing myself.

Juliann giggled and winked at me. "I was just unlocking the door for you, silly."

I forced a smile. "Thanks," I mumbled. Two quick steps and I was in. I paused to bask in the moment as the door gently closed behind me. *I've arrived. I'm standing in the inner sanctum. Not the Holy of Holies, but close.*

Tom Applebee rounded a corner and shook my hand. "Welcome to the staff of First Church, Ellington," he said with a big grin.

"Please, just call me Elmo."

"Elmo?"

"My full name is Ellington Montgomery Jenkins," I explained. "But I've been called Elmo as long as I can remember. And please— no Sesame Street jokes."

He smiled. "Then Elmo Jenkins it is. Let me introduce you to the First Church team. You met our receptionist Juliann. And this first office here belongs to our administrator, Bob 'Big Bird' Stevens."

And so it began.

Tom had to attend a meeting, so after the tour he left me to chill in his office. *Very impressive.* As second-in-command at First Church, he warranted a corner office on the top floor of the Church Administration building. Huge panoramic windows formed two sides of the room providing a spectacular view of downtown from five floors up, high above the intersection of First Boulevard and Main Street.

On my tour, I learned that the fifth floor consisted of only four rooms. The two private office suites belonging to Tom and Dr. Jorgensen, each fronted with separate built-in areas for their executive assistants and visiting guests. The Executive Boardroom, or EBR, and Deacons Lounge occupied the rest of the floor. Perhaps one of the most important rooms in the entire city, decisions made within the EBR over the years had helped shape not only the future of the church, but the direction of the town as well.

Few church members ever stepped foot inside the EBR. A magnificent table made from one continuous piece of solid oak dominated the long, narrow room. Twenty leather chairs surrounded the table, with an additional ring of chairs lining the perimeter along the walls. These outer chairs could accommodate another thirty to forty folks. At capacity, the room could handle at least sixty people.

Tom had told me the deacons met here, filling most every chair. *The old "strength in numbers" game,* I thought. *I bet that's intimidating for the poor staff member who gets called in.* At one end of the room, a door led directly into Dr. Jorgensen's office. On the other end, another door opened into the adjoining Deacons Lounge.

There were no other doors. I asked Tom how they got around the fire code with no doors into the hall. He had laughed. "Every Fire Chief for the last hundred years has been a deacon of First Church. Fire codes have never been a problem."

The Deacons Lounge resembled a stuffy English gentlemen's club. *As if I would know?* My station in life had never afforded me access to anything like it. High-back leather armchairs, a working fireplace, dark wood paneling . . . even a bar, though I hadn't seen any liquor. In my mind's eye, I envisioned years of back slapping, hand shaking, murmured whispering, and of course, plenty of pontificating.

For some reason the Sanhedrin came to mind.

As I waited for Tom's return, I perused the art and artifacts of his office. A plaque on the wall revealed he'd graduated Summa Cum Laude from Slippery Rock University. *Quite humorous considering his line of work,* I chuckled. From his collection of books I could tell he must be quite bright, though I doubted he'd actually read many of them. I even flirted with the idea of asking him a question from Thomas Aquinas's *Commentary on Aristotle's Nicomachean Ethics.* But then I remembered my father's sage wisdom. Dad always said, "Never embarrass the man who signs your paycheck." Tom wouldn't be signing my paychecks, but I figured Dad's wise axiom still applied.

When Tom finally returned, he finished briefing me on the particulars of my job. Basically, I would shadow him for the first several weeks, and he would be my supervisor for the entire six months. I would attend all staff meetings, pertinent committee meetings, and just *maybe* a deacons meeting or two. Since I was already a licensed minister, I would be assigned a sampling of all staff responsibilities, including hospital visitation, funerals, baptisms, weddings, and such.

Finally, he said the words I'd longed to hear all day: "Let me take you down to your office."

I forcefully repressed any show of emotion, but inside I was giddy. I'd never had my own office before. Even the secretaries at First Church had great offices with fancy wood trim and custom-built desks. I knew mine wouldn't be on the fifth floor. Perhaps the fourth floor? Would my window look out on downtown or perhaps back toward the picturesque west horizon? I briefly closed my eyes and imagined a stunning sunset outside my window. We got on the executive elevator, and my ebullient spirit quickly dampened as Tom pushed the second floor button. I fought to regroup. *Well, at least it's not on the first floor.* We exited the elevator and began a series of turns, first walking past the print shop, then the music library and the nurse's station. *Where are the staff offices?* I wondered. Finally, we passed an office. I read the nameplate as we walked by:

Rev. Fred Snooker
Interim Senior Adult Pastor
M-W-F (mornings only)

Snooker. Unfortunate name for a pastor, I thought. Two more turns and we came to a dead end. To our left, was a solid metal door badly in need of a fresh coat of paint. The sign on the door read: UTILITIES/MISCELLANEOUS CLOSET.

Tom turned to me and without a trace of apology in his voice, said, "This will be your office. We haven't assigned office space to any previous interns, but since you'll be performing ministerial duties, I pulled some strings and got you your own place."

He then smiled at me. That special smile. You know, the one that quietly *says I like you, but the fact is you're a punk, and you have to start at the bottom just like the rest of us did.*

He pushed open the door and there it was—my very own *Deluxe Utility Closet.* Deluxe, meaning they supplied it with a six-foot banquet table and one metal folding chair.

And my window? It looked out on a panoramic view, all right.

A panoramic view of the church dumpster.

4

The Horses Rearing

My first week on staff at First Church had gone pretty well. I was systematically getting to know each member of the large staff. Thanks to my nickname, I had to suffer through the obligatory onslaught of Muppet jokes. Nothing new, of course, but when I met Tom Applebee's secretary, I knew the ribbing would proliferate dramatically. Her name? Adrianne Figghie. Yes, that's *Figghie* which rhymes with *Piggy*. As luck would have it, *Miss Figghie* was both single and quite "rotund," if you will. To exacerbate the problem even more, in the right lighting, she bore a slight resemblance to the famed Muppet heroine. I felt awful as she became collateral damage to my humiliation, but what could I do? To her credit, she seemed nonplussed by the relentless wisecracks.

Wednesday morning arrived, and we all gathered for the weekly staff meeting in the first floor boardroom—*not* to be confused with the sacred fifth floor Executive boardroom. A generous supply of donuts, Danish, and coffee covered a table in the far corner. People trickled in, slowly filling the room. I stood next to the coffee pot enjoying a glazed donut and chatting with Adrianne about my list of assignments for the day. I looked up as Thurman Wilson, the youth pastor, casually slipped in from the hall. I knew Thurm from seminary, though he'd graduated a couple years before me.

Thurm spotted me across the room and in his best Cookie Monster voice hollered, "Hey Elmo, could you get Miss Figghie to toss me a cooookkkieeeeeee?"

The room exploded in laughter. I felt my face heat with embarrassment. I turned to apologize to Adrianne, only to discover she had mysteriously slipped away. I started to fire back a witty quip about God's vengeance, when I noticed everyone shuffling to find a seat as Dr. Jorgensen strode through the door. I marveled at the subtle shift in demeanor, from comfortable camaraderie to nervous respect inspired by his commanding presence.

Dr. Jorgensen took his seat at the head of the boardroom table. I quickly discerned the existence of an unspoken delineation by which the staff members seated themselves. Like some type of subliminal pecking order. Apparently, the twelve seats around the table had fixed assignments, whereas the others seem to be filled at random.

My best guess? Seniority rules. The longer you've been on staff, the closer you sit to Dr. Jorgensen. I could only imagine how awkward it must be when someone retired or got fired. Did everyone just move over one seat, like some kind of pharisaical musical chairs or fruit basket turnover? As I dawdled on that thought, I yawned but quickly closed my mouth. *It's your first staff meeting. Stop looking like a schmuck!*

As second-in-command, Tom Applebee took the seat directly to Dr. Jorgensen's right. Fran Bruker, the pastor's long-time secretary, occupied the seat to Dr. Jorgensen's left. I estimated Mrs. Bruker, a widow, to be somewhere in her late seventies. I'd been told her husband died decades earlier, soon after their wedding day and under questionable circumstances. Though she was never implicated in his passing, his suspicious death raised many questions which were never resolved. They had no children, and she never remarried. Quietly living out her life, Mrs. Bruker had served as secretary to the last two senior pastors of First Church.

I have a bad habit of thinking everyone looks like somebody else. I drive my family and friends crazy making these comparisons. Fran Bruker reminded me of Cloris Leachman's character *Frau Blucher* in the movie *Young Frankenstein*—small but stern, with harsh facial features and bad teeth. In the movie, every time someone said the name *Frau Blucher,* you'd hear the nervous whinny of horses rearing off in the distance. Moderately funny in the movie, now it was hysterical.

A couple of days earlier, I'd mentioned this *Frau Blucher* observation to Thurm. We had a good laugh over it, cracking an endless run of jokes along those lines. In hind site? *Bad* mistake. Now, when Fran Bruker's name was announced to read the minutes, I made eye contact with Thurm and the horses reared. I had to call upon every ounce of sheer willpower just to keep from bursting into laughter. Thurm's eyes watered, and I almost wet my pants. Like village idiots, we had opened a Pandora's Box.

As Fran droned on reading the minutes, I began studying the different people sitting at the table. Tom had given me a thorough run-down on each staff person. Harry Simpkins, the minister of music, sat at Tom's right. Tom told me Harry was a piece of work, describing him as a cross between a vaudeville entertainer and professional hockey player. It's widely held that music ministers at large churches tend to be aloof, arrogant, and on occasion, a tad bit prissy. Not Harry. He had a big heart and even bigger personality, but often lacked common sense. Passionate to a fault and not known for being graceful or diplomatic, Harry was indeed quite the character.

Over the years, Harry's crazy escapades had become legendary. Tom told me about the time Harry and the youth pastor *de jour* chaperoned a canoeing trip. While loading the teens back on the bus after a meal break, Harry and the youth pastor got into a heated logistics argument that quickly escalated out of control. Fascinated, the kids watched from the bus as their two leaders engaged in a sanctified fist fight. Two godly men rolling in the dirt with their ordained irreverence on full display.

The poor youth pastor returned to find his office empty and a moving van in front of his home. The beloved Harry survived the incident with a reprimand from the deacons and a few hours of First Church's consecrated brand of community service.

Next to Harry sat Fred Snooker, associate pastor emeritus and now part-time minister for senior adults. Before Dr. Jorgensen arrived, Fred had served as associate to the previous senior pastor, the infamous Dr. Buster Sapp. The onset of dementia had forced Dr. Sapp to retire in his later years. No one knew a problem existed until they discovered Dr. Sapp had been dressing up as an elderly woman and attending the Ladies Missionary Society meetings. The ladies even voted him president-elect of their prestigious women's group before the charade was uncovered. An awkward moment in the otherwise illustrious narrative of First Church.

After the Buster debacle, Fred Snooker stepped boldly into the gap serving as interim pastor while the church searched for a successor. Assuming he would be the next senior pastor, Fred faced bitter disappointment when the church hired Jorgensen instead. A good and decent man, Fred humbly accepted the outcome and stayed on as associate pastor until retiring several years ago. Fred recently rejoined the staff in an interim position replacing Senior Adult pastor Hugo Withers. The elderly Withers had died of natural causes. A colleague found him at his desk, face down in his taco salad.

Looking back across the table, I studied Bob Stevens, the church business manager seated to the left of Fran Bruker. Bob looked like a typical accountant, small in stature, thinning hair, and beady eyes behind black-framed glasses. He seemed nervous to me, like Al Capone's personal accountant must have looked. The annual budget of First Church totaled $11 million, mostly funded through tithes and offerings and special gifts from the town's well-heeled. The church kept another $1 million tucked safely away to be used for more parking spaces should adjacent land ever become available. Forget missions. These folks wanted to park close to the building. Bob Stevens managed all of it. According to Tom, Bob was a man of rigid personal habits. He even took his two-week vacation at the exact same time every summer and always to the exact same location in the Cayman Islands. *An interesting getaway spot for the church bookkeeper.*

Louis Estrada sat next to Bob. To be honest, I found the tall, dark Singles pastor to be rather odd looking. Like maybe he'd spent a little too long in the birth canal. But it takes a special set of gifts to be a minister to singles, and Louis clearly possessed them. First Church enjoyed a wildly successful singles ministry thanks to the impressive program designed under his leadership. As Fran read off the calendar of events for the next several weeks, at least half the entries involved singles activities. Being young and single myself, I carefully noted those that related to my age group. I'd visited First Church in the past, keenly aware of the large pool of single righteous babes in attendance. Hopefully, my new status as a staff member would improve my chances with the ladies. To be honest, I needed all the help I could get.

As Fran finished going over the calendar, I hurried to wrap up my observations of the staff members at the table. Ramona Holloway served as music associate. An attractive woman with scary eyes, she was single and probably so for the long haul. Next to Ramona sat matronly Doreen McGinty, the children's director. Doreen had an unusually soft voice. Almost a whisper, which I presumed came from years and years of yelling, "STOP THAT THIS MINUTE!" Next, Raze Hankins the minister to married adults, and Terry Hankins the college and career pastor. I was betting they were related. Rounding out the table, Bernard Coggins served as head of pastoral care. Bernard played clean-up batter, covering all those tasks the other pastors didn't like to bother with—bereavement visits, counseling, the benevolence ministry, etc.

The second echelon of staff members sat in padded folding chairs around the perimeter of the room. These included the building superintendent, food service manager, preschool director, Thurm the youth pastor, Johnny Rochelle the recreation director, the security director, and a whole brood of secretaries. *There are more people attending this staff meeting than the Sunday morning attendance of about 75 percent of the churches in America,* I thought. *I'm not sure that an $11 million budget is enough.*

When Fran finished, we took a short break. All the secretaries, assistants, and directors were excused, leaving only the upper-level staff in the room. I grabbed my Daytimer and started to leave with the other underlings.

"Jenkins."

I recognized Dr. Jorgensen's voice over my shoulder. As one of his defining characteristics, Dr. Jorgensen addressed everyone by their last name, men and women alike. I turned as the pastor emerged from the hubbub of expensive suits and walked toward me.

"Jenkins," he said again, "just a moment. I'm going to break protocol and have you stay for the rest of the meeting. I've discerned that you're an idea guy. And to be honest, this group of . . ." He paused, subtly scanning the remaining staff members mingling around the room. "A collective . . ." He leaned in, lowering his voice. "Well, let's just call them a collective *brain cramp.* They could use some new, fresh ideas."

Did he just say what I think he said? Did he ask me to stay? I checked the room. *Did anyone else hear this? Surely someone had just witnessed the most significant moment of my young ministerial career.* No such luck. Still stunned, I didn't know what to say. "Uh, sure . . . well, uh . . . why, thank you, sir."

"Just grab an empty chair at the table and feel free to jump right in on the discussions. I'll let everyone know you're here on my invitation as an active participant. Fair enough?"

"Sure. Absolutely." I took a seat.

The door closed, and Dr. Jorgensen led a quick prayer for wisdom, discernment, and brevity. I got the distinct feeling he had a tee-time and didn't want to be late for it. Tom Applebee passed out copies of the agenda. Concise and to the point, the list included just four words or names:

July 7ᵗʰ Agenda:
Strickland
Harvey
Debt
Festival

Whoa. What's with the cryptic agenda? I better start praying for some of that wisdom and discernment.

BOOM! Tom Applebee jumped right in. "We have a vacancy on our Finance Committee. The nominating committee suggested Ansel Strickland, and he's willing to serve. If we approve him, he's in. Comments?"

"Strickland's background check came back clean," Bob Stevens began. "He's been married twice, but his first wife won't be a problem. She remarried and lives in another state. Their children are all adults now. All successful citizens. He has no children with Betty, his second wife. Betty is a faithful volunteer in our church media library. Strickland has worked middle management for Morgenstern-Kimble for twenty-seven years with excellent marks on his annual evaluations. He's bright and stable."

"Any hobbies?" Harry Simpkins asked.

"He's a collector of sorts," Bob responded. "Vintage civil war firearms, old clocks, antique toys. That sort of thing."

"That stuff can get pricey. How does he pay for it?" Harry pressed.

"He makes one twenty-three five annually at Morgenstern-Kimble," Bob continued, "and Betty knocks down another twenty grand as a part-time legal assistant. He appears to manage his money well and has little or no credit card debit."

I fought to keep my composure. I couldn't believe the copious nature of what I was hearing. Weren't we simply discussing the qualifications of a potential volunteer church committee member? It sounded more like the vetting process for a Supreme Court justice.

"Is he a tither?" Fred Snooker asked.

Now there's a reasonable question, I thought.

"Last year, he gave 13.6 percent of his total gross income including benefits to the church," Bob answered. "Another two thousand to other charitable activities in the community."

My head began to swim. I struggled to look attentive, but the intense scrutiny boggled my brain. A sickening thought came to mind. What on earth had they discussed about *me* before I was hired?

Louis Estrada joined the inquisition. "What about his health?"

"It's all good. Very good," Bob stated. "He's a runner. Low cholesterol. Good family history."

I wondered if they'd checked his teeth like prospective buyers of a racing horse. How did they get all this information on the poor guy? I half expected someone to produce his tax returns or latest urine sample.

Out of nowhere, Dr. Jorgensen asked, "Jenkins, what do you think?"

Startled by his question, I made a concerted effort to look contemplative. *How do I play this game? Do I ask something about his views on stewardship?* But then a strange confidence came over me. The finger of God was at work again. His greater purposes for my life were at play, and I felt compelled to go with the movement in my spirit. I paused, then slowly panned the table looking at the faces of people I hardy knew. I turned to Dr. Jorgensen and asked, "What about his faith? We've discussed his good work ethic, his strong exercise regimen, his apparent honesty and integrity. Have these strengths been forged through sheer human will, or are they fruits of a life built upon a sincere faith in God?"

I could only imagine the thoughts floating around the table.

Kid, you are so naïve.

You don't have a clue what you're talking about.

Why are you in here anyway?

After a long pause, Dr. Jorgensen said, "Insightful question, Jenkins. This is one of our most important committees. We need men of strong faith for our leaders. I believe Mr. Strickland to be such a man, but too often we take these things for granted."

Several of the other staff members confirmed Ansel Strickland to be a godly man, then we moved on. I kept my mouth shut for the rest of the meeting. But I did notice a subtle change in the attitude and demeanor of the staff as they discussed the other items on the agenda. When the meeting ended, we stood to leave. Dr. Jorgensen gently patted me on the back without a word. When I turned to acknowledge him, he winked at me with a smile, his way of saying *well done.*

5

The Homemade Pie

I splurged. On my own dime, I had a nameplate made for my office/closet door. With a little effort, I chiseled off the old *Utilities/Miscellaneous* sign and mounted mine in its place. The nameplate was gold with black letters: *Elmo Jenkins – Staff Intern.* I had to admit it was beautiful. Immediately I felt more significant. Someone important once said, "It's the small things that count." With my minuscule intern's salary, the small things were the *only* things that counted. Stepping back into the hall admiring my new nameplate, I had a thought. *Since they assigned me this rat hole for an office, I'm going to do the best I can to make it special. I'll show 'em some creativity!*

To help kick off my renovation program, I enlisted Dunston Jones. Dunston was an old black janitor who had been on the maintenance staff of First Church since way before I was born. Most places would have already put an old guy like Dunston out to pasture. First Church had recently hired an independent cleaning service, but they let Dunston stay on part-time to take care of odds and ends.

Dunston liked me. Most folks at the church paid little if any attention to Dunston, but I would always ask him how he was doing, and he would always respond, "Fine-'n-you?" He would come by my closet, uh, my *office* and tell me colorful stories about fishing. Fishing was his passion. He prided himself as being an expert angler. He had even invented his own special bait and fishing techniques. He once told me his secret to catching The Big Fish. "You gotta hide from 'em. Git y'seff way down low on the bank, or better yet, behind a rock or a tree." He illustrated this for me by crouching behind my table. I would laugh until I cried, but I did take careful notes.

I'd always wanted to be good at fishing, but the truth is I stunk at it. My problem? I couldn't catch any fish. I had vivid memories from a church fishing tournament back home. The whole experience had been an absolute debacle for me from start to finish. I'd borrowed a friend's boat. As I was pulling it out into the lake, the motor jumped off the back of the boat and sank in twelve feet of murky water. We never found it. *Cha-ching.*

With my boat out of commission, I hopped in with the best

angler in the tourney and figured this was the day I would actually catch a fish. We fished all morning, and neither one of us had so much as a nibble. Not even close. To add insult to injury, about noon (the worst time of day for fishing), a boat-load of old local guys pulled up and anchored next to us. They began catching fish, one right after another, using cane poles and bobbers. As I sat there watching them haul in the big ones, I decided it was time to find another hobby.

Dunston was more than just my fishing tutor. He was also my office renovation supply man extraordinaire. That awful view of the dumpster right outside my window? He found a curtain from an unused Sunday school classroom and hung it for me. My door, so badly in need of paint? He located some leftover paint in a storage closet. I may not be a seafoam green kind of guy, but it was a marked improvement. He scrounged up an old area rug that still looked pretty good. It covers most of my tile floor. Later, he showed up with two nice office chairs for any visitors I might have. I have no idea where he got them, and I decided not to ask. Finally, since I didn't have an office phone, he procured an old-school two-way wireless office intercom for me. Those small speaker-type boxes used back in the '70s. He put one on my office table and the other on Adrianne's desk on the fifth floor, so she could contact me whenever needed. This saved me tons of transit time and cell phone minutes. Plus, it came with a special bonus feature enabling me to keep up to date on the latest church gossip. By simply tweaking the channel knob on Sunday mornings, I could tune in the baby monitors installed in the nursery. I could hear every juicy tidbit shared amongst the volunteers rocking those babies. If someone at First Church got a *tummy tuck,* I knew all about it.

In no time, my office renovation was complete. Soon thereafter, Miss Figghie called me on the intercom. "Mr. Jenkins?" There was a lot of static so I adjusted the channel knob.

"Mr. Jenkins?" she repeated.

"Yes, Miss Figghie," I answered in my best pastoral voice.

"Mr. Jenkins, Pastor Applebee has requested that you make a visit out to see Erlene Markham at her home, and he wants you to take one of the other staff guys along with you."

"What time? And what is the purpose of the visit?"

"Noon today. Erlene is the head of our altar counseling room. She's requested a visit, but Pastor Applebee can't go so he's sending you to represent him. She lives at 2346 Oakwood Lane. And, oh yes—Erlene will be providing lunch."

I wrote down the address. "Anything else I need to know?"

She paused. "He did say to watch what you eat."

I laughed. "Thank you, Miss Figghie. Over and out." I clicked off the intercom.

Okay, they're sending little ol' Elmo Jenkins out on an official church visit. It wasn't lunch with the Pope, but it was a start. Papal visits would have to come later.

Since I needed a visitation partner, I invited Thurm Wilson. He wasn't interested until I mentioned the free home-cooked meal. Since it was almost lunchtime, we jumped in my car and headed over toward Oakwood Lane.

Thurm eased down in my passenger seat and closed his eyes. "So who are we going to visit?"

"Her name is Erlene Markham. Do you know anything about her?"

Without changing position or opening his eyes, he simply said, "Oh yeah, I know Mrs. Markham." Then he laughed quietly to himself.

"All right, what's the deal here? What am I getting into?"

Thurm sat up. "You've been in the Sunday morning worship service, right?"

"Yeah, sure. Of course."

"You know at the end of the service when folks come forward to make a decision and Dr. Jorgensen directs them to the counseling room? That little old lady in those funky looking dresses, holding open the door? That's Erlene Markham."

"Oh, that lady. I've heard some wild stories about her."

"They're all true and more. Believe me." Thurm laughed out loud.

"Now I see why Applebee sent me on this visit." I wasn't laughing.

Thurm gave me the whole story. Erlene and her late husband Howard had been missionaries overseas for years. After retirement, they moved back here and got actively involved at First Church. Howard catalogued and archived all the filmstrips used throughout the Sunday school. He kept them in a special media room up on the fourth floor. One day he sat down for a break and never got up. Died right there in the media room.

"Jeez, it sure seems like a lot of people drop dead inside those church buildings. Have they ever checked for asbestos?" I coughed. Power of suggestion, I suppose.

"It's not a burning priority." Thurm laughed at his own failed attempt at humor.

"About Erlene?" I asked, desperate for more information before our visit.

Thurm smiled. "Erlene Markham is one special lady, but a little strange. I think she may have the beginnings of Alzheimer's. She's been in charge of the altar counseling room for several years now. She's good at it, very energetic, very knowledgeable about the Bible, and very persuasive. Erlene's a tiny thing, only about five feet tall and well into her eighties, but she's in much better shape than I am. She'd run circles around you."

"I'm not as slow as I look," I fired back. "I'm in great shape—tight abs, firm glutes."

"Anyway," he continued, "several times a year she'll invite a staff member over to her house for lunch. More to socialize than anything else I suspect. She does have one very peculiar habit, though. She loves to tell off-color jokes. And oh yes, she's nearly blind."

"A small, nearsighted, crazed, perverted, senile, ex-missionary, and I have to go into her house and eat her food," I commented as we pulled into her driveway. "Why do I feel like I'm on a reality TV show? *Visitation Fear Factor.*"

We rang the bell and when she opened the door, Thurm's vivid description of this little senior adult lady was instantly validated. She greeted us in a bright purple and orange house dress. She had short-cropped silver hair with bangs and a bad overbite. Or maybe she was wearing her dead husband's false teeth by mistake. I immediately thanked God that Thurm had come along.

I decided to be cute. "Good morning, Mrs. Markham. I'm Elmo Jenkins and this is my pool boy, Thurm."

Throwing her head back, she laughed a deep guttural laugh. With a smoker's voice, she wheezed, "I know who you boys are. Please come in."

I held the door for Thurm, and he elbowed me in the ribs as he stepped by me. Thick ornate velvet drapes covered most of the windows, making her house dark. We passed lots of French provincial furniture with a few Oriental pieces mixed in as we followed her into her dining room. She had set the table for three.

We hadn't even taken our seats before she started right in. "Tell me, Mr. Jenkins, how do you like being on the staff of our little church?"

"It's a privilege, Mrs. Markham."

"Please call me Erlene if you would, or Miss Erlene if that's more comfortable."

"Miss Erlene, Thurm here tells me you're a retired missionary, and now you give leadership to our altar counseling ministry."

She gave us a toothy smile. "I was, and I am. I've been serving our Lord for almost eighty years and will for the next eighty."

"That's great!" I looked at Thurm with wide eyes. "I understand you wanted to share some church ministry business with us today. Is that correct?"

Studying me for a moment, she looked me right in the eye. "You're new at this, aren't you?"

I blushed. I know I did. "Wh-what, uh, what do you mean?"

"The other staff members always want to eat first and then get down to business. But not you. You want to talk business first. I like that. Okay, business before food. But first you must let me tell you a joke."

Oh God, no! He answered my prayer as my cell phone went off. "Please excuse me," I said as I stepped into her living room. "Now Thurm, he loves a good joke!" I hollered over my shoulder.

The call was from my advisor's office at Harvest Morgan Seminary needing some additional information about my internship. They also wanted to confirm my weekly meeting with my advisor, Dr. Auguste De Villa. Dr. DV and Erlene would get along great—*talk about crazy love.* The call only lasted a couple of minutes. As I walked back into the dining room Erlene was finishing her joke.

"Then the farmer said, 'but I thought she was your sister!'" Erlene croaked, breaking into boisterous laughter.

I glanced at Thurm, his face beet red, his eyes bugging out.

"That must have been some joke," I quipped.

"Would you like me to tell it again?" she grinned.

"No need." I smiled at Thurm trying to compose himself. "I'll get Thurm to tell me on the drive back to the church."

We discussed her church concerns. She stressed the need for more altar counselors, particularly more women and youth. Then she served a delicious lunch she'd picked up at a local delicatessen. She apologized for the store-bought food, explaining she found it difficult to cook these days due to her poor eyesight.

"But I didn't want to totally disappoint you, so I made you my famous peanut butter pie! Even rolled my own crust."

My first bite tasted fabulous. I love homemade pies. I was about to take my second bite when I noticed Thurm making small gestures with his fork, pointing at the crust of his pie. When Miss Erlene turned to ask Thurm a question about his youth ministry, I inspected my own pie crust.

When what to my wondering eyes should appear,
but cockroaches rolled into the crust, oh dear.

I almost gagged. The dead bugs were rolled flat, right into the pie crust. Obviously, Erlene couldn't see well enough to notice these *crunchy additions* to her pie. What was I going to do with the rest of my piece? Smashing it a bit, I moved it around the plate then covered it with my napkin.

We thanked Erlene for inviting us over. She gave us both a big hug and kiss on the cheek, then we escaped with our lives to my car. On the way back to the church, all we could do was laugh about the visit, but Thurm wouldn't tell me her joke. He swore never to repeat that joke to anyone for any reason. Overall, as my first official visit, I thought it had gone well.

Now all I had to do was deliver the piece of peanut butter pie she had insisted we take back for Tom Applebee.

I smiled to myself.

6

The Function

Singles parties. We've all seen them graphically portrayed on television. Beautiful people dancing everywhere. Loud, rowdy music with a gyrating beat. Adult beverages flowing freely. Laser lights flashing through dry-ice smoke. The entire room moves to the music; the noise level overwhelming.

Freeze-frame that picture.

Now remove the loud rowdy music, the liquor, the flashing lights, the dry ice, the dancing, and the beautiful people. What you have left is a Friday night Singles Function meeting in the First Church Fellowship Hall.

A couple of days ago, Singles pastor Louis Estrada slid into my office (now known as *The Closet*) and handed me a flyer for an upcoming First Church Singles Function for twenty-something's. You would like to think this meant for single men and single women in their twenties, but such is not the case. In reality, most of the women attending will indeed be in their twenties, but at least half of the guys will be over forty. I have a theory that the older guys get a pass because they usually drive nicer cars and wear expensive clothes.

Church Singles functions are a genre unique unto themselves. Whereas the popular singles parties that take place nightly in clubs across the country tend to resemble more of a *meat market*, a better analogy for a church Singles function would be a *garage sale*. Some new items, some used items—all looking for a new home and everything priced to move. It's just the way God made us. We're all looking for that special person to share our life with.

Right?

I arrived at Friday night's Singles function on time, but to be honest, I felt completely out of my comfort zone. First, I've never done really well with the ladies. Perhaps I mentioned that before? Second, I'd been there all of fifteen minutes when I spilled guacamole on my white shirt. It looked like I had a bad cold and sneezed green yuck on myself. Great.

In my head, I imagined how this was going to play out.

To pretty girl: *Hi there, my name is Elmo Jenkins. ¿Como se llama?*

Pretty girl: *Sorry, no hablo español, and what's that green crap on your shirt?*

Fortunately, I remembered I had a sports jacket in *The Closet,* and after a quick round trip, the guacamole stain was safely sequestered out of sight.

After a cursory scan, I determined I knew about half the people in the room. Some were staff members like Juliann Roth, the First Church receptionist, and Bonnie St. Hiliare, Louis Estrada's secretary. As far as potential girlfriends go, I didn't stand much of a chance with either of these ladies. Juliann was way, way out of my league. I was actually surprised she was even there. She's drop-dead beautiful, though definitely not a candidate for a rocket science government grant. Bonnie was attractive and very witty, but she was several years older than me. I saw her as fodder for one of the older guys wearing the $1000 leather jackets.

Since we work together, I figured a little small talk couldn't hurt. Juliann and Bonnie were chatting by the buffet table. Pretending to look over the food, I casually approached them. I couldn't help thinking—*why are singles always standing and talking? Why don't they ever sit down? What does this mean?*

I picked up a plate, staying far, far away from the guacamole bowl, and ended up right next to the girls, all the while feigning that I hadn't noticed them there. I might have mentioned earlier I'm not particularly good at this party stuff.

"Hey Elmo," Bonnie said, breaking the ice. "Isn't it kind of warm in here for a wool sports coat?"

Caught off guard, I'm quite sure I blushed. "Well, I, uh . . . well, you see, um—"

"I think it looks nice." Juliann said, coming to my rescue.

"Thanks," I said, regrouping. "Can you all keep a secret—you know, between staff members?"

Serious, concerned expressions crossed their faces. "Sure Elmo, what is it?" Bonnie asked.

I leaned in to whisper. "The reason I'm wearing this very hot jacket is because . . ." I paused for effect. "It's because I spilled guacamole on my shirt." Then, as if revealing a hidden gunshot wound, I slowly opened my coat.

Juliann sighed and slapped me on the shoulder. "I thought it was something serious, silly."

I smiled. "No, really, it's just that I'm not used to eating *inside.*"

They both laughed. For me, this was a good start. A *very* good start.

Still, it happened. That old, familiar, awkward pause. When three adults mildly acquainted, stand there trying to think of something interesting to say.

I fearfully jumped back in. "Do you gals come to these gatherings often?"

Gals? Gatherings? Where did that *come from?*

"I've been coming a lot lately. I'm kind of between boyfriends," Juliann whispered, giggling.

I was beginning to get a read on Juliann. Like one of those model homes on the cover of *Better Homes & Gardens,* she was breathtakingly beautiful on the outside, but quite vacant on the inside. Though she's a brunette, I couldn't help stealing a quick look for blonde roots.

Bonnie took her turn. "As Louis's secretary, I'm obligated to be here and make sure all the bases are covered. I'm really not much into the singles scene.

"Me neither," I said, half-lying. "However, I'd like to get to know some more people my age here at the church."

Our little conversation came to an abrupt close as we were summoned to the middle of the room. Time for the program to begin. The leadership team had placed thirty chairs in a circle. *Uh oh. Kumbaya time?* Thankfully, I discovered this group was more hip than that. Although we did start off by going around the circle and introducing ourselves. Each person had to share one significant thing about themselves. *Swell.*

First up was Art. He worked for UPS and collected Elvis memorabilia. Next came Jerry, a stockbroker who sang in the church choir. Cyndi worked as a loan officer and loved to cook. (It showed.) Debbie was a graphic artist and the reigning state Scrabble champion. (I was at a loss for words.) Nicholas was an anesthesiologist and amateur golfer. We continued around the circle—David, Judy, Ernie, and several others whose names I've already forgotten. Your typical group of church singles, some enjoying the group friendship, others looking for potential dates, most pretty lonely.

Over the next six months, many of these people would become my dear friends.

There's a unique bond that forms in a young singles group. Many of the members are separated from their families by distance, so the group becomes their surrogate family. This type of group is fluid, always changing as new members arrive and existing members either move away or marry. The dynamics of a young singles group are different than, say, a college group where everyone is pushing toward a degree or career. In a young singles group, most of the members are already established in life. They're just looking for fun, friends, and maybe some romance along the way.

We played a few of the regular group games, watched a *Best of Saturday Night Live* DVD from the '70s, then it was food time.

Most everyone had brought a dish for the potluck supper. I had prepared my famous *Elmo Surprise:*

One box macaroni and cheese (the cheapest you can find)
One can of chili with beans (store brand is fine)
One packet grated cheddar cheese (mild)
One small package sliced pepperoni

Instructions: Cook the macaroni and cheese per box instructions and leave in pan. Add the chili and stir until mixed well and heated thoroughly. Pour into an 8-x-8 Pyrex dish and cover with grated cheese, and then a layer of pepperoni. Bake in oven at 350° for 20 minutes. Voila!

Well, I like it. And therein lies the problem with a singles potluck dinner. Most singles are fast food junkies, some never cook. Which means we end up with about twenty casserole dishes, some of which are virtually unrecognizable. Personal favorites, I assume. I chose a healthy portion of *Elmo's Surprise*, some chips (sans guacamole), the always reliable refried beans, Jello, and a Fresca. The person responsible for bringing the drinks brought only Fresca. And he wonders why he's still single?

Finding an empty chair, I sat down with my gourmet meal. To my utter astonishment, Bonnie took the seat next to me. Juliann had exited earlier, so Bonnie was alone. I noticed she wasn't eating.

"Couldn't find anything at the *Buffet Ole'* that motivated your taste buds?" I joked.

"I'm not much for potlucks. I'm pretty finicky when it comes to what I eat." She surveyed my plate.

I took one more bite then set my plate aside. It was just too weird having someone I hardly knew sitting there watching me eat.

"So tell me, Bonnie. How long have you been working here at First Church?"

"Oh, I don't know. Two or three years, I guess. I started out as the church receptionist, then Louis asked me to come be his secretary. The pay was better, so I accepted the invitation. I've been the Singles ministry secretary for going on two years now."

"Are you from around here?

"No, I grew up in a little town in South Carolina. I moved here to attend Bargston College. I graduated with a degree in English Literature four years ago. My plan was to work a few years and save up the money to go back for my masters. The only problem is, I haven't saved up any money, so here I am, a working class stiff at First Church."

I did the quick math in my head. If she graduated from college four years ago, that would make her around twenty-six years old. That was only about a year older than me. I could live with that.

I continued probing. "How do you like working here at First Church?"

She pondered my question for a moment. "It's okay, I guess. Louis is a great boss, and I like working with the Singles ministry. But my dream is to teach and write. Someday, I want to write publishable American fiction and teach literature at a college like Bargston. What about you?"

I decided to break Rule #1 and share my honest feelings with another staff member—albeit an attractive, single, female, interesting, staff member. "At the risk of sounding too pious, I have a sincere desire to serve God with my life, and I'm not yet sure how to do that. I have mixed feelings about working in the church. When I first accepted this internship, it was all about making career contacts and getting an upgrade on my resume. But now it's developed into more of a discovery, or personal journey for me. God is really messing with me on a deeper level than just the day-to-day ministry training I'm getting here."

I looked at Bonnie and immediately wished I'd kept it more superficial. She had that *more-information-than-I-really-wanted-to-know* look on her face. So I took a left turn and lightened it up. "It's been an adventure. Let me tell you about my visit out to Erlene Markham's house the other day."

Several minutes later, my moment with Bonnie was interrupted by Eddie Hughes. Every church singles group has a guy like Eddie. Early thirties, never married, and probably never had a real girlfriend. Yet Eddie fashioned himself as quite the ladies' man. He drove most of the single girls crazy by phoning them repeatedly. Eddie wasn't picky about who he pursued. Tall or short, fat or thin, ugly or attractive, Eddy called 'em all. Several times a year, Louis Estrada would have to sit down with Eddie and ask him to refrain from harassing the single women at the church. Eddie would repent, promise to do better, lay low for a few weeks, then slowly begin making calls again. He wasn't dangerous; just a nuisance.

Eddie had one quirky habit which I found quite humorous. He didn't do it on purpose; it was just part of who he was. Eddie mixed metaphors and confused clichés in the worst ways. He'd approach some poor, unsuspecting woman and introduce himself with a smile. Then, in a futile attempt to be cool or clever, he'd say something stupid or offensive, never even realizing it.

Tonight was one of those nights, and Eddie was about to deliver one of his biggest faux pas of all time.

Eddie burst right into the middle of our conversation. "Hey Elmo. I see you're tying up one of the hottest ladies in the whole church." He coughed. "I mean with conversation, not ropes or anything like that."

Bonnie winced. "Well, Eddie, how are you? Nice sweater vest."

"I'm good, sweetie. Good as gold. What are you two talking about so serious and all?" His eyes widened in his attempt to look serious.

"Elmo was just telling me about some of his ministry training activities here at the church," Bonnie answered.

Eddie smiled. "We've got a great staff, all the way from Dr. Jorgenson down to Dunston Jones. Yes ma'am, they're great from 'throne to throne'." He laughed wildly at his own joke. I didn't get it.

Neither did Bonnie. Eddie must have realized from our blank expressions that we were clueless, so he quickly explained. "You know—Dr. Jorgenson as pastor sits on the royal throne, and Dunston as janitor cleans the porcelain throne. Get it?" He laughed boisterously again. Bonnie contributed a courtesy laugh, but I didn't. It wasn't funny.

He wouldn't go away. "Speaking of the great staff; did you all hear Pastor Applebee's sermon on sexual purity last Sunday night?" And then with Eddie's unique gift of word confusion, he added, "That was some powerful sermon. Yes, sir. It hit me right between the legs!"

No. Tell me he did not just say that! No way.

But the expression on Bonnie's face left little doubt. She'd heard it too.

A moment later, Eddie meandered away to bother someone else. Bonnie, her face still flushed, looked at me and whispered, "Did he just say what I think he said?"

"Yes, I'm afraid he did." We shared an incredulous, esoteric laugh. It took us quite a while to regain our composure.

After dinner, we played a few more silly group games, then the evening wound down. Overall, I have to say I had a good time. I got to know several of the singles a little better. I would do it again.

I didn't think a whole lot more about my conversation with Bonnie other than to reconfirm that Rule #1 was still a good idea. Twice now I'd let down my guard with other staff members, only to regret it.

Collecting my empty Pyrex dish, I grabbed the last Fresca and headed up to *The Closet* to drop off my sports coat. It had been a long week, and I was looking forward to sleeping in on Saturday morning.

7

The Queen Bee

To be totally honest, I had started the internship with a healthy dose of cynicism. When I first decided to pursue a career in church work, I had a focused desire to honor God with my gifts and talents, as limited as they are. My home church pastor had mentored me, given me some training, ordained me, and shipped me off to seminary to hone my skills. I arrived at campus naive but eager. But by the conclusion of the first year, my—shall we say "Salad Days"— had come to an end.

My cynicism about the local church and vocational ministry started subtly, but continued to grow. By the time my internship at First Church started, I had a full-blown jaded view of most ministers, and serious doubts about the effectiveness of the modern church. For me, church work had become more of a career opportunity than a sincere commitment to change the world for God.

Life has a funny way of confirming or destroying our preconceived ideas about things. Through my internship, I was confronting many new situations—some were validating my cynicism, and others were chipping away at it.

My first interaction with Annette May Jorgensen, the senior pastor's wife—aka *the Queen Bee*—did nothing but solidify my cynical perspective. Since Day One, I'd been pulled aside and warned numerous times by other staff to be careful around the Queen Bee. "Greater men than you have been beheaded by her whims," I'd been told. I'm rather partial to my head, so I determined I'd be extra diligent if I ever had to deal with her directly.

Annette May Jorgensen's maiden name was Fitzsimons, as in the wealthy and powerful Fitzsimons family. As you may recall, I met Tom Applebee at the Fitzsimons estate the night of their open house—the night that redirected the course of my life. Annette May Jorgensen was Smitty Fitzsimonses baby sister. Smitty and Horace Jorgensen had been roommates at Yale, and he had introduced Annette May to Horace. They fell in love and eventually married. When First Church began searching for a new senior pastor, Smitty was instrumental in getting Horace hired for the position.

It was obvious, even to a newcomer like me, that the Queen Bee had a serious "entitlement perspective" on life, especially down at the church. In laymen's terms, she got what she wanted with no questions asked.

There are pastors' wives who are notorious for meddling and for power plays. Fortunately for everyone at First Church, Annette May did not care for the minutiae of church work. Subsequently, she stayed out of almost everything with the exception of two or three pet projects per year. Dr. Jorgensen was masterful at keeping his wife at bay concerning situations critical to the life of the church. But when it came to her pet projects, he gave her carte blanche and would consistently take her side in any associated controversy.

Woe to the staff member who crosses Annette May Jorgensen. That miscalculation would be followed quickly by the death fumes of "career suicide."

I had absolutely no desire to go near the Queen Bee's kingdom. But fate had other plans.

My office intercom came to life one afternoon. "Elmo, are you there?" Tom Applebee asked.

"Hey Tom. What can I do for you?" I pulled my feet off my table.

"I have a very special assignment I need you to handle. Our minister of recreation Johnny Rochelle would handle it, but he's out for several weeks with a pulled groin or something."

Who pulled it? I felt like asking, but thought better of it.

"What's involved?" I asked.

"It's some type of Father & Daughter activity . . ." —and then he said it—"that ANNETTE MAY JORGENSEN is organizing."

I was speechless. My worst nightmare had begun. I had nowhere to hide.

"Elmo? Are you there?" A long pause followed. "Elmo? Can you hear me?"

I took a deep breath. "Yes, Tom, I'm here. Must be the intercom cutting out again on me," I lied.

Tom continued. "I've arranged for you to meet with Mrs. Jorgensen and her assistant Betty later this afternoon."

"Here?" I sputtered. "In my . . . *my* office?"

Tom chuckled. "Listen, you've done a fine job fixing that place up, but Mrs. Jorgensen doesn't *do* closets. She'll meet you at four this afternoon in the church parlor." Then he offered some advice. "Just relax and let her run the show. Take lots of notes but don't ask too many questions. The key here is to listen and say, 'Yes, ma'am' often."

"I'll be there." I turned off the intercom. Talk about good days going south. I closed my eyes and began to formulate a strategy. *Okay, okay. This is supposed to be an internship to learn how to work in the church. This is my opportunity to learn how to work with powerful, though problematic people. If I can succeed with the Queen Bee, I can succeed with anyone.*

I arrived at the church parlor at 3:45. I wasn't about to be late for this meeting. Killing the extra minutes, I looked around, admiring the elegance of the exquisite room. Used primarily for wedding receptions, special church-related parties, and an occasional civic event, the parlor's opulence impressed me. An enormous chandelier hung over the middle of the room. Expensive carpet covered the floor. I'd been told all the furniture was custom handmade in Europe specifically for this room. I wasn't sure I was allowed to sit on it, so I just stood waiting.

Betty Darby, the Queen Bee's assistant, arrived first. She introduced herself and said that Mrs. Jorgensen would join us in a few moments. Evidently, the Queen Bee had decided to drop in on Pastor Jorgensen for a surprise visit. *I hope the good pastor isn't over at the country club "visiting the Greens" again.* It was a standard joke amongst the staff. Horace loved to golf.

Betty and I chatted for about twenty minutes while we waited. A very nice middle-aged lady, I wondered if she were paid by the church or by the Jorgensens. I would keep that question to myself.

At 4:20, both double doors gently opened, and Annette May Jorgensen floated into the room.

"Good afternoon," I said, half bowing though not sure why.

"Thank you for coming," she answered, easing down onto one of the overstuffed chairs. Betty nodded at me, then we both took a seat on a couch.

The Queen Bee continued. "And I really appreciate you pinch-hitting for Johnny. I understand the poor man is home nursing a sore foot."

I laughed on the inside, but quietly smiled on the outside. "Oh, it's a privilege and a pleasure for me to fill in, Mrs. Jorgensen."

For forty-five minutes, I listened and took copious notes. Mrs. Jorgensen, who had watched *Oprah* faithfully for years, had seen a recent rerun of an *Oprah* show on the topic of fathers and daughters. The Jorgensens had a fourteen-year-old daughter named Stacey. So the Queen Bee thought how wonderful it would be to plan a special event just for the teenage girls of First Church and their fathers.

She talked about the food. She talked about the entertainment. She talked about the arrangement of the room, the tickets, and the appropriate dress code. She already had a theme in mind: *Behind every great man, there's a great daughter!* There were obvious problems with this theme, of course, but instead of saying anything I just glanced at Betty. She responded with a tight smile, silently telling me to keep my mouth shut. Mrs. Jorgensen continued for another half-hour, filling the air with an expansive list of minute details that you-know-who would no doubt have to work out.

I didn't want to come across as a total lackey, so at one point I jumped in.

"Tell me Mrs. Jorgensen, how many people do you anticipate will attend the event?"

Without blinking, she shot back, "Those are the kind of details I'm expecting *you* to work out, Mr. Jenkins."

That would be my last question of the day.

Mercifully, we finished the meeting and said our goodbyes. I slumped back onto the designer couch and flipped back through my notepad. I had taken eleven pages of singled-spaced notes, most of which outlined action items I would be directly responsible for. I was overwhelmed. This would be a mammoth job. Now I knew what happened to Johnny Rochelle. His groin wasn't pulled. It had been kicked—and exceedingly hard.

I immediately empathized.

Limping back up to *The Closet,* I started making calls using my cell phone. I hoped I'd be reimbursed for the expense. Working until ten that evening, and most of the next day, I still had way too many pages of the assigned tasks to accomplish. Exhausted, I went home and stewed.

Who was this lady dominating my life, with this unbelievable list of mundane tasks, for an event that had absolutely *nothing* to do with me or my ministry training?! And why didn't she assign some of this junk to her paid assistant Betty? I needed some answers, so I gave the injured one, Johnny Rochelle, a call.

"Hello?"

"Hey Johnny, this is Elmo Jenkins, the church intern. I understand you're on the disabled list."

"Well, I tore a thigh muscle playing intramural volleyball at the church Rec Center."

"Yeah, I know. I was pitched one of your assignments—working on a special event with Mrs. Jorgensen."

"Better you than me. My leg feels better already," he laughed.

I wasn't amused. "What's the deal with her? She comes up with some grandiose idea and has me doing literally all the work. And I mean *all* of it. I bet she doesn't even show up for the event."

"She may or may not," Johnny explained. 'That's just how it is with her, Elmo. Believe me, I know. I've worked with—excuse me—*for* her many times. And don't expect much appreciation for your efforts."

"Well, that's bleak," I bellyached. "Any suggestions?"

He hesitated. "I suggest you lose the pity party, suck it up, and do the best you can."

I paused. "All right then, I think I've got it. Good night, Johnny." I hung up the phone. At first, I was ticked, but the more I thought about it, I decided Johnny was right.

I went to bed thinking about the different ways a person could orchestrate a timely leg injury. What does a minister of recreation *do* anyway? . . . zzzzz . . .

The next morning I jumped right in and systematically started knocking out each task on my list. I was a virtual machine—lining up parking attendants, ordering hors d'oeuvres, estimating the number of available seats. I actually started to feel good about the project. Not only was my list almost completed, I also had a feeling this was going to be an excellent event.

While looking through a list of potential deejays, Tom's voice crackled over my intercom. "Elmo? Are you there?"

"I sure am. What's up, Tom?"

"You know that project I put you on for Mrs. Jorgensen?"

"Yeah?" I set down the list of deejays.

"It's been cancelled."

"What?! What do you mean *cancelled?*" I fumed, exasperated. "I've already put in over twenty hours of work into this project!"

"Mrs. Jorgensen ran the idea by her daughter. Stacey told her the idea sucked, and assured her none of the teenage girls would come. So Annette May decided to can the event. I'm really sorry, but just close it down and wrap up any necessary loose ends."

"Okay. Thanks," I said, not meaning it. I switched off the intercom. Sitting there in shock, I felt like the refuse of the rich and famous. If this is what it was going to be like working full-time in a church, I didn't want anything to do with it. Let the kiss-up Johnny Rochelles of the world have this crap. God was going to have to clarify a few things for me. It felt like I was interning at some religious version of the DMV.

I turned the intercom back on. "Adrianne? You there?"

"Yes, "she answered.

"Tell Tom I'm going home for the rest of the day. I've sustained a groin pull."

I clicked off the intercom, then slammed *The Closet* door behind me. The impact knocked my new nameplate to the floor.

Not that I cared.

The Snafu

Even the mailbox case at First Church reflected the staff hierarchy-of-importance. Located in the break room, the case resembled one you might see in a post office with five or six rows of slots. The top row had only two mail slots; subsequently they were quite large—one for Dr. Jorgenson, the other for Tom Applebee. Then, with each descending row, the slots grew progressively smaller, until you reached the last slot on the last row which was barely big enough for a small envelope. This was my slot. It wasn't even labeled. *Oh the subtle humiliation of it all.* So I defiantly made a label for all the world to see as a reminder that bottom dwellers are people too: *Elmo the Great.* Unfortunately, as I attempted to put the new label in place I discovered it was much too wide. After trimming it down to size I was left with *"mo the Gr."* I figured what the heck and taped it up there anyway. At least it would keep them guessing.

If anyone even noticed.

Around ten o'clock on Friday morning, I swung by the mail case to check my slot. Three items of interest and a bunch of religious junk mail crammed my humble slot. After discarding the mailers for *101 Ways to Improve Your Preaching Now on DVD* and *Using Bobblehead Dolls of the Apostles to Grow Your Sunday School,* I was left with:

- The next staff meeting agenda
- A memo from Tom Applebee concerning my assignments
- A sealed envelope with *Elmo* written on the front

I walked up one flight of stairs, then down the hall and into *The Closet* where I flipped on the light and tossed my mail on the table. Normally at this point, I would've taken off my sports jacket or suit coat, but this was casual Friday. One Friday a month the staff is allowed to dress casually. That meant a short sleeved-shirt or perhaps a collared sport shirt, no tie, and casual slacks. On this particular day, I wore Dockers and a blue golf shirt.

Before I could even sit down, Miss Figghie's voice came over my intercom. "Elmo? Are you there?"

I pressed the call button. "Just walked in. What's up?"

She sounded urgent. "We have an emergency. There are one hundred people over at Forest Lakes Cemetery waiting for Deacon Phillip's graveside service to begin."

"Okay. What's the emergency?"

"Dr. Jorgensen is supposed to perform the service, but he's nowhere to be found. We've been trying to track him down for the last thirty minutes with no luck."

"Well, who's going to cover it?" I laughed to myself, imagining Tom Applebee or Fred Snooker having to bust cheeks over there to rescue the situation.

"That's the problem," Miss Figghie stated flatly. "There's no one around today but you."

Uh oh.

I'd never done a funeral before, much less one without any time to prepare. *Think, Elmo, think!* "Wait a minute," I shouted into the intercom. "I just saw Thurm Wilson downstairs. Call his office and have him meet me in the staff parking lot, pronto. We'll get this covered."

Thurm jumped into my car and off we went. I noticed he too was wearing a golf shirt.

"What's the deal?" he asked.

"A bunch of people are over at the cemetery, including one dead guy, waiting for a graveside service, and Dr. Jorgensen is a no-show. Ever done a funeral service?"

Thurm sat up in his seat. "Whoa, where's Horace?"

"They can't find him, and I'm too nervous to speculate. Again, have you ever done a funeral service?" I asked urgently.

Thurm was cool under fire. "Yeah, I've done a few. You open with a prayer, read the particulars about the deceased from the obituary, then read the first part of John chapter 14, followed by the 23rd Psalm, and close with the Lord's Prayer. It's not too hard."

"Great." I sighed with relief. "You've just been nominated to save Dr. Jorgensen's tail."

"No way," Thurm shot back. "I'm in a golf shirt!"

"Sorry Thurm, but your pastor needs you, these people need you, and I need you. I've never done a funeral before! Here's my Bible. Start preparing."

Thurm reluctantly took my Bible, resolved to the inevitable. "*The New Living* translation? Who uses *The New Living* translation?"

"Shut up and start getting ready! We'll be there in no time."

When we arrived at Forest Lakes Cemetery, the people had been waiting a full hour for the service to begin. We apologized for Dr. Jorgensen not being there, we apologized for our casual clothing, we apologized for the late start, then we apologized for apologizing so much. The family members were understanding, but anxious to get on with the service. The funeral director handed Thurm a copy of the program with the obituary included, and he started the service. From my perspective, it went quite well. I was impressed. Thurm hit a home run covering all the bases, and came across very caring, as if he'd actually known these people or spent some time with the family before the service.

I was congratulating Thurm after the service when we were approached by Deacon Phillip's daughter. She thanked us for coming to the rescue, then dropped a bomb on poor old Thurm. Evidently Deacon Phillip's first name was Jacob. He had a twin brother named Jeffrey. Jeffrey attended the service, sitting in the front row. In his rush to get the service started, Thurm had misread the funeral program and eulogized Jeffrey the brother, instead of Jacob, the deceased. All of Thurm's kind comments about a life of service and the welcome reception at the Pearly Gates had accidentally been about a living, breathing man sitting right in front of him in the front row. But the daughter was very gracious, and even shared that Jeffrey was so impressed with Thurm's eulogy, that he had requested him to do it again for his funeral when the time came.

Thurm was mortified. Me? I thought it was hilarious but mostly glad it hadn't happened to me.

The sister handed me a check made out to Dr. Jorgensen for $100, asking me to thank him for all he had done for the family during this difficult time.

How about that. He misses the funeral and still gets a check and a thank you. Man, senior pastors are held in high esteem.

Wonder if he's on the front nine or the back nine?

When we got back to the church, I was informed that Dr. Jorgenson was in his office. Turns out he'd been handling a life-and-death emergency for one of our members at Memorial Hospital. Because the situation had been so touch-and-go, he'd not even been able to check in with the church. I went up to his office to give him the check for the funeral. He graciously thanked me for my role in getting the graveside service covered. He'd already heard about Thurm's snafu, and we both chuckled about it.

Then Dr. Jorgensen told me about the strangest funeral he'd ever participated in. Several years ago, he'd received a call from an attorney out on the west coast. Apparently an old millionaire had died and left specific details about his funeral in his will. If these details were followed precisely as instructed, fifty percent of the dead man's wealth would go to a certain world mission agency. The attorney, who represented this mission organization, called to inform him that the dead millionaire had requested Dr. Jorgensen preside over his burial at sea. He also wanted to be buried in a casket. The man had even listed the exact latitude and longitude for the burial location at sea. For the sake of the mission agency, Dr. Jorgensen had flown out there as instructed, and on the designated day, he joined about fifty other people for a four-hour boat ride out into international waters. It was illegal under the nearest state's law to bury a person at sea in a casket.

Under these unusual circumstances, Dr. Jorgensen performed his regular funeral service, and all was going according to plan until something very unexpected happened. After the family said their farewells, the casket was released over the side of the boat. It floated, refusing to submerge. The family was understandably shaken by the spectacle. The poor funeral directors were perplexed, so they huddled together and formulated a plan. One of the funeral home employees stripped down to his pants, put on a life jacket, then was lowered down into the water. He swam to the casket, opened the lid and let it fill with water. It *still* didn't sink. Some of the family members were beside themselves. Finally, one of the boat crewmen came up with a workable plan. They brought the casket back on board, attached the spare boat anchor to it, chain and all, then threw both the casket and the anchor over the side of the yacht where it sunk to the bottom of the ocean.

"Right there on that boat that day, I vowed I'd never do another funeral at sea," Dr. Jorgensen said.

I left his office wondering what my first funeral would be like and hoping I wouldn't have to don a life jacket.

Back at *The Closet*, I started going through my mail. I browsed the staff meeting agenda for next week. Nothing stood out except for one name: Eddie Hughes. I figured it must be time for one of those periodic meetings with Eddie, telling him to back off harassing the singles chicks. I wondered how long the staff would tolerate Eddie before just telling him to find another church home. Maybe that time had arrived.

Then I picked up the interoffice memo from my supervisor, Tom Applebee. It was attached to a book entitled *Pastoral Ministry for Dummies.*

MEMO:
To: Mr. Ellington "Elmo" Jenkins
From: Pastor Tom Applebee
Re: Evaluation

Elmo,

Since you have now completed the first month of your First Church internship, I thought it appropriate to give you my initial evaluation. So far, I am very pleased with what I see. Dr. Jorgensen shares my opinion. We like your initiative and your ability to cut through the church hype and get to the meat of the situation. You get an A+ for people skills. This has been verified by the relationships you have already developed with many of the staff, and from reports we're hearing about your interactions with members of the church.

On the practical side, we will now be asking you to take on a few ministerial duties. This will add experience to your obvious knowledge base. I have included a copy of the book Pastoral Ministry for Dummies. This thin volume will give you some basic instruction on how to prepare and perform pastoral duties like funerals, weddings, baptisms, etc.

Keep up the great work.
Tom Applebee

I folded the memo and smiled. *Good start, Elmo.* I pretended to pat myself on the back. I set the book aside, but not far. Remembering this morning's emergency graveside service, I knew this "how to" book would come in handy.

The last piece of mail was a small sealed envelope with my first name handwritten on the front. The envelope was pale purple. I hoped it wasn't from a guy.

I opened the envelope and pulled out a note card. It simply said,

Would you consider doing lunch sometime?
Bonnie

At first, I was taken aback. No, to be honest, I was astonished! I'd never received an invitation from a female before. It was courteous, concise, and to the point. But wait a minute. Bonnie was breaking the rules. Wasn't the guy supposed to be the initiator?

I couldn't decide if I was more flattered or more concerned by her aggressiveness.

My contemplation would have to wait for now. It was Friday with much left to accomplish, and the day was already half over.

9

The Indigestion

On Monday morning, I had a message in my wee little mailbox to drop by the office of Bob Stevens, the church administrator. And of course, the yahoo signed it Bob "Big Bird" Stevens. You need to understand Bob is all of five feet four, and that's with double lifts. Since Bob's office was on the first floor right around the corner from the mailboxes, I went there first.

Tapping on the partially open door, I stuck my head into his office. "Hey, has anyone seen Big Bird around these parts?"

Bob looked up from his budget reports and cracked a big smile. "Elmo! Good. Have a seat."

As I sat down in the red leather chair facing his desk, I noticed the paneled wall to my left covered with framed photographs from the Caribbean—specifically the Cayman Islands, Bob's annual vacation spot. Without fully thinking through the implications of my question I asked, "Bob, have you ever read John Grisham's book The *Firm*?"

He jettisoned his smile and stared right into my eyes.

Uh oh. Wish I had that question back.

Bob maintained his stare. *Awkward.* A contemplative pause hung between us. Finally, in a not-so-serious tone, he quipped, "Who's got time to read fiction?" He let out a sinister little laugh. The laugh of a sinister little man.

He quickly segued to the reason for summoning me to his office. "Elmo, we evaluate all interns on an ongoing basis. When we determine that they're a good fit here—dedicated to the task and serious about learning the ropes of local church ministry—we seal the deal. You've reached that point, and I'm pleased to inform you that we're rewarding you with a new laptop computer. It's outfitted with a wireless card and already programmed with access to our church network, including email. Your email address will be elmo-the-intern@fc-online.org. The best news of all is that you get to keep the laptop, even after your internship is over, courtesy of one of our generous members."

"Wow," I blurted out. "Thank you! Will it connect from my clos—" I caught myself. "From my office?"

Bob's big smile returned. "It will not only connect from your office, but from any place in town that provides a courtesy wireless service, including your seminary. You can even connect to our network while sipping snooty coffee at places like Starbucks."

"Man! Thank you, Bob." I took the box from him. "Starbucks? Wow," I mumbled to myself as I left his office.

The time had come. I needed to respond to Bonnie's lunch invitation. What better way to break in my new computer than to send her my first email. Setting the laptop on my office table, I opened the lid. While the laptop booted up, I reviewed what I knew about Bonnie:

1. She was Louis Estrada's secretary and had worked at First Church for two or three years.
2. She had graduated from college and wanted to be a teacher and a writer.
3. She had a quick, witty sense of humor.
4. She was attractive with long brown hair, bright eyes, and a great smile. She must've worn braces because her teeth were all straight and in the correct places.
5. And for some unknown reason, she apparently wanted to get to know me better.

Laughing out loud, I remembered what a nerd I was when it came to this whole dating/girlfriend thing. I'd been on a few dates, but nothing ever came of them. Truth be known, I'd never even kissed a girl. Twenty-five years old and never been kissed. Pathetic. So now I have this nice girl asking me out to lunch, and I'm hesitant. Not because I'm fearful or shy, but because I'm Old School. *Shouldn't I be the one asking her out?* Deciding to turn the tables, I upped the ante. Forget lunch. I would ask her out for a full-blown dinner date.

Launching Outlook Express, I clicked on *Create Mail.* A window opened, and I dove right in.

Bonnie,

Thanks for the lunch invite, but I'd rather take you out to dinner instead. I know it sounds corny, but let's just say I'm kind of old-fashioned. How does Friday night sound? I know a great upscale Cuban restaurant over on Murphy Road —Casa Verdi, which translates, the Green House. Wonderful food and a lush, exotic décor. By the way, they do have a dress code. A sign over the front door says, No Tie, No Taco. *Let me know what you think.*

Elmo

I read back over the email, typed in bonnie@fc-online.org and clicked *Send*. At least, I *assumed* that was her email address.

The email notification chime sounded on my new laptop while I was looking over my hospital visitation slips and planning the rest of my day. *Less than an hour for her to respond. Gotta be a good sign.* Of course, a wise old saying states (and I euphemistically paraphrase), "assumptions make us look like *rear-ends.*"

The return email came from Bonnie all right, but not *that* Bonnie. It was from Bonnie, the First Church librarian. *We have a church librarian named Bonnie?* I didn't even know we *had* a church librarian! I DIDN'T KNOW WE HAD A CHURCH LIBRARY!

I grimaced as I opened the email.

Dear Elmo,

I'm flattered by your dinner invitation, and though I was momentarily tempted to accept it, to be honest, I'm not sure Ralph, my husband of 40 years, would understand.

Something tells me you meant to send this message to Bonnie St. Hiliare. Her email address is bsh3436@fc-online.org. Besides, whenever I eat Spanish food it gives me awful indigestion.

Thanks anyway,

Bonnie Johnstone
Church Librarian

All of a sudden, I had indigestion. Who would've thought—a church librarian with a sense of humor? Now there's an anomaly. I emailed back an apology and resent my invitation to the correct Bonnie.

Sitting there in the shadow of my own embarrassment for a few moments, I pondered the humiliation I would surely be suffering thanks to my email screw-up. Or maybe I'd catch a break and Bonnie-the-librarian would take pity on me and keep this our little secret. The kind of secret held between friends and only ever acknowledged by a subtle smile or mischievous wink.

As I was wallowing in self-pity, a glinting flash of light caught my eye from across the utility closet. Just a pinpoint of light, but extremely bright nonetheless. I could only see it if I held my head just so. Whatever was giving off the light was small, and it was just barely protruding from behind the left corner of an old metal supplies shelf against the wall.

Getting up to investigate, I noticed that one of the curtains had been pushed back, allowing a car windshield in the parking lot beyond the dumpster to bounce the midday sun directly through my window. It reflected off this object behind the shelf. Approaching the shelf, I could now see the corner of something metallic and shiny. I gave it a tug, pulling it free from a crack in the wall. Just an old foil wrapper from a stick of chewing gum. Maybe Juicy Fruit? Double-mint? I started to crumple it up to toss in the trash when I noticed there was some writing on the inside. In blue ink, someone had written,

"I told you that is what he would do. You should have taken my advice. Now you'll have the devil to pay!"

T.B.T.

It was dated May 17, 1959.

That's odd. I was too intrigued to just throw it away, so I put the wrapper in my wallet and made a mental note to drop in on old Fred Snooker.

A knock on my door reverberated around my *shabby chic* walls, startling me.

"Just a second," I said as I walked across the room. Opening the door, I was shocked to find Bonnie. (No, not Bonnie-the-librarian. That would be way too weird).

She smiled. "Hey, Elmo. Got your email."

"And you responded in person," I voiced out loud.

Awkward. We stood there in silence for several seconds.

"Well, are you going to invite me in?" She was still smiling.

"To be honest, I'm not quite sure the correct protocol for a male staff member inviting a female staff member into a church closet."

Her eyes widened as she started to laugh, then abruptly stopped. "You know, you're probably right, Elmo. I'd hate for either of us to jeopardize our jobs over some dumb misperception by a janitor or, I don't know, maybe the church librarian?"

I felt the blood drain from my face.

"Count me in for Friday night. Pick me up at 6:30." She tossed me the aforementioned mischievous wink then delivered her final barb. "I'll *email* you my street address and phone number." And with that she was gone.

I soon discovered that "Bonnie-the-church-librarian" was a charter member of First Church's Gossip Hall of Fame.

Ouch.

10

The Walking Wedgie

Since almost the beginning of my internship, I'd been assigned hospital visitation. Making cold calls on people I didn't know, who didn't know me, was more than a little outside my comfort zone. The staff at First Church not only visited its members who were in the hospital, but also anyone else who either called in requesting a visit for themselves or for a friend or neighbor. Requests even came from out of state asking us to visit folks in our local hospitals. We had nine hospitals in our city, so the staff had divided them into three zones. Each staff member was assigned a zone and a day of the week for making hospital visits. Through a very unfortunate draw, I got Mondays. Hospitals are always *jammed* on Mondays.

After pondering this Monday phenomenon for a while, I formulated a theory. I identified several interesting, though unrelated reasons why so many bodies ended up in the hospital on Monday mornings.

First, I conjectured that most people tend to be more reckless on the weekends. Whether at wild parties or family picnics, people are just more careless about where they put their feet and what they put in their mouths on weekends.

Second, in my opinion, most people hate their jobs. So to enter the hospital on a Saturday would be an abject tragedy. Why? It consumes a day off or even two. Whereas, waiting to enter the hospital on Monday could render *three to five days* away from the office or factory. This alone, I decided, was enough motivation for many very sick individuals to hold on until Monday morning before they headed to the emergency room.

Whatever the actual reasons, I always ended up with a fist-full of visitation slips on Monday morning. The routine was pretty much the same for each visit. Locate the correct room (not always an easy task), identify the patient to be visited, make a brief introduction, an even briefer visit, then close with a quick prayer. Start to finish, five minutes tops. Often the patients were sedated or asleep, so I would pray for them silently then leave my card.

My last visit on this particular Monday was a little more unusual. I found Ramona Muscarella comatose in ICU and very near death. Praying quietly for her and her family, I left my card and exited. Ramona didn't attend our church; she'd simply asked for a visit from a Protestant minister. One of the nurses had called First Church with the request.

Ramona died soon after my visit. I would never have known, except the family saw my card and called the church asking for me to do her funeral. This would be my first official funeral. It would also be a bit more complicated than I would've wished. Religiously, Ramona had been the black sheep in her family. The Muscarellas were Italian Roman Catholics. As in every family member for five generations had been Roman Catholic. For reasons never fully explained to me, Ramona had left the Catholic faith to become a Baptist. She had also raised her kids as Baptists. Needless to say, her conversion to Protestantism created quite a stir for her extended family.

Ramona would be laid to rest at the Italian Gardens Cemetery. I would do the graveside service for her. I figured there might be a dozen people there. Over one hundred showed up. Not familiar with the Italian Gardens Cemetery, I'd never even been to that part of town. The old cemetery looked like something out of a Francis Ford Coppola movie. It was tucked on a one-acre lot, way back in a bad part of the city. There was an eight-foot stone wall around the entire property with big wrought iron gates in the front. To enter the cemetery, a visitor would first have to walk through a mausoleum full of marble-veneered crypts. Huge Italian marble and granite grave markers filled the cemetery, some ten or fifteen feet high. The place had to be at near capacity. It was so crowded, it resembled the back lot of a tombstone/grave marker store.

My first funeral. I was extremely nervous. So nervous, I didn't even realize I had accidentally attached my back suspenders to my boxer shorts instead of my suit pants. Subsequently, I ended up with a two-hour walking wedgie. Further complicating matters, a bad storm rolled in about an hour before the funeral. By the time I arrived, it was an absolute downpour, so we moved the graveside service into the mausoleum.

There I was, this punk Protestant intern doing my very first funeral, jammed into the middle of an overcrowded passageway full of wet, bereaved Roman Catholic Italian-Americans. I kept scanning the crowd looking for Al Pacino. The closed coffin sat in the middle of the mausoleum floor with the mourners tightly squeezed all around it. I stood at the head of the coffin, all eyes on me.

No pressure.

I opened my *Pastoral Ministry for Dummies* handbook (the one Tom Applebee had given me) to the section entitled "Funerals by the Numbers." As I glanced down at the outline, I determined I should make a few comments before I read the prepared service. Such a profound moment under such extraordinary circumstances just demanded a little additional effort on my part.

Silently praying for wisdom, I started quietly. "I did not know Ramona the way you all knew Ramona. I visited with her only once, briefly, right before she died. However, I have since learned that she was a lady of great courage and faith. Though many of you may have disagreed with the choices she made in life, you still honor her here today with your presence. Life is like a grand revolving door. You have people entering it from one side, people exiting it from the other, and the rest of us are inside pushing it around. Ramona has made her break from this life leaving us with the message to keep pushing on."

Then, returning to the scripted service, I completed the funeral.

I decided funerals were not my favorite thing to do, but I was relieved I'd survived my first one. Several of the Muscarella family members came by afterward to shake my hand and thank me, some with tears in their eyes. It was the first time I had provided comfort to some hurting people. It felt good. Perhaps God *could* use me in a ministry capacity.

But, first I had to get home and figure out what was wrong with my boxer shorts.

11

The Intimacy Zone

Friday afternoon arrived, and I was running late. Erlene Markham had made a surprise drop-in visit to *The Closet*. Two hours later, I finally convinced her to head home in order to miss the afternoon rush-hour traffic from the city.

Why they continue to let people her age and frame of mind drive is beyond me. I can just see her looking through the steering wheel, squinting to see if the light is red or green. Yikes.

Exhausted from her visit, I finally made it home to my apartment, but completely out of time to get ready for my date with Bonnie. *What to wear, what to wear. I sound like such a girl. Okay, think. Casa Verde doesn't allow jeans. I'll have to wear a jacket and tie.* I selected khaki Dockers, a white oxford cloth button-down shirt; a "warm and sensitive guy" pastel green tie, and a navy-blue sport coat. *If Bonnie bails on me, I can always hang around at the restaurant and park cars. I'm certainly dressed for the part.*

Time to run down the pre-date Elmo checklist:

Hair just right—check
Teeth brushed—check
Antiperspirant—check
Dangling nose hair removed—check

Okay, gotta go, gotta go, gotta go. I estimated a twenty-five minute drive from my place to Bonnie's apartment, and it was just now six o'clock. This gave me ample drive time to review the Do's-and-Don'ts of a First Date. Though not a comprehensive list, it's just some commonsense ideas I've gleaned from years of suffering through Singles seminars. Picking my favorite relationship concepts, I cobbled them into what I call *Elmo's First Date Strategy*:

1. Be a good listener. Look at your date while she's talking. You must actually *hear* what she's saying instead of formulating your next response.

2. Never pass judgment on her opinions. There will be time for give-and-take on subsequent dates—*if* more actually occur.

3. Don't run your mouth. The Bible says a man of few words is considered wise. Let her form her initial opinion of you based on what you *don't* say.

4. It's not about me. Ask questions about her, her work, her family, her faith. Show genuine interest in her responses. Compliment her clothes and appearance and mean it. Respond to her questions about you in a brief and humble manner. Keep the focus on her.

5. Be a gentleman. Open doors for her, chew with your mouth closed, and avoid vulgar language.

I could feel my confidence rising. Then, in stormed the requisite reality check. I remembered, after all, that I was Elmo Jenkins, a modern-day Barney Fife. Either James Dobson or Dr. Phil would need to come along to hold my hand, and give me play-by-play instructions. Since neither of them would be available on short notice, I decided to give Thurm a call. He could help; after all he had a girlfriend—the lovely Alise. I gave the auto-voice command, "Thurm the Worm," and my cell phone quickly dialed his number.

"Hello?" I could barely hear Thurm over the loud music in the background.

"Thurm, this is Elmo!" I yelled. "Turn off your tunes!"

"Okay, just a second." The music stopped. "Hey, Elmo. What's up?"

"I need some advice, buddy. I'm on my way over to pick up Bonnie for our date."

"The church librarian?" he chortled.

Before I could respond, I heard the loud screeching of tires as the car in front of me slammed on its brakes. Dropping the cell phone, I swerved to the left, just missing a Beamer in the lane next to me. *Whew!*

Retrieving the phone with my heart still racing, I gasped, "Thurm? Are you still there?"

"Elmo! Are you okay? What happened?"

I took a deep breath. ". . . A near accident—*waaaay* too close for comfort!"

"You might wanna check out your shorts." With Thurm, the jokes never stopped.

"Listen, I need you to step out of character for a second and give me some serious advice," I said, almost pleading.

"Sure, Elmo. How can I help?" Before I could respond, he jumped back in. "Sorry, I need to put you on hold for a second. I have another incoming call. It's Alise."

Thurm had programmed his cell to play music for those on hold. As I waited, ABBA sang "Fernando." *Thurm, lay off the cheesy music.*

"Elmo, whatcha need? I only have a minute or two. Alise is

coming over, and I need to power-clean my cave."

"Thurm, I need a little pre-date help. What is it that women really want from a relationship?"

"One word: intimacy. Any time women are surveyed about the relationship stuff, intimacy *always* comes in at #1."

"Okay . . . but what does intimacy actually mean in this context?"

"Elmo, I have no idea. Sorry, but I've gotta run. I'll ask Alise when she gets here." And he hung up.

Yeah, that helped a lot. Looks as if I'm on my own.

Intimacy. Right.

Just what I needed—a "fatal abstraction."

I knocked on Bonnie's door. She stepped out, and I said she looked nice. And she did. She then said I looked nice. And I did. On the drive over to Casa Verde, we made small talk about small things.

Making a snap decision, I let the valet park the car. It cost ten dollars, and I'd have to skip lunch one day next week to cover the extra expense. But first impressions are uber-important. I didn't want to come across as a tightwad (even though that's exactly what I am). Granted, it was a duplicitous move, and even though I consider myself a moral person, I do allow for the occasional small breach.

We were led to a cozy booth near the back of the Garden Room where we had complete privacy. As we settled in, our waitress appeared.

"Buenas noches," she said, smiling. "My name is Maria." She was definitely *not* of Latin origin. "May I get you something to drink?"

"I'd like iced tea with lemon, please," Bonnie said without hesitation.

I'd recently read an article online about the dangers of ordering iced tea in public eating establishments. Evidently, most tea leaves are grown in third-world countries with little or no sanitary regulations. Subsequently, it's imperative that the water be brought to a boil to kill the many different types of bacteria residing in the tea leaves.

After summarizing this issue, I asked Maria, "Do you all boil the water when making your tea?"

"Oh yes," Maria answered with a naughty grin. "We practice *safe tea* at Casa Verde."

"Okay then," I said mildly embarrassed. "I'll have the iced tea also." And we all shared a good laugh, which I considered a good sign. A few minutes later, Maria came back and took our food orders.

It occurred to me—we were about ready to enter *The Intimacy Zone*. I wasn't rattled, just understandably a little nervous. The obligatory greetings, small talk, and food orders had come and gone. Now it was crunch time. Everything would be won or lost during this segment of the evening. Historically, this is where I always fumbled the ball. Which explains why I, Elmo Jenkins, had never kissed a girl. I could never get past this unscripted "Q&A" section of a date without screwing up. I'd either offend my date or totally humiliate myself, taking down the entire male gender with me.

Taking a preemptive tack, I decided to prepare her for the worst. "Bonnie, are you familiar with the song "My Stupid Mouth" by John Mayer? You know, the one about a guy who ruins a dinner date by shooting off his mouth? Yeah, well, John called me before he wrote that song to make sure he got all the details correct."

Bonnie laughed boisterously. "Now, there's a new approach! What is this, some type of pre-conversation disclaimer? So now you can't be held liable for stupid comments, lousy opinions, or offensive remarks?"

"That about sums it up," I said sheepishly.

"Well. It's inventive." She smiled and then her expression turned sincere. "Elmo, just relax. We're both in our mid-twenties; we're past that place in life where we need to impress each other. Look, we have a lot in common—vocationally, academically, spiritually . . . just be yourself. That's the Elmo I want to spend time with tonight."

From where I was sitting, that little pep talk dripped with intimacy. I could really like this girl. A calm came over me unlike anything I've ever experienced on a date before.

Remembering *Elmo's First Date Strategy,* I said, "Bonnie, tell me all about *you*—about your family, your favorite things . . ." I knew she was a writer, so I added, "and tell me about those books you want to write." Then I settled in and worked hard at being a good listener.

The rest of the dinner flew by. We talked about everything. And we laughed and laughed. I kept my foot planted firmly under the table and out of my mouth. Overall, we had a great time.

As the evening concluded and I walked Bonnie up the path to her apartment, I started to get the old nervous stomach again. The end of a first date has to be one of the most awkward moments ever created. Especially for me, since I've never successfully navigated one. The normal guy is always thinking, *Should I try to kiss her goodnight?* The normal girl is thinking either, *I hope he kisses me goodnight,* or *I hope he doesn't try to kiss me goodnight!*

However, Bonnie was not your normal girl. In fact, I found her extraordinary.

When we arrived at her door, I was totally clueless. So I just smiled and said, "Bonnie, thanks for—"

Before I could finish, she leaned in and kissed me. Just for a moment, nothing too passionate, but I know I felt my heart flicker. When she pulled back, all I could muster was, "Thank you." As far as words were concerned, I was done for the evening.

"Elmo, I had a really nice time tonight. Please, let's do it again?" She smiled, then turned and disappeared into her apartment.

I lingered there for an extra moment or two before waltzing back to my car still thinking about her kiss.

Man . . . *too cool.*

12

The Advisor

My Monday morning glee morphed into a frown. I had just opened my email inbox to find 47 messages. After deleting the spam, I had only one legitimate message left, and it wasn't from Bonnie. It came from Tom Applebee:

Dear First Church Staff member,

Just a reminder about our annual Primary Staff Retreat this Thursday and Friday. We will be leaving by church vans from the west porte cochere at 10:00 a.m. One of the main goals of our retreat is team building, so I recommend that all staff members ride in the vans. The retreat will be held at the Golden Stallion Stables and Spa on Highway 320 near Spencer Springs. Horseback riding will be available for those interested. However, Bob Stevens has informed me that our insurance carrier strongly discourages it. Pack light.

Here is a list of those confirmed going and the areas of ministry they represent:

Tom Applebee: Chief of Staff
Fran Bruker: Pastor's Administrative Assistant
Harry Simpkins: Music Ministry
Fred Snooker: Senior Adult Ministry
Bob Stevens: Administrator
Bernard Coggins: Pastoral Care
Louis Estrada: Singles Ministry
Raze Hankins: Minister to Married Adults
Doreen McGinty: Children's Ministry
Thurm Wilson: Youth Ministry
Johnny Rochelle: Recreation Ministry
and Elmo Jenkins: Church Intern

*Dr. Jorgensen will be joining us Thursday evening.

Sincerely, Tom Applebee

There I was at the bottom of the list, but I took comfort in the "and" before my name. Have you ever noticed in movie credits, they always give the main star top billing, but the super-cool, better-known, and more respected actor gets the last spot? And there's always an "and" before his or her name?

... *and Anthony Hopkins*

... *and Meryl Streep*

Well, that was me on this list. At least, that's the way I chose to interpret it. Hey, it could have been worse. They could have asked me to carry everyone's bags.

My intercom beeped and Miss Figghie crackled, "Elmo, are you there?"

"Yes, Adrianne." (I tried to stay away from the whole Miss Figghie thing.) "I'm here."

"Pastor Applebee asked me to remind you that he would like you to give a short report to the staff at the retreat on Friday morning. Nothing heavy, just highlight some of the things you've learned and any suggestions you might have. He also wants you to help with the luggage."

"Got it. Thanks. I'll be ready."

The intercom went silent. I'm convinced God has a great sense of humor. He sure knows how to cook up the humble pie. To be honest, I need a piece of it on a regular basis just for perspective.

Little did I know this staff retreat would be a full dessert tray.

Once a week, I made a quick visit to the seminary to meet briefly with my faculty advisor and bring him up to date on my internship. Due to unfortunate luck or some other bad karma, Dr. Auguste De Villa was assigned as my advisor. Dr. De Villa had been at Harvest Morgan Seminary *way* too long. He chaired the Psychology Department and still taught several courses, but in my opinion, he had succumbed to senility many years ago. Random topics spontaneously sprang to life from somewhere deep down in his demented mind, resulting in obscure and often bizarre lectures. Taking one of his courses was a true adventure. Regardless of the topic, each class turned into a, shall we say, *Detour du Jour*. Still, he had no trouble filling his courses each semester as everyone knew he gave A's to all his students. Even the noblest of seminarians found it too tempting to pass up such an easy GPA boost.

The schedule called for me to meet with Dr. De Villa for fifteen minutes every Monday afternoon from 3:30 to 3:45. Often, he just didn't show up, but as long as I signed in, I'd fulfilled my requirement. Of course, the weeks he went *missing in action* were the best.

"Dr. DV, you're here," I said, sincerely surprised as I sat in the only other chair in his office.

"Well, Mr. Jenkins," he grunted, "I suppose that depends on what you mean by 'here.'" He then cleared the phlegm from his throat and spit into his wastebasket.

Deciding to ignore his psycho-babble, I cut to the chase. "Dr. DV, my internship at First Church is going well. I'm getting lots of hands-on ministry assignments and—"

"I know, I know," he interrupted. "The rich and famous are treating you well—blah, blah, blah. I need you to do a favor for me, Jenkins. I owe old man Snooker $100 from a bet I lost to him years ago. It concerned a land deal I thought Buster Sapp was involved in. Well, it's a long story, and I don't feel like telling it. Anyway, I've finally decided to pay up. That's a long story too, and I don't feel like telling it either." He handed me an unsealed envelope with a hundred-dollar bill inside. "You tell Snooker that now we're even, and I don't want to hear any more of his whining.

"But Dr. DV, I'm not sure—"

"Jenkins, just deliver the dang envelope, and take some advice from your advisor. Don't get sucked into all the *pomp and circumstance* of First Church. Watch your back, watch your wallet, and watch who you trust." He paused, glanced at his watch, took a deep breath, and barked, "I'm late for my next class." Then Dr. Auguste De Villa, esteemed head of the Psychology Department of the prestigious Harvest Morgan Seminary, got up and stormed out of his own office, leaving me sitting in a cloud of Freudian dust.

I elected not to tell him his fly was open.

Driving back to First Church, I couldn't help but wonder what in the world that was all about. I would have to ask Harvest Morgan alumni Thurm Wilson if he had any insight into the Dr. DV vs. Fred Snooker issue. Unfortunately, *The Envelope* would have to stay in my possession until Wednesday morning, since Fred Snooker wouldn't be in his office until then.

My cell phone rang. It was Bonnie. *Yes!*

"Hello?" I answered, pretending not to know who it was.

"Elmo, this is Bonnie. I just wanted to call and say thanks for a great time Friday night."

"I'm glad you called. I've been thinking about you a lot. Through sheer coincidence, John Mayer is in town this Friday night for a concert. I already asked Erlene Markham to go with me, but she turned me down. What do you say?"

"Well, I can't promise you the same quality of jokes Erlene would have brought to the date, but I'd love to be her replacement."

Yes! "I've got that dumb staff retreat on Thursday and Friday.

Which means I'll be cutting it close to get back on time. I'll buy the tickets and let you keep them in case we run late. Is that okay?"

"No problem, Elmo. I'll enjoy the concert—with or without you."

"Thanks. I think? I'll just do whatever it takes to get back, even if I have to pick up and throw the slow moving Fran Bruker into the van so we can vamoose on time." I paused. "Wait, did you hear horses rearing?

"What?"

"Never mind. I'll see you at staff meeting on Wednesday, okay?"

"Will do. Bye, Elmo."

On Wednesday morning before the staff meeting, I stopped by Fred Snooker's office. Fred worked part-time, keeping office hours only Monday, Wednesday, and Friday mornings. I needed to drop off *The Envelope* from Dr. DV, and I also wanted to ask him about the gum wrapper note I'd found in my office.

Fred's office was just a couple of turns down the second-floor hall from *The Closet*. During office hours, he simply left his office door wide open. Many of the First Church senior adults spent several days a week doing volunteer work at the church. They stuffed the bulletins with ministry inserts or helped count the tithes and offerings. Some helped in the kitchen preparing the Wednesday evening family supper. Others sorted bags of donated clothes for the ministry distribution center. These senior souls were in and out of Fred's office continuously. Finding him alone would be rare, but I really wanted some privacy for my questions.

I walked down the hall to his doorway. Sure enough, *The Three Widows* as they were known were ensconced in Fred's office, but he wasn't there.

Emily, Beatrice, and Fanny had all been widows for quite some time. I would guess they were all in their late seventies or early eighties. Though they weren't related, they functioned almost like triplets. They lived together; they dressed alike; they finished each other's sentences, and to the older single men in the church, they were a virtual three-headed terror—and not above stalking. An unfortunate fact of life for Fred, himself a widower.

"Ladies," I said, greeting them with a big smile. "If it's not my favorite troika of warm lovin'. How about a hug?"

"Well, lookie there," Fanny said, smiling.

"It's Ellington!" Beatrice squealed, getting up from her seat.

"He's all mine, girls, I claim him first!" insisted Emily.

"Easy girls, there's enough Elmo for all three of you." We shared a group hug. "Tell me ladies, where's Pastor Snooker this morning?"

Fanny jumped right in. "Well, he excused himself for a trip to the restroom. He always leaves for the restroom about the time we get here."

"It's his morning constitutional," quipped Emily.

"I think he's incontinent," added Beatrice. "Why else would he be running off to the bathroom so often? My second husband Earl was incontinent. What a mess, and oh my goodness, the smell—"

"Pastor Snooker doesn't smell!" Fancy snapped.

"That's 'cuz he goes to the restroom so much," Emily insisted.

I knew this little discussion could go on forever. I also knew Fred was hiding in the restroom waiting for *The Three Widows* to wander off to some other location in the building.

I decided to expedite the situation. "Ladies, don't tell anyone, but before I came up here, I left a box of three dozen Krispy Kreme donuts on the table in the downstairs boardroom. If you hurry, you can snatch one before the staff meeting starts. If anyone asks, just tell them that Elmo-the-Great said it was okay for each of you to have one."

"You don't—"

"Have to—"

"Ask us twice!" answered Emily, Beatrice, and Fanny in that order. They scurried out the door, still bickering down the hall about Fred Snooker's bathroom habits.

I stepped around the corner and stuck my head into the Men's' restroom. "Pastor Snooker, *The Three Widows* have left the building."

A stall door opened immediately and out stepped Fred Snooker closing his Daytimer. "Good morning, Elmo. Are you sure they're gone?"

"Yes sir, I directed them downstairs for a free donut." I held open the restroom door for Fred, and we walked back to his office.

"Sweet ladies, but . . ." he paused. "Thanks for running interference."

"Pastor, may I have a few minutes of your valuable time?"

"Remember, I'm actually retired," he grinned. "You can have as much time as you want."

"Just a couple of things. This won't take long."

Fred was counting on this interim senior minister gig to be short term. After he was pressed back into action following the death of his predecessor Hugo Withers, he didn't even make any changes to Hugo's office. He just moved in, using Hugo's chair, Hugo's desk, even a coffee cup with "Hugo" on the side. We sat in two vinyl chairs at a round table in a corner of the office. Opening my wallet, I handed him the gum wrapper I discovered in *The Closet*. Dated May 17, 1959, it included a handwritten message:

"I told you that is what he would do. You should have taken my advice. Now you'll have the devil to pay!" T.B.T.

Fred spread open the wrapper and read the message. "Well, now there's a find. Where did you get this?"

"It was sticking out from behind one of the shelves in my closet office. I noticed it when the sun coming through the window reflected off the wrapper and caught my eye. Any ideas?"

"Oh, it's a puzzle piece. Looks authentic. It's part of *The Black Toe Enigma.*"

"The what?"

"*The Black Toe Enigma.* It's part of the folklore here at First Church going back almost 100 years. I'm actually the resident keeper-of-the-lore. It's kind of a long and detailed story, which I'm more than happy to share with you. Unfortunately, it will require more time than we have this morning. According to my watch, staff meeting starts in about fifteen minutes. Tell you what. Let me keep this wrapper, and I'll add it to a special album I've helped compile with all the bits and pieces of *The Black Toe Enigma.* When we have more time, I'll fill you in on all of the known details and show you the TBT album."

"That would be great. Just let me know when." I stood up to leave.

"See you at the staff meeting, Elmo. I need one more stop in the restroom. I'm borderline incontinent, and I use a preemptive strategy before any long meetings."

"Oh, one more thing," I added quickly. "Dr. De Villa asked me to give you this." I handed him *The Envelope.* "He said something about an old wager."

He took the envelope, opened it and pulled out the hundred-dollar bill. "Well, son of a—" He caught himself. "That sorry old goat. He's owed me this money for over forty years. The next time you see him tell him thanks for me. And kick him in the—" He caught himself again. "Just tell him thanks. I'll do the kicking myself." He headed down the hall toward the restroom whistling like a man who'd just won the lottery.

13

The Golden Stallion

Thursday arrived. At 10:00 a.m. sharp, we loaded up in two of the sleek First Church vans.

Most churches have a few donated secondhand vans or buses with the bare minimum of amenities necessary to transport people. Not First Church. Their fleet included four regular minivans and four twelve-passenger vans, all fully loaded with the latest available accessories. They also had two full-size Greyhound-style passenger buses. All the vehicles were custom-painted the same color and had matching interiors. Each year, the oldest two vehicles in the fleet were replaced with new models. The ten First Church vehicles were named after the disciples in the Bible (excluding Judas the Betrayer and Thomas the Doubter, of course).

I rode in *Bartholomew* on this cool fall morning. I'd made a conscious decision not to ride in the *John*. It just sounded too much like a *porta-potty* on wheels. Bob Stevens drove *Bartholomew* with Fran Bruker riding shotgun. Thurm and I were in the far back, and Harry Simpkins, the minister of music, rode on the middle bench seat. Harry was a sincere man of the cloth, though cut from a different piece of fabric than most ministers.

Everyone knew at least one Harry Simpkins story. Once, at the annual church picnic at Turnbill Lake, Harry put on a spectacle of a show. Evidently, he fashioned himself quite the expert water skier. So with hundreds of the First Church members picnicking on the beach, Harry wanted to show off his skiing prowess. He'd made arrangements with the deacon driving the boat for a big finish. On the last pass, the deacon was supposed to bring the boat in close to the shore. Harry would let go of the rope and ski right up on the sandy beach to thunderous applause from the adoring church crowd.

When the time came for the big ending and Harry was to let go of the rope, the plan went awry. Fearing the lake was becoming too shallow for his boat, the deacon quickly accelerated toward deeper water. Harry was whipped forward way too fast, hitting the beach at rocket speed. To the delight, then horror, of the hundreds watching, Harry cartwheeled head over foot five or six times before landing on top of the Chairman of the Deacons' sunbathing teenage daughter. She escaped with only disturbed tan lines, but Harry ended up with a broken leg and a concussion for his showboating efforts.

Harry turned toward us. "Hey, either of you guys snore? The rooms at this place sleep three, so we're supposed to buddy-up with two other staff members for the night. Every year on this retreat I get stuck with Stevens and Snooker, and they battle all night long to see who snores the loudest."

"As far as I know, I don't snore. How about you, Thurm?

"Not me," Thurm said. "I've never been a snorer."

"Then it's settled. We'll be the no-snoring room tonight." Then Harry continued, loud enough to make sure Bob Stevens could hear him up front. "That's right. We'll be sleeping like babies tonight in the *No-Snore Zone*."

I could see Bob's eyes in the rearview mirror as they narrowed. Most of the other staff members just tolerated Harry, but for some inexplicable reason, Dr. Jorgensen loved the man. If not for this crucial fact, Harry would've been gone a long time ago.

"Hey, Harry," Thurm hollered over the noise of the van. "Tell Elmo about the time you forgot to bring your song lyrics to that wedding for your solo."

Harry threw his head back and laughed like a wild animal. His eyes grew big and animated. The man had the world's largest mouth. I'd seen him put a whole unpeeled orange in his mouth with room to spare.

He reached over the seat and slapped my leg. "Elmo, you wouldn't have believed it unless you'd been there. See, when I sing solos for weddings, my assistant Carlene places the selected sheet music in a designated blue *Weddings* folder for me. When I arrive at the church for the wedding, I simply swing by my office, pick up the folder on my desk, then take my position on the platform and wait for my spot in the program to sing. I've sung all these wedding songs so many times I know the melodies by heart. I just need the lyrics, particularly for those second and third verses.

"Well, at this wedding last year—" Harry paused to keep from laughing, "At this wedding, I'm standing at my position, and it's my turn to sing; the music starts, I open the file folder, and voila—no sheet music! I actually said 'uh oh' out loud!" Harry then paused for dramatic effect.

Impatiently, I asked, "Well, what did you do?" I glanced at Thurm, who had one of those pre-laugh smiles on his face.

"Elmo, I've been doing this a long time, so I decided just to wing it. There was no problem through the first verse and chorus, but from that point on, I just made up the words as I went along, faking it all the way until I finished the song like a pro. The wedding party was so caught up in the event, they didn't even realize anything was amiss. I thought I'd fooled everyone until one of my choir members approached me at the wedding reception. With a wry smile, she said, "I never realized that song had a verse about tadpoles, butterflies, and sand in your eyes."

His eyes widened even more. "They played a tape of that performance at the annual choir banquet, and people literally fell out of their chairs laughing."

We all shared a good laugh. Harry even had tears in his eyes. I admit it was funny and wished I'd been there to hear it live. Harry's life was a continuous string of outrageous episodes like that, one right after another. I think Dr. Jorgensen kept him around just for comic relief. Harry turned his attention to the front of the van to spend some quality time bothering Fran and Bob.

I dialed down my voice so only Thurm could hear me. "So tell me, what's the deal between Fred Snooker and Dr. De Villa?"

"Oh, that goes way back, and it's really kind of ugly. How'd you find out about it?" Thurm asked quietly.

"Dr. DV is my faculty advisor for the First Church internship."

"Ooh, that's unfortunate." Thurm frowned. "Whose dog did you run over to earn *that* privilege?"

"It's actually turned out to be a blessing because he's rarely there for our appointments. Most weeks, I'm in and out in less than a minute. I'm there just long enough to wink at Bess, his graduate assistant, and sign in."

Thurm smiled. "You know she's—"

"Whatever it is I don't want to know," I interrupted, holding my hand up. "Just fill me in on the Snooker/De Villa *Conflict of the Titans.*

"Okay, but I'm only giving you the short version since we're almost to the retreat center. Plus the long version is just plain boring."

"Fine with me," I said, sliding down in the seat and propping my knees up on the back of the seat in front of me.

Thurm turned sideways to face me and started the grand tale. "Fred and Augie go way back, maybe even as far as high school. They were both very bright and competed for everything along the way. If Fred was Student Council President, then Augie was Captain of the Debate Team. If Augie dated the head cheerleader, then Fred dated the homecoming queen. They both graduated from Cornell, then both attended Harvest Morgan Seminary. They weren't really friends, but it was a good-natured competition, and everyone played fair and by the rules.

"Sometime during the '60s, the screws started loosening a bit in Dr. DV's brain. It was subtle and almost no one noticed, but Fred had spent his entire adult life trying to best the man, and he knew something wasn't right. Fred was the Associate Pastor at First Church at the time and also on the Board of Trustees at Harvest Morgan. When the head of the Theology Department at the seminary retired, the board was considering Dr. DV for the position. Augie was brilliant, and this was the job he coveted. He had the requisite tenure, academic credentials, national reputation, and respect of the rest of the faculty. He was a shoe-in, but Fred intervened and convinced the board that Augie was *not* the right person. Fred suspected Augie might be in the beginning stages of something like Alzheimer's, but he chose not to mention his suspicions to the board. Instead, he passionately argued for 'new blood from outside the seminary' to reinvigorate the program, and he succeeded in persuading the rest of the trustees.

"Fred's actions came out of kindness. He didn't want to embarrass Augie by questioning his mental stability in front of the board. But Dr. DV felt as though he'd been denied his dream job by the jealous machinations of his old rival Fred Snooker. The *Great Feud* had begun.

"Several years later, Fred served as Interim Pastor at First Church. He was also a candidate for the permanent position. Dr. DV worked the phones tirelessly, calling in all his markers to kill any chance Fred had to ever be Senior Pastor. There's been bad blood both ways ever since."

Thurm sighed. "And that's just the short version. They haven't spoken directly to each other for twenty or thirty years."

I sat up in my seat. "Let me get this straight. You have a tenured department head at one of the most highly esteemed seminaries in the country, and you have the second-ranking pastor at one of the most renowned churches in the country, and these guys have refused to speak to each other for almost thirty years?"

"That's the facts," Thurm said shaking his head. "And both are brilliant Bible scholars."

"How do you know all this stuff?"

"Tom Applebee gave me the long, boring version last year when we were on a three-hour flight to California."

An exclusive retreat getaway, the *Golden Stallion Stables and Spa* catered to the privileged few. Privately owned by a dozen of the more *well-heeled* individuals from our state, its board was chaired by Smitty Fitzsimons, who served as the driving force behind the whole development. Famous for its riding stables, the *Golden Stallion* served as home to a former Kentucky Derby winner and several other championship horses. Also available on the prestigious grounds— first class tennis facilities, twenty-seven holes of manicured Jack Nicklaus designed golf, a skeet shooting range, and of course, a full-service spa. The bylaws required all buildings, including the Main Lodge, support structures, and any private cabins built by the club members, to be of luxury log cabin design. The entire property had a rustic ambience to it, though once inside the Main Lodge it felt anything *but* rustic. Think Daniel Boone meets Dubai.

Club membership was limited to three hundred families, but the waiting list numbered in the thousands. Many of the members had built cabins around the property for weekend getaways and summer vacations. The word *cabin* doesn't really do justice as a description for these part-time domains. Some of these log homes were seven or eight thousand square feet in size. Many had huge floor-to-ceiling windows spanning two stories, overlooking the golf course with spectacular panoramic views. Most included separate garages housing up to half-a-dozen vehicles. These were big money, old money, new money, family money, and foreign money people; the operative word here—*money*. And lots of it.

And each year, the primary staff of First Church held their annual staff retreat at the *Golden Stallion*. I thought it rather ironic that the theme for this year's staff retreat was *Sacrifice.*

Harry, Thurm, and I were assigned to a spacious and nicely appointed room in what I would call a *neo-woodsman* motif. No mounted animal heads on the walls, but a weekend hunter would feel right at home. (A mere assumption on my part since I'd never hunted or fired a gun.) The room had only two beds; a full-size bed that matched the other furniture and a single Murphy bed that pulled down from the wall. Harry quickly threw his bag on the full-size bed even as Thurm pulled down the Murphy.

As the reality of the situation slowly sank in, Harry chuckled. "Jenkins, it's a good thing you don't snore since we're gonna be sleeping cheek to cheek." He stepped into the bathroom closing the door behind him.

"Well, at least one of us will be getting some sleep," Thurm said with a smirk.

I winced. "Oh, you're good, Thurm. You sized up the bed dilemma the minute we walked in and staked your claim to secure the best option."

He smiled. "I am fast on my feet, but this time I merely had the advantage of remembering last year's retreat. I'm sure you'll do fine. After all, remember Harry said he doesn't snore."

"Yeah, but a full-size bed for two adult men? That's just wrong."

"Elmo, just give Harry a kiss on the cheek before we turn in, and I guarantee, he'll stay on his side of the bed all night long." Thurm laughed at his own retelling of that tired old joke, then headed back to the lobby.

Whoever invented the full-size bed was a moron. When two adults sleep in a full-size bed, they're basically shoulder-to-shoulder, hip-to-hip. There's no room to turn over, so you have to more or less levitate and spin. Otherwise, you either land on top of the other person or fall on the floor.

I wasn't looking forward to the experience one bit. This had nightmare written all over it.

We had free time all afternoon, so Thurm and I played some tennis. I neglected to warn Thurm ahead of time that I've been banned from playing tennis in forty-five states and Puerto Rico;

mostly for my own safety. Meaning, I dutifully chased around his "winners" for an hour while he scurried after my "losers." But he was a good sport about my lack of tennis acumen. I only heard him laugh out loud a half-dozen times or so.

That evening's dinner was impressive. We sat at tables covered in starched white linen, adorned with expensive European china, Waterford crystal, and real silver cutlery. I shared a table with Tom Applebee, Fran Bruker, and Doreen McGinty, the Children's' Ministry Director. We were given two entrée options: prime rib or spring pheasant. I chose the prime rib which arrived as a thick slice, seasoned and cooked to perfection. Each bite sent my taste buds on a two-week all-expense paid trip to some far-off land. This fine piece of beef was accompanied on my plate by new potatoes marinated in some type of olive oil concoction, then lightly broiled and sprinkled with a spicy Cajun seasoning. Rounding out this exquisite course, fresh steamed kale grown organically right there on the grounds in the Lodge's own garden. Waiters were all about attending to our every dining need. Unaccustomed to this type of attention, I felt a bit pampered, almost embarrassed by all the fuss.

"Well, Elmo," Tom said, breaking the silence, "are you enjoying our staff retreat so far?"

I took two or three more good chews on the beef in my mouth and washed it down with some very sweet iced tea. "Yes, I am. This is one unbelievable facility."

"Yes, it is," he agreed. "When Smitty approached me about having our staff retreat here each year, at first I was hesitant."

"Because of the wrong impression it might give to the First Church membership?" I asked sincerely, though naively.

"Oh no," he chuckled. "I hesitated because of the cost. This elegant meal we're all enjoying is about $75 a plate. And you don't want to know what the accommodations run."

"What changed your mind?"

"That's easy." He laughed again. "Smitty decided to pick up the tab, at no cost to the church budget. A tax write-off for either him or the *Golden Stallion*, I suppose. Bob worked out all the details."

"That's amazing." I reached for another croissant.

Tom smiled at Fran and Doreen. "It's a well-deserved perk for our primary staff members. These folks work long, hard weeks, often with unreliable volunteers, under challenging conditions, and usually with little or no appreciation. Most lay people have no idea how hard it is being a church staff member."

"I've learned that much already," I said confirming his statement. "I even heard a church member ask Thurm the other day what he did for a living during the week. Never mind that the poor guy usually works six days a week, burning the candle at both ends just trying to keep up with the hundreds of teenagers in this church."

"You're right, Elmo. I've always said church staff work isn't for slackers, cowards, or wimps." Both Fran and Doreen nodded their heads in agreement. Tom waved the dessert cart over to our table.

The others selected cheesecake artistically drizzled with raspberry sauce and a sprinkling of dark-chocolate shavings. I topped off my dinner with a smooth piece of French silk pie, and as Bob Stevens would say, a cup of snooty coffee.

After dinner, we were informed that Dr Jorgensen was running late, so our evening session was scrapped. We would start in the morning and incorporate the missed agenda items into the morning's meetings. This worked out great for me on two levels. First, I'd get to spend some time that evening getting to know the other staff members a little better. And second, much to my delight, due to the schedule change my Friday morning presentation to the group was cancelled. Momentarily forgetting about my lousy sleeping arrangements, I thought—*now I can get a good night's rest*. I was jarred back to reality by Harry Simpkins's loud howling across the room over something Lois Estrada said.

Most of us just hung around in the great room for several hours sitting in the cushy chairs and telling ministry anecdotes. We had a good time. Just after 9:00 p.m., I did notice the 50-and-older set start slipping away to their rooms. By 9:15, just us younger folks remained along with Tom and Harry. I also knew from experience that these "early to bed" senior adults would be up at the crack of dawn ready to change the world. They'd be making all kinds of racket while the younger generation was trying to sleep in until the last possible minute.

At about 10:00, Tom stood up, stretched, and announced it was bedtime. Lights out in thirty minutes. We all dutifully headed toward our rooms. Harry proudly reminded everyone he was sleeping in the *No-Snore Zone* this year. Fortunately, Bob Stevens and Fred Snooker had already retired for the night. Sure enough, you could hear them cranking out the hits as we walked by their room.

This led Harry to do a little victory dance as he turned into our doorway. "What did I tell you? The Righteous Brothers are already in there performing their double live album." He let out a boisterous laugh as he grabbed his toilet kit and disappeared into the bathroom.

Thurm and I were lying on our beds and talking when Harry padded back into the room in his stylish silk maroon pajamas with matching eyeshade pushed up on his forehead. For some reason, he reminded me of Ernest P. Worrell. Maybe it was the dim lighting in the room. I was going to spend an entire night in a full-size bed with this guy. An intense shiver shot up my spine. Jumping off the bed, I settled into the one chair in the room.

Harry pulled back the covers and climbed in. He fluffed his pillow then eased onto his back, simultaneously pulling the eyeshade down over his eyes. "Now remember boys, no snoring."

"Good night, Harry," I said, smiling at Thurm.

Thurm and I lowered our voices and continued our conversation. In a few moments, Harry let out a sigh and began breathing deeply.

A minute later he began to snore. At first quietly, but then he floored the pedal, and the rafters began to shake.

It was going to be a long night.

14

The Black Toe Enigma

I arose from bed early. Notice I did not say I *awoke* early. In order to wake up you have to have been asleep. Harry was indeed a master snorer, but that wasn't the problem. I came prepared for that possibility because I always carry foam earplugs when I travel.

I'm from a large family of snorers. Both my parents were robust snorers, and after forty years of marriage, they would actually harmonize as they sawed logs side-by-side in—that's right—a full-size bed. Neither my siblings nor I ever got any sleep on family vacations. My parents would then have the gall to wonder why we were always cranky on those long car rides.

No, I was ready for Harry's snoring. After washing up for the night, I simply jammed in my earplugs and settled in for what I hoped would be a good night's sleep. All went according to plan, and I had just entered into that fuzzy pre-sleep transition zone when— WHAM! Harry kicked me right above my left ankle! It jolted me wide awake, though at first I didn't remember where I was since the room was totally dark. Had there been an emergency like a fire or something? I jerked out my earplugs only to find everything calm and quiet. Except for Harry's snoring, of course.

Man, that was weird. I lay back down, replacing my trusty earplugs. Again I quieted my thoughts and was about to fall asleep when—WHAM! Harry kicked me again! *Surely he's not playing some type of sophomoric prank,* I pondered. I checked. He was still sound asleep.

This happened numerous times during the night at random intervals. I would get thirty or forty-five minutes of sleep, then Harry would kick me through the uprights for yet another three points. I never quite made it to stage five REM sleep.

So when Thurm discovered my disheveled carcass sitting at the breakfast nook the next morning, he found me borderline catatonic.

"Wow, you should consider a transfusion, or maybe an adrenaline shot," he quipped.

"Well, did you get any sleep?" I moved only the minimal facial muscles necessary to form words.

"Not really. Between Harry's snoring and your periodic yelps, I didn't sleep much at all. What was that all about?"

"Harry kept kicking me. And I mean all night long." I yawned.

Thurm smiled. "Restless Leg Syndrome."

"Excuse me?"

"Restless Leg Syndrome," he repeated. "Harry must have RLS."

"You're making that up. You know I'm exhausted, and you think in my weakened, delusional state of mind I'm going to fall for one of your whoppers."

"Not this time, Elmo. This is legit," Thurm insisted. "My grandfather had it. I swear on his humble grave. It usually kicks in at night—so to speak—and people with Restless Leg Syndrome have no control over it. So don't take Harry's kicks personal."

"I just wish I'd known ahead of time. Do you think Harry even knows?"

"He's been married for twenty-five years to the same lady, sleeping in the same bed. He knows." Thurm answered.

"Yeah. I bet she's an amputee by now," I wondered. "Or maybe she wears shin guards under her pajamas."

Even though I was exhausted, the whole thing struck me as quite funny. I took a sip of strong black coffee and shook my head in an attempt to wake up. "Hey Thurm, you got a minute?"

"Sure, what is it?" He pulled up a chair to the table.

I took another hit of coffee then started. "Since I never really made it to a deep sleep last night, I did a lot of dreaming. Most of it's long gone, but I do remember the last dream I had before I got kicked the final time and just got up. Are you any good at interpreting dreams?"

Thurm leaned back and grabbed a pastry from the counter. "I'm no Daniel, but I'll take a stab at it. Tell me about your dream."

"Okay. You know the outside basketball court up on the roof of the First Church Education Building?

"Sure." Thurm nodded his head. "I play in an intramural men's league up there each spring."

"In my dream, I was up on that roof, and there was some sort of children's activity going on—VBS or something. Hundreds of kids were playing on that basketball court with balls and toys and such. And for some reason, there was a big hole in the retaining wall that surrounds the roof to keep people from falling off to the street below."

Thurm interrupted. "Let me get this straight. You and a bunch of children are up playing on the roof of the Education Building, and there's a hole in the retaining wall?"

"Yes."

"Well, what did you do?"

"I wasn't sure what to do. No other adults were around, but there were hundreds of kids running every which way."

Thurm leaned forward in his chair. "What happened next?

"I had to do something fast, or some kid was going to run through the hole and plummet six floors to his death. So I just stepped in front of the hole and held out my arms, hoping I would catch them if they ran toward the hole, to save them from falling." I paused, reliving the scene in my mind. "What do you think it means?"

A serious, contemplative look covered Thurm's face as he just sat there quietly for a moment. Then he finally stood up. "I have no idea what your dream means, Elmo. But one thing I can tell you for sure. It'll never be made into a movie."

"What does that mean?"

"You know," Thurm paused. "Think Holden Caulfield."

Huh? I was just too tired to get it.

"If I were you, I'd take a shower before our first session," he suggested over his shoulder as he headed back to our room. "And don't tell anyone else about your dreams."

Loitering in the Great Room, engaged in assorted casual conversations, our group waited for the morning session to begin. In strode Smitty Fitzsimons and Dr. Jorgensen. Horace had spent the night over at Smitty's palatial cabin, which overlooked the 18th green. No full-size bed for Dr. J. No incessant Harry Simpkins's leg kicks. He looked fresh—the fresh look of a man who'd had a wonderful, uninterrupted night's sleep. But I wasn't bitter. Just tired. Horace and Smitty worked the room shaking hands and doling out morning greetings to everyone.

When they got to me, Dr. Jorgensen put his arm around my shoulders. "Smitty, I'm not sure you've been formally introduced to Elmo Jenkins, our current intern. Elmo here is doing a fine job for us. He even covered my tail when I missed the graveside service for Deacon Phillips." He snickered, "He and Thurman had to do the service dressed casually in *golf shirts*."

"Golf shirts—my kind of guy!" Smitty grinned from ear to ear. "Oh, I remember this young man. He's the one who ate all of the hors d'oeuvres at our Open House last April. I believe you came with my niece Dolly?" he recalled while shaking my hand.

I smiled. "Yes, sir. That's correct. Quite the soirée, as I recall. That's where I met Tom Applebee, which led to my internship at First Church, for which I am very grateful."

"Elmo," Dr Jorgensen said, relaxing his grip on my shoulders. "Smitty here plays an important role not only in the life of our church, but also in the life of our city. I believe he has his finger in just about everything on this end of the state. He's a good guy to get to know."

"Well, nice seeing you again, Mr. Fitzsimons," I said, shaking his hand again. "And thank you for having us here at your beautiful retreat center for a few days. It's a magnificent place."

"You're more than welcome, Elmo. And I hope to see you again next spring at our annual Open House. I'm inviting you now—with or without that rascal niece of mine."

"Wonderful," I said, as they moved on to the next staff member. Of course, I had absolutely no intention of attending that chalky party again. And forget Dolly. I had Bonnie on my mind these days. I made a mental note to call her at the lunch break.

We all settled into our proper places as Tom Applebee started things off with a brief prayer. I have a habit of keeping my eyes open during prayers at meetings and services. It's amazing the things that quietly take place while someone is praying. Today was no exception. While Tom prayed for a productive session, Smitty and Horace whispered back and forth, pointing at Bernard Coggins. Since these were the two most powerful men at First Church, and Bernard was sitting just to my left, I decided I'd better shut my eyes or they might start pointing at me. When Tom concluded his prayer and we all opened our eyes, Smitty was long gone.

I wonder what that was all about.

Smitty Fitzsimons was a deacon at First Church, but he was not and never had been Chairman of the Deacons. Unlike most churches, the Chairman of the Deacons at First Church was mostly a ceremonial office. The real power was to be found in the heads of the different church committees. Smitty chaired two of the most important ones—the Personnel Committee and the Property Committee. Whoever coined the phrase, *"Money brings power and influence,"* surely had Smitty Fitzsimons in mind. Smitty could be the quintessential poster child for that phrase. I had a sneaky feeling whatever had just transpired during Tom's opening prayer didn't forebode well for ol' Bernard Coggins.

In our first session, Dr. Jorgensen gave us the annual State of the Church speech. We learned that giving was up 11% over last year, and that the church now had just over 13,000 members. *With about 10,000 of those people nowhere to be found,* I thought to myself. There is some truth to the supposition that it's much harder to get your name *removed* from a church membership roll than it would be to stroll freely into the Oval Office.

Here I was fighting my cynicism again as Dr. Jorgensen shared the numbers of souls saved and baptized. But all I was hearing was *yada, yada, yada.* How had I become so calloused to the greater purposes of God? Sure, First Church was old school, using old school terminology and old school methods. But people's lives were being changed for the better. The fact is no matter how goofy the local church may get, it's still God's hand-picked vehicle to bring mankind to Himself. So I purposed to lose the cynical attitude and get with the program—or plan, or paradigm, or whatever the latest nomenclature happened to be.

After Dr. Jorgensen finished, Tom discussed the concept of personal sacrifice, particularly related to working in the ministry. He thanked the entire staff for their personal sacrifices, their dedication to the task, and their great team spirit. He then finished the session by presenting two staff awards. Each year the entire staff voted for the *Most Dedicated* staff member and for the *Best Team Player*.

Doreen McGinty won the *Most Dedicated* award for the fourth year in a row. Every staff member at First Church fully appreciated the difficulty of rounding up a hundred-plus volunteers each and every weekend to work in the preschool and children's departments. Doreen spent three to four hours every Saturday evening working the phones and covering all the bases, even though Saturday was technically her day off. Good children's directors are few and far between. A smart church bends over backwards to keep a good one. And First Church was indeed a smart church. The *Most Dedicated* award came with a three-day family getaway weekend to Orlando. Doreen had three kids of her own, so the package was a nice perk for her.

The *Best Team Player* award had to go to a different winner each year, which made last year's winner, Johnny Rochelle, ineligible this time around. Also ineligible: Dr. Jorgensen, Tom Applebee, Doreen McGinty (as this year's *Most Dedicated* winner), and the church intern. That would be me. It may not seem like a big deal, but to be picked by your co-workers as *The Best Team Player* was indeed a huge honor. *The Best Team Player* award also came with the famed and coveted *Mystery Trip* for two. Only Dr. Jorgensen and Tom Applebee knew the destination spot. Last year, Johnny and his wife Sari got to spend a week in Tahiti.

As Tom opened the envelope with the winner's name inside, the anticipation in the Great Room grew thicker than fudge on a sundae. Everyone would joyfully celebrate the winner, but deep down inside they all desperately wanted to win. Tom smiled as he looked at the card. "And this year's winner of the *Best Team Player* award, chosen by a vote of his peers, is—Harry Simpkins!"

"YEEESSS!" Harry hollered. He leapt off the couch he shared with Bob Stevens, spilling coffee all over Bob's tan Dockers. Harry didn't care. He was too pumped with adrenaline. Harry had never won before, though some of the other staff members had won multiple times. The other staff stood to congratulate him

"Chalk one up for the night kicker," I whispered in Thurm's ear.

Lost in the commotion I noticed Bob Stevens—eyes narrowed, futilely trying to towel off the coffee stain on his slacks. Somehow I doubted he'd voted for Harry.

And finally the *crème de la crème*, this year's *Mystery Trip*: a week in Scotland with accommodations at a newly refurbished castle, including tee times at the Old Course at St. Andrews. Rubbing my tender left ankle I tried to imagine what it would be like to play a round of golf with Harry.

I shuddered.

During the break that morning before the second session, I ran into Fred Snooker.

"Elmo," he called, heading across the room toward me. "What do you have planned for the free time after lunch?"

"Thurm asked me to play tennis again, but to be honest I'm looking for an out. There's only so much shame one man can take." I laughed.

"You're that bad?"

"It's actually quite painful to watch."

"No one is that bad," he argued.

"No, I really am," I insisted. "Think of watching your family pet get hit by an eighteen-wheeler."

"Ouch! That *would* be hard to watch." He gritted his teeth. "Well, since you're looking for an excuse, why don't you spend an hour with me? You can invite Thurm to come if you'd like. I brought *The Black Toe Enigma* scrapbook with me. I can explain the story and show you the artifacts. If you're interested, I'll reserve the Crow's Nest. It'll be quiet there."

"Let's do it. Where do I find the Crow's Nest?"

Fred pointed to the elevator door at the end of the south hall. "Just take that elevator all the way to the top. It opens into the Crow's Nest."

The second morning session was a blur. All the staff members presented their proposed budgets for next year. Since I didn't have one, I semi-snoozed through the presentations, staying just lucid enough to look attentive.

Next up—lunch. After a quick gourmet hamburger with French-cut potatoes, I slipped away to give Bonnie a call.

She picked up on the first ring. "Hello?"

"Hey Bonnie, it's Elmo."

"Elmo, I'm glad you called. There's been a development."

A development? Sounds like a new neighborhood or something going in. "I don't follow you."

"The concert is off," she stated matter-of-factly.

Uh oh. What have I screwed up now? "What do you mean the concert's off?"

"Apparently your main man John Mayer ingested some bad sushi or something, and had to cancel his next few concert dates due to food poisoning. What a bonehead," she added, laughing.

I loved it when she threw sarcasm around. Kind of like a good girl's profanity. "Well, crud."

"Let me offer an alternative," she said. "I'll swing by Ticketmaster on the way home from work and get the tickets refunded."

I knew I liked this girl.

"Then why don't you just come to my place for dinner tonight? We can eat and maybe watch a movie. My roommate Peg will be here, but she'll be sequestered in her room finishing her term paper. What do you think?"

"Sounds like a plan. A good plan. They've cut our agenda down some, so we'll be getting back to town around six." I said, realizing I was smiling.

"Then make it seven at my place. Do you like Italian food?"

"I'll enjoy anything prepared by your hands."

She paused briefly. "Well, that was a bit cheesy."

I yawned. "Yeah, you're right. Sorry. I didn't get much sleep last night. But that's another story. Gotta run. I have a meeting with Fred Snooker. See you tonight."

"Bye, Elmo."

The Crow's Nest sat on the pinnacle at one end of the Main Lodge. Shaped like an octagon, it offered a 360-degree scenic view overlooking the entire *Golden Stallion* development. Absolutely stunning.

Thurm and I met in the south hall and rode the elevator together up to the Crow's Nest. We found Fred there waiting for us, holding an old leather photo album.

"Gentlemen, have a seat. Can I get you a cold drink?" he offered.

"No thanks." I looked at Thurm who shook his head.

Fred sat down. "Where do you want to begin?"

"I can't speak for Thurm, but I need you to start at the beginning. I'm intrigued but totally clueless about this big toe thing."

"It's *The Black Toe Enigma*," Fred said, gently correcting me. "Thurm, what have you heard about this?"

"Not a whole lot, Pastor Snooker. I've heard some of the teenagers mention some spooky tooth thing about hidden messages and secret influences. You know, kind of a local *Da Vinci Code* thing."

"Well, *The Black Toe Enigma* was around long before they determined Da Vinci had a code." Fred placed the photo album on the table. "My predecessor, Aaron Spencer, gave me this album sometime in the late '50s. You can see it's quite old. *The Black Toe* legend had been passed along by oral tradition for years until Aaron decided to document it. He chronicled everything he could find out about it and also started collecting what I call the 'TBT Artifacts.' Ninety percent of what's in this album was already compiled before he passed it on to me. I've added a handful of additional artifacts over the years as they surfaced. That gum wrapper you gave me the other day, Elmo, is the first new find in over ten years."

"What exactly is *The Black Toe Enigma*?" I asked.

Fred leaned forward, folding his hands together. "An enigma by definition is ambiguous or inexplicable, and that's what we have here. I can read you the legend and show you the artifacts, but from there your guess is as good as mine. Remember this thing is over a hundred years old—if you believe the legend."

Thurm jumped in. "What does the legend say?"

"Let me just read it to you," Fred said, as he slowly, and carefully opened the album. The first page appeared to be a faded, yellowed piece of paper with several typed paragraphs, obviously typed on an old manual ribbon-style typewriter. Fred had covered the page in plastic to preserve it. He started reading.

The Legend of The Black Toe
Researched and Compiled by Rev. Aaron Spencer
May 16, 1947

Legend has it The Black Toe Enigma began sometime before the turn of the century. It all started with an ill-fated hunting trip. Wiley Smith, Chairman of the Deacons at the time, and another unnamed church member got lost while hunting together late in the fall. An unexpected snow storm caught them off guard while they were many miles away from their camp site. The disoriented hunters stumbled around for several hours in the blinding snow until Wiley stepped through a partially-frozen stream breaking his right ankle and saturating his boot with water, a dangerous predicament in the sub-freezing temperature. The other much younger man took off his own boot and put it on the Chairman's foot, then carried him on his shoulders for many hours until they found shelter.

When rescuers finally discovered Wiley, he was delirious and the other man was nowhere to be found. Wiley could only remember that the young man had saved his life, and that frostbite had caused the other man's toes to turn black. The rescuer never came forward, and for reasons still unclear, Wiley Smith never chose to identify him.

From that time on, the church folk suspected the presence of an anonymous person amongst the flock at First Church who was strong, courageous, and wise . . . and whose blackened, frostbitten toes remained hidden by his right shoe. As Wiley Smith grew older, he would occasionally mention that he'd conferred with The Black Toe. The whispers would circulate, and the legend grew.

And that's how *The Black Toe Enigma* got started," Fred said.

Thurm spoke first. "I don't get what the big deal is. A guy rescues the Chairman of the Deacons and gets frostbitten toes in the process. I mean, I admire his courage, but why are we talking about this over a hundred years later?"

Fred grinned. "It would've been a nice story that ended right there, except for these."

He started flipping through the pages of the album. Handwritten notes signed and dated *The Black Toe* or *TBT* filled the book. Official looking interoffice memos either mentioned something about *The Black Toe Enigma* in the text of the memo, or were simply signed *TBT*. Several church newsletters or newspaper clippings included lengthy stories about *The Black Toe Enigma*. A variety of odd, random items like the gum wrapper I'd found were included as well. Most were dated and included cryptic messages or warnings.

Fred added, "And you have to remember these artifacts were collected over a period of a hundred years."

"So, are you telling us that some church member known only to Wiley Smith, would impart wisdom or guidance through secret contacts or anonymous messages to the leaders of the church?"

"That's one theory," Fred said. "But the range of dates involved would've made our mystery man well over one hundred years old."

"Then what do you think this all means?" I asked.

"To be honest, Elmo, I haven't given it much thought in a long time. Your gum wrapper discovery the other day brought it back to the surface. When I first received this album, I spent quite a bit of time trying to figure out the puzzle. Back then, I concluded that old *Black Toes* was still alive and active in the church. I thought it was my goal to discover who it was. But over the years, I've come to believe that ninety-nine percent of the legend is baloney. And though an actual person may have existed during the '30s, '40s, and '50s going by the code name "The Black Toe," who was covertly influencing the church leadership, he has long ago passed away."

"I can understand how you arrived at your conclusion." I said. "But it leaves many unanswered questions. Why did this really get started? Why did somebody need to act covertly here at First Church? And who has kept the legend alive by planting these artifacts over the years? Just to name a few." I'd obviously been bitten by the *TBT* mystery.

Fred closed the album and handed it to me. "Elmo, why don't you take this for a while and look it over. See what you come up with. I'd be really interested in hearing your thoughts after you've spent some time with it."

The last retreat session came and went, but my mind spent the time elsewhere thinking about the crazy *Black Toe Enigma.* Later, for the two-hour trip back to the church, I chose to ride in the van named *John* with Harry stowed safely in the other van. Negotiating the entire back seat for myself, I slept all the way back to the First Church parking lot.

I may have even snored.

15

The Kiss

Standing on Bonnie's front porch I decided to do one final Elmo checklist:

Fly up—check.
Nose clear—check.
Breath mint in place—check.
Threat of gas—minimal.

I had on blue jeans, my signature flip flops, and an Arizona Cardinals football jersey (a gift). No watch, no rings, no jewelry. I'm not a jewelry kind of guy. Pity the poor girl who ends up marrying me. Perhaps she'll have a family heirloom wedding ring. Now, that would be a twofer.

Ready or not here I come. I pushed the doorbell. I felt really confident about this Elmo/Bonnie thing, and was trying hard not to mess it up. After a minute or so when no one came to the door, I started to lose my confidence. I pushed the doorbell again. *Maybe it's broken, maybe this is the wrong apartment, maybe I'm early, maybe I'm late, maybe I've got the wrong time altogether, maybe she's upset, maybe I ought to get out of here. I'm blushing, I just know it. I'll go back out to my car and call her and tell her I'm lost—which could actually be true.*

I started slowly walking back down the path from her apartment when I heard the door open. *Awkward.*

"Elmo," I heard Bonnie say. "Where're you going, handsome?"

"Well, I, uh . . . well, uh . . . nowhere," I said stuttering, smiling, and blushing all at the same time. "Did you say *handsome?*"

"Yeah, and I meant it."

All of a sudden my confidence returned. Watching Bonnie stand there, leaning against her doorframe, I realized how really attractive she was. Call me smitten, but she was a knockout. She had on old faded jeans with raggedy holes in the knees topped with a navy blue sorority-girl T-shirt with *Got Grace?* written in big white letters. *Now there's some subtle evangelism,* I thought. She'd tied up her long brown hair in a ponytail, and she wore just a wisp of makeup. But what made Bonnie so beautiful were her eyes—her big, bright, beautiful eyes, the perfect blend of green and blue.

"What you got there, Elmo?" she asked, looking at the DVD in my hand.

"It's *The Princess Bride,* one of my personal favorites," I said as I stepped back up onto the front porch. "I thought it might be fun to watch after dinner."

She leaned forward and whispered the movie's most famous line into my ear.

"Ah, I see you're a *Princess Bride* aficionado." I smiled.

She smiled back as she led me into her apartment. "It's one of my favorite movies too."

"I should've known." I closed the door behind us. "Wow. You have a really nice apartment, Bonnie. Cool furniture."

"Most of the good pieces belong to my roommate Peg. I want you to meet her."

We walked down a short hall and around a corner into a small apartment-size kitchenette. Peg was pouring herself a bowl of Cinnamon Toast Crunch cereal.

Bonnie introduced us. "This is Peg Leahy, my roommate and best friend."

Peg looked up from her pouring and set the milk carton on the counter. She extended her hand to me. "Well, if it's not the Dread Intern Elmo," she said with a wink.

I shook her hand laughing, "I see that every occupant of this apartment has seen *The Princess Bride.*"

"I grew up in the Sudan," Peg explained. "It was one of only six videos my family owned. Our copy was dubbed in French with English subtitles. I've watched it literally hundreds of times."

"Wait a minute," I said, "I recognize you from seminary. Didn't we have a class together last winter?"

"Systematic Theology to be exact." Peg chuckled. "I was there the infamous day you tried to sneak out early and accidentally stepped in the hood of that girl's coat, ripping off the fur collar. What a scream. Whatever happened with that?"

"Oooh, that was indeed a day of abject embarrassment, though it does seem kind of funny looking back on it now. It cost me $25 to get her coat repaired, and Dr. Edwards made me write a ten-page paper on ethics." I quickly pivoted, "So you lived in the Sudan?"

"Yes, my parents are missionaries there, and once I complete my degree at the seminary, I'm heading back."

"One of my best friends is in the mission degree program at Harvest Morgan," I said. "His name is Jamie Fulton. He's a black guy about six feet tall and kind of thin, but don't tell him I said that. He's leaning toward Africa when he graduates."

"I've met Jamie. Nice guy. I believe he's thinking about going to the Ivory Coast. Well, kids, I have a term paper to finish." She picked up her cereal bowl and headed toward her room. "Enjoy your dinner and the movie. It's a classic."

Bonnie had cooked a wonderful dinner. This was a pleasant surprise since singles often take a minimalist approach to meals. A married mom with several kids might prepare a meat or main dish, three or four side dishes, a small salad, some sort of bread with butter, and a homemade dessert—all in large quantities in case unexpected guests show up at the table. Add even more for the requisite leftovers, an important staple in a hungry family, and she'd prepared quite a lot of food. Whereas a single person will prepare one dish, often out of a box or a can making just enough for that meal, then wash it down with a can of Coke followed by a tasty pint of Ben & Jerry's finest.

Bonnie had outdone herself by making a three-cheese lasagna, a Caesar salad, and hot, buttery garlic bread. Of course, she served the obligatory cans of Coke—after all, we're both single. She'd covered their *little bitty* kitchenette table with a red and white checkered tablecloth. She'd even set the table with *cloth* napkins— I'm not kidding you! I felt like I was in *Lady and the Tramp*. The final touch— a candle in the top of an empty Sangria bottle with a wicker bottom. I half expected Peg to reappear, red cummerbund in place, with a starched towel over her arm.

To be honest, I was a bit taken aback by her efforts. "What's the special occasion?"

"You Elmo. *You're* a special occasion," she said, misquoting a Marlon Brando line.

"I can see you're a romantic, meaning I'm probably in big trouble. I, like most American males, have no clue what being romantic means."

She laid her hand gently on mine, "I think your naiveté is actually quite charming. Would you mind blessing our food?"

"Sure." I then closed my eyes and stumbled through something no doubt both grammatically and theologically inaccurate, but I did hammer home the *Amen* with gusto. When I opened my eyes looking for some kind of affirmation, Bonnie was smiling one of those *you're-cute-even-though-you're-a-dufus* smiles.

The meal was wonderful. And that's right; we topped it off by sharing a pint of Ben & Jerry's *Chunky Monkey*.

"Bonnie, what do you know about *The Black Toe Enigma?*" I asked casually as we ate our ice cream.

"I have no idea. It sounds like some type of serious though puzzling athlete's foot condition."

"Clever," I said scraping the carton for the last remnant of ice cream. "Actually, you aren't very far off the mark. It has to do with cryptic messages left over the years in various places around the First Church buildings, supposedly left by some mysterious church member who had frostbitten toes."

"Do you know how stupid that sounds?" She stood to start clearing the table.

"I would normally agree, except Fred Snooker loaned me a

scrapbook full of what he calls *The Black Toe Enigma* artifacts. These are actual bits and pieces of evidence collected over the last hundred years."

"Well, what are you going to do with it?" Bonnie asked, placing the last dish in the fridge.

"I'm not sure, but just think how much fun it would be to solve a century-old riddle." I could just sense Bonnie didn't share my enthusiasm on the subject. *I would have to go the TBT journey alone.* I changed subjects. "Hey, let me load the dishwasher."

"That would be great," she said, wiping off the table.

A few minutes later we sat down on the futon in her living room, making small talk and easing back into the old *intimacy zone*. I admit it. I'm *completely* intimidated by the intimacy thing.

Bonnie ran her fingers through the hair over my right ear. "Elmo, I'm really starting to like you. A *lot*. And I think you like me too. I want to get to know you better." She paused. "I've made some premature assumptions in past relationships that led to hurtful outcomes, but I'd like to think I've learned from those mistakes."

I smiled at her. I hadn't had sufficient opportunities to make many relationship blunders, but intuitively I understood what she was saying.

"So tell me, why are you studying for the ministry?" Her question seemed sincere.

"Okay," I said, relaxing my posture, lifting my left arm on the back of the futon, softly touching her shoulder. "Here goes. In my late teens, I started listening for the first time to the messages from the pulpit. Up until that time, I only went to church because my folks expected me to. One Sunday it just started to make sense. Our pastor told stories about guys in the Bible who had the same kinds of doubts and feelings I was having. Yet God still used those guys to literally change the known world.

"Then one day our pastor invited me out for lunch. He said he sensed something special about me, and wanted to know if I would be interested in being discipled for a year. I thought about it for a few days and decided why not. Pastor Ron was cool, and he treated me like an adult. I liked that. I was about halfway through college at the time and still living at home. So we met once a week in the Student Union lounge at my college for about an hour. It seemed pretty lightweight at the time. He'd throw out some question about the Bible, or faith, or spiritual growth, and we'd just discuss it. He'd let me ask questions then give me Bible-based answers. I began to better understand who God was, and that the world didn't revolve around me, and that God has a purpose for my life. Like the Psalmist said, *God had ordained my days before they ever came to be.*"

As I was telling my story, I watched Bonnie closely. I wondered how she'd respond to this bare-my-soul kind of conversation. She appeared genuinely interested, smiling and nodding in approval at the right times.

"After I finished college, I felt a tug in my spirit that perhaps God wanted me to use my gifts and skills, as meager as they are, in some kind of ministry service. With Pastor Ron's encouragement, the seminary seemed like the natural next step.

"And that brings us up to today."

"Elmo, I suspected you had a deep serious side," she said, "but I haven't seen much if it before."

"Yeah, I tend to be more of a life-of-the-party, cut up kinda guy. I guess it helps conceal my insecurities or something." I said feeling uncomfortably transparent.

"Me too," Bonnie offered. "I'm actually quite shy. I know I might've seemed kind of aggressive with you, but to be honest, I had to work up my courage. There was just something about you I liked from the first time we met, and I couldn't shake it."

Flattered, I felt my heart start to soft-shoe around in my chest. And then I did it, surprising even myself—I leaned over and kissed Bonnie. It seemed so natural. She responded, putting her arms around my neck . . . *and man, were her lips soft and warm* . . .

I'd waited for this moment for a long, long time.

"Ta Da! The term paper is finished." Peg's shouted from her room.

We were too focused on each other to pay any attention. Too focused to hear her door open and the footsteps coming down the hall . . .

Peg rounded the corner, caught us kissing, and in her best *Vizzini* voice demanded, "Knock off the lip-lock, I mean it!"

We broke our embrace and I quickly rhymed back, "You wouldn't have known if you hadn't seen it!"

All three of us laughed until it hurt. Finally, after catching my breath, I asked Peg if she wanted to join us for the movie.

"Sure would," she said, plopping into an easy chair. "You all can just rub noses some other time."

We could and we would.

16

The Big Top

Show Time!

As a church staff, everything we did focused toward the Sunday morning worship service (also known amongst us insiders as under *The Big Top*). A large percentage of the congregation knew nothing about First Church apart from its Sunday morning worship service. For many, this service became an integral component of their Sunday morning routine. For others, it held no more significance than, say, a weekly television program they might watch regularly. Dr. Horace Jorgensen, Harry "The Night Kicker" Simpkins, Tom Applebee, Erlene Markham, Louis Estrada (on announcements), and whomever else might be on the platform that day, would mysteriously appear. Each service included some talking, some singing, some preaching, then all the actors would fade back into the unconscious minds of the members as they scurried back out to their cars.

It was a cardinal rule (no Catholic sarcasm intended) that the Sunday morning worship service start promptly at 10:30 a.m. Yet, of even greater importance at First Church, the Sunday morning worship service always, and I do mean *always*, ended by 11:30. This rule had been mandated through decree by the Deacon Board. Most of the other downtown churches started at 11:00 and finished around noon. By ending at 11:30, First Church members had a full thirty-minute jump on getting to the best restaurants for lunch. According to Tom Applebee, several hundred folks attended our Sunday morning service just because of the early start time. For a staff member to cause the Sunday morning service to run late violated this sacred principle, and guaranteed that poor soul a slot on the next Deacons meeting agenda. Not a happy place to be.

After losing a staff member or two over this sacred time issue, and realizing that the Deacons were indeed serious about it, Dr. Jorgenson put in place some helpful tools. First came *The Clock*. Think Mission Control at NASA. *The Clock*, measuring four feet wide by one foot tall, displayed the time in large white digital numbers. Mounted dead center on the front of the balcony, the accurate time was impossible to miss when you stood in the pulpit. Only those on the platform could see it. So it wasn't a distraction for the congregation in the pews, except for the occasional teenager turning around to check the time. During the Sunday morning worship service, per Dr. Jorgenson's instructions, *The Clock* ran backwards— a countdown starting at sixty minutes. With ten minutes left in the service, the numbers changed from white to red and the seconds also became visible for *The Countdown.*

Dr. Jorgensen timed his messages to end before the numbers on *The Clock* turned red. Otherwise, the service would run late, and the Deacons would howl. As an added precaution, he had trained the sound man to flash a bright white light from the sound booth—twice when he had five minutes to go, and once again with one minute left. Over the years, Horace had become the master of a concise summation. Each Sunday morning he would wax eloquently for twenty-four minutes, spinning all kinds of deep philosophical webs, asking penetrating spiritual questions, and challenging the saints to take the narrow road in life. Then, when the white light flashed from the sound booth indicating the sixty-second warning, Dr. Horace Jorgensen would somehow answer every posed question and tie up every loose end. He would finish by inviting those who would like to meet God or move their membership to First Church to join him at the front of the sanctuary.

Upon hearing the words ". . . move your membership," Harry Simpkins would spring to his feet, simultaneously whirling toward the choir in one fluid motion. He would signal them to stand, signal the organist to begin playing, then spin back around just in time for the first downbeat to lead the congregation in the first, second, and fourth verses of *Just As I Am* or *I Surrender All.* I always felt sorry for those poor third verses of hymns . . . all dressed up and no place to go.

If Dr. Jorgenson was the master of the closing summation, Harry was the royal wizard of the closing song. Always in total control, he would wind down everything just in time. If they were running way behind, he'd cut a verse of the hymn. If they were running just slightly behind, he'd pick up the tempo of the song. If they were slightly ahead, he would merely repeat the chorus one more time at the end. This was a fine art, and Harry was the *artiste most excellenté.*

During the invitation, Dr. Jorgenson would stand at the head of the center aisle and greet folks coming forward. He would then pass them off either to Tom Applebee or Louis Estrada, who would walk them over to the counseling room door and turn them over to Erlene Markham. Erlene would then escort them into the counseling room, where trained counselors waited to get their information and answer their questions.

These last ten minutes ran like a well-oiled machine. With just one minute left, Harry would bring the music to a close, and Dr. Jorgensen would close in a brief prayer. By the time the members turned to leave, *The Countdown* was complete. *The Clock* simply flashed *Have a great day!*

I found myself tossed into this tightly-orchestrated intrigue one autumn Sunday morning. Louis Estrada had been called out of town for a family emergency, so Tom Applebee informed me that I would be doing the announcements in his place.

"Elmo," Tom began, putting his hand on my shoulder. "The time has come for you to move up to the next level."

I knew immediately what that meant. "What will I be doing under *The Big Top*?" I asked with a nervous smile.

"You'll be giving the standard announcements and also acknowledging the winners of our Sunday School High Attendance Day. I'll provide you with all the necessary details."

"I'll be there, and I'll be ready," I asserted, acting more confident than I felt.

"Just remember that even though there's some license to vamp off your notes, time control is critical on Sunday mornings. Any overage on our part up front in the service means that Dr. Jorgensen and Harry have to tap dance at the end."

No pressure. "I fully understand, and thank you for this opportunity, Tom."

One of Tom Applebee's responsibilities at First Church included overseeing the Sunday school program. The preschool, children, youth, college, and single ministers and coordinators all ran their respective Sunday school classes, and merely reported their attendance numbers to Adrianne Figghie each Sunday morning. Adrianne then compiled those numbers along with the attendance figures from the forty or so adult classes that met regularly on Sunday mornings at First Church. The *Final Number* would be totaled at the last possible minute to allow time for stragglers, then sent to Tom Applebee's Blackberry just in time for him to make the Sunday School Report at the beginning of the worship service. I would liken his announcement of the *Final Number* to the closing bell of the New York Stock Exchange. Though most members rarely attended Sunday school, the savvy First Church membership knew that a good *Final Number* meant all was well at the church.

Legend has it, one year a redeemed bookie named Benny "Quick Hands" McDonald who attended First Church, fell into temptation, taking bets on the *Final Number* each week. But this side game came to a screeching halt when it was discovered he'd been manipulating the *Final Number* by sending carloads of his old drinking buddies to Sunday school classes each week in order to pad the total. Benny had put a whole new spin on Sunday school evangelism, but alas, in the end it didn't pay off . . . too much of a gamble.

The Adult Sunday School Department at First Church operated under the leadership of a volunteer named Alex Leichhardt. In my opinion Alex was a full-blown schizophrenic. First clue? By day he worked at the Corp of Engineers; by night, he became a used car salesman. On one hand he was this precise, pragmatic, logistical genius; on the other hand, he'd sell a full-sized Hummer with spinners and the ultimate tow package to a widowed grandmother with only one arm. He was supposedly married, but no one had ever seen or talked to his wife. If he had any kids, he never mentioned them. This unique mix of personality traits made Alex the quintessential Adult Sunday School Director, and he excelled at it.

First Church held to a well-accepted set of church growth axioms. They believed:

1. A growing church is a healthy church.
2. The best growth comes through the Sunday school.
3. New groups or classes grow much faster
than existing ones.

To Alex Leichhardt these meant one thing: the more new adult Sunday school classes, the healthier the church. So he set his face like flint to the task of creating new "units" as he called them. It's always amazed me how the church growth gurus can somehow use mathematical formulas to accomplish spiritual goals. I wonder if that's why the book of Numbers is in the Bible. Just a thought.

Every autumn, First Church would have a *Sunday School High Attendance Day*. The goal—to bring in as many people as possible to attend Sunday school on that given day, with the intent that some might just stick around. The planning meetings began in late summer. Several lay members, along with Tom, Alex, and me, comprised a special committee to come up with this year's *Sunday School High Attendance Day* theme. Alex would come up with a list of ten possible themes and bring them to our first meeting.

After introductions and a few general comments, Tom jumped right in. "Alex has prepared a list of ten themes for us to consider. Our goal tonight is to select one of these ten for this year's theme. Alex, how did you come up with these themes?"

Alex straightened in his chair "Well, Tom, I sent out a survey to all of our adult Sunday school teachers and department leaders asking for their suggestions for this year's theme. I received back forty-three suggestions. After removing the prank entrees and the downright silly suggestions, I ended up with about twenty useable themes. Several of these had been used before, or were similar to previous themes, so I culled them out, leaving about fifteen on the list. I then ordered them in a 'best-to-worst' list and kept the top ten for our discussion this evening." He then gave each of us a copy of the list:

1. Choose to honor God by being in Sunday school this year.
2. Sunday school at First Church—there's no better place to be.
3. Let's set a new world's record in Sunday school this year.
4. Do you attend Sunday school at First Church? If not, why not?
5. Make friends, meet needs, attend a Sunday school class!
6. Sunday school: one small step for man, one giant step for First Church.
7. Sunday school—it's the place to be!
8. You can do better. Go to Sunday School.
9. Sunday school. Just do it!
10. What the world needs now is YOU in Sunday School.

Alex gave everyone a few minutes to look over the list then added, "These are in random order, just so you know."

"Well done," Tom said smiling. "I see several great possibilities for us on here. Let's each pick our top three favorites by putting an X in front of them, and then we'll total them to find a winner."

Personally, I thought they were all pretty lame with the exception of number nine, but then again I'm a big Nike fan. We ended up with, *Sunday school: one small step for man, one giant step for First Church.* I envisioned Tom Applebee promoting this by climbing down the pulpit in a space suit. He could have wires attached to simulate the low gravity on the moon, and they could alter his voice to make him sound as if he were speaking on a low wattage transistor radio.

"Now that we have a theme," Tom said, "all we need is a numerical goal. Remember, it needs to be big enough to present a challenge, but not so big that it's self-defeating."

I wonder how many times he's used that line in the past. Somewhere out there Peter Drucker was smiling.

Tom continued, "We've been averaging between sixteen and seventeen hundred in Sunday school so far this year."

Several numbers were bantered around until someone suggested two thousand, a number we could all agree on. I suggested making it "2001" to stay with the space motif created by our theme. They loved the idea. I noticed Tom looking off into the distance as if in deep thought. I just knew he was picturing himself in that space suit climbing down from the pulpit.

Alex took over from there, and ran with it from that day forward. Other than sitting in on a few more meetings, I wasn't very involved in the campaign. But I could see Alex really kicking up some dust. He may have been a competent engineer, but when it came to sales, he kicked into a whole new gear. He designed and posted slick four-color posters all through the church buildings for the *High Attendance Day*. He used an actual photo of an Apollo lunar module with the campaign theme spelled out in stars streaking across the sky and the American flag in the background. It inspired even me. He put together a phone tree to make sure every member at First Church received at least two calls to invite them to Sunday school on High Attendance Sunday. Each member also received two postcards with a big *2001* printed on the front and the theme on the back. He held several meetings with his teachers and directors, most of them resembling those Amway rallies with all the whooping and hollering, and gift giveaways, and special awards, and standing ovations. They too were inspiring. I'd been told that First Church had never failed to hit a high attendance goal since Alex had become director. I made up my mind that if I ever owned my own company, the first person I would hire would be Alex Leichhardt.

The excitement and intensity built for weeks. By the time the *Sunday School High Attendance Day* arrived, the whole church was abuzz with expectation. And somehow, it had fallen upon my shoulders—the lowly church intern—to announce the *Final Number* and the winning adult class with the biggest increase.

That Sunday morning, as I sat down in one of the throne-like chairs on the platform, Tom handed me my list of announcements. He whispered a reminder that he would cue me when it was my turn. I'd watched Louis do the announcements numerous times, but it's totally different when you're sitting on the platform looking out at three thousand plus faces. Shifting uncomfortably in the big chair, I glanced at the list in my hands. There were the two standard announcements; one about the tear-off prayer request flap in the bulletin, and the other about the correct parking lot protocol.

And there it was. The *Final Number* for this year's *Sunday School High Attendance Day*. My hands began to tremble. At this moment, only three people in the world knew this number: Adrianne, who had tabulated it; Tom, who had just received it on his Blackberry; and now me. I felt like Ryan Seacrest. As I regained my composure, I realized Alex had really outdone himself. Yet again I was impressed by this unique man's superhuman ability.

While I waited nervously for my turn behind the big oak pulpit, Miss Geraldine Fitzsimons O'Leary wowed the congregation with her boisterous rendition of *His Eye is on the Sparrow*. They always wheeled out the rotund Miss O'Leary on important Sundays. Not only because she was the undisputed queen of the money note—able to hold a high C for minutes on end—but also because she was Smitty

Fitzsimons's *other* sister. Meaning, she was Annette May Jorgensen's sister and thereby, the Pastor's sister-in-law. You get the idea. Nepotism at its finest.

Geraldine had been briefly married when she was quite young. But the marriage ended tragically when her husband, an older foreign gentleman, died suddenly in his sleep. Her sorrow was tempered by his billion-dollar estate which she inherited upon his death. She never remarried and kept his legal name, though she insisted on being called Miss O'Leary. When her mother Lady Estella passed away, Geraldine assumed her role as matriarch of the Fitzsimons family. She made sure her much younger siblings Smithson and Annette attended the finest universities and were given every opportunity to succeed in life. Smithson, affectionately known as Smitty to all his friends and family, proved to be gifted in the area of business, and assumed responsibility for managing the Fitzsimons's numerous enterprises. This freed up Geraldine to attend to all the necessary social duties befitting her station in society, a role in which she both delighted and excelled.

As Geraldine hit the last refrain high and hard, the congregation rose for the obligatory standing ovation. Tom reached over and touched my arm.

"Elmo, you're up next as soon as the music fades down."

I cleared my throat, swallowed, and sat up on the front edge of my chair. Then, as Geraldine took a subtle bow and glided off the platform, I stood and quickly approached the pulpit with my notes firmly in hand.

Standing there surveying the sanctuary while the crowd was settling back into their seats, I had a calm spirit come over me. I quietly thanked the Lord for it. Sticking to the script, I asked everyone to find their bulletins, then explained about the tear-off prayer request form. Next, I encouraged them to patiently follow the correct parking lot egress procedures, thus assuring the quickest and safest possible exit for all.

Then it was time for the big announcement—the *Sunday School High Attendance Day Final Number*. I asked Alex Leichhardt and his leadership team to stand. Then I asked all of the Sunday school department directors and teachers to stand. Finally, I asked everyone who had attended Sunday school that morning to stand. I guessed about sixty to seventy percent of those in attendance were standing. Alex, Tom, and even Dr. Jorgensen all beamed. As the excitement continued to build, I reminded everyone of this year's theme and our goal to have "2001" in Sunday school attendance.

I paused briefly for dramatic effect, then took a deep breath and said, "And the *Final Number* for this year's *Sunday School High Attendance Day* is—2,764!"

Audible gasps arose from both the congregation and the choir loft, followed by a spontaneous outbreak of cheering and hugs throughout the sanctuary. Alex was beside himself. He worked the crowd like a man who'd just won a seat in Congress. In a most unusual and out-of-character gesture, Dr. Jorgensen gave a very surprised Tom Applebee a big hug. It was a special moment, and I let it continue for a minute or two, even though *The Clock* glared at me the whole time. *Harry Simpkins will just have to tap dance later at the end of the service.* I smiled at the thought.

Finally, I quieted everyone down and asked them to take their seats. Time had come for the announcement of the adult class with the biggest increase in attendance for the day. The entire membership of the winning class would be treated to dinner at Ruth's Chris Steakhouse. Another one of Alex's ideas that had apparently paid off—*big time.*

I held up my note card and as the room grew quiet I announced, "This year's winner is—the Young Married class!"

An outburst of screams and laughter to my left erupted as about three dozen twenty-something's jumped up and started "high-fiving" each other. The rest of the congregation gave them a nice courtesy applause.

And then, for reasons I still do not fully understand, I tagged on an ad-lib, saying, "And we all know how hard it is to get the Young Marrieds out of bed!" Of course, I *meant* to add "on Sunday mornings," but in the excitement of the moment, I left off those three critical words. I didn't even realize my gaffe.

The organ kicked in with the prelude to the next hymn, and I strolled off the platform glad it was over, but generally pleased with my presentation. That was until Thurm grabbed me in the hall and repeated what I had just said, between his outbursts of laughter. After my initial shock wore off, I had to laugh too. It was an honest mistake. What could they do to me anyway? Move my office into a closet?

I told Thurm to take a hike, then I headed off to find Bonnie for an affirming hug. Maybe even a kiss if I were lucky.

17

The Hospital Visit

Monday, Monday, Monday, it's already Monday again. Church work is basically a six-day work week. You work Monday through Friday like everybody else, but then you also work Sunday. Yet it's generally accepted that Sunday doesn't count as a work day, based on the theory that even if you didn't work at the church, you'd be there anyway. Forgotten in this assumption is the fact that Sundays are easily the most demanding day of the work week for those in ministry, often lasting from seven in the morning until nine at night. Our *High Attendance* Sunday had been one of those long, grueling Sundays, so Tom Applebee told the entire staff to take Monday morning off. I knew I liked him.

Swinging by the church at noon, I picked up my hospital visitation slips. Typical Monday, meaning I had ten visits to make, spread out over three different hospitals. Since I'd been making these visits for months now, I'd become rather efficient at getting in, getting it done, and getting out. Ten visits would take a little over two hours. No sweat. That gave me more than enough time to make my weekly appointment with Dr. De Villa at 3:30.

Things were moving along briskly as planned until my last visit. The hospital slip listed the patient's name as Justin Kryder, age 23. His name had been turned in by a friend who attended First Church. A notation indicated he'd been hospitalized due to severe chest pains. *Wow*, I thought. *He's kind of young to be having heart problems.* Still, I planned to pop in, introduce myself, pray with Justin, and slip out. But even before I found his room on the fifth floor, I sensed God laying the groundwork in my spirit for something else.

When I arrived at Room 537, I found Justin sleeping peacefully on his back. Standard protocol for this scenario dictated that I leave my card and not wake the patient. As I gently placed my card on his bedside table and quietly turned to leave, I heard a faint whisper.

"Thank you."

I wasn't even sure he had actually spoken, but when I turned back around, his eyes had opened.

"Well hello, Justin. I'm Elmo Jenkins from First Church. I thought you were sleeping. Sorry, I didn't mean to disturb you."

With the slightest smile, still whispering he said, "That's all right."

He had a gentle face, but with sad eyes. He actually looked much younger than twenty-three, maybe sixteen or seventeen. He sat up and leaned back against his pillows. "I've never been to First Church," he said with a little more volume. "Isn't it that big church downtown? I've seen it on television several times. I don't do church much."

"Yes, First Church is downtown, and I guess it's pretty big. A friend of yours who attends there asked us to stop by," I said, checking his hospital visitation slip again. "But I'm sorry, I don't have their name."

"That's okay. I appreciate you coming. I've been here a week, and you're my first visitor."

"Really?" I said, sincerely surprised. "Don't you have any family here in the area?"

"My mother and father both live here, but they don't get along, and I'm not close to either of them. As far as I know, they don't even know I'm here in the hospital." I couldn't detect any emotion in his voice.

"What about friends?" I asked.

"Oh, I've got a few," he stated, "but I didn't want to bother them with my problems. They've got enough of their own."

"Justin, it says here you're experiencing chest pains. Do they have any idea what's causing them?"

"It's really more of an ache," he said looking at my card. "Mr. Jenkins, are you a minister?"

"Please call me Elmo. I'm really more like a minister-in-training. Though I do all the same stuff the regular ministers do. I just get paid less."

Justin smiled.

"Any idea what's causing your chest to ache?"

"Well, I know I look young, but trust me, I've already lived a lifetime. There's been lots of heartache."

"Oh really," I said stepping closer to his bedside.

He continued. "Yeah. I've run into so many dead-ends in school and family and relationships, and they all hurt, bad. Most of the time I just feel like Bono."

"Bono?"

"You know, the U2 song where the guy still hasn't found what he's looking for?"

"Do you mind if I pull up a chair?" I asked.

"No, not all."

From my perspective, it seems like in today's world, at least in the U.S., there aren't that many open doors to talk to people about God. But Justin had just kicked one wide open, and I wanted to take all the time he needed to answer any questions he might have about faith.

"Justin, what exactly is it you're looking for?"

Who knew that a Bono song could spark a discussion for a

young man to open his life to God? We talked for almost an hour, and I believe with all my heart that Justin made a sincere commitment to follow Christ. Promising to be there for him as he started his new adventure of faith, I gave him my cell phone number. I also made a mental note to talk to Louis Estrada when he got back in town to follow up on Justin with some of the young singles.

At 3:30 on the nose, I strode into Dr. DV's outer office.

"Hey Elmo," Bess said, looking up from her book. "Don't forget to sign the ledger."

I signed the page. "Is the old man here today?"

"Not yet, but he's supposed to be here any minute." She smiled as she carefully placed her bookmark in her textbook and closed it. "Just have a seat."

I sat down as an awkward silence filled the room for several moments.

"I understand you're dating Bonnie St. Hiliare."

Was that a statement or a question? "Wow. Where did you hear that?"

"Peg Leahy and I have several classes together."

"Oh, Bonnie's roommate, Peg, yes. Nice lady. Funny sense of humor."

A gossip's smile crept across her face. "She said she caught you all kissing,"

I felt a blush spreading. "Well, if she said that it must be true."

How did I ever get into this conversation, and how was I going to get out of it?

Suddenly, Dr. De Villa burst in with a flurry, coming to my rescue. I stood as he rushed by me. "Afternoon, Dr. DV."

"Jenkins, is it Monday afternoon already? Dang it, where has this day gone?"

Following him into his office, I closed the door behind me. He immediately made a phone call as I took a seat and waited my turn.

Dr. De Villa's office was quite small with no windows. Floor-to-ceiling bookshelves filled three walls, each slammed full with thick, ancient volumes. His library included tomes on Theology, Psychology, Sociology, and several other "-ologies" that I couldn't pronounce. The thick accumulation of dust suggested that most if not all the books had not been touched in many years. He had set aside two shelves for his collection of bowling trophies, all shapes and sizes. Apparently, he'd been quite the bowler. The trophies appeared free of dust, as if they'd been dusted or at least handled recently. *Curious . . .*

It seemed to me like some form of heresy for theological texts and bowling trophies to occupy the same bookcase. I always thought most bowlers were predominantly of the blue-collar bent, not world-class academicians. Yet Augie broke all the molds for seminary professors. Maybe something deeper explained it; something I was missing. Perhaps he mentally painted each bowling pin with the face of an adversary then mowed them down without mercy. I could easily envision Fred Snooker's face on the head pin, taking the first crushing blow with each new rack.

Dr. DV slammed down the phone. "Morons!" He looked up at me. "Don't even ask."

Not sure how to respond, I said nothing. Something told me this would not be a happy meeting. Or so I thought.

Then Dr. DV, famous for his dramatic mood swings, slowly fashioned a big grin and calmly asked, "What did he say?"

Clueless. "What did who say?"

"Old Fish Face Snooker. What did he say when you gave him the envelope?"

"To be honest, sir, he appeared quite incredulous, but very pleased."

"Good, good." Dr DV came around and sat on the front of his desk. "But what did he say, my young Jenkins?"

"Well, he mentioned that you had owed him that money for over forty years, and he said to be sure to thank you for him the next time I saw you."

"Jenkins, my boy, you have done well, and you shall be rewarded." He paused to ponder, fist against his chin. "Tell you what, you may skip our meeting next week."

Crud! I was hoping for my own envelope with a hundred bucks tucked inside.

He smiled. "Please tell the old man he's been on my mind a lot lately."

I smiled back, "I will. And thank you, sir."

"Now about your internship. Bess tells me you have a girlfriend at the church . . ."

18

The Memo

A single piece of paper occupied my mailbox on Tuesday morning—a memo.

MEMO
From: Fran Bruker
To: Elmo Jenkins
Re: Golfing with Dr. Jorgensen on Thursday

Dear Elmo,

Dr. Jorgensen has requested that you join him for a round of golf on Thursday morning. Denton Persay, one of Pastor's regular Thursday foursome, had to cancel this week. Dr. Persay is a heart surgeon and has a bypass procedure scheduled that morning. Bring your clubs here to the church at 8:00 a.m., and you'll drive over to the Echelon Country Club with the Pastor. Your golf and lunch will be provided courtesy of Smitty Fitzsimons who will also be playing.

Sincerely,
Fran

Though I stink at fishing, and I'm scary bad at tennis, I'm actually a pretty decent golfer. Dr. Jorgensen and I had spent a few minutes at the staff retreat talking about golf, which probably accounted for the invitation. The Echelon Country Club rivaled Augusta in pedigree and prestige. A chance to play such an exclusive course was quite a perk.

I played on the golf team in high school. I wasn't the best player on our team, but I was good enough to fancy the idea of someday playing golf professionally. God must have had other plans, because I never received any scholarship offers to play golf in college. But I still loved the game. Needless to say, Fran's memo came as great news. I couldn't wait until Thursday morning.

In my brief tenure on staff at First Church, I'd already discerned that nothing transpires without a reason—especially if it takes four to five hours of Dr. Jorgensen's time. Throw Smitty Fitzsimons into the mix, and I could guarantee something was cooking. So I thought it wise to run the memo by Tom Applebee for his opinion and seasoned advice.

Adrianne told me I could find Tom up on the roof of the Education Building. I found him sitting at one of the picnic tables in the covered recreation area with his laptop open. Adrianne had told me that on nice days, Pastor Applebee would often steal away to the roof to escape from the phones so he could get some work done.

As I got off the elevator and walked across the basketball court toward Tom, I observed a large patch in the retaining wall. A hole had been repaired—a really *big* hole. Remembering my dream that night at the staff retreat, I visualized myself standing in front of that gaping hole trying to keep the children from falling off the building. I'm not one to give a whole lot of credence to the significance of dreams, but now I was intrigued. I made a mental note to Google *Holden Caulfield* and find out what Thurm had meant.

Tom must have noticed me studying the retaining wall. "Now there's a story," he said, reaching out to shake my hand. "What a day that was."

I toyed with the idea of telling him about my dream, but thought better of it. "Don't tell me. Some 300-pound deacon missed a lay-up and crashed through the wall?"

"Actually, it was a lot more exciting than that." He laughed. "They had one of those mini sky-bucket contraptions up here to mount the court lights up on the light poles. The worker jumped out of it to get something and forgot to set the brake. He turned around just in time to see it smash through the retaining wall and go over the side of the building—sky-bucket and all."

"Oh my!" I exclaimed. "That's *six floors down* to the sidewalk below. Did anyone get hurt?"

"Fortunately, no one was below at the time. But Harry Simpkins's brand spanking new Mustang wasn't so lucky." Tom grinned from ear to ear as he momentarily got lost in the memory of the fateful day. Then discarding any pretense, he laughed out loud. "You see, Harry had just bought it. He'd only had it a couple of weeks. Brand-new red Mustang, fully loaded . . . a bit of a pride issue at play there. And even though we provide free parking for the staff right across the street, Harry decided to park his new car along the curb and pay the meter several times a day. He babied that thing and was worried the doors would get nicked-up if he parked next to other cars, which in all fairness probably would have happened.

"Well, that sky-bucket contraption fell right on top of Harry's new car smashing it to smithereens. The impact turned on the car's CD player at full volume, playing none other than Harry's personally autographed copy of *Air Supply's* greatest hits, to the delight of the small crowd that had gathered to see what had happened. It was surreal, and poor Harry was undone. The rest of us felt bad for him, but I have to be honest— it was also *hilarious*." He laughed again, clearly enjoying the memory.

"We were just relieved that no one was injured or killed. You know, Elmo, someone ought to write a book about Harry and all his adventures. But enough about Harry. What can I do for you?"

I sat down across the picnic table from Tom. "I need some advice." I handed him the memo from Fran and asked, "Any ideas what this is all about?"

Tom smiled as he perused the memo. "Looks to me like you're in for a round of golf."

Hoping for more here . . .

He handed back the memo. "I don't play golf. Bowling is my sport of choice."

Bowling. Again. I was going to have to rethink my attitude toward bowlers. "Ever bowl with Dr. De Villa?"

"No, but I understand he was quite the bowler back in his day."

I stood back up to leave. "So you think there's nothing more to this round of golf than just a round of golf?"

"No," Tom said, closing his laptop. "I didn't say that. It'll be golf first and foremost. Our pastor is very serious about his golf game. But I'm sure there's some secondary agenda; though to be honest I have no inkling what it might be. Just go and have fun. Those four guys have played golf together almost every Thursday morning for years. Be prepared for a small wager of some sort. Oh, and don't be shocked—Dr. Jorgensen always smokes a stogie when he golfs. Pray you ride in the other cart.

We headed back across the court toward the elevator. "Who are the other two guys who play in the group?" I asked.

"Well, let's see. The memo said Denton Persay, the heart surgeon, won't be there. Be glad. Denton's a great guy, but he plays golf angry. And it's not pretty to be around. So that leaves Smitty Fitzsimons, and the fourth member of the group is Hartzel Wiley Smith, the IV."

"As in the great-great-grandson of Wiley Smith, the legendary former Chairmen of the Deacons?" I could hear the excitement in my own voice.

Tom stopped walking and looked at me with astonishment. "How have you found the time or the desire to read back through a hundred years of First Church history?"

"I'm energetic, but not at that level," I admitted. "I heard about Wiley Smith from Fred Snooker."

Tom chuckled. "Ah. *The Black Toe* lore." He pushed the elevator button. "Then you'll definitely want to ride in Harty's cart on Thursday. He knows all about *The Black Toe Enigma*. By the way, did Fred show you that scrapbook?"

The elevator doors closed us in.

As I rounded the last corner of the second-floor hallway on the way to my office, I ran into Dunston Jones. He was pushing one of those non-electric carpet sweepers picking up lint from the hallway carpet.

"Hey, Dunston. How you doing?

"Fine-'n-you?" he said with his famous big grin.

"Do you have a minute? I'd like to ask you something."

"Sure."

"Great." I patted him on the back as we walked into *The Closet* together.

In the middle of my table, I found a paper plate with a dozen chocolate chip cookies covered with Saran wrap. A lavender envelope rested on top of them. Setting the card aside for later, I picked up the plate of cookies and removed the plastic wrap.

"Dunston, would you like a cookie?"

"No thanks, Elmo. I already had one. Miss Bonnie gave it to me when I let her in here 'bout ten minutes ago. Now that's mighty fine!"

"I know. I love fresh chocolate chip cookies," I mumbled as I munched down on one.

"No, I mean Miss Bonnie is mighty fine. I don't know how you ever got her to pay any attention to your sorry grill, but if you have any smarts at all, you won't let that one get away."

"Well, Dunston," I said, pretending to be taken aback, "thanks for the advice."

He nodded. "You're welcome."

Changing topics, I motioned for him to take a seat, and I sat down in the other vinyl visitor's chair. "Dunston, you've been here at First Church for a long time."

He nodded again. "That's right."

"Longer than most of the other current staff members?"

"That's right too," he answered with another nod.

"Then, you probably know more about what's happened within these church walls than just about anybody."

"I s'pose that's possible," he said. "But not everything. Only the Lord knows all that's gone down in this place."

"Okay. We've determined you've been here a very long time, have known many people, and probably know as much or even more about what has gone on here than anyone else, correct?"

He seemed flattered. "Well, I guess that's 'bout right."

"Then All-Knowing Dunston Jones, what can you tell me about *The Black Toe Enigma?*"

He seemed startled. "The black toe what?"

"Enigma. You know, the, uh, mystery or uh, puzzle—*The Black Toe Mystery.*"

He stood up. "Do you mean that crazy folktale about the guy

with the frozen foot?"

I also stood. "Well, yeah."

Dunston burst out laughing as he headed for the door. "Sorry, man. I gotta get back to work." I could hear him laughing all the way down the hall.

Well, that didn't work out the way I'd planned. But something struck me as a bit odd. Dunston was never in a rush to get back to work.

Ever.

19

The Brouhaha

Wednesdays had become my odds-and-ends day. Wednesday morning was the best time to catch a few minutes with Fred Snooker. And, of course Wednesday morning always included the obligatory weekly staff meeting. It was also the one day of the week Bonnie and I could have lunch together. I would then spend the afternoon covering various ministry assignments Tom Applebee had assigned me that morning.

On this particular Wednesday, right before staff meeting was about to begin, Tom pulled me off to one side and asked me to set aside some time in the afternoon to visit Jeremy Cantor. He handed me a slip of paper with Jeremy's phone number and address. He casually added, "Be careful."

For months now, I had been doing funerals, making home and hospital visits, doing some counseling, and helping with benevolence cases. But I had never been warned to "be careful." It caught me completely off guard. *Why would he say that?*

In marched Dr. Jorgensen, and our weekly staff meeting started. Since it had become a known and accepted fact that Bonnie and I were dating, we would sit together during the first part of the meeting. At first, Thurm and friends ribbed us about it, but after a week or two, no one even seemed to notice us.

Bonnie and I had developed a special set of cryptic symbols to communicate during staff meetings. Using these silly doodles, we would make commentary on, satirize, or even filet the different people participating in the meeting. For instance, when Bernard Coggins would drone on and on about something while no one listened, Bonnie would draw a horizontal line with a big hook on one end. It conjured up the image of a vaudeville stage manager giving the hook to a failing actor and yanking him off stage. When Dr. Jorgenson would start randomly eliminating agenda items or cutting people off prematurely, one of us would draw a golf tee to represent a pending tee time he was up against. When Harry Simpkins would get his mouth way ahead of his brain, we would draw a picture of a kicking leg or just write *RLS*. The key to our secret language was to stow away our laughs, then relive them over lunch several hours later. Kind of like retelling or quoting the funny lines from a favorite movie while standing about with your friends. Some things are just funnier the second or third time around.

But this week Bonnie missed the real fireworks. About twenty minutes after the secretaries and directors had been dismissed, Harry Simpkins and Bob Stevens got into a first-class row. Thurm once told me these two mixed it up pretty good at least two or three times a year.

Noticing earlier how unkempt and sleep-deprived Harry looked, I had written *RLS* on Bonnie's notepad. Maybe his wife had decided to kick him back after all these years. An hour or so later, about halfway through Bob's weekly budget/expense update, Harry erupted.

"Bob, my church debit card isn't working again," Harry huffed, obviously exasperated. "I waited in line twenty minutes yesterday to buy some choir music only to have my church debit card declined."

"Well, you know why, don't you?" Bob said with a smirk.

"No, Bob; why don't you tell me," Harry's sarcasm, sharp and pointed. "By the way," he said, turning to the other staff members, "is anyone else having problems with their church debit card?"

"No, Harry, they're not," Bob said curtly. "And the reason they're not is because *they* follow the rules, unlike someone we all know and love."

Harry's face began to redden. "What are you talking about, Bob?"

"I'm talking about receipts and expense reports. You know, those pieces of paper you never bother to turn in?" His voice amping up with each word.

I sketched a small hammer on my agenda sheet. My father used to say that every toolbox has to have a hammer. Bob Stevens filled that role at First Church with no pretense. He hit hard and fast. Damage control would come later.

Harry stood up, leaning over the table toward Bob, waving his extra-large hands in the air. "I forget a receipt now and then, and you cut off my debit card without even telling me? Am I to understand that I was horribly embarrassed yesterday in front of about fifteen people, just so you could try to teach me some kind of obtuse lesson about your stupid procedures?!"

Harry was a big man, with big hands and a large mouth; physically, he could be extremely intimidating. Bob, on the other hand, was small in stature but tough as nails on the inside. And he would have none of Harry's bravado. Not one bit.

Bob leaned back in his chair. "Harry, why don't you just sit down and start following the rules, then we'll see if we can get your card reactivated."

Harry exploded. "Listen, Island Boy, I don't take this kind crap from anybody!"

Dr. Jorgensen had endured enough. "Harry, sit down. I'm requesting that you two stay after the meeting and work out your little problem. Let's move on. What is our next item on the agenda?"

"Our next agenda is our upcoming *Spirit of Grace* conference," Tom Applebee answered, fighting back a smile.

"Well, that's ironic," someone mumbled. Instantly, the room broke into boisterous laughter, totally wiping away any leftover tension. Harry laughed the loudest, and even Bob Stevens attempted a smile.

A church staff is a lot like a nuclear family. There may be a lot of inherent stress, and even the occasional disagreement or two. But when all is said and done, mutual respect and purpose win out. And for the most part, everyone's got everyone else's back. True, even at First Church.

I met Bonnie for lunch at the Fourth Street hotdog stand. The weather was cool, but not cold. My mother would call it *sweater weather*. We ended up eating on a park bench on Main Street near the downtown mall. Following our new Wednesday tradition, we talked back through the facts and faux pas of the morning staff meeting. I gave her an animated play-by-play reconstruction of the Simpkins/Stevens brouhaha.

"I cannot believe that Harry called Bob *Island Boy!* Oh, that's choice." She took a swig on her straw.

"It's the God's honest truth. Just ask Thurm. He'll confirm it."

"You know, it's amazing that Harry has kept his job all these years. If First Church were a pirate ship, any one of the other pirates would have already slit his throat."

"Interesting choice of analogies—First Church as a pirate ship." I smiled, "How far can we stretch that?"

"Let's see," Bonnie jumped right in. "Pirate ships usually have a captain with an inflated ego and well-developed sense of self-importance."

"Oh, that's good," I said. "My turn. Okay, pirate ships are known for collecting and hoarding gold."

"Oooh, that's good too! Let me think . . . how about, pirates are always looking to build or commandeer bigger ships?" She winced a little.

"No, I get it. That works. How about this—the pirates had a captain named Black Beard, and we have a deacon named *Black Toe.*"

"Elmo!" she scolded abruptly. "Please, not that black toe stuff again."

Bonnie didn't share my enthusiasm for solving *The Black Toe Enigma*. I don't know if it was a girl/guy thing or just a Bonnie/Elmo thing, but we didn't see eye-to-eye on the subject. But what do you do? I wasn't going to let my fascination with Old Frozen Foot hinder my relationship with Bonnie. On the other hand, I wasn't going to let Bonnie's indifference keep me from solving the puzzle. I just needed to be more careful not to cross the two streams.

"Bonnie, one more thing." I put my arm around her waist as we walked back toward the church.

She smiled back at me. "Sure."

"Please tell that loudmouth roommate of yours to be more discreet about you and me. I had to suffer through some rather personal interrogations about our relationship from both my seminary advisor and his fruity student assistant."

"Oh, Elmo, I'm sorry."

"No, no, I'm not upset. And it's not your fault. Just tell Peg to cease-and-desist, or I might be forced to put her on *The Rack of Pain*."

"*As you—*"

I kissed her before she could finish as our Wednesday rendezvous came to a sweet close. *La fin.*

Jeremy Cantor wasn't really active in our church or our Singles ministry, but he would show up on occasion. This had been his pattern for the last several years. Jeremy was different. He rarely smiled, but I wouldn't say he was sad. Evidently he'd been deep into hallucinogenic drugs at one time, but as far as I knew, he'd beaten his addiction several years ago. That experience or something equally intense left a discernable hole in his personality. He was never a problem, but the church had a hard time ministering to him or even getting through to him. Yet he kept coming back. Probably just lonely.

Jeremy liked me. He told me I was different from most ministers he'd been around, like I wasn't even a minister. I didn't know if that were good or bad. From the first time I'd met Jeremy, I'd felt led to get to know him and give him a little extra attention. He always seemed a bit out of place but earnestly wanting to belong.

So when Tom Applebee asked me to visit Jeremy, I accepted the assignment without hesitation. Granted, I had a check in my spirit due to Tom's unexpected warning, but I forged ahead anyway.

Jeremy had recently moved to the Lancashire Apartments which were located in a transitional part of the city. Probably not a good place to visit after dark, but in mid-afternoon, I didn't think twice about it. I'd been there once before with Louis Estrada, so I knew right where he lived—Apartment 217 on the second floor.

I was still thinking about Harry and Bob's tiff when I parked my car on the street and started making my way up the first flight of stairs. Approaching Jeremy's door, I could hear some type of New Age music playing inside. If I had to venture a guess, I'd say that it was Yanni—not my personal favorite. I knocked firmly on the door twice. He immediately responded.

"It's unlocked. Come on in."

Opening the door, I turned a quick left, then a quick a right, and entered his living room. Jeremy appeared relaxed, sitting in the middle of his couch, leaning back with his legs crossed. He had on a suit and tie, which I found strange since all I'd ever seen him in were jeans.

"Hey Jeremy."

He looked up. "Elmo. I'm glad it's you they sent over. Grab a seat."

I plopped down on the love seat. "What's with the suit? Did you have a job interview or something?"

"No, I was at the funeral home."

I sat up and leaned forward. "Did someone you know pass away?"

"Nah, I was just making arrangements."

"For your parents or a relative?"

"No, my parents both died when I was quite young."

"Then who—"

"I want you to have something," he said, cutting me off. He reached under his coffee table and pulled out one of those enormous white family Bibles they give you at the funeral homes. The kind that's so heavy you have to grab it with both hands. "I want you or the church to have this." He slid it across his coffee table to me.

I paused. "Jeremy it's beautiful, but I believe these are supposed to be kind of a family keepsake. To remind you of the person who died."

"Yeah, I know." He half smiled. "But I'm not gonna be needing it."

That's when I noticed it. On the couch beside Jeremy, a gun protruded out from under a throw pillow. A pistol of some kind. My heart stopped. I tried to force myself to stay calm, but I failed.

Jeremy looked genuinely concerned for me. "Elmo, what's the matter?"

Having never been trained for this scenario, I wasn't sure what to say. So I instinctively defaulted to being direct. "Jeremy, what's the gun for?"

"Oh, I don't know. I've been doing a lot of thinking lately."

"What kind of thinking?"

"You know, just thinking."

I had no idea what his intentions were. I didn't know if the gun were loaded. I didn't know his psychiatric history. He seemed so totally relaxed, not stressed in the least.

"Have you ever done this type of thinking before?"

"Not really."

"So, this is *new* thinking?"

"Yeah, I guess so."

I almost asked what triggered these thoughts, but I caught myself. "When did you start thinking this way?"

"Not too long ago."

"Okay, *why* did you start thinking this way?"

"If I tell you, you'll think it's stupid."

"Probably not. Try me."

"It's because of a girl."

"No, that's not stupid! Can you tell me what happened?"

"Well, we met at work. Her name is Gracie, and we really liked each other. I looked forward to seeing her every day. And then one day she was gone." Jeremy started to tear up, then he started to sob.

"Where did she go?"

"I don't know," he said between sobs.

I hurt for Jeremy. It was heartbreaking, and I didn't know what to say. So we just sat there in silence as he cried quietly.

A few moments later I heard the front door open, and in rushed a middle-aged woman I'd never seen before, followed close behind by Tom Applebee. I let out a sigh of relief. The women sat down on the couch next to Jeremy and gave him a big hug. He melted in her arms. I quickly reached across the coffee table and snatched the gun from under the pillow. I stood up and handed it to Tom Applebee, my hand shaking uncontrollably.

Later, out on the sidewalk, Tom and I pieced together what had happened. Tom put his hand on my shoulder. "Elmo, I am so very sorry about sending you into that situation alone. I should've known better, but I let myself get distracted by a church staff issue this morning and didn't fully think through my decision."

"Was the gun loaded?" I asked flatly, swallowing hard.

"No."

Taking a deep breath, I released the air slowly. "How did you know to come over when you did?"

"That lady is Jeremy's older sister. She raised him. The funeral home director called her and said Jeremy had just stopped by to ask about buying a cemetery plot. He'd listed his sister as the next-of-kin on the application, so they had her number. She was concerned and called the church. We got here as quickly as we could. Fortunately, it looks like you had it under control."

"Nothing could be further from the truth. I'm just seriously thanking the Lord I didn't witness a suicide . . . or get shot myself. I'll definitely have to go home and change my boxers before tonight's service."

Tom smiled. "Take the night off, Elmo. Tomorrow too."

"Thanks, Tom. I'll take you up on tonight, but tomorrow is my golf outing with the Pastor and Mr. Fitzsimons. After this, tomorrow should be a cakewalk."

"You're probably right. Then we'll see you Friday."

20

The Echelon Country Club

Enjoying an absolutely gorgeous fall morning, I leaned against the trunk of my car waiting for Dr. Jorgensen to arrive. Eighteen holes of golf were just what I needed to clear my head after yesterday's traumatic event. And getting to play at the Echelon Country Club— icing on the cake.

Dr. Jorgensen was never early, but he was also never late. I found it uncanny. So at 8:00 right on the nose, his silver Lexus SE rolled into the staff parking lot.

The tinted window on his driver side slowly rolled down. "Good morning, Jenkins. Just throw your clubs in the trunk." The trunk slowly opened on his cue.

I loaded my clubs as instructed and shut the trunk, then ran around and hopped in the passenger side of his car. "Thank you, sir, for this invitation. This is a real treat for a lowly church intern."

"I'm glad you could come," he said as he patted me on the shoulder. "This course is a real treat for anyone who can manage to get on it. If it weren't for Smitty, even with everyone I know in this town, I wouldn't be able to play there. It's very exclusive."

"Man, that is exclusive. *Uber*-exclusive." I laughed. "Thank you, again."

"You're welcome, but you should really thank Smitty. He's picking up the tab for both of us." He pulled out onto Main Street and headed east. "Tom Applebee tells me you had quite an experience with Jeremy Cantor yesterday afternoon. He said considering the situation, you handled yourself very well."

"Whew," I exhaled, shaking my head. "Definitely a learning experience. God was gracious, and what a relief that Tom got there when he did. What will happen to Jeremy?"

"His sister checked him into the psychiatric ward at St. Michael's Hospital. They'll evaluate him for a few days, then he'll probably move in with her for a while and start regular counseling. I would also suspect they'll set him up on some type of ongoing medication."

I buckled my seatbelt. "I got the impression that whole scenario yesterday was caused by the sudden loss of his girlfriend at work."

"Unfortunately that's not the real story." He continued. "The girl at work had recently been transferred to a different department at a different location because she'd filed a harassment complaint against Jeremy. There *was* no relationship, except in his mind. It's really a very sad situation."

"Well, it was obviously very real to him. I feel for him. Have you seen this type of thing before? You know—guns, potential suicide, that kind of thing?"

"Anyone who's in full-time ministry for any length of time will have his share of those touch-and-go situations. It can't be avoided. There are a lot of needy people out there, and sometimes they just don't know how to deal with their feelings.

"We have a couple in our church right now, super people. I'll call them John and Betty. I consider them friends. John is a dry alcoholic, hadn't had a drinking problem in over twenty years. Last summer, I got a call from Betty asking me to come over ASAP. She said John had a slip-up and they were in a big fight, and she needed me to help with him. So I hustled over there and found them screaming at each other. John was very inebriated. I got them to sit down and stop the yelling, then I tried to get to the bottom of the problem. After about five minutes, things seemed to be calming down when all of a sudden John pulled out a double barrel shotgun from under the couch. First he pointed it at Betty and then at me, and back and forth for what seemed like an hour of pure panic. Finally, their precious eight-year-old daughter, who was awakened by the commotion, came out of her room and said, 'Daddy, what's going on?' John took one look at his daughter, put down the gun and said, 'Pastor, I'm so sorry.' The good news is, Betty forgave him, he got back into an AA group, recommitted his life to God, and they turned it around. As far as I know, he hasn't had a single relapse since."

"Were you afraid?" I asked.

"You bet I was afraid! I sat there praying and re-confessing every sin I could remember. I mentally put my house in order and started trying to wrap my brain around the idea that this could be my last day on Earth. But I also had the assurance that no matter what happened, my future was secure in God's hands. That's one big advantage we have over non-believers—we know the future is secure no matter what happens to our bodies. Understanding that simple fact makes situations like the one both you and I went through more manageable." He paused for a long moment. "But don't be too concerned about it, Jenkins. Those types of scenarios are really quite rare."

Now there was some good news.

106

I guess I didn't fully comprehend what Dr. Jorgensen meant when he used the term *exclusive* in referencing the Echelon Country Club. Not knowing what to expect, I wasn't prepared for the level of service we received. As we pulled into the main entrance, we had to pass through a security gate. The security guard gave both of us a special navy-blue urethane wristband. Each had our last name and the date embossed on it in white raised letters. Dr. Jorgensen said all guests are required to wear these wristbands while at Echelon. We drove down a winding road lined with huge oak trees for about a mile or so, before dead-ending into a horseshoe driveway that curled up to the front of the plantation-style clubhouse. A gigantic front porch stretched across the entire width of the building. White rockers graced the porch, swaying randomly in the breeze. Beautiful flowers, chrysanthemums, sedum, and aster were everywhere.

Dr. Jorgensen pulled his car to the designated spot, and we got out. A valet took the car from there. An attendant greeted us with frosted glasses of fresh-squeezed orange juice and informed us that Mr. Fitzsimons was waiting for us in the guest lounge. Once inside, we walked past the entrance to the Pro Shop. I noticed a small counter sign: *Guest greens fees billed to member's account.* It's a good thing Smitty was paying, because I would've had to sell my car to do so.

Smitty sat at a small table in front of a large window overlooking a pond with three identical fountains, and of course, it was surrounded with colorful flower beds. He stood as we arrived.

"Horace, Ellington—top of the day to you, gents!"

We all shook hands. Dr. Jorgensen had told me this wasn't Smitty's regular club; he just kept a membership here for business reasons since it was close to downtown.

Smitty smiled. "Elmo, I'm so glad you could join us today. It should be a great day for golf. And the Thursday Mediterranean Buffet is always the best lunch of the week."

"Thank you so much for inviting me, sir. I hope I don't embarrass myself too much on the course."

"Don't concern yourself with that," he quipped. "Old Horace is a pretty good golfer, but Harty and I are high handicappers. Speaking of Harty, he's running a little late this morning, so he'll meet us at the first tee. Elmo, you'll be riding with Harty. Horace and I have a special golf cart that's retrofitted with ash trays for our cigars."

"Great," I said, meaning it on several different levels.

After a plate of fruit, Gouda cheese, and a croissant, we were escorted to the Guest Locker Room. We each had our own locker; our names engraved in white on a navy blue nameplate. When I opened the locker, there were my old golf shoes. They'd not only been cleaned up, but polished and outfitted with new soft spikes and new shoe strings. They hadn't looked that good since I bought them several years ago. Also in the locker, a new Echelon golf towel with my name stitched on it in blue. Plus a dozen complimentary Titleist golf balls with my name printed on them above the Echelon logo. To top it off (so to speak), they'd also provided an Echelon Country Club fitted golf hat. How they got my hat size, I'll never know. I don't even know what it is. I put on my golf shoes and new hat, grabbed the towel and golf balls, and followed Dr. Jorgensen out to the cart area. Two carts awaited us, our clubs securely loaded on the back. They'd been cleaned, of course. Even the golf bags sparkled.

I felt like Prince Charles. Everywhere I turned someone asked, "May I help you with that, Mr. Jenkins?" or "Is there anything I can get for you, Mr. Jenkins?" I hadn't been this pampered since I was in diapers. To be honest, all the attention got old pretty fast. Maybe the rich and famous just get used to it after a while.

Sure enough, Hartzel "Harty" Wiley Smith IV was waiting for us on the first tee, a Starbucks *Venti Caramel Macchiato* in his hand.

"Hey boys! Sorry I'm late, but I just can't get cranked up in the morning without a big ol' cup of coffee with lots of sweet stuff in it." Harty smiled really big then took a big chug.

The upper-crusters didn't seem bothered that he was late. Not in the least. These rich folks sure knew how to relax.

"Harty, have you met Elmo Jenkins, our current church intern?" Smitty asked.

"No I haven't, though I've probably seen you around the church." He smiled as he shook my hand.

"Nice to meet you," I said.

"Looks like it's you and me today against the tobacco lobby," he cracked. "Maybe we'll get lucky and their brown lungs will slow them down a bit."

Harty didn't smoke, but you could tell he loved to eat. You might say Harty had a *hardy* appetite. He weighed at least two hundred and fifty pounds, maybe more, and stood only about five feet eight inches tall. I would guess he was in his early forties. Dr. Jorgensen had told me he was into commercial real estate and quite good at it. I imagined he brought a lot of his clients out here to the Echelon Country Club to seal the deal. I bet it worked.

Harty turned toward me, whispering so the others couldn't hear him. "You any good?"

I whispered back. "Sometimes, but not always. I'm kind of streaky."

"Listen. I'm going to challenge these cigar-sucking rubes to a little contest just to get their blood pressure up a bit. Don't worry about the money. I've got it covered, win or lose."

"Okay," I whispered. *No pressure. Yikes!*

Harry turned back toward the other cart, speaking louder this time. "Me and the kid here would like to challenge you cigar lovers to a little wager."

Smitty stepped out of the cart, his stogie tucked in the corner of his mouth. "Bring it on. What's the bet?"

"Our cart against your cart, an eighteen-hole best ball match, one hundred dollars a person, winners take all."

Smitty smiled broadly and looked back at Horace. Horace looked at me. I nodded. He then nodded at Smitty who turned back to Harty. "Let's do it."

I promptly shanked my first drive sideways into the parking lot causing Harty to choke on a mouthful of his macchiato. Thankfully, after a few holes I settled down and we played competitively.

Completing the front nine, we were only one hole down. I noticed the cigars were now nowhere to be found. The other cart seemed to be paying a lot more attention to the match. Conversely, in our cart, Harty and I were more relaxed and getting to know each other a little better.

"Harty, I've been told you're related to the infamous Deacon Wiley Smith."

"Yep, he was my great-great-grandfather, but he died long before I was born."

"Fred Snooker told me all about *The Black Toe Enigma* there at First Church. He said Wiley Smith is a central character in that legend. I'm sure you're familiar with *The Black Toe* story?"

Harty chuckled. "Oh yes. I know all about it, believe me."

"Well, Fred has challenged me to solve the puzzle, so I'm hoping you can shed some light on the whole thing."

"I can solve if for you in four words—a bunch of hooey."

"Harty," I pleaded, "I'm keeping us in this golf match. The least you can do is throw me a few bones about *The Black Toe* thing."

"All right, all right." He stopped the cart. "Here's the straight poop. These are the only verifiable facts in the whole thing. One—my great-great-grandfather Wiley Smith did get lost while hunting in a blizzard, and when they found him, he was near death and delirious. Two—he was Chairman of the Deacons at the time. Three—he was never quite the same after that. Four—he was aided during the storm by someone, but because of the trauma, he could never remember who it was. Five—he was a key a leader at First Church for many years, and during that time accepted advice and counsel from many different people, most of which was given in confidence. Six—as he got older, he suffered a stroke making his speech slurred and hard to understand. The stroke also made him a bit crazy. Seven—it was during the last period of his life that *The Black Toe* thing got started."

"Wow," I blurted out. "It almost sounds as if you had to write a paper on the topic for a college class."

"Close. A speech for my Public Speaking class. Got an A-plus on it," he said with pride. "Now can we get back to the task at hand and focus on taking these boys down?"

"Yes we can," I said. "Onward to the next tee."

Finding my stride on the back nine, I started parring every hole. By the 14th hole, the match was all tied up. Smitty and Pastor made a great team. If one messed up, the other one got a par. My partner Harty was all over the course. He hadn't helped our team at all on the back nine. He needed his dozen Titleists and a few more the way he was losing golf balls, but it didn't seem to bother him. I actually quit paying attention to his shots as I focused on the match, trying to keep us in it. When we arrived at the 18th tee, the match was still all even.

The 18th hole was a short par 4 with a lake down the left side of the fairway and dense woods along the right. Smitty went first and promptly hit two balls into the lake. He called it quits for the day, and went back to his cart for a few last puffs on his cigar. Dr. Jorgensen hit a good drive, but pushed it a little right and it kicked into the trees. I'd been driving well most of the day and piped this one right down the middle of the fairway. Harty was the last to tee off, hitting a big banana slice that started out way over the lake but curved back across the hole, clipped a tree, and bounced back onto the fairway. For his second shot, he hit a low rolling ball that ended up about ten yards short of the green. Dr. Jorgensen was partially behind a tree and had to play out short of the green, ending up about fifty yards away.

I held all the cards. All I had to do was put this hundred-yard wedge shot somewhere in the middle of the green, two-putt, and we would more than likely win. Unfortunately, my adrenaline level was too high, and I hit my shot over the green and behind some shrubs. Dr. Jorgensen then calmly stepped up and hit his third shot landing it about a foot away from the hole. He'd have a tap-in par. In about two minutes, the whole situation had reversed itself. Now Harty and I were scrambling to get a par and not lose the match.

Assessing my unplayable position behind the shrubs, I didn't see Harty step up quickly and hit his chip from in front of the green, but I heard his holler a few seconds later. That rascal had chipped in for a birdie to win the match. I looked up and saw him doing cartwheels across the green. Not an easy task for a man with his build. Dr. Jorgensen just shook his head as he walked back to his cart. I couldn't see Smitty from where I was standing, but I imagined he was probably eating the rest of his still-smoldering cigar. Harty ran over and gave me a big bear hug nearly squeezing the air out of me. What a finish. I figured Smitty would never invite me back out for golf again.

As we were turning in the golf carts, Smitty walked over and handed Harty two crisp one hundred dollar bills and patted him on the back. No words were spoken. The big guy had carded a pretty ugly golf score at well over one hundred, but he made the one shot that counted to win the match. I love golf for stuff like that. I'm convinced that's why so many bad players keep on playing. It takes just one good shot like that to bring them back again, to waste four more hours and spend a lot of their hard-earned money.

Harty walked over to me sporting a huge grin. He put the two one hundred dollar bills together, folded them once, and handed them both to me. "Take your girlfriend out for a nice dinner. You just made my week."

"Are you sure?" I asked.

"Oh yeah," he grinned, slapping me on the back.

We had a good laugh. The kind of laugh that only the winners enjoy.

The Mediterranean Buffet was as good as Smitty had bragged it would be. It featured a variety of shellfish dishes, many sautéed in different wine sauces, complemented by generous mounds of fresh fruits, numerous cheeses, and hot-out-of-the-oven breads. Harty had an appointment, so he couldn't join us for lunch. His loss. Dr. Jorgensen, Smitty and I were seated at a table on the rear terrace of the clubhouse that looked out over the 9th green and surrounding lakes. It was beautiful, and I was hungry. We loaded our plates, said grace, and began the pleasant task of eating the mouthwatering food. Discussion over the main course remained light. We shared a good laugh over Harty's golfing skills and concurrent antics. After the dessert cart had delivered its best and the cappuccino had been served, the conversation turned more serious.

"Elmo," Smitty began, "you've probably conjectured that there was more to today's invitation than just a round of golf."

"Yes sir, I had a feeling that was the case."

"You're a sharp young man, Elmo. I like that about you. When will you be finishing your degree at Harvest Morgan Seminary?"

"This internship at First Church is my last requirement. I've already completed all my class work. So unless I get a bad evaluation from Tom Applebee, I'll be graduating in December."

Smitty laughed as he glanced over at Dr. Jorgensen. "From what Horace and Tom tell me, you're doing a great job. I'm sure that will be reflected in your final evaluation."

I found it interesting and a bit disconcerting that Smitty was doing all the talking while Dr. Jorgensen just sat there passively. Then again, maybe I was misinterpreting the situation. Maybe Dr. Jorgensen had instructed Smitty what to do and say, and Smitty was merely following orders. Similar to how Tom Applebee ran the church staff meetings while everyone knew that Dr. Jorgensen was really the one in charge. A curious leadership style, almost like that of a CEO or even a monarch. That thought gave me a chill.

Smitty continued. "First Church is a great church. Has been for over a century. That said, those of us in leadership are concerned the old girl is starting to show her age to some degree. Our membership is aging. To be frank, we feel our methodology and approach to the local church in today's world just isn't as effective as it used to be. We've all suffered through enough Peter Drucker-type seminars to understand how large organizations go through bell curve life cycles."

Did he say Peter Drucker?

"Horace and I and our other leaders have discussed this thoroughly, and we've decided we will not idly sit by and watch First Church go the way of the dinosaurs. We want to be proactive and help get the First Church ship back on course, to remain effective in our town and in our world."

I was reeling from metaphor overload, desperately needing another hit of coffee with two shots of espresso this time.

"Elmo, let me get straight to the point," Smitty continued. "After you graduate, we would like you to consider joining our church staff full-time." He paused, watching to see how I would react.

His statement caught me totally off guard, and it probably showed. "Well, thank you sir. But in what capacity?"

"The key word for our church's health into the future is *transition.* If you agree to join our staff, we'll be creating a new position just for you—Assistant to the Pastor." Your sole responsibility will be to research and oversee a First Church transition strategy designed to take our church into the future. It won't be easy, but we feel as though you have the skill set and personality necessary for the job."

"Wow." And I meant it. "Mr. Fitzsimons, I'm honored that you'd even consider me for any position at First Church, much less one of such importance. I know Dunston Jones is retiring, and I thought maybe that was the position you might be offering me."

Smitty turned toward Dr. Jorgensen with a puzzled look.

"The old janitor who's retiring next month," Dr. Jorgensen explained. Then they both laughed

"To be honest," I continued, "it's a lot to think about."

Dr. Jorgensen took over for Smitty. "We aren't expecting you to give us an answer today or even for a while. We just wanted you to start thinking about it and praying about the possibility. You would be answering directly to me, and you'd have a lot of freedom and resources available to you. The bottom line is, either First Church starts reaching and assimilating younger folks into the life of our church, or there won't *be* a First Church to worry about twenty-five years from now."

I promised to pray about it and get back to them in a few weeks. God had just laid a huge opportunity in my lap, but I wasn't sure I was up to the task. Fortunately, I had time to get some good counsel.

Dr. De Villa would be no help whatsoever. But I could call my home church pastor, and I would ask for Fred Snooker's sage advice on the idea. I also wanted to run it by Bonnie and get her thoughts. In the short time I'd been around Bonnie, I'd already discovered her to be quite wise for her age and worth listening to.

21

The Gaffe

HELP! Somebody please help!"

Bonnie was trapped in a car upside down with water rising all around it. Two of us tried to free her—me and Johnny Moran. But we needed help! As I scrambled around trying to find a way to get Bonnie out, I thought, *This is so odd. I haven't seen Johnny Moran since I was in junior high school.* In fact, he still looked like he did in junior high. Then I realized that Bonnie wasn't trapped in an automobile—it was some sort of train or subway passenger car. When I looked closer, it wasn't even Bonnie. It was an old friend of mine named Marlene. From in the distance, I could hear this ringing sound. It would ring, pause, then ring again, getting louder and louder each time. I was dazed and confused and getting more confused. The rising water, the loud ringing, the screams from Bonnie, or Marlene or whomever it was . . . louder, higher, louder . . .

BAM! I woke up in a rush to the sound of my phone ringing.

"Yeah?" I yawned into the phone while glancing at my clock. It read 7:30. *On a Saturday morning? This had better be good.*

"Elmo, this is Juliann. Pastor Tom asked me to call all the ministerial staff requesting them to be at church for an emergency meeting at 9:00 this morning in the Executive Boardroom."

I yawned again, bigger this time. "Wow, the EBR? Someone must've died or been arrested or something."

"I really don't know what's up, Elmo." Juliann sounded way too chipper for this early on a Saturday. "Gotta run."

"Wait, wait—Juliann, could you do me a favor? Would you mind asking Pastor Tom to roll the meeting back to, say 11:00? After all, it *is* a Saturday morning, for Methuselah's sake."

"Come on, sleepyhead. Rise and shine," she said with her signature giggle. "I have a half-dozen more calls to make. See ya."

As I hung up, I got ticked. We get one morning off a week and now this.

"What could this possibly be all about?" I grumbled as I dragged my dog-tired carcass toward the shower. And I wasn't about to shave. If they had a problem with it, they'd just have to get over it.

I'd only been in the Executive Boardroom on one other occasion—just a brief stop on my first day guided tour with Tom Applebee. But since that day, I'd heard many a tall tale concerning the "goings on" inside this hallowed room. I had no idea how accurate these stories were, but if you accepted them all as totally valid, the EBR had to be one of the most important rooms in the country—no, make that *the world*.

I arrived early at 8:45, very surprised to be the first one there. If it hadn't been for a hand-drawn sign (*This Way* with an arrow to the left and a pink happy face—thank you, Juliann), I would've thought I was in the wrong building. To get to the EBR, you had to first navigate the Deacons Lounge. Its polished oak door stood open with another one of Juliann's cheery directional signs taped to it. I fished around the Deacons Lounge hoping to score a strong cup of hot coffee, but came up empty. On the bar countertop, Juliann had provided chilled apple juice box drinks and slices of raisin bread. I kid you not. Some poor schmuck was going to marry her one day for her great looks, then regret his decision the first time she prepared food for him.

Snatching up a juice box, I headed for the EBR and plopped down on one of the perimeter chairs. Over the next fifteen minutes, they all trickled in, most with coffee in hand from Starbucks or McDonald's or wherever.

Note to self: when Juliann is in charge of refreshments, pick up a cup of coffee on the way in.

And for the record, I didn't notice anyone gnawing on a piece of raisin bread.

As expected, Dr. Jorgensen arrived precisely at 9:00 with Smitty Fitzsimons in tow. I casually glanced around the room taking inventory of those in attendance. It appeared to be the entire ministerial-level staff of the church, except—uh oh—no Bernard Coggins. My mind darted back to the incident at the staff retreat when Dr. Jorgensen and Smitty were obviously discussing something about poor Bernard during a prayer. Perhaps the fruit of that discussion had ripened and fallen from the tree, taking old Bernard down with it. Dr. Jorgensen's opening sentence immediately confirmed my suspicions.

"We've asked Bernard to clean his office," Dr. Jorgensen said with a touch of sadness.

I expected an audible gasp or some collective show of emotion by the staff, but no one made a sound. *Very odd.* Everyone in the room knew the phrase *to clean his office* meant he'd been canned, but they were all so stoic about it. I was taken aback.

To fully comprehend the workings at First Church, you had to develop the astute ability to read between the lines. Direct orders were communicated both verbally and in writing, but the real agenda could most often be found in a nuance or subtlety. An integral part of this intrigue included the liberal use of euphemisms. For instance, any use in any context of the word *stragglers* meant we'd all better start getting our tails to meetings on time. A staff member's name used in the same sentence with the phrase *not-cuttin'-it* meant he was in serious jeopardy of being asked to *clean his office*. If a staff member weren't pulling his weight in a particular ministry area, the entire ministerial staff would get a general "pep talk" on the subject with the clear implication that someone in the room was *not-cuttin'-it*. Each staff member then had to discern if he or she were the culprit and what needed to be done to *get it fixed,* another oft-used code phrase.

Why things weren't more straightforward puzzled me, but it probably had something to do with the First Church mystic. The place had something of a *secret society* ambience about it.

So everyone sitting in the EBR immediately knew that Bernard Coggins had been fired and was long gone.

When I first started my internship, Thurm had explained the exit protocol First Church used when terminating a staff member. When I heard the procedure delineated, I assumed it had been borrowed from the corporate world. Of note, Dr. Jorgensen never participated in any staff dismissals. By staying disconnected from the process, he reasoned he could still be available to the individual as their pastor if needed. The great irony rested in the fact that *he* had been the one who initiated the dismissal proceedings in most cases.

First, the staff member's supervisor and the Chairman of the Personnel Committee would call in the poor chap for a meeting. In this meeting, he would be advised of his termination and the reasons why, most commonly a sub-par job evaluation (translated – *not-cuttin'-it*). He would also be informed that no appeal process would be offered. They would then produce a severance check based on the fired employee's tenure and a "termination agreement." Of course, for the fired employee to receive the check, he had to first sign the agreement. By signing the agreement, the staff member pledged not to pursue legal action against the church. The fired staff member always took the check.

He was then escorted off the church property, with instructions to come back the following day *after hours* when a Personnel Committee member would stay with him as he cleaned out his office before permanently leaving the premises. It seemed cold and efficient, but it was actually designed to minimize the fallout with the rest of the staff. The severance checks were usually quite generous. The staff leadership made themselves available to help the terminated staff member find another position in another church better suited to his skills and abilities.

The fact that we had all been called in to the EBR meant this was no normal dismissal. We all liked Bernard and knew him to be a diligent worker, faithfully covering some of the most tedious and difficult ministry tasks. Which made his dismissal all the more puzzling.

"Friends, I'm sorry we had to call you back down here on a Saturday," Smitty began. "But it was imperative that we have this meeting before tomorrow's services, so you would all be fully informed in case you're queried about Bernard's sudden departure. I'm not at liberty to share the reason for Bernard's dismissal, but I can say that it was not the result of poor work performance or because of a sexual indiscretion. Bernard has some personal issues to work out, and we will be helping him get the necessary counseling to deal with those issues."

Thurm, seated next to me, pointed to a doodle he'd drawn in his Daytimer. It looked like a couple of horses running in tandem. I had no idea what it meant.

Smitty continued. "If you are asked about Bernard, please simply respond that he left for personal reasons and we wish him well. Nothing more, nothing less. Any questions?"

Harry jumped right in. "Who'll be covering his responsibilities, like the Benevolent ministry and such?"

"Fred Snooker has graciously agreed to fill in until we find a replacement for Bernard."

Yeah right, I thought to myself. *They either offered Fred a boatload of cash or kidnapped his beloved parakeet Peppy, threatening to kill the bird unless he agreed.*

I realized Fred wasn't at the meeting. I figured he might be mapping out an escape route across the Canadian border with Peppy in tow, even as Smitty was speaking.

Finally, Dr. Jorgensen closed us in prayer, we filed out of the Executive Boardroom, and that was that. I grabbed a couple pieces of raisin bread to eat on the way home—*yes I do eat raisin bread*. I rode the elevator down with Thurm.

"What's with the horse doodling?" I asked with a mouth full of raisin bread.

He looked and me and somberly said, "They caught Bernard at the horse track."

In the silence that followed as the elevator quietly descended, no horses reared off in the distance, and no one even considered laughing.

The Sunday morning church services went well. Bernard's sudden departure created quite a buzz, but the damage appeared to be contained. Crossing the street to my car, I heard someone call out my name. I turned to see Tom Applebee waving me to come back. Crossing back over, I met him under the side porte-cochere.

"Elmo, we just realized Bernard was scheduled to handle the baptisms at the evening service tonight. I need you to cover those. Is that okay?"

I gulped. "Well, uh, sure. When and where?"

"Just be at the baptismal room at 5:30. Erlene Markham will meet you there to assist. She does these every week, so she can fill you in on what to do. I'm sure you'll do fine. Oh, and by the way, don't wear long sleeves."

He disappeared back into the church before I could tell him I'd never actually performed an official baptism before. Oh well.

One of the required pastoral training courses at the seminary dealt with the practical skills necessary to be a pastor. I'm not sure if it had an official title or not, but I called it the "Dip 'em, Marry 'em, & Bury 'em" Guide to Pastoral Care. Part of the instruction included two full class periods in a swimming pool to practice baptizing each other. I'm not referring to the aspersion/sprinkling routine. No, we're talking a full-court body slam down under the water, over and over again. Drowning each other for the Lord, amen!

Believe it or not, to immerse someone correctly is actually a fine art. First, you have to decide if you'll take them down to the right or to the left. Contrary to popular myth, this has nothing to do with a church's theology. It's more of a personal preference. I'm a switch-baptizer—I go both ways, though I have a better percentage of success from the right side.

It's very important to instruct the individual being baptized to bend their knees when they go under. Otherwise, both of you may end up on the steps out of sight from the congregation. It's the old baptismal disappearing act. Another problem occurs when some people are more buoyant than others. What if they don't go all the way under? What if the face or nose stays dry? Do you have to do it again? Will this impact their spiritual walk? These are questions I never found answers for.

Back at my apartment, I kicked off my shoes and slacks and fell back on my bed staring at the crack in my ceiling. I'd heard horror stories about baptisms going awry. I didn't want my first experience to be added to that Top Ten list. I briefly considered calling in sick, but eventually decided to forge ahead and, in the famous words of Michael Jordan, "just do it." It couldn't be that tough. I figured there might be one, maybe two people show up to be baptized. Surely, I could do that without screwing up.

As instructed, I showed up at 5:30 in the baptismal room.

Erlene showed me the booklet given to everyone who comes to be baptized, highlighting the major points she would be going over when the candidates arrived. What she neglected to tell me was tonight's number of scheduled baptisms—seventeen! A modern-day First Church record.

After Erlene's brief but informative talk, *(I kept praying she wouldn't curse)* the guys headed off to the men's dressing room and the ladies to theirs. Fortunately we had plenty of baptismal robes. I located the special stall just for pastors in the back of the men's dressing room. There, I found the waders. Whereas the folks being baptized were required to wear a swimsuit or a T-shirt and shorts under the baptismal robe, the pastors usually wore fishing waders over their clothes, so they could quickly get back to the service after the baptisms were done. Unfortunately, no one had bothered to inform me about the small, pinhole leak in the wader's left boot. So I simply slipped off my shoes and jumped into the heavy rubber pants, topping it off with the official white pastor's gown used specifically for this function.

According to established procedure, the minister doing the baptisms goes into the water first, and makes a few general comments to the congregation before he invites down the first person to be baptized. At Tom's cue from the platform, I slowly waded into the water and took my position. The house lights dimmed as the baptistry lights were brought up. About halfway through my opening comments, I realized I had two problems. First, I immediately began to feel my left sock get squishy as the left boot of my waders began slowly filling with water. The second and perhaps more critical problem was the water in the baptistry. It was nowhere near warm. Not exactly ice-cold, but definitely cool. Someone had forgotten to turn on the water heater in the baptistry, most likely one of Bernard Coggins' jobs as overseer of the Baptism ministry. Or perhaps I was the victim of one of Erlene's infamous and often bizarre practical jokes. Either way I quickly calculated that the cool water probably wouldn't be that big of a problem for those getting baptized. After the initial shock, they'd only be in the water for a minute or less. It might even add some energy to the proceedings.

On the other hand, I would be standing in less than comfortable water temperatures for at least fifteen minutes or more. I wondered if hypothermia would come into play. I could see tomorrow's headline: *First Church Intern Drowns While Performing Baptismal Service.* Then there would be a mug shot of Erlene Markham with the caption explaining she was last seen boarding a plane for Montenegro . . .

Alas, in the end it wasn't the cold water or the leaky waders that made this event memorable. No, it was my ever-dependable bad habit of screwing up my words when under pressure. Actually, I'd performed like a champ up until the last person. And then, well . . .

The seventeenth person to be baptized was Katie Cotese. Katie was the twenty-one year old daughter of one of the newer couples at

First Church, Burt and Marion Cotese. Katie had flagrantly flown through the rebellious teen years but recently turned her life around. She was now actively involved in our Singles ministry under the watchful eye of Louis Estrada. Katie was a super young lady. But there was one unique characteristic that made her stand out—literally. Katie was eight months pregnant.

By the time Katie came down the baptistry steps, I had no feeling remaining in my left leg below the knee. Not even phantom pain. I felt like Captain Ahab in search of his missing peg leg. The gown hid Katie's bulging abdomen, but most folks in the church knew about her pregnancy and her single status. They were glad she had turned her life around and started attending church, and thankful she was going to keep her baby.

I reached out and took her hand, helping her into position.

"Our last candidate tonight is Katie Cotese. Many of you know Katie and her parents, Burt and Marion." I turned to face her. "Katie, have you accepted Jesus as your Lord and Savior?"

Katie smiled at me and then at her parents sitting out in the congregation. "Yes, I have."

I was cold, I was sore, and I was ready to wrap this thing up. I took a deep breath. "Katie, my sister in Christ, I now *pronounce* you—"

I stopped mid-sentence. A wave of quiet, astonished laughter rolled quickly across the sanctuary. I hung my head momentarily, disbelieving my own gaffe. "Uh, I mean . . . Katie, I now *baptize* you in the name of the Father, the Son, and the Holy Spirit." And I dunked her.

As she came up out of the water, the organ kicked in with *Blessed Assurance,* and we escaped stage left.

"Katie, I am *so* sorry! I—"

"Don't say another word, Elmo," she said, cutting me off. "It was an honest mistake, and it's no big deal." She gave me a big hug and headed off to the ladies locker room to change.

I really appreciated her attitude, but I knew it would not be so easily forgotten by my co-workers or the church membership in general. I would be ribbed about this for weeks or even months.

It would be included in my obituary one day. I just knew it.

22

The Pity Party

Monday morning arrived. I planned to lay low trying to minimize the abuse I would receive because of my "I now pronounce you" mistake. I hoped Bernard's surprise departure would provide me some cover. Knowing that Juliann would not be a problem, I walked right in the front door intending to sweep by my mail slot then slither up the back way to my office.

"Buenos Dias, Senorita Juliann," I greeted without breaking stride. "Abra la puerta, por favor."

"Ah Elmo," she said pushing the buzzer to open the door. "You know I don't know Spanish."

"I think you know more than you think you know. Gracias!" I dove into the break room, pleased to find it void of any other staff members. The one correspondence in my bottom slot was from Louis Estrada. He asked me to drop by his office first thing. *Oh boy, here we go.* I winked at Juliann as I snuck out of the break room and around the corner toward Louis's first floor office. His door was cracked, so I knocked then stuck my head in.

"Don't tell me Katie's parents have demanded my head on a platter."

Louis looked puzzled. "What? Uh . . . oh. No, not at all. Though that was an unfortunate slip of the tongue. I also heard they forgot to heat the water for you. Tough first baptism, huh?"

"You aren't just kidding." We both laughed though mine was a bit forced. "What can I do for you this morning, Louis?"

He motioned for me to take a seat. "Since you've participated a few times with our young singles, you know what a great group of people they are. As long as I plan structured events with plenty of supervision, everything goes well. But to be honest, there's a real lack of leadership from within the group. Normally, that's manageable, but every once in a while something comes along that requires someone from within the group to step up and take charge. The annual First Church Fall Festival Skit Night is one of those events. As you know, each ministry age group of the church is supposed to perform a ten-minute sketch that Sunday evening. I've been waiting for one of the young singles to jump in, but so far I've come up empty. So I'm asking if you'd consider standing in the gap and pulling this thing together."

I leaned back in my chair and thought for a long moment. "Skit night is what—two Sundays away?"

"That's correct."

"And the sketch only has to be ten minutes long?

"Correct again."

"Do you have a script?"

"No."

"Is there a theme?"

"Yes, *The Ten Virgins.*"

"What?!" I about fell over backward in my chair.

Louis laughed boisterously. "I'm just joking. The topic is yours to pick."

I regrouped. "I know—we can do a sketch on the rapture and call it, *Up, Up and Away.* We could have several singles planted in the audience tied to black ropes and at the given time, have them slowly start rising into the air."

Louis didn't laugh. "Now, don't get too carried away." He missed his own pun. "This is to be performed in front of the entire church family and respectful of all views on eschatology."

Now I laughed out loud. "Where's your sense of humor? I was kidding. Really! I tell you what, Louis old buddy. I'll do this, but you owe me lunch at the Executive Club across the street."

He grinned. "Well Elmo, I believe in some parts of the country they call that *extortion.*"

I smiled back. "Yes, they do, and it's darn good work if you can get it."

This time we both laughed.

When I finally got to *The Closet,* I found a note pinned to my chair.

> *You can't hide forever, Waterboy.*
> *—Thurm*

I guess it's inevitable. I knew I'd have to suffer grief from Thurm on this baptism thing, so I decided to just get it over with. I would take my medicine like a man. I headed toward the south stairwell that led down to his office.

Before hitting the stairs, I made a brief stop at Fred Snooker's office. Fred wasn't in, but his door was unlocked. I decided to leave him a note asking him what would be a good time for us to get together. I needed about thirty minutes or so. I wanted to discuss more about *The Black Toe Enigma,* but I also wanted to ask him about the rift between him and Dr. De Villa. Using Thurm's technique, I pinned my note to his chair, then quietly closed his door. I stepped back into the hallway and headed for the south stairs.

Thurm hung up his phone just as I got to his office. He looked as if he'd just been told his mother had died.

"Thurm, what's the matter?"

He looked ashen. "Do you mind shutting the door?"

I closed the door then took a seat on his couch. "What's going on?"

He came around his desk and sat in his wingback chair. "That was Alise. Evidently, she wants to call it quits."

"What do you mean, call it quits? You mean breaking up? What's the deal? You guys are perfect for each other."

Thurm let out a tired sigh." Well, that's kind of what I thought too, but she sees it differently. This has actually been coming for a few weeks now. As a thick-headed, card-carrying member of the male gender, I just thought if I ignored the problem it would take care of itself."

I sat up on the front of the couch. "If you don't mind me asking, what's the problem?"

"Elmo, you're one of my best friends, and I know I can trust you. But I still need to say this. Please don't share any of what I tell you, even with Bonnie. I'm still hoping to turn it around, so I don't want to do or say anything that might further complicate the situation."

"I promise anything we talk about will not leave this office. I would expect the same from you if the scenario were reversed. So what's going on?"

"Well, it's a pretty common issue. We've been dating for a couple of years now, and she's ready to move it to the next level. And, well, I'm not sure I'm ready to go to the next level."

"Okay, Thurm, bear with me. I'm pretty new at this relationship stuff. What exactly do you mean by 'the next level'?"

"It's basically black and white. She wants to get engaged, she wants to get married, she wants to settle down and start a family."

"Yikes. I see your dilemma."

"I mean, I like the lady. No—I love the lady. What's not to love? She's gorgeous, she's smart, she's employed, and for some inexplicable reason, she loves me. At least, I thought she did."

I stood up and started pacing. "Then what's the problem? Marry her, start a home, make babies. How old are you? Twenty-six, twenty-seven? Remember, your biological clock is ticking."

"You Bozo. That's a women's phobia." He momentarily smiled. "I just don't know if I'm ready to pick out curtains quite yet."

"Well, you really need to pray through this one. Let's be honest; you're not going to find a whole lot of Alise-quality ladies coming your way at this point, and you're plenty old enough to settle down."

"Fortunately I've got some time to think it through. She's going to be out of town for a couple of weeks on some type of job-training junket. When she gets back, we'll talk it out and see what the future holds."

"Sounds like a good plan. Anything I can do to help?"

Thurm stood up. "Well, since you asked—yes there is. But it has nothing to do with my love life. I'm holding an *all-nighter* for my middle-schoolers on Friday night. I could sure use your help. It'll be here at the church in the Youth Room and also up on the roof recreation area. Your job will be supervision. You won't have to prepare anything. I'm short a couple of chaperones, and I could really use a few more."

"Excuse me, did you say all night?"

Thurm laughed. "Yes, that's right. *All night.* Haven't you ever participated in an all-night youth event?"

"To be honest, I don't believe I've ever stayed up all night. You mean, like no sleep? Who *does* that?"

Thurm continued to laugh as he sat down behind his desk. "Oh yeah. It sucks for the adults, but the kids just love it. Be here Friday at 10:00 p.m. Dress comfortably and drink lots of fluids."

"Why lots of fluids?

"Oh, I don't know. I always just throw that one in there for free. Seems like good advice for just about anything . . . except maybe a two-hour staff meeting."

He was still laughing at his own joke as I headed back up the stairs. *Well, at least he's laughing.*

An eventful morning so far. Roped into organizing a Single's skit. Roped into chaperoning an all-nighter. What's next? Tom sending me out to the suburbs on a bicycle to distribute religious magazines door to door? I got chills just thinking about it. Besides, I don't even own a white button-down shirt. *That's it. I'm going to stay right here in The Closet the rest of the day.*

"Elmo?" Adrianne crackled over the intercom.

"Yes, Adrianne. What can I do for you this morning?" *Did I just say that?*

"Pastor Tom gave me your hospital visitation slips for today, and he also needs you to cover his as well. The Mayor asked him to participate in the ribbon-cutting ceremony for the new Battered Women's Shelter opening over by the city library. First Church made a sizeable contribution to the project, and we'll be providing volunteer counselors, so the Mayor thought it would be nice for Pastor Tom to be there."

"No problem. Thanks."

"Oh, and Elmo, you might want to get an early start. I've never seen this many slips on a Monday before."

"Thanks for the heads up, Adrianne. I've always liked you, but please excuse me as I have to go now and kill myself."

"Tough morning, huh?" she fired back. "Well, if you decide to go through with it, please let me know 'cause I've gotta give the slips to somebody. Bye."

I guess we can conclude that Adrianne does not have the spiritual gift of sympathy. Or would that be a spiritual fruit?

I flipped open my laptop and launched Outlook Express.

Dear Bonnie,

Hope you're having a good day. No, make that a great day. You deserve a great day just for putting up with me. Allow me to whine for a moment if you will, and please, no sympathy. Just because I'm crying like a little girl, doesn't mean you should treat me like one.

Well, it's Pile It on Elmo Day. What? You didn't get the memo? Everyone else must have. That communist boss of yours put the strong arm on me this morning to be in charge of the Young Singles skit for Fall Festival Skit Night. He threatened to fire you if I said no. What was I going to do? Actually that's not true. I like Louis, and he didn't use you to leverage his request at all. Anyway, I'm really going to need someone to help me with it—hint, hint?

Then Thurm shot our Friday date night all to heck. He drafted me to be a chaperone for a youth all-nighter. You'll just have to catch up with me Saturday morning over at St. Michael's. I'll be in the ICU. Just look for the multiple IVs, the oxygen mask, and perhaps an eye patch

Then Adrianne decided to pick today to break the Guinness World Record for most hospital visitation slips in one day. I'll be finishing those just in time for the Friday all-nighter, again concluding over at the ICU

This concludes my whine and cheese fest. Hope you enjoyed the rant. Gotta run—I can hear the sick and infirmed calling out my name.

Now where did I put that stethoscope . . .

Love, Nurse Elmo

23

The Espresso

Cue the theme song:

<u>*Captain's Log; Starbucks,*</u>
<u>*Date: Wednesday, October 27th*</u>

After successfully navigating through two days of galactic debris spewed from the exhaust ports of the mother ship USS First Church, I'm now patiently waiting at the remote Starbucks Fourth Street station for Archives Officer Lieutenant Fred Snooker to arrive.

I'm such a geek, but hey, somebody's gotta be.

Fred agreed to meet me at Starbucks, but only after I swore to him it was okay for someone over seventy to hang out there. Besides, I'm banking on his senior adult discount so I can upgrade to a Venti.

"Hey, Pastor Snooker, over here."

"Hi Elmo. So this is what the inside of a Starbucks looks like. Cool!" he said, smiling.

"You threw that 'cool' in there for my benefit, didn't you?"

"Caught me."

"Thanks for coming. I hope Starbucks isn't too much of a culture shock. We can meet at Waffle House next time if you like."

"Cool."

"Okay, enough of that!" I refocused him. "Pastor Snooker, I'd like to spend some time going over *The Black Toe Enigma* stuff, but first I need to ask you a couple of personal questions if that's okay?"

"Elmo, at my stage of life I'm willing to discuss just about anything. The tougher the question, the better. If my blood pressure kicks up a little, that's actually a bonus. Good for the old circulation."

"Okay; as you know Dr. De Villa is my Seminary Internship Advisor. And as you may remember, he asked me a while back to deliver you an envelope."

"Why, yes I do," he said, folding his arms across his chest.

"I've been told by someone I'd rather not name about the *feud*—for lack of a better word—between you and Dr. De Villa. Do you mind

126

giving me some insight into that situation?"

Pastor Snooker straightened in his chair and put his elbows on the table. "I have no qualms in discussing that, but why the interest?"

"For starters, I have a tremendous amount of respect for you. You've not only become a good friend, but I also depend on you as a ministry mentor. Dr. DV, as we both know, is somewhat of a nut case, but he is my advisor and seems to have taken a genuine interest in me. At first, I dreaded our weekly meetings, but he's grown on me over time. But also, it seems Dr. DV and I spend most of our time nowadays talking about *you*."

"About *me*?" he said taken aback.

"Oh yes. It all started with that envelope I delivered to you. Ever since then, he asks about you every week."

"Really? What type of questions?"

"Caring questions—how's your health, what are your kids doing these days, what ministries are you involved in, etcetera. He seems sincerely interested, as if inquiring about a dear old friend."

Pastor Snooker grinned. "He's probably just plotting my assassination."

I laughed. "No, I think he's had some kind of change of heart, and he's reaching out to you through me."

"Well Elmo, I hope that's true. Our situation hasn't been a feud so much as a vendetta from him against me. I'm sure Thurman told you that I recommended the seminary pass over Augie and hire someone else to be the head of the Theology Department."

"Wait a minute. How did you know it was Thurm who told me?"

"Just a guess, but thanks for confirming it. I guess I'll be slashing *his* tires tonight."

"What?"

"It's a joke, Elmo. Even us old toots have a remnant of humor left. Anyway, Augie never understood my motivation for doing that, though I tried to explain it to him. So he went on a twenty-year mission to exact his revenge on me. I believe he even thinks he harpooned my chances of becoming the First Church Senior Pastor. But Smitty Fitzsimons had pushed hard for Horace, and that's actually what ended any hope I had for the position."

"Maybe you should slash Smitty's tires instead."

"No, I have no hard feelings toward Smitty, or Augie for that matter. God had me right where He wanted me. I have no regrets whatsoever. As far as reconciling with Augie, I'm very open to that, but he will have to initiate it. After all, he's the one with the grudge. If you feel led to be the peacemaker between us, that's great. Just let me know what I need to do."

Just the answer I was hoping for. "Pastor Snooker, with your permission I'd like to follow up on the positive signals Dr. DV has been sending out, and see if he really is interested in burying the hatchet, so to speak."

"You have my permission and my blessings on your efforts. Just keep me informed if you will."

"Will do," I said reaching for my TBT folder.

"Hey, would you like some coffee? My treat," he asked hopping up out of his chair using that standard senior adult maneuver that proclaims: *Hey—I look and feel better than my age!*

"Let me warn you," I cautioned, "the coffee at Starbucks is slightly more expensive than other places."

"No problem, Elmo. I'm loaded these days," he said with a rich man's grin. "They offered to double my salary if I'd take on Bernard Coggins' duties, at least until they find a replacement. What could I say but yes? What can I get you?"

"In that case, and since we'll be discussing the *Black Toe* lore, I'll have a Caramel Macchiato Venti. That's what Harty Smith drinks."

"Whatever that is, it sounds good. I'll just get two." He shuffled off to place our order.

That gave me a minute to touch base with Bonnie. I called the church office, and Juliann answered. "First Church, the church that cares for you; how I can direct your call?"

I tried to disguise my voice, but I'm no good at it. "My, what a pretty voice you have, missy. This is Mr. B. B. Wolf. Is Little Red Bonnie-hood in?

"Elmo, you silly. She's at her grandmother's house—duh?" She giggled. "One moment," she added, then sent my call through to Bonnie's office.

"This is Bonnie, how can I help you?"

"Elmo Jenkins, the boy who cares for you; how can I direct your call?"

"Very funny. What's up?" She sounded busy.

"Just confirming our lunch date. Are we still on for noon at Chili's?

"Looking forward to it."

"Good. Unfortunately, it's going to be a working lunch. You've got to help me pull this Singles skit together. Can you bring some of the Whispering Creek drama notebooks with the funny sketches they use in their Sunday morning services? Maybe we can adapt one of those."

"Will do. See you there. Bye"

Pastor Snooker came back with two drinks. "Boy, you weren't just kidding about the pricey coffee. I could get a steak and potato dinner at the Sizzling Sirloin for the cost of these two coffees."

"Yeah, but that's not *cool.*" I smirked.

"Touché." He sat back down. "Okay, what have you discovered about *The Black Toe Enigma?*"

I opened my *Black Toe* file folder. "To be honest with you, Pastor, I'm befuddled. The deeper I dig into this stuff, the more questions I raise. But I'm not giving up. I talked with a few of the old, old-timers. I blackmailed Harty on the golf course to get some input. I even ran it by Dunston Jones, but basically, I've come up empty. The fact of the matter is, other than this old notebook and your knowledge on the subject, there's not much left to go on. I've put together a timeline based on what Harty told me, the dates in the TBT notebook, and any other info I could come by through old church letters, bulletins, and such."

"Well, that sounds intriguing. Let's see what you have," Pastor Snooker said as he leaned over to look at my notes.

The Black Toe Enigma Timeline

1891 – Wiley Smith becomes Chairman of the Deacons. He
      remains chairman for fourteen years.

1898 – He gets lost in a blizzard but is saved by another
      unnamed church member (possibly a deacon)

1921 – Wiley Smith has a debilitating stroke and becomes
      wheelchair-bound. He develops slurred speech, yet
      he continues to participate in the Deacon Meetings.

1925 – *The Black Toe* story begins to circulate within the
      church.

1928 – The earliest known *Black Toe* artifact surfaces; a
      Sunday church bulletin with a handwritten message
      on the back: "See you at the usual spot. 3:00 p.m.—
      The Black Toe." It was discovered in Wiley's papers
      after he died.

1929 – Four artifacts.

1930 – One artifact.

1933 – One artifact.

1936 – Wiley Smith dies. Several *Black Toe* artifacts found
      amongst his papers and files.

1937 – One artifact.

1939 – Article in Sunday Times detailing the *Black Toe* story.

1941 – Two artifacts, including an official church office
      memo signed TBT.

1944 – Aaron Spencer becomes First Church Associate
      Pastor

1946 – One artifact.

1947 – Aaron Spencer creates *The Black Toe*
      Notebook/Album.

1949 – One artifact.

1950 – An article in the church paper by Aaron Spencer
      entitled *The Black Toe Enigma*. In the article, he asks
      anyone with information about the *Black Toe* story to
      please come forward. No one does.

1954 – One artifact.

1958 – Fred Snooker becomes the First Church Associate
      Pastor.

1959 – Onc artifact.

1964 – Two artifacts.
1975 – One artifact.
* Four artifacts discovered after 1975, but all were dated
pre-1975. This includes the gum wrapper I found in my
closet office dated 1959.

Pastor Snooker leaned back in his chair sipping his coffee.
"Honestly, Elmo, I'm impressed. This had to take some time to
compile."

"A little, but it helps me better understand the whole picture.
There are some interesting conclusions we can draw just from this
timeline. For instance, if this anonymous church member were
twenty years old when he got caught in the blizzard with Wiley
Smith, and he died in 1975—the last year on the TBT timeline—he
would've been ninety-seven years old when he died. When you first
told me about *The Black Toe Enigma,* I assumed it had to involve
more than one person, based on the time span. This timeline has
proven that assumption wrong.

"I checked the First Church funeral records for 1975. The
pastoral staff performed eighty-nine local funerals that year, sixty-
seven of them for First Church members. Out of these sixty-seven
dead members, thirty-two were men. Of these thirty-two men, six
were over the age of ninety-five. Four of the six were life-long First
Church members, and three of them had been deacons."

I showed him my notes on the three deacons.

1. Randolph Hitchcock who died at the age of ninety-nine.
2. Snuffy Newton who died at the age of ninety-eight.
3. And William Sinclair Jr. who died at the age of ninety-eight.

"If I were a betting man, which I'm not, I would bet that old
black toe belonged to one of these three *fellas.*"

Pastor Snooker smiled. "Son, you're in the wrong line of work.
You have plumb missed your calling. You should be in forensics. I
can see it now: *Elmo Jenkins CSI.*" He started laughing so hard I
feared he was going to cough up his pacemaker.

"Pastor Snooker," I said, calmly patting him on the shoulder
while nodding assurances to the other startled coffee drinkers. *Yes,
we've got it under control.* "It's really not *cool* to be too rowdy in a
Starbucks. It breaks the accepted decorum. Pretend we're in a
library."

He wiped his eyes. "Sorry. What exactly do they put in this
coffee?"

Uh oh. "Did you order any extras?"

"Well, the kid with the nose ring suggested espresso, so I said,
'Give me a double.'"

Now I really *was* worried about his pacemaker. "I tell you what;
why don't you just let me have your Venti cup there, and I'll get you a

glass of water. Just sit tight and think about your Happy Place for a few moments. I'll be right back."

"Excuse me," I said to the kid behind the counter with the nose ring. "Could I get a glass of water?"

"No problem."

"By the way, why did you give that old guy over there two hits of espresso?"

"That's easy. He said for five dollars he wanted a bang for his buck."

I grabbed the glass of water. "Thanks, just be ready to call 911 if I give you the signal." I walked the water back over to Pastor Snooker.

"Archives Officer Lieutenant Fred Snooker, can you hear me?"

Pastor Snooker shook his head. "What did you say?" He took a big gulp of water.

"I said, how are you feeling?" I sat back down at the table.

"The water is helping, thank you. Where are—I mean, where were we?

"We can do this some other time if—"

"No, no," he stopped me. "I'm fine. Sorry for the outburst. Some coffee. I'm just going to stick with the water if that's all right." He paused for a couple of deep breaths. "Okay, let's continue. What other conclusions have you drawn from your research?"

"Well, there's one small problem with my lone shooter theory. I'm no expert, but it appears to me that the handwriting on the various artifacts changed over time. As if they were written by two, maybe three different people. It's really hard to be certain, because many of the older samples have degraded pretty badly. I also factored in the possibility that if it were just one perpetrator, his handwriting could feasibly change as he aged."

"Well, again I'm impressed. You're using a more technical strategy than I did. I spent more time trying to decipher the cryptic messages on the artifacts."

I sat up in my chair. "So you must have assumed that the legend was true, and you were just trying to find out whom the person was?"

"Yes, but more than that, I was trying to figure out the *why* and the *what*. Why the subterfuge, and what did it all mean? I struck out on both questions, so after a couple of years it became more of a hobby just to see if any more artifacts could be found. Basically, a glorified Easter egg hunt."

"Thank you, sir. That's what I'll do next. I'll list all the artifact messages then cross reference them to check for common words or verses, and see if it leads to anything." I shoved all my notes back into the TBT folder.

Pastor Snooker downed what was left of his water. "Elmo, I think it's great that you've taken an interest in *The Black Toe Enigma*. But don't let it consume you, and don't spend an inordinate amount of time working on it. Remember, the main reason you're here at First Church is to learn about ministry."

We got up and walked toward the exit.

"Oh, I know," I said. "I think I have everything in its proper perspective. I just love solving puzzles. It keeps my mind sharp. Listen, I think you'd better let me drive you back over to the church. I'd hate for you to get a ticket for driving under the influence of strong coffee."

We wcrc both laughing as he held the door open for me. That is until he hurled on my shoes.

Not cool.

My watch read 12:15. *I know I told Bonnie noon at Chili's.*

Certain scenarios in life are full of lousy moments. One of these occurs when you're meeting someone for a meal, but they don't show. It almost always goes down like this. You bust your tail to get there at the agreed-upon time. The restaurant is starting to get crowded, so you make the stupid decision to go ahead and get a table. When the waitress comes by, you explain that you're waiting for someone. You go ahead and order your beverage, but ask to wait on your food order until the slowpoke shows up. It's immediately awkward as you sit there alone nursing a sweet tea, while watching everyone else in the now-full restaurant enjoying a great time with their dinner mates. Then you start to second-guess yourself. *Am I at the right place? Did I get the time wrong? Is this the wrong day?*

The waitress comes by again, and you plead for more time knowing she wants to turn the table. Then you start getting that sick feeling. Did the other person forget? (Always a big self-esteem kick in the head.) You dread calling to remind the person because then *they'll* get embarrassed, and it all gets even *more* awkward.

Then you get mad. *Why don't folks write things down? It's downright inconsiderate!* Now you're hungry, but eating alone sucks. But you've tied up this poor waitress's table for too long, so you order something to go, double-tipping out of guilt, then eat in your car. The rest of your day is basically screwed on several levels. You still haven't accomplished whatever you were getting together for in the first place. So it'll have to be rescheduled, risking a repeat of the trauma. You now have unresolved bad feelings and trust issues with the other person. They're embarrassed and end up apologizing too much, which makes you feel like a jerk.

You get the idea.

So there I was, sitting on the precipice of the aforementioned scenario. And I was not happy about it. I tried Bonnie's cell phone. No answer. I tried her office. She wasn't there. The people in the restaurant lobby waiting for a table were giving me the evil eye. Fuming, I contemplated leaving. Twenty minutes later, Bonnie finally arrived. Preparing to lower the boom, I took one look as her sweet smile and decided to let it go. *Oh, the restraint of a saint!* After all, I desperately needed her help on this skit project, and if we were to get into a fight, I would most assuredly end up doing it solo.

"Elmo, I'm so sorry!" She slid into the other side of the booth. "I got ambushed by Erlene Markham in the church parking lot and had trouble extricating myself from her grasp."

I smiled. "Oh, I know that pain."

Bonnie laughed. "She told me this story about these ancient Greek virility statues that had moving—"

"Stop right there!" I put my hand over her mouth. "I've already had to sneak down the street to the confessional booth at the Catholic church to purge myself of the guilt I carried due to one of her stories. One more of her sordid tales and I'll have to start carrying rosary beads."

She carefully removed my hand from her face. "Hope you washed your hands."

"I always wash my hands. By the way, I tried your cell phone two or three times, but got no answer."

"The battery is dead." She hung her head in mock shame. "Sorry again."

"Okay, I'm over it. Let's move on. Did you bring the skit books?"

"I did."

"I'm starving, so let's order then get right to it."

"You go ahead. I just want a Coke."

"What, and skip the world-famous Southwest Egg Rolls?!" I didn't believe her.

"The students from the pastry college brought by samples of their goodies to the church office, and I've been nibbling all morning."

She then proceeded to describe to me in careful detail each of the specialty pastries. Bonnie expresses herself well, but when she talks about food, she takes it to another level. Whereas in normal conversation her hands play a minor role, when she describes different dishes of food, her hands take over—outlining shapes, sizes, and illustrating textures. It's an endearing quirk I've unofficially labeled *Food Hands*. And the best part is she doesn't even realize she's doing it.

BAM! My egg rolls arrived, saving me from any further culinary play-by-play descriptions. While I inhaled my lunch, Bonnie flipped through the Whispering Creek skit books.

"Here's a possibility," she said, placing the open book on the table. "It's about Peter, James and John arguing with each other. They've borrowed Jesus's car but lost his car keys, and they're frantically trying to find them, all the while blaming each other for losing the keys. Looks like a humorous take-off on the New Testament story about the keys to the kingdom. It ends with them finding the keys and the narrator saying 'They all drove off in one accord.' What did you think?"

"I think it sucks on about three different levels, not the least of which it ends with an old and overused preacher's joke. Besides, we need something to involve more singles and both genders. Next."

"Okay, Mr. Spielberg. How's this one about a church camping trip? The title is *It's Not All About Me.* It calls for a cast of twelve, both men and women. The synopsis states: 'Twelve selfish church members start out on a weekend camping trip, each looking out only for themselves. Fighting for the best seats on the bus, hoarding the snacks, using all the hot water, etc. But they're all drawn together by some humorous adversity. By the end of the skit, they've learned to serve each other.'"

"Now that sounds promising. Do you mind if I take a sip of your Coke? My glass has been empty for at least ten minutes. I think our waitress must be off molting somewhere."

Bonnie handed her glass to me and closed the skit book. "Looks as if you'll need two male and two female leads. The others are all extras with just a line or two."

"Perfect," I said before I drained her glass. "Why don't you schedule the Fellowship Hall for us on Sunday afternoon for our first practice—say 4:00? Also put together a flyer to hand out to the Young Singles Department Sunday morning, then we'll get the ball rolling on this thing."

"Anything else, mein Führer?"

"That was harsh."

"No, this is harsh." She reached across the table and snatched my last egg roll. Two quick bites, and it was gone.

"Dang."

24

The All-Nighter

Coffee at Starbucks, egg rolls at Chili's, but I had saved the best for last—Wednesday Night Family Suppers at First Church featuring Martha's homemade yeast rolls. The bread of the angels. Martha Ross had been the First Church cook for over fifty years, but she didn't look a day over fifty. Only five feet tall, she ran the church kitchen with an iron fist, yet somehow managed to be very warm and friendly. A true kitchen matriarch, if you will. She was known city-wide for her delectable yeast rolls.

I'd figured out the perfect strategy for Family Night Suppers, arriving about ten minutes before the serving lines closed down. When the kitchen closed, Martha would make the rounds handing out any leftover rolls. Everything she cooked was delicious, but her rolls were simply manna from heaven.

I found Thurm sitting alone finishing his meal. "Hey, Thurm. Got room for one more?"

He scanned the six other empty chairs at his table. "Sure, Elmo. For you, we'll make room."

He looked tired.

Setting my tray on the table, I sat down. "I've been meaning to ask you something for some time now. You're the only Thurman I've ever met. How'd you come by that name? Was it your father's?"

"No, my dad's name was Earl. Everyone called him Big Earl. That is until he died of cancer a few years back. He was a good guy."

"So where did the inspiration for the name Thurman come from?"

"Big Earl was a huge lifelong New York Yankee's fan, and Thurman Munson was one of his favorite players."

"The guy who died in the plane crash?"

Thurm popped one of Martha's rolls into his mouth. "My dad cried like a baby when that happened. Absolutely heartbroken. It was a sad day around the Wilson house."

"Speaking of sadness, you look pretty low." I patted him on the shoulder.

Thurm hung his head. "Things have hit a low point with Alise. In fact, we officially broke up. Indefinitely. Chalk one up for male stupidity."

"What's the deal?"

"There's no deal. It's game over. I'm a free man, even though I don't want to be."

"Give it some time. She'll come back around, you'll see. You're one of a kind." He looked as if he were drowning, so I changed the subject. "What's the agenda for the big middle school all-nighter this Friday?"

"We start at 10:00 p.m. with some games in the Youth Room. Then at midnight, we'll have all the pizza they can eat followed by a two-hour movie. Then it's free time up on the roof recreation area—basketball, skate boards, dodge ball—you know, kid games. Then ice cream and another movie, and it winds down by 7:00 in the morning. It's a very full night, and when it's over you'll be extremely tired."

I started to complain about how this all-nighter messed up my date night with Bonnie, but I bit my tongue in light of his current situation. "I'd like to say I'm looking forward to this gig, but to be honest I'm not."

Thurm didn't hear me. He was too busy trying to get Martha's attention to bring the bread tray our way. Unfortunately, by the time she made it to our table the "manna from heaven" had all been distributed.

"Sorry boys," she grinned, "can I get you a cracker?" She disappeared into the kitchen laughing out loud.

Fridays were usually fairly quiet at First Church. Though theoretically a work day, most of the pastoral staff members never came in on Friday. Giving them the benefit of the doubt, I assumed most were either at home preparing for their weekend ministries, or perhaps had meetings or appointments scheduled off-site. This reality often made my Fridays quite busy, having to cover many of the pastoral bases at the church in their absence. By 5:00 on most Friday afternoons, I was exhausted.

With the all-nighter kicking off at 10:00, I knew I needed a strategy or I'd never make it through the night with my body intact. I decided I'd knock off a little early if possible and try to snag a two or three-hour nap before heading back to the church at 10:00. Sure enough, I stayed swamped all day with several benevolent interviews, two committee meetings, and an emergency run to the hospital to check on Miss Fanny Stutson (one of *The Three Widows*) who had fallen and broken her hip. Of course, the other two widows, Emily and Beatrice, were there and beside themselves with anguish. You would've thought all three ladies had broken their hips. And to top it off, Erlene Markham spent the afternoon at the church, so I had to play "duck and run" all afternoon to avoid being drawn into one of her epic conversations.

Limping home about 4:30, I wolfed down a spaghetti and meat balls frozen dinner while watching *Headline News*. My cell phone rang. Bonnie's name flashed on the screen.

"Hey, Bonnie. What's up?"

"You want to grab something to eat?'

"Sorry, I just ingested a frozen dinner, and now I'm heading to bed."

"That's probably not a bad idea. Gonna be a long night for you."

I yawned. "Sure you don't want to join the all-night party?"

"Nope, Peg and I are going to see a chick flick. By the way, I've talked to several people who chaperoned all-nighters before, and they all say the same thing."

"Which is?"

"It's eight long hours of intensely wishing you could go home and go to bed. About fours hours in your legs begin to ache, and then your head starts to hurt, and—"

"Okay, okay, I've got it, thank you very much. No more horror stories."

"Peg's beeping me. Gotta run. I'll call you tomorrow morning."

"Oh no you won't!" I threatened, but she'd already cut me off. If she calls in the morning, I'll have to think up some evil way to get back at her. *I could give Erlene her cell phone number. Oh yeah.* No, that would be cruel and unusual punishment.

I needed to get three or four hours of sleep, but it was only 5:30 in the afternoon. What to do? The situation called for a Baptist cocktail, which every good teetotaler Baptist knows is a shot of Nyquil. Not the recommended dosage up to the designated line on the plastic cup. No, we're talking 'bout fillin' that sucker right to the top of the rim, then lettin' her burn all the way down.

Night, night.

Sleep time is fast time. I awoke at 9:30 that evening with a profound question at the forefront of my mind. *Where did the idea for all-nighters come from in the first place?* I envisioned a group of rational adults in some sort of meeting as they planned their youth calendar. Then the resident moron jumps in, "Why don't we have all the kids come down to the church and spend the whole night running around crazy and screaming and destroying the furniture? Yeah! Yeah, that would be fun." And then the idea spreads like the Ebola virus, maiming and killing adult chaperones from one end of the country to the other, eventually finding its way to my doorstep. I would like to meet this moron and lay hands on him. For prayer, of course.

Arriving at the church at 10:00, I was already tired. A throng of middle schoolers had assembled in the Youth Room on the third floor. Estimating about seventy-five kids in all, I counted only six chaperones. It looked to be a long night.

"Hey, Thurm!" I shouted above the racket. "Where do I pick up my body armor?"

"Elmo! You made it! I had my doubts."

"So did I. Where do you want me?"

"Just hang around the back of the room and look forbidding. We'll be playing some group games for a couple of hours, then the pizza arrives at midnight. If you need any help, just ask one of the other chaperones. They've all done this before. And Elmo, thanks for doing this. It means a lot to me that you're here."

They've all done this before. Great. I'm stuck all night with a bunch of masochists. Finding a padded chair in the back of the room, I kicked my feet up and tried not to fall asleep. By the time the pizza arrived, fatigue had overwhelmed me, but the kids were just getting cranked up. Two caffeine-enriched Cokes later with a slice of pepperoni pizza, and I was back in top form. But then the movie started. Some Disney drivel with dancing and singing animals sent the sleep fairy my way for an up-close-and-personal-visit.

When the movie ended, Thurm herded all of us up to the rooftop recreation area. There was a full-length basketball court, some ping pong tables, and other assorted game areas. A six-foot retaining wall topped by a three-foot chain-link fence surrounded the entire roof. The chaperones were instructed to make sure the kids didn't do anything stupid. They might as well have asked us to solve world hunger.

"Let them run and play hard," Thurm said. "Just don't let it get out of control."

"Sure, whatever you say," I responded. "By the way, where are the chaperone's Tasers stored?"

"Funny," Thurm yelled over his shoulder as he disappeared down the stairwell.

I had a sneaking suspicion he was stealing away for a thirty minute nap somewhere hidden and quiet. I didn't blame him.

One of the other chaperones organized a game of dodge ball and the evening took a sudden turn for the better. I mean, where else can a young adult man throw a rubber ball as hard as he can against the stomach of a bratty thirteen-year-old middle school boy and get *cheered* for doing it? It was the modern-day version of the Roman Coliseum. Now I knew why these other adults were repeat chaperones. Let the games begin!

Twenty minutes into the game, I was still having fun when I realized that even the chaperones were taking a turn in the middle as the target. Meaning, these little punks were going to get a chance to exact their revenge on *me*. Yikes! When my turn came, I figured that dodging the weak efforts of these prepubescent rug rats would be no problem for an agile, fleet-footed gazelle like me. Who knew these

4'10" crumb-crunchers all had arms like Peyton Manning?

I nimbly dodged their first several throws until a small, quiet boy nicknamed Cujo chose to bypass my stomach, rifling a rocket that reached light speed just as it impacted my face. SLAM! I could hear the sickening sound of rubber slapping flesh. I saw stars . . . and noticed everyone stopping dead in their tracks. The place got quiet, but only for a moment as the ball bounced right back to Cujo. He caught it, bounced it a couple of times, and gleefully taunted, "Who's your daddy now?"

The game resumed as I staggered over to a folding chair and sat down. Since my vision was still a bit blurred and my ears were ringing, I didn't notice who was occupying the seat next to me. Eddie Hughes must have slipped in late during the dodge ball game. After a few moments, he blurted out, "Elmo—man, you took that one right in the chops! Bet that stings."

I recognized his voice immediately. "Eddie, what a surprise. Hey, it's a Friday night. I would've guessed you'd be out on the town with some hot lady." I held an unopened can of Coke from the ice chest against the bridge of my nose. It didn't help.

"Well, I made a few calls, but you know the Shriners are in town this weekend. Everyone was already tied up."

"Really?" *I bet he made a few calls. In fact, I bet he'd been making calls all week long.*

Eddie handed me a dish towel wrapped around some ice. "So when nothing panned out, I decided to come over and give Thurm a hand with his all-nighter. It's hard to pass up free pizza."

"You've worked these things before?"

"What can I say? I'm a regular. It's a whole lot better than sitting at home alone, watching *M.A.S.H.* reruns and eating a chicken pot pie."

"Eddie, you're one of a kind."

Adolescent screams cut our conversation short. Glancing up, I saw two middle school boys standing on top of the retaining wall. I couldn't believe it.

"Hey! Get down from there!" I yelled, still aching from my dodge ball smackdown.

I recognized one of the boys as Cujo. "Hurry!" he cried out. "Somebody help! Scotty's falling off the building!"

Both Eddie and I sprung to our feet and raced toward the wall where the boys stood. Halfway across the basketball court, I realized a third boy was up there—hanging from the *outside* of the chain-link fence topping the wall. Hanging on for dear life.

Cujo was now in full-blown panic. "I told him not to do it! I told him not to do it! He's gonna fall, he's gonna fall! Quick, somebody help! He's gonna fall!"

The other boy up there was bent over the fence holding onto Scotty's shirt with all of his might.

"Eddie, quick—give me a step up!" I shouted. Eddie bent over, interlocking his fingers together and forming a toe hold for me. I stepped into his hands and reached up as Eddie boosted me higher until I was able to get both my hands on the top crossbar of the chain-link fence. Using the momentum of Eddie's lift, I pulled myself up onto the wall and quickly handed Cujo down to the other adults below.

It was a precarious perch as the wall was only four or five inches wide from the base of the fence to the edge. There wasn't much room to stand or maneuver.

Scotty was hanging onto the crossbar with both hands, his feet dangling down the outside wall of the building six floors above the street below.

"Son," I spoke to the boy holding Scotty's shirt. "What's your name?"

"Chris, sir."

"Chris, I'm going to lean over the fence and grab Scotty by his belt, then pull him back over the fence. As soon as I get hold of his belt, I want you to let go of his shirt and turn around and jump back onto the basketball court. Do you understand?"

"Yes, sir."

I spread my feet apart and dug my shoes up under the bottom of the fence.

"Eddie, you and a couple of the other guys grab onto my ankles and don't let go for nothing!"

"Got it, Elmo."

Fortunately, Scotty wasn't a very big kid. As soon as I felt the guys hands grip onto my ankles, I leaned over the fence. The crossbar caught me right at my waist. I grabbed his belt with both hands—my heart pumping full force.

"Okay, Chris, you can let go. Now get outta here!"

He released his grip on Scotty's shirt, wheeled around, and someone helped him down off the wall.

I silently prayed for strength. "Okay, Scotty, we're gonna get you back over the fence, but you've got to trust me and help. Okay?"

"Okay."

"Scotty, on the count of three, I'm gonna pull you up. I'll need you to pull up too, then I'll swing you over the fence and some folks on the other side will be there to catch you. Okay?"

"Okay."

"Here we go!" I yelled to Eddie and the others. "Get ready for him!"

"I'm scared!" Scotty croaked.

"So am I, but we can do this if we work together. One, two, three!" And I pulled him up with every ounce of my strength. Either Scotty was lighter than I'd estimated, or I was super jacked-up on adrenaline, because he came up and over the fence more quickly and easily than I'd expected. I released him in mid-air and the chaperones safely caught him. However, my twisting move threw me off balance, and with my feet pinned down by Eddie, I fell backward toward the basketball court headfirst.

Then everything went black.

The next thing I knew, two EMTs were strapping me to a stretcher. As they secured me, I looked up at the retaining wall and realized I'd just pulled Scotty over the exact spot where that big hole had been patched. *Man that's just too weird.*

Then I drifted off into unconsciousness.

In my dream, I had this huge, heavy boulder lying on my head. I couldn't move, and it started to really hurt. So I opened my eyes and found Bonnie staring at me.

"Whoa, what's going on here?" I asked.

She smiled. "What, no eye patch?"

"Huh?"

"Elmo," she said, gently pushing my hair off my forehead. "You're in St. Michael's Hospital. You fell off the retaining wall last night and hit your head on the court. You've been unconscious for the last fifteen hours."

"Man, do I have some headache."

"The doctors say you have a mild concussion. You're lucky. From what I understand, it could've been a lot worse. Eddie Hughes broke your fall and his arm while doing it. He checked out this morning. He'll have to wear a cast for a few months, but he wasn't too upset about it. He mumbled something about 'sympathy dates.' From what I heard, you are *both* heroes."

Looking around the room, I noticed several bouquets of flowers, some balloons, and even a couple of gifts. "What's with all the flowers and stuff?"

"You've had quite a few visitors. They all got to see you drool in your sleep. I even have video."

"Great," I said under my breath. "What visitors? Like from the funeral home?"

"No, you big lug. Let's see. The big bouquet over there is from Scotty Lichen's mother, the kid you pulled back over the fence. She also brought you some restaurant gift cards, which we can certainly use at a later date. She was very, very grateful for what you did. She's also grounded Scotty—I believe she said for the next decade.

"The balloon bouquet is from church staff. Several of them have come by to check on you—Tom Applebee, Fred Snooker, Juliann, Louis, and of course, Thurm. He left the gift bag."

"What's in it?"

Bonnie picked up the green and blue bag and went through it. "Looks like a bag of assorted *Jelly Bellies*, a get well card, and a copy of *The Catcher in the Rye*."

"Do you mind reading the card to me? My vision is still a little blurry."

"Sure." She opened the card.

Dear Elmo,

I'm so sorry about last night and you getting hurt and all. But you're now officially my hero. Your quick action most likely saved Scotty Lichen's life. You are indeed a modern-day Holden Caulfield, so I got you your very own copy of The Catcher in the Rye. *You're also a modern-day Daniel, my friend. I've gained a new respect for the prophetic nature of your dreams. As a matter of fact, I recently had a dream about winning the lottery, and I'd like to discuss it with you when you get a minute.*

Get well.
— Thurm
P.S. Enjoy the jelly beans!

Bonnie closed the card. "What was that all about?"

"Oh, just some Elmo/Thurm esoterica." I did a redirect. "When do I get out of this joint?"

"The doc was just waiting for you to wake up so he could examine you once more. And then, unless you're hemorrhaging from the ears, we should be able to get out of here. He did tell me you should avoid cliff diving, bungee jumping, mud wrestling, and of course, no driving of heavy machinery. At least for the first week or so."

I pretended to be indignant. "Then what am I supposed to do with my time?"

"For starters, sit back and let me feed you your dinner. We'll start with these tasty puréed green beans and corn. Open wide." Bonnie gave me a wicked Nurse Ratchet smile as she jammed the greenish concoction into my mouth.

Yum.

25

The Cold Shoulder

It felt good to get back to the safe confines of my apartment. Thanks to several healthy doses of Tylenol 3, I was lights-out for the rest of Saturday and slept in Sunday morning—with Tom Applebee's blessing of course. My goal was to limp into our first skit meeting at 4:00 Sunday afternoon. After all, we only had a week to pull this thing together. And I theorized the Tylenol 3 would make it easier to tolerate some of the goofy singles I knew would show up for the skit practice. And goofy they were.

Eddie showed up cast and all, and of course wanted to be in the skit. What could I say? The guy may have saved me from serious injury or even death. I figured, what the heck, and gave him one of the non-speaking parts.

Since we would only have ten minutes for the skit, we had to edit it down to one scene. The rest of the story would be filled in with narration which I would do. In addition to the narration, we had four main speaking parts; two guys and two girls. The other eight players only had a few lines, if any. They would be basically be just moving props.

The afternoon's tasks included assigning the different parts, handing out scripts, discussing set props, and setting a rehearsal schedule.

To pick the players, I assessed those in attendance and chose Debbie Jesper (the state Scrabble champion) and Charlise Maldune (an English teacher) for the female leads. For the guys, I selected Bob Druthers and Bob Rickets. In hindsight this was a stupid mistake on my part. Later, during rehearsals I would call for "Bob," and both guys would answer at the same time, causing endless confusion and time loss. I selected the other eight players, including a part for Bonnie, then handed out scripts. We decided to practice both Friday and Saturday evenings back here at the church. Eddie would head up a team to find campground props for our skit, and we all agreed on the type of clothes to wear.

After practice, Bonnie and I headed toward the parking lot. All in all, the meeting had gone pretty well. At least, I thought so. We had a good script, and we were on track to put on a good performance. But when we got into my car to go get a bite to eat, I realized there was a problem. Bonnie didn't say a word. This usually meant she was upset about something.

"What's wrong?"

"Nothing."

"I know better, now come on. Out with it," I said impatiently.

"You know, Elmo, you can be a real jerk at times."

"Excuse me? What are you talking about?" I was hungry, my head still hurt, and I honestly had no idea what her problem was. But I could tell she was really angry.

"You just blew me off with the skit assignments. I helped you pick out the skit and rewrite it, I volunteered to help you pull this thing off in one week, and I get assigned a part with one line, which states—and I quote—"the toilet paper is too rough.""

My defenses went up. "Hey, I was just trying to give everyone who came a chance to participate. If you wanted one of the main roles, you should have said something about it before the meeting. It's not fair to bust my chops over it now."

Then I got *The Bonnie Look*—or stare or whatever it was—with the always accompanying sarcasm. "Okay, Mr. Coppola, you're on your own with this one." She got out of my car, slammed the door, and stormed off.

"Whoa . . ." I said, channeling Keanu Reeves.

It was all I could think of to say.

Bonnie wouldn't answer her phone, so on Monday morning I dropped by the Singles office to see her. What did I get for my extra effort? An ice-cold shoulder. Figuring life was just too short for this kind of crap, I decided to let her stew on it for a while. I had bigger fish to fry. Still, it bugged me.

After lunch, I dutifully stopped by St. Michael's Hospital for a follow-up examination, where I learned that my brain was still intact. The doctor quipped that my hat size might be one or two sizes larger from the swelling. I promised to postpone any fitted hat purchases indefinitely. Noticing that the good doctor sported an Echelon Country Club wristband, I figured he had a collection of fitted hats.

After parking my car in the church staff lot, I noticed a man digging around in the dumpster behind the Education Building. As I approached him, I called out, "Excuse me, sir, are you looking for anything in particular?"

He stopped foraging for a moment and flashed a grimy smile. "One man's trash is another man's treasure." He resumed rummaging around. His right arm boasted a large "Sid" tattoo in murky blue-green Old English letters. He clutched several half-empty bags of chips in his dirty hands.

"My name is Elmo, and I work here at the church. How about you hop out of there and I'll take you inside and get you a plate of food. They serve lunch every day for our volunteers. We can even set you up with a fresh set of clothes if you like.

"No, son, you just go on 'bout your business. I'm not interested in goin' into your church, and I'm not interested in hearin' 'bout your religion."

"But—"

"I said not interested," he snapped. "Comprendo?"

As I climbed the stairs up to my office, I couldn't shake the image of Sid clinging to his scraps of garbage, turning down the invitation to a plate of real food. It painted such a vivid picture of the church in today's world—holding out the Bread of Life and being dismissed by people violently clutching their "trash" while rejecting God's love.

It reminded me of a conversation I had with a good guy named Billy back at my home church. Billy asked me out to lunch one day to talk about spiritual matters. He'd been dating one of the single ladies in our church, and seriously thinking about giving his life to God. But he was reticent. In his skewed view of Christianity, it meant losing personal freedoms, and he had several "habits" he didn't want to give up. I explained how faith in Christ was all about freedom, and that if he truly committed his life to Christ, he would have total freedom, even in those areas he'd mentioned. But I also made sure he understood that once a person makes the commitment, God has a unique way of reordering their priorities. Often, those old habits don't seem as important anymore.

When I got back to *The Closet*, Bonnie was sitting in my chair. No homemade chocolate chip cookies graced my desk.

"Hey," I said, plopping down in one of my other chairs. "What's up?"

After a brief dramatic pause, she responded. "It really hurt my feelings when you skipped over me in the skit assignments yesterday. But I thought about it, and in all fairness, I should have said something ahead of time."

She's apologizing. I can't believe it.

I could've let her hang out to dry for a few minutes, but I was weary of the whole thing. "Listen, I'm sorry for being such an insensitive dolt about it. I have a latent genetic defect in my discernment skills, but there is good news. Charlise called me this morning and begged off her part. She said she'd rather have one of the smaller roles. So I just figured I would switch you two. I would've told you earlier today, but alas—well, that's another story . . ."

She smiled. "Now I feel like a jerk."

"Good. This means you'll be able to empathize with me since I regularly play that role with gusto."

Her smile and her sarcasm returned. "And you play it oh so well."

145

Monday afternoon rolled around which meant a ten-minute drive over to the seminary for my mandatory weekly meeting with the Dr. DV.

Now that Pastor Fred had kicked open the door of reconciliation, I began searching for a cogent strategy to convince Augie to participate in a face-to-face meeting with his long-time adversary. This wasn't going to be easy. Or so I thought.

The seminary campus teemed with activity as the fall semester wound down. The ancient oak trees adorning the main drive exploded with brilliant orange, red, and yellow leaves. I loved this beautiful old campus, and I felt a tinge of sadness knowing my days here at Harvest Morgan were all but over.

When I entered the outer office, Bess was nowhere to be found. *Probably out gathering gossip on some poor unsuspecting ministerial student.* Dr. DV's door was closed, so I knocked on the door, three quick blows in a staccato rhythm.

"Who is it?" he grunted.

"Elmo Jenkins," I answered firmly through the solid wooden door.

"Come in, Mr. Jenkins," he said without hesitation.

When I opened his office door, I found him sitting with his back to me rifling through papers on his credenza. As I stepped into his office, I was immediately assaulted by a virulent, pungent aroma that could be only one thing: flatulence. But on this occasion, a flatulence that most assuredly emanated from the very bowels of hell. My eyes burning, I suffered immensely as I wobbled toward his desk, careful to breathe only through my mouth. This was no ordinary odor. No, this propane had obviously percolated in the old man's colon for quite some time before gaining purchase and exploding into his small office instantly vaporizing all flora and fauna as it rushed to permeate the confined space.

He turned slowly as a huge grin stretched across his face.

He knew I knew.

I knew *he* knew I knew.

Neither of us spoke. He paused for an extra-long moment, clearly enjoying my torment.

"Jenkins, let's go for a walk," he said. "I need some fresh air."

"Me too," I gasped, thanking God under my breath.

Exiting the main doors we strode slowly along the cobblestone pathway fronting the Theology Building. To our right in my line of site just over Dr. DV's shoulder was the historic and esteemed Campus Rotunda Building fashioned after the Jefferson Monument. I did a double-take. The resemblance astonished me—the domed roof identical to the curvature of Dr. DV's bald head. As if he'd surely posed as a model for the building's designer. I kept this observation to myself.

Stirred from my musing by Dr. DV's familiar phlegm gurgle and spit, I broke the silence. "Dr. De Villa, according to my internship calendar, this is our last meeting. I want you to know how much I've benefited from your guidance. I've gained a tremendous amount of respect for you along the way, and I want to thank you for everything you've done for me."

The old man cleared his throat again. "Jenkins, we both know that's a bunch of flowery nonsense. I'm one miserable internship advisor. I know it, and you know it. I do it because it's part of my job description—period. That said, I've grown to like you. I believe you have a bright future in whatever you pursue, and I'm not just blowing pig manure when I say that."

He had an interesting way of delivering a compliment.

I slowed my pace. "I do have one last favor to ask. This may be way out of line but here goes. I've asked Pastor Snooker if he'd be open to a sit-down meeting with you to talk over old grievances and clear the air. He said yes, and he said it without hesitation. Would you also consent to such a meeting?"

Dr DV sighed. "You know, young man, in past years such meddling would have been a poor career decision on your part. But I'm in a bit of transition as of late. Some would call it a softening of long-held convictions about certain issues. A bit of a renaissance I think. Fred has been on my mind a lot lately. Maybe it has to do with the growing need to tie up loose ends as I enter the *swan song* phase of my life. It's not widely known yet, but this is going to be my last year at the seminary. I don't see it as retirement; no it's more of a *fading off into the horizon.*"

He stopped walking and turned toward me. "Sorry for the rambling. I've been experiencing a touch of melancholy these last few months, and that's a new experience for me. Expressing myself along these lines has always been difficult. To address your question—yes. Tell Fred I would indeed like to meet with him. Perhaps we can get together after the graduation ceremony. I'm assuming he'll attend your commencement?"

"I believe he is planning to be there, but I'll confirm that, then let Bess know. Finally, before I go, I have one last question. I have to know about your bowling trophies. How did you ever get into bowling?"

A delighted smile broadened his face. "Well, Mr. Jenkins, that's quite a long story. But if you don't have to rush off just yet, I'd be more than happy to tell you all about it . . ."

26

The Bowling Ball

My First Church internship would be over in just a few weeks. I'd fulfilled most all of the assigned requirements necessary to get full credit, so my last couple of weeks at the church looked to be pretty light work-wise. I could relax some and enjoy the ride, which was nice. Popping into Bonnie's office Tuesday morning, I surprised her with a bouquet of flowers. The look on her face let me know it was worth every penny I'd spent on them.

"Elmo, you are indeed developing into a romantic." She beamed.

"With God, all things are possible," I quipped, thrilled with her response. "Listen, I have an idea for tonight if you're open to it—a fun way to kill several birds with one stone, or ball in this case. Dr. DV gave me his beloved bowling ball yesterday! He can't bowl any more due to a bad back, and he wanted me to have it. I thought it would be fun to go bowling tonight and try it out. I've also been looking for an opportunity to get Thurm out of his apartment. He's been in the major dumps since he and Alise broke up."

"Sounds like fun, though I'll have to cancel my Amway meeting."

"Your what?!" I gasped.

"Easy boy, just kidding; I'm not a multi-level type of girl. How 'bout I see if Juliann would like to join us? Do you think Thurm would mind?"

"Why would he? As long as we don't slip up and call it a double date. Let's shoot for 7:00 at the Happy Lanes and Grill. It's automated so you don't have to keep your own score."

"My kind of place. I'll pick up Juliann, and you bring Thurm. That way it'll be casual and relaxed for everyone. By the way, Elmo, can you bowl?"

"About like I play tennis and fish, but don't worry. I'll try not to injure anyone."

I'd made an appointment to see Tom Applebee in his office at 10:00, so I took the executive elevator up to the fifth floor. When I walked into Tom's outer office area, Adrianne called me over to her desk.

"Elmo, you've gotta hear this," she said, barely suppressing a laugh. "I just pushed the ON button on the intercom to call you and remind you about your appointment with Tom. You must have left your CALL button on. Take a listen."

Dunston Jones was singing *Sitting on the Dock of the Bay* with all his gusto. He must have been sweeping up my office. He sounded rather good, singing in a mellow baritone voice.

"Well, who knew old Dunston could sing like that?" I said.

But what I was really thinking? *How many times have I inadvertently left that CALL button down, letting Miss Figghie eavesdrop on me? Dang. Payback for all those times I'd listened in on the nursery ladies.*

"Elmo," Tom stood in the doorway to his office. "Come on in."

I winked at Adrianne. "Now don't you tell Dunston you heard him crooning, and I won't tell Pastor Tom what I've heard when you've left *your* CALL button down." Her jaw dropped, and her face turned pale. Now I was the one suppressing a laugh. As I closed Tom's door, I winked at her one more time.

"Elmo, have a seat. What's on your mind?" he said, smiling.

I eased into one of his leather chairs. *Man, what a nice piece of furniture.*

"Pastor Tom, I know I have a scheduled Exit Interview in a few weeks to wrap up my internship here at First Church. But today, I'm here to ask your opinion and advice on the full-time position the Personnel Committee has offered me starting the first of the year."

Tom swiveled sideways, leaning his chair back and putting his hands behind his head. "To be honest, Elmo, the idea for the new position actually started with Horace and Smitty. They didn't wrap me in until the third conversation or so. There's been concern for some time now that First Church was aging, and in danger of going the way of so many other great churches that just dry up through attrition. We really had no strategy or plan to correct this problem until you came along. Horace feels—and I concur—that you are a 'prototype,' for lack of a better word, for the kind of young, energetic, outside-the-box, yet grounded individual that we need to help First Church succeed where other long-standing churches have failed.

"It's a huge win-win opportunity for you. You'll get to innovate and take risks, and at the same time have the full support of the leadership of the church. A lot of the sharp young guys coming out of the seminaries are trying to recalibrate their churches for the future with no mandate from their church leaders or membership. More often than not, they get eaten alive, disillusioned in the process, and in many cases kicked out on their heads.

"Here, we have a unique situation. An old, established, historic church that really wants to turn the corner."

I leaned forward and put my elbows on Tom's desk. "I know it's an incredible opportunity, but I'm just prayerfully wondering if I'm the right man for the job. Or if I'm even up to it. Wouldn't it make more sense to find someone who has more seasoning, more actual church staff experience?"

Tom wheeled his chair around to face me directly. "Elmo, you proved your capability to us all these last six months. I wish some of our other guys had your enthusiasm and work ethic. Personally, I think you would be a tremendous success in this new role, but ultimately, the decision has to be yours. Only you know what's best for you and your future. It's a big job, and I hope you say yes, but I will support your decision either way."

My afternoon schedule was open so I swung by *The Closet* and picked up a few things, including *The Black Toe Enigma* album and my folder of TBT research. I figured I would head back to my apartment and spend some time analyzing the different TBT artifacts to see if there were any clues in them.

I dropped in on Thurm on my way out. "Hey, buddy."

He was working on some lame-looking poster for one of his upcoming youth events. "Hey, Elmo. What's up?"

"You know, you should take some of your staff 'continued training' allowance and take a few classes in graphic arts or something. You design some dog ugly posters."

"If you accept that uppity-up staff position you've been offered, perhaps you can convince Smitty and friends to finally okay a secretary for me and Johnny. You know youth ministers get no respect—"

"Uh oh, here comes the whining again—not! Subject change. We're going bowling tonight."

"What? No, Elmo, I can't—"

"Yes you can, and you will," I said firmly. "I know you don't have any plans, and you can just TiVo *American Idol* and watch it later."

"How'd you know I watch *American Idol*?"

"I learned all kinds of weird stuff about you from the kids at the All-Nighter."

"No."

"Oh yeah," I said with a big grin. "Anyway, the real draw is that I'll be bowling with Dr. DV's championship bowling ball which he gave me as a graduation present yesterday. He told me he had won over one hundred trophies with that ball."

"Elmo, I've seen you play competitive sports. Does the bowling alley have good insurance?"

"Now there's the Thurm I love. Yes, I have limited bowling skills, but it should be fun watching me flounder. And by the way, Bonnie and maybe Juliann will be there also."

"Why Juliann?"

"Bonnie wanted to invite a friend along. And hey, you and Juliann are just friends. Remember, no agenda, no regret. I'll pick you up at 6:30 sharp."

When I got home I threw my stuff on the coffee table in the living room and headed to the fridge for a—you guessed it—can of Coke. The only other items in my refrigerator were a jar of grape jelly (not jam) and a bag of mozzarella cheese sticks. I grabbed one of those as well. Ah, the unencumbered life of a young single man.

Back on my couch, I took a bite of cheese and a swig of Coke then grabbed the TBT album. I took out the stack of artifacts with the intent of writing down each message and doing an analysis of them as a group. From the pile, something caught my eye. It was rounded with a scalloped edge. I didn't remember seeing it before. Pulling it from the pile, it appeared to be a cardboard coaster or something similar. A message written on it said: *Just let it go. TBT*

There was no date. *How could I have missed this one? Oh well.* But then I flipped it over and about fell off the couch. It was a coaster all right—a coaster from the Echelon Country Club. My mind started spinning. Where did this come from? How did it get here? This must be some type of practical joke, but whom from? *Who would have access to this type of coaster?* I jotted down the possible perpetrators.

The list was short:

Smitty
Dr. Jorgenson
Harty Smith
Tom Applebee (maybe?)
Thurm (possible, but why?)

I quickly eliminated Harty as a suspect. He wouldn't have had access to the TBT album. And why would he play a joke on me? He didn't even really know me.

No way Dr. Jorgensen would have done this. We'd never discussed it, and he was no practical joker. Smitty, ditto.

That left Tom Applebee and Thurm. It had to be Thurm. Tom was a fun-loving guy, but he had much bigger concerns to deal with. I couldn't imagine him taking the time for this type of prank.

As I pondered this new turn of events, I stared at the pile of artifacts. I pulled out the one dated 5-5-1975. The message was written on an interoffice memo slip of paper which was originally probably white, but now a faded, tannish yellow color.

The cryptic handwritten message simply stated: *That's not a good move.*

I had no clue what that meant or what it referred to. What caught my eye was the 'g' in the word *good*. The shape was unusual, almost like a curved, elongated figure eight. I reached for the Echelon coaster and flipped it over. Sure enough, the 'g' in the word *go* was identical. I'm no handwriting expert, but it sure looked as if these messages were written by the same person. And since the Echelon Country Club was only a few years old, it meant these two messages were written decades apart. That eliminated Thurm and Tom.

What the heck was going on here? Why write a message on an Echelon coaster? I was more confused than ever.

I picked Thurm up at 6:30 sharp. He wore a bowling shirt. *No way.*

"Who owns a *bowling* shirt?" I said, embarrassed for him.

"I used to be in a church bowling league. It's an expensive shirt, and I never get to wear it, so I thought why not? Besides, it matches my bowling ball bag and shoes."

I laughed out loud. "So you have an entire matching bowling *ensemble.*"

"So what?"

"I bet you also have one of those Spandex bicycling outfits with matching helmet and gloves."

"Sure do."

My mocking tone flew right over Thurm's head. Maybe the joke was actually on me in my cargo pants and sweatshirt.

'Thurm, I have to ask you something straight out, and I need you to be totally honest with me. Did you plant a new clue in the TBT album?"

"I have no idea what you're talking about. I've only seen that stupid book the one time—at the Staff Retreat. What's going on?"

"Well, as you may remember there were a lot of clues, or 'artifacts' as Pastor Snooker called them, in *The Black Toe Enigma* album. Since then, I've been spending a lot of time doing a kind of forensic study of all the material in the album."

"Why?" He seemed incredulous.

"Because I want—no, I *need* to get to the bottom of this hundred-year-old mystery. It's just the way I'm wired. I like working and finding solutions to challenging problems or puzzles." I felt a bit frustrated by his ambivalence.

"Okay, okay. Don't get all huffy on me," he said, straightening up in the passenger seat of my car. "What's this about a new clue?"

"Up until today, the most recent artifact had come from 1975. Then out of nowhere this afternoon, I found a new artifact written on the back of an Echelon Country Club coaster. Which means it can only be a few years old."

"Hey Elmo, did I ever tell you I saw Jack Nicklaus play an exhibition match at the Echelon Country Club?"

"You know what, Thurm? Just forget I even brought it up. Look—we're here, and there are the girls waiting for us. Is Juliann wearing a poodle skirt?"

Thurm checked his hair in the mirror. "What's a poodle skirt?"

"Maybe you two *do* belong together . . ." I mumbled, shutting the car door behind me.

I bumped into Louis Estrada in the break room Wednesday morning.

"Hey Elmo, how's the Young Singles skit coming along?"

"I think we're in good shape. The skit is written, and we've already had one meeting to assign all the parts and prop-making responsibilities. We have two rehearsals planned this weekend to finalize everything."

"Sounds great. Bonnie tells me you had a rough time at the bowling alley last night."

"Yeah, well, the bowling ball was a gift from Dr. DV, and it was *extremely* heavy. I had trouble keeping my fingers in the holes custom-cut for his big hand."

Louis chuckled. "Did you really knock over one of the planters?"

"Unfortunately yes, and I'm afraid it went downhill from there."

He continued to chuckle as he walked out of the room. "See you at staff meeting."

Making my way up the back stairs, I headed for Pastor Snooker's office. As I rounded the corner, I could see *The Three Widows*— actually only two of three (Miss Fanny was still home recovering)— had just left Fred's office and were headed back to the volunteer room. I cracked the door to the men's room and whispered "All clear!" And just like always, Pastor Snooker emerged with his Daytimer, and we walked back to his office.

"Pastor Snooker, I had my last meeting with Dr. DV this week, and he agreed quite amicably, to meet with you for the purpose of making amends."

"Splendid, Elmo! You are a true peacemaker!" he said, all smiles.

"Dr. DV suggested sitting down right after the conclusion of the commencement service over at the seminary."

"You let him know that would be just fine. I'll look forward to it."

"On another topic" I segued, "there has been a new development with *The Black Toe Enigma.*"

"Oh, really?" Fred replied as he sat down behind his desk.

"This showed up in the TBT album this week." I handed him the

Echelon coaster.

"Well, isn't that interesting. Any idea who did it?" he asked.

"I thought it might be Thurm pulling a practical joke. But I asked him about it, and I'm convinced he had nothing to do with it. And here's where it gets really weird." I handed him the 1975 artifact. "Notice the similarity of the handwriting between the two, look at the 'g' in both messages."

His eyes widened. "You're absolutely right. This could be the same person. Or, perhaps the new one was forged?"

"I suppose." I laid the TBT album on his desk. "Pastor, I've decided to give up the chase. I've had fun working on it, and it helped me learn about First Church's history, but I'm facing some very important decisions right now, so I need to turn *The Black Toe Enigma* back over to your faithful hands."

"I'm not at all surprised, Elmo," he said pausing for a reflective moment. "But kudos to you for resurrecting the search, even if only for a while. I too have invested a lot of time over the years in the ol' TBT. Maybe next year's intern can build on your work and bring the journey to its conclusion. I, for one, would still like to know what really happened," he said with a touch of remorse.

"Me too. Let me know if there are any new developments, okay?"

"I will," he said with a smile. "Let me walk with you to staff meeting."

Thurm was back in true form. As I walked into the first floor Boardroom, I noticed an announcement filling the whiteboard on the far wall:

> *Elmo Jenkins sets Modern Day Record for most gutter balls in one game of bowling. Team Guinness en route to validate.*

It would be yet another long day . . .

154

27

The Skit

I'd like to say skit rehearsals had gone well, but that wasn't the case. I'd begun to realize that most young singles are just too carefree. It's not that they're irresponsible—okay, maybe *some* are—but they don't seem to value attention to detail and schedule that you find among older and/or married people. Meaning, both nights we got started late, each night some key player was missing, and few of them had prepared ahead of time. You get the picture. We weren't ready, but the show must go on.

The Sunday evening service at First Church was called *The Family Hour.* No children's or youth programs were scheduled during this service in order for families to sit together in church at least once a week. Wisely, "the powers that be" agreed to leave the nursery open.

On Sunday evenings, staff members were still required to wear a coat and tie, but members were encouraged to dress more casually. Even so, some of the old-timers still wore their Sunday best. If I agreed to accept the position as Assistant to the Pastor, one of the first issues I would address would be the dress code. To the eyes of my generation, the only people who still wore suits on the weekend were ministers and undertakers. And let's face it—when people equate going to church with going to a funeral, there's a problem. Definitely *not* a good way to reach the young. But that's a battle for another day.

Six skits would be performed with the young singles in the last slot (their choice). We grouped up in the Green Room and awaited our turn.

Eddie Hughes raised his hand and quieted the room, then looked at me. "Okay, Captain Pep Talk, give us our marching orders."

I stood up. "All right, gang. In light of our less-than-sterling rehearsals, we've decided to go the improv route. Though Eddie and Jesse made some rather . . . *interesting* props, we've chosen to go with a bare stage. Each of you will have a flashlight."

Eddie walked around the room distributing flashlights.

I continued. "We'll stay with the basic structure of the original skit—a church group on a campout that learns how to put others first. I'll start with the narration, and when I'm done, you all walk up on stage and start interacting. It's okay if you use some of your original lines, but be sure to speak naturally and not stilted in your delivery. Also, remember this is a *church* service. Don't let your ad-libbing embarrass us all. Especially you, Eddie."

"Got it," Eddie whispered from the corner of the room, pretending to zip his mouth. I knew it wouldn't stay zipped for long.

The Super Seniors had just finished some dreadful version of *The Love Boat,* and they were being wheeled off the stage (literally) with several oxygen tanks in tow.

And then it was our turn.

Tom Applebee, the emcee for the evening, stepped up to the mic. "And now, last but not least, our Young Singles group. The title of their skit is: *Kumbaya and Other Camping Horror Stories.* A nice courtesy laugh floated across the audience as he handed me the mic.

"Oh the joys of camping," I began. "The bugs, the heat, the dirt, those wonderful porta-potties, the rain, the snakes, the bears—I could go on, but you get the idea. Into this environment of warmth and love, what do we as churches do? We send unsuspecting people. Busloads of people who hardly know each other. We send them waaaay out into the woods away from every known convenience so they can 'share' with each other, build camaraderie, and have fellowship." I turned to stage right. "Here come some happy campers now."

Bonnie, Debbie, Bob and Bob, Eddie, and the rest of the cast filed in.

"Why did the Singles Director drop us off out here in the middle of nowhere and then leave with the bus?" Bonnie asked with appropriate distress.

One of the Bobs answered, "Oh, Louis always spends the night at the Hampton down the road on these trips. He says he needs a good night's rest before driving the bus back home tomorrow."

I snickered. *Louis will never believe that was ad-libbed.*

"I'm thirsty!"

"I'm hungry!"

"I'm scared"

"Who's in charge?"

"Well, that would be me." Eddie stepped forward.

Uh oh. I clenched my teeth.

"Why are *you* the leader?" Debbie asked.

"Because I have the bag of food."

"You've got my vote."

"I'm thirsty!"

"I'm hungry!"

"I'm scared!"

"Would you all pipe down?" Eddie shouted with authority. "You're all whining like a bunch of girls!"

"We *are* a bunch of girls," the whiners said in unison.

"Oh, yeah. I see that," Eddie responded, a bit befuddled. "Okay, let's get organized. Bob and Bob, you guys pitch the tents over there, and you whining girls set up the food table over there. I'll build a campfire right here in the middle with my one good arm."

"Why do the guys always have to do the grunt work?" the Bobs said together.

"Why do the girls always have to prepare the food? Huh?" one of the girls retorted.

"I'm thirsty."

"I'm hungry."

"I'm scared."

Eddie, now totally immersed in character, threw his head back and screamed, "QUIT YOUR COMPLAINING!"

At that split second, a bolt of lightning crashed outside the church, so close I wondered if it might have hit the steeple. Thunder boomed through the auditorium, shaking the stained glass windows, and simultaneously knocking the power out on the entire church facility. Everything went pitch black. Gasps and screams filled the auditorium, then suddenly the room went completely silent.

Now what!? I thought. The emergency exit lights at the back of the auditorium flickered on but remained dim.

Bonnie had the presence of mind to click on her flashlight and point the beam up toward her face. She took one step toward the audience, who were now sitting in the dark. "I'm sorry for whining, Eddie. Here, let me help with the food."

And then another flashlight clicked on. "Here, let me help you."

And another. "I'll get the tents all set up."

One by one the flashlights came on until everyone was working together to set up the camp. So cool. Very spontaneous.

How are we going to end this thing?

Then BAM! Louis Estrada burst into the front of the auditorium with a bright Coleman lantern, "Is everyone all right?" he shouted. Louis had been counseling someone in another part of the building when the lights went out, unaware of what was happening on stage.

"Louis, did you remember to bring back the bus?" Eddie yelled back, still in character.

The audience roared at poor Louis's expense as the young singles filed off the stage, and the emergency halogen lights finally brightened to full power. Many of the members in the audience thought the whole thing had been staged.

But the young singles knew better. They took off to Applebee's to celebrate with some *real* food and fellowship.

Man, was I glad that was over! Forget Applebee's. I took off to celebrate with some real up-close-and-personal Bonnie time.

28

The Wrap-Up

I believe it was Yogi Berra who once said, "It ain't over 'til it's over."

Well, it was almost over. How'd I know? They had scheduled the fat lady, Geraldine Fitzsimons O'Leary, to sing for my last Sunday morning under *The Big Top*. Probably just a coincidence, but for me, it put the final fork in the pie for my internship at First Church.

With Friday came a long list of tasks to accomplish, including cleaning out *The Closet*, signing a few papers for Louis, meeting with Tom for my Exit Interview, and several other miscellaneous items. I'd asked Dunston to come down and help me get all the furniture and other office accessories put back where he'd found them.

On Wednesday, the staff had given me a nice party during staff meeting, and presented me with one of those giant going-away chocolate chip cookies. And who knew it was possible, but not a single Sesame Street joke. Either I'd gained their respect, or else they'd just grown tired of embarrassing me. Who knows. But they all chipped in and gave me a new leather briefcase—even though I'd told them I only wear boxers. Go figure.

My graduation commencement exercises would take place at Harvest Morgan Seminary on Monday morning at 10:00. For reasons not fully understood, I had been chosen to represent the graduating class and give the final remarks at the close of the ceremony. They probably couldn't find anyone else willing to do it.

Most of the church staff had promised to come to my graduation. I felt as though these folks had become my new family, and many of them would probably be lifelong friends. Only a few people at the church knew I'd been offered a permanent position on the staff, but word was starting to get around. No surprise there. Churches are notoriously bad when it comes to gossip. Ironic, isn't it?

I still wasn't sure what to do about the job offer. The seminary placement office had been sending out my resume, and I'd been contacted by four other churches to interview for a variety of positions. A church in Birmingham needed a Singles minister, and one in Orlando had an opening for a Youth minister.

I'd even had a call from a Chairman of Deacons named Slim from a small town in Texas looking for a pastor. "Son, what would it take to get a city boy like you to come to West Texas?"

"How about the oil and minerals rights under the church property?" I quipped. He thought I was serious. Probably not a good match.

Someone knocked on my door. "Come in," I called. The door opened, and my favorite janitor walked in. "Hey Dunston, how're you doing this morning?"

"Fine-'n-you?"

"I'm great, and I sure appreciate you coming down here to help me close up shop. By the way, when is *your* last day at First Church?"

He smiled real big. "Two weeks from today."

"When did you start working here?"

"Why, I believe it was the first week of 1969. Yessir, yes that is correct."

"Wow—you've worked here a *long* time! What happens now for ol' Dunston, and how will the church ever function without you here?"

He looked at the floor. "Oh, I don' know. They'll make do just fine. You know, 'specially with that fancy new cleanin' service that's takin' over. And me, you'll find me down at the lake fishin' most ever' day, I s'pect. You should come out there some time and learn a few things."

"I just might do it," I said, laughing. "Will I have to get down low behind the bank like this?" I slid down behind my table just peeking over the edge.

Dunston stiffened his back. "Laugh all you want, just 'member I'm the one eatin' fresh fish sam-a-gis' ever' day!" he said proudly.

"Hey, I'm just kidding. In my eyes, Dunston, you may just be the best fisherman in the world."

His smile returned. "Could be true, I s'pose."

"Dunston, this is my last day in my off—uh, this *closet,* so we'll need to return all this stuff back to its rightful place."

"No problem. I know right where everythin' belongs. I'll take care of it. I would like to keep that nameplate that fell off yo' door. I have me a collection of doorplates from most the folks I've worked for here over the years, and I'd like to add yours to the collection."

"Well, I'd be honored for you to have it! It's right over there on that metal shelf against the back wall. His request humbled me.

"I'm mighty thankful, Elmo. Now, I've got somethin' for you. I know you're graduatin' Monday, so's I wanted to give you a little somethin'." He pointed a weathered finger at me, his expression serious. "Don't you ever forget that a good education is a *privilege* and comes with a responsibility to *pass on* what you learned." He pulled a sealed envelope from his back pocket with "Elmo" written on the front. "Now, don't be gettin' too excited. It ain't money, but you'll be mighty happy when you see what's inside. But you got to promise me you won't open this envelope 'til after you graduate. You hear what I'm sayin'?"

"Yessir, I promise." I took the envelope from his hand. "Dunston, I don't know what to say. Thank you. Getting to know you has been one of the highlights of my time here. And I really do want to go fishing sometime. No, scratch that. I want to go 'catching' with you sometime."

He smiled his biggest smile yet. "Well, I'm yo' man for that!" We both had a good laugh, and I gave him a big ol' hug.

My exit interview went well. Tom gave me mostly high marks, and lots of good suggestions for the areas he thought I could improve in. He reviewed the job offer from the Personnel Committee with me, this time including the salary and benefit numbers. If I took the job, I wasn't going to get rich, but it would still be a great starting point for someone like me, coming right out of school. I told him I would have a decision for him on Monday. He promised this time I would get a real office with real furniture and a full-size mail slot. What more could a guy want?

The fact is, you don't go into church work to get rich. Granted, some senior pastors of larger churches probably make what most of us would consider big salaries. In reality, most church workers—including most pastors of smaller churches—make paltry salaries, and in many cases have to work a second job just to pay their bills. The rewards come in other forms, like seeing lives change for the better. That doesn't mean it's not hard, particularly on the families. For those choosing a life in vocational ministry, there's one cliché that is absolutely valid: *No one ever said it would be easy.*

After many hugs and goodbyes and a few tears (mostly mine), I walked alone across First Boulevard toward the staff parking Lot. These past six months had gone by so very fast. I remembered sitting in my parked car that first day not knowing what to expect. I'm ashamed to admit it, but back then I was intimidated and uncertain—not only about the internship, but also about my future. I had deep, unanswered questions in my soul about ministry and those who made a living doing it. But to my surprise, quoting Forest Gump here, "God showed up," and over the last six months, my cynicism about the "church" had gradually turned into hope.

I got excited seeing lives changed for the better! To see families reconciled. To see people pull together in time of great need. To see strangers with little in common become good friends. The church is a place where these types of things really happen. Sure, there's still some politics and posturing, but those are just minor sideshows to what happens under *The Big Top* then floods out into the community each week.

As I walked, I felt a rekindling of those feelings that led me into ministry training in the first place. This is what I wanted to do.

Slipping onto my front seat, I shut the car door. I sat there for a moment pondering events from the last six months.

BAM! Something whacked the roof of my car.

"Yo, Elmo!" Eddie Hughes hollered. "You coming or going?"

"I'm on my way home." I yawned. "Today was the last day of my internship, and it's been exhausting trying to wrap things up."

"You coming back for the Singles function tonight? I'm in charge of the entertainment. I'm headed there now to set up my Karaoke machine. I'm giving it a special twist. Everyone has to dress up like the original artist of the song they're singing. I call it 'Eddie-oke.' He beamed. "I'm doing Elvis. Already had the outfit."

"Somehow I just knew that would be your choice. Just a wild guess. Sorry, Eddie, but I can't make it tonight. I need to spend some time working on my speech for my graduation ceremony. Bonnie will be there tonight, of course. She's in her office now working on the nametags or something."

"Bummer. Your loss, man. Well, y'know what—*wise men say* . . ." Eddie started singing (badly). And with that, he was on his way toward the church, the white jumpsuit with gold embroidery slung over his shoulder.

I'd picked the best possible night to skip the Singles get-together, but Bonnie would fill me in on the details. We had a late dinner date at the Roadhouse Grill. Somehow I knew she would skip her turn at "Eddie-oke," much to Eddie's chagrin.

Bonnie dragged her bones into the restaurant about 10:00 after a thirteen-hour work day. I know that seems late for dinner, but hey—it's Friday night; we're singles in our mid-twenties with no place else to be, and we have tomorrow off. So why not?

The way I see it, the older a person gets, the earlier they "call it a night." Folks in their twenties don't get started on Friday or Saturday nights until at least nine or ten o'clock—unless, of course, they married young and have several children to tend to. By the time you turn fifty, you're getting ready for bed by nine or ten o'clock. And since most senior adults eat dinner at four in the afternoon—the always popular *Blue Plate Special*—they're ready to hit the sack at seven.

"Hey, hun. I bet you're tired, I know I am." I gave her a kiss on the cheek, and we sat down at a booth.

"Not too bad," she said, pushing her hair back from her face. "Laughing at some of those singles making total *rear-ends* of themselves jolted some life back into me. Juliann even told me that Eddie had his *chest waxed* today so he could wear that hideous Elvis outfit! Oh my gosh, if only somebody had the foresight to video his performance and upload it to YouTube, it would go viral in a flash. With the support of all the Elvis wackos in the world, Eddie might just become the next William Hung."

"Please—whatever you do, *don't* encourage him along those lines. He's already insufferable as it is."

"What? I would have thought for sure you'd want to be his manager/life coach/wardrobe mistress—"

"Stop the madness!" I pleaded mockingly, cutting her off.

I sat there quietly watching her laugh. I loved it when she laughed, and she laughed a lot. She was so much fun to be around. I mean, she had her off moments, we all do, but Bonnie was special. And then it hit me. Right there in that noisy restaurant I realized it had really happened. I'd fallen in love, and I was completely undone by it. Like the lines from the Benjamin Moody song, *Back to You* . . .

Back in the beginning,
Love was overwhelming,
Feeling for the first time . . .

This was all a new experience, and I liked it.

She turned serious, "Are you sad your internship has come to an end?"

"Yes and no. It's been super fun and a great learning experience. But it's part of my seminary training, and I'm ready to move on with my life."

"So then, what's next?" she asked.

I took her hand. "Now that you've had a while to think about it, what's your opinion concerning the position I've been offered by the church? Would it be weird to have me there on staff full-time? What if we ever broke up—would that be too awkward?"

She looked right into my eyes. "I hope we never break up, Elmo. I like you that much—no, I *love* you that much. I really do. I'm just not going to give you my opinion about the job offer because I don't want to sway your feelings one way or another. Though I will fully support whatever decision you make. I believe you'll succeed wherever you decide to work."

"I respect that," I said, squeezing her hand. "I'm going to take the rest of the weekend to think and pray about it some more, then finalize my decision. I've promised Tom I'd let him know Monday."

I pivoted. "Now to the really important stuff. Let's order some food."

29

The Decision

"The disciple who abides in Jesus is the will of God, and what appears to be his free choices are actually God's foreordained decrees." — Oswald Chambers

True to my word, I spent the weekend alone. I did attend the Sunday morning worship service and sat with Bonnie, but after lunch I came back to my apartment. I allotted plenty of time for reading the Bible, particularly Proverbs, trying to glean some insight from one of the wisest men whoever lived. I also devoted quite a bit of time to prayer, earnestly looking for some direction. How to know God's will in a decision is one of the great spiritual questions of all time. This question has been answered in a variety of ways by some very intelligent men over the centuries, most way smarter than me. Mostly, I was just looking for some peace—no burning bush, no sun standing still, just some peace. By Sunday night, I'd found it, ready to forge ahead.

When Monday morning rolled around, I couldn't have been more excited or anxious. My parents drove in for the ceremony, and I could tell they were very proud. Especially my mother. The bratty kid she'd prayed over for all those years was going into the ministry. She positively glowed.

I spotted most of my new friends from First Church in the audience, cheering me on. Before the ceremony began, I had just a minute with Dr. DV who shared that he and Pastor Snooker had spoken briefly and would be meeting for lunch after graduation. He thanked me for my diplomacy, and I have to admit, I felt gratified. I also met up with Tom Applebee and gave him my decision about the church's job offer. He seemed to understand and took it well.

Bonnie pulled me out of line to encourage me and give me a kiss. Thankfully, she didn't tell me to "break a leg" because I probably would have done so, trying to please her on some subconscious Pavlovian level.

I sat with my 137 fellow graduates at the front of the middle section of the auditorium, positioned dead last in the lineup. Not because I was the dumbest or the smartest, thank you very much. But since I'd be speaking at the close of the program, this would place me on the platform at the appropriate time.

If you've ever gone through a graduation ceremony, you know it can be quite tedious waiting for your turn to walk the platform and grab your diploma. As last in line, I had some time to kill, so I took out the envelope Dunston had given me for a graduation gift. I'd promised not to open it until I graduated, but I reasoned that *technically* I'd already graduated. The "walk" just symbolized the achievement, right? Then again, with that type of reasoning, perhaps I'd be better suited for a career in politics . . .

Opening the envelope, I pulled out a handwritten note along with a gift card for $10 at the Bait & Tackle Shop on Stone Lake. I guess he planned to take me fishing after all. His note read:

Dear Elmo,

I know the secret to the black toe thing. I'd been told 'bout it way back when I first started at the church. It's just some stupid thing started by the janitors long ago.

The way I heard it, old Deacon Smith used to have a nickname for one of the janitors whose real name was Joe Thomas. Deacon Smith called him "Black Joe." Joe was a black man, and that's just how they did things back then. Fact is, Joe and Deacon Smith was good fishin' buddies. Good friends. One day, Deacon Smith had him a bad stroke and couldn't walk or speak right no more. Mrs. Smith, she was sickly herself, so on Sunday mornin's Joe would pick 'em up in his car—help ol' Deacon Smith into his wheelchair and even sit with 'em in church. Then after the service, he'd take 'em back home and have lunch with 'em. He did that pretty much ever' Sunday 'til the old man died.

See, after his stroke, Deacon Smith would mumble when he tried to speak, and people just didn't realize he was tryin' to say "Black Joe." All's they heard was "black toe." Somehow it got all tangled up with that snow storm story, and then some of them fool-hearted janitors decided to have a little fun with it. They started hidin' those stupid messages. Then the dang thing kinda just took on a life of its own.

It be the janitors' special secret, passed on from generation to generation with one of them guys taking turns to "stoke the fire" ever' now 'n then with a new note or some such.

I never had much use for all that shenanigan, but I kept those feelin's to myself. I figured now, being as I'm retirin' with the cleanin' service takin' over, it's time to spill them beans about that whole black toe thing.

So there you goes. Now you know. Happy graduation.

Dunston

P.S. I saw you was lookin' into this stuff, so I put that coaster in yo' book hoping you'd catch on. I pulled it outta Pastor's trash can. That message—that be my doin'.

I couldn't believe it. First Aaron Spencer, then Fred Snooker, me of course, and a whole host of other folks—we'd *all* been totally fooled by the maintenance staff—and for decades and decades! A practical joke of gargantuan proportions! I could only imagine the laughs those janitors had shared through the years whenever they'd hear the different pastors and staff talking about *The Black Toe* mystery, or when that article in the city paper came out about it. Pastor Snooker would be beside himself.

I couldn't help but smile.

The last row of graduates filed across the platform. My turn had come. I had just enough time for a final pre-speech Elmo checklist:

Notes in hand—check
Fly closed—check
Shoes tied—check
Voice clear—"Test, test." —check
Nose clear—check

As I climbed the steps to the platform, Dr. McGregor began his introduction.

"And finally, our last graduate this morning is Ellington Jenkins. Ellington is receiving his Masters of Religious Education and has been chosen by his peers to deliver this year's closing remarks."

I walked up to the podium just a tad nervous. Cap and gown firmly in place, I looked out on the audience, so many of them I knew.

How did I get here?

Then I began my remarks slowly, deliberately.

"Thank you, Dr. McGregor. Nothing could've surprised me more than to be told I'd been chosen to give the final remarks at this year's seminary commencement service. I am greatly humbled by this opportunity.

"Today's graduates, those seated together here at the front of this auditorium, are the new world-changers. Some, you will become familiar with by name as they move into high-profile ministries and agencies of our world. Others will minister in total obscurity in the far outer reaches of our globe. But all of them will be of equal importance to the ministry of Christ. We celebrate their achievements today."

A warm and extended round of applause arose spontaneously

from those in the audience. Even some cheers.

As it died down, I continued. "When I came to Harvest Morgan Seminary, I came searching. Today I leave with purpose. When I arrived at the seminary, I arrived uncertain. Today I leave with a confidence anchored in faith. These changes did not happen overnight. In my case, it took the full force of the program and a huge portion of God's grace to bring me to this place today. I'm sure many of my fellow graduates would admit to a similar experience.

"The Old Testament tells us, 'Where there is no vision the people perish.' As one representing all of my fellow graduates, I would like to thank the seminary staff, the faculty, the trustees, and all those who support the seminary for giving us the chance and the encouragement to seize that vision. To boldly become the world-changers God has called us to be."

Another round of applause broke out, and some of the gowned graduates actually stood out of gratitude to the school and the faculty.

"On a personal note, I would like to thank my family. Without your love and support, I would not be standing here today. And for all of you who have mentored me in the faith along the way, my victory today is your victory as well. A special thanks to Tom Applebee and my new family at First Church who took me in and changed my life. By the way, I said yes." As I looked out at them, I couldn't help grinning. "See you all in January."

To my right, Harry Simpkins shouted out, "All right!" followed by Fran noisily shushing him. I smiled and continued.

"This has been quite a day for a young man like me. Not only am I graduating from seminary, but I've also accepted my first full-time church position. I've seen two dear friends start the process of reconciling their friendship after thirty years of feuding. And I have finally, *finally* found out the truth behind *The Black Toe Enigma*. For most of you that means nothing, but for others in this room, it represents the answer to a one-hundred-year-old mystery. Pastor Snooker, I'll give you the details on that later." He waved with a smile, obviously pleased.

"And now, if you'll indulge me just one last item. Moments like this, full of confidence, adrenaline, and excitement are rare and must be maximized to their fullest. With that in mind, I share the following. One of the unexpected benefits of my internship at First Church was my acquaintance with Bonnie St. Hiliare. God took pity on me and brought this angel into my life, and I know now that I love her more deeply than life itself."

I stopped for a moment, fixing my eyes on her beautiful face. "Bonnie, at the risk of rejection in front of all of these people, and with the deepest humility and resolute sincerity, I need to ask you a question today . . ." I stepped to the side of the pulpit and dropped to one knee, locking my eyes on Bonnie's once again. "Would you be my wife?"

A sudden hush fell over the auditorium. Then Bonnie slowly rose from her seat, her eyes glistening, focused solely on me. For a moment, she said nothing. My heart pounded. She bowed her head briefly then looked back up at me, a tear escaping down her cheek. Then, with the sweetest smile I've ever seen, she quietly responded with three words I'll never forget.

"As you wish."

The room exploded with cheering and applause. Though I was tempted to do a jumping fist-pump, I chose instead to just blow her a kiss. I would wait for a real one later. A deep sense of accomplishment and peace swept over me. So much had come to fruition in one grand moment. As I stood there drinking it all in, I'm pretty sure I felt God's hand resting gently on my shoulder.

The crowd quieted down and returned to their seats. I had one more thing to say.

"I can see now this is going to be a day to remember."

And it was.

In a well-furnished kitchen, there are not only crystal goblets and silver platters, but waste cans and compost buckets— some containers used to serve fine meals, others to take out the garbage. Become the kind of container God can use to present any and every kind of gift to his guests for their blessing. 2 Timothy 2:20-21 (MSG)

BOOK TWO

1

The Metaphor

A bell rang out over the murmur of the crowd as I tugged against the rope holding my hands behind my back, firmly to the stake. The air, thick with the stench of sweat and smoke, caused me to gag and cough. I'd been stripped to the waist, and the coarseness of the wooden pole gnawed into the flesh of my exposed back. The pain was excruciating.

The large pile of kindling beneath my feet elevated me high above the rabble. I surveyed their dirty faces, ten to fifteen people deep in all directions. All eyes were on me. They'd come for a cheap thrill, a visceral jolt, hoping to add a small portion of meaning to their meaningless lives.

A squire, wearing what looked like balloon culottes and tights, stepped forward and unfurled a parchment scroll. He shouted out to the gathering:

> *Hear ye, hear ye. By order of the First Council under the leadership of Cardinal Fitzsimons, we today bring judgment against one Friar Jenkins for sedition against First Church and its people. After exhaustive interrogations, we have concluded that this man sought to change our great church and its venerable way of life. His actions and words threaten the very sacred traditions by which our church was founded and is even to this day sustained.*

> *We did not take lightly the responsibility of this somber task. After careful, assiduous consideration the First Council has decided our only viable course of action is to excise this cancer from our midst. And so today we gather, not with joy, but with sadness to condemn this man, Friar Jenkins into eternity through fire.*

. . . through fire? That got my full attention. "Hey, wait, wait . . . WAIT!" I pulled harder at the rope binding my hands.

The bell rang a second time intensifying the urgency, electrifying the crowd.

Cardinal Fitzsimons rose from a throne-like chair at the center of a crudely fashioned platform. "I'm afraid the time for appeals has come and gone. At the third ringing of the bell the fire will be lit and you, Friar Jenkins, will indeed burn to death. May God save your soul."

The crowd morphed into a mob.

"Start the fire."

"He's so smart—let him try re-educatin' the devil!"

"Change us, will he?"

"Why wait for the bell?"

"To hell with his new methods!"

"Let him burn!"

"And burn those drums and guitars while you're at it!"

Wait just a minute . . . drums and guitars? I sat up in bed. The bell rang a third time. It was my cell phone.

I yawned, "Hello?"

"Hey, good lookin'. You outta bed yet? This is a big day, and you don't want to be late."

Bonnie's a morning person. If we're gonna get married, we'll have to dial that down a notch or two.

"Nah, I was dreaming. No, make that a nightmare." I eased back down on my pillow. "The First Council under Cardinal Fitzsimons was burning me at the stake. You should have seen the pants this squire dude had on."

She laughed. "Elmo, you and your dreams. You haven't even started your new job, and you're already worrying about it in your sleep. It's actually quite pathetic." She laughed even louder.

"Thanks for the sympathetic ear." I quickly sat back up. "Hey, do you think it could be a metaphor?"

She muted her laughter, but I could feel her smirking. "What, the guy in the fussy trousers?"

"No, no, the whole dream about me being torched for introducing and promoting change." I paused as a shiver raced up my spine. "Man, I hate it when dreams become metaphors. As a matter of fact, I'm over metaphors all together. I wish people would just say straight out what they mean and skip all the symbolic double talk."

"Here's what I think," she said, her laughter now totally gone. "I think you need to get your over-analyzing fanny out of bed and into the shower, or you're gonna be late for one of the *most important days* of your young life!"

I hopped out of bed. "Okay, okay. I'll see you at church. Love ya. Bye." I hung up the phone.

I thought I knew Bonnie St. Hiliare pretty well when I asked her to marry me, but I'd grown to believe she just might have a touch of schizophrenia. One moment she was Bonnie—my beautiful, warm, encouraging fiancée; the next moment she became my mother telling me to get out of bed or my boss showing me how to do my job. On rare occasions she even transformed into the lady DMV clerk with a mustache telling me to take a number, shut my mouth, grab a seat, and wait my turn.

But this time she was absolutely right. My new job as "assistant to the pastor" officially kicked off in about two hours. I needed to be there early, well-nourished, and ready to hit the ground running.

I still remember it like it was yesterday—the afternoon Dr. Jorgenson and Smitty Fitzsimons offered me the job.

"If you agree to join our staff, we'll be creating a new position just for you. Your main responsibility will be to research and oversee a First Church transition strategy designed to take our church into the future. The bottom line is that either First Church starts reaching and assimilating younger folks into the life of our church, or there won't be a First Church to worry about twenty-five years from now."

By saying yes to the new position I took on a huge responsibility ergo the nightmares. Yet I felt God leading me to accept their offer, so if I get burned at the stake, *que sera.*

Oswald Chambers, who once famously said, "reach beyond your grasp," also wrote:

> *Jesus says, I have come for the man who knows he has a bigger handful than he can cope with, who knows there are forces he cannot touch; I will do everything for him if he will let Me. Only let a man grant he needs it, and I will do it for him.*

That's the man I want to be, and today is that day.

As I prepared to shave, I glanced down and noticed rope burns around both my wrists. *Uh oh. Stigmata alert . . .*

Weird. I was taking these dreams way too seriously.

2

The New Office

While driving downtown it occurred to me that almost a month had come and gone since my First Church internship had concluded. It almost felt like I was returning from a sabbatical. My internship seemed like a fading memory. This time I would walk in the front door as a full-fledge staff member. Would the other staff members see me differently now? Not a chance with this bunch. I'd still be the punk kid fresh from seminary and green behind the ears.

The most significant and immediate change would be geographic—my new office. Yep, you heard me correctly. I'd been assigned a real office! No more closets for ol' Elmo Jenkins. Dr. Jorgensen and Associate Pastor Tom Applebee had big fancy offices up on the top floor of the Education building. Pastor Fred Snooker and my former office, known affectionately as *The Closet,* were both located on the second floor. The offices of Harry Simpkins and Ramona Holloway were conveniently housed in the music suite behind the sanctuary, while the office for Recreation Minister Johnny Rochelle resided in the recreation building. I didn't know the exact location of my new office, but I figured I'd be somewhere near the rest of the mid-level grunts on the first floor of the Education building. That would be perfect.

After deftly maneuvering into the staff parking lot, I locked my car. The universally acknowledged rule of thumb when parking downtown was "lock it or lose it."

Pausing for a moment, I inhaled a deep breath of the choice metropolitan air—part carbon monoxide, part odor of the hordes, with a wisp of phosphorus mixed in from the factories across the river. Ah, the city life.

Brimming with excitement and anticipation, I jogged across First Boulevard toward the side entrance of the church. I may have even skipped once or twice, but don't tell Bonnie. She thinks skipping is reserved for "pansies." And I sure don't want my future bride to think I'm a pansy. That's all I need—my own color-coordinated broom and apron with an embroidered "milquetoast" insignia. Nope. Not gonna happen.

Once across the street, it was two quick skips—um, I mean steps—then under the porte-cochère, up the stairs, and into the outer lobby/vestibule/narthex, or whatever you prefer to call that first room off the street.

I gathered myself, then stepped nonchalantly into the church office reception area. A blonde secretary stood making photocopies with her back to the counter. When she heard the door close behind me, she turned around and squealed.

"Elmo! You're back!" Juliann reached across the counter and gave me a big hug.

"Juliann! You're blonde!" I stood there stunned.

"Yes, it's true." With one hand on her hip and the other poofing her hair, Juliann giggled. "After all these years, I finally decided, what the heck. Everyone likes it. They say it fits my personality to a 'T'—whatever that means?" She giggled again.

Truer words had never been spoken. I smiled. "It really looks great," I said. And it did.

Juliann was one of those naturally beautiful people. She had been a professional model or dancer or something in her younger years. It's one of life's greatest injustices. Most of us have to pay hard-earned money for products to try to enhance our appearance while a few others actually get paid simply based on their God-given good looks. That'll be one of my top ten queries for God when I get to heaven one day.

"Any idea which one of the offices I've been assigned to?"

"Elmo, I've been asked to hold you up out here until they're ready. I think there's a surprise in the works," she said with a wink.

"Fair enough. Can you at least tell me if it's on the first floor with the rest of guys?"

"Sure. I believe it's Sparky's old office."

"Sparky?"

"Oh, he must have left before you started your internship. He was the middle school pastor. He got fired for—" Juliann paused. A nervous smile formed as her face reddened, followed by several seconds of awkward silence. With her bright red face and her big blonde hair she looked like *Sunburn Barbie.* "Anyway, he's been gone for about a year." She coyly turned away, busying herself with some photocopies.

"Juliann, I'm going to run up to *The Closet* for old time's sake. Just have somebody come for me when they're ready. Thanks." I stepped back out in the hallway, wondering what that was all about.

Sadly, The Closet was once again just a utility room. Things never stay the same. It would probably be home to the new intern when he arrived next summer. Since Dunston Jones had now retired, the new intern would be on his own to decorate the place. As a seasoned veteran of The Closet, I suppose I could throw him a few tips on how to furnish it on a zero budget.

Walking inside, I flipped the switch and the overhead fluorescent light buzzed to life. I pulled the door shut behind me. Fluorescent lights aren't very *feng shui*. I'd learned that from Bonnie. Of course, until I met her I thought *feng shui* was some type of sushi. Then again, I'm a card-carrying member of the Moron Patrol.

Walking around the small room, I contemplated just how much had changed since my six months in this humble grotto. I'm now the assistant to the pastor, no longer the "Dread Intern Elmo." I'm engaged to be married. I'm a seminary graduate. I have my own real office . . . somewhere. And the most astonishing development of all? Juliann's now a blonde. What's the world coming to?

These were indeed changing times. What I really needed now more than anything was direction and encouragement. So I decided to take a few moments to pause and pray for some divine wisdom. I'd spent quite a bit of time in this closet during my internship seeking God's help, and I'd need His help now more than ever.

After ten or fifteen minutes someone tapped on the door.

"Elmo? You in there?" Ah, the familiar voice of Thurm Wilson, Youth Pastor and my best friend.

"Come on in, Thurm."

He stepped inside. "Elmo, dude, I know you love this closet, but wait until you see your new digs. That Bonnie sure has a way with arrangement and décor. I need to-have her spend a little time with my office. You know, to make it more *feng shui*."

"Did Bonnie say that?"

"Yep."

"Do you know what it means?"

"Nope."

"Yeah, just what I thought." I couldn't help but laugh. I loved Thurm like a brother. "Hey listen, before we go downstairs I need to ask you something."

Thurm's eyebrows inched up. "Sure, what is it?"

"The new and improved Juliann started to tell me about Sparky and why he left. Then all of a sudden, she got embarrassed. It was really awkward. That's why I decided to come up here. What's the deal with Sparky? If I'm going to be in his old office, I'd like to know if he's a convicted ax murderer or something worse."

He smiled momentarily before turning serious. "Elmo, since you're my close friend and you'll be in his old office, I guess it's appropriate to fill you in. I'm going to tell you something that's extremely confidential. Only a few people know about it. The only reason I'm in the loop on this one is because I supervised Sparky."

I patted him on the shoulder. "As you know, I'm not good at many things, but I'm a champion when it comes to keeping a confidence."

Thurm nodded, then seemed to choose his words carefully.

"Walter 'Sparky' Sparkman came to First Church to be our middle school pastor after serving six or seven years as a youth minister in a great church about an hour from here over in Jackson Falls. He had good credentials, great references, a clean record—at least we thought he did. And he connected really well with teenagers, especially middle schoolers. Which, by the way, is a tough crowd. I interviewed the guy myself, and he was impressive and very likeable. It's hard to find good middle school workers. We were all thrilled."

"Okay, if he's such a great guy who checked out fine and did a super job with the kids, what happened?"

Thurm winced. "This is where Juliann comes in. You know she's only been a believer for two or three years. Before that . . . well, let's just say Godly living wasn't one of her top priorities."

I leaned against the closet wall. "Now you've lost me."

"Turns out Juliann was born and raised in Jackson Falls. For a short time in her late teenage years she worked as an exotic dancer in one of the men's clubs there."

I gasped. "You're kidding, right?"

"Oh, it's true. She was upfront about it with Tom Applebee before he hired her here at the church. And remember, that happened long before she became a Christian."

"Wow," I said, flabbergasted.

"Juliann joined our staff six months after Sparky came, and that's when it got interesting. He didn't recognize her, but she recognized him immediately."

"No way, not from the—"

"Yes sir. She had seen him in the club on numerous occasions—and that was when he was on staff as a youth minister there."

I was incredulous. "How'd he get away with that?"

"Don't know."

"Well, what happened?"

"She didn't want to say anything at first because she didn't want to lose her new job and didn't want to see Sparky get fired. Finally, conviction got the best of her, and she told Tom about it."

"That had to be awkward for everybody." I slid down the wall and sat on the floor.

"First Church is proactive and very thorough when it comes to these types of situations. I mean, these were career-altering allegations. Before they brought Sparky in for questioning, Tom hired a detective agency to investigate. Not only did they corroborate Juliann's story, they also discovered Sparky had been quietly let go from a previous church for the same issue."

Indignant, I quickly stood back up. "Quietly let go? What does that mean?"

"Elmo, it happens all the time. A staff member gets caught doing something wrong and is fired quietly because the church, hoping the guy has learned his lesson, doesn't want to see him get kicked out of ministry forever. There are also churches that don't want to be embarrassed or tainted by the incident. So again, they keep it quiet. I didn't say it was right. I just said it happens."

"How did First Church handle it?"

"They don't mess around here. He was terminated immediately, told to clean out his office, and instructed to pursue another line of work. Tom informed Sparky the church retained the services of that same detective agency to keep tabs on him indefinitely, and if he applied for any other ministry position, First Church would intervene with his background information."

"Whew. Kinda wish I didn't know all of that now, moving into his old office and all."

Thurm threw his arm around my shoulder as we started walking back down the hallway. "Don't worry. Thanks to Bonnie the office doesn't look anything like it used to. You'll be impressed. I guarantee it."

"Is the blindfold really necessary?" I complained as I tried to peek under the cloth covering my eyes.

Bonnie pulled it even tighter and tied it in back with a double knot. "Come on Elmo, be a good sport. You can touch up your hair later."

I did have a reputation for being a bit prissy about my hair. "Okay, okay, I'm on board now. Let the procession begin."

The buzzer blared as Juliann pushed the button to open the door between the reception area and the inner office suite. With my eyes covered, I tried to identify the perpetrators by their voices and laughter, these interlopers comprising the cadre of new office-christeners. I could hear Bonnie, of course, as well as Juliann, Thurm, Fran Bruker (Dr. Jorgenson's secretary), and—uh oh. Please God, not Erlene Markham! I reached for the blindfold, but Bonnie grabbed my hand.

"No you don't, Ellington Montgomery Jenkins."

Dang. She sounds just like my Mom.

"Did I hear Erlene off in the distance?" I whispered to Bonnie.

"Yep."

"Did you invite her?"

"No, but she came anyway, and she brought you an impressive office-warming present. Gird your loins." She laughed.

"*Please* tell me you're joking. Ha! I know. That's Ramona doing her spot-on Erlene impersonation. You all are just makin' sport of me."

"Wishful thinking, my love. Now shush. We're almost there."

"S U R P R I S E!" the gang shouted as Bonnie removed the blindfold.

Wow! Thurm was right—my office looked amazing! Near the door, a fabric loveseat and matching high-back armchair were situated around an Oriental rug. Toward the back of the office sat a handcrafted oak desk and a red leather desk chair. Behind the chair, a credenza and matching wooden bookcases lined the back wall.

No overhead fluorescent lights here. Illumination came from four separate lamps. A tall halogen lamp, nestled in the corner behind a ficus tree between the loveseat and chair, gave the room a soft glow. An ornate black lamp with gold markings lit the credenza behind the desk. A small table lamp gave light on the bookshelf, and a green banker's lamp on the desk provided plenty of light for my work area. The incandescent lighting made it seem more like a home library than a church office.

Cool.

It all seemed so *feng shui* except for . . . wait a minute. In the back corner stood a three-foot high stone statue resembling something you might see on Easter Island.

"Bonnie?"

"That's from Erlene," answered my fiancée.

"Erlene?!"

"Hi Elmo!" Erlene cackled from the hall. "I knew you'd like it! It's an authentic fertility god statue. It'll be a great conversation starter when new folks visit your office."

"Bonnie!" I croaked.

"I've got some great ideas concerning Erlene's 'unique' and generous gift. We'll talk later. But now it's time to celebrate."

Juliann brought in a tray of muffins followed by Thurm with a pitcher of lemonade and paper cups.

"Elmo," Juliann said with a giggle, "I made these bran muffins myself just for your new office party!"

I held up one of the muffins and turned to the group. "Bran muffins—God's gift to the colonically-challenged."

Thurm could not resist the set up. "Elmo, that was moving."

"Stop it, you two," Bonnie scolded as we both guffawed.

The office looked great, and the welcome party was a nice touch. Bonnie had outdone herself, and even had it all paid for by the church. *Attagirl!*

Now I just needed to find a subtle way to lose that silly fertility statue. Why? I would soon be married, and I sure didn't want to wake up one morning and find Bonnie preggers with twins. Double yikes!

3

The Dormant Thorn

The rest of my first day back at First Church had been consumed with filling out all the necessary paperwork—annuity applications, insurance forms, W4s, etcetera—for church administrator Bob "Big Bird" Stevens. I also hauled all of my personal stuff into my new office including my less-than-stellar library of just sixteen tomes. Most of the books were leftovers from seminary; many with long, impressive-sounding erudite titles. They were just for show, of course. I hadn't read them the first time around. Why read them now?

Once everything had found its proper place, I sat behind my polished desk, in my new red leather desk chair, surrounded by Bonnie's atmospheric lighting. I felt significant, even important. Granted, these were carnal feelings, but as it was my first day, in my first full-time ministry position, in my first "real" office, I decided a momentary smidgen of pride could be tolerated.

It had been a good first day.

Tuesday morning I hit the ground running. By picking up two dozen *Krispy Kreme* donuts on the way in, I figured I could quickly rekindle old friendships and win over any potential new enemies. Nothing says "I'm back and you'll be glad I am" better than a complementary *Krispy Kreme* donut.

After depositing the sweet treats on the break room table, I surveyed the mail case on the far wall. Ah ha! Another sign that ol' Elmo was moving up in the world. My mail slot had climbed from last on the bottom row to fourth slot on the second row from the top. A sign beside my old mail slot read: *Place your 3rd class trash here.* I chuckled, thinking that sounded like the title of a country music song.

Thurm came flying into the break room and grabbed a donut. "Mornin', Elmo."

"Hey! I just brought those in, and no one saw me. How'd you

know they were here?"

"Pro bono food news travels quickly on the first floor." He jammed another one into his mouth.

I bristled. "What, are you comin' off a fast? Take it easy and leave some for the others. There's a strategy in play here."

"Okay, okay. I get the picture. Got milk?"

"Thurm!"

"Never mind," he said, wiping his mouth with a paper towel. "How'd your first day back at the church go?" He took a seat at the table then belched. Thurm was, after all, a youth minister.

"Went well, I think. Got all moved in. Finished all of Big Bird's red tape. Even had a visit from two of the Three Stooges, otherwise known as Erlene Markham, Eddie Hughes, and Harry Simpkins. Eddie nicknamed my office *The Taj Mahal,* which I like and will probably call it from now on. Or I may just call it *The Taj* for short. Sounds kind of like a hip dance club, don't you think?' I attempted to moonwalk across the tile floor but tripped, almost knocking over the water cooler.

Thurm laughed. "Man, you are some kind of dangerous around water coolers. Whatever happened with the one you smashed at the bowling alley?"

"I got a letter from the bowling alley manager. He agreed not to charge me for the damage if I agreed to sign a waiver never to come back. I even had to get it notarized. Can you believe it?"

"You bet I can. Remember, I was there that fearful night." He laughed again. "Elmo, I say this with all sincerity—stick to golf. When you attempt to bowl or play tennis, it quickly devolves into a public safety issue."

"You're probably right." I joined him at the table and snatched a donut from the box. "Speaking of property damage or public safety issues, where's Harry been hiding?"

Thurm snickered quietly. "He took off a few days to recover from his latest mishap, but he'll be back next week."

"I've really missed the Harry Simpkins stories," I said, laughing. "I've decided my next book is going to be about him."

"Elmo, you haven't written any books."

"It's just a figure of speech, Thurm. Though you should know I'm keeping lots of detailed notes. One day sometime in the future I may write a book about First Church. This place is resource-rich when it comes to colorful narrative and anecdotal material."

Thurm sat up in his chair. "Will I be in it?"

"Buddy, you'll be one of the stars. Now tell me what happened to Harry."

"Well, it's funny, and it's not funny." He paused for dramatic effect. "Actually, it's only funny because it happened to Harry. Like all of his other infamous escapades, he'll eventually have a good laugh about this one, but first he needed some time to get over the trauma."

"Okay, you've now piqued my interest. Spill the beans, or I'm pulling the box of donuts off the table."

"Easy, anxious Annie. I'm getting there. Just allow the suspense to build organically." He paused again. "This year we had our annual church staff Christmas party over at Tom and Charlene Applebee's house. As always we started with a Saturday brunch followed by a game of Dirty Santa. Big fun. Harry's wife Trixie had to be out of town on business, but Harry let it be known he'd just come to the party solo. Surprisingly, Harry didn't show up. Dirty Santa just isn't the same without Harry knocking over people and furniture trying to get the best gift.

"Sunday morning, still no Harry. Now we were all concerned. Turned out Harry spent the night in the lockup over at the county jail."

"What?!"

"It was all a big misunderstanding, but traumatic for everyone just the same."

"What happened?"

"Evidently Harry stopped at an ATM on his way to the party. As you know, Harry's had trouble in the past with his debit card. He couldn't get the ATM to work, so he popped it with his fist a couple times out of frustration. An off-duty police officer had just pulled into the bank parking lot and witnessed Harry's rant. On a whim, he called in Harry's license tag number and lo and behold, he found an outstanding warrant for Harry's arrest. They might have been able to work it all out right there at the bank, but the officer did a search of Harry's car and found a clown mask and a gun. So they hauled him off to jail."

"Either you're doing some serious embellishment here, or you're making the whole thing up."

"Oh no. It's all true. The clown mask belongs to our children's ministry. Harry had just borrowed it for a trip to the pediatric wing at St. Michael's Hospital, but hadn't returned it yet."

"What about the gun?"

"It's Harry's gun. No big surprise there. He'd received a phone call Friday evening from his elderly parents who thought there might be a prowler in their backyard. So Harry grabbed his gun, jumped in his car, and went over to check it out. Turned out to be nothing, but he inadvertently left the gun in the car when he got home."

"Okay, what about the arrest warrant?"

"A long time ago Harry used to live over in Woodward County. As luck would have it, there are several people by the name of Harold Simpkins living there."

"You mean there's more than one Harry Simpkins?"

"Yep, and apparently one of them bounced a personal check for $12.73 at a 7-Eleven. Thus the warrant. The stars had all aligned, and Harry spent the night in the slammer."

I stood up and pushed my chair under the table. "I get it. Harry's upset at the ATM, and before they can get to the bottom of the warrant mix-up, they find the gun and the mask—right there in a bank parking lot. Unbelievable!"

Thurm shook his head. "Poor Harry. Before they got it all straightened out, he spent the entire night in a holding cell with fifteen other guys. Mostly drunks and thugs."

"That had to be frightening."

"Oh, he was terrified, but you know Harry. By morning he had several of his cellmates promising to come to church. That is, in three to five years," he added, chuckling.

I slid the box over to him. "Thurm, have another donut. You've earned it."

And of course he took two. "What's next on the agenda for *Mr. Assistant to the Pastor,* your greatness," he said with his mouth full.

"Enough with the sarcasm. I'm actually kind of nervous about the whole thing. I have a meeting this afternoon with Dr. Jorgenson. He's supposed to give me my marching orders."

He patted me on the back. "Listen, you're gonna do great. Just let him do most of the talking and be sure to say 'yes sir' a lot. And for heaven's sake, stay clear of his water cooler."

Riding alone on the executive elevator rising gently toward the top floor, I took several slow, deep breaths trying to calm my nerves. My meeting with Senior Pastor Dr. Horace Jorgensen would set the agenda for my entire next year. We'd be breaking new ground for First Church, and any time you dig in a new place you're never quite sure what you'll find.

I walked into his outer office area where Fran Bruker, his long time secretary-slash-assistant, gave me an oversized, toothy smile. She appeared to be totaling numbers using one of those old school adding machines with a crank handle.

"Fran, did your calculator break again?"

"Now, Elmo, be nice. You know I don't like all those new fangled contraptions. This machine has worked faithfully for me for years, and I have no intention of deserting it now."

If Fran's response was any indication of the "resistance to change" quotient here at First Church, this could turn out to be one painfully long year.

"Fran, you know I'm just messing with you. You use whatever works best for you and do it with gusto." I walked over and sat down in one of the guest chairs to wait for my audience with the pastor.

I didn't wait long. Dr. Jorgensen's office door opened, and out he walked with an elderly gentleman in a 1950-ish style three-piece tweed suit. I stood up and smiled.

"Jenkins, I'd like you to meet someone special. This is Mr. Sturgis Weaver. Mr. Weaver has been an important member of First Church for many, many years. He was Chairman of the Deacons the first year I started here and is still one of our deacons today. He just dropped in to say hello."

I reached out and shook his hand. "It's an honor to meet you, sir." The strength in his handshake amazed me. He had to be at least eighty years old, yet he had the grip of a young man.

"Jenkins, grab a seat in my office. I'm going to walk Mr. Weaver to the elevator."

"Yes, sir."

Scanning Horace's large and fully-appointed office, I noted there were no fluorescent light fixtures. Just as in Tom Applebee's office, two large panoramic windows looked out onto the city, though in this office they were covered with sheer translucent drapes. This gave the room a soft, indirect light which was accentuated by strategically placed lamps. I wondered if Bonnie had ever seen his office.

Whereas I own sixteen books, his library consisted of at least sixteen hundred volumes and maybe more. I rationalized the difference in my mind. I was young; he was old. I went to a small state college he went to Yale. He, a world class theologian; me, just four weeks removed from a utility closet. It was what it was.

An impressive, if not incredible collection of photographs filled a side wall. All double-matted in expensive frames. The most prominent was a signed photograph of Horace and President Reagan sitting in this very office. *Whoa!* Another featured Horace with President Clinton on the golf course. Others with Billy Graham, both George Bushes, Arnold Palmer, Jack Nicklaus, Tony Dungy, Kurt Warner . . . you get the idea. The man knew people.

I noticed a sitting area on the opposite side of the room from his desk. A leather couch and two high-back armchairs circled an ornate marble-top coffee table. Easing into one of the arm chairs, I waited for Dr Jorgensen to return. Leaning forward with my elbows on my knees, I prayed once again for wisdom and to find favor in my pastor's eyes.

In a few minutes Dr. Jorgensen reentered the room slowly closing the door to the outer office behind him.

"My apologies for the late start, Jenkins. Sturgis dropped in unscheduled, of course, which is his usual modus operandi."

Uh oh, he's using Latin phrases. My Latin skills were anemic. I hoped Dr Jorgensen would keep it to a more plebeian language like basic English. "Does Mr. Weaver drop by often?"

"Four times a year like clockwork. He just wants me to know he's still around and still has an eye on me. Of course, he's all saccharine platitudes. It's just a little dance we go through, necessary from his perspective."

"So this dance, as you refer to it—has it gone on for a long time?"

He settled in the other armchair and crossed his legs. "Let me fill you in on the entire story. It's a great example of what you and I will be confronting as we look at the needed changes for the future here at First Church.

"I became the pastor of First Church as a young man who'd just graduated from Divinity School. My only previous experience had been pastoring a small church on the weekends while I attended Yale. The transition here was difficult.

"As I'm sure you've heard, the former pastor, Dr. Buster Sapp, had to be forcibly retired due to the onset of Alzheimer's disease. A good friend of Dr. Sapp's and the leading layman in the church at the time was none other than Sturgis Weaver. With Buster's abrupt departure, a leadership vacuum developed overnight, and Sturgis picked up the reins and rescued the day. So he felt entitled to play a major role in the selection of the next pastor. Sturgis wanted to bring in what's referred to as a 'step-aside' pastor. Meaning, hire a minister who'd preach on Sundays and do weddings and funerals, but leave the business of the church to the board of deacons under the direction of Sturgis Weaver.

"Fortunately for all of us, a group of younger deacons coalesced around Smitty Fitzsimons and thwarted the machinations of Mr. Weaver and his cronies. So the church experienced a regime change of sorts, and I hired on to lead the church into a fresh new direction.

"Though their plans were defeated, Sturgis and his like-minded friends stayed on the deacon board to become a silent but not very loyal opposition. They patiently lay in the reeds like water snakes waiting for the right moment to strike. Every few years they rear their ugly heads only to recede back into the tall grass. In reality, only the sheer personality and people skills of Smitty has kept them at bay all these years.

"In my mind, Sturgis is a thorn in my flesh lying dormant beneath the skin, but a thorn that will fester again someday and cause me a great deal of pain. Unless, of course, he dies first and goes off to bother the Lord instead."

Yikes, back-to-back metaphors. I shifted my weight trying to get more comfortable. "Wow, that's a lot or pressure to live and work under."

"It's actually quite common and just part of the territory. W. A. Criswell, the legendary pastor of First Baptist Church Dallas, spoke often about a group of deacons that pre-existed him at the church and gave him fits for his entire forty-seven years as pastor there."

"How do you handle knowing there are folks in your church who oppose you in such a manner?"

"Jenkins, as you will learn, anytime you are faithful to your calling and pursue doing significant things for God you will face opposition. It's guaranteed. I believe with all of my heart that God allows this to occur to force us to trust in Him totally and not in our own natural abilities. These challenges also build our faith and create strength—spiritual muscle to make the hard choices and do the right things as a leader.

"And that brings us to you and what I want you to do here at First Church for the next year. This is a big church, and like a big ship it turns slowly."

Metaphor number three. I smiled. "Yes sir."

"So we're going to take it slow. *Nihil boni facile factu.*"

Uh oh. "I'm sorry, Pastor, but my Latin's not very strong."

A grin rolled across his face. "*Nihil boni facile factu.* 'Nothing good can easily be done.' I would like you to spend the next full year observing, and listening, and researching, and evaluating, and building a comprehensive plan with suggested steps we should take as a church. The steps should be accompanied by delineated action items necessary to accomplish the steps, as well as the projected outcomes the steps will bring.

"Do a series of interviews with a crosscut sampling of our leadership and laypeople. And I also want you to hit the road and visit some of the churches that have made successful transitions."

"I think I understand. Sort of a *carpe annum.*"

He laughed out loud. "'Seize the year.' Very good. That's actually what I'm tasking you to do. I'll expect quarterly updates on your progress, but I'll not need anything in writing until the end of the year. I also want you to continue on with your pastoral responsibilities just like during your internship. Tom will be your supervisor for those duties." He stood and I followed his lead as we walked toward his door.

"Jenkins," he patted me on the back, "it's really good to have you as part of the team."

"Thank you, sir. I'm very pleased to be here."

I stepped out of his office. As he closed his door behind me, I heard him quietly chuckle. "*Carpe annum . . .*"

The Secluded Booth

Arriving late, I saw Bonnie wave from across the crowded restaurant before disappearing around a corner way in the back. Working my way over to her, I realized the room appeared to be L-shaped. It went straight back from the front door then took a left turn into a narrow section of booths. I joined Bonnie in one of the back booths. The high-back benches and the niche-styled location of our booth sequestered us away from the other diners and made for some welcomed privacy. This restaurant booth would become our special getaway place for an intimate meal or serious discussion. After all we had a wedding to plan.

The Lucia Café, a family-owned and run restaurant known for its fabulous sandwiches and homemade potato salad, had been highly recommended by Tom Applebee and others. It also had quite a reputation as a hangout for piano virtuosos. I'd noticed the upright piano against one of the walls as I entered, but at that time it stood silent and I didn't think much of it.

"Sorry I'm late. I've only been to this part of town a few times, and the one-way streets threw me a curve or two, and—"

"And you forgot to write down the address?" She grinned.

"Uh, yeah." I had to smile. We'd only been engaged a month and she was already completing my sentences.

"Well, hon, are you getting back into the swing of things at the church?" Bonnie asked casually while looking over the menu.

"Other than my new main assignment from Dr. Jorgensen, not much has changed. I even got stuck with Mondays on the hospital visitation schedule again."

She peeked over the top of the menu at me with a raised eyebrow. "Remind me again why Monday is the worst day to do hospital visits?"

"To be honest, it's not really that big of a deal. But I'll tell you what is," I said with a touch of grit in my voice. "You've got to help me figure out a way to get that stupid fertility statue out of my office. It sits there all day long while I'm trying to work staring at me with those creepy iridescent eyes." I shivered.

"Come on, Elmo. It can't be *that* bad. What are you ordering?"

I felt a bit bothered by her nonchalant response. "After all, you're partly responsible for 'that hideous beast' being in my office in the first place."

She closed her menu and slowly laid it on the table, obviously exasperated. "First of all, nice attempt at trying to wedge in a C.S. Lewis reference, but his novel is actually entitled *That Hideous Strength*. Secondly, Erlene just walked in your office and sat the silly statue down. What was I supposed to do? Hand it back to her and say no thanks? Finally, regardless of what she told you, it's not authentic. Have you picked it up? It weighs all of about five pounds, and it's made out of some type of plastic alloy. She probably picked it up at *Fertility Statues 'R' Us*. If it bothers you that much, just haul it down the hallway and stick it the janitor's closet. Now, what are you ordering?"

"That was not a C.S. Lewis reference by the way, and I'm having three of those mini-hamburgers." I felt my jaw clinch ever so slightly. "I'd ask to have my buns toasted, but you've already taken care of that."

With narrowed eyes, Bonnie stared me down for just a moment before bursting into laughter. "I'm sorry, Elmo. I'm really sorry. I've had kind of a tough day, and I guess I brought some of the angst to dinner with me. Forgive me for my terse response."

I laughed back and blew her a kiss. "You're forgiven. I'm gonna take your *savoir-faire* advice and stuff Ferty into the janitor's closet first thing tomorrow morning. Then she can glare at Mr. Clean all day."

"Ferty?"

"That's my nickname for the fertility statue."

"Cute. Whatcha gonna tell Erlene?"

"I don't know yet. I'll think of something." I let out a long sigh. "Okay, now that we've both sufficiently vented, let's change the subject and discuss a more meaningful topic. One that just might lead to some serious smooching later this evening."

"Impressive segue. You're such a romantic." She laughed sarcastically. "I'm game. What did you have in mind?"

"Let's talk about our wedding," I said with a big grin.

"Hold it. Have you been reading that *How to Make a Woman Happy* book again?"

I blushed just a tad. "If I had, would that be a bad thing?"

She laughed again. "No, I guess not. But it almost feels like you're cheating on a final exam or something."

"Just look at this way—and I hope this isn't a metaphor. You're marrying a man who doesn't speak English, so he's studying hard on the outside to learn the language so he can understand what you're saying. Si?"

"Si. Then I'd say that man has about a 90 percent chance of scorin' a few meaningful kisses later this evening."

"Only 90 percent?"

"The other 10 percent allows for the always-present possibility that the aforementioned *hombre* screws up and says something *estúpido* or *ofensiva* killing the proverbial *momento*. Tu comprendo?"

"Sí. Yo comprendo." We both laughed.

"Let's order. I'm starving." She waved over the waiter as someone started playing the beautiful theme from *Romeo and Juliet* on the piano.

As we sat there enjoying our dinner and discussing our wedding plans, the piano player continued to play, though out of our line of sight. At first the songs were mellow and light, but as the evening progressed the playlist transitioned into ragtime and jazz. The piano player was tearing up the keys, and after each song the appreciative dining crowd responded with boisterous applause.

I joined in clapping after a fantastic Scott Joplin number. "That's some piano player."

Bonnie waited for the applause to die down. "It's probably one of the music students from Bargston College, my alma mater. It's just down the street."

I think we probably both envisioned a tall lithe college kid with long skinny fingers and slicked-back hair. So I about fell down when we rounded the back corner to leave. There on the piano bench sat this middle-aged, matronly woman in a sleeveless brocade dress and gold flats just eating up the keys! Her large girth forced her forearms to run parallel to the keyboard. I seriously doubted she could see her hands. But man could she play.

I asked the cashier, "Who's the lady on the piano?

"Oh, that's Lucia. She owns the place." She grinned. "She'll be here all week."

The morning sun ushered in a beautiful day, and to top it off, it was casual Friday. I love casual Fridays. No coat, no tie, no suspenders, just a pair of khakis and a long-sleeve oxford cloth shirt. No golf shirt this time. Too cold outside. I would roll the golf shirts out sometime later in the year.

The first item on Friday's agenda was the relocation of Ferty to the hall closet. I know it sounds cruel, but I grabbed her by the head. That's really all there was to her—a very big head, a tiny little torso, and little bitty feet on a small pedestal. Just like Bonnie said, she weighed only about five pounds. I flipped her upside down and sure enough, I found a *Made in China* sticker on the bottom.

Surely this had to be some type of sordid practical joke perpetrated on me by Erlene. Then again, maybe not. All kinds of this strange stuff filled her house from her many years spent overseas as a missionary. And after all, she was certifiably two parts crazy. Either way this statue would soon be in the slammer.

Walking down the hall with Ferty under my arm, I passed Thurm's office.

"Yo, Elmo. Whatcha you doing there?"

"I'm moving Ferty to the janitor's closet for the indefinite future."

"Ferty?"

"That's my nickname for this fertility statue."

"Clever. What are you going to tell Erlene?"

"Excuse me. Déjà vu? Haven't we had this conversation already?"

Thurm shrugged. "Not that I remember. Why're you moving her? She poop on your carpet or something?" He laughed at his own joke.

"Okay Sir Jokes-a-lot. Why don't you keep her in *your* office for a while? I'll tell Erlene we have shared custody."

"No way, man. The last thing I need is a fertility statue around my youth group. I've got enough trouble keeping the boys and girls apart as it is."

"Then she's headed for an extended stay in the janitor's closet. If Erlene asks you about the statue, just play dumb. That is one of your spiritual gifts, isn't it?"

I found a nice empty corner in the closet and placed Ferty there. She didn't say anything, but I knew she understood it was for her own good. I promised to look in on her from time to time. Then I did an Elmo Idiot Check. Standing there in the janitor's closet, talking kindly to a three-foot-tall plastic fertility god statue, I realized that anyone walking down the hall could easily come to the conclusion I'm a total idiot. So looking both ways, I hightailed back to my office and crossed item number one off my list of tasks for the day. That felt good.

There are several different approaches available for managing your daily agenda items, or what's commonly called the To-Do List.

In the first method, the person prioritizes his tasks in their order of importance, then starts with the most important and works his way down the list. The most inherent drawback with this approach is that often the most important item takes the longest. Consequently, none of the other items get completed. So he starts each day with a longer list of items to do, and before long he's totally overwhelmed. As the stress amps up, he notices his hair falling out. His skin becomes gray and pasty, and his wife is spending way too much time with her Watusi instructor.

So he changes his approach and starts prioritizing his tasks from easiest to most difficult, starting with the easiest. Now he's making some serious headway as he checks off items one right after another. He sharpens his pencil. Check. He reloads his Scotch tape dispenser. Check. He organizes his desktop. Check. And on and on. By the end of the day he's completed 90 percent of the items on his To-Do List and feels pretty good about himself. That is, until his boss calls and wants to know where the reports are he requested last week. *Uh oh.* The reports were one of the more difficult tasks on his list that he never quite got around to. His boss wasn't impressed with his sharpened pencils or neat desktop, and he gets fired. Subsequently, he takes a job as a Watusi instructor teaching the dance to women whose husbands use the first To-Do List method.

In church work, so much of the agenda is driven by the old nemesis—the tyranny of the urgent. Someone's dying in the hospital, someone's marriage is breaking up, someone's kid has run away from home, and so on. Before the onslaught of cell phones, many ministers wore beepers just like doctors used to wear. This is one of the main reasons for the high level of stress for those of us in church ministry. We're always one phone call away from just about anything. And it can come at any time, day or night.

The key is to strike a balance between the urgent and the practical. This is a skill that takes time to develop.

As I sat at my desk I again prayed for wisdom. I needed to be able to give a majority of my time and creative energy to constructing the First Church transition strategy. But I also needed to be spontaneous and available to the people of the church who needed me—for just a word of encouragement or a listening ear.

It had been a busy week, and it would indeed be a busy year. Looking forward to the weekend, I dove back into my To-Do List.

Now where's my pencil sharpener?

5

The List

My new position at First Church came with a simple mandate. Well, at least it *sounded* simple: to help First Church make the necessary transition to relevancy for my generation. To be candidly honest, this was going to be anything but simple.

As Bonnie and I sat in the sanctuary waiting for the Sunday morning service to begin, I concluded that most Sunday mornings at First Church were fairly routine, if not predictable. My generation hates predictable. The Sunday worship service (dubbed *Under the Big Top* by many on staff) basically followed the same format week after week, year after year, decade after decade. You get the idea. The church already had two tires in a rut and the other two were on a very slippery slope. To my demographic, the whole feel and temperament of the morning service could easily be encapsulated in one salient adjective: boring.

Consequently, anyone under the age of thirty lived for that moment in the service when someone broke protocol, ordered off the menu, wandered off the reservation, or drop-kicked the monkey. Ergo, screwed up. We yearned for something, *anything* different for a change. We knew all too well that real life is always funnier than anything we might contrive. And that life is funniest when it catches us off guard, surprises us, or breaks us out of our ordinary routines. This is what we hoped for each Sunday morning.

This particular Sunday we got lucky at poor Ramona Holloway's expense. The morning service had droned along as usual until it came time for the solo. After the offering, Ramona Holloway was to sing one of those cheesy Bill Gaither standards from the eighties. But on this blessed morning there would be a much welcomed twist.

Ramona Holloway, a nice lady and a very talented vocalist, had attended the Julliard School of Music on a full vocal scholarship—a fact she proudly let everyone know and often. Many of the less sophisticated members of the church actually thought Juilliard was Ramona's last name due to the way she introduced herself.

"Hello ma'am, my name is Billy Suggs."

Ramona's response, always the same. "Charmed. Ramona Holloway, Julliard School of Music 1991."

"Nice to meet you, Ms. Julliard".

You get the idea.

Ramona had been Harry Simpkins' assistant for over a decade. Her job included responsibility for all of the children and youth choirs, managing the soloists and the many different ensembles of the church, and most importantly, keeping Harry out of hot water—a huge task in itself.

Harry had invested thousands of dollars in accompaniment tracks on cassette tapes for the worship service soloists. While the world moved on from cassettes to CDs and mp3s, Harry decided to stick with the tapes as long as possible due to the past expense. And this short-sighted decision provided the foundation for Ramona's ultimate Sunday morning humiliation.

As I fidgeted in the pew, Ramona quietly stepped to the front of the platform. She gently lifted the microphone from its stand while simultaneously nodding to the sound booth to start the cassette track of her song. She sounded great and her solo progressed normally until the last chorus. Unbeknownst to Ramona or the sound engineer, when planning the service, Harry had taken home the accompaniment cassette tape for Ramona's solo to preview it. He then inadvertently left it in his car where it sat for hours in the hot afternoon sun—a death knell for cassette tapes.

As Ramona began the last chorus, the accompaniment tape warbled ever so slightly, dropping the pitch of the track about a quarter of a note. You could see a wave of concern roll across Ramona's face as she vocally slid down to follow the pitch change. No harm, no foul. After all, she was a pro, though I seriously doubted she ever had training at Julliard for this scenario. A moment later the tape slowed and the pitch dropped again. Ramona tried valiantly to stay with it while giving the sound engineer a jumbo stink eye. Though not his fault, he would get his ears pinned back after the service; you could tell he knew it by the sick look on his face.

Finally, mercifully, the tape chirped one last time and stopped entirely catching poor Ramona halfway through the last line of the chorus. Like a vanquished champion with her head held high, she finished the solo a capella but in a key that was a full step- and-a-half below where the song had started. It was indeed a bravo effort and the congregation knew it, giving her a robust ovation as she turned red-faced and stomped off the stage.

I made a mental note to stay clear of Ramona Holloway, Julliard School of Music 1991 for at least a week.

An unofficial, unwritten list of the top five All-Time Greatest Sunday Morning Worship Service Screw-Ups had been passed down by oral tradition from staff to staff. Over the years, this came to be known simply as "The List". At staff retreats or out-of-town seminars, The List would often surface during late night conversations . . . those times when everyone's tired and a bit giddy, and laughter comes easy.

Coming in at number five on The List: Dr. Buster Sapp's take on a classic Bible verse tongue-twister. Dr. Sapp, deathly ill with the Bubonic Plague or some other malady that was popular during his day, was preaching on the "The Importance of Avoiding the Fiery Darts of Satan." Forty-five minutes into his sermon and burning with fever he stepped to the front of the platform to dramatically drive home his theme one more time. With what strength he had left, he shouted, "At all cost, avoid the—" Well, let's just say he interchanged the first letters of next two words creating quite a stir. That infamous slip of the tongue held the number one position on The List for many years.

At number four, longtime church organist Sigmund Newt literally closed down a Sunday morning service with his foot, or more specifically his shoe. Sigmund, an avowed bachelor and one of the first known metrosexuals, had an ongoing love affair with shoes. The sheer enormity of his shoe collection purportedly rivaled that of Imelda Marcos.

On this momentous Sunday morning he wore an expensive pair of Gucci loafers with an unusually narrow heel. The morning service had progressed according to plan with no noteworthy distractions until the closing organ benediction, some boorish Baroque number. First Church loved the classics. As Sigmund pulled out all the stops, hammering home the song's crescendo, one of his fussy shoe heels got stuck between two of the bass pedals, sustaining a low B-flat. No matter how hard he tugged or twisted, the Gucci shoe held steadfast with the bass note blaring. An exasperated Pastor Jorgenson finally stood and used hand gestures to signal the stupefied congregation that the service was officially over and they could leave.

Sigmund had been quite humiliated by the whole sordid affair and purportedly "teared up" when informed by the organ repair technician that his designer shoe was a total loss.

Number three on The List: the Case of the Domino Deacons.

As noted earlier, the Sunday morning worship service at First Church incorporated numerous traditions that had been in place for many decades. One such tradition concerned the manner in which the church took up the offering. Though not officially listed in the church bylaws, the universally accepted, unwritten rule mandated that only deacons were allowed to participate in the collection of the Sunday morning tithes and offerings. No ushers, no staff members, and—heaven forbid—no women. Why? One word—tradition. Some things never change.

This helps explain why First Church had so many deacons. The large attendance of Sunday morning worship services necessitated twenty or more men to effectively navigate the offering collection. The deacons at First Church were a serious bunch, and each year they elected a Sergeant of Arms, respectfully referred to as "The Sarge." It was his responsibility to enlist the requisite number of deacons to carry out the offering each Sunday morning.

The offering plate served as the collection device of choice at First Church. In the early years of the church, these offering plates were fashioned out of wood, usual stained myrtle. Later, the church switched to plates made out of metal with a gold finish which were lighter and more durable—making them perfect for flying like Frisbees. How do I know this particular fact? That's a story for another day. Let's just say I have no idea how the stained-glass window in my home church got cracked. *No* idea.

I've visited lots of different types of churches in my life. Some of these visits were with friends or family members, others as part of my seminary studies. I always pay close attention to the type of offering receptacle a church has chosen to use. You can tell a lot about a church by their choice of collection devices.

Churches using the offering plate are usually Protestant, traditional though not liturgical, and evangelical but probably not contemporary. If a double-handled velvet bag or pouch is used for the collection, you are more than likely sitting in an Episcopal or Lutheran church with a traditional or high-church bent. The double-handled bag has always been a concern for me since I spent some time as a child magician and had a similar device with a hidden compartment. I'm of the opinion that the terms "tithes and offerings" and "hidden compartment" should never be found in the same conversation or collection device.

If the church ushers start passing buckets around, you are almost assuredly in a contemporary church of some kind—with or without a denominational affiliation. I've even seen Kentucky Fried Chicken buckets used in some churches. The KFC buckets add a subliminal benefit by encouraging church members to stick around for the after-church picnic.

But hands down, my favorite collection apparatus is the basket on a pole favored by many old-school Catholic churches. The usher literally extends the pole with the collection basket on the end down the pew, then draws it back to the aisle, person by person. This leaves no chance for fast-handed teenagers to pilfer God's money. Through basket movement and positioning, the seasoned usher can encourage each member of the flock to participate in the offering, if you catch my drift.

One more tidbit. If ushers take up the offering two or three times during the course of the service, you are probably worshiping in an ethnic congregation or perhaps an old school Pentecostal church. Be prepared to be there for several hours.

This brings us back to the Domino Deacons of First Church, number three on The List of the All-Time Greatest Sunday Morning Worship Service Screw-Ups. It occurred one Sunday morning, around the time when Al Gore was inventing the Internet. The deacons, under the watchful eye of The Sarge, had queued up at the front of the sanctuary for the morning offering. Standard procedure called for ten or more deacons to line up on each side of the center aisle up front, facing the platform, standing shoulder to shoulder. The Sarge would hand each deacon an offering plate. They would all bow their heads as Pastor Jorgensen, standing in the center between them, prayed for the offering. This routine, or one very similar to it, had taken place without incident every Sunday morning for over a hundred years at First Church.

Until one ill-fated day. That morning, one of the newer deacons, Cletus Jenkins (no relation), had been pulled over for speeding on his way to church. This made him late for his offering assignment. Since this was his first time to take up the collection, he didn't want to let down The Sarge. So Cletus waited patiently until Pastor Jorgenson began the offertory prayer, "with every head bowed and every eye closed." Cletus then sprinted in from the front side door intending to slip—albeit belated—into the line of deacons unnoticed. His plan would have worked except that he tripped over a microphone cord at the last moment and plowed full force into the last deacon in line. This knocked down the entire row of deacons in sequence like so many wounded toy solders. As the men fell in a heap, they all dropped their metal plates creating quite a racket, awakening the church flock from their prayer.

Dr. Jorgensen opened his eyes to see half the deacons sprawled around his feet, then quipped to the puzzled congregation, "It appears some of our deacons have today become Pentecostals."

Cletus was subsequently reassigned to the homeless ministry.

Number two on The List created quite an eventful morning. On the fourth Sunday of every month, First Church baptizes its new believers. If done during the morning service, the baptism is scheduled to follow the choir special and right before Dr. Jorgensen's sermon. The baptistery at First Church is centered just above the top row of the choir beneath the stained glass window.

Before his (unfortunate) departure, Bernard Coggins headed the pastoral ministries at First Church. It was his responsibility to make sure all the necessary details were taken care of before each baptism. One beautiful fall morning on the fourth Sunday of the month, Bernard went down his pre-service checklist and discovered that the baptistery needed additional water added before the service. He turned the faucet to the "slow fill" position and made a mental note to check back on it thirty minutes later. He had done this procedure countless times before. Unfortunately, Bernard was called away to a life and death emergency at the hospital, and totally forgot about the water running in the baptistery.

Ordinarily this would not have been a problem since the staff member doing the baptisms would show up, see the water was on, and simply turn it off. But as fate would have it, only one baptism had been scheduled that morning, and due to an illness, it had been canceled at the last minute. So the water, unabated, slowly continued to fill the tank.

Now Harry Simpkins liked baptism Sundays because he had Horace's full permission and blessing to do an extra-special choir number. For that particular Sunday morning he decided to go all out and hired an orchestra. He wanted a big song with a big sound and even enlisted Geraldine Fitzsimons O'Leary for the solo. She would guarantee a huge, window-shakin' finale to the choir anthem. But unbeknownst to Harry, trouble was brewing.

The water in the baptistery continued to rise, slowing inching up the glass panel separating it from the choir loft. In fact, it rose so slowly that no one noticed. When the choir stood for their special, the top row of choir members obscured the congregation's view of the baptistery. After the orchestra and choir kicked into full volume, no one seemed aware of the water cresting the top of the glass panel and spilling over.

Across the back wall of the choir loft near the floor, a planter stuck out from the wall four or five inches. Only used on special occasions, the planter was empty that particular day, serving as a make-shift collection trough for the overflowing water. As the choir members joyfully sang on, the planter began to fill up. Unfortunately, the planter was designed to hold lightweight artificial plants—not gallons and gallons of heavy water.

As the song crescendoed with the orchestra, choir, and Miss O'Leary in ecstatic overdrive, the planter burst releasing the water. A powerful wave the full width of the choir loft ran through the stunned choir members, across the platform, and into the orchestra pit where it doused the poor instrumentalists. The congregation gave a standing ovation after the spectacular finale, assuming Harry had once again delivered a legendary finish. But reality quickly sunk in as everyone on the stage scrambled for higher ground. Church organist Sigmund Newt sat on his organ bench with his feet raised high to protect his precious shoes from the torrent.

Coincidentally the name of the choir anthem that morning was "Come Thou Fount of Every Blessing."

The church installed an overflow drain in the baptistery the following week per a deacon board directive.

And finally—the number one All-Time Greatest Sunday Morning Worship Service Screw-Up. Ta Da! And yes, you guessed it. The star of this unforgettable moment would be none other than Harry Simpkins.

A few years back, the church started providing all of the staff platform participants with wireless Lavaliere microphones. Each staff member would arrive in the sanctuary thirty minutes before the service to put on this wireless mic for a sound check. The sound booth technician would make the necessary adjustments and then simply mute that mic on the soundboard until the service started.

The staff member would continue to wear his microphone and go about his regular Sunday responsibilities. When his turn came to speak in the morning service, the sound tech would simply un-mute his mic. The arrangement worked flawlessly with one exception—Mr. Zeke Nardozza.

Zeke capably ran the sound booth at First Church for more than forty years. Now an old man with hearing loss, he had reluctantly relinquished his sound booth duties to a couple of young techno geeks. In his prime Zeke had been a top sound engineer for RCA records. He even named his son Nipper after the famous RCA dog. Though now retired from church sound board duty, Zeke still liked to hang around the booth for old time's sake. The new guys didn't seem to mind.

One Sunday morning before the service, when the young techs had slipped away for a moment, Zeke decided to do a little soundboard tweaking of his own. In the process, he inadvertently un-muted Harry Simpkin's wireless microphone. The snafu went unnoticed at first since Harry was sitting quietly in his office looking over some memos. But then he stepped into the men's restroom to use the urinal and started singing a silly little ditty called, "The Joys of an Empty Bladder." Harry had no idea his mic was live. Thanks to Zeke's meddling, Harry's adlibbed solo was broadcasting in the sanctuary where a large number of church folks sat waiting for the service to begin. Harry did everything with gusto, and this impromptu concert was no different.

The joys of an empty bladder,
Downloading fluids I no longer need,
The joys of an empty bladder,
Oh why did I wait so long to pee!

Then, the venerated sanctuary—the century-old sacred auditorium where worship was about to commence—was filled with the loud crashing sound of a urinal flushing.

One of the young sound techs rushed back into the booth and dove across the soundboard to re-mute Harry's mic as Zeke quietly slipped out the back and headed for his car.

As Harry took his seat on the platform, unaware of his little broadcast, Dr. Jorgenson leaned over with an extra wide smile and needled him saying, "Hope you washed your hands."

All of the services at First Church are recorded. It didn't take long for one of the young sound guys to add a drum track and some auto-tuning to Harry's restroom song, then upload it to YouTube where it became quite the sensation.

Once again, Harry was the talk of the town.

6

The New Guy

Arriving at church about fifteen minutes before the Wednesday morning staff meeting, I quickly discerned a noticeable buzz around the office. Harry's back! Normally everyone would drag into the staff meeting at the last possible moment, but not this morning. No one remained in the first floor offices, having all rushed to the boardroom to hear Harry's tall tale. I figured *what the heck* and flipped my valise on my desk and scurried over to join them.

When I entered the boardroom, it was standing room only. I literally elbowed my way into the room and ended up in one of the back corners. Harry sat in Dr. Jorgensen's chair at the head of the table giving a colorful, wonderfully embellished, play-by-play account of his jail experience. With his signature ostentatious hand gestures, Harry was painting a vivid picture of his arrest, booking, and incarceration.

The room was jam-packed. *Who are all these people?* Looking around, I noticed the regular staff members, as well as the cleaning service employees, the counting committee, the Rec Center staff, the Thrift Shop volunteers, and even the Three Widows. *Did I miss a memo or something?*

I turned my attention to Harry's animated presentation.

"Then they made me strip down to my boxers!" His face morphed into a wild *can-you-believe-it* expression.

"Oh, my goodness!" blurted Beatrice, one of the Three Widows.

"Trust me, ladies. I'm fifty-seven years old—it ain't that exciting!" Harry laughed boisterously.

"Well, I'm eighty-two," Beatrice wisecracked, "so at fifty-seven, you're like a stud teenage boy to me!" The whole room exploded in laughter.

"Thanks for the ego stroke, Beatrice, but wait until you hear this. They made me put on one of those tangerine-colored County Jail jumpsuits. And you know what? It fit good, and it felt good. I even asked if I could keep it when they released me. It'd be great for working in the garden or mowing the lawn. Then again, my neighbors might flip out if they saw someone in my backyard wearing a bright orange 'County Jail' jumpsuit. They might call the coppers on me!" He flashed another grin and added, "Then it would be back to the joint." Harry rocked back and unleashed the raucous laugh of a freed man. I had to admit he was funny. Ol' Harry had the whole room in the palm of his hand. We were all laughing; some were even crying from laughing so hard.

Harry raised both hands to quiet the crowd. "Then they put me in this holding cell. I'd say it's no bigger than this room with benches around the walls. There were probably twenty or so other guys in there. All colors and sizes. Some were sleeping off the booze; others just sat there looking at the floor. Nobody made eye contact."

"Were you scared, Harry?" someone asked.

"Scared out of my mind. I'd seen way too many *CSI Miami* shows!"

"What happened next?" someone else asked.

Harry's eyes grew wide. "After a few minutes, I noticed the two biggest, ugliest, scariest guys in the cell were chit-chatting and looking and pointing in my direction. I thought, 'Oh no, *now* what?'"

Harry slowly stood up. "Then the biggest one started slowly walking toward me." Harry started backing up with a terrified look on his face. He was milking this story for all it was worth. "He backed me up against the wall . . ." Harry crouched, pausing for dramatic effect.

"Then, in a gruff voice, he said, 'Hey, old man, aren't you one'a them weddin' singers?'"

"I swallowed hard and said, 'Yes. Yes, I am?'"

"He shot back, 'I thought so. Lefty said I's just blowin' wind, but I knew. You sang at my kid brother's weddin' last year. You ain't half bad.'"

"He went by Spike, and we became fast friends. He, his ugly and quite smelly friend Lefty, and I hung out the rest of the night. They were actually great guys. They'd been out drinking and got arrested for jumping off a roof into a swimming pool. It just so happens, it wasn't their roof or their pool. I guess you could say they made quite a splash." Back went Harry's head again as he laughed like a frat boy at the end of an all- night kegger.

"It's good to have you back, Harry."

"We love you, Harry."

Harry sat back down wiping his eyes. "Friends, it's good to be free."

A round of amens circled the room, then someone shouted, "Dr. Jorgensen's coming!" The crowd quickly dispersed.

Bonnie and I resumed our practice of sitting together during the first part of the Wednesday morning staff meetings. Our esoteric game of cryptic note-taking, along with some oh-so-subtle footsies helped cut the boredom.

Fran, in her usual, perfectly flat monotone, read the list of church calendar activities for the upcoming week. Dr. Jorgensen then warmly welcomed Harry back, and the staff responded with enthusiastic applause.

But not everyone joined in. Not a big fan of Harry's, Bob Stevens quickly launched into some budget numbers for the new year, prematurely cutting off any lingering adulation for Harry Simpkins. A sly maneuver, and one not missed by Harry who responded by giving Bob the evil eye treatment.

Ah, the joy and intrigue of the Wednesday morning staff meeting at First Church. It was good to be back.

The secretaries, managers, and coordinators were released when we took a small break before the upper level staff regrouped for the second part of the meeting. The brain trust remaining for this second portion included Dr. Jorgenson, Tom Applebee, Fran Bruker, Harry Simpkins, Bob Stevens, Louis Estrada, Fred Snooker and yours truly.

As usual, Fran handed out a cryptic agenda. This week's agenda consisted of five topics for discussion:

Home Missions Week
Budget Promotion
Spring Series
Carpe Annum
The New Guy

On Sunday, Dr. Jorgensen had mentioned in the hallway that our "transition" discussion might come up at the staff meeting on Wednesday. Unfortunately, I had fixated on the "might" part of his comment and never dreamed it would actually be an agenda item—a precarious rookie error. Now, while the others discussed the first three items on the agenda, I feverously attempted to formulate a five point presentation of my transition plans.

But my scrambling was all for naught. When agenda item number four arrived, Dr. Jorgenson jumped right in, took the ball, and ran with it.

"Jenkins and I had a productive meeting last week discussing what he'll be focusing his time and energy on for the next year. He has coined the term 'Carpe Annum' as a theme for his project."

Harry interrupted. "Excuse me, Pastor. I believe I remember something about us declaring the staff meetings a Latin-free zone."

Dr. Jorgensen laughed. "If I recall, I think that was solely your idea, Harry." He glanced around the table. "Carpe Annum. Anyone?"

Fred Snooker smiled at me. "I believe that would be 'Seize the Year.'"

Harry shot back. "How do you say seize the lexicon?"

Dr. Jorgenson resumed control. "I've asked Jenkins to spend the entire year observing our church and researching other churches that have successfully incorporated new trends and effective ministry approaches. I want him to give special focus to what works well with young adults.

"In deference to his Carpe Annum project, I'm asking all of you for total cooperation with his requests for interviews and access to your leaders and program details."

"Carpe will do," Harry quipped.

Since I hadn't prepared, I was thrilled I didn't get called on, but the Carpe Annum thing had just been my lame attempt to use a Latin phrase. Now I'd be printing it on t-shirts. Talk about losing control early on in a project.

Dr. Jorgensen moved quickly to the last agenda item. "As you all know, losing Bernard Coggins from our staff left a huge hole, and I really appreciate Fred Snooker pinch-hitting until we could find a permanent replacement for Bernard."

"It's been my pleasure to help out, Pastor," Fred added, chipper as always.

Dr. Jorgensen continued. "The pastoral ministries have been running so well with Fred in charge, I've been tempted to let it go on as is indefinitely. Yet in all fairness to Fred, who is technically retired and also serving as our interim senior adult pastor, I thought it best to pursue someone permanent. Besides, I didn't want to have to answer to God if Fred headed to heaven early because he was overworked by First Church."

We all laughed, though Dr Jorgensen rarely used humor in these meetings. That's what he kept Harry around for.

Louis Estrada jumped in. "I'm assuming from the agenda that you've found someone. Is he from within the First Church family?"

Dr. Jorgensen smiled and winked at me. "Actually, in the spirit of Carpe Annum, the Personnel Committee decided to reach outside the box to fill this position. We've hired Theodore Wendel to be our new pastoral ministries pastor."

"Why does that name sound familiar?" Harry asked, scratching his head.

"He usually goes by Ted. Most of you probably know him as Father Ted." Dr. Jorgensen then paused, waiting for us to connect the dots.

After a long moment Harry stood up, "Not the Father Ted from the TV commercials?"

"The very same." Dr. Jorgensen smiled again. "Ted recently retired after pastoring the Hickory Street Cathedral for the last thirty years and was in the market for a new day job. We've been friends for a long time, so I asked him if he would be interested."

Fred raised a brow. "He's from a completely different denomination than First Church. How did you walk *that* through the Personnel Committee?"

"We interviewed Ted extensively and discovered that we agreed on all the main doctrinal issues. Any disagreements over minor issues were insignificant, and he pledged to fully support the First Church way of doing things."

Everyone around the table seemed either stunned or befuddled. Bob Stevens asked, "Will he to be allowed to continue doing the TV commercials?"

Dr. Jorgensen laughed. "Sure. It can't hurt to have a local celebrity on our staff. Worship service attendance will go up 5 percent immediately."

"This is great!" Harry clapped his hands together. "When do we get to meet him?"

"Right now. He's out in the hall." Dr. Jorgensen directed Tom to step out and invite Ted in.

The Hickory Street Cathedral was a large mainline denominational church on the opposite side of downtown from First Church. It too had played an important role in the development and life of our city, and had recently celebrated its 100th anniversary.

Theodore "Ted" Wendel, aka Father Ted, started out as the associate pastor at Hickory Street. After five years, he took the reins of the church when the former pastor retired. He served faithfully as senior pastor until his recent retirement. Ted Wendel, now in his mid-sixties with snow white hair and gentle demeanor, was beloved by both his church and city.

Due to his unique rich voice, Ted had been approached several years ago to do a series of radio spots for a local charity. The commercials were so well received, the station manager hired him to do their Public Service Announcements. From there it blossomed into a second career in both TV and radio.

His Father Ted moniker arose from his most famous series of TV commercials for a local tire company. Ted, dressed in a monk's robe and sandals, would look into the camera and say, "When driving on life's highways, you know who you can trust—Royal Tires."

Virtually everyone in town, young and old alike, knew Father Ted from the TV spots. Since retiring from Hickory Street, he'd become the face of Royal Tires. In robe and sandals, he often made appearances at store openings and trade shows to pose for pictures and sign autographs. Ted was a bona fide local celebrity.

Tom Applebee opened the hallway door, and Ted Wendel strode into the board room with confidence in his step and a matching smile on his face.

We all stood as Dr. Jorgensen shook Ted's hand. "Take this seat here by me." He pointed to the chair where Tom had been sitting. Tom slipped around the side of the table and grabbed the seat next to mine. Dr. Jorgensen patted Ted on the back. "Ted, why don't you take a few minutes and tell us about yourself, your family, and also your ministry background."

"Thank you, Pastor. And thank you all for such a warm welcome. Let's see, where to begin? I'm a graduate of Asbury

Seminary with a PhD in Theology. Asbury is also where I met my wife Patty who's an epilepsy counselor-slash-yoga instructor. She likes to say she's a 'fits-ness' professional."

We all laughed, even Bob Stevens. I could already tell Ted and I would hit it off. Maybe we'd even become good friends.

He continued. "Patty and I have two grown sons, and both are in full-time ministry. Both graduated from Florida State, an epic scar on my legacy since I attended the University of Florida."

Another plus. I'm also a big Gator fan.

"As I'm sure you're aware, I retired not long ago after thirty years as the senior pastor of the Hickory Street Cathedral. Pastoring there was my life's work, and I have a book full of wonderful experiences and ministry accomplishments vividly imprinted in my mind from my years there.

"And finally, there's my alter ego, Father Ted. He's my 401K, if you will. And yes, it's okay to call me Father Ted. A lot of folks do. That's about it. Are there any questions I can answer?"

"Ted, I'm Louis Estrada, Minister of Singles. What are your favorite hobbies?"

"Nice to meet you, Louis. Well, I'm a voracious reader. Mostly non-fiction. I read everything from Dietrich Bonhoeffer to Pete Wilson and anything in between. I also play a little golf, but by far my favorite avocation is bowling."

I couldn't believe it. Another bowler? Maybe it was a generational thing. "Father Ted, I'm Elmo Jenkins. Have you ever bowled with Dr. Auguste De Villa?"

"Augie is a long-time member at Hickory Street. We bowled together on the same team in the city church league for many years. We won four straight city championships together back in the day. Augie threw the bowling ball harder than anyone I've ever played with. Two or three times a game they'd have to send someone down the lane to try find a missing pin after one of his throws."

"Oh, I can totally believe it. The man has huge hands. So which of you was the better bowler?"

"In our prime we were both really good. I hold the distinction of being one of the few people to ever bowl back-to-back games of 300 in tournament play. And we *still* lost that match to a charismatic Korean church. What a night. Every time one of their teammates threw a strike, the whole squad would jump in the air and start celebrating. We couldn't tell if they were shouting in Korean or glossolalia! We never figured out which." He turned to Dr. Jorgensen. "Pastor, how do you tell if a person is speaking in tongues if you're not familiar with their native language?"

Totally caught off guard by the question, Dr. Jorgensen just shook his head and shrugged. "I have no idea."

I looked across the table and thought Harry would fall out of his chair, he was laughing so hard. Since our staff tended to skew toward the stuffy and staid, Ted Wendel was a perfect addition. I looked forward to getting to know him better. I also wanted to pick his brain for help with what was apparently now known as The Carpe Annum Project.

7

The Relish Tray

Sometimes it seems like the most dangerous place to be found in life is minding your own business. It's like you become this uber-magnet for others to dump their excess trouble onto. It would be far better to be out mixing it up with somebody or turning something over. But no. There you are, right where you're supposed to be, not bothering a soul.

That's the trap I had just fallen into. Tom Applebee came to the first floor fishing for someone to dump on. Anyone would do. And of course, there I sat at my desk on time sharpening my pencil. I could've lollygagged and been late or stopped at the Krispy Kreme to feed my sugar habit. But no. I was right where I was supposed to be.

"Morning, Ellington. Got a minute?" Tom said with a smile way too large for the early hour.

"Sure, Tom. Come on in," I said, as I put a check beside "sharpen pencil" on my To-Do List. "What's up?"

"First, let me compliment you on your office décor. This is the first time I've been in here since you moved in. The incandescent lighting really gives it a warm, almost homey feel. Your idea?"

"Nope, all Bonnie."

"That bodes well for your future home together. By the way when's the big day?"

"We've not firmed that up yet, but somewhere in the neighborhood of the next three to four months."

"That's great. If there's anything I can do to help just let me know."

"Will do. Thanks."

I knew he was making small talk, waiting for the right moment to drop the hammer on poor ol' Elmo.

"Where's this statue I've heard everyone taking about—your exquisitely exotic and controversial gift from Erlene?"

"It's safely stowed away in the janitor's closet and will only see the light of day when I know Erlene is going to be around."

Tom laughed. "That bad?"

"Well, I'm no authority on fertility statues, but I prefer not to have it in here staring at me all day."

He smiled. "Speaking of Erlene, I need you to do a favor for me today."

Here we go.

"I'm supposed to take Father Ted over to her house this afternoon so they can get acquainted. Since he'll be overseeing both the altar counseling and baptism ministry, he'll be working weekly with Erlene. Unfortunately, I can't make the appointment because Dr. Jorgensen asked me to join him in his office at two-thirty this afternoon. Evidently Sturgis Weaver and a few of his allies have scheduled a meeting with Horace, and he wants me to be there as his wing man. To be honest, I'm not looking forward to it.

"Anyway, I need you to pick up Ted in the reception area at two. Don't worry, there's no lunch included this time," Tom said with a wry chuckle.

"I've got it covered. By the way, I think Father Ted was a great hire."

"Oh yes, a stroke of genius. He'll do great here unless there's a backlash."

"As in Sturgis Weaver?"

"You catch on fast. I'm sure Ted will be discussed thoroughly up in Dr. Jorgensen's office this afternoon . . . just about the time you're saying no to Erlene's relish tray for the third time."

Locking my office door, I headed for the church office reception area. The hallway clock showed two o'clock on the nose. I could hear Juilann giggling as I neared the front.

"Father Ted, I've never met a real live celebrity before."

"Juliann, it's nice to meet you. But I'm no celebrity. I just willingly take people's money for standing in front of a camera in a dumb outfit while reading words off a cue card. It's actually more like stealing."

Juliann grinned. "That's no dumb outfit. It's what monks wear, silly."

"Um, you know, you're right. They sure do." Father Ted sounded a bit flummoxed, which happens frequently when talking with Juliann.

She leaned in with a serious look on her face. "Do you know why there are no locks on a monk's door?"

Ted looked up at me, then looked back at Juliann as he shook his head. "No idea."

"Because then they would need *monk-keys.*" Juliann burst out giggling.

Ted laughed. "Miss Juliann, I believe you just made that up."

She winked. "I did, but don't tell anyone."

"Sorry to break up the frivolity," I interrupted, "but Father Ted, we need to vamoose."

We headed through the church foyer and across First Boulevard.

"Juliann's a very pretty girl, but I think I see why she's still single," Ted said with a chuckle as we got in my car.

"She's actually brighter than she puts on. The silly act is almost like a defense mechanism she's developed. Probably the result of getting hit on ten times a day, every day of her life. That beauty thing cuts both ways."

"Very true, Ellington, and a very mature opinion for someone your age. I'm impressed."

"Careful, I'll fool ya on occasion." I pulled out, merging into traffic.

"Tell me a little bit about this lady we're going to visit. I was told her name is Mrs. Markham?"

"Erlene Markham to be exact. One of the most unique people I've ever met."

Ted put on his seatbelt. "Unique in what way?"

"In every way, really. She lived with her husband on the foreign mission field for most of her adult life. They served in difficult spots like Cambodia, Laos, and even Namibia. Since they had no children, they would fold into the local culture full bore. Eat the food, wear the clothes, speak the language. They retired back to the states, then her husband died a few years ago. Maybe all those years in the bush combined with her old age have caused her to be the way she is."

"The way she is? What do you mean?"

"Oh, you'll see soon enough. She's only about four-foot-ten, but she's a real firebrand, a veritable ball of energy—bad haircut, bad false teeth, bad eye sight. Incredibly whacked-out sense of humor, which is often very off-color. Yet she loves the Lord, loves the church, knows her Bible, and is good with people. She's quite the paradox."

"Sounds like it," Ted said. "I've known a few just like her over the years." He laughed as his gaze grew long, no doubt reminiscing.

I continued. "I've learned to accept that just about anything can happen when Erlene's around. The other day she had me pinned in a hallway corner going on and on, cackling about something, when all of a sudden the upper plate of her false teeth came flying out of her mouth and hit me right in the chin. Hard enough to draw blood."

"What did she do?"

"Continued her story as she nonchalantly reached down, picked up her teeth, stepped over to the water fountain to rinse them off, popped them back in, and never missed a beat. I was so traumatized by the flying teeth attack I had nightmares for a week."

"Oh my! Now there's one I've never heard of."

"She's a piece of work, all right. And since we're going into to her house, just be prepared. I won't even tell you what happened the last time I went there. You'd make me turn the car around."

"Ellington, I've been doing this ministry thing for a long time. I think I've seen just about everything, but I'm always open for a new adventure. It's the Vin Diesel in me. So let's do it."

We pulled into her driveway then walked up to the front porch. I rang the bell. Stepping back, I assumed a bit of a defensive position with my feet. Father Ted gave me a puzzled look.

"Just instinctive, I guess. Or perhaps it's the fear of the known."

As the door slowly opened we were accosted by the strong, acerbic smell of burning incense that literally bellowed out of the house. You could see the haze floating in the air. When the door fully opened, Erlene stepped out of the shadows in a shimmering red kimono topped by a jet black wig of some sort. Father Ted gasped. But me? Seasoned Erlene veteran that I am, I played it cool.

"Miss Erlene, I see you've pulled out your Thursday best. What's the special occasion?"

She bowed. "I've never had a movie star in my humble home before. So I thought it best to dress to impress."

"Well, mission accomplished! Miss Erlene, I would like you to meet Ted Wendel, our new head of pastoral ministries at First Church."

She looked up at Father Ted with a full smile, teeth in their proper place for the time being. Relaxing my defensive posture, I looked over at Father Ted. As I waited for him to say something, I realized he was dumbstruck. So I jumped back in.

"Tom wanted to be here today, but got called into a special meeting at the last minute so he asked me to bring Ted over to meet you."

She bowed again. "Please, please come in."

Overwhelmed by the incense-infused air, we headed toward her heavily draped sitting room. I calmly patted Father Ted on his back, silently assuring him that everything was fine.

There's usually only one reason people burn incense or light a scented candle when having guests in their home—to mask the real odor. When you live there full time, you become acclimated to the smells of your house. It all smells normal to you. But then you go away for two weeks on vacation and come home only to realize there's a special aroma associated with your abode. With this in mind you make a special effort to scent the air when visitors come around as a normal courtesy. Unfortunately, with her aging olfactory glands on their last piston, Erlene had gone way overboard with this common practice. We could hardly breathe.

Erlene displayed quite a contrast in cultures as she sat on her French provincial loveseat dressed in her Japanese attire. Ted and I sat down on the matching couch in the dimly lit room.

"Tell me, Elmo," she asked with her all too familiar raspy voice. "Do you like the fertility god statue I gave you?"

I forced a smile. "It's become the water cooler topic of the month at First Church. I nicknamed it Ferty," I said, glancing at Father Ted who stilled appeared to be in a fog. Literally.

Erlene flipped her head back, laughing. "I told you it'd be a conversation starter! It often takes something unusual or unexpected to break the ice between people. You know that's where humor comes from—the unexpected. Speaking of humor, have you gents heard the one about the eunuch and the rabbi? A eunuch goes in to see a—"

I cut her off. "Miss Erlene, to be honest it's quite stuffy in here. Do you think maybe we could move out to your back porch? It's a beautiful day outside, unusually warm for this time of year."

"Why sure. You boys go ahead on out there. I'm going to stop by the fridge and get the relish tray I've prepared for our little get together."

Oh boy.

Erlene's screened-in back porch was nicely furnished with several wicker settees. We each grabbed a seat.

"Father Ted, you okay?"

"Yes, I believe so," he said, coughing. "I think maybe the heavy incense triggered some sort of hashish flashback from my rowdy Peace Corp days. The fresh air is definitely helping."

I lowered my voice. "Listen, any food Erlene serves up will be suspect, so choose wisely. She served Thurm and me a pie with bugs in it last year."

Ted's color was returning to his face. "Not an issue for me. I grew up on a farm, so I've eaten more insects than a bull frog."

"All right. Just remember you were duly warned."

Erlene stepped out from the house carrying one of those divided cut glass serving dishes.

"Miss Erlene, you didn't have to go to any special trouble for us."

"Are you kidding me, Elmo? Nothing but the best for my new friend, the movie star. This is my world-famous relish tray. Tom Applebee's personal favorite."

I chuckled quietly to myself.

Father Ted finally spoke. "Miss Erlene, thank you for being such a nice hostess. My, my, what all do you have there?"

She flashed a toothy grin and lowered the glass dish so we could see its contents. "There are fresh-cut radishes, both green and black olives that have been soaked in Shōchū, bamboo shoots, Betel nuts from Papua New Guinea—careful, those can turn your teeth red—pickled okra, and pickled peaches."

"It's a virtual international cornucopia." I wisecracked.

Ted took a cocktail napkin from Erlene and selected two or three items from the tray, then quickly popped an olive in his mouth. "Mother of pearl, that's delicious!"

"It's the Shōchū," Erlene cackled. "Anything soaked in Shōchū is pretty dang good. Elmo, what're you havin'?"

"Miss Erlene, though I'm mighty tempted, I'm afraid I must take a pass this time. I've had a few stomach issues as of late, with the new job and all. I'm having to be extra careful what I eat."

Her face turned serious. "Now Elmo, don't be a pansy."

She just called me a pansy. I can't believe it.

"No, Miss Erlene. I really do need to take a pass, but thanks anyway."

She persisted. "How 'bout just one Betel nut?"

"No thank you!" I said tersely for the third time. Somewhere across town in a meeting, Tom Applebee was smiling.

As our meet-and-greet progressed, we talked about the altar counseling ministry, and the baptism ministry, including the infamous story of the day the baptistery overflowed.

Ted asked Erlene all about her days on the mission field. She shared some fascinating anecdotes, even speaking some Khoisan, the language with all the clicks and clacks. Man, how would you ever learn that stuff?

Erlene then peppered Father Ted with questions about his work in TV and radio. At one point she even asked him if he'd ever gone "commando" under the monk's robe, to which Father Ted adroitly responded, "Only on my birthday." Erlene laughed so hard, all of the neighborhood dogs started barking. I noticed Ted raised his hands to shield his face in case any teeth went airborne.

We said our goodbyes, Ted snatched a few more relish tray items for the road, and we skedaddled.

We turned on to the expressway for the trip back downtown. "Congratulations, Father Ted. You survived your first pilgrimage to the Temple of Erlene unscathed. Well, that is unless you get food poisoning."

Ted smiled while gnawing on a bamboo shoot. "I like exotic food. I'll try just about anything once."

"What did you think of Miss Erlene?"

"Once I regained equilibrium after the initial incense overload, I had a great time. Oh, you're right. She's a strange duck, but most of that's probably cultural with a sprinkling of hardening-of-the-arteries thrown in for good measure."

"Well, there you go. One thing you can count on, she keeps her bases covered. She'll be where she's supposed to be when she's supposed to be there, and always prepared. Bernard pretty much just let her run both the altar counseling and baptism ministries. He would just make the pastoral appearances when needed."

"My kind of arrangement. But enough about Erlene. I understand you're engaged to be married. Is that correct?"

"Yes sir, we're getting married sometime this spring, though we don't have a firm date as of yet. Her name is Bonnie St. Hiliare, and she's Louis Estrada's secretary. We met at the church."

"That's great, Ellington. Marriage is a wonderful institution. Patty and I've been married over forty years, and I still love her like the first day I met her."

"Forty years. Wow. If you had to encapsulate the secret to your long and happy marriage, what would you say?"

A big smile stretched across his face. "Oh, that's easy. Just remember three simple words: Put It Away."

"Sorry, I'm not following you. I tend to struggle with relationship concepts. Can you break it down for me?"

"The marriage concept of Put It Away works on many different levels. The first is literal, and you have to decide early on to be intentional about it. Simply stated, if you get something out of a drawer or cupboard, you put it away when you're finished with it, back where it belongs. It's really a metaphor for common courtesy. Treat your spouse with consideration and respect and always do a little more than is expected. If both partners follow this simple rule, years of frustration and angst can be avoided."

"Okay, okay. This is good stuff. Please continue."

"Ellington, when you're single your main concerns are for your own needs and desires; your own well-being and enjoyment. When you get married, you have to put that perspective away and make your desires and attitudes subservient to what's best for your marriage and your spouse. You have to learn how to say 'no to me' and 'yes to us.' This isn't an easy transition, particularly when you're young. But it's critical to a long term, fruitful relationship. Some would call it being mutually submissive."

As we pulled into the church parking lot, my head was spinning. It's not that Father Ted's advice was overly complex or difficult; I just found it revolutionary to my current way of thinking.

"I've really enjoyed getting to know you a little better today, Father Ted. And thanks for the great marriage insights. If you're open to it, I'd like to discuss this topic again if we could. For now you've given me plenty to ponder."

"Count me in. You seem like a sharp young man. If I can be of any help in any area, you just let me know. For now I'm headed home to try to wash the smell of incense out of my clothes. I'm also starting to think there may be a big ol' cup of Pepto Bismol in my near future."

I laughed. "Don't say I didn't warn you."

The Rock Star

Several weeks had passed and over all, everything seemed to be progressing normally. I spent Sundays walking the halls observing the different classes and groups. I'd ask random church members informal questions about the church.

Do you like your class? What would you change?

Do you like the worship services? What would you change?

How often do you attend?

Do you invite others to church? Do you bring others to church?

Do you consider the church visitor-friendly? What would you change?

You get the idea. I also made sure they always had the opportunity to give their opinion concerning change.

The responses were enlightening, and I kept copious notes which I would compile and analyze. Though I hated my statistics class in college, I finally had to admit I'd become a numbers wonk. *Ouch*. Early on, I decided empirical evidence would be the best way to present my conclusions at the end of the year. Thus, the number crunching marched on.

One Sunday after making my rounds, I stepped back into my office, known officially now as The Taj, to read over my notes. After a minute or two I started getting that creepy feeling you get when you think someone's watching you. I slowly scanned my office looking for any irregularities, and then—ah ha! Staring right at me from the corner of the room was Ferty. Those spooky-tooth, iridescent eyes peeked out from the shadows between the loveseat and the wingback chair.

How'd she get back in here?! Had to be Thurm. I rang his office. "Okay, dude. Very funny. When did you put her back in here?"

"When did I put who in where?"

"Don't play coy with me. You got me, and I admit it was funny, but it's time to fess up."

"Elmo, I've no idea what you're talking about."

"Come on, Thurm. You got Ferty out of the closet and planted her right back in The Taj, right?"

"If you're talking about that stupid statue, I haven't laid eyes on it since the day you carried it past my office door."

I knew he was telling the truth. If it'd been his prank, he'd be bragging about it. Thurm's hubris knew no limits.

"Elmo, it could be anybody. You've been shooting your mouth off about putting that thing in the closet for weeks now."

He was right. Unless the perpetrator voluntarily came forward, I might never know who did it. I decided not to mention the situation to anyone else. On Monday I'd simply hide Ferty in some obscure, remote location in another part of the church facility. And that would be the end of that tomfoolery.

Hanging up the phone, I checked my email inbox. I found the usual spam for things like household products or hot stock investments, an email from my folks, and some First Church notices. Then one new message caught my eye. The subject read "Long time no see. Jason M." I clicked to open it.

Hey Elmo,

It's been a while. My bad! Too busy—way too busy. Anyway, I'm going to be in your town on Tuesday and Wednesday of next week and thought we might do lunch. If you're up for it, just pick a place and let me know when and where. Of course, some of my entourage will be tagging along and the spot will need to be private. It'll be great to catch up since it's been—what? Two years since the last time we got together? Wow, time flies.

Let me know if we can pull this off.

Your friend,
Jason McKenzie / OOTB

I met Jason McKenzie when I was a twenty-year-old junior in college. I'd been elected (unchallenged or I wouldn't have run) to the student council as the Media Events Coordinator. Several of the small colleges in our end of the state went together and booked Jason's band *Out of the Blue* for a one-night concert. Normally a group as hot as *Out of the Blue* sticks to the larger metropolitan areas, but their manager just happened to be an alumnus of our college. She cut us a special deal which allowed us to offer the concert tickets at a price most college kids could afford.

As event coordinator, I made the arrangements for the band's food, transportation, and lodging while they were in town. I ended up riding in the limo from the airport with Jason and a few of his crew, and we became fast friends. He wasn't your typical rock star at all. Unassuming and unpretentious, he just didn't fit the mold. If you hadn't seen him on television or heard him on the radio, you would've thought he was just another college kid.

The concert went great, and afterwards we stayed in touch. He seemed to relish our friendship because it was outside the crazy circle of his celebrity life. We had little in common other than our age and our faith. He often told me how challenging it was living the life of a believer in the music business. I think he liked how openly we could talk about God and faith and life when we got together.

Over the years we'd gotten together a handful of times, usually when he was doing a concert somewhere close by. He would send me two free tickets, always on or near the front row. After the concert, my date and I would join him and some of his gang for dinner. Pizza. Always pizza. Great fun! Getting a righteous babe to accompany me was easy once I explained our evening would include a chance to meet Jason McKenzie. Inexplicably, follow-up dates never seemed to materialize.

I hadn't heard from Jason in a few years, so this was a welcomed surprise. I knew just the place and would make the arrangements on Monday. I decided not to tell Bonnie and instead, have her meet me there and surprise her. I knew she probably liked *Out of the Blue,* though I'd never mentioned my friendship with Jason. Nearly every girl in the country over the last decade had grown up squealing to their music and putting *OOTB* posters on their bedroom walls. This was gonna be a fun afternoon.

My phone rang.

"Elmo, you there?" As part of her job responsibilities, Juliann manned the front desk and the switchboard on Sunday mornings.

"Yeah, what's up?"

"There's someone here to see you."

"And who might that be?"

"It's Eddie Hughes. Okay if I send him back?"

"Check him for weapons and if he's clean, let him through."

"Elmo, you silly. He's on his way." I heard the door buzzer followed a few moments later by a knock on my door.

"Who is it?"

"Whatta ya mean who is it? It's Eddie."

"Eddie who?"

"Eddie Hughes! Come on, Elmo."

"Okay, come on in. You can't be too careful these days with Erlene lurking around."

"Huh?" He flopped down on my loveseat.

"Never mind. What can I do for you, Eddie?"

"Actually, it's what I can do for *you!*"

Uh oh.

"I came by to personally give you and Bonnie an invitation to a little get-together I'm having at my new place next Friday night," he said with an uber-grin.

"New place?"

Eddie sat up straight and bobbed his head with pride. "That's right. Me and my new roommate have moved into the Terracotta Condos on Winchester Avenue."

"Movin' up in the world, are we? Who's the new roommate?"

"His name is Jimmy "Cornbread" Jackson. I met him at the World Gym."

"I didn't know you worked out."

He laughed, leaning back in the loveseat. "I don't. I service the gym's Biz-Hub."

"Wait a minute—Cornbread Jackson? Wasn't he the punter for the local semi-pro football team?"

"Yep."

"He's the guy who completely whiffed on a punt in the playoffs last year."

"Yep."

"Then he picked the ball up and tried to run with it and got the 'cornbread' knocked right out of his name."

"Yep, that's the guy."

"No wonder he's at the gym. What's he doing, full body rehab?"

"He's actually retired from football now. He's a local businessman. He'd purchased the condo and was in the market for a roommate. I hated to leave my garage apartment. Lots of great memories there, but I needed to change it up. Besides, I figured living with a pro football player in a condo on Winchester Ave would be a big upgrade on my profile with the ladies."

"Well, every little bit helps. What's Friday's get-together all about?"

"Oh, just having some friends over to see the new place and meet Jimmy."

His tone and body language portrayed a touch of evasiveness.

"Can we bring anything?"

"Not necessary. We'll be serving refreshments."

"Let me run it by Bonnie, and I'll let you know."

"Great. Hope you can make it."

"We'll see." I was already brainstorming viable excuses for missing this little gathering.

"Hey Elmo, did you hear about Madonna?"

"The singer?"

"Yeah, you know she lives most of the year over in England. The word is that she got saved and is now attending Bible College in London."

"What?"

Eddie stood up. "Oh yeah, she's even got a new song out called 'Like a Spurgeon.'"

"Get outta my office!"

Cackling boisterously at his own joke, Eddie wandered back off into the church to find and torment some of the single gals using his infamous S&P technique—Stalk and Pester.

I had an uneasy feeling about his Friday night party. Something was askew, but I couldn't put my finger on it.

Still, it would be fun to meet Cornbread Jackson. I'm actually amazed he's still alive after the hit he took in that playoff game. *Ouch!* No wonder he retired. I would've.

After church was over, I swung my car up to the curb by the south entrance. Bonnie emerged from under the porte-cochère wearing a white dress with navy blue trim.

I whistled. "Hey sailor, new in town? Or would that be sailorette? No, that's not very PC. Oh, just get in the car."

She hopped in. "What are you babbling about?"

"Never mind. I just spent some time with Eddie Hughes. Guess I haven't given my brain adequate time to deprogram. Whatcha hungry for?"

"Louis and Jane E. have invited us to join them at Cracker Barrel. The one over by the Interstate where it crosses the river."

"Sounds like fun. Hey, do you happen to have your calendar with you?"

"I just swung by my office on the way out and grabbed my Daytimer. What do you need?"

"There're a couple of social items I need you to block out for next week. I have an old buddy from my college days who's going to be in town on Tuesday, and I'd like you to meet him. We haven't firmed up the time or place yet, but could you check with Louis and see if you can get some time off Tuesday afternoon?"

"That won't be a problem. Louis is out of town Tuesday through Friday at a Singles leadership conference. Some place in North Carolina. Starts with an R. Ridgeline? Ridgemont? Ridge-something. Anyway, I'm good for Tuesday. What else?"

"Tighten your seatbelt."

"Why?"

"Eddie has invited us to a party at his new condo on Friday. Actually, he called it a get-together."

"Eddie has a new condo? Wow, office equipment repair must be thriving."

"The condo belongs to his new roommate, which is a long story in itself. My main concern is the nature of the 'get-together.' Eddie was very vague."

"I'm sure he's just showing off. I wouldn't worry about it. He's probably invited every single girl under the age of thirty in the church hoping a few show up. You know Juliann will be there. She loves parties."

"I hope you're right. I just hate being set up, especially by friends. Oh, speaking of Juliann, she told me today she attended ballet school and graduated the top of her class. Would that make her the *ballet-dictorian*?"

Bonnie laughed. "Yep, you've definitely been hangin' with Eddie."

9

The Stents

Some people prefer to mix it up and do things differently each time. Their credo would be *la variété est le piment de la vie*—"variety is the spice of life." I, on the other hand, am a creature of habit. My personal life philosophy: if it ain't broke don't fix it. I live by routine. Every morning I set my alarm so I can hit the snooze button exactly three times before I get up. Why have a snooze button if you don't use it? I'm of the opinion that if the snooze button isn't the first part to go bad on your alarm clock, you've dramatically underutilized it.

I shave and shower, get dressed, and eat exactly the same way each morning. I eat the same brand of cereal pulled from the same location on my shelf poured into the same kind of bowl. For some, routine is boring. For me, it adds structure and comfort. It streamlines the decision-making process, freeing up needed brain cells for the more important and complex choices in life.

Unfortunately, when my personal lifestyle philosophy is applied to the local church, the results are disastrous. The younger the church's demographic, the greater the carnage.

I received a vivid reminder of this somber truth while driving to work one day. Whereas Thurm drives to work using a different route each morning, presumably to elude any potential Arab terrorist attacks, I travel the same way each day according to my routine. Thus, I had become quite familiar with all of the landmarks along my drive to the office.

On the edge of downtown stood one such landmark—a beautiful gray stone church complex taking up almost a full city block. The main structure had to be at least seventy-five years old. The magnificent building with traditional architecture stood proud and sturdy. There was only one problem. The church was now vacant and for sale.

At some point in the past, the building most likely housed a thriving congregation doing life together, making a difference, and changing the world for God. But over time it had become irrelevant. Now it was just an empty building.

Adding injury to insult, the church had recently been razed, reduced to a vacant lot used for Saturday flea markets and overflow parking.

As I sat in my car waiting for a red light to change, I looked at that vacant lot where a towering stone church once stood and thought, how did that happen?

When I arrived at First Church, I swung by the break room and checked my mail slot. I found my hospital visit slips from Miss Figghie and a note to call Tom Applebee when I got in.

Juliann came into the break room and retrieved an apple juice box drink from the mini-fridge.

"Morning, Elmo," she said as she frantically tried to jam the little straw into the drink box.

"Here, let me help you with that," I said. "I grew up on these things. It's all in the wrist." I noticed she stood by nervously patting her hands together as I inserted the straw. I handed back her drink box. "Tell me Juliann why do you drink apple juice instead of coffee like everyone else?"

She took a rapid-fire anxious gulp. "Coffee makes me hyper," she said, giggling.

"You? Hyper? No . . . really?"

She slapped me on the shoulder. "Bonnie told me your 'ballet-dictorian' joke, but I didn't get it. Sorry."

"That's okay, it wasn't that funny. Hey listen, are you going to Eddie's party on Friday night?"

"I wouldn't miss it. Eddie told me that football player Johnny Whitebread is gonna be there."

It wasn't easy, but I resisted laughing out loud. "I think you mean Jimmy 'Cornbread' Jackson."

She smiled. "That's the one. I've never met a r-e-a-l football player before."

"Eddie didn't happen to tell you what the party was all about, did he?"

She took another draw on her box drink. "No, but he did say they'd be serving refreshments."

"Yeah, he mentioned that to me too. Hmmm. Listen, gotta run. You have a good morning." And I hit the door.

I slid behind my desk and called Tom's office.

"Tom Applebee's office, this is Adrianne. How may I help you?"

"Hey, Adrianne. This is Elmo. Tom around?"

"Just a second, Elmo. I'll connect you."

"Thanks."

A moment later, Tom was on the line. "Ellington, thanks for checking in. While you're making your hospital visits today, I need you to check in on Smitty Fitzsimmons over at St. Michael's. They discovered some blockage in his arteries last week, and he's having a couple stents put in today. Horace is out of town and I'm tied up with a personnel problem, so I need you to make the visit. Why don't you take Ted along so he can get acquainted with our hospital protocol. Plus, Ted's known Smitty for many years."

"What time?"

"He's having the procedure late this afternoon so anytime before, say, three o'clock should be fine."

"Will do."

"Thanks, Ellington."

After an hour or so, I'd whipped through the first several items on my To-Do List, including making arrangements for lunch with Jason McKenzie on Tuesday. I knew Café Lucia was closed each afternoon between two and four, but I also knew the staff was there preparing for the evening meal. I got lucky. Lucia just happened to be in when I called. When I explained my need for a private lunch and mentioned that Jason McKenzie would be there, she cut me a deal. We could come at two after they closed their doors to the public, but only if Jason agreed to play a few songs for her and her staff. I knew he wouldn't mind, so I went ahead and booked it, then fired off an email to him with the details.

Now for the morning's most important task—relocating Ferty to her new digs over in the utility closet behind the baptistery. This operation had to be totally clandestine to guarantee that her move wouldn't end up being another roundtrip. As part of the plan, I had procured a black garbage bag from the office janitorial closet.

"Sorry, girl, but I've got to wrap you up in this here bag. Trust me. This move is good for both of us."

I admit it did feel a little creepy talking to a statue in the dim light of my office as I dropped her into a black plastic garbage bag. I could almost hear the narrator from the Mystery Channel say . . . *Little did Jenkins realize the chain of events he was setting in motion, and the horrific consequences that would rain down upon him and everyone he held dear.* Cue the macabre music.

I paused as a shiver ran up one leg and then down the other. Maybe this wasn't such a great idea. I shook my head. Time for another Elmo Idiot Check. *It's just a statue. It's just plastic. It's just some kind of weird ritualistic practical joke. Be a man and get on with it.*

I slowly opened my door, looked both ways, then stepped out carrying my contraband in a bag. And it happened—just as it *always* happens, forcing a quick moral decision. Doreen McGinity came around the corner.

"Mornin', Elmo. How's it going? Whatcha got in the bag?"

I yielded to the expedient. Forgiveness would have to come later. "Just some garbage I'm taking out to the dumpster."

Dang. I hate lying, even on small things. And I knew I would end up finding Doreen and apologizing for not being totally truthful. This was a foregone conclusion.

But for now I needed to complete my mission. Making my way to the utility closet behind the baptistery without further incident, I stashed Ferty away. Leaving her in the bag, I located a great spot behind some stacked boxes of old hymnals. From the looks of it, they'd been there for at least fifty years. Mission completed, I let out a relieved sigh.

As I searched for Doreen to free my soul from the guilt of lying, I ignored the voice of the Mystery Channel narrator in my head taunting me about Ferty; explaining in grisly detail my impending demise.

"Fitzsimons, please?" I winked at the pretty nurse behind the nurse's station counter.

"Which one?' she said, with a strong southern twang.

"Excuse me?"

"Are you looking for Dr. Fitzsimons or Mr. Fitzsimons?"

"Huh?"

Father Ted jumped in. "We're looking for Smithson Fitzsimons. We're from his church."

She smiled and pointed. "Room 716. Down around the corner on your left. By the way, I love your commercials."

Father Ted smiled back. "Why, thank you." And off we went down the hall.

"What's with the double Fitzsimons mumbo jumbo?" I asked quietly.

He laughed. "Smitty's cousin Raul is a heart specialist here. I'm sure he's probably doing Smitty's stent procedure."

"Raul?"

"His mother was Castilian."

"Oh."

As we rounded the corner, we found Jerome, Smitty's driver-slash-valet-slash-bodyguard sitting in a chair by the door to Room 716.

"Hey, Jerome. Is Mr. Fitzsimons available for a visit?"

He stood up. "Wait here, please." He disappeared into the room.

A few moments later the door opened. From behind the curtain we heard, "If it's not two of my favorite people. Please, come on in."

We walked into the room past the curtain, and there he lay—Smithson Fitzsimons, the man and the legend—all propped up on pillows. Wearing silk pajamas under a fancy velour robe with his initials embroidered on the pocket, he also wore a white scarf around his neck which tucked into his robe. A pair of color-coordinated velour slippers sat on the floor next to his bed. Ah, the perfect picture of the rich and famous. And to top it all off, a huge stogie stuck out the side of his mouth. Ironic for man with a heart problem.

"Pull up a chair, boys," he said with an oversized smile.

"Why, Smitty, I didn't know they allowed smoking in the hospital?" Father Ted laughed.

"Oh, they won't let me light it, even though I paid for most of this building."

"Hello, Mr. Fitzsimons," I chimed in. "It's good to see you again. I wish it were under better circumstances."

"Now, don't you go worrying about me. Raul tells me this is just a precaution. He says I have the heart of a teenager. Evidently I've just eaten too much red meat and too much ice cream over the course of my lifetime. So now they're just needing to ream out my pipes real good."

"How many stents are they putting in? Father Ted asked.

"Two, I believe. Maybe more later if that doesn't get the job done. I'm very fortunate to have a cousin who happens to be one of the best stent doctors in the country. But don't tell him I said that cause I'll never hear the end of it.

"Speaking of talent—Ted, don't ever play golf for money with young Ellington here. He fleeced ol' Horace and me for a hundred spot each last fall over at the Echelon."

"Now, now. As I recall Harty Smith is the one who made the winning shot." I laughed. "And what a shot it was."

Smitty chuckled. "Oh, I'll never forget it. How can I? Harty brings it up every stinkin' Thursday when we get to the eighteenth green. I have nightmares about that shot."

We all laughed. Then I segued, "Mr. Fitzsimons, did I see Sturgis Weaver getting on the elevator a few moments ago?"

"Why, yes, you did. He came by to pay me a visit. Did his vintage suit give him away?" He grinned. "Ellington, are you familiar with the saying, 'keep your friends close and your enemies closer'? Well, Sturgis is both. I've known him since my boyhood days, and I really do consider him a friend. But when it comes to First Church polity and politics, we don't see eye-to-eye. Sturgis Weaver put the 'old' in old school, and he's stubborn as the day is long."

"I've only met him once, up in Dr. Jorgensen's office. I just remember he had a very firm handshake for a senior citizen."

Smitty grinned. "That's probably because Mr. Weaver's the reigning state arm wrestling champion for men eight-five and older. He owns several lumber yards here in town, and the man still occasionally puts on the gloves and helps his guys unload the logs. Strong as an ox, as they say."

Okay that's just a simile or two, but he's getting dangerously close to dropping a metaphor, and Smitty's king of the metaphors.

Smitty turned his attention to Father Ted. "Well, how do you like working at First Church?"

"It's been great. Everyone's been so helpful and kind, and it's good to get back to ministering to people."

"We're very fortunate to have you on the staff. If anyone in the church—staff or layperson alike—gives you any trouble, you let me know and we'll nip that in the bud."

That was an idiom. We're still metaphor free.

"Ted, has Ellington told you about his Carpe Annum program?"

Father Ted busted out laughing. "Say that again?"

Smitty looked confused. "His Carpe Annum program."

Father Ted laughed again. "Oh! Carpe annum—as in, 'seize the year.' I thought you said carpe *anum.*"

Smitty looked at me then back at Father Ted. "Well, what does that mean?"

Father Ted smiled. "Now you know why Latin isn't spoken anymore. Euphemistically translated, carpe anum means 'grab your butt'."

Our raucous laughter filled the room, no doubt spilling into the corridor and even entertaining those at the nurse's station.

10

The Surprise

Arriving at Café Lucia at 1:45, I took a seat in the back and waited for the lunch crowd to clear out. Lucia brought me an iced tea.

"I really appreciate you working with us on this. It's very hard to find a private place for Jason and his friends to catch a meal. Here—he provided me with his Gold Card number to give you. He said to add twenty-five percent for your gratuity."

She smiled. "Now, remember your part of the deal. Before you all leave, he has to play a few of his songs for us. I've invited a few friends. Don't worry, we won't let them in until you all have finished your lunch meeting."

I forced a smile. "Shouldn't be a problem." At least I hoped it wouldn't be. I wondered what she meant by a few friends?

I called Bonnie. "Hey, girl! Are you still going to be able to make it to lunch?"

She sounded tense. "Just got out of a secretaries' meeting with Tom Applebee. They fired Jackie Hightower, Bob Stevens' assistant. She's allegedly been gossiping about some church members' tithing records, and it got back to Tom. Let's just say the succotash hit the fan."

"Ouch. Did Tom come down on the rest of you?"

"Tom's a great guy, but he was all business today. By the way he acted, I have to assume he caught heavy flak from some very unhappy church members. We spent a full hour going over the employee manual and making sure we all understood what each section meant. Absolutely grueling."

"Well, do you still have enough juice left to come over and have lunch?"

"Looking forward to it. I really need a break. In fact, I think I'll just take the rest of the day off. It'll be 2:30 or so before I get there."

That'll be fine. Just call me when you park, and I'll make sure someone up front knows to let you in."

"Remind me again about your friend—an old high school buddy or something?"

"Kind of. Jason's a guy I met while attending college. I'll introduce you when you get here and fill in all the details. See you in a little while. Love ya."

"Backatcha. Bye"

The last lunch patron slipped out a little after two. Lucia locked the front door and pulled down the window shade. About ten minutes later someone tapped on the front door. As I walked over to let them in, I could see it was George, the band's driver and quasi-bodyguard.

I opened the door. "George, great to see you."

He gave me a big bear hug. "Elmo. It's been a while. You look good."

"I see you're still a schmoozer after all these years."

"Goes with the territory," he chortled.

"Where's our boy?" I looked over his shoulder.

"They're waiting in the car for my signal. We play this little cat and mouse game everywhere we go. Jason's just radioactive. Once he steps out in public everything heats up quick. You'll see. What's the paparazzi like around here?"

I laughed. "This isn't New York or L.A. I doubt they even know what that word means in this town."

"Oh, you'll see. I guarantee it." He waved to a silver Lexus with dark tinted windows. The doors opened and out stepped three people, one with a hoodie pulled up over his head and big sunglasses. They made their way to the front door and quickly slipped inside. George locked the door behind them and stayed right there to monitor the parking lot.

Down came the hood, off came the glasses, and there he was— the world-famous Jason McKenzie.

"Elmo Jenkins, my golly look at you! All-grow'd-up and fit as a fiddle. Long time no see!" He gave me a big hug then messed up my hair with his hands. "Now, *that's* more like the Elmo I know."

Jason was ADD before ADD was even cool. Always moving, always smiling, always joking.

"I see you haven't changed one iota. Does the world of rock music just freeze you in time or something?"

"It's the adrenalin. It keeps you young, then one day you wake up and you're like fifty or something. That won't be a happy day." He cut loose with a rowdy roar.

Jason turned to his companions. "Let me introduce you to today's posse. You know George, of course. This here is Lopez McGill. Cool name, huh? Lopez is a publicist for our record label. And this is Art Jones. He's a regional entertainment promoter for your part of the country—you know, music shows, wrestling matches, monster trucks, that type of thing. He also produces all your semi-pro home football games.

"Really? Art, you wouldn't happen to know Jimmy 'Cornbread' Jackson?" I asked.

Art's face flushed red. "Oh, I know Jimmy. The bum blew our playoff game last year. Cost me a thousand bucks on a lost bet, and it got him kicked off the team."

"Any idea what he's doing these days?"

"Don't know and don't care as long as he stays retired."

Lucia stepped out of the kitchen.

"Jason, this is Lucia. She's the owner of this fine establishment. She went way out of her way so we could have some privacy this afternoon and enjoy one of her world- famous sandwiches."

Jason took her hand and looked right into her eyes. The man was a pro when it came to his fans. "Thank you so much, Lucia, for helping us out today. Elmo tells me that you've requested a couple tunes later which I am more than happy to accommodate—with one condition. I understand that you're a fabulous piano player. Would you mind playing a song for us while we have our lunch? I'd be most grateful."

She blushed. This matronly restaurateur, easily in her mid-fifties was under Jason McKenzie's spell. *Unbelievable.*

"It would be an honor Jason. Do you prefer any particular style of music?"

Out came his million-dollar smile. "Do you know any Gershwin?"

"Oh yes. He's one of my favorite composers. How about 'Someone to Watch over Me'?"

He gave her a hug. "That would be fantastic!"

I stood there dumbfounded as I watched her scurry into the kitchen like a teenager who had just met Ringo Starr.

Art, George, and Lopez grabbed a table near the front while Jason and I sat at one near the rear of the dinning room.

"Thanks for doing a couple songs for Lucia." I tossed Jason a menu.

"Ah, it'll be fun. I do this kind of thing all the time."

"I do need to warn you. She said something about inviting a few friends."

"Won't be a problem. Mark my word, they'll all be middle-aged ladies. It's actually a weird phenomenon. We've got all these tweenagers who come to our concerts, but they're too young to drive so their moms come along. So lo and behold, we have this whole demographic of middle-age women who are big fans."

We ordered grinders with a side of Lucia's world-famous potato salad. We played catch-up like old friends do when they haven't seen each other for a while. I asked about his parents, he asked about mine. He wanted to know all about my new job at First Church and, of course, about my upcoming wedding. I asked about his band and his recent and very public breakup with his girlfriend Jennifer.

As we ate our sandwiches, Lucia played the Gershwin tune. I watched closely as Jason sat there stunned at her proficiency on the keys. He begged for an encore, and she played Mason William's *Classical Gas* to which we all responded with an extended standing ovation. Jason thanked her and gave her another hug.

While they were talking about her musical background and training, my cell phone went off. Bonnie had arrived. I signaled to George and he unlocked the front door to let her in. As she entered, I could see a large number of folks had gathered outside. She thanked George and headed toward the back. I could tell she was flustered, so I walked up to meet her.

"You all right?" I helped her take off her coat.

"What's with the crowd outside? I had to elbow my way through to get to the door. There are even photographers."

George smiled at me. "Told ya."

"It'll make sense here in just a moment. I promise." I kissed her on the cheek.

Behind Bonnie, Jason had finished his conversation with Lucia and was walking our way.

"Bonnie, let me introduce you to my good friend, Jason McKenzie." I turned her around just as Jason got to us.

"Hello, Bonnie," Jason said, extending his hand. "It's a pleasure to meet you."

Bonnie shook his hand. "Well, it's nice to—" She snapped her face back toward me. "Did you say *Jason McKenzie?*"

Jason, still holding her hand, smiled. "I'm afraid he did."

Bonnie released Jason's hand and covered her mouth as her jaw dropped. For a few seconds, no one said anything as she studied Jason's smiling face.

"Wait a minute." Bonnie laughed. "Elmo, this is one of your lame practical jokes, isn't it? Come on, Thurm's around here somewhere with a video camera." She scanned the room with her eyes. "Where is he?"

She turned back to Jason who was suppressing a laugh. "You're good, by the way. You could make a living as Jason McKenzie's body double. You have to forgive Elmo here. He thinks he's Ashton Kutcher."

Jason grinned. "Actually, Ashton Kutcher's a friend of mine. We're snowboarding buddies. He's stayed at my place in Estes Park numerous times."

Bonnie tilted her head and gave me a what-the-heck's-going-on-here glare.

I had to laugh. "Okay, this just hasn't gone the way I'd envisioned it. Bonnie, please have a seat and let me rewind and start over."

The three of us sat down at the table.

"This is no prank, and this is indeed the *real* Jason McKenzie. I met Jason in college when I helped organize one of his band's concerts. We've stayed in touch over the years, but I haven't seen him in quite a while. There's no Thurm with a camera, there's no wannabe Aston Kutcher . . . just you, me, and Jason. Honest!"

Bonnie thought for a moment then quickly regrouped. She turned to Jason. "Since we're starting over, Jason, it's very nice to meet you. Please just pretend the last five minutes never happened."

Jason laughed. "No way. Your reaction has been the highlight of my day, maybe my whole week."

Bonnie looked puzzled. "I don't understand?"

"See, when I'm in public, I'm forced to spend all my time behind the silly persona that is Jason McKenzie. So it was totally refreshing when you looked me right in the eye and just blew me off. *Totally* refreshing. Even if you did think I was just some no-account look-a-like actor."

"So you're saying you're not really a diva after all?"

"Not even close. But when you're lucky enough to catch some notoriety for a few years, it comes with a price. The public builds this image of you then pressures you to be that person. But that's not who I am. I'm really a lot more like your boy Elmo here. Which is probably why we became friends."

"Yeah, but you sing a *whole* lot better than he does."

"That's God's honest truth," I had to admit, laughing.

We spent the next half hour visiting. Jason shared some incredible stories from the road and how his faith kept him steady when the world swirling around him was out of control. Bonnie shared about her dream to be a writer and perhaps teach creative writing at the college level. And then our time together was up.

Jason gave us each a hug before slipping onto the piano bench and directing George to let 'em in. A crowd of about two hundred people filed in and sat around the tables or stood around the perimeter. They were very well-behaved. Just as Jason had predicted, most of them were middle-age women with a few daughters tagging along.

He spun around on the piano bench facing the crowd with a big grin.

"Welcome to the Café Lucia impromptu *Out of the Blue* all-requests mini-concert!" And with that, he performed some of the band's most popular songs with verve and vigor. Twenty minutes or so later he was whisked away by George. As the cameras flashed, he dove into the silver Lexus and was gone.

I put my arm around Bonnie's waist as we waved goodbye from the sidewalk. "Now, *that* was fun."

Bonnie laid her head on my shoulder. "Any other people from your past I need to know about? Any chance you know Brad Pitt?"

11

The Tripod

Friday mornings at First Church were unusually quiet because most of the ministerial staff members weren't in the office. Since Father Ted had now joined the staff to handle all pastoral ministries, Fred Snooker cut back his office schedule to Mondays and Wednesdays only. I missed my Friday morning talks with Pastor Snooker. These casual conversations had played a beneficial role in my development during my internship.

Good church staffs operate much like a healthy extended family. The older more experienced staff members take the newer ministers under their wings and nurture them through the overwhelming challenges they often confront. First Church had a nice blend of young, median, and older staff members.

My desk phone rang. "Good morning," I said in an earnest yet early-morning-appropriate tone.

"Morning, Elmo," Juliann responded. "We have a gentleman here who needs to talk with a minister, and Father Ted isn't in yet. Can you come out front?"

"Is this a benevolence case?"

"Possibly."

"I'll be right out. Have him wait in the conference room and check with Bob Stevens to make sure we have some food vouchers available if needed."

"Will do. Thanks, Elmo."

The disheveled man I found slouched down in a conference room chair looked to be in his mid-forties. He wore an expensive suit, but its crumbled appearance suggested it had been slept in more than once.

"Hello, I'm Elmo Jenkins, one of the ministers here at First Church." I shook his hand. "How can we help you today?"

"To be honest, I'm not sure. My name is Chester LaBarre, and my whole life is now officially in the toilet. I've been wandering around on the streets for a couple of days, and I when I saw your church I figured, what the hell. I have nothing left to lose, so here I am."

I started to request that he avoid using profanity, but then I reasoned the last thing this poor fellow needed was a sanctimonious lecture.

Sliding into a chair at the table, I silently prayed for wisdom. "I tell you what, Chester. Let's start at the beginning, okay?"

I sat there and listened attentively as the man shared how his life had totally unraveled.

According to Chester, a year ago he had it all—a beautiful wife, children, a home in the burbs, a stable six-figure job, and all the amenities that life could offer. And then the world conspired against him and systematically, each of the aforementioned blessings was diabolically torn from his grasp. He was a broken man stripped totally of pride, arrogance, self-sufficiency, and hope. In a weird way I simultaneously felt both sorry and thrilled for him. Sorry for his great loss and the subsequent pain it had wrought; thrilled he had chosen to step into a church for help.

He said he'd only been in a church two other times in his entire life. Once for a friend's wedding and once for the funeral for a family member.

"Chester," I said, "It's no accident that you wandered into our church. God loves you and has a purpose for your life. I believe in a God of new beginnings, and I believe you can start your life anew. With God's love and care, you can put things back together, but this time with God involved."

The door to the hall opened and Father Ted walked in.

"Mornin', guys. Mind if I join you?"

I smiled. "Please do."

Chester sat up. "Hey, you're the guy who did my Aunt Betsy's funeral last year. You said some very meaningful things to me and my family that day."

That seemed to open a door. Ted, Chester, and I spent quite a while talking about life and about God.

When it was all said and done, Chester bowed his head and invited Christ into his life. He promised to come by once a week to visit with Ted, and we supplied him with a Bible and some devotional books. We also hooked him up with a men's group of new believers who were going through a discipleship study.

Material needs were not an issue for Chester. He had a new job starting in a few days and lived in a downtown apartment. He just needed emotional and spiritual support. Both Ted and I committed to being there for him.

Chester appeared to be a changed man as he stood and gave both of us an extended hug.

So far it had been a good day.

I began scheduling interviews for the Carpe Annum project. Deciding to start with a sampling of the staff, I selected:

Doreen McGinty, Children's Ministry Director
Thurm Wilson, Youth Pastor
Harry Simpkins, Minister of Music
Louis Estrada, Minister of Singles
Raze Hankins, Minister to Married Adults

I wanted these interviews to be less structured and more "stream of consciousness" oriented. I wanted to reach below the pat answers, those standard answers we all usually give to standard questions. With that in mind, I decided to keep the names of any staff members interviewed anonymous in the final report. I theorized this would make it easier for them to be candid with their responses.

Once the staff interviews were complete, I would move on to a series of interviews with selected laypeople from the church. I wanted to talk to at least one person from each age group. An ambitious undertaking, but with the better part of a full year to accomplish the task, I knew it could be done. Remembering that I had to work around my ministerial duties and requisite meetings, I set an attainable goal of two interviews per week. This would allow ample time for compilation and analysis.

Someone knocked on my office door.

"Come in."

"Mornin', Elmo," said a smiling Fred Snooker as he poked his head in from the hallway. "Do you have a minute to spare for an old man?"

"You bet. Come on in, Pastor. I thought you were taking Fridays off now that Father Ted's on board?" I stepped around my desk to shake his hand, then directed him to have a seat in my wingback chair. I sat down on my loveseat.

"Oh, I'm not here on church business. I came to ask you for permission and a favor in regard to a new project I'm undertaking."

"Okay, what's the new project?"

"I've decided to write a book. It's something I've always wanted to do. Now that I have the time and a great idea, I'm ready to get after it."

I smiled. "That's fantastic. What's the topic?"

He leaned forward in his chair. "Here's where I need your permission. I've decided to write a book about the Black Toe Enigma."

"Really?"

"Yes, and I'm pretty exited about doing it. I spent so many years searching for the answer to that mystery, and now that it's solved I want to make sure it's not forgotten."

"Why do you need *my* permission?"

"Your interest and zeal last year helped revive the quest which ultimately led to the truth coming out."

"I enjoyed the research, but it's Dunston Jones who gets all the credit for stepping forward and revealing the secret. He could have easily let the truth die with him."

"True. That's why I've already talked to Dunston, and he's agreed to let me interview him for the book. What I need from you is permission to use your notes and the charts you created."

"Permission granted, but there's really not much material available other than what's already in the TBT binder. It may be a very short book."

Fred chuckled. "Oh, I'm just going to use the Black Toe Mystery as a story arc. There's a plethora of great First Church anecdotal material from the last hundred years to draw from to complete the narrative. It'll end up being a coffee table history of First Church with photos and everything."

"Wow, that'll be cool. What's the favor you need from me?"

"I'd like you to write the Foreword."

I hesitated. "I'm honored, but why me? Why not Dr. Jorgensen, or Harty Smith, or even Dunston?"

"Because it was your passion and tenacity that revived the search. Without you, it never would have been solved. I'm convinced of that. I'd be lying on my deathbed wondering about the mystery man with the frostbitten foot."

"Well, it will be an honor, then. When do you need it?"

"No big hurry, but the sooner the better. My editor is a bit prickly."

"Your editor?"

"Here's the kicker. Dr. De Villa has agreed to be my editor."

"Whoa . . . are you sure that's a good idea?"

"Now that Augie and I are friends again, thanks to your fine work, it seemed like a natural choice. He's actually a top-shelf editor, having edited numerous educational texts over the years."

"Who knew? Good for you guys. I'm sure it'll turn out great. If possible I'd like to get a signed first edition copy for a keepsake. I may even use it to a start a collection of signed books like Rick Warren does. I've got plenty of room since my current library is quite small. And unlike Dr. De Villa, we both know I'll never need any shelf space for bowling trophies."

"Or tennis trophies," Pastor Snooker added. We both laughed.

"I'm going to miss our Friday chats. But while I've got you here, mind if I ask a personal question?"

"Fire away."

"All of a sudden, everywhere I turn, I'm either hearing about or seeing Sturgis Weaver. I don't remember hearing his name mentioned last year, but I now understand he goes way back, even to the days of Dr. Sapp. I'm assuming you're well acquainted with the man. How about giving me some of your savvy insight into what's going on?"

"He's a cicada," Snooker said as his eyes narrowed.

"I'm sorry, I don't understand?"

"A cicada is a flying insect that lies dormant in the ground for up to seventeen years at a time. Then it loudly emerges creating quite a mess for a few weeks. Then it vanishes for another seventeen years."

"Is that a metaphor or a simile?"

Dr. Snooker's eyebrows rose and his eyes widened. "Well, I don't rightly know. Why?"

"Eh, it's not important, but I understand what you're saying. Sturgis Weaver has reemerged and is stirring things up. How often does this happen?"

"About once a decade or so. Maybe a half-dozen times since I've been at First Church. It usually plays out the same way. He picks some issue that's gotten stuck in his craw. He rallies his troops and they storm the castle, so to speak, usually in a deacon's meeting. He's soundly defeated, and like the cicada he disappears for another eight to ten years. Then the cycle repeats itself."

"So what's your advice to a new young staff member during this cicada outbreak?"

"Oh, I wouldn't worry about it too much. The heads Sturgis is after have a much higher pay grade than either you or me."

Friday night finally arrived. I still had a lingering suspicion about Eddie's get-together, but I just couldn't put my finger on why.

I picked up Bonnie on the way. When I arrived at her apartment, I jumped out and opened the car door for her. *What are the chances I'll be hopping out to open her car door in a few years? If I turn out like most other married men, the chances are little to none. Why is that?*

"Hey, beautiful." And she was. Skinny jeans. Oversized muted-red sweater. Long brown hair hanging ever so gently on her shoulders. "You look great. Let's just stay in and skip the party."

"Now, Elmo. Don't you want to meet George 'Buttermilk' Jones?"

"No, no, it's Jimmy 'Cornbread' Jackson. Why can't anyone remember the dude's name? It's cornbread. Cornbread, for Pete's sake! It just can't be that hard."

"You seem a bit tense, sweetie. Everything all right?" She massaged the back of my neck.

"To be honest, I'm somewhat concerned about the nature of Eddie's party. But the massage is helping. Like I said, let's just stay in."

"Elmo."

"Please?"

"There'll be ample time for massages later. Put the car in drive, put your size 12 on the gas pedal, and let's go. We promised, so let's fulfill our obligation to a friend."

"Dang. All right, all right. Like cattle heading to the slaughter house, they unknowingly marched on . . ."

"What's with all the drama? Have you been reading Tolstoy or something?"

"Nah, I just hope I'm wrong."

We turned off Winchester Avenue into the Terracotta Condominiums parking garage and deposited our ride in the visitor's area. As I stepped out of the car, I knew immediately we were in an upscale facility. If living here didn't help Eddie with the ladies, nothing in this material world would . . . which was, in fact, a distinct possibility.

Riding the glass elevator up to the thirteenth floor, I stole a quick embrace and a kiss. Something about looking out over the city skyline at dusk from a moving glass booth a hundred feet above the ground fired up my ardor. Or maybe it was just Bonnie's skinny jeans.

Bonnie knocked firmly on the door marked *1313*. Eddie greeted us, looking dapper and relaxed in his coordinated black shirt and slacks, with almost a Johnny Cash vibe. He'd either had some wardrobe coaching from Cornbread Jackson, or perhaps the Terracotta mystic had just taken hold. Regardless, both Bonnie and I marveled at the new Eddie—that is, until he opened his mouth and reality came crashing back down to earth.

"Elmo, where'd you pick up this hot mama? Dig the sweater."

"Why, thank you Eddie," Bonnie said while elbowing me in the ribs, effectively cutting off any inappropriate response I was apt to mutter. "Nice place you have here."

"Let me give you the tour," Eddie said, putting his arm around my shoulder.

We took a right turn through the kitchen where Eddie had enlisted Juliann to help with the refreshments. He may have gotten good advice on what to wear, but he totally dropped the ball on the food and drink. Juliann was filling miniature plastic cups, the kind you use to gargle mouthwash, with either Kool-Aid or possibly Crystal Light.

Uh oh. Black outfit. Kool-Aid in plastic cups. I hoped Eddie hadn't gone all Jim Jones on us.

The "quaint" cups of beverage were complemented by a large Tupperware bowl of trail mix and a paper plate stacked with cheese cubes, each skewered by a red toothpick. So much for the highly-touted refreshments.

"Looks like we'll be heading to Casa Verda as soon as this *faux-fiesta* winds down," I whispered in Bonnie's ear.

Once through kitchen, we took a left into the living room area. A dozen or so people sat around the room on couches and chairs. I recognized a few of the faces from the First Church singles group, but I didn't know most of the folks. That's when I noticed them all looking intently at slick four-color travel magazines and luxury home brochures.

What's wrong with this picture?

Over in the corner, a tall, muscular guy stood looking over a collection of three-by-five cards. Mensa rocket scientist that I am, I quickly discerned he must be the infamous Jimmy "Cornbread" Jackson.

Wait a minute. The pieces began falling into place. Cheap refreshments. Travel magazines. Three-by- five cards . . .

Still, one crucial component was missing. Hoping against all odds, I slowly scanned the room.

Ah no! There, standing against the far wall—a tripod and its insidious counterpart, the dreaded flip chart!

"Eddie, excuse us for a second. I need a word with Bonnie." As I pulled her back into the kitchen, I lowered my voice. "We've been had."

"What are you talking about? We just got here."

"I'm talking about a tripod, a flip chart, a sales pitch—the multi-level vortex!"

Bonnie turned to Juliann who continued filling the stupid little cups. "Hey, Juliann, did Eddie tell you what we'll be doing tonight?"

"No, but I did overhear him and Jimmy talking. Isn't Jimmy cute?" She giggled.

I butted in. "Focus, Juliann. What were they talking about?"

"Oh, something about a presentation and commitment cards, and such."

I winced. "I knew it, I knew it, I knew it. Let's skedaddle."

Bonnie the Rock gave me a squeeze. "Elmo, you need to man up here. What are we talking about, maybe an hour? Just suffer through this and then we'll go grab some dinner. Okay?"

"All right, but only because you've insisted."

We walked back into the living room and sat down on a couple of folding chairs in the back. Bonnie flipped through one of travel magazines, but I just sat there silently, selfishly praying for a miracle. *Let's see. There could be a storm with a power outage— meeting over. Or there could be a HVAC malfunction—meeting over. Or there could be a bomb scare and they would have to evacuate the building—meeting over.*

Eddie stepped to the middle of the room and called for everyone's attention.

"I'd like to thank y'all for coming tonight. I hope you've enjoyed the fine refreshments and the camaraderie. I'd now like to introduce to you my roommate and friend, Jimmy 'Cornbread' Jackson."

I'm not sure why but we all applauded when Jimmy stepped up to speak. Then, before he could get his tripod and flip chart set up, my miracle arrived. My cell phone went off! I apologized as I stepped into the kitchen to take the call. I'd forgotten I was the First Church minister on call for weekend emergencies. They needed me to make a hospital visit pronto. *Yes!!!* I waved both Bonnie and Eddie into the kitchen just as Jimmy began his pitch.

"Eddie, I'm really sorry. I'm the minister on call, and I'm needed over at Mercy Clinic. We're going to have to go ahead and leave early. Thanks for inviting us. You have a great place here."

"No problem, guys. I'll just get you for the next one. Bye." His condo door closed behind us.

I grinned as we headed for the elevator. "Oh, no you won't!"

12

The Acoustic Venue

"**I**'ll just sit here in the visitor's area while you make your visit. I inadvertently walked out of Eddie's get-together with one his travel magazines. It'll keep me occupied. Take all the time you need," Bonnie said as she took a seat.

I proceeded down the corridor to the hospital registration desk. "Hello, I'm Elmo Jenkins from First Church. We received a call that one of your patients requested a ministry visit."

The nurse smiled up at me. "Just a moment, Reverend Jenkins. Let me check the request log for you."

I didn't get called "reverend" very often, probably because of my age. I stood a little straighter, though I'm not sure why. Her nametag read *Nurse Durkin*. Boy, that sounded familiar, but I couldn't think where I'd heard it before. It really bugs me when I can't recall stuff. Like it's right there, but I just can't find the words to say it. *Bummer.*

She glanced up again. "Here we go. Mr. Dunston Jones in Room 107. Just down the hall behind me. It's after visiting hours, so you'll have him all to yourself. He had a crowd in there earlier. Sounded like they were having a revival."

"Yep, that would be Dunston. What's he in for?"

"He had a minor stroke. Says here there's no permanent damage and he'll be treated with medication and released, probably tomorrow."

"Thanks for the info. One more thing, if you don't mind. Is Durkin a family name?"

She laughed. "The answer to your real question is *The Tooth Fairy*."

"That's it! The old radio program." I blushed. "You've been asked that question before, probably many times. Sorry."

"Oh no, I think it's funny. I get that query about once a week, ever since I married David Durkin last spring. I'm sure it'll get old one day. I'm just glad my husband's last name wasn't Ratched."

"I bet," I said, as we shared a laugh.

I tapped on the door and stuck my head in Room 107. "Anybody home?"

Dunston sat up and smiled. "Man, look what d' cat's done drug in here. Elmo Jenkins. Mighty fine to see ya. Come on in, son."

I stepped into his room. "Dunston, how are you?"

"Fine-'n-you?" he said with his famous big grin.

"Did you make yourself sick fishin' too much?"

"Elmo, you knows better. You can't fish too much. Fishin's good fo' you. Helps you re-lax."

"Yeah, that's what I hear, though it's never had that effect on me."

"It will, it will. Once da lake warms up, you 'n me'll go do us some catchin' and then we'll do us some eatin'. Fish samiches, o'course."

"I look forward to it. Just give me a call when you're ready."

"I'll do it. I promise."

"Great. Listen, what happened for you to end up here at Mercy Clinic?"

"Oh, I's been havin' some dizzy spells and all. Took me a couple falls. Fell in da lake once. Wasn't too deep, but musta scared da fish real good 'cause I didn't catch a'nuther resta' d'day."

"Dizzy spells? Wow."

"Yep, and I fell again dis mornin'. So the misses said, 'Enough of dat mess,' and she hauled my sorry hind-end up here to da clinic. You know, to get it all checked out and such."

"She did the right thing. They'll probably put you on some blood thinners and maybe some blood pressure meds. You'll be back at the lake before you can say fish-or-cut-bait."

"I s'pose you're right."

I helped Dunston adjust his pillows. "Pastor Snooker told me you're going to help out with his new book."

He chuckled. "Dat's right. I'mo get some of d'old janitors together—Red, Johnny D, maybe Sonny. We'll have Pastor Snooker over and spill de beans 'bout da whole dang thing. Have us some big fun."

"I'm sure it will be."

I spent another ten or fifteen minutes with Dunston, mostly listening to him tell First Church stories. Then I prayed for him and slipped out.

Back in the corridor I found Bonnie at the desk chatting with Nurse Durkin. A couple minutes later, we headed for the parking lot.

She gave me a kiss on the cheek. "What's ya hungry for?"

Casa Verde was jammed, so I made an executive decision, and we headed for Café Lucia. We got lucky and were seated at our favorite secluded booth in the back.

"How's Dunston?" Bonnie asked, slipping into the booth.

"He's got some circulation issues. Old man stuff. They'll put him on meds, and he should be fine."

"Will he still be able to fish?"

"They couldn't keep him from it. He'll die at that lake one day, happy as a clam, and no one will be surprised."

"Think he'll still take you fishing out there?"

"Yeah, that's what he says, and I hope he does. I'd like to do 'some-catchin-n-some-eatin' at least once in my life."

Bonnie laughed. "Ah, you're too funny. Speaking of eatin', hand me one of the menus, please?"

"Yes, ma'am."

She looked over the menu. "I had a nice conversation with Nancy Durkin."

"The nurse?"

"Yes. She got married around this time last year and told me all about her wedding."

"Really? You girls. Can't leave you alone for a minute. What'd she say?"

"They had their wedding in what she called an 'acoustic venue'."

I closed my menu. "An acoustic venue?"

"The way she described it, they wanted their ceremony to have a vintage feel to it. So, they found this old turn-of-the-century church out on State Road 253 about twenty minutes from town. The church is actually a registered historical site. There's not been an active congregation there for many years. She said they have this cool amphitheatre out back that's cut into the side of a small mountain. It has natural acoustics, so there's no need for mics or speakers. It'll seat up to a hundred people, and everyone can hear every word that's spoken or sung."

"What if Mother Nature shows up uninvited?"

"She said the old church sanctuary is a great back-up in case of bad weather."

I could tell this acoustic venue idea really piqued Bonnie's imagination. I wanted our wedding to be something special. Weddings are one of those top-tier life events—especially for the ladies. Many girls dream about and plan for their weddings starting at an early age.

Most men on the other hand, myself included, are clueless when it comes to this special day. We know we're supposed to be there and preferably on time. We know there are customized, often expensive clothes to be worn. There're usually a couple of rings involved, again often expensive. There are parents and friends to include, and something about a cake. Beyond that, our brains begin to swell. So, like all good future husbands, we just do what we're told and stay out of the way.

Now, ask us about the honeymoon, and we know every single detail with razor sharp clarity. This is an immutable fact.

This gender disparity shows up again after the wedding when it comes to, say, something like shopping. A man can easily spend four hours walking up and down hills with a forty-pound golf bag on his shoulder. Yet, if he goes to the mall with his wife, his legs grow weak after only twenty minutes, and he needs to either sit for an extended period or go home for a nap. Go figure.

I reached across the table and took Bonnie's hand. "I like the acoustic venue idea. Why don't we drive out there one afternoon and check it out?"

She squeezed my hand and looked back with loving eyes. I knew I had just hit a home run. A rare and wonderful experience for me, but I was learning.

Since I now had some momentum, I decided to stay on the offensive. "If we go this acoustic venue route, what if we also wear vintage clothing? How cool would that be to dress up like a couple getting married in the Roaring Twenties, or even the Civil War era?"

She paused for a pensive moment. "You know, that might be really cool. We could have all our wedding photos done in sepia tones, giving them that old-timey look. Kind of an antique motif."

"Where do you find old clothes like that?" I took a sip of iced tea.

"We'll have to check out the costume shops in town, or maybe the Starwood Neighborhood Playhouse. I bet Father Ted knows some people who could help."

Now I was the contemplative one. "What do you think about Father Ted doing the service? We've become friends, and he's been counseling me on some of the finer points of married life."

"I think that's a great idea. I like Father Ted. Normally, I would have defaulted to Louis since he's my boss, but I've been to a few weddings he's officiated, and . . . well, let's just say weddings aren't his strong suit."

"Okay, we've got the place, we've got the clothes, we've got the preacher. Now, what about the music?"

"Whoa. Elmo, I know you're a decisive guy and you like to aggressively pull the trigger, but you need to slow down and take a few deep breaths. We're planning our wedding, not shopping for a new lawnmower. These are just concepts we're talking about. You have to ruminate on the ideas and let them develop slowly. The process of planning a wedding is just as important as the wedding itself. And it can be just as much fun."

I felt a bit patronized. "As a man, I simply don't understand what that means. And did you just compare our wedding planning to a cow chewing its cud?"

Bonnie's raised an eyebrow. "Perhaps you need another session with Father Ted?"

"Ouch? The Queen of Sarcasm has returned and with a vengeance."

She raised both hands. "Time out. It's been a long day for both of us, at the end of a long week. We got a good start talking about the wedding, but I suggest we table that discussion for now. Do you concur?"

"Yeah. And sorry about the Queen of Sarcasm comment."

This time she reached across the table and took my hand. "I'm sorry too about the Father Ted quip. I have an idea. Let's get our dinners to go and head back to my place for some kiss-and-make-up snuggling."

I smiled. "I definitely understand what that means, and I concur."

13

The Lost Key Ring

Life flew by. Hours turned into days, days turned into weeks. Things were becoming routine, which I liked, of course. But it does make time move faster—at least in my opinion.

We took a trip out to see the old church on Route 253. Bonnie loved it for its ambience and setting. I loved it because it was free! You only had to pay a small maintenance stipend for the janitor. So naturally, we booked it.

Bonnie warmed up big time to the vintage clothes and photo concept, so the planning and implementation phases moved into warp drive. I wisely stepped out of the way and let her run with the ball.

Back at First Church, my staff interviews progressed well. I'd also begun calling other churches around the country that had taken a similar path as ours to get their feedback. I scheduled on-site visits to several of the more helpful. I was amassing a large quantity of valuable data, but I still had a long way to go.

Most Monday mornings I'd be one of the first staff members to arrive at the church office. Sundays were grueling, so Tom Applebee more or less looked the other way on Monday mornings, allowing the ministerial staff to drag in later than usual. But I'm fastidiously routine-dependant, so I usually made it there on time.

On this particular Monday I arrived before anyone else. Flipping on the break room light, I snatched my mail from the slot and headed up the dark hall to my office.

After walking into my even darker office, I pulled the chain on my desk lamp, tossed my mail on my desk—and jumped straight back three or four feet screaming like a little girl! There in the murky glow of my office, sitting in my desk chair with her spooky-tooth eyes glistening in the dim light was Ferty! I couldn't believe it. How could . . . where did . . . who knew . . .? Complete sentences eluded me.

After a long moment of reflection, I shifted quickly from embarrassment to anger. Whoever was behind this prank had played with my mind for the last time. I jerked the stupid plastic statue out of my chair and marched straight out to the church dumpster to throw the dang thing away for good.

Before I read Ferty her last rites, I had a thought. *These things are clearly inexpensive. A smart, committed prankster could easily have purchased two or three of them to prolong the joke on ol' Elmo as long as possible.* So I flipped her upside down and with my pocket knife, I carved the words *Nice Try.* If she showed up in my office again I would simply check for my carving and quickly know how this charade was being perpetuated.

Giving Ferty a kiss on the cheek, I tossed her into the dumpster fully expecting that to be the end of it. Well, to be truthful, I really *hoped* that would be the end of it, but I had legitimate doubts. I was obviously dealing with a fiendish mastermind.

Back in the Taj, I began my day as always by sharpening my pencil and going over my To-Do List. I had a few hospital visits to make before lunch. Then I would meet Bonnie for a hotdog over on the downtown mall. My afternoon agenda looked fairly normal with the exception of my interview with Raze Hankins, our minister to married adults. A necessary interview, but to be honest, one I would rather skip.

First Church staff members and brothers Terry and Raze Hankins were a modern day Jacob and Esau. Terry and Raze were the sons and only children of the infamous itinerant evangelist—and occasional snake handler—Ezekiel Jedediah Hankins. Their father died (from a snake bite, as you probably surmised) when they were still quite young. Their mother, a quick study in spousal selection snafus, then married an older widowed Baptist pastor named Leon Pasquale. Pastor Pasquale, as he was lovingly referred to by his small number of congregants, raised the boys on conservative theology and conservative life choices.

Terry, like Jacob in the Bible, was the younger and more street clever of the two brothers. Full of life, everything always seemed to go his way. Raze, not unlike Esau, tended to be more impulsive and brooding, often quietly seething over his younger brother's victories and exploits.

Both Hankins boys attended Pensacola Christian College and after graduation worked in various ministry positions before finding their way to First Church. Terry arrived first, serving as the college-and-career pastor. He quickly excelled in that capacity, becoming a rising star on the church staff. Several years later, when the position for minister to married adults came open, Tom Applebee jumped at the opportunity to hire Terry's brother's Raze.

At least, that's what most folks think.

Actually, Raze had bounced around working in several different churches, always leaving just as the ax was perched to fall. He had been out of work for quite some time when Tom hired him as a personal favor to Terry.

How do I know all this about the Hankins brothers? Thurm told me. How does he know? I have no idea.

On a talented staff of precise, hard workers like Bob Stevens, Tom Applebee, and Ramona Holloway, or creative and energetic minds like Harry Simpkins and Louis Estrada, Raze Hankins was an odd fit. He kept to himself, rarely interacted at staff meetings, and basically stayed focused on his area of ministry. Maybe he'd learned from his previous church position failures to just keep his head down and his mouth shut.

On top of everything else, I could tell Raze didn't like me, probably because of my quasi-flip demeanor.

Figuring a neutral location would be a wise choice, I scheduled Raze to meet me in the conference room at three o'clock, then I prayed for wisdom. I'd have to deal with him later, but for now I had other tasks to accomplish. I grabbed my hospital slips and my jacket, and hit the door running.

Cool but comfortable. That's how I described the fresh air as Bonnie and I found an empty park bench to eat our Hebrew brand hot dogs.

"You know, since these are Hebrew hot dogs, you have to eat them from right to left," I said with an erudite flair.

"I can only assume that's some type of linguistic humor, which I don't get since I don't read Hebrew."

"It's never too late to start. Hebrew, unlike English and the other Latin-based languages, is written from right to left." *Oh, the seminary pedigree.*

She wasn't impressed. "What is this, Elmo's Hebrew 101? Okay, smarty-pants. Say I open a book written in Hebrew, but I don't even know what Hebrew looks like. What difference does it make if I try to read it left to right, or right to left?"

"Technically none, I guess, but—"

"Stay with me. Since I've already established that I don't know what the Hebrew language looks like, and concordantly I don't know how a Hebrew hot dog looks any different from other brands—" She paused. "Are you still with me?"

I scratched my head. "I think so?"

She pushed on. "Then it really doesn't make any difference if I eat this hot dog from left to right or right to left, does it?"

"What is this, Bonnie's Logic 101?" I laughed. "One thing I do know. If you don't stop prattling on and on, I'm going to eat *both* of our hot dogs."

She narrowed her eyes. "Reach out your hand for my hot dog and you'll pull back a stub," she said with a raspy, sadistic laugh.

When you're young and in love, everything's funny. Even the stupid stuff. You just *enjoy* each other's company. How else do you explain three-hour phone calls or two-hour snogging sessions? So why, after a few years of marriage, does it turn into twenty-second phone calls and a kiss on the cheek—if you're lucky? I didn't want our life together to be that way.

"Subject change." I washed down a bite of hot dog with a sip of coke. "I forgot to tell you about my latest 'You Just Won't Believe It' episode yesterday morning at church."

"What happened?"

"You Just Won't Believe It," I said in a deep radio announcer's voice, channeling my inner Tooth Fairy narrator.

"Okay, I got that part. Now what actually happened?"

I stood up to add some gravitas to my storytelling. "Six weeks ago on a Sunday morning I was hanging out after church at the Visitor's Welcome Desk in the foyer."

"You mean *the vestibule?*"

"No, I mean *foyer*. The word *vestibule* bothers me."

"Well, it's better than *narthex*. That sounds like something you should spray on bugs."

Exasperated, I put my hands on my hips. "Do you want to hear the story or not?"

"Yes, yes." She smiled. "Sorry."

"Anyway, remember I'm at the Visitor's Desk when all of a sudden Rob Holbrook comes rushing up to me all a-fluster and froth."

"Cute phrasing."

"Bonnie."

"Again, sorry."

"Rob has lost his key ring and he's frantic. He says the ring holds his house keys, his businesses keys, and his car keys. His wife has a backup set with her, but she only has keys to their house and car. He shows me her key ring because they drive some spiffy foreign number and the ignition key is big and clunky—very-odd looking. He figures, in case they're turned in, I can identify them as his because of the unique car key. I promise to call him if his keys turn up. Well, they don't and I forget all about it."

I paused to let the drama build.

Bonnie leans forward on the park bench. "Okaaaay. Then what happened?"

"You Just Won't Believe It!" I repeated in my deep radio announcer's voice.

"ELMO!"

I snicker. "Anyway, so yesterday—remember now, this is six weeks later—Jess Albright comes up to me holding a set of keys and says, 'Any idea who these belong to?' I take one look at the keys and I'm gobsmacked. It's Rob Holbrook's key ring, clunky ignition key and all!

"Jess proceeds to tell me that he owns six sport coats which he wears to church on a six-week rotating schedule. He put on the coat Sunday morning—the one he would've worn six weeks ago—and discovered the key ring in his pocket.

"Evidently, Rob must have been at the Visitor's Welcome Desk that fateful morning, talking to someone and laid his keys on counter. Jess, who volunteers behind the desk, must have inadvertently scooped up the keys thinking they were his and put them in his coat pocket. Where—"

"Where they hibernated for six weeks," she gasped. "Ouch! Have you called Rob?"

"Yep. Poor guy. For security reasons he'd been forced to have the locks at both his house and his business changed. Though when I called, he seemed genuinely happy to discover what had happened."

"I bet," she said before finishing off her last bite of hot dog.

"Cue the music . . . ta da, ta da da da, ta da. And that's another 'You Just Won't Believe It'. Until next week, I'm Elmo Jenkins."

I sat back down. "I'm considering using that radio voice when I do my wedding vows. What d'ya think?"

"I think you're an insufferable spaz. Speaking of weddings, have you had a chance to ask Father Ted if he would officiate ours?"

"Yes, and he said he would love to. There is one caveat, albeit a beneficial one. He requires that we go through three premarital counseling sessions with him."

"Sounds great."

"Whew. I assumed—which I know you should never do—you'd be all in for the sessions, so I went ahead and agreed to them."

"I'm all in. Just let me know when and where."

"Wonderful!" I gave her a big wet kiss on the cheek.

"Easy, fella," she said, laughing while she wiped off her cheek.

We started walking back toward the church arm-in-arm. "Let me tell you what happened with Ferty this morning. . ."

14

The Tirade

For two hours each Wednesday morning the first floor conference/ boardroom comes alive with budgets and debates, agendas and calendar dates. For the remaining one hundred sixty-six hours each week, it sits mostly vacant except for an occasional special meeting or interview.

I flipped on the lights and sat down at the conference table. The clock on the end wall showed two fifty-five. I spent a few moments perusing my Carpe Annum folder. I also said a prayer.

At five after three Raze Hankins walked in.

"Raze, come on in and have a seat." I directed him to a chair at the conference table. "Hope you're having a good day."

He semi-smiled as he took a seat. "It's okay, I guess."

"I really appreciate you taking the time to talk with me today."

"Didn't know it was optional. How long will this take?"

"Not too long. I promise. Let me explain what we're trying to accomplish with all of these staff interviews."

"We're?"

"Let me rephrase that. Dr. Jorgensen and Mr. Fitzsimons have given me the task of gathering information that will be used to help formulate a strategy for the future of First Church."

"Were the deacons involved in the launching of your little initiative?"

I was taken aback by the implication in his question. "Well, Raze, to be honest I don't know. Since both Dr. Jorgensen and Mr. Fitzsimons are active in the deacons' meetings I'd have to assume—"

"Ah, never mind. Let's just get on with it." He leaned back in his chair and crossed his arms.

"Raze, if this isn't a good time we can reschedule for another day."

"Nope, I'm here. Let's just do what we gotta do and move on."

I closed my folder sensing my normal methodology wouldn't work well with Raze. I wondered if he was attempting some sort of stress interview technique on me.

Dr. De Ville used to talk about these situations in his seminary psyche courses.

He would say, "If you ever find yourself in the middle of a stress interview, here's what you should do. Stay calm at all costs. No matter how hard the other person tries to intimidate or aggravate you, keep your cool. Then stand up and walk around as you talk. This changes the dynamic of the interaction and puts you in a position of power over the other person who's sitting."

So I stood up and started pacing a bit. "Raze, how long have you been a staff member here at First Church?"

"I'm not sure why that's relevant, but I've been here a little over five years."

Ignoring his defensiveness I forged ahead. "Okay. And what are your major areas of responsibility on the staff?"

"I'm in charge of the entire married adult Sunday School program. I recruit and train the teachers. I order the curriculum. I coordinate the necessary space for rooms and make sure all the bases are covered each Sunday. I meet individually on a regular basis with each teacher for encouragement and instruction."

"How many married adults attend Sunday school here at First Church?"

"We average around twelve hundred in our married adult Sunday School classes each week."

He was proud of that number. I could tell by the way he said it. So I stroked his ego. "Wow, that's a lot of folks studying the Bible. Of those twelve hundred people, how many would you say are over the age of fifty?"

"I don't know, Jenkins. Off the top of my head—maybe sixty-five percent."

The high percentage startled me. "You're telling me that two thirds of the married adults here at First Church are over the age of fifty?"

"Yes, of those married adults who attend Sunday School. That's what you asked, wasn't it?" He sounded a bit testy.

"This is going to be tougher than I thought," I mumbled, thinking out loud to myself.

He bristled. "Just what do you mean by that?"

"The goal of this whole Carpe Annum thing is to figure out how to make First Church relevant not only for the current membership but also for the next generation coming up behind it."

He stood up, all in a huff. "I can tell you for a fact that the members in my program like things at First Church just the way they are. These people have attended faithfully and given sacrificially to First Church for years. They've earned the right to keep the church just the way they like it. They won't tolerate any gimmickry or slick changes just for the sake of being culturally acceptable."

I could almost see steam coming out of his ears. "Easy, man. Why the anger all of a sudden? If I've offended you, I didn't mean to and I'm sorry."

Ignoring my apology he continued his tirade. "Regardless of what your powerful friends are up to, you need to understand there's talk among the members, and many of them are unhappy with the situation."

"Raze, I've no idea what you're referring to. Can give me some more specifics to help me better understand the problem?"

"You've been out of seminary what—less than a year? No wonder you're clueless. When you've been around as long as I have, you learn to see the writing on the wall. As a matter of fact, here's an Old Testament clue you can chew on." He marched over to the white board and wrote: *Mene, Mene, Tekel u-Pharsin.*

Then he wheeled around and blew out of the conference room slamming the door behind him.

I sat back down at the table. After a long moment of contemplation I opened my Carpe Annum folder to the schedule of staff interviews and put a check mark by the name Raze Hankins.

Are we having fun yet?

Back in my office I opened my laptop and looked up *Mene, Mene, Tekel u-Pharsin.* I discovered it was the famous Aramaic "writing on the wall" from a story found in the Old Testament book of Daniel. It literally translates:

> *God has numbered the days of your kingdom and brought it to an end; you have been weighed on the scales and found wanting; your kingdom is divided and given to the Medes and Persians.*

Ouch! At least he knows his Bible. I decided to give his younger brother Terry a call. We'd gone to lunch a couple times, and he seemed like a sharp, genuine, even-tempered guy. Perhaps he could help me understand what had just happened.

"Hello?"

"Hey, Terry. It's Elmo. Got a second?"

"Sure, whatcha need?"

"I just did a Carpe Annum interview with Raze, and it was pretty rough. I know he's your brother, so if I'm out of line here let me know."

"No, you're fine. What happened?"

"Raze seemed defensive from the minute he walked in the room. Then after just a few questions, he got hotter than a car hood on a summer day. He finally just stormed out. Does he have something against me?"

"Don't take it personal, Elmo. Raze has a bad temper. Believe me, I've got the scars to prove it. It's gotten him in trouble in the past, but he's done much better here at First Church. For the first time he seems to have found a position that suits his abilities and one that he likes. He's probably worried that any changes coming down the pike, like Carpe Annum, are going to mess up his current arrangement here. That said, he hasn't mentioned any such concerns to me."

"Thanks, Terry. That explains a lot. The way he was talking made it sound like we had a full blown membership putsch on our hands. Now I see he's just concerned about his job. I get that."

"Membership putsch?"

"Think *Mutiny on the Bounty, or Moby-Dick.*"

He laughed. "Aye, our old friend Captain Ahab and his unhappy crew. Arrgh!"

"Hey listen, Terry. I really do appreciate the candid insight. Thanks." And I hung up the phone.

One thing was for certain. Some of the First Church faithful were murmuring, and they were a long way from being convinced of the need for any Carpe Annum strategies.

Arrgh!

15

The Triangle

The curtains parted and out he stepped in all his glory.

"That may be the funniest thing I've ever seen," I said, literally falling off my chair laughing.

"Remember, Elmo, I'm doing this as a 'big' favor. And don't forget, a good best man is hard to come by these days."

I couldn't help myself. "Thurm, after the wedding is over, I think you ought to consider buying that outfit. It really accentuates your manly tone and panache."

"Not gonna happen. Remind me again what era these clothes are from?"

"Somewhere between 1900 and 1910.

"And why did you pick that particular time period?"

"That's easy. They were available. A play about Teddy Roosevelt just finished its run at the Starwood Neighborhood Playhouse, and they said we could borrow whatever we needed from the show's wardrobe for the wedding. Yes, that's right—for *free.*"

"So you got the venue for free, the clothes are borrowed, and Father Ted is doing your ceremony—"

"As a wedding gift." I smiled a miser's grin.

"How 'bout the ring?"

"Heirloom. Her great-great-grandmother's."

"Wedding cake?"

"Made and given as a wedding gift by Martha, the First Church cook."

"Music?"

"Ditto. Ramona Holloway."

Thurm was beside himself. "Elmo, you've gotta pay for *something*. Dang! It's your stinkin' wedding, for Pete's sake."

"Says who?" I asked, laughing out loud.

"I dunno. It just seems like a wedding should be expensive. What about the wedding dress?"

"Bonnie's roommate Peg is making it. She's a world-class seamstress. Peg grew up on the mission field and made the clothes for her entire family. And of course, she's doing it as a wedding gift."

Thurm threw up his hands. "Okay, I give up. You win. Kudos to you. By the way, why is Ramona singing at the wedding and not

Harry?"

"I asked Harry first and said he would love to do it, but he's going to be out of town at some evangelism training seminar. Funny, I never took Harry to be an evangelism intensive type of guy."

Thurm chuckled. "He didn't used to be until last year when he read a book by Arthur Blessitt."

"Is that the guy who carried a cross around the world?"

"That's the guy. After reading his book, Harry developed what he calls GPS Evangelism."

"What?"

"See, Blessitt is a strong advocate for the use of Chick tracts."

"Chick tracts?"

"They're like a *Four Spiritual Laws* tract but on steroids with scary cartoons. Blessitt recommends finding creative ways to get these tracts to lost people. You know, like leaving them in public restrooms or including one in each bill payment you mail in."

"Okay, I get that. But what is GPS Evangelism?"

"After reading Blessitt's book, Harry wanted to come up with a unique way to give out some of these Chick tracts. He lives out in the Craggie Canyon area south of town. There's a lot of high hills and elevation out there. Harry's house sits on scenic Avalon Trace Road. Sometime last year the county permanently closed a section of Avalon Trace just past Harry's house. They put a barricade at the top of a hill and one at the bottom and bulldozed the asphalt in between them. It had something to do with the road being too steep to qualify for insurance coverage. The problem is, no one ever told the knuckleheads at GPS that Avalon Trace is no longer a through road. So every day people drive by Harry's house like lemmings following their GPS only to be stopped by the barricade. They back up or turn around, clueless how to get to the other side of Avalon Trace.

"So Harry ordered a whole box of Chick tracts with directions to the other side of Avalon Trace printed on the back. On weekends he sits in a lawn chair in his front yard sipping a big ol' iced tea. He waves at the cars and trucks as they go by, knowing full well they'll return in a moment. Most stop and ask for directions, at which time Harry introduces himself, explains what happened to the road, and gives them the Chick tract with the directions on the back. Then he sends them on their way with a 'God bless you'. And there you have GPS Evangelism."

"Wow, that's really thinking *waaay* outside the box."

"Here's the amazing thing. He's had a handful of people come back to his house to ask questions about the tracts, and some have even prayed to receive Christ. You know Jeff and Tonya Cornelius?"

"Sure."

"That's how they became Christians and started coming to First Church."

"GPS Evangelism. Who knew?"

"Elmo, can I take this monkey suit off now?" Thurm tugged at the tall collar. "It fits just fine."

"Sure, but we need to have them let down the pants a few inches. You've got a high-water thing goin' there, buddy."

"You two have a seat over on the couch. I'll be with you in just a minute," Father Ted said as he wrapped up a phone conversation.

"How'd the fitting go?" Bonnie whispered.

"Everything fit great except for the length of the pants. I figure men a hundred years ago were just shorter than we are today."

"Elmo, you do know the costumes were made just six months ago for the play, right?" She needled.

"Oh, yeah, right. Six months ago. Well, then I guess male actors must be shorter. Generally speaking, of course."

"Actually, that does make some sense—small stature, big egos. It's all about compensation these days."

Father Ted hung up the phone. "Sorry about the call. That was Erlene. Easily the strangest woman I've ever met. She just rambles on and on. Something about a blind cowboy and a three-legged donkey. I choose not to remember the rest."

He stepped around his desk. "How are the 'engaged ones' this afternoon?"

We both stood up.

"Great!" Bonnie said, giving him a hug. "Father Ted, thanks for being part of our special day. This really means a lot to me."

"I'm good too," I said, shaking his hand.

"Oh, I enjoy doing weddings, especially when I know the couple. Please be seated."

"How many weddings would you estimate you've officiated over the course of your years in ministry?"

"Ellington, I lost count long ago, but it's hundreds upon hundreds. Which is why I now require some counseling sessions before every ceremony I do. In my younger years I'd just show up for the rehearsal and off we'd go. I soon discovered that approach to be a disservice both to the couple and to my ministry."

I smiled at Bonnie. "We're both very interested in hearing what you have to tell us. And we're committed to doing whatever it takes to help our marriage start off as strong as possible."

"Wonderful. Then let's get started." A sincere smile warmed his face. "Over the course of our three sessions, I'll be talking about the many different facets of married life—spiritual, emotional, physical, financial, and much more."

"Will we be tested on the material?" I asked with a grin.

He laughed. "Not by me, but you'll tested by each other many times over. I guarantee it."

"Okay, let's do it." I squeezed Bonnie's shoulder.

Father Ted took us each by the hand. "I'd like to start with a prayer. Father God, as we talk today I pray for an extra special portion of Your wisdom. I offer this young couple up to You, Ellington and Bonnie, and ask that You place Your hedge of protection around their hearts. May their love for each other be grounded in their love for You. Help them as they start this journey together to be kind and generous and patient with each other. May their love form a bond as strong as steel but as soft as silk. In the beautiful name of Jesus, amen."

"Father Ted, that was very special," Bonnie said with moistened eyes. "Thank you."

"Is this where I say I do?" I quipped, prompting a quick, stern glance from Bonnie. "Well, a sense of humor is important too; right, Father Ted?"

He laughed. "Save your I do's for the ceremony. But you're correct. A sense of humor is a critical component of any healthy marriage relationship. You have to be able to laugh together in order to really love together."

"Whew, *that's* a relief." I leaned back on the couch.

"But of much greater importance will be your ability to grow together in your faith. That's why today we'll be talking a little geometry." Father Ted reached for a yellow pad.

"Geometry?" Bonnie asked.

"That's right, geometry." He sketched something on the pad. "Your marriage is not a duet, it's actually a trio." He flipped the pad around to show us he'd drawn a triangle. "The persons in your marriage trio are Ellington, Bonnie, and God." He wrote *God* at the top point of the triangle, *Bonnie* on the bottom left point, and *Ellington* on the bottom right point.

"Now, we're going to be talking a lot this afternoon about this simple drawing and how it relates to your relationship. The main point that I'll illustrate over and over again is that the closer you two get to God, the closer you'll grow to each other." He drew an arrow from *Bonnie* up the side of the triangle toward *God*, and a similar one from *Ellington*. "Notice, when you both move closer up the triangle toward God that the space between you grows smaller."

If my memory served me correctly, I'd done rather poorly in geometry in school. But his illustration made perfect sense. As a matter of fact, everything Father Ted said that afternoon made a lot of sense. Melding our two lives into one was a monumental undertaking, and I needed all the help I could get. Bonnie and I both were thankful for his years of experience and seasoned advice.

Dr. Jorgensen had asked me to stop by his office sometime and give him a Carpe Annum update. After our session with Father Ted, I gave Bonnie a goodbye kiss and headed up the executive elevator. At the second floor the elevator doors opened and Tom Applebee stepped in.

"Hello, Ellington. I bet you're on your way up to see Horace."

"Yes, sir. He asked me to drop by when I got a chance. What brings you slummin' down to the lowly second floor?"

He chuckled. "Spoken like a former second-floor tenant. Since Miss Figghie's out, I came down to drop off some budget reports at the print shop in preparation for next week's deacons' meeting."

"What's up with Adrianne?"

"I guess you haven't heard. Miss Figghie's out sick with food poisoning, though it doesn't sound serious. Evidently she ate some bad pork."

"You're kidding." I laughed out loud then caught myself. "I'm so sorry. It's just the whole Elmo-Miss Figghie-Muppet thing. Miss Figghie . . . bad pork? Never mind. But I hope she's gonna be all right."

Tom thought for a long moment then smiled. "Oh, you're right. Miss Figghie getting sick after eating pork. Though I see the humor, I suggest we keep that thought between you and me. Agreed?"

"Agreed."

We stepped out of the elevator onto the fifth floor. "Tom, there's one other thing. Do you have a minute?"

"Sure." We walked into his outer office and he closed the door. "What's up?"

"As you know, I've been interviewing the different staff members as part of the Carpe Annum project. That process was motoring along quite well until I crashed and burned while interviewing Raze Hankins. He walked in angry and left livid. His bad temper I can live with, but what concerns me is something he alluded to. He implied that there existed a group of First Church members who are very unhappy with our current leadership. It came across almost like some type of threat."

"Thanks for bringing this to my attention. I've heard some similar rumblings. Sturgis Weaver has been active lately, and that always means some behind-the-scenes maneuvering is going on. I'll be meeting with Horace and Smitty before next week's deacons' meeting, and I'll be sure this topic is discussed."

"Thanks for giving me a few minutes of your time."

He shook my hand. "You're welcome."

As I turned to leave I noticed him looking over my shoulder out the window.

"Sorry, Ellington. I'm afraid your door of opportunity for seeing Dr. Jorgensen this afternoon has now closed." He pointed through the window in the direction of the staff parking lot five stories below.

I watched as Dr. Jorgenson, dressed in *knickers* of all things, placed his golf clubs in the trunk of his car.

Yet again, he was headed off to *visit the greens* . . .

16

The Consecrated Carnival

I tightened my grip around the large pole, pulling down against the upward force, utilizing the full weight of my body and all my strength. And I prayed, hard. If I somehow managed to survive this traumatic scenario I was going to . . . well, to everyone watching I would be the calm, collected leader they needed me to be. I would perform due diligence making sure everyone was safe and accounted for, and then I would nonchalantly slip out the back of the carnival tent, drive over to Harry Simpkins' house, and burn it down.

Why? The genesis of my angst had been birthed six weeks earlier in a seemingly unremarkable staff meeting. The official agenda that day was utterly benign and rather brief, in fact. But therein lies the problem. When you have forty minutes of business to transact, but a full hour of time allotted, a pocket of time remains wrought with danger, intrigue, and risk. For the seasoned captain these uncharted waters can provide great opportunity for invention. In just such unscripted moments, concepts like wireless communication and micro-processing were conceived.

A quality leader like Horace Jorgenson or Tom Applebee might use these twenty extra minutes to milk the creative juices of their senior staff to produce a fresh and innovative idea. They would then lead the group to stretch and bend and expand this new idea into something wonderful and useful; not only to First Church, but to all of mankind. A lofty pursuit, granted, but nonetheless necessary to maintain that all-important "edge" that makes an organization relevant in a changing world.

Unfortunately on that fateful day, both Horace and Tom were out of town and the task of moderating the staff meeting fell to the aforementioned Harry Simpkins. Harry handled the agenda items with no problem, but during that critical closing twenty-minute segment of free thought and exchange, an idea emerged so insidious, so pernicious, that it should have been quickly dispatched to the outer reaches of Siberia. But no, Harry was in charge and he liked the idea. No—he *loved* it. Big time.

I don't remember which boneheaded staff member conceived the concept, but that's actually irrelevant. Once it found its way into the demented mind of Harry Simpkins, all hope was lost. The idea? First

Church would hold an annual carnival. A *country carnival*, to be exact. There would be country western music—gospel-tinged, of course. There would be clogging, and I'm not talking about your drain pipes. There would be livestock and carnival games, and of course a huge tent. Why a carnival? Harry reasoned that First Church needed an opportunity to, how do you say—"let its hair down." After all First Church had a widely held reputation for being a high-brow, upper- crust, straitlaced rich church with no crumbs in the carpet. As Harry envisioned it, an opportunity existed for the church to "reach across the tracks" to the rest of our community.

At the time I thought, what's next? A tractor pull? Or even better, a professional wrestling match? I just didn't get it, or perhaps I had subtly become a snob. But it didn't matter what I thought because the tsunami named Harry Simpkins had already been turned loose and wouldn't be denied.

The following week Harry, who was all amped-up like an atomic particle collider, convinced Pastor Jorgensen that a country carnival was a grand idea, and the planning and preparations began in earnest.

First Church rented the vacant city block that had once been that beautiful stone church on the edge of downtown. We also procured a gigantic carnival tent to be erected in the middle of the vacant lot and surrounded by different carnival booths and games. Each Sunday School class was assigned a booth. The kitchen staff was directed to come up with lots of carnival-type food. So Martha went out and found a waffle cone maker, a cotton candy machine, a snow cone machine . . . you get the idea.

Someone recruited a couple farmers from Jackson Falls to bring over some of their calves, ponies, and piglets. We even rented a few of those old-school carnival rides like the Scrambler and the Tilt-O-World—carnies included. Of course, then we had to hire special security to keep an eye on the carnies.

For the big service under the carnival tent, Harry called in some of his small town markers and brought in Righteous Eddie Bisket and the Skillets, the Singing Hickson Family featuring Slappy Pappy, and for the show-stopper (or would that be stomper?)—the Clogging King Brothers all the way from Vinita, Oklahoma.

First Church Sunday School director extraordinaire Alex Leichhardt took charge of getting the word out to the community. He convinced one of the local billboard companies to donate three billboards for the event. Alex then recruited Father Ted to be the face of the ad campaign dressed in some silly Howdy Doody outfit. He also organized teams to canvass the adjacent neighborhoods and projects to hand out flyers detailing the First Church Country Carnival.

Harry beamed. It would be his show of shows. Unbeknownst to the rest of the staff (with the exception of Dr. Jorgenson), Harry Simpkins had a secret avocation. Several times a year he would slip away to another part of the country and become Tex Larimore, county western singer. He had quite a following in places like Nevada, Wyoming, and Idaho where he would do shows in small towns singing the great country western standards of George Jones, Merle Haggard, and Buck Owens.

Harry, who grew up watching *Gunsmoke* and *Rawhide* on black-and-white television, had a deep passion for the country western genre. After graduation from high school, he'd planned to move to Nashville and chase his dream of becoming a country western singer. But Harry's father, a prominent attorney, would have nothing to do with such foolishness. He packed up Harry and shipped him off to some Ivy League school to study environmental policy and other mundane disciplines. To his credit, Harry fought for and won the right to pursue a minor in music, but at the time, the only options available at his blue blood college were of a classical persuasion. His country music career had to be put on hold.

Of course life is full of unexpected curves. During his senior year Harry attended an Intervarsity retreat and his life was irrevocably transformed, spiritually speaking. Returning from the retreat he immediately began preparation for ministry. Four church positions later, he landed at First Church, though he never totally forgot his country music dream.

Several years later, while doing a revival in a small church in central Tennessee, he was introduced to some people from the country music business. This led to some conversations that then led to the creation of his alter ego, Tex Larimore. With Dr. Jorgensen's blessing, Harry quietly began his second career.

Harry had never been able to find the appropriate venue for introducing his Tex Larimore persona to the stuffy black tie crowd at First Church, which explains why he'd been so gung ho about the carnival idea from the start. He'd simply add Tex Larimore to the slate of performers and wow the amazed crowd with his crooning. Then all things would once again be in equilibrium for the world as Harry knew it.

The big day arrived. As a staff we'd been instructed to wear something Western. For me that meant blue jeans and white long sleeve shirt, an old brown vest I'd inherited from my grandfather, and a string bolo tie with a turquoise and silver clip. Bonnie wore a jean skirt with a plaid blouse and a bandana around her neck. It all seemed a bit silly but fun at the same time.

Arriving early I helped set up chairs in the big tent. Later I caught up with Bonnie as she worked the cotton candy machine. I got a sticky kiss.

I raised an eyebrow. "I see somebody's been nibbling away at the profits."

She gave me a dieter's backslidden smile. "I had to make sure this stuff was safe—you know, for the kids."

"Right."

"Now, if you were *really* my true love, you'd go get me one of those funnel cakes," she purred while batting her eyelashes.

"Nice try, Cleopatra, but I love you too much to bring you fried grease on a stick covered with sugar. How 'bout I take you out for some real food after this hootenanny winds down?"

"Killjoy."

"It is what it is. Anyway, I saw Juliann here with Jimmy Cornbread Jackson. Are they dating?"

"Not really. She just brought him as her show pony."

"Show pony?"

"When Juliann goes to an event where she knows there'll be a lot of single guys hovering around, she usually takes along a show pony. As she defines it, a show pony is an attractive male platonic friend who keeps the other guys at bay. She told me Jimmy's really not her type, though they've become friends since Eddie's multilevel get-together."

"Oh, what a night that was. I remember our harrowing escape all too well." I feigned a shiver. "Sorry, babe, gotta run." I gave her a hug. "Evidently they need some shovels over at the farm animal pen."

"See ya," Bonnie said, wedging a fluff of cotton candy into her mouth. "Watch where you step."

Due to Alex Leichhardt's superlative work, we had a huge crowd. People were playing games, riding rides, eating corn dogs, and many of them were from the adjoining neighborhoods. I'm a big enough man to admit when I'm wrong, and I was dead wrong about this country carnival. It was a bona fide success.

When the time came for the big event under the tent, we were at full capacity with every folding chair filled and folks standing around the inside perimeter.

Someone thought it would add to the countrified atmosphere of the program if one of the calves was placed up on the stage during the performances. What appeared to be great theater went south when the calf—as my granny would say—*shooy'd* all over one of the Clogging King Brothers' boots as he waited to perform. Interestingly enough no one ever fessed up to the "calf on stage" idea. Thurm later quipped that he thought the clogging number really stunk. Literally!

As the musical portion of the program progressed, I began to notice the wind had picked up and the roof of the tent had begun to bellow up and down a bit. Thurm came and got me from my seat and we joined a group of deacons and staff members outside the tent for an impromptu emergency meeting.

The weather change had caused a concern for safety because the tent poles were being lifted and moved with each gust of wind. Several in the group argued that we should shut down the program and send the folks home. Harry wasn't about to let that happen. Revivals and circuses had successfully operated in tents for years and so could we, he argued. He recommended we simply assign a deacon or staff member to each tent pole to hold it down during any gusts of wind. A terse debate ensued but the thicker heads prevailed, and we all marched off to man our tent poles.

So there I sat bear-hugging the bottom of this thirty-foot wooden pole while suffering through the Singing Hickson Family's greatest hits. Every few minutes a breeze would kick up, and I'd just clamp down on the tent pole holding it in place. After about half an hour, things got a little more interesting as the wind kicked it up a notch. During a prayer by Fred Snooker I watched in amazement as the tent pole ten rows in front of me lifted poor Bob Stevens up in the air and sat him down on the lap of a very startled senior adult woman—who promptly slapped him.

By the time Harry took the stage as Tex Larimore, the wind was gusting continually. In my opinion we were on the verge of a catastrophe. It took all the strength I could muster just to keep my tent pole on the ground, and I could tell the other guys were struggling too. My anger grew steadily as I listened to Harry's rendition of "An Okie from Muskogee." If the tent collapsed and people got hurt the blame for the debacle would lie squarely at Harry's feet. Bonnie looked my way from across the crowd, and I could see panic in her eyes. I tried to signal her to leave, but with my hands locked to the pole I failed to communicate my message.

On stage Harry appeared oblivious to the impending disaster. Lost in the world of Tex Larimore, impervious to the howling wind and the wobbling tent, Harry sang on. I began to pray in earnest for a divine intervention—for my own sake and for the physical safety of all those around me.

As often happens, rain follows wind, and oh, how it rained—a virtual downpour! When the heavy rain hit the top of the canvas tent, it generated an explosion of noise. Poor Harry's coming-out concert was washed away in sound and water. Little rivulets cascaded through the tent as everyone scrambled for their cars.

There were many lessons to be learned from our first annual Country Carnival, both good and bad. I knew we'd do it again, but I could guarantee we'd do a better job monitoring the weather.

I also made a mental note to recommend keeping a shovel up on stage in the future.

17

The Slammer

About the time I arrived at college, all of the wise instructions I had received from my parents over the years began to take hold. Whereas my room at home had always been a mess, at college I hung up my clothes and kept my room neat. Everything in its proper place. I also became more careful with my money and my time. I wisely chose with whom and where I would hang out. I even made a conscious effort to avoid waste by taking shorter showers and limiting my food servings to only what I knew I would eat. Much of my parents' advice simply become part of my DNA.

Back home Mom would always say, "Turn off the light if you're not using it." So I learned to click the lights off when I left my room. This habit followed me into adulthood, and I subconsciously turned off lights if they were not in use. If no one was in the break room when I left, I would turn off the light. If no one was in the restroom when I left, I would turn off the light. On more than one occasion I stranded some poor soul in one of the stalls with his pants down around his ankles, engulfed in total darkness.

Harry nicknamed me The Light Watchman. I won't tell you what I nicknamed Harry after the carnival tent debacle.

Late one Thursday afternoon when most everyone had left for the day, I was going down the hallway and of course turning off the lights.

"Ellington?" Father Ted's now familiar voice rang out from around the hall corner.

"Yes, sir?"

"Can you come here to my office for a second before you leave?"

I walked down the hall and around the corner, stepping into Father Ted's office. "What's up?"

"You wouldn't happen to have a few hours available tomorrow morning, would you?" he asked with a warm smile.

"Sure. What's going on?"

"I'm visiting an old friend over at the penitentiary, and I'd like you to come along. I'm inviting you for two reasons. One, I always like to take along a wing man when I'm making a prison visit. There's strength in numbers. And two, I thought it would be a good chance for you to get some training in these types of visits."

"Sure, what time?"

"I'll meet you in the staff parking lot about eight. It's a good forty-five-minute drive out there. That will get us back here before lunch."

I stepped back into the hallway. "Okay, then. I'll see you in the morning. I've got a few more lights to turn off, then I'm meeting Bonnie for dinner over at Café Lucia's. You're welcome to join us."

"Thanks for the invite, but I've got Eddie Hughes coming in for a meeting. Tom asked me to talk to him about leaving the single girls here at the church alone."

"Good luck with that," I said, laughing as I headed back down the hall. "You'll need it!"

The drive from First Church over to Café Lucia's only took about fifteen minutes. As I walked in, I noticed the restaurant was practically empty. The reason for this aberration quickly became apparent when I realized the piano had gone missing. In its place hung a sign: "Sorry, Old Joanna is out this week for repairs." Talk about a cultural mash-up. The restaurant was owned and operated by a middle-age white woman with a Spanish name who played an upright piano nicknamed in Cockney slang.

Ah, the American melting pot at its finest.

Bonnie had already ordered our sweet teas as I slid into our booth. We sat across from each other—not very romantic, perhaps, but much better for conversation.

"Harry just called and said you left a couple lights on."

"What? No he didn't."

"Gotcha," she said, laughing. "I'm sorry I just couldn't resist."

"So it's gonna be one of those nights, is it?"

"Unfortunately no. We've got a lot of pre-wedding business to discuss. But before we jump into the lace logistics, I've got some good news to report."

"Really? I like good news, so lay it on me."

Her eyebrows went up. "'Lay it on me'? What, have you been trolling sixties TV shows again?"

I rolled my eyes. "Touché. Now, come on. What's the good news?"

Bonnie took a hit on her straw. "Louis overhead me talking to Juliann about our frustrations in trying to find an affordable house to rent. He said when he and Jane E. got married they rented a home from one of Smitty Fitzsimons' companies, and Smitty cut them a deal on the rent. So Louis made a few calls and voila! I have a list of three homes for us to look at and all are less expensive than we budgeted for."

"I knew I liked Louis. Remind me to give him a kiss the next time I see him."

"Elmo," she paused, eyes narrowing. "If you kiss my boss you'll be honeymooning alone."

"Okay, then I'll just make that a hug. Whew, that was close." I pretended to wipe the sweat from my brow.

"Very funny, dear. Now try to stay focused. With the wedding only a couple of weeks away, we're in somewhat of a time crunch. Let's try to visit all three of these houses on Saturday and make a decision."

"Sounds like a plan. I've already lined up Thurm and his pickup to help me move. I figure once we sign a lease, I can go ahead and move my stuff over and set up a beachhead. It should only take one or two trips. Then after the honeymoon we can rent the biggest moving van we can find to move your stuff over." I winked at Bonnie.

She didn't wink back. "Elmo, about the honeymoon . . ."

Uh oh.

"I've been thinking. Since you haven't accrued any vacation time yet, we'd have to cram our honeymoon into a long weekend. We both deserve better."

I smiled. "You're absolutely right. And to be honest, I've had the same thought, but didn't know how to broach the topic. What d'ya suggest?"

"How about let's just stay in town and spend the night at the Esquire Plaza or the Pinnacle House? Then we can save up our money and next fall when your vacation days kick in, we can take a real two-week honeymoon to some exotic place."

I reached across the table and squeezed her hand. "Now, there's an excellent idea. It kind of depressurizes the weekend so we can focus our energies on the wedding."

Bonnie smiled. "You took that better than I anticipated. I'm glad we see eye-to-eye on this. Now we won't have to rush off after the ceremony and can spend some time celebrating with our family and friends." She seemed genuinely relieved.

"Wonderful. Okay, let's run down the pre-wedding checklist." Bonnie opened a folder with a happy face sticker on the front.

Did I mention previously that weddings and their planning are uber-significant to the ladies? I fully get that. It also helps that I'm a checklist-loving guy.

"What's the status on the rings?" Bonnie asked while perusing the list.

"The jeweler told me both your heirloom wedding ring and the band we picked out for me will be sized and ready on Monday. Tuesday at the latest."

"Check."

I love it when she says that.

"Peg finished my wedding dress yesterday, and she's now working on the alterations for her and Juliann's vintage bridesmaid dresses. How about the guys?"

"We've all been fitted, including Father Ted, and they're ready to be picked up anytime." I smiled because I knew I was ahead of schedule.

"Well done. Why don't you go ahead and pick them all up next week and then hand them out to your guys at the rehearsal? That will minimize the risk of a lost or misplaced outfit come Saturday morning."

"Smart idea. Check?"

"Check!"

"Do you mind if we go ahead and order. I'm starting to get *the sugar shakes.*"

"Elmo, have you fallen off the wagon again?"

"Okay, okay. Yes, I admit I ate some jelly beans this afternoon. What can I say? I'm addicted to them. But then so was President Reagan."

She laughed. "Nice try. Was that transference or misdirection?"

"Does it matter since you obviously didn't buy it?"

"Listen, you big lug. I love you, and that's *all* of you, including your arms and legs. I don't want to see you develop diabetes and start losing your limbs to the disease. Capiche?"

"Yeah, I get it. Maybe I can find a candy eater's support group somewhere. It's just that my inner child thinks everyday is Halloween."

"Now, Elmo . . ."

"All right, I promise to do better. Really."

Sheesh. I signaled for the waiter.

We split a panini with the works and settled in for an evening of finalizing the details. Our wedding plans were all coming together and we were both excited about our special day. Unbeknownst to Bonnie, I had also orchestrated a wedding day surprise, and it was all I could do not to tell her about it.

The crisp morning air greeted me with the heavy scent of honeysuckle, but the idyllic moment was lost to distraction. I'd never been to a prison before, and I felt both anxious and curious as I drove downtown to meet Father Ted. It's just that none of my friends or family members had ever been in jail. My perception about prisons had been entirely formulated from watching TV shows and movies, and the portrait they painted was both ugly and frightening.

In college I played on a freshman intramural basketball team called the SQUIDS (Spiritual Quick Underclass Individuals Devoting to Scoring). The SQUIDS were invited to play an exhibition game against the guards over at the Juvenile Detention Center. We played the game on a court inside the facility with the rowdy juveniles in the stands on both sides. Getting into the building required us to go through several gated checkpoints and even a pat down. The whole process was surreal.

We'd been recruited by a local youth counselor named Skinny Taylor who happened to be a former NBA player. Skinny joined our team for the exhibition game. The guards were good, but Skinny was better and he easily made up for the rest of our team's deficiencies. As the tight game progressed the place got louder and louder, and the kids were all pulling hard for the guards. Toward the end of the game one of our players caught an intentional elbow in the nose, followed by some pushing and shoving, then absolute bedlam. As the decibels soared we were hustled out of the building with our arms over our heads for protection. All of us were quite shaken up. Skinny apologized profusely. It was a scary experience—and those were just juveniles.

Father Ted pulled into the staff parking lot right behind me driving his shiny red Dodge Viper—his retirement present to himself. A Dodge Viper can go up to two hundred miles per hour, and I had a sneaking suspicion Father Ted had hit that speed on more than one occasion. After slipping into his passenger seat, I subtly pulled my seatbelt extra tight. I considered asking him if the Viper had a passenger side airbag, but what good is an airbag when you smash into something going two hundred miles an hour?

"Morning, Ellington. I really appreciate you taggin' along for this visit. It normally takes about forty-five minutes to get out there, but the sky is clear and the wind is low, so who knows? We just might shave a few minutes of that ETA," he said with a wink.

Oh boy. I should've brought a backup pair of boxer shorts.

I tightened my seatbelt even more as he eased out into traffic.

"Father Ted, do you know Raze Hankins very well?"

"I've only had one brief conversation with him and that was concerning a hospital visit he needed me to make. Why?"

"Well, it's pretty obvious the guy doesn't care much for me, and I'm not sure what to do about it."

"If it's not your fault don't do anything about it. One of the hardest lessons to learn in ministry and in life in general is that you're not going to be liked by everyone. Especially when you're a leader and a decision maker. The key is not to take it personal— which can be very hard sometimes. There'll always be some people you just have to manage around. Raze could be one of those people."

"Yeah, I guess you're right. Raze is just a hard one to manage around."

Father Ted smiled. "I met his father once when I was about your age."

"Really? Ezekiel Hankins, the evangelist and infamous snake handler?"

"That's right. Ezekiel Jedediah Hankins, the man and the legend."

"How'd that happen?"

"Several of my Asbury college buddies and I would often listen to this radio program from the Appalachian area in eastern Kentucky. It was a live broadcast of the Sunday morning worship service of a Pentecostal church in some small mountain town. We just got a kick out of listening to the ol' boy preach. And preach he did.

"One week they announced that Ezekiel Hankins would be there the following Sunday for revival and he would be bringing his snakes. So a few of us decided to go and see it for ourselves."

"Wow. What happened?"

"It was much a longer drive than we anticipated and we got there after the service had already begun. So we ended up sitting on the back pew. Ezekiel preached for over an hour. He was actually pretty good.

"Then the praise and worship segment of the service started. People were singing and dancing in the spirit, some were speaking in tongues, and some were on the floor either slain in the spirit or just rolling around."

"What were you guys doing?" I asked excitedly.

"Oh, we were into it, hands raised, singing at the top of our lungs—mightily praising our God. Then all of a sudden out from under the front pews came several wicker baskets of vipers. We were spellbound watching the folks up front handle those snakes. And then it happened."

Father Ted was telling the story so well, I felt like I was there with him. "What happened?"

Father Ted looked at me with terror in his eyes. "People started handing the snakes to the people behind them! Those vipers were quickly working their way to the back where we were standing."

"Uh oh!" I blurted out loud. "What did we—I mean, what'd you all do?"

"After a moment of panic we realized that the folks rolling around on the floor weren't handling the snakes, so all four of us immediately hit the deck."

"Oh, man. What a great story." I felt my body relax.

Father Ted chuckled. "It was quite an experience all right. We hung around after the service for the potluck dinner, and that's where I met Ezekiel Hankins. He was very nice and seemed like a pretty normal guy to me. But the best part of the day was the homemade pies. Delicioso!"

"I understand he died from a snake bite," I said.

"That was just a widely circulated rumor. He died when his car was struck by a train someplace out west."

We'd reached the outskirts of town and the Dodge was now traveling at least ninety miles per hour—maybe more. And did I mention we were on a two-lane road?

Yikes.

"Tell me about the guy we're going to visit."

"Hugh is a longtime friend. He was an elder in my former church for many years. Great guy. One of the best."

"Why's he in prison?"

"It's quite simple, actually. He hired the wrong guy."

"Really?"

"Yep. Hugh owned a small brokerage firm. One of his employees got busted for insider trading, and Hugh got sent up to the big house with him. Hugh claims he had no idea what the guy was up to, and I believe him. But the judge determined that since it was Hugh's company, he was negligent for *not* knowing. Subsequently he got eighteen months to two years in the slammer. He's been there for about a year now. I try to get up to see him every other month or so."

"That's too bad." The uber-tight seatbelt squeezed my voice up almost an octave higher than normal. "With all the bad guys that are running loose, you hate to see a good guy get locked up like that. How's he managing?"

"It's no picnic, but God's been looking out for him. He's got a great cellmate. A guy named Casper Loggins. Casper's been in for a while. He owned a fishing business and got into some type of row with one of his competitors. Eventually he got so mad he blew up several of the other guy's fishing trawlers. He's known in the joint as 'The Tuna-Bomber.' The other inmates don't mess with a guy like Casper, so they leave Hugh alone too."

"Wow." I laughed nervously. "Nothing like hearing a Ted Kaczynski anecdote while riding in a fast-moving sports car driven by a senior adult who often dresses up like a monk, and on our way to the penitentiary. Hey, who needs Flomax?"

Father Ted guffawed as he grabbed the steering wheel firmly with both hands. "Elmo, you're truly one very funny guy. Now let me show you what this baby can *really* do." He stomped the gas pedal and off we zoomed.

And yes, I whimpered like a frightened child all the rest of the way.

We parked in a spot next to a sign that read (I kid you not):

Reserved for Priests and Priestesses,
 Pastors, Rabbis, Imams, Brahmins,
 and any other religious ministers.

Talk about political correctness run amok. Geez.

After some brief questioning by a guard and a pat down that would make any TSA agent proud, we were finally let inside.

"Now, I've got to warn you. Hugh decided not to shave or cut his hair during his stay here, so don't be shocked when you see him.

He's got kind of a Jerry Garcia-meets-Charles Manson thing going. I think he believes this wild look helps protect him from the other prisoners."

We stepped into the visitors' area which was nothing more than twenty picnic tables spread around a large room with a high ceiling. Several convicts were already there visiting with either friends or family members. Two guards walked the room with two more looking through a large glass window high on the far wall.

Father Ted filled out a small request form and walked it over to one of the guards. The guard picked up a phone and relayed the information from the form up to one of the guards behind the window. A few moments later we heard a message over the prison PA system.

"Please bring Prisoner Bongus, Cell C2473 to the visitors' area. Repeat, please bring Prisoner Bongus, Cell C2473 to the visitors' area."

Barely holding back a laugh, I leaned over our table. "Your friend's name is Hugh Bongus?"

"Yes, why? Do you know him?"

"No, it's just that . . . well . . . is he a big guy?"

"Not really. Why do you ask?"

"I mean, with a name like . . . oh, it's nothing."

Five minutes later the door opened and in walked Hugh Bongus. The irony of his name was immediately apparent. Hugh looked to be about five-six and maybe a hundred and fifty pounds. Ted's description—spot on. He could easily pass for Jerry Garcia's half brother. He gave Ted a big hug.

"Hugh, I'd like you to meet my fellow pastor, Ellington Jenkins."

He shook my hand. "Nice to meet you, Ellington."

"Just call me Elmo. Nice to meet you too."

We all sat down. Father Ted smiled. "I see you've got new uniforms."

Hugh laughed. "Yes, we do. Out with the stripes, in with the denim. It's actually a fabric test program for Nike, but you won't find their *Swoosh* anywhere on these jumpers."

Father Ted's expression turned serious. "How are you holding up?"

"I don't know, about as good as can be expected, I guess. Like Morgan Freeman once said, 'Prison time is slow time.' It's a lot like the feeling you get when your airplane gets put on gate hold. You're just sitting there waiting for them to finally open the dumb door and let you off the dang plane."

"Did you get the books I sent over?"

"Yes I did, and thank you." Hugh pulled his long hair back into a two-fisted ponytail. He tied it if off with a rubber band.

Father Ted chuckled. "Man, your hair is really getting long."

Hugh flashed a big smile and looked at me. "I'm actually slowly going bald. So I decided to just let it grow out one more time. My hair's farewell tour, if you will."

We all laughed. At least he still had his sense of humor. I sat there and just listened as these two dear friends talked. Hugh had not only started a Bible study that was well-attended, he'd also led Casper Loggins, the ol' Tuna Bomber himself, to Christ and was disciplining him.

Most people don't realize that much of the New Testament was written by Paul while he was in prison. I admired Hugh for choosing to turn what others would consider an unjust, crappy situation into compost for good. I wondered if I would've responded the same way.

Wrapping up the visit, we said our goodbyes and climbed back in the Viper. Needless to say, we were back to the church in a flash. I excused myself and made a quick trip home for a wardrobe change.

Enough said.

18

The New Manse

I must have had my knees locked, or maybe Thurm had tightened my cummerbund too snug. Whatever the cause, I obviously had a circulation issue and felt light-headed due to the lack of blood reaching my brain. Fighting off the urge to faint, I patiently waited for Bonnie to walk down the aisle. Over my shoulder I asked Thurm to spot me if I fell, but my eyes remained transfixed on her as she walked in a gentle staccato rhythm. Left then right, left then right. So beautiful, so elegant. I did find it a little strange that she seemed so far away and didn't appear to be getting any closer . . .

In my periphery I took note that we were indoors, so I assumed the weather must have turned ugly. *The groom is always the last to know.* Briefly breaking my focus on Bonnie, I surveyed the room. Something was amiss. The ceiling seemed too high and the room too big. And who were all these people? *I hope they all brought gifts.*

I turned to ask my best man about it, but it wasn't Thurm. It was Prince Harry, bushy red hair and all.

"Hey, where's Thurm?"

Prince Andrew smiled while firmly patting me on the back. "Who's Thurm?" He chuckled. "Just relax, mate. It'll all be over soon."

I turned back just as Bonnie arrived at the altar. "Bonnie, they've taken Thurm away, and I don't know where!" I began to weep. *Not good. Not good at all.*

Handing off her bouquet to Pippa—*Pippa?*—Bonnie grabbed my shoulders and started to shake me. Gently at first, then with greater force. "Elmo!" I heard her voice, but her lips weren't moving. *Odd.* "Come on, sugar, wake up. You're dreaming again."

My eyes finally opened. I was sitting on Bonnie's sofa. The TV was playing a DVD of *The Royal Wedding.* Bonnie sat next to me eating popcorn and dabbing her eyes.

"I just love this wedding."

I yawned, stretching my arms. "I thought we were watching the *LOST* Season 2 DVD."

"We were until you fell asleep forty-five minutes ago. So I switched over to the *Royal Wedding.* Don't you just love her dress?"

"Yeah, the dress, right. Um, it's late so I better head out. I'm working til noon tomorrow then taking the afternoon off before the rehearsal at six-thirty. That will give me time to tie up any loose ends."

"Sure, okay," she whispered without looking away from the TV. Bonnie was lost in Royal Wedding LaLa Land. I'd seen this condition before.

I kissed her forehead and let myself out. The next several days would be quite busy, and I obviously needed some serious sleep. Alas, this would be a good night for a Baptist cocktail (otherwise known as N.T.T.R—Nyquil-to-the-rim).

Full of Friday morning vim and vigor, I arrived at the church office thirty minutes early. I planned to expedite my To-Do List for the day and slip out before lunch. There would be no pencils sharpened this morning.

Swinging by the break room I snatched my mail from its slot. Several newsletters from other churches, a brochure for bowling lessons—had to be from Thurm, the jerk—the obligatory cache of junk mail, of course, and finally, a sealed envelope with no writing on it.

When I got to my office I plopped down in my desk chair and casually swung my feet up on my desk. In the soft light of my office, I studied the unmarked envelope before picking it up. It appeared to be a greeting card. Probably a wedding gift of some sort from a church member. But why wasn't it addressed?

Time was of the essence, so I cut my analysis short and ripped open the envelope. On the front of the card in letters cut out from different magazines it stated, "I'm Always Watching You." *That's weird.* When I opened the card, it started playing that creepy, repetitive song from the Hitchcock movie, *Psycho.* Scrawled in blood red letters it said, "Nice try." And there inside were several Polaroid shots of Ferty. One with her sitting in the backseat of my car, another with her on the front porch of my apartment. The last was a picture of her sitting on top of some building downtown with First Church visible in the background. A Harvest Morgan Seminary beret adorned her scary little head.

No one saw me carve the words "Nice Try" into Ferty's base. And no one, I mean *no one* saw me throw her in the church dumpster. *What's going on here? Somebody's spending a whole lot of time managing this prank. And what's with the Harvest Morgan beret?*

The only Harvest Morgan beret I'd every seen was on the credenza in Dr. De Villa's office. The beret had to be a red herring— no way Dr. DV was involved in this. Thurm, Erlene, Harry, Ted—who could it be? Maybe all of them? I jammed the card and photos into my desk drawer. The answers to those questions would have to wait until after the wedding and honeymoon.

Grinding my teeth, I decided to go ahead and sharpen a pencil or two. All the way down to the eraser.

Argh!

Completing a condensed, though productive morning, I slipped out early as planned. After my final bachelor's lunch of tuna fish, Doritos, and a Coke, I set my face like flint toward my destiny of married bliss. By the way, why is it called "tuna fish" and not just tuna? We don't say salmon fish or trout fish or grouper fish? Hmm?

I spent the afternoon completing Elmo's Pre-wedding Checklist:

Haircut—check.
Nose and ear hair trimmed—check
Fingernails *and* toenails clipped—check
Shoes shined—check.
Overnight bag packed—check.
Clean underwear—double check.
Footie pajamas—check. (Just kidding. Really.)

Earlier in the week I had relocated with my small cache of worldly possessions into our new rental house on Platypus Place. Typical young single guy that I am, I hadn't yet acquired much stuff, at least by American standards. Of course, my austere situation had been greatly exacerbated by the fact that until recently, I had no money. None. Nada. A somewhat desperate scenario that most middle-class students face upon graduating from college.

Our first home. I thought it most appropriate to name the new manse, and since it resided on Platypus Place I decided to simply call it *Bill.* Of course, I did this knowing full well that Feng Shui Bonnie would quickly rename it upon her arrival—probably something more stuffy and aristocratic like . . . *Leonesse.*

While Bonnie would decorate the inside of the house all prim and proper, like most husbands I would be assigned lawn duty, garbage detail, and grill responsibilities. According to most marriage traditions I was supposed to participate in the inaugural "picking out" of the curtains, but I had preemptively deferred that honor to Bonnie. Though I saw this gesture as a diplomatic if not generous move on my part, she saw it as merely "obvious common sense."

Ouch!

At least I would be king of castle for another day or two, and in this reality I would revel mightily. And so, with brazen bravado, casting all health concerns to the wind, I reached for my stash of jelly beans.

(Umm, let's just keep this whole jelly bean thing between you and me, okay?)

Though we would be getting married at the old historic church out on State Road 253, we decided to have our rehearsal in the chapel at First Church. I'd call it a joint logistics decision. More convenient for everyone involved.

After the rehearsal we'd all retire to the Governor's Room at the Metropolitan Dinner and Dance Club for the customary rehearsal dinner. Unfortunately, there would be no dancing at this festive get-together of family and friends. Dancing was frowned upon for First Church staff members—unless of course it was a square dance, which just didn't seem to fit the occasion *or* the venue.

This dinner, per tradition, was arranged and paid for by my wonderful parents. The Club is owned and operated by a prominent First Church family. They cut my parents a deal. Sweet.

Finally I'd finish off the evening by spending a few hours celebrating with my friends. As a First Church staff member, a bachelor party in the traditional sense was out of the question, but I still wanted to have some fun with my homies. Someone suggested bowling, but since I'd been banned for life from the local bowling alley that idea was quickly and summarily dismissed. We settled on laser tag—a virtual male testosterone lollapalooza.

Since the wedding was scheduled for eleven the next morning, we couldn't prolong our celebration for too long. But I felt it necessary to spend some time with the boys—a final rite of passage into my new life as a married man.

And that was the schedule for the rest of the day.

Since I had several hours to myself before the festivities began, I decided to hit my knees and spend sometime with the Lord. I had a lot to be thankful for—a blessed past and a bright new future. I also needed divine guidance and wisdom to be the husband Bonnie deserved, and to be the spiritual leader God intended. I thought about Father Ted's triangle of faith and how I deeply wanted our marriage and our home to represent Christ well. I knew God would be with us there at the altar in the morning, and I was grateful beyond words that He would be.

Now well past midnight, I lay in bed exhausted but unable to sleep. It had been a long and wonderful day. The rehearsal went well with Father Ted making sure we all knew where we were supposed to stand and what we were supposed to say. He shared several funny stories from some of his previous weddings, and we laughed until we cried. He assured us that our ceremony would be incident-free.

The rehearsal dinner couldn't have gone any better as our two extended families melded seamlessly in a night of fun and fellowship. Erlene Markham made a surprise visit and presented Bonnie and me with a special "nuptials" version of her infamous relish tray. She also led a toast to us, most of which I cannot repeat here. I thought my mother would die right there on the spot.

The laser tag was a blast, highlighted by another unforgettable Eddie Hughes' moment. Evidently Eddie tagged some big guy's girlfriend one too many times and almost had his laser gun permanently implanted in his lower intestines.

Good times. So much so that my elevated adrenalin level was keeping me from falling asleep. I decided to count myself to sleep and for some reason Prince William and Kate came to mind. In my mind's eye I started counting the wedding gifts at the Royal Wedding. It took a while, but I could finally feel myself getting sleepy.

One thousand two hundred thirty seven, one thousand two hundred thirty eight, one thousand two hundred thirty nine . . .

Man, they got a lot of gifts . . .

19

The Big Day

I've overslept on numerous major occasions in the past, and I wasn't about to let that happen this time. Before bed I set three different alarms—my bedside clock, my cell phone, and even the oven timer in the kitchen. They all worked and I got up on time, but it took me fifteen minutes to figure out how to turn off the stinkin' timer on the oven. Oh well.

First item on my agenda: call my best man. Thurm was famous for his "catch a few more winks" morning routine. His phone rang twenty-three times, but I wasn't giving up. Not today.

A sleepy voice finally answered. "Yeah?"

I disguised my voice. "Is this Mr. Thurmand R. Wilson, holder of lottery ticket number 3545678?"

I could almost hear his brain clicking as the synapses all fired up at the same time. "Well, yeah, maybe. What'd you just say?"

"Mr. Thurmand R. Wilson, this is indeed your lucky day! If you can produce lottery ticket 3545678 you will instantly become the world's newest multi-millionaire."

I could tell he was now fully awake. Mission accomplished. "What was that winning ticket number again?" He yawned noisily. "Hey, wait minute. My middle initial isn't R. Do I still win?"

"Really? Our mistake. Sorry for calling so early and thanks for playing the lottery." I hung up and laughed out loud.

My phone immediately rang back. "Good morning, Thurm."

"Nice one."

"Sorry, but I needed you wide awake and ready for action."

"Okay, you got me. What are my marching orders?"

"We need to get there about thirty minutes earlier than planned. It looks like the weather is gonna be nice, so we'll be moving the harpsichord from the old church building out to the amphitheatre for the wedding. It takes four guys to carry it."

"Harpsichord?"

"Yep. Since we're doing an acoustic service with an early twentieth-century motif, Ramona asked Sigmund Newt if he would play for the wedding. He said yes and even offered to bring along his beloved antique harpsichord. It was delivered to the old church yesterday."

Thurm yawned again. "I thought Siggy had retired and moved to San Francisco?"

"He did, but evidently he recently moved back. Ramona said he's now playing organ out at some Unitarian church in Craggie Canyon."

"Speaking of music, how many solos are you having? I went to a wedding last month where the soloist did his entire double-live album. We were all dying before it was over."

"Don't worry, just two solos. Ramona's singing one, then a friend of ours is also singing. You don't know him."

"Sounds good. I'll pick you up in an hour. It'll take that long to get this silly costume on."

"You're a good friend, Thurm. Just remember the zipper in the pants goes in the back, so go light on the fluids."

I've been to a lot of weddings, even officiated a few. Every wedding is different, distinctive unto itself. Even though the components of most weddings are similar, something sets each ceremony apart from all the others. Maybe it's the personalities of those involved. Regardless, each wedding is truly unique.

Still, I've noticed there are some common denominators in every wedding. The bride is always beaming or glowing, as though ready to burst with ebullient joy. The groom, on the other hand, often looks like he's in a trance. That-deer-in-the headlights mode.

I have a theory (which I will never share with anyone) that at some point in a relationship a woman begins to emit a "wedding pheromone" of sorts. Once this process begins, the hapless male begins a subconscious process that culminates in the aforementioned trance. By the time the effects of this pheromone have worn off, he finds himself married and mowing the yard, taking out the trash, and cleaning the grill.

Of course, this is just a theory.

Some men appear to be immune to this wedding impulse. Father Ted told me that at one wedding he performed, the groom and the best man were waiting in a side room for their cue to enter the sanctuary and start the proceedings. At the last possible second the best man turned to the groom and asked, "Are you sure you really want to go through with this?" To which the groom responded, "You know, I don't. Let's get outta here."

They took off leaving Father Ted the unenviable task of breaking the bad news to the unsuspecting bride and everyone else.

In light of my never-to-be-mentioned theory I did a quick assessment of my frame of mind. I wasn't anxious, I wasn't nervous, I wasn't even very excited. Ha! I was in the throes of the male wedding day trance. I knew it. But coming now from an experiential perspective, I finally understood why this happens. I was calm, I was focused, I wasn't fearful—and most important, I wasn't second-guessing my decision to get married.

Now it all made sense. With a smile I simply yielded to the phenomenon and started getting dressed.

The amphitheatre had built-in seating for a hundred people which we supplemented with another hundred folding chairs borrowed from First Church. The platform, hewn from the side of the mountain that framed the amphitheatre, was stone. The audience bench seating formed a semi-circle around the platform. Majestic oak trees lined the perimeter, their branches forming a high canopied ceiling over the seating area. The perfect venue for an outdoor wedding.

There were no steps. The wide middle aisle gently ramped upward to the platform. Peg and Juliann would make their way down the aisle followed by Bonnie, escorted by her father. There, my groomsmen Thurm and Louis would be waiting beside me. Father Ted would make a few introductory comments, then Bonnie's Dad would turn her over to me.

We spent quite a bit of time practicing this father-daughter exchange. When Bonnie's sister Jan got married, her father accidentally stepped on the back of her long veil, snapping her head back and knocking over one of the candelabras. After putting out the small fire they resumed the wedding without further incident. All was forgiven but the snafu was singed into everyone's memory. We thought a few extra minutes rehearsing his handoff would be time well spent.

Fire safety would not be an issue at our wedding. Since we would be outside we opted against candles. Instead we went with numerous wicker baskets of colorful fresh-cut zinnias. Bonnie's bouquet was made entirely of daisies. With the vintage clothing and colorful flowers, the setting had a bit of a California vibe.

We hired a photographer who specialized in antique-style portraits and pictures. Most of the pictures would be taken before the wedding so our guests wouldn't have to wait around afterward to visit with us. Bonnie planned to use the photos in a magazine-format wedding portfolio to give family and friends. The sepia-toned product would look like a vintage publication from the early twentieth century. Very cool.

The guys in the wedding party started trickling in around a quarter til ten. The girls would not get there until right before the wedding. I hadn't seen the wedding dress, of course, but I heard it looked fabulous.

While we got the harpsichord situated, some of the family members and friends decorated the platform. Did I mention Bonnie loves fresh flowers? Baskets of fresh flowers were everywhere. It looked like we were getting married in the middle of an allergy medication infomercial.

Finally, with everything in its proper place, we rounded the corner into the homestretch. Sigmund took his seat at the harpsichord to play a mini-concert of the classics for those arriving early. Thurm, Father Ted, Louis, and I found a quiet spot for last-minute reflection and good ol' boy camaraderie.

"How're you feeling? Father Ted asked while patting my back.

"I'm good. I'm actually very relaxed considering that my bachelor's head is queued up in the matrimonial guillotine."

"Off with his head!" Father Ted cackled.

"Off with his head!" Louis seconded.

"Okay, I'll be honest. Maybe I'm a *little* nervous."

Father Ted smiled. "That's to be expected. I know I was before I married Patty—mostly out of fear for her father. The man was a behemoth whose favorite food was steak tartare. He also had six fingers on his left hand."

"What the heck is steak tartare?"

"Raw beef or horse meat," Louis piped in.

"Oh great. Not only am I nervous, now I also have a queasy stomach."

Thurm stepped back. "If you hurl on my costume I'm not paying to get it cleaned."

"What's with you guys? Aren't you supposed to be calming me down, reassuring me that it's gonna be great? That I'll do just fine?"

They looked back and forth at each other then all spoke at the same time. "Nah, nope, not gonna happen. Nice try though." We all laughed.

Walker Wilkins, the wedding photographer, came around to our secluded spot. "Okay boys, time for a few photos." He grouped us in several poses. "Remember, for this time period you want to keep your backs straight, shoulders back, and give your head a small tilt. And *no* smiling. The cameras back then took a while for the film exposure so the folks being photographed had to stand real still for several minutes. That's why all the photos from back then look so staid and stilted."

As we were all posing stiff-backed with heads tilted, I spotted Bonnie's mom's van arriving. My view was obscured by the tree line, but I caught a glimpse of the girls scurrying into the church building, presumably for last minute primping and such.

Walker finished our photo shoot and headed over to capture the ladies.

The launch sequence had begun. There was no turning back now.

Father Ted and the guys put their hands on my shoulders and prayed for me to be a godly husband, to be patient and kind with Bonnie, and for the service to go well. It brought tears to my eyes.

I peeked around the corner. The amphitheatre, now crowded with family and friends, buzzed like a beehive with conversation.

Father Ted got my attention. "It's time." He signaled Sigmund who finished the song he was playing. The audience settled down to a whisper and focused toward the platform. We quietly strode out and took our positions, now looking toward the back of the amphitheatre. Father Ted nodded to Sigmund again, this time to signal him to start playing Bach's "Jesu, Joy of Man's Desiring."

At that point, everything seemed to start moving in slow motion. There was something intoxicating about the sound of the harpsichord playing that iconic song in the outdoor majesty accented by the fresh spring air. My sensory world became surreal.

It reminded me of the first time my parents took me to the county fair. As a young boy, the sights, the sounds, and the smells overwhelmed me. That's how I felt standing there waiting for my bride to appear. For the rest of my life, I knew certain sounds and smells would immediately bring my mind back to this moment in this place. And I would smile.

As the music played, Peg slowly stepped around the corner then up the aisle. Juliann followed, eventually taking her place beside Peg at the front. Sigmund paused ever so briefly . . . then modulated, continuing Bach's familiar melody with the splendor it deserved, calling down heaven and all of God's angels with it. Then, as Bonnie emerged from the old church building, those in attendance rose as one.

Someone once said a woman never looks more beautiful than on the day of her wedding. On this day Bonnie was the quintessential validation of that phrase. Pure radiance.

Her long auburn hair was woven in a loose French braid, accented with baby's breath beneath a veil of antique lace.

And her dress . . . her dress was *stunning.* Peg had designed the cream-colored original in the style of the early 1900s using delicate fabrics cut from three vintage wedding gowns. The dress, covered with antique lace adorned with tiny pearls, fit my bride perfectly, its moderately long train flowing gracefully to the ground. She carried a sweet bouquet of daisies and baby's breath in one hand, the other tucked around the arm of her father as they slowly made their way up the aisle.

Absolutely breathtaking.

I smiled, remembering my dream. Then as now, I found my eyes transfixed upon her. I quickly turned to make sure it was Thurm standing behind me, not Prince Harry.

Thurm gave me a huge smile and patted me on the shoulder. All was as it should be.

The first part of the ceremony was a blur to me. The hand-off from Bonnie's dad occurred without incident, Father Ted did a super job, and Ramona sang a tender version our favorite Dave Barnes song, "I Have and I Always Will." We exchanged rings, shared our vows, prayed, and then before the pronouncement, Father Ted announced, "We have one more song before we present the bride and groom for your approval."

From the far side of the platform, Jason McKenzie walked toward us carrying his acoustic guitar. Dressed in black jeans and a long-sleeved button-down black shirt, he gave us a big smile as gasps trickled through the audience. Bonnie's eyes went wide, looking first at Jason then back at me. *No way,* she mouthed.

"I can't believe it!" someone in the back loudly whispered. "That's Jason McKenzie!"

Jason stepped to the front of the platform and pulled his guitar over his head with the strap resting on his shoulder. Then he quietly played the strings and looked out into the crowd. "When Elmo asked me to sing at his wedding, I was honored. I've known him for a long time, and now I know Bonnie too. They're dear friends." He smiled then chuckled. "Let's be honest. Elmo Jenkins getting married proves miracles still happen."

Everyone laughed.

"Elmo sent me some lyrics he'd penned and asked if I would put them to music for today. Well, I did, and I like this little song so much, I'll probably sing it at my own wedding—if *that* ever happens." He chuckled again.

"Just tell me when and where," a young woman shouted. The audience roared again.

Jason smiled, letting the laughter die down. "The name of this song is 'As One'."

A special gift from You, Lord,
A bond of love that we can share.
Today we start brand new,
A dream come true within Your loving care.

The oneness of our love for You, Lord.
We lift our lives together, we give ourselves to You.
The marriage of our souls to You, Lord.
The love You gave for two,
We're giving back as one, as one.

Together we will serve you,
And in Your name do what we can.
With Your love in our hearts,
Now we can start to understand Your plan.

The oneness of our love for You, Lord.
We lift our lives together, we give ourselves to You.
The marriage of our souls to You, Lord.
The love You gave for two,
We're giving back as one, as one.

Jason finished the song, then turned and quietly walked off the side of the platform.

Father Ted stepped forward and in his booming baritone voice stated, "I now pronounce you, husband and wife—Mr. and Mrs.

Ellington Jenkins. Ellington, you may kiss the bride."

And oh yeah, did I ever!

We held the reception right there in the old church. Jason hung around for just a minute or two, saying he needed to catch a plane or something. But I knew he was being gracious, not wanting to be a distraction. I thanked him, gave him a hug, and let him slip away.

There was cake, there were toasts, then Bonnie tossed her bouquet. All the normal post-wedding merriment you'd expect. And a good time was had by all.

We were both glad we'd decided to postpone the big honeymoon so we could hang around and visit with everybody. The custodian finally kicked the last of us out around three in the afternoon.

What a day! Totally exhausted, Bonnie and I headed to our suite at the Esquire Plaza.

And that's all I'm gonna say about that.

20

The Grill

She sketched a whistle on the top of her notepad and pointed to it with her ballpoint pen.

I grinned.

"Someone's nose is whistling," Bonnie whispered in my ear as Fran went over the church calendar.

Another Wednesday morning staff meeting; the first since our wedding. I reconnoitered the crowded room. It was faint, and you had to concentrate to hear it, but there was no doubting it. Someone's nose was indeed piping out a tune. This had happened before, several times in fact, and it always seemed to be a different person.

The secret to identifying the nose whistler was to match the person's breathing pattern to the sound. After a few minutes of observation, I decided to put my money on Bob "Big Bird" Stevens. I wrote "BB" on her notepad. Bonnie glanced at Bob for a long moment then penned the letter "C" on the pad and circled it—our secret code meaning she concurred. She suppressed a chuckle as she doodled a smiley face on her pad. We would laugh about Bob's Greatest Hit later at lunch. Alas, another intriguing staff meeting mystery solved. Our little cryptic game playing help cut the monotony. These meetings were known to skew toward the mundane.

As the opening segment of the staff meeting wound down, Tom Applebee stood to make an announcement. "For the first time in over fifty years, we now have a husband and wife serving at the same time on our First Church staff."

A small round of applause broke out spontaneously. Bonnie and I were both caught off-guard by the announcement, and I'm sure it showed on our faces.

Bob continued, "For such an historic union, we as a staff deemed it most appropriate to grace each of you with a special gift of our love and friendship. We took up a collection and as Aaron, the older brother of Moses would say, 'out of the melting pot' comes a pair of silk pajamas for Bonnie along with some bath salts, scented candles, and a day trip to the spa for a massage, manicure, and pedicure."

Doris McGinity presented Bonnie a gift bag with all the goodies inside. All the ladies in the room oooed and aahed over the gifts, while the men simply looked befuddled. I figured if she got the spa treatment, maybe I would get something cool like a golf weekend away or tickets to a pro football game.

Bob turned to me. "And for our beloved Elmo—" he paused while grinning, then clapped his hands twice. The door flew open and in came Thurm pushing . . . *a grill?* I fought to look excited. It was shining, it was black, and it even came with the requisite weapons of war—grill tools. I smiled as I attempted to acknowledge my gratitude, but I knew as every other married man in the room knew, grilling is hard work. Let me rephrase that. Grilling is hot, dirty, greasy, and dangerous hard work! Which is why most single men don't own a grill. That's what steakhouses are for!

Case in point. After the meeting I grabbed Thurm. "Hey man, thanks for wheelin' in the grill. You got a minute to show me how it works?"

"Sorry Elmo. I don't own a grill and I have no idea how this one works, but don't worry. Yours came with this thick manual of instructions."

I bet.

Don't you just hate it when gifts come with a new job attached?

Alone in a dark room (or maybe a cave?), I was afraid. Not sure how I'd arrived in this dank and dark place, my instincts were screaming, "Be still! Be quiet!" Danger lurked nearby. Someone or something shared the darkness with me. Did they know I was there? Did they mean me harm? My fear intensified as something touched my arm. The aroma of cooking meat filled my nostrils causing a paralyzing terror like I'd never experienced before. Something warm and moist nuzzled my ear. My demise was imminent and I knew it! The VCR in my head queued up my entire life to flash before my eyes . . .

And then it spoke. "Hey honey, I brought you a surprise."

The slow insidious voice was feminine and strangely familiar.

It spoke again. "I couldn't remember if you favored bacon or sausage so I made some of both."

I opened my eyes just as Bonnie gave me a good morning kiss.

"You okay? Dreaming again?"

I yawned with a big stretch. "Yeah, but you rescued me. How sweet. What's this about bacon?"

"I brought you breakfast in bed." She propped up pillows so I could sit up against the headboard.

I'd never been served breakfast in bed before. I gave my new wife a hug. "Have I told you today how much I love you?"

"No, but then you just woke up. And I'm very glad that you do."

She gave me another kiss. Then, quoting Inga from *Young*

Frankenstein in a thick Romanian accent, she said, "Da feeling's moochall."

Ah, the life of a newlywed. Awakened with a kiss. Breakfast in bed. Even time for a little "roll in-za hay" as Inga would say.

Later that morning as we folded laundry, I asked, "Tell me, my love. How would you like to spend our Saturday?"

She ran her hand through her soft auburn hair, pulling it away from her face. "How about we hit the flea market and treasure hunt for some cool antiques for the house? Jane E. found an old chicken coup there last week. She cleaned it, painted it, then turned into an *awesome* coffee table."

"Okay, sounds like fun. You know me. If there's a bargain to be had, I'm all in."

"Then let's pick up some steaks and fixin's at the grocery store so we can try out our new grill tonight," she said, excited.

"Sounds like a plan."

Since we now owned a new grill, I might as well learn how to use it. After all, lots of guys find grilling to be a fulfilling, even manly way to spend their weekends and evenings. I'd always thought that men who loved to grill were probably from the same demographic as those who loved to bowl. But who knows, maybe grilling was one of those activities that transcended my cultural stereotyping.

I surprised myself. "Let's kick it up a notch and invite over a few friends over to help break in the grill. What d'ya say?"

"That's a great idea, but it's kinda late to be asking people over. They might already have plans in place."

"I know Thurm will be available and interested, and I bet Juliann will too. Of course, you can't *just* ask those two or it'll look like we're matchmaking."

"You're absolutely right. You finish up the laundry, and I'll make a few calls."

"It's called a pig trough," I said as we set the weathered wooden box on the back porch. "Thanks for helping me carry it around back."

Thurm scratched his head. "Where did you get it and *why* did you get it?"

"We got it for a dollar this afternoon over at the Flea Market. Bonnie's gonna use it for a flower box. You might remember from our wedding that Bonnie loves flowers."

"Yeah, I recall there were quite a few flowers in attendance that day." Thurm chuckled. "I see you got the new grill all set up, so you must have figured it all out. Good job, Elmo."

"You know, there's a reason this grill came with a thick user's manual. It took me over an hour to get it all put together correctly.

Then I had to individually test each connection for gas leaks. There's even an extensive checklist you're supposed to repeat each time before firing it up. Just out of curiosity, besides the grill, what other potential Elmo gift ideas were discussed?"

Thurm held his thumb and forefinger close together. "We came *this close* to giving you a La-Z-Boy recliner instead of the grill."

I gasped. "Why oh why did you all change your mind?!"

"Doris overspent on Bonnie's gifts so we had to *downgrade* you to the grill. Tough break. But hey, this is a top-of-the-line grill. What're ya cooking up tonight?"

"So I lost the La-Z-Boy to a *pedicure?* Dang. Oh well. We were gonna break in the grill with steaks tonight, but then our little party guest list proliferated, so—using your term—we had to *downgrade* to hamburgers."

"Who all's coming?"

"It started out being you, Juliann, and Peg. Then Juliann invited Cornbread Jackson and he's bringing Eddie Hughes along. So there'll be seven of us."

"Sounds like fun." Thurm looked over my shoulder. "Speak of the devil, here comes Eddie now."

"Hey, dudes and dudettes, anybody home?" Eddie yelled as he burst through our side gate.

"Just us boys out here," I yelled back.

"Hey Eddie, love the hat," Thurm teased. "Is that made of black velvet? You trying to channel some Justine Timberlake?"

He missed the slight. "Yeah, man, and dig this—it's reversible."

"Where's Cornbread Jackson?" I asked.

Eddie grinned. "He stopped off at the condo to pick up his tripod."

"What?! No!"

"Come on, man. I'm just kidding ya. There'll be no presentations tonight. That is, unless you invited us over to sell us some Avon or Mary Kay?" Eddie guffawed like a drunken sailor. Personally, I didn't see the humor.

Thurm came to my rescue. "Eddie, I see you've brought your best material tonight."

Eddie wiped his eyes. "Sorry, guys. I couldn't help myself—especially after watching Elmo squirm that night over at my place when the tripod came out. Whew, that was some funny stuff, dude."

"All right, enough of the multi-level chit-chat. Where's Cornbread?"

"He's picking up Juliann on his way over." His eyebrows arched. "Whoa, Elmo, nice grill, man. I've personally never owned one. Are they easy to use?"

"If you ever get married you'll have one. Guaranteed. And a lawnmower, too." I opened the grill lid. "Is it easy to use, you ask? If you fastidiously follow every step in the owners manual, it takes about three days to cook some hamburgers."

Eddie cackled. "Mister married man, already whining about household chores. Listen, you better count your blessings. They don't make many fine ladies like Bonnie anymore, and you're dang sure lucky to be married to her."

"Now Eddie, you almost sound as if you've been receiving some PR money from said wife," I feigned shock.

"He's right, Elmo," Thurm jumped in. "You're truly blessed."

I laughed. "I guess what goes around comes around. Here I am being tutored on the finer points of marriage by two single guys. Boys, mark my words, when you all get married my wedding gift to you will be a grill." I brandished the grill fork. "And if either of you ever start lecturing me on childrearing—"

Bonnie popped her head out the sliding glass door. "Hey, guys! Elmo, ready for the burgers?"

The burgers came out great, so I had to assume you get top-of-the-line food with a top-of-the-line grill. That concept flew in the face of my buy-cheap philosophy. Then again, I realized many of my premarital philosophies were in fact evolving.

Jimmy Cornbread Jackson turned out to be a great guy. Not what I expected at all. I'd been around him a couple times before, but we'd never had a real conversation. He seemed to be a decent person with a smart head on his shoulders, and a believer to boot. It also looked like he'd taken a real shining to Juliann, and that she was, in fact, warming up to him. Together they looked like an airbrushed couple on the cover of *People* magazine. If marriage is in their future I hope they don't ask me to perform their ceremony. I avoid doing weddings like the plague. All it takes is one classic Elmo screw- up and I've blown up some poor couple's most important day.

Thurm had to leave right after dinner to attend to some youth crisis, but the rest of us settled into a rowdy game of Scrabble. Bonnie and I teamed up as did Juliann and Cornbread. That left Peg and Eddie going solo. Eddie must have skipped English classes in school because he attempted some outlandish words. Peg challenged and nailed him on every single one of them. Growing up in the Sudan, she'd been home-schooled, and it showed.

It was a fun night and special for us to have friends over for the first time. Bonnie obviously had the gift of hospitality, and it didn't hurt that she was also a great cook. The guys were right—I was blessed to have her as my life's partner. I looked forward to building a lifetime of memories with her. God had been incredibly gracious when He brought her into my life.

The phone rang, startling me as I sat at my computer checking my email. Bonnie was in the shower, so I hopped up to go answer it. The clock read eleven seventeen. Awfully late for a phone call.

"Hello?"

"Elmo, it's Thurm. I'm really sorry about calling so late, and even more sorry because I have to ask you for a favor." He sounded stressed.

"What's a matter?"

"I need your help. That call I got tonight was about a kid in my youth group. His name is Terrence Jennings, and he's a senior over at Bellcore High School. He's actually one of my leaders. Turns out he's been hiding a drug problem—crack, I think—and it all came unglued this evening. I'm been over at his house since I left your place, and it looks like we're going to have to check him into rehab."

"How can I help?"

"He's from a single-parent home, and his mom needs to stay home with his two little sisters. I need someone to help me get him over to the Nelson Clinic."

"What's his address? I'll be there as soon as I can."

Thurm flopped into one of the plastic chairs lining the walls of the Nelson Clinic Rehab waiting area.

I patted him on the back. "What did they say?"

"They'll accept him into the program, and a good portion of the cost will be covered by his mom's insurance. They're processing him for entry now."

"His mom is single with three kids. How will she pay the balance? Rehabilitation can get pricey."

"I've already talked to Father Ted, and he believes we can use some of the First Church benevolence fund to help them."

I was surprised to see Thurm fighting back tears. I could tell he was fatigued and emotionally exhausted. "Hey man, you okay?"

He looked at me with sad, moist eyes. "You just pour your life into these kids. You pray over them. You give them Godly counsel. You celebrate their victories. And on nights like this, you mourn their defeats."

"Can you tell me what happened with Terrence?"

He took out his handkerchief and wiped his nose. "It's a familiar tale. A lot of these kids have church friends, and they also have school friends. Terrence let a few of his school friends cajole him into trying crack one time, and that's all it took. He was hooked. He's been doing it for quite some time now, leading a double life and fooling everyone. One day he said he read in his Bible about how God sees what others don't—the stuff in a man's heart. He was wracked with guilt and tonight confessed the whole story to his mom.

"I'm proud of him for coming clean," he continued, "but I hurt for him and his mom. He's got a tough road ahead. I told him to have hope. To believe in *Jehovah-Rapha*,—the God who heals." Thurm chuckled. "Of course, then I had to explain to him about the different names of God in the Old Testament."

I laughed too. "That's the Thurm I love—never one to miss a teachable moment." I put my arm around his shoulder and gave him a side hug. "I love you, brother, and so do the kids in your group. First Church is lucky to have you working with our teens. C'mon, let me buy you a cup of coffee."

21

The Gypsy Fleas

Our first two months of marriage had been spectacular. The extended honeymoon period had been very, very sweet. It was all "yes, dear" or "what can I get you, honey?" or "don't worry about it." We were living in a virtual utopia. Sir Thomas Moore would have been proud.

Then one day Bonnie—um, I mean *we*—decided to get a dog. At first I pushed back vehemently against the idea, making the obligatory rational argument concerning such a precipitous decision. There were the cost concerns, carpet concerns, noise concerns— well, you get the idea. I made my case with passion, grounded on a thousand years of scientific fact, and undergirded by irrefutable common sense.

Not at all impressed with my reasoning, Bonnie remained undeterred in her desire to acquire a furry little critter. To be honest, she seemed a bit *stiff-necked* about the whole ordeal. We even had what I would term "an extended tiff" over the matter. I began to appreciate the full irony of the fact that by marrying Bonnie St. Hiliare, I had legally removed the word "saint" from her name. After all, it's just a name. Or is it? I didn't even consider the potential ramifications at the time, but now I hoped this wasn't an uh-oh moment.

Yikes.

Alas, the irrepressible forces of nature (aka Bonnie) won out, and a tiny black ball of fur named Colby bounded into our heretofore pristine home. Colby, an unusually gregarious dog, invited a family of gypsy fleas to come home from the pet store with her. These gypsies were a small family when they arrived; so small, they quietly slipped in the door unnoticed. By the time they made their malfeasance known, their number had exploded into to a formidable dynasty seven generations deep with grandiose plans to homestead every square inch of our house.

We quickly moved to DEFCON 3.

"What's taking so long? The pet store is only ten minutes from the house?"

"Elmo, I can't hear you. The place is jammed with people and their dogs, and of course, they're all barking at the same time."

"Remind me again why I was selected to stay here a Flea Central while you got to escape to the relative safety of the No-Bite Zone?"

"Nope. Didn't hear that either."

"How 'bout this. Colby fell off the counter into the garbage disposal while I was cleaning the dishes. It's quite gruesome, really."

"I heard that, and it's nowhere near funny."

Dang.

She did a redirect. "I need you to do me a favor. Fish my tan blouse out of the hamper and throw it in the wash on gentle. I repeat, ON GENTLE."

Great. I make one laundry mistake and now every time laundry is mentioned I get CAPITAL LETTERS.

Bonnie raised her voice above the din of the barking dogs. "I need it for the staff wives monthly Chef Salad Soiree tonight at the Estrada's."

"Will do. Just hurry home with a big can of bug spray or something. These fleas have already turned my day into a circus."

"Very funny. I'll get there when I can. You hold down the fort and keep Colby out of trouble. See ya!" And she was gone. With a flip of the wrist I slid my phone across the kitchen counter.

I'd been tasked with keeping Colby out of trouble, so what were my options?

1. *The Calming Biscuit.* An eighth of an Ambien rolled into a piece of white bread. Goes down easy and the pooch is out like a light for several hours. Of course, this option is wrought with risk in that PETA would surely find out, and I would end up spending a fortnight or two with Michael Vick's husky former cellmate. Not gonna happen.

2. *The Quarantine.* This involves sequestering said pup in Bonnie's closet (with the light on, of course). My reasoning here being that this option limits potential damage to a smaller percentage of our possessions. Unfortunately the stuff in harm's way is all Bonnie's. Well, someone has to take a hit for the team, and it might as well be her. On second thought, this could dampen her enthusiasm for *other* facets of our relationship. Probably not the best option.

3. *The Distraction.* This is where you take the mutt's favorite chew toy and tie it to her tail. This can keep her distracted for quite some time with the added entertainment benefit of getting to watch her spill around the room, all awhirl and tumble. Of course, here too, there's the possible PETA complication once gain raising its ugly head. (See #1).

4. *The Paddock.* This is where you toss the little bundle of joy into the dirty clothes hamper. There she can romp amongst the dirty laundry and have a grand old time. If there are any unfortunate accidents with fluids and such, there's no problem since the clothes are going to be washed anyway. Then again, this could lead to a problem with both Bonnie *and* PETA.

What's an Elmo to do? Here's an idea with merit. Just let Colby run wild and worry about damage control later when Attila returns. *Que sera.*

So instead of concerning myself with the dog, I thought about taking a nap. But then I remembered that lying down would be exposing myself to a full frontal attack by the gypsy hordes. The sofa had already fallen into enemy hands. Napping there would give the carnivorous sub-creatures with their uber-gymnastic skills an easy access to choice cuts of Elmo flesh. I had no intention of becoming a meat 'n' three.

Since I still had control of the high ground—which I refused to relinquish without a dog fight (no offense, Colby)—I decided to stretch out in my desk chair. With my feet up on my credenza, I was safely above the gypsy carnage and debauchery below.

Or so I thought.

I'd only been surfing the web for a few minutes when it happened. While reading an enthralling article about one of the Kardashian's recent trip to the hardware store, my eyes suddenly refocused from my computer screen to a point right in front of my face. This happened just in time for me to see a gypsy flea reach the apex of its leap from my keyboard toward my shirt. Instantaneously, I performed an evasive maneuver, back-flipping Jackie Chan-style out of my chair. While simultaneously releasing noxious counter measures in the form of, well—I'll just leave that to your imagination.

This was war! I needed Munitions Sergeant Bonnie Jenkins home, and I needed her NOW, armed to the teeth!

Someone once said fleas are like third-world terrorists. Now I know why. You have to bomb your house to get rid of them.

After three flea baths and about a hundred bucks worth of anti-flea powders, lotions, and meds (that's right—*one hundred dollars*), I found myself driving over to Thurm's to spend the night with the mutt in tow. Thurm wanted me to sign a waiver guaranteeing no fleas were taggin' along. Instead, I just promised him we were clean, though I didn't really know that for a fact. Since we'd flea-bombed the house, we needed to spend the night elsewhere. Bonnie would stay the night over at the Estrada's after the staff wives' Chef Salad Soiree wound down. She and Louis's wife Jane E. had become best friends after we got married. (Her full name was Jane Elisabeth Estrada, but everyone called her Jane E., and that's how she signed her name. Weird, huh?)

Thurm met us in his driveway.

"Cute puppy. What's that contraption she's strapped into?"

I grabbed Thurm by both shoulders, holding him firm. "Thurm, listen to me as your friend. For the love of Godiva chocolates—never,

never, *never* agree to a dog. No matter how much your lady begs, no matter how much she pouts, just be a man and stand your ground. That contraption is an *I Wuv My Dog* car safety seat, and it cost me one hundred and twenty-nine dollars." I gave him a good shake. "Thurm, are you hearing what I'm saying?"

"Yeah, yeah, I'm listening. But don't worry, Elmo. I prefer cats."

"What?!"

He shrugged. "You know, cats? Those animals that purr and clean themselves?"

Now normally I would have taken Thurm to task for such a lame proclamation, but the day had run long and I felt a bit peckish. "I'm hoping you have some food in The Cave. I'm starving."

Thurm had named his bachelor duplex The Cave. The other side was home to some boneheaded Czechoslovakian guy named Krun. His colorful neighbor fashioned himself as quite the up-and-coming country singer. Thurm had to buy industrial-strength ear plugs because Krun stayed up half the night practicing his Garth Brooks covers. At first, the thick Eastern European accent on Garth's famous songs was pretty funny. Now it was just a plain old nuisance.

With Krun crooning and Colby dancing, I was looking at a long night with limited sleep. And of course, tomorrow was Sunday, my busiest day of the week.

As far as food, typical single guy that he was, all Thurm had was some white bread and a week-old package of bologna. Against my better judgment, being hungry, I ate it anyway and hoped my old nemesis *Sal Monella* wouldn't be joining me for dinner.

Bonnie looked forward each month to the staff wives' Chef Salad Soiree. A special camaraderie had formed amongst this group of ladies.

There are unique pressures and stresses experienced by the families of those in the ministry that most church members simply cannot relate to or come close to understanding. Helping people through times of bereavement, illness, loss, relationship problems, and spiritual issues can create an intense day-to-day emotional drain on a minister. Often, by the time he gets home at the end of the day, he is physically and emotionally empty, making it difficult to meet the needs of his family. Marriage to someone in full-time ministry is a special calling all unto itself. The wife must often pick up the slack caused by the demands of her husband's ministry.

The Chef Salad Soiree, formally called the Gospel Girls, had originally been started by the pastor's wife, Anna Mae Jorgensen, when she was much younger. Several years later she had a falling out with one of the other staff wives and never again attended. The monthly get-together continued after her exodus, though on a more informal basis. These women shared a lot in common and the monthly Soiree was an opportunity for them to support each other and vent about the frustrations they all faced. Since the staff continually changed, the composition of this group did also. Incorporating the new wives into the group had never been a problem.

Until now.

"Elmo, I know it's late. I hope I didn't wake you."

"Nope, there's not a whole lot of sleep going on over here," I said, jerking the phone charger cord out of Colby's mouth. "Colby says hi."

"I'm really sorry about the hassle with the fleas and all. I'm also—wait. What's that awful noise in the background?"

"That's Thurm's neighbor Krun absolutely murdering Garth Brook's song 'Friends in Low Places'."

"Wow, that awful racket is actually someone singing?"

"Only if you meant to use the word *singing* in a very liberal big picture type of context. In that case, the answer to your question would be yes. And get this. Thurm says Krun practices almost every night."

"Is Krun his first or last name?"

"I have no idea. I never thought about it before."

"How does Thurm ever get any sleep?"

"He dropped a wad of cash and bought these special *Black Out* ear plugs. They look more like headphones to me. Of course he only has one pair, so Colby and I are suffering through Krun's eponymous live album."

"You made that up."

"Okay, I am a bit delirious from sleep deprivation. Maybe I'm having a Krun-induced flashback to the sixties or something. All I need is a purple lava lamp and some phosphorescent posters to complete the experience."

"I'm sorry, Elmo, but I'm just too tired tonight to fully appreciate your whacked- out sense of humor. Besides, I actually called to talk to you about something else."

I winced. "I'm open to discussing anything as long as it does not involve adding any additional creatures to our home."

Bonnie lowered her voice. "No, this is actually more serious. I think we have a mole."

"Oh, man that's all we need," I said, raising my voice. "Another rodent and this time it's the kind that tears up the lawn!"

"What? No, silly, not *that* kind of mole."

"Then what are you taking about?"

"I'm talking about a mole or snitch in our staff wives group."

"Huh?"

"Apparently one of the staff wives has been breaking our circle of confidence and passing things shared within our group to some of the deacons."

"Now, how do you know that?"

Bonnie was almost whispering now. It was a good thing Krun had decided to take an intermission, or I wouldn't have been able to hear her. She paused for a long moment. "I really don't want to discuss the specifics over the phone, but I would like you to keep your eyes and ears open. You're good at figuring out this type of stuff. You should also know Sturgis Weaver's name was mentioned. I'll fill you in on the rest of the details tomorrow. Try to get some sleep and give Colby a goodnight kiss for me. Love ya."

I hung up the phone. *Try to get some sleep.* Right. My head hit the pillow just as Krun started up his second set. Lying there with my eyes wide open, I watched as a gypsy flea moon-walked to the music across my pillow. I decided not to mention this flea incident to Thurm. He would know soon enough.

22

The Stones

First Church buzzed with typical Sunday morning exuberance while I sat sequestered in my dimly lit office contemplating a faster way to imbibe caffeine. Staring at my third cup of coffee I fought to bring all of my senses back online. Altogether, I figured I'd had two hours of sleep the previous night.

After a gentle knock my office door opened and Bonnie stepped inside closing the door behind her.

She gasped. "Whoa, you look like the insomnia fairy was breakdancing on your face all night."

My bloodshot eyes rotated in her direction. "Morning, love. Sorry for the disheveled appearance. My masseuse, my hair and makeup person, and my-life coach all called in sick this morning." I forced a small smile.

She laughed as she stared at the three empty coffee cups on my desk. "I take it the caffeine hasn't kicked in yet. Oh, but it will."

"Here's hoping."

"What are the bumps all over your face?"

"I believe the technical term for them is flea bites. I think I'll just lie low in here this morning."

"Probably a good idea, and sorry about the fleas. Hopefully bombing the house took care of the problem." She walked over and gave me a kiss. "Does that make it feel any better?"

"No, but I forgive you anyway. Listen, I had quite a bit of time to think last night, and I figured out who your gopher is."

"Gopher? What are you talking about?"

"You know, the snitch you mentioned."

"Oh, you mean the mole."

"Yeah, yeah. Your mole is Mary Beth Hankins."

"Raze's wife?"

"Yep."

"Why Mary Beth? She never says two words in our staff wife get-togethers."

"Yes, but she talks to her husband, and he's got a chip on his shoulder about First Church the size of the non-planet formerly known as Pluto."

"And how do you know this?"

"I've had multiple run-ins with Raze. Once he candidly told me there was a group of 'long time members' that were very unhappy with the direction of the church."

"Seriously?"

"He basically told me I needed to back off my Carpe Annum initiative and mind my own business. It came across like a threat which is how I believe he intended it to."

"He does seem like a sour sort. Does this have any connection to Sturgis Weaver?"

"I think it does, but who really knows? Raze has a long history as a troublemaker. For that matter, so does Sturgis Weaver."

"Thanks for the input. I'll run it by Jane E. and Charlene Applebee and see what they think." She reached in her purse and pulled out a Five-Hour Energy Drink bottle. "Here, drink this. That and the coffee you've already ingested should have you up and flying around like Superman in no time. Sorry though, it won't help with the bumps on your face. That humiliation you'll just have to grin and bear. Just tell everybody it's my fault."

"Oh, I will." I blew her a kiss as I felt the caffeine starting to take hold. "Now, where's my cape?"

On the way home from church I stopped at a corner landscaping store called Got Stones. At one time it had been a gas station, but that business had closed years ago. Recently it reopened, providing landscaping stone, rock, yard ornaments, and such. Piles of different types of stones and rocks were spread out all over the property, along with a few pallets of colored river slate here and there. The lot was partially surrounded by a chain-link fence, but no gate existed. It didn't seem very secure, but I guess they figured, who steals rocks?

Our new house didn't have a walkway from the back porch around to the side garage door. So I had decided to put in some path stones. When I pulled my car onto the lot at Got Stones, an old boy in overalls was sitting in a chair under the awning of the old gas station building. As I got out of my car he hopped right up and came over to greet me.

"Howdy, can I help ya with sumpun'?" His crooked smile revealed that most of his teeth had gone missing.

I explained my plan, and he showed me several different types of path stones available there on the lot. His name was Bucky, and he seemed knowledgeable about the different pathway options. I picked a style I liked, and we decided I would need about ten of them to accomplish my task. He helped me load them in my trunk.

"Thanks, Bucky. How much do I owe you?"

"Well, our credit card gismo's all broke. Have cash?"

"No problem."

He gave me that crooked smile again. "These here stones are two dollars apiece plusin' tax and you got ten of 'em. Let's just call it an even twenty bucks." I noticed him studying my face closely.

"They're flea bites." I handed him a twenty-dollar bill.

He croaked. "I wuz guessin' 'skeeters. I bet they itch sumpun' fierce."

"Oh yeah. Thanks again for the help, Bucky." I hopped in my car and headed home for a late lunch and a long nap. With the extra weight in the trunk, my Nissan drove like a low-rider. I smiled the whole way, pleased with myself because the cost was so much less than I had expected.

The following Saturday I got up early and went to work on my new pathway. By noon it was nearly complete, but I came up short. After a quick lunch with Bonnie and Colby, I drove back over to Got Stones to get three more path stones so I could finish the job.

I parked my car next to the path stones I needed and walked over to the old gas station building. I didn't see anyone outside, but the front door stood propped open so I just walked in.

A middle-age woman behind the counter smiled as she hung up the phone. "Can I help you?"

"Yes, thank you. I need to get three more of those gray path stones." I pointed through the window at the stack next to my car.

"Okay. Is there anything else we can get for you today? Perhaps a driveway marker?"

"No, but thanks for asking." I handed her a ten-dollar bill.

She looked at me and smiled again. "I'm sorry, but those gray path stones are five dollars apiece, so your total will be fifteen dollars plus tax."

The higher price caught me by surprise. "Did they recently go up in price?"

"No, that's what they've always cost."

Exasperated, I said, "I bought some of those here just last Sunday, and they were only two dollars apiece."

"I'm afraid you're mistaken. We've always charged five dollars each for those. That will be sixteen thirty-five with tax."

She was clearly wrong, but I decided not to make a fuss. I handed her a twenty and got my change.

Her smile was back. "Do you need some help loading those?"

"No, but thank you." I turned to walk out.

I heard her shut the cash register drawer. "By the way, we're not open on Sundays. Never have been."

What?! Then it hit me and I had to laugh. I guess ol' Bucky can just use my twenty to get his tooth cleaned.

In many ways, the first year of marriage can be the most difficult as two people adjust to each other's domestic idiosyncrasies and proclivities. But it can also be a great time of unlimited joy and laughter before the stresses of life move in full force. During the "salad days" of a young marriage, you even have permission to lovingly laugh at each other without causing offense.

Our new home came with hardwood floors. We had received several nice area rugs as wedding presents, but much of the bare wood remained exposed. To me, one of the downsides to hardwood floors is the noise. Whereas a carpet absorbs sound, wood reflects it causing it to reverberate around the room.

Bonnie and I were both raised in middle-class homes, so we grew up used to cost-cutting strategies. Like using a fan at night instead of running the AC and unnecessarily cooling the whole house. Fans at night also provide plenty of white noise. This makes it easier to sleep, particularly if you live by a noisy road or railroad tracks.

At the foot of our king-size bed, we placed Bonnie's cedar hope chest. Since spring had turned to summer and the nights were warm, we placed a square box fan on the cedar chest to keep us cool. On most nights this setup worked like a charm, but fate's wry sense of humor had other things planned for one particular evening.

The night had started out as usual with our now-established bedtime routine. Bonnie got the bathroom first as she cleaned up for bed, then it was my turn. Afterward, we prayed together, kissed goodnight, and it was lights out by eleven.

Somewhere around two in the morning in the dark stillness of the night, the box fan on the cedar chest at the foot of our bed, for reasons not yet fully understood, decided to take a dive. Like the famed cliff divers of Acapulco it leaped out over the cliffs, assuming the beautiful silhouette of a swan. But unlike those graceful and talented cliff divers, our fan hit the hardwood floor with a belly-flopping bang that was surely heard two blocks away.

Abruptly awakened by the sonic boom, Bonnie sat right up in bed and screamed into the darkness, "MAMA!" (I kid you not.)

I laughed so hard, tears were running down my face. So did she, initially, until the potential humiliation implications of her childlike yelp convinced her brain to move into intense damage control mode. She threatened me to within an inch of my life to keep quiet about the "Mama incident" as it's now referred to. Yet, here I am writing about it.

It happened, I was there, and no creative rewriting of history or aggressive denial campaign will ever alter the veracity of the event.

And what of the poor misguided, misunderstood box fan you ask? It was banished to the back of the closet. Fodder for a future garage sale. Just another tragic tale about a household appliance yielding to temptation and suffering the consequences of its ill-conceived actions. A sad tale indeed.

23

The Belated Gift

The warm moist air accosted my face as I stepped from the plane into the jetway. It had been a long, exhausting three days, and I was happy to be back home.

Bonnie met me in airport luggage area with a smile. "Welcome home."

I gave her a big extended hug. "Hey, beautiful."

"You look tired and your eyes are all red," she said sounding concerned.

"I just woke up. I slept the entire three-hour flight—from takeoff til touchdown. Some Goth-looking teenage girl sitting in the middle seat elbowed me when I woke up and said, 'Thank *gaaawd* for earplugs.' So I'm assuming I must've snored the whole way back. I'm not use to sleeping sitting up."

"I wouldn't worry about it. If she's truly a Goth babe, it'll just give her something else to rag about to her friends. Y'know, to help validate her anti-social ideals."

"You're terrible." When it came to sarcasm Bonnie was a five-star Ninja assassin.

We grabbed my suitcase and headed for the parking lot.

She popped open the trunk. "How was the Church on Castle Ridge?"

"Impressive. Very different. It had the feel of a college campus. Of course, the median age of the membership is about twenty years younger than First Church."

"Did you get some good ideas for your Carpe Annum report?"

"Yes, I did. I took about twenty pages of notes. The place was really cool. You enter the church through what they call the Atrium. It's this huge room with a three-story ceiling populated with chic coffee bars and food kiosks. There are tables and couches spread all around. It's very welcoming, but not confrontational. Volunteers circulate the Atrium wearing red vests with "Ask Me" on the front and back. Very unique."

"It does sound cool," Bonnie said as we pulled up to the toll booth. "By the way, how's the Carpe Annum report coming along?"

"It's about seventy-five percent complete. This Castle Ridge trip was my last off-site visit, and boy, I'm glad. They've all been grueling.

I've finished all of the staff interviews and have only a handful of member interviews left to go. Then it's all about compiling, culling, editing, analyzing, formulating, and publishing."

"Oh, that's all?" She laughed out loud.

"Granted, there's still a lot of work to do, but it's the analyzing and formulating that I enjoy the most."

"When's it actually due?"

"As you know Dr. Jorgensen gave me a year, but my goal is to have it on his desk November first. That will allow him a few days to digest the material and the recommendations before the November deacons meeting. Then if he and the deacons approve, the full Carpe Annum report could be presented at the annual church business meeting in December."

"Wow, no pressure. If there's anything I can do to help just let me know."

"I'm glad you offered. I'll definitely need your keen eye for help with the editing and proofreading."

"Willing and available."

"Wonderful." I leaned over and gave her a kiss on the cheek. "What's been going on around here while I was gone?"

"Same ol', same ol'. "Let's see . . . our newlywed Sunday school class is working over at the Crosstown homeless shelter this month. I signed us up to serve breakfast on the second and fourth Saturday morning. Hope that's okay?"

"That's great. Matter of fact, one of my Carpe Annum recommendations is for First Church to get more involved in service to the downtown community. Research has shown that younger Christians are very interested in what they term 'social justice.' They want to attend a church that isn't afraid to get its hands dirty helping out the less fortunate. I know it sounds like a cheesy, clichéd metaphor, but its true—First Church needs to be less of a country club and more of a hospital."

"Good luck selling that. It's probably quite accurate, but you're gonna have to grow that philosophy through the new folks coming in. The current gang attends First Church because it's clean, safe, and non-threatening. It'll take a miracle for most of those folks to have the change of heart you're talking about."

I smiled. "Oh, you're absolutely right, but you have to start somewhere. I've already been praying for just such a miracle, and I believe it can happen."

"Welcome back, Elmo. Did you have a good trip?"

"Yes I did, Juliann. Thanks for asking. Do I have any messages?"

She handed me a pile of slips. "And Harry wants you to come by his office sometime. He's got something for you."

"Really? For me?"

She leaned in and whispered, "It's for you *and* Bonnie. I think it might be a belated wedding gift," she said with her signature giggle.

"Is it a new car?" I faux-gasped.

"No, silly." She scurried off to make some copies or something.

Back in my office I began to unpack my travel gear. I've discovered there are basically two main approaches people take when returning from a trip, whether it's a business trip or a vacation in the county.

Approach number one assumes that before you left, everything in your room or office was in its appropriate place. After all, you'd spent valuable time and energy organizing your things so they'd be easy to find when needed. Quickly restoring everything to its proper place upon your return efficiently facilitates your reentry back into your day-to-day routine. Whether it's a suitcase or a notebook, you simply put it back where you found it when packing for your trip.

Approach number two asks, "Why waste time unpacking when important tasks needing your attention have piled up while you were gone? There will be time for unpacking later." So your bulging briefcase or jammed suitcase is merely opened for easy access, then you hit the ground running. The problem with this approach is that before you know it, a week or two have gone by and you still haven't unpacked. Eventually you just get used to living or working from your unorganized pile of stuff. This less disciplined approach can lead to a less efficient life.

An extreme example of this approach was exemplified by a roommate I had in college named Steve. Though he didn't start out this way he got to the point where none of his clothes ever made it back into a closet or drawer. His wardrobe had devolved into a dirty pile and a clean pile. He dressed from the clean pile each day. When the dirty pile got too large he would scoop up the clothes and launder them, then simply add them back to the clean pile. His approach was inefficient on many different levels. Unfortunately, his studies followed a similar pattern and he eventually dropped out of school and went home.

Striving to be Mr. Efficient, I took approach number one and put away everything I had taken on my trip. It felt good. Feng shui had been restored to the Taj.

Afterward, I headed over to Harry's office to see what this wedding gift mystery was all about.

After the pastor, the music minister almost always gets the second best office in the church. Why? In many churches, the minister of music (or "music minister") achieves something of a sanctified rock star status, particularly with the people in his immediate ministry—choir members, instrumentalists, soloists, and ensemble singers. If he's also a gifted singer, this adulation extends beyond the music ministry family to the general congregation at large. With such popularity comes clout and when tenure is attained, the minister of music is rewarded. The reward? His chance to realize the ultimate dream—the fulfillment of the golden hope that every church music minister longs for. He gets to redesign and renovate the music suite in accordance with his own vision. Oh, happy day!

Harry got his shot at this task several years ago. It's rumored he got so excited, he even chirped some Latin—*Carpe Renovati!* He indeed seized the project with Harry Simpkins' signature fervor and zeal.

Though a small budget line item had been set aside for this music suite renovation, most of it was actually underwritten by designated gifts. To church business managers like Bob "Big Bird" Stevens, the term *designated gift* is a vulgar profanity. Bob would say, "Designated giving to church budgets is akin to graft in a capital development program—totally repugnant."

For some reason church music ministries seem to be quite susceptible to this type of "consecrated extortion." As a prime example, most churches often receive designated gifts for ministries like drama teams or hand bells—even if they don't currently have these programs. In this regard First Church was no different.

Harry had been working behind the scenes for years asking folks to designate part of their First Church giving to the CMSRP (church music suite renovation project). Bob Stevens complained bitterly about Harry's continued subterfuge and its budget implications, but Dr. Jorgensen turned a deaf ear to Bob's complaints. Coincidently, Geraldine Fitzsimons O'Leary, the pastor's sister-in-law and favored church soloist, was a major contributor to the CMSRP fund.

Thus, when the day came to break ground on the renovation project, Harry had amassed enough cash to buy, renovate, and flip the state of North Dakota.

These days, the expression "spare no expense" is rather common, but the term originated with Harry Simpkins. He built a five-tiered choir rehearsal room with top of the line padded chairs for one hundred and fifty singers. Choir members had their own individual lockers in the special-designed, climate-controlled robe room. Each locker housed four different choir robes, each with its own color and style.

The renovated choir suite included a fully functional recording studio used by the soloists and ensembles for practice and for making song tracks to use in the worship services. In addition, Harry designed and built a state-of-the-art music library. Choir members could even check out iPads which included digital song sheets and separate recordings of their individual parts, be it soprano, alto, tenor, or bass. When completed, the renovated music suite was so impressive, it would have made Sir Elton John giggle with glee.

Yet Harry saved the best for last—his office. When it comes to church budgets, if a staff member does not spend all the money allocated for a particular project, someone else will. There is no rollover from project to project or year to year. Use it or lose it. Harry took this fact to heart. By the time he was done, his spacious office rivaled that of Liberace or perhaps Donald Trump.

As I neared the music suite, located in a hall behind the sanctuary, I could hear a commotion. I stuck my head in Harry's office doorway and there was Harry, lying face down on the carpet, banging his fists and kicking his feet like a bratty preschooler who'd been denied an ice cream cone. Ramona and Skip, one of the sound guys, stood by shaking their heads.

"I've been raped! I've been raped! I've been misused and abused!" Harry ranted.

Ramona looked up and noticed me standing in the open doorway.

I smiled. "Okay, then. I'll just come back at a better time." I turned to leave.

With a wry smile, Ramona responded, "No need to leave, Elmo. Harry's just throwing a little tantrum. I think he's about done."

"Hey, Elmo," Skip said calmly as he headed out the other door, obviously unmoved by Harry's outburst.

Harry rolled over on his back, wheezing. "Come on in, Elmo. I'm just venting a little frustration."

I slowly approached the peculiar scene. "What happened?"

"Harry's new state of the art sound system software has been acting up again," Ramona deadpanned. "Which is odd since it was very, *very* expensive," she added with heavy sarcasm.

Harry sat up. "And it's a total piece of crap. Those boys over at Satellite Sound sold me a bill of goods! Man, I just *hate* getting screwed over."

"I'm the same way," I empathized, helping Harry back on his feet. "It ticks me off when I get taken by somebody."

Ramona frowned. "Think I'll just slip out and let you boys have your bellyaching contest without me." She sighed as she headed back to her office.

Harry sat down behind his gigantic desk. "Sorry about that. Every once in a while this job just gets the best of me. Anyway, thanks for coming by."

"Sure. What's up?"

"As you're well aware, I had to miss your wedding, which I've been told was fabulous and really unique. Trixie and I got you and Bonnie a gift, but it's been sitting here in my office for months. Totally my fault. Sorry again." He reached into one of his desk drawers and pulled out a square, wrapped package about the size of two shoe boxes.

"Thanks, Harry. This is very kind of you and Trixie. I'll just wait and let Bonnie open it when I get home. You know how brides are about wedding gifts."

Harry chuckled. "Yes, I do. Listen, I understand you just spent a few days out at the Church on Castle Ridge. Did you happen to meet their associate pastor, Reeves Huntington?"

"Sure did. Seemed like a very nice man."

"Oh, he's the best. We were on staff together many years ago when I was about your age. We're good friends, kind of like you and Thurm. I have many, many great memories with Reeves.

Harry's eyes grew wide. "One time we both signed up for a training tour of Israel. The trip was free if you agreed to later sponsor and lead a group of your church members for an official tour of Israel. We were both on staff at a small Baptist church at the time. We ended up taking the training tour with twenty-five Episcopal priests—twenty-four men and one woman, to be exact.

"Now back in the day, at least in our denomination, to be a woman in a pastoral position was taboo. The lady didn't bother me a bit, but she rubbed old Reeves the wrong way, especially on the eleven-hour flight over there.

"My doctor had given me a bottle of mild tranquilizers to help with sleep on the trip because of the dramatic time difference. We arrived in Jerusalem about eight in the evening. The plan was to have a late dinner together as a group then go to bed. But because of the time change, we were all wide-awake. Our body clocks were telling us it was noon. So I gave Reeves a couple of my tranquilizers, and the dingo took them before dinner.

"About half through the meal I realized we had a problem. Reeves starting behaving like he'd downed a quart of whiskey. Exacerbating an already awkward situation, right across the table from Reeves sat the female minister. He began asking her a lot of extremely pointed questions about the validity of women leading men. Very obnoxious and *totally* out of character for him. The lady's face got redder and redder. Finally she reached a breaking point and threw her dinner roll at Reeves before storming off. The rest of the Episcopalians appeared to be shocked momentarily, then they all broke into boisterous laughter. Turns out they didn't care much for the woman either.

"Now, these guys didn't know that pastors in the Baptist denomination don't drink alcohol. They just assumed Reeves had imbibed too much liquor. The real irony was that most of them were heavy drinkers and spent much of the trip sampling the local concoctions."

"What happened with Reeves and the lady?" I asked.

"Oh, he apologized the next morning, but there was a definite chill between them for the rest of tour. How I wish I had a video of that night at the dinner table in Jerusalem. It was absolutely hilarious! One of those priceless moments you never forget."

As I walked back to my office with Harry's wedding present under my arm, I pondered what it would be like to room with Harry on a ten-day tour. After a moment of reflection I concluded—*not gonna happen in this lifetime.*

After saying hi to Father Ted and Thurm, I sat down back at my desk and reached for my To-Do List. I found a folded piece of note paper taped to the page. When I opened it, I saw it was on Bonnie's personalized notepad. In typed letters it said: *Meet me on the roof for a newlywed surprise—XO XO.*

To say the least I was intrigued. As a recently married young man wouldn't you be? I slipped out the back door of the church office and skipped—that's right, *skipped,* so just get over it—to the elevator. Riding up the lift to the rooftop area, I wondered what my saucy young bride was up to. A little smooching on the clock might be just what the doctor ordered after my three-day trip away.

Then I had a chilling flashback. My last visit to the roof ended with a trip to the hospital and a concussion. I would need to be more careful this time. The elevator doors opened and I stepped out on the rooftop basketball court with great anticipation. No Bonnie. Was she hiding? I slowly walked the perimeter, looking behind the vending machines and picnic tables, but alas I found myself all alone. Or at least I thought so.

Up on top of the retaining wall, perched right on the exact spot where I had taken my fall, was none other than Ferty wearing that dang Harvest Morgan beret.

Not again?!

Walking over to the wall, I reached up and grabbed the obnoxious statue. A note was taped to the front, again from Bonnie's personalized notepad. It said, "Will you catch me if I fall?" For a moment I considered chunking it over the wall, but with my luck, it would crash down on my car six floors below, giving even *more* pleasure to my invisible tormentor.

I decided to quit playing the game. To put out a fire you take away its oxygen. I would take away the prankster's thrill. Instead of throwing Ferty away again, or driving her across town to some remote landfill only to have her show back up, I would just take the stinkin' statue home. Then at some point in the distant future when the perpetrator had either moved away or been institutionalized, I would quietly dispose of Ferty. In the meantime perhaps the psychopath behind this whole ordeal would get bored and find someone else to annoy.

Smiling at my new strategy, I picked up the Harvest Morgan beret and sailed it out over the wall and into the city air. It caught the wind and disappeared over a building two blocks away. A fitting, symbolic end to this foolish episode . . .

I hoped?

24

The Fishing Hole

The fall morning air felt cool on my skin as I opened the trunk of my car to throw in my fishing gear. *Uh oh.* Harry's wedding gift smirked at me from inside the trunk. I'd forgotten all about it. Oh well, it'll be a nice Saturday morning surprise for Bonnie. Out came the gift and in went the tackle before I slammed the trunk shut. Walking the gift into the house, I smiled to myself. *Chicks dig wedding gifts. Woohoo!*

Bonnie and Colby were awake but still lying in bed, so I carried the package into the bedroom.

She yawned. "I thought you were going fishing with Dunston?"

"I am, but first—TA DA! I discovered this in the trunk and thought I would bring it in before I left. It's a belated wedding gift from Harry and Trixie." I sat it on the bed grinning.

"Belated? I'll say. They should have just held on to it and gave it to us for our first anniversary. And let's remember who it's from, so don't get too excited."

Colby attacked the box yanking off the bow.

I handed the gift to Bonnie who was now sitting up in bed. "Okay, open it and let's see what Harry conjured up. I'm just hoping it's not a companion for Ferty."

"You still think he's the one behind your prank?" she said, ripping off the wrapping paper.

"He's currently my top suspect, but I have several potential perpetrators. Mark my word—I'll eventually find out who's behind it."

Bonnie opened the box and pulled out what looked like an upside-down wicker basket. She immediately started laughing.

"I'm confused. What is it, and what's so funny?"

"Harry may or may not be your prankster, but he's definitely the king of the re-gifters." She laughed again.

"I don't get it."

"This, young Ellington, is an Asian vegetable steamer, probably manufactured somewhere in Hong Kong. Basically it's a piece of junk. Think Ronco with an Oriental flare. The idea is to place it over steaming vegetables to keep the steam in and continue to cook them, supposedly making them more delectable."

"How do you know all that just by looking at it?"

"Because originally, it was a gift Louis and Jane E. received at their wedding. Then I saw it again at the staff Christmas party two years ago when Harry won it playing Dirty Santa. Now it's made its way to our humble abode." She fell back against the pillows, laughing some more.

"I know what it'll be good for." I put it over Colby and laid a pillow on top.

"Now Elmo, remember what happened when you put Colby in the clothes hamper?" Her laughter now gone.

Yikes, two nights on the couch. I quickly pulled the basket off the frisky pup.

I gave her a quick kiss. "Gotta run. Don't wanna keep ol' Dunston waiting. Remember he promised me some 'catchin'' and some eatin','' and today's the day. I just know it!"

The day couldn't have been nicer, with clear cloudless skies, no wind, and the temperature warming up to about seventy degrees. The calm water on the lake looked like glass as it reflected the trees and the green hills off in the distance. We set up shop on a narrow outcropping of rocks jetting out into a small inlet off the main lake.

"Is this the best spot?" I asked like an obvious amateur.

"Oh, we juz gettin' started," Dunston said. "We gotsta catch us some live bait." He pulled out a piece of white bread and started tearing it into small pieces.

"I thought you made your own bait. Some secret formula that the big fish just can't resist?"

He smiled. "Tha'z partly true. But you has'ta start w'da live shiner. You put dat little fish on yo hook and then you dips 'em in my special sauce 'fo you casts him out in d'lake. The magic's in the sauce. Ain't no secret to it."

He dropped a handful of bread pieces into the water by the rocks and almost immediately, minnows started nibbling on them. Then Dunston dipped his fishing net into the water and scooped up a dozen or so shiners. He did this four or five times until the bait bucket was teeming with the tiny squirming bait fish.

"Okay, what's in your special sauce?" I asked

"Oh, nuthin' special." He threw his head back and laughed, then laughed some more.

"Then why do you call it your special sauce?"

"Come on now, Elmo. I's just funnin' wid'ya. My fish bait sauce is very special. See, I's sittin' by this here very lake one day quite a while back, and I's thinkin' to myseff, 'What do big fish eat dat makes 'em so big?' Then I's thinkin', 'What do big people eat dat makes 'em so big?' That was easy—fried food and sugah. So'z I went home and stirred me up sum bacon grease and sum brown sugah inta sum olive oil. Then I dips one a'my shiners in d'stuff and casts him out on da lake and caught me a *three- pound bass* in less'n a minute! An I ain't lying. I's been using dis special sauce ever since." He held up an old pickle jar full of brown viscous-looking stuff.

I jumped up. "I'm ready. Let's do this!"

"Now, just hold on, Sir Elmo. We'll catch us sum big'uns, but not til later. And then, o' course, we'll lets 'em go."

"Let 'em go?! What about the 'catchin' and the eatin'?"

"Oh, you never eat da big'uns. You put 'em back so's you can catch 'em again 'nother day. I've caught some of dem big bass so many times I gives 'em names. They like friends to me. Though I'm not so sure they feels da same ways about it." He chuckled.

"Then which ones do we eat?"

"Elmo, you gots eatin' on the brain! Miss Bonnie not let you eat yo' breakfast or sumpin'?"

"Oh no, nothing like that. You just have to understand in my many attempts at fishing during the course of my young life, I've never had any success. No photos of me holding my trophy catch, no fishing success stories to exaggerate to my friends, and never, *ever* any catchin' and eatin'. Ever."

"Well then, Elmo, today's yo lucky day. We'z be eatin' Bluegill samiches' in just 'bout an hour."

Dunston took me over to his favorite Bluegill hole on the east side of the lake. He showed me how to bait the hook with a piece of hotdog, and sure enough, in less than five minutes I'd caught two fish! Thirty minutes later we'd caught so many we were just throwing them back. Dunston selected two from the catch and put the others in his cooler to take home. He showed me how to filet them, and in no time they were sizzling on his hibachi grill.

"Let's da eatin' begin," he cackled as he handed me my fresh fish sandwich on white bread slathered with mayo.

And man, was it good! "Tell me, Dunston. How many years have you been coming out to this lake to fish?"

He smiled real big. "I's been fishing dis pond since I's 'bout yo' age. Use'ta fish here wit' my brothers, but they both up 'n moved away."

"So you've spent quite a bit of time out here alone?"

"Oh no, this is where I spends time wit' da Lord. I loves goin' to church and all, but out here it just me, Him and His creation."

"Really?"

"Dat's right, and I does lotsa prayin' when I's out here fishin'. When you first show'd up at da big church I done prayed fo' you a lot. Wadn't so sure you was gonna make it."

"To be totally honest, Dunston, I wasn't so sure I was going to make it either."

"But juz look at you now, Mr. Assistant to da Big Dog hisself. And all married up to a fine lady like Miss Bonnie. Man, you juz de cat's meow."

"Thanks for the prayers. Between you and my mom's prayers,

you must have tilted the Lord in my favor."

"You mighty welcome," he said reaching back for his tackle box and the jar of fish bait dip. "Now theyz other days me and de Lord, we juz kinda hang out wid nots a whole lotta talkin'goin' on, if you knows what I mean."

"Yeah, I think I do."

He handed me the fishing poles to carry. "I figure, ya know, wid da Lord's buddies all bein' fisherman that He shorely *wet a line* a time or two Hisself."

"That makes sense to me. And you know what? I bet He ate lots of fish samiches."

"Oh my, yes!" He laughed as he got up. "You knows He did. Okay now, The Right Rever'nt Jenkins, iz' time to go and catch us a big un."

We walked over to a shady spot where several big boulders were perched right on the edge of the bank under some tree branches that hung lazily out over the lake.

"Da big ol' fish likes a'hangin' out in da cool water under dese here trees. When da shiners swim by, dey juz gobbles 'em up."

"So all we have to do is drop our line into the shade and they'll take the bait?"

"Nope. If dey see ya, dey won't bite nuthin'. Like I use'ta tell you back at da big church, you gotsta hide from 'em. Then deys believin' it safe ta come on out 'n eat."

So we got low to the ground and snuck up behind the boulders. Dunston signaled for me to be quiet. He put one of the shiners on my hook then dipped it into the jar of special sauce. Then very slowly, he raised my pole up over the boulder and with a flip of his wrist, he cast the little fish about ten feet out into the lake. He handed me the pole.

"Holds on tight," he whispered. "Watch da end of yo' pole. Let da big daddy fish swallow da shiner whole. Then snap yo' pole back to set da hook."

It sounded easy, of course, but anyone who's ever fished knows it's not. It's all about feel and timing, and that takes practice to develop. So I kept jerking the pole either too quickly or too hard. Dunston, consummate and patient angler that he was, would simply re-bait my hook and encourage me. Finally, after about an hour it happened.

"Whoa! Dunston, I got one! I got one!" My pole was bending so much I thought for sure it would break. "What do I do now?"

"Juz give 'em a little line and let him tucker hisself out."

My reel buzzed as the line flew out.

"Now, slowly, very slowly starts to reel 'em in."

We walked around the boulders to the edge of the bank. The poor fish was pulling hard against the line, fighting for his life. Don't ask me why, but at that very moment in my mind's eye, I saw myself as that fish pulling hard against God's will for my life. I quickly refocused on the task at hand, making a mental note to explore that metaphor another time. Then the line went slack.

"Oh, man, did I lose him?"

"Nope, Mistah Fish's juz takin' a break. You juz keep on reelin' in. It'll be easier now, he's pretty darn tired."

I was the one who was pretty darn tired. This was hard work! After reeling in for another few minutes, the fish finally surfaced near the bank and Dunston scooped him up in his fishing net.

"Mighty fine, Elmo! You done hooked ol' General Grant. He weighs 'bout four pounds."

"Why do you call him General Grant?"

He held up the bass and pointed his face toward me. "'Cause I thinks he kinda looks like him. Don'tcha think?"

"Well, maybe, if he had a beard and hat."

He started laughing. "Elmo, you busts me up sumtimez. You wanna snap a picture 'fo we lets him go back to his b'ness?"

"You bet I do! Otherwise Thurm will say I made the whole thing up." I leaned in next to Dunston and held my cell phone out while he stretched out ol' General Grant in front of us. *Snap!*

Then I watched as Dunston released the fish back into lake. I imagined the bass was thankful for his freedom, but I'm sure he muttered a few choice fish words over his shoulder as he headed back out to deeper water.

Think about it. How would *you* like to get pulled into shore by a hook in your lips two or three times a year?

25

The Beret

Dr. Auguste De Villa had retired in the spring with a huge display of pomp and circumstance. Former students from all over the world made the trek back to Harvest Morgan Seminary for the ceremony. There was even a former U.S. Senator in the audience.

Since Dr. DV had taught at the seminary for over forty years, the trustees allowed him to keep his campus office after his retirement, a rare honor not unlike retiring a player's number in the world of professional sports.

Since I'd learned from Fred Snooker that Dr. DV was a top-shelf editor, I decided to ask him to take a gander at my first Carpe Annum draft. Knowing you should never drop in on someone with Dr. DV's volatile personality traits, I called ahead and made an appointment. The wisdom of that decision become apparent when I arrived and discovered that Bess, his long-time student assistant, had finally graduated and moved on with her life. His new assistant—an obvious battle ax in every sense of the word—would have quickly dispatched me for not having an appointment.

Her nameplate read Agnes. A portly woman in her mid-sixties, Agnes wore an eyepatch and was in desperate need of a breath mint. After sitting in the small outer office for several tense minutes, inhaling the bad-breath-infused air, Dr. DV called over the intercom for me to come in. Without a word, Agnes eyeballed me the whole way though his doorway, which I quickly closed behind me.

That was creepy.

Dr. DV's office had not changed one iota since my last visit almost a year ago, with one glaring exception. The Harvest Morgan beret that once prominently adorned his credenza had gone missing.

Interesting.

"Well, if it's not ex-intern Ellington Jenkins in the flesh. It's a pleasure to see you, boy. Have a seat." A huge smile spread across his weathered face. Gone were the old crumpled suits and horrendous ties. Now he wore a pair of casual slacks and a pullover sweater. Think Bill Cosby in the eighties.

"Dr. DV, I know you're a busy man, so thanks for seeing me on such short notice."

"Jenkins, I'm a retiree. I've got all the time in the world."

"I see Bess is no longer with you," I said, pointing over my shoulder toward the door.

"That's correct. Since I was retiring, she decided to go ahead and complete her degree and get the 'dell out of hodge', so to speak." He guffawed loudly before coughing two or three times and hocking into his waste basket. Nothing new there.

"Who's the new gal?"

He leaned forward lowering his raspy voice. "Scary huh? She just showed up one day. I'm not sure where she came from, and I don't know how to ask her about it. Personnel said they didn't send her over. I'm not even supposed to have any paid help." His eyebrow rose sharply. "It's all a great mystery." A faux-frightened expression covered his face just before he broke into a guttural laugh—which, of course, culminated with another hearty cough and spit.

"Speaking of mysteries, what happened to your Harvest Morgan beret?" I asked, while nodding toward his credenza.

"Oh, that's no mystery. They had a seminary auction last summer and asked us all to donate items to be auctioned off. The money all went to a mission church in Central America sponsored by the seminary. So I gave them a few items including that old beret. I was flabbergasted when I heard the dang cap fetched twenty-five dollars."

"Did they keep a list of everyone who bought the items? Like, for tax purposes?"

"I'm not sure." He pushed his intercom button. "Agnes, check with the business office and see if they took note of who bought my Harvest Morgan beret at last summer's auction. Thanks." He clicked off his call button. "Why all the interest in that old hat?"

I snickered. "That's a long story which I don't mind sharing, but some other time. The real reason I'm here is to ask a favor."

"Okay, what do you need from a worn-out old seminary professor like me?"

I took a deep breath. "My main assignment at First Church has been to research and develop a report on how the church can transition successfully into the future—specifically addressing the need to be more effective with the younger demographic. I've spent the better part of this year doing interviews and making observation visits to other churches. I've just completed my first draft. Would you be willing to read through my draft and give me suggestions for ways I can improve it?"

"Jenkins, I'd be honored. If it's anywhere near as good as that 'Foreword' you composed for ol' man Snooker's book, I'm sure it will be just fine. Send it over. I'll be glad to give it a read-through. Though I will tell you, I'm a pretty tough old-school editor, so don't be offended by my suggestions."

"That's exactly what I want. Don't hold anything back."

Dr. DV's face and tone turned serious. "Ellington, there's another reason I'm glad you dropped by. I received a strange phone call a couple weeks ago from an old nemesis of mine. This man used to be a trustee here at the seminary, and he's a real pain in the rear. He wormed his way onto the board by making several sizeable donations over the years. Since we never got along, his call caught me completely off-guard.

"At first he just asked about me and how my retirement was going, throwing in some general questions about the seminary. Then he wanted to know if I had been your internship supervisor. When I said yes, he started asking some rather personal questions about you. Based on my past experience with this guy, I quickly discerned he was up to no good, so I abruptly ended the call. It really ticked me off. We lost several good, godly teachers here at the seminary due to that old hairball's shenanigans."

"His name wouldn't happen to be Sturgis Weaver would it?"

"One and the same, so I guess you're not all that surprised by what I just told you?"

I smiled. "No, I'm not. Hardly a week goes by that I don't hear his name mentioned. And it's always bad news."

He frowned. "Weaver's probably fifteen years my senior, so he's bound to be an old, old man, but apparently he's still robust. Whatever he's up to, don't take him lightly."

Agnes blared over the intercom. "Dr. De Villa, the business office says your beret was bought at the auction by a First Church staff member. That's the only information they could find."

"Thank you, Agnes." He clicked off the intercom. "Well, there you go. Now before you leave, I want to hear the rest of the story about that stupid beret . . ."

Driving back to the church I passed a stranded car on the side of road. A man had the hood up looking at the engine. As I approached I thought about stopping to help, but I talked myself out of it. After all I was in nice clothes, I had appointments to get back to, and . . . you know how it goes. But God wouldn't let me off the hook, so I did a u-turn and circled back. By the time I got back to the car, the man had the hood down. He was sitting in the driver seat. I pulled up next to him.

"Anything I can do to help?"

He smiled, "Thanks for stopping. It was just a disconnected vacuum hose. Once I hooked it back up, the car starting running normal again. I'm good to go now, but thanks again for offering help." He pulled back on to the road and drove off.

Sometimes I think God orchestrates situations like that one just to test my obedience. Maybe He simply wanted me to respond to the prompting of His spirit. Once I did, the situation resolved on its own.

I don't know a vacuum hose from a sparkplug wire, but that wasn't the point. God just wanted me to say yes to Him. Unfortunately, many times I ignore such promptings, or worse, I say no. But not today, and I received that special joy that only comes from being obedient.

I knocked on Father Ted's office door. "Gotta a minute?"

"Sure, Elmo, come on in."

I slouched into one of his chairs. "I need some of your savvy advice."

"Okay, how can I help?"

"There's an old man in this church, a longstanding member who, from what I can tell, is inciting a rebellion of sorts. I know this happens in churches all the time, but in this particular case I appear to be the catalyst of his ire."

He came around his desk and eased into his other guest chair. "Why would he be upset with you?"

"I don't think it's me personally, but it's what I represent—which is change. I'd imagine you're on his hit list as well." I sighed quietly.

"Okay, let's back up and break this thing down a little more. Every organization has disgruntled members, all churches included. And most church members who've been attending for any length of time usually dislike change to some degree. Why? Because folks find comfort in continuity and change breaks that continuity.

"We used to have a rule of thumb at Hickory Street Cathedral. All Adult Sunday School classes had to move to a different room every two years. We didn't want anyone becoming too comfortable and claiming ownership for their space. They needed to know the room was just a tool for spiritual growth and recruiting new folks for Bible study.

"That being said, as a pastor you have to be very circumspect when dealing with unhappy parishioners. So who are we talking about? Anybody I'd know?"

"Sturgis Weaver."

"Ah, Mr. Weaver. That explains a lot."

"So you know him?"

"I used to do the radio spots for his lumber yard. Yep, he's one tough old coot. I didn't know he attended church here. He must not come on Sunday mornings."

"He probably doesn't, but he's very active in the deacons meetings—at least he has been recently from what I've been told. The way I understand it, he's never liked Dr. Jorgensen's way of doing things. So every few years he attempts a mutiny which is subsequently beaten down by Smitty Fitzsimons and his supporters on the deacon board. After some blood-letting and hand wringing, equilibrium is reestablished and everyone plays nice for a time. Then at some point Sturgis Weaver's angst again reaches critical mass and the cycle starts all over again. This is no way to do church! Come on!" I'd become very frustrated with this whole ordeal.

Father Ted hung his head. "I'm afraid the scenario you just delineated is much more common in local churches than most laypeople would ever know."

I stood up and started pacing. "I guess what I really need is some direction. I feel like I've been busting tail all year working on a strategy and a plan that could ultimately implode the church. Talk about counterproductive."

Father Ted leaned back in his chair. "Here's the deal. I fully understand your frustration, but if we're both being honest, the outcome is not your concern. That's totally in God's hands. As hard as it is to fathom, maybe God *wants* to implode this church. Plow under the old stock and plant seed for a new harvest. Listen, it's absolutely no fun to be on the boat when God sinks it, but it's virtually impossible for any of us to grasp His bigger plan.

"My advice is to turn in the best report you can develop, and then let God do with it what He will. If the winds of influence change and some of us get burned at the stake, so be it."

He was right and I knew it. "Maybe I should invest in some asbestos underwear."

Father Ted laughed. "That's thinking outside the box-er shorts."

26

The Invitation

Now Colby was a smart dog, but not in the traditional sense. She was street smart and clever—more like a cat in that regard. There would be no rolling-over or playing dead for Colby. No, she used her considerable wits for far more mischievous undertakings.

One day, as I began to make my lunch the phone rang in the other room. I'd just laid out two pieces of bread on the kitchen counter to build a sandwich. As I sprinted to take the call, I noticed Colby sleeping peacefully on our couch. The back corner of our couch butts up against the end of our kitchen counter. This had never been an issue before because one, Colby didn't get up on the back of the couch, and two, she never got into our food. After all, she had her own stinkin' food that cost a small fortune.

After returning from the rather lengthy call, I resumed the preparation of my lunch. But there was just one problem. The two slices of bread were nowhere to be found. I second-guessed myself, wondering if I'd actually laid them out. Yes, I definitely remembered opening the loaf and getting out the bread, but where did the slices go? There were no crumbs on the counter. I checked Colby and found her curled up on the couch, sound asleep. Still, I just knew she'd gobbled them up, but I had no proof.

Colby's subterfuge occurred around our home on a regular basis, and rarely did we ever catch her in the act. She loved to snatch and hide random items. Her kleptomania knew no rhyme or reason. A slipper, or the remote control, a book, or maybe a washcloth would simply vanish. Usually, but not always after a thorough search we would discovery the item in her latest hidden cache of stolen goods.

This is how I found the invitation. Our mail, delivered through a wall slot, fell into a wicker basket on the floor beneath it. Colby would occasionally cull through our daily mail delivery and select one or two letters to steal away to her secret stash de jour. One day while searching for my wireless mouse, I found the invitation in the guest room closet along with several other missing household items. It had been there over a week.

Bonnie and I had been officially invited to join the Jorgensens, the Applebees, and the Estradas at the home of Geneva and Smitty Fitzsimons for a dinner party. Thanks to Colby's fine work we had missed the deadline to RSVP. That left me the embarrassing task of calling Smitty to explain how our dog hid the invitation which led to our late confirmation. Boy, did I feel middle-school small. I'm sure he probably hung up the phone and thought, *man that was lame.*

The dinner party had been scheduled for November first, the same day I would be submitting my final report in writing to Dr. Jorgensen. A superb coincidence.

Having visited the Fitzsimons' estate once before, I knew the food would be fabulous and Bonnie would be blown away by the opulence of their home. I also knew that any dinner with Anna Mae Jorgensen and Geneva Fitzsimons at the table would have stilted conversation—polite and cordial, but less than engaging. We'd cross that bridge when we got to it.

Meanwhile back at the house, on that particular Saturday, Bonnie was gone for the evening to the monthly staff wives Chef Salad Soiree. Trophy husband that I am, I figured I'd power-clean the grill. Stepping out into the garage to procure my wire brush, I decided to check on Ferty. Since I'd brought her home and incarcerated her in my garage, the heinous prank had come to an end. Still, I checked on her regularly to make sure she hadn't made a break. I'd yet to uncover the identity of the prankster, and no one had voluntarily come forward to confess. So some uncertainty still remained.

After reading an article in *Science* magazine, I developed a theory that there might be a tracking device implanted in Ferty's plastic alloy. It could be as small as a pencil eraser. That would explain how the perpetrator kept finding her and slipping her back into my office. But for now, that little irritation seemed to be on hold. Still, I double-checked the chain and padlock securing her to the water heater.

You can't be too careful with these things.

The days flew by as the first of November approached. After receiving my draft report back from Dr. DV along with his fabulous suggestions, I had Bonnie proofread the edited version. It was now time for a trip to the second floor print shop.

Lucky Wu ran the First Church print shop. Lucky was an immigrant. His mother was Korean while his father came from somewhere else along the Asian Rim. Lucky used an old-style offset printer that probably ran on steam originally. We're talking *very* old school. First Church was paper and ink intensive, and all of it was produced in-house by Lucky and his ancient offset press. Tom Applebee had told me the church planned to go digital when Lucky retired. He implied that it would actually be a sad day because Lucky's work was so good.

Lucky, though in the U.S. for many years, had never learned to speak English, though he seemed to understand it well. He communicated using two phrases and two phrases only—"yes sir" and "will do." These two phrases were augmented with wild, ostentatious hand gestures and crazy facial expressions.

Lucky cooked and ate his lunch in the print shop every day, and he always had Kimchi. Basically, Kimchi, a Korean favorite, is a mix of rotting vegetables. His entree of choice emitted quite the nasty fragrance.

Visiting the print shop at First Church was like taking a side trip to Chinatown in San Francisco. Upon entering the shop, the warm sticky smell of ink accentuated by the even stronger smell of Kimchi would accost you like a karate chop to the olfactory glands. For days afterwards that pungent smell would still be lingering in your nose.

"Hey Lucky, got a minute?"

"Yes sir," he said, emerging from the back room were the offset was running.

I opened my folder and spread out my report. There were one hundred and fifty pages of text, graphs, charts, and photos. The report was extensive and complicated. Per print shop manual instructions, I had included all of the necessary color separations.

Lucky quickly rifled through all of my pages. I noticed his finger rapidly tapping up and down on one of the charts even as his eyes narrowed.

"What, did I leave out something?"

He pointed again to the chart and then placed one of his hands on top of the other. He quickly repeated this maneuver several times.

I finally got it. "Okay, I see now. You need another separation for that page."

"He smiled flashing his Kimchi-stained teeth. "Yes sir."

"I'll have that to you this afternoon. Lucky, on the first run I only need about twenty copies. Can I have them by Thursday?"

He flipped back through my pages. "Yes, sir."

"Just let Juliann know when they're ready. Thanks a bunch." I shook his ink-tarnished hand.

He smiled again. "Will do."

I stepped back out into the hall ran for the nearest open window to get some fresh air. All I could smell was fermented cabbage.

Bonnie and I took our time strolling over to the downtown mall for our weekly hotdog lunch date. The city was experiencing an Indian summer, and it was absolutely gorgeous outside.

She handed me the mustard. "I had coffee this morning with Jane E. and Charlene Applebee."

I handed her the catsup. "Oh yeah?"

"After we kicked it around for a few minutes, we all agreed that just as you said, Mary Beth Hankins is the one who's leaking like a sieve."

"Are you sure? She seems so sweet."

"Oh, we don't think she's maliciously spying on us or anything even close to it. We suspect she's innocently sharing our group discussions with Raze not realizing he's in turn feeding the information to others."

"You're probably right. What's the plan?"

"Charlene's going to meet individually with each of the other staff wives and explain the situation. We'll just keep our discussions superficial until this mess has all blown over."

"Very wise. I'm duly impressed." I kissed her on the cheek."

"To be honest, Charlene's the one with all the wisdom here. She's been around First Church long enough to have seen it all. Sturgis Weaver is a widower. Apparently his wife made him look like a cub scout when it came to behind-the-scene dealings at the church. She was legendary for her machinations and maneuvering. She drowned in their swimming pool a couple years ago. Not everyone believes it was an accident."

"Wow, this church has more intrigue than the Bill Clinton White House."

Bonnie arched a brow. "Interesting comparison. But let's talk about something else. Now that you have some vacation days, where would you like to go for our honeymoon?" She took a swig of the Coke we were sharing.

I smiled. "What would you say to the Cayman Islands?"

27

The Dinner

Lucky wasn't lucky for me this week. Thursday came and went and my reports still weren't printed. Late in the afternoon I made another foray up to his Kimchi lair. Lucky promised, via enthusiastic gestures, that I would have the reports first thing Friday morning as soon as the ink had time to dry fully.

Talk about cutting it close. I had a ten o'clock appointment with Dr. Jorgenson to present him with my Carpe Annum report. Needless to say, I was on pins and needles all night and didn't sleep well.

Bonnie, on the other hand, slept like a baby. How do I know? Because I lay there all night long watching her sleep peacefully, like someone without a care in the world. Irritated and exhausted, I was tempted to wake her up just out of spite. Or maybe it was envy. It would've been a stupid move for either reason because I'd just be adding another stressful situation to my already overloaded plate.

Fortunately, my dear friend Mr. Adrenaline greeted me Friday morning, and I didn't feel too bad. With such an important day ahead, I guess my brain must have called down to the adrenaline gland and asked him to pull some overtime. Or so I imagined.

Of course, that meant come Saturday morning, I would be rendered catatonic—which just might get me out of mowing the lawn if I played my cards right.

But that would be tomorrow's scheme. Back to the task at hand: Carpe Annum Friday.

I arrived at my office on time and five minutes later, someone knocked on my door.

"Come in."

The door swung open and in walked Juliann with a box from the print shop. There was no writing on the box, but I knew it came from the print shop because of the rancid odor.

"Here are your reports, Elmo. Where would you like me to put them?"

"Thanks, Juliann. If you don't mind, take all the copies out of the box and stack them over on the credenza. Then please get that smelly box out of here. And take some advice from a close friend— you might want to consider spritzing yourself.

"Elmo, you're so silly. She stepped into the hall and closed the door behind her. I could hear her making sniffing sounds. She spoke back through the closed door. "Elmo, is it really that bad?'

"Just consider the spritz," I said laughing.

The Carpe Annum Report looked great. Lucky Wu might not speak much English and he might smell like a sour cucumber, but man could the guy run a printing press.

I placed two copies of the report in my valise, then decided to spend some time in prayer before my meeting with Dr. Jorgenson.

At a quarter til ten, I headed down the office hall toward the executive elevator. Some of the staff members cheered me on from their offices as if I were a Roman Emperor heading off to war. Except for Raze Hankins, of course, who simply glared at me and shook his head as I walked by. Whatever.

Excited but calm. That's how I characterized my frame of mind as the elevator advanced slowly toward the fifth floor. I had worked toward this day nonstop for ten full months.

The bell rang signaling the fifth floor, and the elevator doors slowly opened.

Ahhhh! Sturgis Weaver stood before me, waiting to get on the elevator. I was dumbstruck as a cold shiver jolted up my spine.

Though startled at first, he actually seemed pleased to see me. "Well, well, Mr. Jenkins. Good morning." A sly grin slithered across his face. "The pastor and I were just talking about you." His grin intensified.

I fought to regroup. "Good morning, Mr. Weaver. Nice to see you again." *I lied— big time.* I reached out my hand and there it was, that phenomenally firm handshake. Way too strong for someone his age. Dare I say *demonically* strong?

I stepped off, he stepped on, and the elevator doors mercifully closed behind me. I could feel myself trembling. *Wow. Talk about the unexpected.*

My meeting with Dr. Jorgensen went great. I presented him with the two copies of the report. He quickly perused it, making several very positive comments and promised to study it extensively before our next meeting. The other copy would go to Smitty Fitzsimons.

I mentioned that I had bumped into Mr. Weaver at the elevator. He confirmed that the old man had stopped by for his quarterly check-in. Unannounced, of course.

He reminded me about the dinner party that evening at Smitty's. He'd heard about our dog stealing the invitation. He said he and Smitty had shared a good chuckle over that one. I chose not to tell him that's what really happened.

We said our goodbyes and I elected to take the stairs back down to my office. I wasn't about to risk another interaction with Sturgis Weaver. I was much too young for a heart attack.

The Fitzsimon's tri-level mansion rested on a sleepy hillside sequestered in the middle of fifteen hundred acres of rolling countryside north of town. Bold, brass letters embedded in a stone sign at the gated entrance to the estate read *Our Country Home*—and what a home it was. Sixteen bedrooms, nine bathrooms, and garage parking for twelve vehicles.

We rode together with Louis and Jane E., sitting in their backseat.

"So, you've been to Smitty's house before, Elmo?" Louis asked as he pulled up to a guard house at the main entrance. He signed a clipboard handed to him by the security guard.

"Yes, for his spring open house several years ago."

Jane E. turned, addressing us over her shoulder. "How'd you score an invitation to one of those parties? I thought those were only for the high rollers."

"I went as the 'show pony' for his niece, Dolly Ehler. She ditched me right after we got there. That humiliation took a while to recover from."

Jane E. laughed out loud. "Serves you right for going out with Dolly in the first place. That girl's nothing but trouble. Maybe the most self-absorbed person I've ever known."

I bristled. Her comment was a little too personal for my taste. Jane E. could be that way. "Um, excuse me. One, we weren't going out. I simply let her talk me into going to her uncle's open house. Two, how do you even know Dolly in the first place?"

"Now, don't get all riled up, Elmo Jenkins. Bonnie, give your *show pony* a chill-pill, will ya?" Jane E. laughed again.

"Smitty and Geneva used to bring Dolly to First Church," Louis piped in. "She came to some of the single functions. But to be honest, we were all glad when she dropped out. She created a lot of problems within the group."

Jane E. couldn't resist. "Sounds to me like God saved you from a big heartache and delivered you safe and sound to our sweet Bonnie."

Bonnie pinched me hard signaling me to keep my big mouth shut.

Note to self: Politely turn down any future invitations to ride with the Estradas.

Louis parked the car, and we walked up to the main entrance. Another security staff member let us in the front door where we were greeted by Smitty and Geneva. The Jorgensens and Applebees were already there. Geneva led us all on a guided tour of their home which was spectacular.

Smitty pulled me aside as the others walked through the pool area. "Ellington, Horace showed me your Carpe Annum report. *Very* impressive. I'm anxious for the three of us to spend some quality time discussing the report and its implementation. Horace also invited me to sit in on your follow-up meeting with him next week. I believe we are on the cusp of some truly exciting days for First Church." He slapped me on the back. "Well done, son."

The weather was still nice so we dined out on their veranda. We had our choice of salmon or lobster with a half-dozen delectable side dishes to choose from, and fresh bread made right in their kitchen. For dessert we selected from a variety of bread puddings and cobblers. *Yum.*

As I predicted, conversation around the table was light and cordial. Even Jane E. kept her sharp tongue properly stowed away in its sheath. After dinner the women retired to the sitting room to talk about . . . well, whatever women talk about in sitting rooms. The men moved out by the pool where Dr. Jorgensen and Smitty lit up stogies. The conversation quickly turned serious.

"I got a call from Sturgis Weaver this afternoon," Smitty said just before taking several puffs on his cigar. "He's pretty concerned about all the Carpe Annum stuff."

Dr. Jorgenson concurred. "Yes, he mentioned those same concerns to me this morning when he dropped by. He appears to have quite a bit of misinformation, but he also knew some things he *shouldn't* know, at least not yet."

I leaned in. "May I say something—and if I'm out of line just let me know and I'll keep my novice observations to myself."

Smitty flicked his stogie to shake off some ashes. "Please do, Ellington. The more information we have about this little problem, the easier it will be to resolve."

"I really hate to accuse anyone of anything, especially since they're not here to defend themselves, but I honestly believe Raze Hankins is an integral part of the problem. He's all but told me on several occasions that he's in league with a segment of disgruntled First Church members. The staff wives also suspect that Raze has been getting confidential information from his wife and passing it along to those disgruntled folks. Tom can confirm both of these claims. If there's an information leak from within the staff, there's a good chance it's coming from Raze."

Smitty turned to Tom Applebee. "Tom, do you have anything to add?"

Tom leaned back, crossing his legs. "Charlene told me just this week that there's a concern about Raze's wife, and Elmo and I have had several discussions about Raze's lack of enthusiasm for the Carpe Annum project. If there's a connection between these issues and Sturgis Weaver's troublemaking, I don't know. You tell me."

Smitty stood up and walked over by the pool. "As we all know, Mr. Weaver pulls this crap about every six or seven years. I think it's reached the point now where it's time to shut down this foolishness. I'll make a few calls. At next week's deacons meeting we'll confront Sturgis and his cronies and try to put an end to his latest rebellion." Smitty began blowing smoke rings as he turned to gaze out over his pool.

322

Dr. Jorgensen put out his cigar and was about to speak when a loud splash got our attention. I turned to see Smitty lying face down in the water. At first I thought it was some kind of odd practical joke, but then someone screamed, "Call 911!"

Tom and I jumped in the pool. We quickly lifted Smitty out of the water, but he was unresponsive. Louis began CPR as the women came rushing out of the house. Poor Geneva took one look at Smitty's wet, lifeless body and immediately fainted. She fell hard onto the pool's stone decking, badly gashing her head. People were running in every direction, all yelling at the same time for someone to bring blankets, towels, and ice.

It was thirty minutes of pure panic mingled with overwhelming despair. Louis continued CPR until the ambulance arrived, but Smitty never breathed on his own again. He was pronounced dead at the hospital from massive coronary failure.

None of us there could believe what had just happened. I kept thinking, surely this is just another one of my bad dreams, but it wasn't. We were all devastated by Smitty's death and shaken by the horrifying manner in which it occurred.

So much so, that we all missed the distant rumblings of the coming tsunami that his passing had created.

28

The Funeral

When a wealthy and prominent citizen dies unexpectedly, their funeral takes on a life of its own—even to the point of becoming a spectacle. Such was the case for the wake of Smithson Constantine Fitzsimons. Isn't it interesting how you rarely hear a person's middle name used unless they've died—or assassinated someone famous?

Smitty's service was held the following Monday morning in the sanctuary of First Church. The large crowd filled every available seat with the standing room only in the back, spilling into the church foyer and even out onto the street. The crowd was peppered with the city's rich and influential. All significant politicians, business owners, entertainers, religious leaders, and high-level civil servants were in attendance.

Geneva sat on the front pew with her two sisters-in-law, Anna Mae Jorgensen and Geraldine Fitzsimons O'Leary. Both of Geneva and Smitty's children had died many years ago, one off at war and the other from leukemia.

More than a dozen people took the podium to speak at the funeral, many of them representing the numerous charities Smitty had funded over the years.

Midway through the service Miss O'Leary brought everyone to tears with her visceral rendition of "It is Well with My Soul".

Dr. Jorgensen, Smitty's best friend, closed the service with a touching tribute to a man who had given so much to both First Church, the community, and to mankind in general.

The funeral lasted over two hours. We were all exhausted by the time it wound down. A dinner served by Martha and the First Church kitchen crew was served in the fellowship hall for family members and close friends. Several staff members and our spouses sat at a table off to one side where we quietly discussed the ramifications of the last several days.

"I don't know how you replace a guy like Smitty and all he meant to this church." Thurm said while munching on one of Martha's yeast rolls.

"The obvious answer is that you can't." I responded. "Smitty leaves not only a huge hole, but a dangerous leadership vacuum as well. If there's a lesson here for the future, it's to spread around the key leadership roles. If someone goes down then others are there to pick up the slack."

Louis lowered his voice. "What happens now to your Carpe Annum initiative?"

"As far as I know we're still on track. Dr. Jorgenson asked me to come in early on Thursday morning to go over the report and review the feedback from Wednesday night's deacons meeting. I assumed he scheduled me in at eight o'clock that morning so he could squeeze me in before his Thursday golf outing. But now that Smitty's gone, I seriously doubt he'll be golfing on Thursday."

Thurm smiled. "Oh, I don't know. Maybe he and the others will still play their regular round as a tribute to their old friend."

"You may be right. Maybe he'll invite me to play. A round of golf would sure help ease the stress. It's been brutal around here these last couple of weeks."

Louis laughed. "Are you kidding? The stress is brutal year round at First Church."

"Better gird your loins, boys," Tom Applebee said as he approached our table. "I fear the First Church stress level is about to go into overdrive for a while."

"Oh, great. In that case I need some comfort food." I snatched two of Martha's rolls off the serving plate.

We all shared a nervous laugh.

Smitty's sudden departure had cast a pale over the church office. Like zombies we were all trudging around, just going through the motions. By late Wednesday afternoon, I was more than ready to punch out and go home. The Wednesday night Family Dinner and Prayer Service had been cancelled due to a HVAC problem.

Due to my schedule, Bonnie would usually get home about an hour before I did. Some nights we would go out and catch a bite, and other nights she would make dinner. If she cooked, I would do the dishes. If I cooked, she would do the dishes. Due to several poor culinary efforts on my part, I usually ended up doing the dishes.

On this particular Wednesday she'd prepared vegetarian meatloaf, mashed potatoes, and broccoli. *Is vegetarian meatloaf even possible?*

We sat down to eat.

"Elmo, you don't look so good."

"If truth be known, I'm *not* so good. I haven't slept much in the last week. I know I shouldn't worry, but I'm still fearful that all the hard work I've put in over the last ten months is precipitously close to getting flushed down the toilet."

"Hey listen, your report came out fantastic, and I'm very proud of you. The deacons are reasonable, God-fearing men. You know when Dr. Jorgensen gives the presentation tonight he's going to give your report his full endorsement. The rest is in God's hands."

"Sweetheart, I know you're speaking the absolute truth, but I'm afraid exhaustion has robbed me of my ability to see things clearly. I really do want to step away from my doubts about this, but I'm finding that difficult to do."

She pulled her chair up next to mine and began massaging the back of my neck. I felt myself start to relax.

"That's nice. Keep it up and I may even forgive you for making *vegetarian* meatloaf."

Bonnie laughed, her eyes dancing. "I've got an idea. Why don't we clean up the kitchen, and then . . . how about you join me for a nice warm bath. Whatcha think?"

I smiled. "Well, I *was* gonna clean the grill, but I guess I can change my plans."

"Yeah?" she whispered, nibbling on my ear.

"Oh yeah . . ."

Big day. BIG day. And I slept much better, thanks to my sweet Bonnie.

I left the house extra early so I could spend some time praying in my office before my meeting with Dr. Jorgensen. Apparently fate had another agenda. I ended up sitting in a traffic jam for thirty minutes due to a bad accident on the expressway. So I had my prayer time right there in my car. After all, I was just inconvenienced. The poor people in the accident just had their lives dramatically altered or maybe even lost. I prayed for them too.

By the time I finally arrived at the church, I ended up going straight to Dr. Jorgenson's office. There was no time to talk to any of the other staff, so I had no idea what to expect after last night deacons meeting.

As I rode the executive elevator up to the fifth floor, I contemplated the possible outcomes. One, the deacons embraced the Carpe Annum report and I would soon be given marching orders to start the implementation phase. Two, they sent the report back to be revised based on their suggestions. Or three, they rejected it outright. I was hoping for outcome number one, could live with outcome number two, and had no clue what to do with outcome number three.

I stepped out of the elevator and strode *faux confident* into Dr. Jorgensen outer office. I started to say a cheery hello to Fran but her desk was empty. *Well, that's odd.* Dr. Jorgensen's door was closed, so I just took a seat. As I waited I wondered if he would be in his usual suit and tie or perhaps his Echelon golf shirt. The answer to that question came quickly as his door opened and he stepped out wearing a long sleeve oxford cloth shirt with no tie.

"Morning, Jenkins. Please come on in."

I followed him through the door as he led me into his office. He took a seat behind his desk, so I eased into one of the two leather wingback chairs facing his desk.

"Sorry I'm a few minutes late, sir. There was a pileup on the expressway."

"Yes, I heard about that on my car radio. Hope no one was hurt too seriously."

He culled through several folders on his desk until he came to his Carpe Annum folder. He pulled out a copy of my report and leaned back in his chair flipping through the pages. This went on for several minutes. If his facial expressions were any indication, he liked what he saw. He pointed to the chart numerically displaying the correlation between age and a person's propensity toward making a decision for Christ. Finally, he closed the report and gently placed it back on his desk. He folded his hands with a heavy sigh.

"Ellington—"

He never calls me Ellington . . .

"This is a superb piece of work. You provided everything we asked for and more. Before he died, Smitty told me we were very fortunate to have chosen you for this assignment. He felt as though you were destined for great things in life, and I have to say I agree with his assessment."

I was taken aback by his praise. "Thank you, sir. That's most encouraging—especially coming from Smitty and from someone of your stature."

He chuckled as he turned, wistfully looking out his window at the city below. We sat there in awkward silence for what seemed like a long time.

Finally, still looking out his window, he said, "It's a shame, really. This church is poised to do great things well into the future, and . . ." He turned back toward his desk and picked up my report. "and this is such a good plan, but we have a small problem."

"A problem, sir?"

His smile couldn't mask the sadness in his eyes. "Unfortunately . . . we've both been fired."

29

The Business Meeting

I limped into Bonnie's office, still in a daze.

"Elmo! Honey, what's the matter?" She came around her desk and enveloped me in her arms, pulling me close.

"Apparently I'm now unemployed." My own words sounded hollow in my ears.

"What?! What do you mean?" She led me over to sit in her visitor's chairs.

"Horace just told me that the deacons voted last night to fire him, Harry, Fran, Father Ted, me—and even Lucky the printer. He even referred to it as the 'November Massacre'."

Bonnie looked dumbstruck. "I don't understand. Why did they— *how* could they fire . . . they *fired* Pastor Jorgenson? Is that even possible?"

"Evidently." I stared at nothing, my mind reeling. "I guess I should clean my office, huh?"

"Now, just wait a minute. There has to be more to this situation than we know."

Louis busted into the office. "Elmo! Thank goodness—I've been looking for you."

"I guess you heard?" I said as Bonnie squeezed my hand.

He smiled. "You're not fired. At least not yet!"

I bolted up from my chair. "What?"

"You heard me right. I just came from a meeting with Tom Applebee, Bob Stevens, and the personnel committee. It appears Mr. Sturgis Weaver didn't thoroughly do his homework before making his power play last night."

"What do you mean, Louis?" Bonnie asked, also standing up.

"The First Church bylaws are very clear on the correct procedure for terminating an employee. For staff ministers, a recommendation has to come directly through the personnel committee in writing to which the deacons can approve or disapprove. As for the pastor, any termination requires a church vote."

"Wow." Bonnie blew out a sigh of relief. "So you're saying as of right now, neither Elmo nor anyone else has been fired?"

"That's correct, but just for the time being. The situation is still fluid and extremely tenuous."

328

This new information was starting to sink in. "What happens next?" I asked.

"There's to be a special called church business meeting Sunday evening after the worship service in the sanctuary. Anyone who wants to speak will be given that opportunity, then a vote of confidence will be taken for Dr. Jorgensen. If he gets a simple majority of the vote, everything goes back to normal. If he loses, he'll be asked to resign. Then it gets precarious for all the rest of us. It all hinges on that vote."

This was indeed a fortunate turn of events. Suddenly, it felt like a cool breeze reenergized my spirit. I startled Louis with a hardy hug. "These next few days are going to be intense, but there is a silver lining." I smiled. "The Sunday evening service will have its best attendance of the decade."

Louis laughed. "You're absolutely right. It'll be standing room only. I guarantee it. Sturgis and his boys are probably dusting off the old church directories as we speak and burning up the phone lines. You'll see First Church members who haven't attended in *years*."

"I've gotta to know. Why do they want to fire Lucky the printer?"

Louis smiled. "Who knows? If I had to venture a guess I'd say it has something to do with that unique *fragrance* emanating from all our printed materials."

I laughed. "Man, that's the truth."

As Louis headed off to find Father Ted, I kissed Bonnie on the lips. "I'm back from the dead, I'm refocused—and I'm hungry! Let's go grab an early lunch."

"Yeah? Whatcha have in mind?" she asked.

"For some bizarre reason, I have a hankerin' for Asian cuisine."

The term "church business meeting" has been known to strike terror in the heart of many a church minister over the years since Jesus renamed Simon *the Rock*. It's at the church business meeting that the parishioner (aka the layperson) gets to question the decisions of the ministerial staff.

It's important to remember that a large percentage of the churches in the world only have one staff member—the pastor. Too many times these poor guys flying solo have taken it on the chin in these meetings. But even in a church with a large staff like First Church, a business meeting can be a fearful event.

Consequently many churches have moved to limit the number of church business meetings held each year to the minimum necessary to transact church business. The operative theory behind this strategy—fewer meetings means less conflict. Over the years First Church had whittled down their number of church business meetings to just one annually.

Of course, all churches allow for the infamous "special called" business meeting. These rare meetings deal with the urgent, the time-critical, the expeditious, or anything else falling under the general category of "emergency." First Church had not held a special called business meeting in over a decade.

The air coursing through the halls of First Church that Sunday morning felt supercharged with electricity. Around every corner, the flock was huddled into small groups anxiously discussing the *church politic*.

Validating his great inner strength of character, Pastor Jorgensen chose not to use the pulpit to lash out at his opponents or even defend himself. Instead he preached on having the faith of a child and how much Jesus loved to spend time with the children. In light of the current circumstances, his message was poignant, moving many to tears.

At the end the service Tom Applebee encouraged everyone to come back for the evening service which would be followed by the special called business meeting. In an almost-humorous coincidence, it was foreign missions week at First Church. The evening service would be featuring several of the church's retired missionaries, including Erlene. They would be showing slide presentations about their work on the foreign field. Sadly, under normal conditions this mission service would be poorly attended. Tonight, in an uber-ironic twist, the auditorium would be jammed to the gills. Erlene would be absolutely thrilled. I winced at the thought of her with a live mic and prayed she stayed on message. *Oh boy.*

After lunch Bonnie took Colby to the dog park, so I decided to take a nap. My futile efforts to sleep were sabotaged by my mind which was spinning like a gyroscope. There would be no rest for the weary this afternoon.

Instead I utilized my time alone to pray. I prayed for Dr. Jorgenson. For him to have a double portion of God's wisdom and grace in dealing with his adversaries. After all, this was no surprise. He had predicted that his "dormant thorn" would one day fester again, and fester it did.

I prayed for Sturgis Weaver. I prayed he would see through his personal pet peeves about First Church and grasp the bigger picture. I prayed he would understand that as Christians we could agree to disagree on the nonessentials, but needed to pull together on the main issues. To me, these included reaching a lost world for Christ and inspiring these new believers to grow spiritually. Who got the credit was unimportant and who held the controls was secondary.

I prayed for the members of the church. The world is littered with collateral damage caused by this kind of church discord. Many people have given up on the church entirely because of the hurt they've endured due to a church split or splinter. This is truly one of the great tragedies of the Christian era.

Again I had to remind myself of God's sovereignty. No matter what the outcome, He was ultimately in control of the situation. How thankful I was for this immutable truth.

As predicted the sanctuary was filled to capacity. The retired missionaries, pumped up by the large crowd, had run the evening service long by more than half an hour. By the time Tom Applebee called the business meeting into session, the whole room appeared to be fidgety.

Tom was all business. "I want to remind everyone here that this is a church meeting and not a political convention. Treat each other with kindness and respect. As moderator I will not tolerate rudeness, interruptions, yelling, name-calling, et cetera. Does everyone clearly understand the rules? Let me know that you do by saying amen."

The congregation responded affirmatively.

Bonnie and I sat on the back row with several other staff members. We were all nervous. Much was at stake.

Tom continued. "In accordance with the rules for a special called business meeting as delineated in our church bylaws, we will be dealing with only one item of business this evening. At the conclusion of an open period of discussion, we will have a vote of confidence for Pastor Jorgensen. Any church member is allowed to speak, but there will be a three-minute time limit for each speaker. There are microphones available in each aisle and we ask that all speakers use a microphone so that we can all clearly hear you. I now call our special business meeting to order. At this time you are free to move to the microphones. I will signal you when it's your turn to speak."

Louis had been correct. There were quite a few faces in the crowd I'd never seen before. I spotted Sturgis Weaver sitting on the front row with several members of his posse. A dozen or so folks scrambled to queue up at the mics. I silently prayed, and I knew many others were doing the same. Dr. Jorgensen appeared stoic, sitting in his normal chair on the platform. I wondered how I would feel if I were in his position. Of course, my future at First Church was indeed tied to his, but I was prepared for either outcome.

A middle age, nondescript woman was the first to speak. "Dr. Jorgenson, I'm not quite sure what all of the fuss is about, but I want you to know that my family and I love you. I'll forever be indebted to you for leading my sons and my husband to Christ and baptizing them. God bless you."

Dr. Jorgensen acknowledged her with a smile and a nod.

A freckle-faced middle school girl with braces spoke next. "Dr. Jorgensen, my name is Betsy Rollins. The seventh grade girls Sunday school class asked me to come tonight and represent them. They wanted you to know that we all love you and thank you for being our pastor."

This is turning into a love fest. I smiled. I was pretty sure I could hear Sturgis Weaver's teeth grinding.

But then the other shoe dropped, metaphorically hitting the floor with a resounding thud.

"Excuse me, Tom. Over here, please." Don Kruger, one of Weaver's cronies, stood at the mic on the far aisle waving both hands.

Tom acknowledged him. "Yes, Don, go ahead."

"It is a sad day when you have to recommend that your pastor step down. But I'm afraid that day has arrived. For many of us this has been a long time coming. It's not that we don't like Pastor Jorgensen. He's a fine man, but for the sake of First Church we need to make a change. Those of us who have sacrificed and faithfully supported this church for decades are not in agreement with the direction he wants to take us." He held up a copy of the Carpe Annum report.

Yikes. I gulped. Bonnie patted me on the leg.

Don continued. "Too many institutions in today's world have given in and conformed to the latest fad, trying to ride 'change' to relevance and success. First Church has thrived over a hundred years by sticking to what works and by taking care of its own."

He held up my report again and waved it around. "This plan *threatens the very sacred traditions by which our church was founded and is even to this day sustained.*"

I couldn't believe my ears. His denouncement was verbatim from my dream!

Suddenly it all made sense. My dream had been a metaphor. I knew it! I checked my wrists for rope burns and was relieved there were none. That would have been *way* too weird.

Don finished his three-minute diatribe and took a seat up on the front row with the rest of the Weaver minions. Like a returning Roman legion, they were falling into formation for the victorious final march up to the throne. For them, this meeting was just a formality. The die had already been cast. And to be honest, the overall direction of the evening seemed to be favoring their opinion.

For the next half hour, church members rose either to praise Dr. Jorgensen or to list his perceived shortcomings. It was uncomfortable, it was ugly, and from my perspective, it was so totally unnecessary. A pall of gloom hovered over the crowd and it wasn't pretty. We all felt it.

Complicating an already tense situation, the air conditioning stopped blowing. All of the climate control functions at the church were handled by a computer system. The regular Sunday evening schedule called for the AC unit to quit at eight-thirty. No one had thought to reprogram it for the special business meeting. With a room overflowing with agitated church members, it didn't take long for the BTUs to skyrocket. Even after Bob Stevens did a manual override, the poor AC units just couldn't catch back up and overcome the heat being generated in the room. We were all sweating.

Mercifully the last person had their say. Before the vote, Tom gave Dr. Jorgensen an opportunity to speak. I was actually surprised that Sturgis Weaver didn't protest, but nothing was said. He must have had a very high level of confidence that he would prevail no matter what Horace might say.

Dr. Jorgensen rose slowly from his chair and calmly walked to the podium. Before saying anything, he paused for a long moment and scanned the room looking at the many different faces in the pews. He wore a gentle smile, but the deep sadness in his eyes remained.

Slowly but deliberately, he began. "A great man once wrote these words about our nation. Tonight I read them with our church in mind." He took a piece of paper from his pocket and unfolded it.

> "'We have been the recipients of the choicest bounties of Heaven . . . but we have forgotten God. We have forgotten the gracious hand which preserved us in peace, and multiplied and enriched and strengthened us; and we have vainly imagined, in the deceitfulness of our hearts, that all these blessings were produced by some superior wisdom and virtue of our own. Intoxicated with unbroken success, we have become too self-sufficient to feel the necessity of God's redeeming and preserving grace.'

Signed, Abraham Lincoln.

"In praying about tonight's meeting, God reminded me of these words and how they applied to me as your pastor. And I must confess to you, the kind and generous people of First Church, that I had indeed become too self-sufficient, too clever in my own mind. I have repented of this sin and asked God for forgiveness for my arrogance and pride. And now I ask you for the same forgiveness.

"It's the responsibility of a pastor to lead by example, to set a tone of dependence upon God. From now on I intentionally choose to make this the guiding principle of my ministry, be it here or wherever God chooses to place me.

"I now realize that First Church too, under my leadership, has fallen prey to self-sufficiency and pride. Somewhere along the way, comfort has become more important than challenge, safety more important than service, and ease more important than evangelism. Yes, we're the biggest church in town. Yes, we have the largest budget and the nicest buildings. Yes, we wield influence throughout the community. Do these accomplishments really matter to the greater purposes of God? A resounding no! Then the question that bears asking is: are we striving to reach a lost world for Christ? Period.

"There's been a lot of consternation thrown around this evening concerning the Carpe Annum project, and the impact it would have on the First Church way of life. The truth is, whether I'm your pastor or that task is given to someone else, First Church needs to get back on God's track. We need to refocus on those who need God, those who need help, and those who need grace. It is truly not about me, it's not about us; it's about God's purpose for this church and for each of your lives.

"These may be the last words I ever say as your pastor. And if that is your choice and God's will, so be it. I will graciously accept that outcome.

"I close with this challenge. Reach beyond yourself, your needs, your stuff, and seize the greater purposes of God. Allow Him to work *through* you, not just *for* you.

"It's been a true joy being your pastor."

With that, Dr. Horace Jorgensen walked off the platform and headed to his office. Perhaps, for the last time.

30

The Honeymoon

Raising my finger to my lips, I alerted both Father Ted and Thurm to remain quiet. We held our breath as we crouched down between some bushes and an old stone wall in a small open air courtyard. We were dressed like monks. Why? I have no idea, but I could feel the cool breeze rustling up my bare legs. I silently thanked the Lord for my gender.

A burly guard with a three day beard strolled leisurely by, cradling an old bolt-action rifle while whistling some lively tune. Ensconced in the shrubbery, we remained unnoticed. When the guard disappeared around a corner, I signaled the guys and we slipped low profile into the decrepit building.

After a brief search we located multiple rows of prison cells, but strangely they were all disproportionably small—only four or five feet tall at most. Inside each cell were children, teenagers, and even young adults all reaching out to us for help, for liberation. Methodically, we opened each cell and set each prisoner free handing each of them a pamphlet as they scurried away.

I glanced down at one of the paper booklets we were distributing and noticed it was a Chick tract with a drawing of Harry Simpkins on the front—dressed like Tex Larimore. The tract was written in Latin, but surprisingly I could read it. Its title? *How to Know God.*

Thurm handed me a walkie-talkie and speaking with a woman's voice said, "Elmo, you have a call, but if I were you I would wake up first before taking it."

"Thurm, dude, what's with the feminine voice?"

"Elmo, wake up!"

Startled, I sat up in my chair as Bonnie handed me the phone. She walked off shaking her head and laughing at me.

Taking a sip of my fruit tea with a colorful little umbrella stuck in it, I listened intently to the operator's instructions. "Thank you," I said, "and yes, I accept the call. Hello?"

"Elmo! You're a hard man to track down. Where in the heavens are you?"

"Jason McKenzie! I'm impressed you found me! You must've bribed my parents with concert tickets again."

"Your mom's become quite the negotiator. I even had to throw in a couple of backstage passes to get this phone number. Where are you guys, on the moon?"

"Not quite. I'm actually talking to you from a satellite phone while lounging on the deck of a sailboat anchored in the bay of a small deserted Caribbean island."

"Yeah, right." I could hear him snickering.

"I'm afraid it's oh so true, my skeptical friend." I laughed out loud. "Bonnie and I finally got around to taking our long awaited honeymoon."

"You're in the *Caribbean?*"

"We sure are. Bob 'Big Bird' Stevens, the administrator at First Church, is letting us stay at his condo on Grande Cayman Island. He only visits here in the summer, so it was available. He took pity on us poor newlyweds and let us stay here for free."

"Well la-de-da, if it's not lifestyles of the poor and infamous! By the way, how do you like the married life, ol' buddy?"

"It's good. Okay, actually it's wonderful. We're still adjusting to being with each other on a full-time basis, but it's all good. It really helped a lot going through the pre-marital counseling sessions with Father Ted. Men and women are just so dang different in so many ways. I'm still on a sharp learning curve when it comes to recognizing and meeting Bonnie's needs."

"You got that right. Women are from a different planet."

I chuckled. "It does seem that way sometimes. But man, it sure is nice having someone who cares about your day, your hurts, your needs. Like, for instance, when you get *fired.*"

"What!? Do you say you got fired? I thought everything was going great."

"It's a long story, and I know you're a busy man—"

"C'mon, now. Don't even try to give me that junk. This is Jason you're talkin' to. Besides, I'm sitting in the back of my tour bus on a three-hour junket to who-knows- where, so I've got all the time in the world."

"All right, all right. No need to get all up in a snit. I just didn't want to burden you with my little challenges. But you're right—what good are friends if you can't emotionally *vomit* your stuff on them occasionally?"

"Hey, hey, remember I'm riding in the back of a bus here, so let's just stay away from any more hurling references. And for the record, I'm not in a snit. I just care about you guys."

"Whoa, sorry, I forgot all about your motion sickness issues. Anyway, yeah, I got fired all right. There was a brief coup at First Church."

"At a church? Whoa!"

"Not only did I get the boot, they also fired the senior pastor who'd been there forever, his long-time assistant, the minister of music, Father Ted, and even the printer. It was like the climax of a Martine Scorsese movie—a veritable bloodbath."

"What caused it?"

"A perceived change in the balance of power. The most influential lay leader in the church who was also the biggest supporter of our pastor died unexpectedly. The wolves he had perennially kept at bay temporarily seized control of the deacon board and the carnage was unleashed. Fortunately, the church body rallied behind Pastor Jorgensen and the coup failed. Our jobs were then reinstated."

"That's a relief."

"No kidding." I laughed. "Here's the real kicker. The whole uprising was sparked by little ol' Elmo Jenkins and his Carpe Annum project."

"Seriously? Even though you were doing just what you were told to do?"

"Yes, sir. The underpinning of the discontent at First Church predated me by many years, but my work became the catalyst for the actual revolt."

"Wow—no double wow! What happens now to the report you spent all that time and energy working on?"

"Here's where a sad story takes a turn for the good. Kind of a 'plan B' from the Lord. At first, of course, the project was dead in the water. But when the whole situation at the church turned around, my report was back on track. Dr. De Villa, my former supervisor at the seminary, had helped me edit the report, and he asked for permission to run it by several of his publishers." I paused to take a sip of my fruit tea.

Jason, famous for his ADD, blurted out, "Well? What happened?"

"That's the best part of the whole shebang. One of the big publishing houses purchased the rights to the report, and I got a big fat advance check."

"You gotta be kidding me? And the church let you keep it?"

"Oh, yeah. That's when Bonnie and I decided to take our honeymoon to the Caribbean. And that, my friend, is where you found us today."

"Good for you guys. Elmo Jenkins, a published author! Who'da thought?"

"No kidding. Went right to my head. I'm even considering writing a novel about my experiences at First Church. Who knows it might just get published one day."

He chuckled. "Sounds like you have plenty of source material."

"Hey, Jason, Bonnie and I have basically been out of touch for awhile, but I did see something about your band flash across the screen at a restaurant. Did one of the guys get sick or something over the holidays?"

"That's also a long story and really traumatic—in fact, I'm still not ready to talk about it. But I promise I'll fill you in completely at some point in the future. I will say the silver lining to that debacle is a young lady name Hannah Brooks. Mom introduced us at Christmas, and—well, let's just say I'm head-over-heels. Whenever you and Bonnie wind down your Caribbean adventure and come home, we'll all get together. I know you'll love Hannah. She's *amazing.*"

"Jason, that's great. You deserve the best. Just please don't ask me to sing at your wedding. Unless you need to clear the room quickly for something else."

He hooted. "Elmo, you're some piece of work. One more question then I'll let you get back to your honeymooning. Whatever happened with that crazy wild-eyed statue thing that kept showing up in your office? Did you ever get to the bottom of that?"

"Interesting that you ask. We just resolved that little problem once and for all last night. I still don't know who was behind it, and I may never know. We brought the fertility god statue which I named Ferty with us on our trip down here. Late yesterday afternoon we sailed out to deeper water and buried Ferty at sea. We lit some candles and sang a song or two, then weighed her down with rocks and tossed her over the side. It was really quite touching."

"Now Elmo . . ."

"Okay, maybe I exaggerated just a bit. But we did weigh her down and toss her overboard offshore. So good luck to whoever's been retrieving her and putting her back in my office."

Jason laughed again. "Yeah, I think that'll probably take care of it. You know I just may have to write a song about Ferty. Don't forget Donovan had a big hit back in the day with a song called 'Hurdy Gurdy Man'."

"Now Jason . . ."

"I'm just kiddin' ya, man," he said, cackling. "Elmo, I love ya, brother, and it's been great catching up. Give Bonnie a kiss for me and let me know when you get back to the states, okay?"

"Will do."

"See ya and God bless."

"You too."

Turning off the phone I reached for my glass of fruit tea taking a big swig, I let the sweet liquid swirl around my mouth for a while before swallowing. *Ahhh . . .* a warm breeze rolled over me as I lounged there for a long time, looking out over the water and reminiscing about my life.

Later Bonnie emerged from the boat cabin carrying a package. She bent down and gave me a kiss.

I smiled up at her. "What's up?"

"I took a power nap. It was absolutely wonderful. The gentle motion of the boat on the water makes for great napping. Who was that on the phone?"

"Jason McKenzie. He just wanted to catch up. He said hi and sends his love. By the way, he's got a new girlfriend. I think he said her name was Hannah or something like that. We'll have to pick up a couple of tabloids to get the real story," I said, laughing.

"Good for him." She smiled real big. "I've got a surprise for you. This came before we left, but I decided to wait and give it to you when we got here." She handed me a UPS box.

"What is it?"

"Open it and see."

I tore open the box and found a book inside. On the cover, standing on the steps of First Church was Pastor Snooker and Dunston Jones shaking hands. It was titled *The Legacy of the Black Toe*. At the bottom of the cover it said, "Foreword by Elmo Jenkins."

"How about that!" I opened it up and started thumbing through the pages. "Thanks, sweetie."

She gave me another kiss. "I'm gonna change into my swimsuit and take a dip. That okay with you?"

"Sure, sure." I continued looking through Fred's book.

Another five minutes went by and suddenly I heard a blood-curdling scream from down below in the cabin. I flew out of my chair and sprinted down the steps into the sleeping quarters. Bonnie was frantically jumping up and down with her hands over her mouth. Her face was white as a ghost.

There, in the middle of the bed, dripping wet and covered in seaweed, sat Ferty!   I couldn't believe my eyes.

"What—how the . . .?"

Bonnie screamed again and I went into full-fledge panic mode, my adrenal glands jumping to warp speed. Rushing forward, I grabbed Ferty and sprinted back up the stairs stumbling several times before I reached the deck. My heart was pumping hard and fast against my chest. The intensity of the situation paralyzed my ability to make a decision. I stood there running in place, clutching the wet and slimy statue. Finally, not knowing what else to do, I ran to the back the boat and threw Ferty as hard as I could out into the water, almost falling overboard in the process.

As I leaned against the railing trying to calm down and catch my breath, I could hear muffled giggling. I turned around to find Bonnie—videoing me with her iPhone?

"Bonnie? What's going on here?"

A sinister smile darted across her face. "Let's just say you married a girl who just *loves* a well-planned, long-term, perfectly executed practical joke."

No Way.

31

Epilogue

There are extraordinary moments embedded in our daily lives that rise above the rest of the humdrum. The first bite of a delicious meal. That fresh, clean feeling after a shower. A soothing wind brushing across your face before a storm. The moment your head hits the pillow after a long hard day.

This was one of those special moments. I sat on the beach with Bonnie watching the setting sun explode the Caribbean sky with an array of brilliant colors . . . panoramic swatches of orange and red, yellow and violet. A cool dusk breeze brought relief from the lingering warmth of the day. I held her close, her head lying gently against my shoulder. No words were spoken as we simply allowed God's majesty to wash over us.

My thoughts wandered to the previous year; the euphoric heights and the gut-wrenching lows.

Joining with Bonnie for life had been the crescendo moment. Finding someone who loved me with grace and strength, regardless of my numerous flaws, was truly a miracle from God. That our relationship was grounded in our mutual love for Christ gave us both a confidence that we could weather the difficulties and accentuate the joys of a lifetime together. All practical jokes aside, I felt blessed to have her as my wife.

I was still processing my feelings concerning the upheaval at First Church. My post-traumatic thoughts were not of anger, but more of sadness. Why the rancor? Why the ugliness? Why do churches have these problems? To my young mind it all seemed so counterproductive. I just didn't get it.

My sudden though brief unemployment had also led me to appreciate just how precious and tenuous life's circumstances are. With a wife and hopefully some kids in the future, it was hard not to worry about the precarious nature of my vocation. It was easy to conclude that there are no certainties in this life.

Yet as I sat there watching the magnificent sunset unfold, I was again reminded that God's ways are higher than mine. Smiling, I pulled Bonnie closer and determined to simply yield my uncertain future into the able hands of the Father—the awesome Painter of the sky.

Your constant love reaches the heavens;

Your faithfulness touches the skies.

Show Your greatness in the sky, O God,

and Your glory over all the earth.

Psalm 57:10-11 (GNT)

BOOK THREE

THE OLD MAN AND THE TEA

McMILLIAN MOODY

ELMO JENKINS BOOK THREE

1

The Old Man

Kranky's Coffee Shoppe opened its doors for business long ago during the formative years of our city. Located at 107 Main Street in a small storefront across from city hall, it seemed out of place shoehorned between two enormous, forbidding skyscrapers in the heart of downtown.

Over the years, several attempts were made to close and tear down the old greasy spoon. Thankfully, each challenge by the money-grubbing speculators had been beaten back by the local antiquities juggernaut. Ultimately, after a lengthy legal battle, Kranky's became an official historical landmark protecting its future once and for all.

The iconic coffee shop remained in the family of Kranky Calhoun, the original proprietor for many generations until recently purchased by Buddy Skipbow. As you might suspect, Kranky—known for his signature cantankerous demeanor—was quite the curmudgeon. Whereas Buddy, the new owner, was the nicest guy on the planet. Since I stopped in at Kranky's two or three times a week for coffee and small talk, Buddy and I had become good friends.

Buddy had this endearing, silly habit of speaking in rhymes.

"Morning, Buddy. How's the coffee today?"

He flashed his famous smile. "Freshly ground, the flavor's sound."

"Give me a large one, please."

"I'll get you a cup. It's coming right up."

No "grande" or "venti" falderal at Kranky's. Your choices were all American—small, medium, or large.

While waiting for my order, I glanced toward the back of the dated eatery. As usual, there sat an old man alone in the last booth reading a book. Virtually every time I came into Kranky's, I noticed him there by himself, reading. Just like clockwork.

I'd fought the temptation to introduce myself for months, but now my relentless curiosity would not be denied. It had to be today. I slowly approached his booth.

"Excuse me." My words were swallowed up by the noisy din of the busy room.

The old gentleman in a faded wool sports jacket and plaid shirt looked up from his reading. "Yes? Can I help you?"

"I apologize for interrupting, but I've actually come by to say hello."

"Really?" He raised a wrinkled brow. An awkward moment ensued.

I forged on. "I stop in here regularly for a 'cup of Joe' on my way to work. While waiting in line, I've often spotted you reading in this same back booth. I guess you could say I've become intrigued and have recently felt compelled to introduce myself. So again, I apologize for the intrusion."

He scanned my face with a wary eye. "I don't suppose you're trying to sell an old man a product he doesn't want or need?"

"What? Oh, no, I'm not a salesman." I laughed. "Unless you consider a minister to be a salesman."

His worn face broadened into a wide grin. "Some folks might, but not me. Please have a seat." He gestured for me to sit down.

I slid into the other side of his booth. "My name is Elmo Jenkins. I work at the big church two blocks up the hill. Thanks for your kind hospitality."

His open book appeared to be written in a foreign language. When he closed it, I realized it was a Bible. An ornate antique lace bookmark protruded from the top of its pages.

I continued. "I'm a person who follows a pretty rigid personal routine, so when I noticed you reading here at the same time every day, it piqued my interest. If you don't mind me asking, how long have you been coming here to Kranky's?"

He studied me for a moment. "For a while, I suppose. You mentioned you drink coffee. I prefer a hot cup of tea in the morning." He cradled his cup in withered old hands. "Helps this ancient mind of mine wake up, if you know what I mean."

"Oh, I do. My brain may still be quite young, but my morning coffee helps to bring all my senses online."

He slid the Bible to one side. "Tell me, Reverend Jenkins, how long have you been a minister?"

"Not long, really. I started at First Church as an intern, but now I'm the assistant to the senior pastor, Horace Jorgenson."

"Horace Jorgensen. Yes, yes, I've heard of him. Word on the street is he's a good man."

"I think so. He's been a big help to me as a young man in the ministry."

"Good for him. Well then, Reverend Jenkins, do you like working in a church?"

"Please just call me Elmo. I haven't gotten used to all the *Reverend* jazz as of yet. Let's see, do I like working in the church? Yes and no. I enjoy helping people, though it can be draining. I especially like reaching out to the folks who are often overlooked or lost in the crowd. I sincerely believe the church is making a difference in people's lives, and being part of that is gratifying. Conversely, I absolutely hate church politics."

The old man chuckled. "Church politics? Now, wouldn't that be an oxymoron?"

"You'd like to think so, but unfortunately, it's an ever-present reality in most churches."

"Really? Interesting. Church politics—who knew?" He stared off into the distance as if contemplating a new concept and its implications.

"Well, I'd better get back to the church office, or they'll find someone else to take my spot. It was nice meeting you, and I hope to see you here again." I got up to leave. "By the way, what's your name?"

His friendly grin returned. "The name is Elijah Enoch, but you can just call me Eli."

I smiled back. "Then Eli it is." I grabbed my coffee cup. "One more thing. I noticed you were reading your Bible. What's your favorite part?"

He flashed an ebullient smile. "Oh, I like it all."

After winking at Juliann, our church receptionist, and collecting my mail, I plopped down in my red leather desk chair. My brief conversation with Eli had placed a burr in my spirit. The old man obviously spent hours reading his Bible. My paltry chapter a day suddenly seemed embarrassingly insignificant. I reasoned he was obviously retired and had unlimited time. Naturally, he would be looking for something to fill his mornings. But I knew I was just rationalizing my lack of commitment to God's word. *Dang, a new spiritual challenge. No rest for the weary.*

Thurm poked his head in my office. "Morning, Elmo."

Glad for the distraction, I motioned him in. "Come on in and kick your feet up for a spell. Tell me what's going on in the world of Thurm Wilson, youth minister *per eccellenza*? And what're you doing down here? I thought you were taking the day off."

"I am, kind of, but I needed my iPad. I'm finalizing some details for the high school all-nighter coming up this Friday."

I started to raise my hands in protest.

He quickly allayed my fears. "Don't worry, Elmo. I'm not here to ask you to be a chaperone. After what happened last time, I've given you a lifetime exemption."

"Thank God. Hallelujah! And yes, I unconditionally accept the exemption."

"I figured you would," he said, laughing.

"Is the all-nighter going to be here at the church again?"

"Not this time. We'll be over at *The Barge*."

"The Barge?"

"The Barge. You ever been out to the River Marina?"

"Sure, a few times."

"Do you remember that old abandoned barge that's tied up near the entrance to the inlet?"

"Yeah, I think so. Wait a minute. You're not taking kids out at night on that old piece of floating flotsam, are you?"

"Yeah, but it's not what you think. A high school buddy of mine bought the old barge and converted it into a fun center. It's got a game room, putt-putt golf, ping-pong, pool tables, and a great meeting room. It's really nice."

"Seriously?"

"Yep. So, I'm helping him out by renting it when I can. He's trying to market *The Barge* to churches, schools, local businesses, and even civic organizations—for parties, company socials, after-school events, and such."

"Wow. I'm always amazed at the innovative ideas people come up with. Capitalism at it's finest. And *The Barge* is indeed a great name. Hey, has he thought about pitching it to the folks over at the synagogue?"

Thurm's eyebrows rose. "I don't know. Why?"

"It'd be a great place to have a—*barge-mitzvah*."

"E-l-m-o!"

"Sorry. I couldn't resist."

"That's awful!"

"It is, isn't it?" I laughed. "Subject change. What's up with your T-shirt? Are all those stains keepsakes from your last middle school food fight?"

"Nah. Just an old shirt I kick around in."

"Oh no you don't. You're not getting off that easy. What happened?"

"Well, it's kind of embarrassing."

"We're friends, aren't we?"

"Okay, okay. But this is between you and me. All right?"

"Of course."

Thurm sat down on my love seat. "You know how I'm always looking for a new way to lose a few pounds? I hate dieting. Just hate it."

"Who doesn't?" I glanced briefly at my jar of jelly beans.

"So I was watching *Duck Dynasty* the other night and—"

"You're kidding me, right?"

"Oh no. It's my favorite show. Right up there with *American Idol.*"

"You're truly one of a kind, buddy. So you're watching TV and . . . ?"

"And a commercial comes on for *The Wonder Fork.*"

"*The Wonder Fork?*"

"*The Wonder Fork.* It's a specially designed fork that keeps you from eating too much."

I laughed again. "What, is the fork so big you can't get it in your mouth? Now there's an innovative idea." I reached for my jelly bean jar and grabbed a handful.

"No, man, it's more sophisticated than that." His voice betrayed a growing irritation with me.

"Sorry, sorry. Please, go ahead and tell me how it works." I clenched my jaws fighting the urge to laugh.

He sat up on the edge of the love seat. "It's really a pretty neat idea. See, most people eat too fast. Consequently, they eat too much. When you eat slower, you tend to eat less because you feel full before your plate's empty."

"Okay, I get that. Where does *The Wonder Fork* factor in?"

"*The Wonder Fork* has a small motor built in; kind of like an electric toothbrush. It also has a motion sensor. The sensor keeps track of how many times you lift your fork per minute. If you eat too fast, the motor kicks in and the fork vibrates in your hand. Theoretically, it signals you to slow down. So you eat less."

"All right. That makes sense. But how does that translate into, let's see—one, two three . . . *seven* stains on your T-shirt?"

Thurm's face reddened. "Well, I haven't quite gotten the hang of using the dumb thing yet. Maybe it needs to be calibrated or something. If the motor kicks on while I'm raising the fork to my mouth, the food goes flying everywhere—most if it landing on my shirt as you've so duly noted. It's a *wonder* they're selling any of the dang things."

We both had a good laugh. I patted him on the back as he got up to leave. "Maybe you should refrain from buying any more gizmos while watching *Duck Dynasty*. That just sounds like a recipe for disaster, y'know?"

"You're probably right." He waved as he headed out the door. "Later, Elmo."

A thought occurred to me as I sat back down. *What's next—The Wonder Knife?*

I shivered. *Ouch. That could be a hurty . . .*

2

The Vacuum

After a couple late-afternoon meetings, I headed home for a quiet evening with Bonnie, and Colby the wonder dog. Church staff members usually work three or four nights a week doing training events, attending meetings, or doing visitation. Evenings at home are precious and greatly cherished.

Our dog Colby is fearless. She chases anything without hesitation. Our backyard has two large oak trees chock-full of acorns. Consequently, the neighborhood squirrels congregate daily behind our house. It reminds me of the 1950s when all the greasers who couldn't find work would just hang outside the corner drugstore killing time. That's our backyard—a throng of loitering punk squirrels with nothing better to do.

When you're young, married, and broke, you look for cheap entertainment anywhere you can find it. Which is why I often get Colby all riled up and then release her into the backyard surprising the unsuspecting squirrels. There's always momentary mass rodent bedlam as they trample each other scampering for higher ground. Colby is fast, but the squirrels are much faster and never in any real danger. I'm not even sure Colby would know what to do if she ever caught one. But boy, it's fun watching her try. She has a special gait she reserves exclusively for chasing squirrels, kind of a bounding motion. This little game never gets old.

There's one thing Colby is deathly afraid of—our vacuum cleaner. She'll run for cover even before we turn it on.

Whereas Colby fears the vacuum, Bonnie hates it. The power cord isn't long enough. The cord is always tangled. The bag is full, and we're constantly out of replacement bags. The attachments are lousy or have totally gone missing. To Bonnie, these are more than just inconveniences. They're personal.

I figured she must have been forced to run the vacuum as a child before her parents would ever let her eat. That's how intense her negative feelings are toward this common household chore. Fortunately for me, her angst does not extend to any other necessary tasks around the home.

Being the Nobel laureate in psychology that I am, I quickly discerned that this vacuum cleaner issue was merely an anomaly. I cogently forged a plan to minimize the fallout each weekend as we cleaned the house. My brilliant solution? I simply volunteered to do all the vacuuming. In my spare time, I began crafting my Nobel Prize acceptance speech.

One day, God must have been experiencing a bit of Old Testament nostalgia, because he unleashed a legion of black flies into our peaceful neighborhood. They were everywhere, by the thousands. No matter how careful your coming and going, droves of the pesky insects would still end up inside the house. They dive-bombed the table during meals. They buzzed incessantly inside the windows. Which begged the question—*if they want out so badly, why did they come inside in the first place?*

At first, I did what any respectable head-of-the-household would do—I swatted them by the dozens. After a while, my bloodlust was assuaged. But I realized the fly swatter wasn't the most efficient way of eradicating these nettlesome creatures. I turned to the one feared and hated machine in our home that was up to this grisly task—our vacuum cleaner! With a little creativity, the vacuum hose attachment made fly elimination quick, clean, and easy.

The plague of the flies lasted for weeks. I'd simply pull out the trusty vacuum cleaner several times a day and *voila!* No flies! Even Bonnie gained a new respect for the vacuum and sadistically renamed it the *Grim Sweeper*. In an ironic twist, God had used a Mosaic plague to bring freedom and peace to the Jenkins household.

The phone rang. "Hello?"

"Hello, may I have a word with Mr. Elmo Jenkins?" asked a tentative male voice with a British accent.

"This is Elmo. How can I help you?"

"Right. Elmo, this is Lopez McGill. We met when Jason McKenzie visited, over at the Lucia Café."

"Sure, I remember. You work for his record label."

"Well, I did 'til I got canned last week. Seems one of the bloody rappers at the label had a cousin who needed a job and the rascal got mine."

"Sorry to hear that."

"Securing a new job is the least of my worries, which is why I rang you up. I desperately need to visit with someone about a personal issue. Since you're a chum of Jason's, you must be a decent fellow. I also recalled that you were a vicar or priest or some such. Do you think you could spot me some of your time next week?"

"Sure, Lopez. Just call the church and have them schedule a time for you to come in."

"Actually, would it be possible for us to meet up at a different location? Perhaps an eatery or pub?"

"That'd be fine. Are you familiar with Kranky's Coffee Shoppe?"

"Yes, downtown. I know it well. The record label's regional office suite is in the high- rise next door."

"Okay, then. I'm available either Tuesday or Thursday morning.

What works best for you?"

"Either's fine."

"Then I'll see you at Kranky's at 9:00 on Thursday morning."

"Right. I really appreciate this, Elmo. Cheerio."

I walked into the kitchen where Bonnie was setting the table for dinner.

She smiled. "Who called?"

"A guy named Lopez McGill. He was one of the guys hanging out with Jason the day you met him over at Café Lucia's. The guy with the British accent?"

She shook her head. "Sorry, I don't remember him. That day was kind of a blur. Why'd he call you, and here at home?"

"He remembered that I was a minister. It sounds like maybe life has thrown him a few curves. He needs someone to talk to."

She gave me a quick kiss on the cheek. "Well, you're a good choice."

"Thanks, sweetie. What's for dinner?"

She paused. "Elmo, I know you love fried chicken, smashed potatoes, and yellow corn floating in butter. But tonight we're having tofu, raw broccoli, and avocado wedges."

I forced a smile and lied. "Yummy."

Bonnie was on this health-food kick, and as a good husband I went along without complaining. At least not out loud. To keep my sanity and pacify the needs of my male ego, I always ordered something greasy or sweet when out with the guys for lunch. We had a lunchtime edict: *What's eaten at the table stays at the table.* To be honest, I suspected the wives knew of our dietary malfeasance. Why? Because in every secret society, there's always one member who leaks like a sieve.

And if one wife knew, they all knew.

We sat down to eat dinner and I took Bonnie's hand. "Dear God, thank you for this...uh...um...food. And for my sweet wife Bonnie and for your love and care. Amen."

I opened my eyes, and Bonnie was smirking. "Way to cover your tail with the 'sweet wife' bit."

I feigned shock and addressed the dog. "Why Colby, I believe she just questioned my sincerity."

Bonnie took a bite of tofu. "Now darling," she purred sarcastically, "I would never question your sincerity or your integrity. By the way, what did you have for lunch today?" she asked, her eyes blinking at me.

Uh oh.

3

The Interloper

Her name was Canasta Langanelli, and I knew the first minute I met her she was trouble. She was short with dark hair, dark eyes, and an olive complexion. She was confident, fleet of foot, feisty, and conspicuously manipulative. Canasta was the long-awaited Youth/Recreation secretary whom Thurm had been campaigning for.

Thurm was thrilled. I was wary.

As Tom Applebee stood to introduce her to the rest of the First Church staff, I was keenly aware that her arrival had already created quite a buzz among the clerical staff. Tom was usually a good judge of character, but in my opinion, he'd faltered badly with this particular hire. I suspected he would eventually reap the whirlwind for his inexplicable lack of discernment in bringing Canasta on board.

Tom smiled as he addressed the conference room full of people. "Before we take our break and let the support team members slip back to their desks, I would like to introduce our newest staff member." He gestured for Canasta to stand. "As you all know, we've been looking a long time for just the right person for the new support position for our youth and recreational ministries. It will take a high level of energy and unique skill set to succeed in this new position. The Personnel Committee and I feel strongly that Canasta is the perfect fit for the role. She comes to us from Bargston College where she earned a degree in business innovation—with a 4.0, I might add. She was also president of the Bargston student body for her final two years."

The staff gave her a warm round of applause. As the meeting broke up, several of the secretaries went over to personally welcome Canasta to the staff.

The DNA of a clerical or support staff at a large organization is complex, and the inner workings are often fraught with intrigue. The support staff operates behind the scenes as "an organization within an organization," with its own set of unofficial rules and protocols. These shadow societies are usually led informally by a woman of long-standing tenure within the organization. In a successful support staff, everyone knows their place, everyone knows their position in the pecking order, and *everyone* plays by the rules. This allows the organization to run smoothly on a day-to-day basis.

On occasion, the support staff apple cart will be shaken or even toppled as an interloper emerges. Most often a new employee, this rogue individual is either unaware of the unofficial rules, or willfully chooses to ignore them.

This is the role Canasta Langanelli chose to play at First Baptist.

And the way I saw it, this did *not* portend well.

"Elmo," Juliann said, calling me over to the receptionist desk. "I've got a phone message for you." She handed me the note. "He said he was calling from New York City . . . oooh!"

"Thanks, Juliann" I headed down the hall then stepped into my office and closed the door behind me.

Who is Castor McMullan? I dialed the number.

"Brown & Brewster, how can I direct your call?"

Ah, my publisher.

"Castor McMullan, please."

A few seconds passed.

"Elmo, thanks for returning my call. We haven't met, but Mr. Hillard asked me to give you a call and set up a time for you to fly to New York and meet with our editors, marketing staff, etcetera. Of course, we'll be covering all your expenses."

"New York City. Wow. I've never been there before."

"Really? Well, I'll make a note to have your driver show you some of the sights on the way in from the airport."

"Driver?"

"Yes, he'll pick you up at the airport and bring you to our main office here in Manhattan. Parking is non-existent here in the city, so a car rental is out. And you put your life at risk when you use a NYC cab." He said chuckling.

"How long will I be there?"

"Just for a day. Then you'll be bunking in one of our guest suites here at the main office building. They're very nice. We'll have you back on your way home the next morning."

"Sounds great."

"All right then. Pull out your calendar and let's hard code a date for your visit."

Bonnie and I walked to the downtown mall for lunch. *Hot dog Wednesday* had become part of our regular midweek routine. To save time, we took a shortcut through an alley which was home to several seedy business establishments. Since it was midday, safety was not a concern. As we walked past the entrance to an adult bookstore, the door flew open and out stepped Erlene Markham, almost knocking me down.

She smiled a toothy grin. "Hi, Bonnie! Sorry about that, Elmo. I didn't see you. These old eyes of mine just aren't what they used to be."

Caught off guard by the awkward situation, I was at a complete loss for words.

Bonnie, always cool under fire, responded. "Hi, Erlene. Picking up some new reading material, are you?"

Erlene's head bobbed as she cackled like an inebriated hyena. "No! No, it's a new ministry I've started." She continued guffawing.

"Huh? What new ministry?" I asked.

Erlene reached into her purse and pulled out a handful of Chick tracts. "Harry Simpkins gave me these, and I thought—what better place to hand them out than this nasty dive!" she said, pointing over her shoulder.

I was incredulous. "Erlene, you're telling us you just waltzed into that porn shop and started handing out gospel tracts?"

"Where's the fun in *that*?" She cackled again. "No, I'd sneak up behind a customer as he looked at the merchandise, and say, 'Gotcha!' Every single one of 'em jumped at least three feet into the air. Hilarious! After they calmed down, I'd pat them on the back and give them one of Harry's tracts. Then I'd tell them, 'God loves you.'"

"How'd they respond?"

"To a man they thanked me and took the tract. Who knows? Maybe God will show mercy and save a few of them."

I chuckled. "Erlene, you are one gutsy lady."

"How'd you handle all those trashy pictures and products in there?" Bonnie asked, with her best yucky facial expression.

Erlene grinned. "Oh, that stuff is nothing. Back in Africa they used to—"

"Miss Erlene!" I jumped in. "Sorry to interrupt, but Bonnie and I have to scoot, or we won't make it back to the church office on time. I have to be back for a group . . . uh, staff . . . uh, well, you know, a meeting thingy." We made our escape.

As we rounded the corner toward the downtown mall, Bonnie snickered. "A 'meeting thingy'?"

"I admit that was lame, but I was a bit flustered. I just couldn't handle another one of Erlene's sordid tales from Africa. Not today."

"Why's today any different?"

"Oh, I don't know. I'm having kind of a blue-goofus day, I guess."

"Really? What's going on?" She gave me a side hug as we walked.

"There's this troubling accumulation-of-doubt cloud gathering over my head, and I fear it's about to rain down on me."

"An accumulation-of-doubt cloud? Hmm. Part of my job description as a wife is to listen to your hurts and fears and help where I can. It's part of the written contract all wives sign."

"Yeah, now that's funny." I gave her a kiss on the cheek.

"It's true. Seriously."

"I know ladies are good with the sharing and support stuff, but that comes harder for guys. And the last thing I want to be is a Donnie Downer ruining your day."

"Come on. Give me a shot," she said, her smile sincere. "What's bothering you?"

"Okay, here goes. For starters, ever since the infamous *special called church business meeting,* there's been a subtle change in the atmosphere and demeanor in our staff meetings. The trust level has been diminished, and the guys are more guarded with their comments and opinions. The camaraderie has been irreparably damaged.

"Poor Raze Hankins. You know he's not one of my favorite people, but he's literally a dead man walking. His brother Terry told me Raze has been feverishly working the phones trying to line up a new position. He knows the axe is positioned to fall any day. I can tell myself it's not my fault, but I still feel partially responsible for the whole mess.

"And then there are my pastoral responsibilities. The thing is I'm still discovering how to be a 'minister' and all that goes along with that. It's a steep learning curve. Take my meeting with Lopez McGill tomorrow morning. What do I say to him? I kinda feel as if I'm winging this ministry thing, making it up as I go along.

"Finally, there's the self-doubt I'm feeling about the book publishing ordeal. The boys up in New York are all jacked up and working at warp speed, and I'm just not sure I'm ready to step into that world."

I slipped my arm around Bonnie's waist. "So, there you go. You asked, and I told. Funny, saying it all out loud makes me feel like I'm neurotic."

Bonnie smiled, brushing my hair back off my forehead. "I didn't hear any neurosis. Those are honest, legitimate feelings. The kind we all have."

"Yeah, but— "

"You're right, Elmo. The church dust-up wasn't your fault. Raze has no one to blame but himself. It's actually good that he's moving on. Better for him, and better for First Church.

"As far as the book stuff, I'm not sure what to say. Just try to enjoy it for what it is, and don't let the New York wonks push you around. It's your book, after all. A culmination of almost a year of hard work.

"When it comes to the ministry stuff, you're selling yourself short. You have *great* people skills; you have the training, and you're compassionate and caring. Just lean into the Lord and trust him in the new ministry situations. You've done pretty well so far."

We queued up in the hot dog line. "I know you're right. It's just hard to bridge the disconnect between what I know is true and what I feel. Just talking with you about it seems to have helped some."

"Anytime, sweetie. And hey, don't forget Philippians 4:6—be anxious for nothing."

"Thanks."

We paid for our hot dogs and grabbed our regular bench.

"Bonnie, tell me something. How is it that we're on a healthy eating regimen, but we're still allowed to eat a hot dog once a week? Next to the donut, a hot dog is probably the unhealthiest food on the planet."

She feigned shock. "I never intended for us to be *dog*-matic—"

"Oh, *that's* funny. I bet you've had that one loaded up and ready, just waiting for me to ask that question. C'mon, haven't you?"

"I'll never tell." Bonnie grinned while taking a sip of coke. "Hey, this'll make you smile. Jane E. dropped off some books for Louis at the church office this morning. She was headed over to Wal-Mart, so I asked if I could tag along. I needed to pick up some printer cartridges.

"As we were walking down one of the store aisles, there was this grandmother pushing a toddler in a stroller. When we got closer we got a whiff of something *nasty* in the air, as if junior was about to load his diaper. Just then the old lady leans down and says to the kid, 'I'm afraid someone's made a *fluffy*.'

"And without breaking stride, Jane E. says with her signature sardonic flair, 'Trust me ma'am, that ain't no *fluffy*!'

"The old lady looked up and gave us both the full-court stink-eye as we walked by. It took everything I had not to laugh out loud. I almost swallowed my tongue! We turned the corner and then laughed 'til it hurt. I laughed so hard I may have even fluffied!"

Bonnie and I both laughed 'til we had tears in our eyes.

Just another reason why I love our Wednesday lunch dates.

But then it happened. The classic mustard packet mishap. Attempting to dress her hot dog, Bonnie squeezed the packet too hard, and the mustard shot sideways all over my khaki slacks.

"Oops?" she said nervously.

"*Oops?*" As I drove home to change my pants, I remembered one of my college psychology classes. The class was taught by Dr. Dave Skaer—pronounced like the word "scare." Yep, I had a psych class taught by a guy named Dr. Scare. Spooky, huh?

One day in class, we discussed the concept of *oops*. In particular how the concept related to the way we treated other people.

Dr. Skaer explained that most people were easier on themselves than they are on others. He gave an example from his own marriage. His wife, while on the phone, had backed their car over their mailbox, damaging both the car and the mailbox. He was upset and ready to read her the riot act when he had a profound thought.

What if I had backed over the mailbox? What would I have said? Oops.

We all have the tendency to let ourselves off the hook much easier than others. This has huge implications in our relationships, but it can be a neutron bomb in a marriage.

Take our little mustard calamity, for instance. There we were laughing, enjoying each other's company, and bam—Bonnie carelessly shoots mustard on my slacks. Oh, it was an accident all right, but I'm of the opinion that most accidents can be avoided with a little forethought.

In times past, I would have scolded her harshly, pointing out the grand inconvenience she'd just created for me. I would have reminded her that clothes cost money and that my slacks were probably ruined—blah, blah, blah.

Now, let's assume I'd been sitting there by myself and spilled mustard on my pants. Most folks would not pitch a fit berating themselves for being stupid and ruining their clothes. Their most common response? *My* most common response?

"Oops."

Then I would wipe off my pants the best I could. I would finish my hot dog. Later, I would tell Bonnie that Mr. Nimblefingers dropped mustard all over his slacks. *Que sera.* She'd probably laugh at her klutz husband.

So, when Bonnie shot mustard on my pants and said "oops," I reacted just as if I had done it myself. She apologized, helped me clean up, and we finished our lunch. Afterward, I headed home for a quick wardrobe change. Consequently, there would be no arbitrary relationship fissure to be resolved later that evening.

It took a while for me to integrate this 'oops' concept into my marriage, but it had already saved me substantial heartache.

Thank you, Dr. Skaer. Wherever you are.

The Surprise

As I walked into Tom Applebee's outer office, I noticed his wall clock read 8:15 a.m. "Hey, Adrianne. Is Tom available for a quick visit? I know he's been out the last several days, so if he's too busy I can come back."

She smiled. "Mornin' Elmo. Let me check and see."

While she rang Tom's inner office, I walked over and glanced out the window. From five stories up, I could easily see Kranky's Coffee Shoppe down the hill. I wondered if Eli was there drinking tea and reading his Bible.

Adrianne hung up the phone. "Tom said come on in."

I tossed her a wink. "Thanks, Adrianne." I opened Tom's door and stepped inside.

Tom sat casually at his desk sorting through his mail. "Morning, Elmo. What can I do for you on this beautiful morning?" He smiled and reached for his coffee cup. "Would you like some coffee?"

"No thanks. I wanted to report back to you on the visit you asked me to make Monday afternoon with the guy who's home recovering from back surgery."

"Yes, Danny Satterwhite. Good guy. How'd it go?"

"Well, it was interesting."

Tom sat up in his chair. "How so?"

"I was in my car coming back from a hospital run when Adrianne called me with Mr. Satterwhite's address. Since I was only a few blocks from his neighborhood I decided to just go ahead and make the visit right then. I parked my car on the street and walked up to the front door and rang the doorbell. I'd say it was around three in the afternoon. I waited a few minutes, and no one answered. So I rang the bell again. I'd no sooner stepped back, when the door flew open and there was a whirl of color, motion, and sound, which concluded with a loud 'SURPRISE!' yelled in a heavy Spanish accent. There, standing in the open doorway before me was a short, plump, middle-aged Hispanic woman in a very revealing negligee. She froze, I froze, and we both just stood there with our mouths gaping open not knowing what to do next. Then, after an awkward and embarrassing moment, she slammed the door in a flurry of angry Spanish.

"I looked again at my handwritten note with Danny Satterwhite's name and address. It was obvious to me that the senorita wasn't Danny, or at least I hoped she wasn't? Fearing she might call the police and not knowing what else to do, I scurried back to my car and got the heck out of there."

Tom looked at me, clearly bumfuzzled. "Elmo, do you have that paper with Danny's address on it?"

I dug it out of my pocket and handed him my hand-scratched note. He rifled through a stack of memos from Adrianne until he found the one he was looking for. He compared it with my note and immediately burst into laughter.

"Elmo, I'm not sure who's to blame here, but Danny lives on Elm Court, and your note has him on Elm *Place*. Son, you were at the wrong house." He leaned back in his chair and continued laughing, which was uncharacteristic for Tom.

I thought about it for a moment, then joined in the laugh fest. I had to admit, it was pretty funny. I guess I'm just lucky I wasn't wearing a postal uniform. Mucho Yikes!

"Over here." I waved Lopez over to my table by Kranky's front window. As he worked his way toward me, I checked the back booth for Eli. His table was empty.

"Good morning, Elmo. Thank you for meeting with me."

I stood and shook his hand. "My pleasure, Lopez. Would you like something to eat or maybe a cup of coffee?"

"No, I've already had my brekkie, but I would fancy a cuppa hot tea?"

Tea, tea, what's with all these tea drinkers? I signaled for the waitress.

"Before we get started, you have to tell me about your name. It's very unique."

He laughed. "Yeah, I've heard that one before. Not much to it really. My mother is Spanish—Maria Lopez. My father is Irish—Donny McGill. I was born in London, so they covered all their bases and christened me Otis Lopez McGill.

"So you go by your middle name? Why not? How long have you been in the States?"

"Moved here when I was but a wee lad of sixteen and quickly started going by Lopez. I discovered right away that Otis wasn't too popular with the American ladies."

I laughed. "Really? Who knew? But then, neither is Elmo."

He smiled. "Speaking of the ladies, that's why I requested a speck of your time for a chinwag."

I was taken aback. "Okay, but you need to know up front when it comes to the opposite sex, I'm no authority. Not even close."

"Maybe so, but you're a church guy, and that's where I'm badly needing some advice."

I took a big chug of coffee. "Fair enough. Fire away."

He smiled. "For some reason—perhaps it's the accent—girls have always taken a fancy to me. Getting dates has never been a problem, and I've taken full advantage of that advantage. T'was almost a game for me, and thus I've never truly loved any one filly. Until I met Shantel and everything changed. She was different from anyone I'd ever dated. Most of the women I see are dodgy party gals I've met in the clubs. But not Shantel. I got to know her down at the corner laundrette by my flat."

"Your flat?"

"My apartment."

"Got it." I called the waitress over for a coffee refill. "So does Shantel work at this laundr . . . er, laundromat?"

"Oh, no. She does her clothes there every Saturday morning—which is how I met her. You see, normally I'm out with the dry cows on Friday evenings. The last thing I'd be doing on Saturday morning is washing my clothes. But one Friday three or four months ago, I had a bad bellyache, so I stayed home and hit the sack early. By nine on Saturday morning, I was up and bone-idle, so I decided to do my laundry."

"Wait, out with the dry cows?"

He grinned. "Y'know, so late that it's early."

I chuckled. "I'll have to remember that one."

"Anyway, that's where I met her, and I've been courting her ever since."

I leaned back in my chair with my hands behind my head. "So what's the problem?"

"The problem is I love her so much, but she won't marry me because I'm not a churchgoer. It's against her beliefs. I'm gobsmacked! I need your help."

"Okay, I think I get the picture."

I spent the next hour explaining to my new British friend why it's important for both partners in a marriage to be believers. I also encouraged him to avoid the dishonest route of pretending to become a Christian just so Shantel would marry him. That was the quintessential recipe for marital frustration and heartache. As I shared the gospel with Lopez, I noticed Eli sitting in his booth. Strange, I didn't seen him slip into the coffee shop. At one point we made eye contact, and he smiled.

Lopez and I agreed to meet again and discuss more of what it meant to be, as he called it, "a churchgoer". We said our goodbyes.

I was late for an appointment back at the church, so I didn't have time to go by and visit with Eli. I waved as I left, but he was consumed with his Bible reading and didn't see me.

Walking back up the hill toward First Church, I concluded that my "chinwag" with Lopez had gone quite well—whatever that meant?

A late-model sedan honked and pulled up beside me. The windows were tinted so I couldn't see inside. The passenger side window slowly rolled down. "Hey Elmo, you want a lift up the hill?"

"Well, good morning, Father Ted. What's with the Buick?" I asked as I climbed in the front seat. "Where's your red Viper?"

"Sold it."

"Why?"

"Bought a boat."

"You're kidding?"

"Nope."

"But—"

"I know, I know. All that best-day/worst-day malarkey. I'm semi-retired, I'm healthy, and I've always wanted a boat. All I needed was the cash."

"So out with the Viper and in with the boat."

"Exactly."

"Did you tell the Lone Ranger?"

"Huh?"

"You know, the Lyle Lovett song?"

"Lyle who?"

"Never mind. Tell me about your boat."

"She's a real beauty—a sailboat. And yes, she's red."

"Ever done any sailing?"

"Oh sure. Remember, I was the pastor of a well-heeled metropolitan church for three decades. Many of my parishioners had sailboats and took me out all the time. For some odd reason, a sailboat is a 'must-have' for rich white people."

"Yeah, I've noticed that. Almost like it's a requirement. Whereas in the hood you have to have 'street cred' to be accepted, at the country club, you have to have 'nautical cred'—to include the obligatory America's Cup official slicker," I quipped.

"True, true." Father Ted croaked. "Anyway, it'll make for fun weekends for Patty and me. You and Bonnie will have to join us sometime."

"Sounds like a good time." I said as we pulled into the First Church parking lot. *I hope he sails his boat more safely than he drives. I guess I'll be wearing two life preservers that day . . .*

"Tell me, Elmo, how's married life going?"

"We're doing well—with one exception."

"Really? What's that?"

"Are you familiar with tofu?"

"Oh boy, the ol' healthy diet routine. Don't worry. In my

experience, that's just a phase that comes and goes periodically. Something to do with varying dress sizes and such. I've learned always to keep a bag of chips hidden away for emergencies."

"Now, there's some good advice." We walked across First Boulevard. "Subject change. Have you ever met or heard of a senior adult gentleman here in town named Elijah Enoch?"

He thought for a moment. "No, I'm not familiar with that name. Should I be?"

"Oh, I don't know. Just an old guy who spends quite a bit of time in the back booth down at Kranky's. I'd noticed him there on numerous occasions, so I introduced myself the other day. Seems he sits back there every day drinking hot tea and reading his Bible. And here's an odd note. I got a quick look at his Bible while it was open, and it appeared to be in Aramaic."

"Really? Maybe he's a retired seminary professor. Could even be a rabbi. You should ask Dr. De Villa or Pastor Snooker if they know him. Why the interest in the ol' boy?"

"I'm not sure. I felt strongly compelled to introduce myself, and when I did, I felt an even stronger connection with the man. Weird, huh?"

"No, not really. My advice is to befriend him. Who knows? Maybe he's got something to say that you need to hear. I've learned God reaches us, and God teaches us through other believers. Anyone who spends that much time reading his Bible has to have some profound insights to share. Next time I'm down there, I'll look for him."

"Thanks, that'd be great. So, what did you name your boat?"

5

The Dream

I stumbled into the kitchen with one eye closed and one eye somewhere near half-mast. One of my slippers had gone AWOL on my trip from the bed to the coffeemaker, a dereliction of duty I didn't fully appreciate until my bare foot hit the chilly kitchen floor. Yeeow. My need for caffeine was so intense I manned-up and pushed through the icy pain.

Last night I'd astutely set my coffeemaker to auto-start at 6:00 this morning. For a change, I'd even remembered to load it with coffee grounds. As I poured myself a mug of the steaming hot elixir, I was pleased with myself for finally getting it right this time.

In my stupor as I forged through the morning haze into the kitchen, I hadn't noticed Bonnie. She sat quietly at the breakfast nook sipping grapefruit juice and reading the news on her laptop.

"Morning, Elmo."

After a micro-moment of startled panic, including a small jump, I breathed deeply and grunted back. "Mornin', love."

"You're coffeemaker wasn't plugged in, so I plugged it in and turned it on. Hope it turned out all right."

"Grrr."

"Did you say something, sweetie?"

"Oh, nothing. Just some self-flagellation. Punishment for an episode of premature self-congratulations." I plopped down at the table, and Splenda'd-up my coffee.

"My, that's a mouthful of big words for so early in the morning. Which tells me your brain is alert and obviously way ahead of your body. Which means you just woke up from one of your epic dreams. Which means—"

"Okay, okay, I get it." I gulped down some coffee.

"Well, am I right?"

"Yes dear, I was dreaming. Any other breaking news this morning?"

"Now come on. I love the fact that you're a prolific dreamer. It's part of what makes you that special, warm, and interesting guy I fell in love with. And I really do enjoy hearing all about them. So tell me, what was on the Elmo dream channel last night?"

"Funny." I sat up in my chair, the caffeine clearly breathing new life into my tired bones. "Some nights I dream all night long, but I usually only remember the last one before my alarm goes off. The last dream this morning, as Ned Ryerson would say, 'was a doozy'."

Bonnie got up and poured herself a cup of coffee and then refilled my mug. "You had a dream about *Groundhog Day*?"

"What? No . . . no." I added more powdery sweetener to my mug. "Ahhh. Morning coffee. The liquid of life."

Bonnie closed her laptop. "Okay, then what was your dream about?"

I closed my eyes and tried to remember the details of the dream. "Let's see. Harry Simpkins and I were in an elevator car that had stopped or jammed or something. We were just sitting there waiting.

"To kill the time, Harry says, 'Elmo, what's your favorite parrot joke?'

"That's easy,' I say. 'A guy named Wally goes into a pet store to buy food for his cat. The pet store owner has this big parrot that sits up on its perch next to the cash register and talks to the customers. While Wally's waiting at the counter, the parrot starts insulting him, calling him all sorts of vile names, impugning his character. Wally tries to ignore the obnoxious bird, but the parrot is relentless in his humiliating attack. Wally's ticked off, but he keeps his cool and makes his purchase. After all, he reasons, it's just a dumb bird.

"'A month later, he's back for more cat food, and the same thing happens. The parrot belittles poor Wally, calls him names, and even insults his family. The owner seems oblivious to the situation which makes Wally livid. Again, he quietly makes his purchase and leaves, but he stews about it. Wally's your classic passive-aggressive.

"'So, when he gets home he fires off a hotly-worded email to the pet store owner. He tells the owner he does not appreciate the parrot insulting him, calling him names, and impugning his character. He says if the owner doesn't rein in the bird and make it stop, he'll start buying his pet supplies elsewhere. He'll also tell everyone he knows to avoid that store.

"'The pet store owner jets back an apology, and shares that the parrot has been disciplined and will no longer be a problem. He offers Wally a free bag of cat food as a gesture of good faith.

"'Wally feels vindicated and immediately heads back to the pet store to pick up his free gift. As he walks into the store, Wally notices the parrot eyeballing him, but true to the owner's word, the bird remains silent. The owner is tied up with another customer, so Wally patiently waits at the counter. The whole time he's standing there the parrot is staring him down, but says nothing. Finally, Wally can't take the bird's glare any longer and turns to the parrot and says, 'What?!'

"'The parrot casually checks to see what the owner's doing, then leans over and whispers in Wally's ear, '*You* know.'

"Well, Harry guffawed like a circus clown then mumbled something about staring down Bob Stevens during the next staff meeting, then telling him, '*you* know.'

Bonnie interrupted. "You told a joke in your dream?"

"Yeah, and get this—it's one I'd never heard before."

"Really? What happened next?"

"After Harry calmed down, he said, 'Elmo, that was good but here's a better one. A guy goes to a pet store to buy a parrot. The store has one for sale named Pete, but the clerk warns the man that Pete's previous owner was a sailor, and the parrot picked up some bad language from him. The man isn't concerned because he's successfully trained parrots before, so he takes Pete home.

"'The man painstakingly spends the next several weeks training Pete what he can and cannot say around the house. Everything is going smoothly until the man forgets to feed Pete one morning, and the bird goes hungry all day. When the man comes home from work, Pete lets him have it with some choice sailor profanity. The man is stunned, having never heard such vile language, and warns Pete if it happens again he'll be severely punished. Pete apologizes and everything again runs smoothly for a while.

"'Lo and behold, one day the man slips up again and forgets to feed Pete. The parrot responds by lambasting him with another ugly tirade. For punishment, the man decides to put Pete in the freezer for thirty minutes. He figures a sampling of arctic weather will teach the tropical bird to mind his manners once and for all.

"'After thirty minutes the man opens the freezer door and asks the parrot, "Well? Have you learned your lesson? There will be no more swearing in this house!"

"'To which the parrot responds, "Oh yeah, I got that. But what I really want to know is—what did this poor turkey in here do?"'

Bonnie laughed out loud. "That's hilarious! Had you ever heard that one before?"

"Nope."

"How's that possible?"

"Don't know, but the dream really got strange after that."

"How so?"

"We're still laughing when the elevator doors open and in walks Erlene Markham. She says, 'You boys think that's funny, let me tell you about—'

"'No! Wait!' we both screamed, but when I looked back it was no longer Erlene. She'd morphed into Al Gore, and he was rambling on about the dangers of cell phone batteries overheating, a phenomenon he called *Mobile Warming*. He started yelling, "No one's listening! No one's listening!" and he frantically started pushing the elevator emergency buzzer button. That's when I woke up and turned off my alarm."

Bonnie laughed again. "On the Elmo Dream Fujita scale, I would give that a 3.0." She took a sip of coffee. "You usually try to learn something from your dreams. What's your takeaway from this last one?"

"An EDF-3, hmm? I guess that's fair. What did I learn? One –

never, ever get on the same elevator with either Harry Simpkins or Erlene Markham. And two – cell phones are destroying the ozone layer. Who knew?"

She deadpanned. "On that second point I'm afraid you would have to consider me a mobile warming skeptic."

I feigned distress. "See? Just like Big Al said, 'No one's listening! No one's listening!'"

Bonnie rinsed her coffee cup and placed it in the dishwasher. "Okay, enough foolishness for one morning. Time to get ready for work. We don't want to be late!"

Thurm asked me to help him carry some boxes over to the CLC—aka our Christian Life Center. This was our recreation center and domain of recreation minister Johnny "the pulled groin" Rochelle. The CLC occupied part of the same city block as the other First Church buildings, but didn't connect directly to them. You had to walk out of the Education Building, down the sidewalk, then into the CLC.

Par for the course, the First Church Christian Life Center was top of the line. It included a full-length basketball court with a parquet floor, two racquetball courts, and the requisite squash court. *Who plays squash anyway?* A ceramics studio with built-in kiln. A state-of-the-art workout area with all the latest exercise machines. Plush locker room facilities, including both a sauna and a cold plunge. And get this, a four-lane bowling alley in the basement.

No concrete slab with net-less basketball hoops and a tetherball pole for First Church. When they decided to build a recreation center, it would either be Olympic venue quality or nothing at all.

Thurm's new secretary, the infamous Canasta Langanelli, also had her office in the CLC. She split her duties between Thurm and Johnny. Her office location was inconvenient for Thurm, but he was so happy to finally have clerical help, he wasn't about to complain.

It was a beautiful clear day as we walked down the sidewalk carrying the boxes of youth materials.

"Spizzerinctum!"

"What?"

"Spizzerinctum!"

"Elmo, what are you taking about?

"Thurm, I've come to the conclusion that it takes spizzerinctum to successfully survive working on a church staff."

"Okay, you've got me. I have no idea what a spizzerinctum is. It sounds like some obscure surgical procedure to remove a suspicious polyp from your large intestines."

"Have you been watching *Grey's Anatomy* again? It's not a medical term, you doofus."

"All right, then what does it mean?"

"It's one of those words that's easier to feel or experience than define."

"I need something more tangible."

"Okay, how about vim and vigor, determination, zeal, verve, uber-chutzpah."

"Uber-chutzpah? Where do you come up with this stuff?"

"Don't miss the point here. To be a long-tenured, effective, engaged church staff member takes determination, nerve, and zeal. Otherwise, you burn out like a solid rocket booster and crash back to the earth. Let's face it; you need spizzerinctum to survive in the ministry."

"How are you gonna fit that on a T-shirt?"

"Thurm, I'm serious. I've given this quite a bit of thought. As staff members of First Church, we face pressures and stresses that are unique to our profession. So unique that most of the membership of our church have no idea what we deal with day to day and week after week."

"You're right, but face it—that's what we signed on for. Doctors face the stresses of managing their patients' health. Police officers face the stresses of keeping the public safe. We face the stress of helping people spiritually as they do life and all that goes along with it. It's a noble profession."

"Oh, I agree wholeheartedly. I'm just saying it takes an extra portion of spiritual determination to be an effective minister and still have a balanced, whole life."

Thurm opened the front door of the CLC. "Spizzerinctum."

"Spizzerinctum indeed, my languid friend."

"Languid?"

"Look that one up later when I'm out of punching distance."

Johnny and Canasta's offices were located on the second floor, so we hit the stairwell door and made our way up. We deposited the boxes on a table in Canasta's office. She wasn't there.

"So, where is the little gadfly?"

"Elmo, would you be nice? She's probably out running some errands for Johnny. What's your problem with Canasta anyway?"

"I can't put my finger on it, but I just have a check in my spirit about her. I'm really not trying to be unkind. You just be careful. If there's truly a problem, it'll surface soon enough."

"Man, I have no idea what you're talking about. She's bright, very bright. She's energetic to the point of being gung-ho. She's conscientious and hardworking."

"You're probably right. I tend to be overly cautious sometimes. But from my perspective, the jury is still out on Miss Langanelli. Time will tell."

Thurm closed the office door as we stepped back out into the hall. "Did you know Father Ted bought a sailboat?"

"Yeah, he told me. Had to sell his Viper to pay for it."

"Did he tell you who bought the Viper?"

"No. Someone I know?"

"Yep."

"Someone here at First Church?"

"Yep."

"Someone on staff?"

"Yep."

"Oh, no! Not Harry?"

"Nope." Thurm laughed.

"Whew. For a minute there, I thought the Great Tribulation had just begun. Then who bought it?"

"Big Bird Stevens."

"You are *kidding* me! The man is a bean counter with a visor and wire-rimmed glasses. They don't drive Vipers."

"They do now."

"Whoa. Now wait a minute. Bob's a church administrator. How can he afford a Viper? It's not like he already owns a condo in the Caymans."

"Got me. That's not my business. Maybe he's a Donald Trump when it comes to his personal finances."

"Was that hyperbole intentional?"

"Hyper what?"

"Boy, I bet Harry's chewing nails." I chuckled. "Wednesday's staff meeting should be interesting."

"Yeah. By the way, what's the big staff meeting announcement gonna be? No one seems to have any clue about it."

"No idea. We'll just have to wait and see. I did hear that Raze Hankins resigned this morning. He's taking a position at some historic old-school Baptist church in Georgia."

"Really? Well, that's where he needs to be. I hope they get a good guy to take his place."

"From what I understand, they're not planning on replacing him, at least for now. Tom Applebee is going to take over his responsibilities with the Adult Sunday School classes. Evidently, that used to be part of Tom's job back in the day. Tom's very diplomatic, and he needs to get in there and repair some of the damage Raze did, particularly with the older classes. In my opinion, some major healing still needs to take place. There are still lingering wounds from the attempted coup."

"Sounds like a smart plan, and Tom's the right guy for the job."

"We'll see."

"Hey Elmo, before we head back over to the church office, wanna slip down to the basement and bowl a game or two? I brought my body armor."

"Oh, that's cold. Even by your standards."

6

The Campaign

On Wednesday, we awoke to a beautiful, clear morning with the birds chirping energetically outside our window. The day had finally arrived for the big announcement we'd all been hearing about.

Though Bonnie and I both worked at First Church, we drove separately each morning because I often had to stay later than she did. The secretaries were expected to be on time and at their desks when the day officially began. The different ministers tended to trickle in as the morning progressed. Was it fair? Probably not, but that's just how it was.

The first-floor conference room slowly filled with staff as Bonnie and I sat there chatting, waiting for the meeting to begin.

"Eddie Hughes dropped in to visit Louis this morning," Bonnie said as she opened her notepad.

"Really? How's Eddie doing? I haven't seen him in a while."

"Evidently, pretty well. Jimmy "Cornbread" Jackson has trained Eddie to be his front man. He sends Eddie into a town to rent a room and run some newspaper ads. Then Cornbread rolls in and makes his presentations. They've become quite the team."

I shivered. "The new Batman and Robin of multi-level marketing. I guess I'll need to up my Kryptonite dosages."

"Wrong superhero, dingo."

"Whatever. Just keep those flip chart cowboys and tripod hillbillies away from me. Even the thought of one of those meetings makes me break out in hives."

"Speaking of hives, Eddie showed me his new body art." Bonnie grinned.

"What?! Eddie got a tattoo?"

"He sure did. He said something about it adding 'street cred' to his appearance, and that the younger chicks dig 'street cred'."

"Younger chicks." I laughed. "That guy's a trip. No, make that a round trip to Lala Land and back."

Bonnie laughed. "Here's the kicker. He had the word *Excellence* tattooed on his forearm in a script font."

"So what's the big deal?"

"I didn't have the heart to tell him, and apparently no one else has either, that the tattoo artist left out the first 'c'."

"The tattoo is misspelled?!"

"Oh yes."

"That's more than a little ironic considering the word he chose. And Eddie doesn't realize it's misspelled?"

"Nope." She shook her head.

"That's rich, and sooo Eddie."

"It's really not a big issue though," Bonnie's said as her gift of sarcasm kicked in. "The caliber of chicks he's trying to impress won't even notice the misspelling."

We had to mute our laughter as Dr. Jorgensen entered the room, followed by some guy in a fancy suit with slicked-back hair.

Tom Applebee called the staff meeting to order. "We're going to change things up a little bit this morning and dispense with our normal routine. Fran will put a copy of the minutes from last week and the church activities calendar in your mailboxes. I'd now like to turn the meeting over to Dr. Jorgenson."

Dr. Jorgensen stood up—something I'd never seen him do in a staff meeting. "As everyone here knows, our church is in the beginning stages of a big transition. From now on we'll be planning our programs and strategizing our ministries with the next generation in mind. A major component of this effort will be the renovation of the First Church facilities. Most of our interior space has looked the same for the last fifty years. If we're going to be successful in our efforts to forge into the future, we must update our church plant.

"The deacons, in conjunction with our Building Committee, have been working tirelessly to formulate a plan for this renovation. I've seen some of the drawings and artist renderings, and I can tell you that you're going to like it when it's done. There'll be an extended period of inconvenience for everyone as we execute these changes, but in the end, it will be well worth it."

As Dr. Jorgensen continued waxing eloquently about the building renovation project, I studied the man with the slicked-back hair. *Who is this guy?* Expensive pinstripped suit with color-coordinated handkerchief and tie. Pat Riley hair cut. I guessed him to be in his mid-forties, but who knows? A little hair dye here, a little Botox there; he might even be in his mid-fifties.

I looked down at Bonnie's notepad. She'd written, "*Who's the suit with Horace?*"

I took her pad and wrote, "*I don't know - Brad Pitt maybe?*" I could feel her chair vibrate as she suppressed a laugh at my *Meet Joe Black* reference.

At the other end of the room, Dr. Jorgensen was about to drop a bomb.

"Now, to accomplish all of these grand plans, I'm going to need your help. We'll need to raise the necessary funds to make these renovations, and as you'll see, it's not going to be cheap. As of today, we're officially launching a capital fundraising program called *For the*

Future We Build. The First Church Building Committee has determined we'll need to raise ten to fifteen million dollars to complete the entire renovation package."

The conference room when into collective shock, as if the air had been sucked from the room instantaneously.

Now, your normal leader would've been caught off guard by such a visceral reaction, but Dr. Jorgensen wasn't your normal leader. He'd not only anticipated such a reaction he'd prepared for it. He calmly paused and allowed everyone to start breathing again. Then, with a pre-planned, Reagan-esque chuckle he wryly proclaimed, "Oh, it's a lot of money, but you know what? We serve a big God, and we work for a big church, and by golly, we're going to raise every necessary dime!"

He turned to the *slickster* in the pinstripped suit. "With that goal in mind, we've enlisted the help of the premiere fundraising company in the Northern Hemisphere. Let me introduce you to Mr. Lancaster Hicox. Mr. Hicox is the senior vice president for Church Capital Development at Johnson-Maynard-Stubbins LTD New York and London."

As Joe—I mean Brad—I mean *Lancaster*—began his presentation, with (you guessed it) a tripod and a flip chart, my mind quietly slipped away to a safer place. I'd have to get the details from Bonnie later.

Though raising money to build and renovate church buildings is part and parcel of every church, very few pastors relish the thought of having to do it. No one likes asking for cash. So somewhere back in the annals of the local church, the concept of bringing someone in from the outside to do the asking was conceived. Brilliant idea. This provides cover for the pastor, especially from that segment of the congregation that bristles every time money is mentioned from the pulpit.

The cold hard truth is that only a small percentage of any church membership roll is regular, consistent, substantive givers. These folks are commonly known as tithers. Most folks who attend church contribute, but often sporadically. There is also a sizeable group of members who give nothing. Nada.

But there's something about constructing a new building, or renovating a sanctuary, or buying new property, that puts people in a giving mood. Funding the day-to-day operations of a church, of which a substantial portion goes to salaries, often fails to motivate a large number of the membership to give. Whereas building a new two-story Family Life Center will have them enthusiastically asking their neighbors to chip in. *"You know, for the kids."*

Initially, outside fundraisers were former pastors with a gift for motivating congregations to participate in these special efforts. Over time, church fundraising—borrowing heavily from the secular business world—developed into a science with formulas and algorithms. Out went the preacher buddies who owed you a favor and in came the wonks, the motivational speakers, and the banker types.

Typically, when a fundraising program begins, the congregation is dissected and analyzed by income, giving records, special gifts, attendance, leadership capability, and even personality types. Based on this research, each individual or family unit is ranked and categorized by potential capital gift capability. Next, they are put into groups, which are prioritized from the highest potential givers to the lowest. A strategy is then developed to maximize the number of pledges from each group or category.

Okay, it's true. I have a smidgen of cynicism when it comes to this professional church fundraising stuff. In the greater scheme of things, these programs tend to be effective and help local churches successfully build buildings and launch ministries. But I can't help thinking that it diminishes the role of the main Player in the process which, in my novice opinion, is God. You know—the great Creator, Sustainer, Redeemer, and in light of this discussion, Motivator.

Ultimately, any misgivings aside, I am, in fact, a consummate team player. So I will dutifully take my packet, make my visits, twist a few arms (spiritually speaking), and help First Church meet the grand goal. I have to remind myself that, after all, it was my recommendations that started this whole transition into the future facilities upgrade business in the first place.

Just please don't ask me to use a tripod and a flip chart in my *For the Future We Build* home meetings. Even a devoted team player has his limits.

Back in my office, I set my *For the Future We Build* packet *waaay* over to the side of my desk. I then surveyed my tasks for the day— emails to answer, appointments to schedule, memos to read, etc.

To task or multi-task? That is the question. There is a raging debate these days concerning the most proficient way to utilize your time. Some so-called experts say you should pack each minute with as many tasks as you can simultaneously accomplish to maximize your production. Other know-it-alls suggest limiting your tasks to one at a time and focusing on the quality of your effort using all of your skills to maximize the outcome.

I say it's both. The approach should be determined by the task itself, factoring in the desired outcome.

I was pondering this concept on a recent Saturday morning as I prepared to make a pitcher of iced tea. It takes four minutes to heat up the water in the microwave and another four minutes to let the tea bags steep—a total of eight minutes. What to do with those eight minutes?

I could channel Charles Bronson and be Mr. Majestic leaning

against the kitchen counter, arms crossed all macho style, contemplating the world and my place it in while daydreaming of busting heads and taking names.

Or, I could be Mr. Domestic and use the eight minutes to multi-task by knocking out some household chores. In eight minutes, I could take out the trash, refill the soap dispenser, empty the dishwasher, and score big points toward a possible Bonnie Bonus Round later.

Conversely, when I'm having my prayer time, I need to focus on it alone—avoiding the temptation to check my email, send a text to a friend, or jot down a note for a later task.

Sometimes, doing several things at once can lead to the wrong outcome. For instance, you should *never* send out a sensitive or personal email while you're distracted. Like, *uh oh.* "Bonnie, I'm so sorry. I just accidentally forwarded the video of your colonoscopy to the entire church staff. Oops?"

Or never, ever carve the Thanksgiving turkey while watching TV. "Hey Bonnie, didn't I have ten fingers?"

And ladies please, *please* don't put on your eye makeup while driving down the interstate while talking on your cell to the co-worker you'll be sitting next to all day. Who, by the way, is also driving and putting on her makeup while she's driving and talking to you. *Yikes.*

But when done wisely, multi-tasking can help you be more efficient with your time.

Someone knocked on my door. "Anybody home?"

"Father Ted, come on in. How's my favorite sailor-man?"

He took a seat. "Things are good, though I haven't gotten around to taking out the new boat yet. But I will."

I moved to the love seat across from Father Ted. "I understand you sold your Viper to Bob 'Big Bird' Stevens. Word has it he was last seen somewhere near Corpus Christi crossing the board going 150 miles per hour."

Father Ted chuckled. "Well then, he needs to take his foot off the brake."

We both laughed.

"Anyway," he continued. "I wanted you to know I dropped in at Kranky's this morning for a cup off coffee and I looked for your friend Elijah."

"And?"

"There was no one in the last booth, but there was an old man in the next-to-last booth. So, I figured that might be him."

"Did you talk to him?"

"I sure did, but it wasn't Elijah. His name was Rufus McGee, and I'm guessing he was probably homeless."

"Was he drinking hot tea and reading a Bible?"

"No, he was drinking coffee and reading a newspaper. I'm not sure he was totally lucid."

"Why?"

"Well, he was holding the newspaper sideways as he read. When I asked why, he said he was ambidextrous—which he defined as having two left eyes. The conversation degenerated from there, so I won't bore you with the details."

"Two left eyes? Wow. Reminds me of that stupid dog show movie where the guy has two left feet and wears two left shoes."

Father Ted winced as he stood. "Sorry I missed that one."

"I really appreciate you giving it a go," I said, standing. "If you're at Kranky's again Eli *always* sits in the back booth, and he *always* drinks tea."

"Now that you mention it, hot tea sounds good. I think I'll go make myself a cup. I may even try reading sideways. Who knows, maybe I'll learn something new."

I laughed. "I'm not too familiar with this hot tea phenomenon. I've always been a coffee drinker, but everywhere I turn lately it seems people are drinking hot tea. Though, I do enjoy iced tea."

"Tea has been around forever," Father Ted added, grinning like a high school egghead. "But it was first grown in America in the late 1700s. Iced tea became popular with the onset of refrigeration."

"How do you know so much about tea?" I asked.

His grin grew into a smile. "I have a favorite niece named Lucy, who's an author. She writes stories centered around vintage tea cups. She's my source for all things tea."

And he was out the door.

The Big Apple

Bonnie lay quietly sleeping as I kissed her on the cheek and slipped out of the dark bedroom. I was headed to New York City for my overnight junket to see my publisher, Brown & Brewster. I planned to drive myself to the airport and leave my car there overnight so she wouldn't have to make two trips.

Unaccustomed to being up so early, I fumbled around the dimly-lit kitchen trying to procure a cup of coffee. Naturally, my coffeemaker failed me yet again, so I decided just to stop for a cup on the way to the airport. I had plenty of extra time built into my schedule.

The quickest route to the airport from our house went through downtown, so I decided to drop by Kranky's to placate my caffeine needs.

As I drove in the darkness on the nearly deserted streets, I sensed the anxiousness welling up inside. This whole publishing gig was way outside my comfort zone. I berated myself for agreeing so quickly to have my book published. I'd allowed the advance money and the recognition to cloud my better judgment. But there'd be no going back now. As Bonnie would succinctly say, it was time for me "to put on my big boy pants" and do what was required of me.

The sun hadn't risen yet, but Kranky's was already hopping. The city's early birds were up and buzzing. As I chatted with Buddy Skipbow, I was surprised to see Eli there in his booth. I waved as I grabbed my coffee then headed back to say hello.

"Morning, Eli."

"Morning, Elmo. What brings you in here so early?"

I took a seat on the other side of the booth. "I'm on my way to the airport and needed some coffee. I see you're still drinking tea as always."

"Yes, sir. Where you headed?"

"New York City."

"Really?"

"Yep. It's my first trip to the Big Apple. My publisher's flying me up there for a meet-and-greet with the editors and staff."

"You're an author? I'm impressed. Tell me about your book."

"My first assignment at First Church was to do research and

then write a report and some recommendations for the church. The goal of the project was to help the church better understand how to reach the next generation. It grew from there."

"Sounds interesting." A gentle smile warmed his face. "Must have turned out pretty good if it's being published."

"It was a lot of hard work, but Dr. Jorgensen was pleased, and the church is moving ahead with most of the recommendations. But—"

"But?"

"I enjoyed the research and the writing, but this publishing thing has thrown me a curve." I stared at my coffee. "I'm just not sure I have the requisite skill set to pull it off."

"So, it's a confidence issue?"

"Yeah." I paused. "I guess it is."

Eli patted his Bible and set aside his antique lace bookmark. "When I think of confidence problems, I'm always reminded of Gideon hiding in that old winepress. He was a young man not unlike you, Elmo. God had a job He needed Gideon to do, but Gideon wasn't sure he was up to it. God patiently reminded Gideon that He had given him the necessary skills. And God let Gideon know He had his back. Ultimately, a great victory was won.

"Elmo, it sounds like your research and your book may be needed by other churches. Go to New York City with the confidence of knowing that God has your back."

And right there in the rear booth at Kranky's, Eli prayed for me.

The terminal was congested and noisy as I cradled the phone against my shoulder.

"No Bonnie, I'm not sure why they routed me to the Long Island Airport. They're supposed to send a limo to pick me up and drive me over to Manhattan. There's an ethnic-looking guy, dark curly hair, mustache, holding a sign that reads 'Rev. Jennings'—I have a sneaking suspicion he's my ride. I'd better go. Love ya. Give Colby a hug for me. I'll call you tonight when I get to my room. Bye."

I approached the guy with the sign. He looked to be in his mid-thirties, leather jacket, tight slacks, cocky stance . . . as if he'd just stepped out of *Saturday Night Fever*.

"Excuse me. Are you with Brown & Brewster?"

He shook my hand. "Yeah, you musta be Reverend Jennings. You're a younga fella. I was expectin' someone who looked, y' know, kinda like the Pope or maybe a Cardinal or somethin'."

"Oh, I *am* the Pope; this is just my incognito traveling attire."

He laughed out loud. "A minista with a sense of humor. Who knew?"

"By the way, my name is *Jenkins*, not Jennings. And let's skip the 'reverend' bit. Just call me Elmo."

"Ahhh, just like the little red guy on TV! Dat's easy to rememba. Me, I'm Sergio. Y' know, like the golfer, or the spaghetti western guy."

"Okay, Sergio. Nice to meet you. Where to?"

"We're parked out front, close to the building in the handicapped spot." He covered his mouth with his hand and whispered. "I use my cousin Gino's handicapped sticka. Got his foot caught in a garbage disposal. It's a long story."

"Ouch!" I responded, following him out of the terminal with an oh-so-subtle, vicarious limp.

I'm not sure what I was thinking when I was told a "limo" would pick me up, but my definition was obviously too narrow. Sergio led me to a late-model emerald-green Chevrolet Impala—all but the right front fender, that is, which was white. I threw my carry-on in the back and hopped into the front passenger seat.

"You must be new at this?" he said as he pulled out into traffic.

"What do you mean?"

"You sittin' up here with the driver and all. Most of the stuffed shirts I pick up for this outfit sit in the back."

"Okay, you got me. This is my first trip to New York City. Do you work for Brown & Brewster?"

"Nah, I'm just an emergency backup. They own two or three of those fancy stretch limos with staff drivers. They only call me in a pinch when their cars are all tied up. You must be pretty low on the totem pole."

"I'm not even *on* the totem pole. Heck, I haven't even *seen* the totem pole."

"Y' know, Elmo, you're a pretty funny guy. A real smart-alex."

"You mean smart-aleck?"

"Yeah, as I said—a real smart-alex. I like dat. Are you like some sorta' religious comedian or somethin'?"

"No. I'm just a lowly assistant at a big church who did some research and wrote a report. The folks at B&B got a hold of my report and decided it might make a good book and voila—here I am riding with you."

"Well, how 'bout dat. They told me to show you around on the way in. You in a hurry?"

"Nope, I'm on your clock."

"Then shazam! I'm gonna give you the jumbo tour of the Big Apples sites." He leaned toward me and lowered his voice, speaking out of the side of his mouth. "You see, d'ey pay me *per mile*." He threw his head back laughing. "Let's start with Yankee Stadium—the house dat Ruth built. Dat is 'til they tore the ol' sucka down."

And off we went.

Several hours later, Sergio dumped me off on the curb at Brown & Brewster—literally. He barely stopped the car long enough for me to get out with my bag. I tossed a twenty-dollar bill in the passenger window for a tip as he sped off.

We'd driven by so many places I'd lost count, but mostly what I saw was traffic and kamikaze cab drivers. *How do these people live this way?*

After watching Sergio's faux-limo disappear around the corner, with black smoke pouring out of the tailpipe, I pivoted around and looked up. Over the entry etched in gigantic gold letters was the name Brown & Brewster. I estimated the building to be around forty stories tall with an art-deco motif.

I stepped through one of the turnstiles into a huge marble lobby three stories high. There were small stores around the perimeter of the lobby that sold gifts, coffee, or cookies, and of course a large B&B bookstore.

I asked the Asian lady behind the general information desk where to find the B&B offices. She pointed toward the express elevator in the far corner of the lobby next to the bookstore. I thanked her and headed in that direction. I stepped inside and rode alone. The elevator's rapid ascent made my stomach queasy reminding me of my roller coaster rides as a child—fond memories of family and ecstatic fun.

At the thirty-seventh floor, the elevator doors opened, and I walked out into the Brown & Brewster waiting area. In sharp contrast to the building's airy first-floor lobby, this room had a low ceiling and dim indirect lighting. The walls were paneled in polished oak with inserts of elegantly framed fabric. With its plush carpet, expensive couches and wingback chairs, the ambience was that of a private library in a wealthy man's home.

The receptionist sat behind a polished oak counter facing the elevator doors. Her name plate read *Chrlzv*. I had no idea how to pronounce it. She spoke with a heavy European accent, and she was gorgeous. Back home, Juliann was beautiful, but compared to Chrlzv, Juliann looked like one of Cinderella's stepsisters. This beauty had to be a model when she wasn't working at B&B. She took my name and told me to take a seat, which I did. I didn't wait long.

"Ellington?"

"Yes?" I looked up from my magazine.

"Hi, I'm Castor McMullan. We spoke on the phone. Welcome to New York. I hope your travel went well."

When I stood, I realized Castor was at most five feet tall on a good day. "The flight was great, the ride in from the airport was . . . interesting." I laughed as I shook his hand.

"Sorry about that. It seems all of our regular limos are in the shop for some type of emissions leak recall." A wry grin stretched across his face. "You appear to have made it here with all of your extremities still intact."

"Nah, the ride wasn't bad, and Sergio gave me the two-dollar tour on the way in. But I see what you mean about the cabbies. It's kill-or-be-killed out there."

"Sergio drove you in? Really? I thought he was still in prison."

"What?"

He slapped me on the back. "I'm just kidding. Come on back and let me introduce you to some people."

Exhausted, I relaxed in the B&B boardroom sipping cappuccino and waiting for Castor to take me to my room for the night. I'd just survived four hours of meetings with very energetic people who all talked fast and often at the same time. The onslaught overwhelmed my poor *red state* mind.

I was dumbfounded by the realization that the hectic, intense, Red Bull pace I'd just witnessed was the normal daily B&B experience. Forget about the rat race. These people worked like cheetahs on steroids. Their employee turnover rate had to be catastrophic.

Hmm. Perhaps they weren't people at all, but androids covered with life like human skin and hair. *Publishing terminators.* I shivered at the creepy thought.

It had been a long day, and apparently I was a little punchy. I poured another cup of coffee then closed my eyes and daydreamed of still waters and cool breezes.

"Ellington?"

Stirred from my musings, I almost dropkicked my cappuccino. "Yes?"

"Sorry, didn't mean to startle you," Castor said with a smile. "We're done here so grab your gear, and I'll take you up to your room."

I followed him to a staff elevator just beyond the boardroom entrance.

He opened the elevator with a key. "You've lucked out. Several of the regular rooms are being re-carpeted so you'll be staying in the Executive Suite."

"Sounds fancy."

"Oh, it is." He pushed the button for the top floor. "This is where all the company bigwigs stay when they're in town. A lot of celebs and politicians have slept in the suite as well. Meaning, I wouldn't carve your initials in the cherry paneling if I were you."

"Don't worry. I won't touch a thing. As long as it has a bed, I'm good." I yawned. "I'm exhausted. You guys wore me out today."

"I believe your meetings went well. I really like the title they came up with for your book—*Change is Good*. Has a bit of a Michael Douglas Academy Award vibe to it."

"It's growing on me, but I'm not so sure about all the merchandise stuff. Why do we need book accessories like bracelets, and badges, and T-shirts and such?"

"That's just how it works in publishing these days. B&B loses money on the front end due to production costs and promotion. But they make it all back and more on the back end with merch sales, foreign translations, audio books, etc."

The elevator door opened quietly, and we stepped out onto the roof. A glass-covered walkway led to a cul-de-sac of room doors. The view from the roof was breathtaking. Manhattan at dusk from forty floors up in all directions. Absolutely stunning. I couldn't help myself—I gawked.

Castor gently elbowed me. "Pretty cool, uh?"

"Oh, yeah. Wow."

He opened one of the doors. "Wait 'til you see inside."

I stepped in and surveyed the room. It wasn't super large, but oh my . . . floor-to-ceiling windows on two sides, beautiful cherry paneling on the other walls adorned with numerous original paintings. Several large skylights in the ceiling, and a round king-size bed. Yes, that's right—a *round* king-size bed.

And oh, what a view.

Castor handed me the key. "This works on both the room door and the elevator in case you decide to go out. You'll find several menus on the table there from some of the finest restaurants in New York. We have a special arrangement with them for room service to our suites. Simply call the number listed on the card with the menus. I highly recommend Corton. Try the wild striped bass. *Magnifico*."

"Castor, I have a pretty plebeian palate. There wouldn't happen to be burger joint close by, would there?"

He laughed as he turned to leave. "Take the main elevator down to the fourth floor. There's a T.G.I. Fridays. I'll let them know to expect you."

After a shower and a steak burger and fries, I fell back on the king-size bed and called Bonnie.

"Hey, beautiful."

"You remembered to call. I had my doubts."

"Are you kidding? I miss you *terribly*. This place is a madhouse. I'd much rather be there with you and the dawg."

"I miss you too, sweetheart. Tell me about your day."

"Let me start off with where I am right this moment. You would love this. As a matter of fact, if they bring me back, you're coming with me."

"Oh, really?"

"Yes, really. You won't believe this place. Due to some room renovations, they put me up in the B&B Executive Suite. As we speak, I'm lying on a *round* king-size bed looking out on the New York City skyline from forty stories high. It feels as if I could just reach out and touch the Chrysler Building or the Empire State Building."

"Wow, Elmo. That's too cool."

"And get this. There's a guestbook. Are you sitting down? Here are some of the folks who've stayed here and signed the book. Henry Kissinger, Colin Powell, Tony Dungy, Michael Jordan, Elizabeth Dole, Chuck Colson, George Lucas, and wait for it . . . George Clooney. The list goes on and on."

"Oh my, I sure hope they changed the sheets," Bonnie said laughing.

"Now, Bonnie."

"Just kidding. So? Are you going to sign the book?"

"Nope. I thought about it, but God put a check in my spirit. I've already been fighting the pride and ego battle all day. And I'm sorry to say I lost that challenge a few times. I'll be spending some time tonight on my knees tying to regain my perspective on this whole publishing thing. It's God's church, and it's God's book. I'm just privileged to play a small role in the whole process."

"I'm thrilled to hear you say that. I totally agree. When you get back, let's spend some time praying together about it. Okay?"

"Okay."

"Reverend Jennings? Over here."

"Sergio! Good morning. Somehow I just knew we'd meet again. I guess I'm still hugging the bottom of that totem pole."

"I'd get ya bag for ya, but I've hurt my back. Do ya mind?"

"Not at all. I have the strangest feeling you're taking me all the way back out to the Long Island Airport. Am I right?"

"A comedian and a mind reada. Who knew? Here's your plane ticket."

"How're we doing on time?"

"We're ahead'a schedule, so we'll be takin' the long route," he said with a wink.

"I know, I know. 'D'er payin' ya per mile'."

And off we went leaving several poor pedestrians in a cloud of black smoke.

8

The Microwave Syndrome

"**I** spent twenty minutes trying to calm Juliann down this afternoon," Bonnie said as she placed the soy burger on my whole wheat bun. "Sprouts?"

"Why not?" I forced a smile. "Am I allowed to use condiments? And did you say this is goat cheese?"

"Free-range goat cheese, to be exact."

"Something tells me that *free-range* means it actually cost a whole lot more. What's wrong with Juliann?"

"She had another run-in with Canasta."

I relocated most of the sprouts off my burger to a remote safe place on my plate. "Is there a problem between those two?"

Bonnie took a swig of her carrot juice. "Canasta talks down to Juliann, and it's really starting to get on her nerves."

"Really? I'll be the first to admit that Juliann's not the sharpest knife in the drawer, but she doesn't have a mean bone in her body. I've never seen her mad at anybody."

"Well, she was spitting fire this afternoon. She even used some rough language—leftover from her pre-Christian days, I'm guessing."

"Wow. What's Canasta said to her?"

"It's not what she's said, it's *how* she's saying it. Extremely patronizing. I worry that Juliann's going to go all postal and slap her one of these days, then lose her job."

"Hmm. That could well be Canasta's plan."

"Plan? What do you mean?"

"I'm not sure. I've had my suspicions about Canasta from the beginning. There's just something about her that's put my *suspectors* on high alert."

"Wait a minute. 'Suspectors' isn't a real word."

"Oh yes, ma'am. It's plural for *suspector.*"

"What's a suspector?"

"Someone who suspects."

"Elmo, have you been studying that stupid Scrabble dictionary again?"

"Yes, ma'am. You know I have a standing challenge with Debbie Craven for a one-on-one, mano-a-mano, scrabble match to the death. If she ever *mans-up* and agrees to play me I want to be ready."

"You need to let that one go, big guy. You know she doesn't do battle with friends. And even if she did, she's the stinkin' State Scrabble Champion. She'd carve you up like an Easter ham."

"Yeah yeah, right. Anyway, where were we? Oh. Canasta. Just keep an eye on her. Who knows, she may be angling for total office dominion."

Bonnie smirked. "Let's just keep that theory between us *suspectors* for now. Okay?"

"Okay, but—"

"No buts. Now, would you like a carob cookie for dessert?"

Oh, boy.

The next morning, I found Thurm up on the rooftop recreation area of the First Church Education Building. He was cleaning up after the previous night's middle school activity."

"Wow, looks like a bomb went off up here."

He laughed as he picked up more trash. "Just a day in the life of a typical youth pastor. What brings you up here?"

"I need you to tell Canasta to take it easy on Juliann."

He set the trash bag down. "What do you mean?"

"Bonnie told me Canasta's been treating Juliann pretty badly, talking down to her. Juliann is really upset by it all."

"Seriously?"

"I'm afraid so. And I hate to tell you this, but some of the other office ladies have been complaining about Canasta also."

"Really? What kind of stuff?"

"Maybe she's just inexperienced in working on a large, long-established support staff. She's obviously Type A, and used to being in charge. Just sit her down and tell her she needs to earn the ladies' respect instead of ordering them around."

"Okay, I'll see what I can do."

"You might want to include Johnny in your meeting with her."

"Good advice. I'll do just that."

"Enough dark matter for one morning. Can I help you clean up?"

"That'd be great. Grab an empty trash bag over there on the picnic table."

I shook open a plastic bag and started picking up empty juice boxes and candy wrappers. "How's the Wonder Fork treating you these days?"

Thurm frowned. "I sent the stupid thing back to the moron farm and got my money back."

I laughed. "Yeah, that idea seemed a little far-fetched to me. What's your new plan?"

"I think I'm gonna try the Costco cardio program."

"Huh? That's a joke, right?"

"Nope, it's a real weight-loss plan. There's an interactive website and everything."

"All right then, how does it work?"

"First you have to be a Costco member."

"Makes sense."

"Then, you know how gigantic those Costco stores are?"

"Yeah, so?"

"You take your grocery list, which includes all the items from the recommended eating plan—and all available at Costco."

"Of course."

"Then you get your grocery cart and start walking briskly around the inside perimeter of the store."

"Briskly?"

"Yes, briskly. After each lap around the store, you are allowed to add one item from the list to your basket. When your list is complete and your grocery basket is full, you're done. If you've followed the plan correctly you will have walked two full miles."

"Briskly?"

"Briskly."

"Okay, but how do you lose the weight?"

"Well, along with the walking you have to eat a healthy 2000 calorie per day diet. Plus drink six eight-ounce glasses of water daily."

I chuckled. "Don't forget the exercise you'll get walking *briskly* back and forth to the men's room all day."

"Funny."

"Thurm, have you ever noticed that no matter what the weight-loss program is, albeit pills, supplements, liquid shakes, group support, exercise contraptions, or routines—they all include the proviso, 'With this program you are guaranteed to lose weight if done along with a healthy low-calorie diet'."

"Well, yeah."

"Why not just skip all the extracurricular falderal, cut to the chase, and just eat a healthy low-calorie diet?"

"Too boring, I guess. The same reason most folks don't eat plain vanilla ice cream."

"Hmm. Interesting that you used a food analogy. Anyway, let's wrap up this trash detail."

"Briskly?"

"Briskly."

Ducking into the break room to get my mail, I was surprised to find Harry Simpkins there.

"Hey, Elmo."

"Harry, what brings you over to the lowly first floor of the Education Building?"

"One word—coffee. The music suite's coffeemaker is on the fritz again. But can I get that tightwad Bob Stevens to replace it? Noooooooooo!" He tapped his foot anxiously while waiting for the coffeemaker to finish brewing.

I decided to needle him a bit. "Maybe you could bribe Bob with a gift or something, to 'grease the skids' toward getting a new coffeemaker. Perhaps some racing gloves for his new car."

Harry grunted. "Yeah, I heard about that, and I don't want to talk about it." He slapped the side of the coffeemaker. "Come on, come on, COME ON!"

Juliann entered the break room and headed for the fridge. "Everybody all right in here?"

I smiled at her. "Yes, ma'am. Harry's just stealing some of our coffee."

"That's if the dang thing will ever fill the dang pot!" Harry slapped it again.

"It takes two minutes and thirty-four seconds to fill a pot," chirped the ever-chipper Juliann. "I timed it."

"Finally." Harry grabbed the coffeepot and lit out of the room in a flurry of muffled complaining.

Juliann turned to me. "What was that all about?"

"I call it the *Microwave Syndrome.*"

"Elmo, I have absolutely no idea what that means."

"Juliann, think of it in these terms. Say you live five miles from the grocery store. When you need food, you hop in your car, and fifteen minutes later you're buying groceries. One day on your way to the grocery store you get stopped by a train. You're delayed five additional minutes. The whole time you're waiting for the train to pass, you're irritated by the delay. You forget the fact that before cars were invented, a five-mile trip to the store could take a whole day.

"Or how about the student who's working on a research paper for a class assignment. Because of a slow internet connection, it takes him thirty more minutes to look up and download the necessary information for his paper. He's peeved by the delay. He's forgotten that before the Internet, he would've had to motor over to the library, look up books in an archaic card file system, find the books in the library stacks, then search through the books for his information. A process that could take hours.

"But the quintessential example of this phenomenon is the microwave. Whereas in the past it might take twenty to thirty minutes to cook or heat food in a conventional oven, the same outcome can be derived with a microwave oven in less than two minutes. Yet we stand at the microwave tapping our toe impatiently waiting for those two minutes to conclude, frustrated by how long it's taking.

"Which is why I say today's world suffers from a serious case of the Microwave Syndrome."

I noticed Juliann's eyes were totally glazed over.

"Oh . . . okay." She smiled as she reached into the fridge, got her boxed drink, and headed back to her desk.

Note to self: Limit details when talking with Juliann and focus on more concrete topics like the weather and fashion.

9

The Bluebird

"**E**lmo, quick! Hurry or you're gonna miss him!"

"What, what are you taking about?"

"The bluebird!" Bonnie's voice overflowed with excitement.

"The blue what?"

"The bluebird I was telling you about—he's back. Look right there on that tree limb by the light post."

"What's so special about a Blue Jay?"

"Not a Blue Jay—a bluebird."

"Bluebird, Blue Jay. What's the difference? It's just a dumb bird."

"I've never seen one with such brilliant blue feathers. I bet he's set up shop in the old birdhouse out back. He's probably on the prowl for a lady friend. Let's name him."

"Well, if he's looking for love, I suggest we call him Don Juan."

"No, no. Look at him. He's *so* soft and kind and beautiful. Let's name him Francis after Saint Francis of Assisi."

"Fine with me. Frank, it is. Now can I get back to my TV show?"

"Sure. I'll let you know if a momma bird shows up."

"Great," I said, smirking all the way back to the sofa.

An hour later Frank was back.

"Bonnie, something keeps hitting the front door. Do you mind checking?"

"Hey, it's Francis," she said. "I guess he just wanted to say hi."

I hopped up to take a look. "Oh, man. Bonnie, look! He's pooped all over our porch railing. He's even gotten it on our front door!"

"He must be seeing his reflection in the glass and thinks it's another bird. Bluebirds can be very territorial. He's just trying to chase the other bird away."

"Okay, that's good and fine. But that still doesn't excuse him for pooping all over everything. Sheesh."

"Elmo, you better hose that off before it dries."

I stepped outside to rinse away the bird dookie and Frank was on me like a duck on a June bug. I immediately morphed into Tippi Hedren screaming with my hands over my head and face. I dove back into the house. "Soft and kind and beautiful, eh? I think we have a problem."

I hit the Internet and did a little research. I discovered that during mating season, the male birds get an extra dose of testosterone. This tends to make them more aggressive as they try to protect their nest and their offspring. As part of this jacked-up frame of mind, the bird will often attack windows or mirrors; anything that reflects back his image.

We soon surmised that due to some freak act of nature, Frank had surely received two or three times the normal dose of testosterone. He wasn't concerned with his image in the window. Noooo . . . he wanted to run us off the property! Forget the old birdhouse in the backyard. He wanted our house!

The bird was uncanny. Look out any window and there was Frank—taunting you, daring you to come outside. He would tap dance all over our skylights, giving us the evil eye the entire time, and leaving behind numerous bird droppings. And oh, the unspeakable things he did to our poor defenseless cars.

I downloaded an article that suggested hanging a cardboard cut-out of a black crow. The theory was that the smaller bird would see the cut-out, think it was a predator, and consequently leave your house alone. Since I was fresh out of black crow cardboard cut-outs, I decided to make one. A little cutting, a little coloring, a little electrical taping, and an hour later I had a piece of cardboard that slightly resembled the silhouette of a black bird. That is if you were looking at it from fifty yards away at dusk with serious cataracts. Bonnie gave me a lukewarm thumbs-up, so I decided to give it a try.

I sent Bonnie to the back door to create a diversion. Wearing my swim goggles over my eyes and a black hoodie over my head, I darted out to the front porch. Like Jack Flash, I hung the faux black crow from a string and jumped back into the safety of our house. Bonnie's diversion had worked; after a quick eye and finger count, I appeared to be unscathed.

The black crow cut-out gently twisted in the wind. An hour went by with no Frank sightings. No banging on the front door. No tap dancing on the skylights.

We had solved the problem!

Or had we?

I decided to check the front porch one more time. Lo and behold, Frank was sitting on the porch rail calmly watching the black crow cut-out spinning in the wind. And yes, St. Francis left numerous calling cards all over the porch.

When the sun rose the next morning, we got a good look at the full extent of the damage. There was bird dookie all over the front porch, both cars, both skylights, and even on the black crow cut-out. How could one bird poop so much? Perhaps Frank had the bird flu. Bonnie didn't see the humor in my theory.

As the morning went along, we soon realized Frank was no longer looking in our windows. I waited another hour, then bravely went outside fully prepared to be ambushed by the sadistic bluebird, but nothing. I reconnoitered the outside perimeter of the house, but Frank was nowhere to be found. I checked the old birdhouse in the back, but it was vacant. Maybe Frank had indeed found his lady love, and she refused to live in that dump of a birdhouse. All I found were two brilliant blue feathers left on our back stoop. Had Frank left them there as a token souvenir from our epic battle the previous day? Or perhaps it was a victor's final taunt aimed mercilessly at a vanquished opponent.

There was one final possibility which I chose not to share with Bonnie. Just maybe the large tomcat sunning himself at the base of the birdhouse pole held a clue.

10

The Tabouli

As the secretaries and managers left the conference room to return to their desks, I snatched a muffin and refilled my coffee cup. I'd noticed an odd tension in the room during the opening portion of our staff meeting, and it lingered as we began the executive staff session.

Mentally, I worked my way around the table trying to discern where the problem lay. Bob "Big Bird" Stevens seemed to be his normal nervous self. As the smallest man in the room, Bob always looked apprehensive, like he was just waiting for someone to kick his tail.

Harry Simpkins appeared distracted, his mind obviously elsewhere. Doodling furiously on his notepad, he would occasionally pause to look up as if searching for that one missing, elusive detail.

Louis Estrada looked alert and attentive, but his wife Jane E. must be out of town. He had trimmed one of his sideburns significantly shorter than the other. Jane E. would never have let that walk out of the house.

As usual, Father Ted seemed happy just to be alive as he sat there with a smile on his face. I figured he was probably fighting the urge to daydream of sailing on a placid lake.

Dr. Jorgensen, as his usual stoic self, had that classic look that says, *Let's get on with this because I've better things to do.* Nothing new there.

Of the regular attendees, that left—*uh oh*—Tom Applebee. Tom was always steady, but on this day, I detected a hint of agitation simmering just below the surface of his demeanor.

When Tom circulated the agenda for the meeting, the fermenting issue quickly became apparent. The second agenda item listed right after the church picnic—Canasta Langanelli.

Gulp.

Tom cleared his throat. "I've invited Johnny Rochelle to join us today since he heads up the annual church picnic. Johnny, why don't you take a few moments and bring us up to speed on this year's picnic?"

As Johnny launched into his spiel about the annual event, I made a conscious decision not to let the impending dust-up concern me. Instead, I let my mind drift back to a conversation I'd had with

Thurm over a year ago concerning Johnny. It seems Johnny Rochelle had been destined to be an all-star major league baseball player almost from birth. His father, Lefty Rochelle, was a major league Hall-of-Famer. His mother had been a collegiate All American softball player.

Johnny's baseball skills were evident early on as he starred on every youth team he played on, all the way up through high school. He was a first-round draft pick coming out of college, and played infield on a handful of minor league teams. Then, inexplicably his baseball career stalled. When he finally realized he'd never play a game in the majors, he walked away from baseball. He vanished into a world of depression, narcotics, and malaise.

A few years later, he met an angel named Sari. Sari saw something in Johnny no one else did. She developed a deep love for him, and saw him through recovery and ultimately restoration.

Growing up in the church as a pastor's daughter, Sari had a strong faith in God. She slowly, gently led Johnny to the Lord. He was a changed man. After Sari's father mentored him for a year or two, Johnny felt called to the ministry. Several years at seminary and several churches later, Johnny found his way to First Church.

Tom thanked Johnny for his presentation and excused him. Then the tabouli hit the fan. Tom's face reddened as he rose slowly. I'd never seen this side of him before, and I wasn't sure how to react.

He spoke in curt, measured phrases. "It's been brought to my attention . . . that there has been an unkind, back channel of criticism . . . circulating around the church offices . . . concerning our newest employee, Canasta Langanelli. . . . This type of destructive . . . rumor-mongering will not be tolerated here at First Church. . . . Anyone caught participating in this unsavory activity . . . will be disciplined or terminated."

What?!

I didn't believe my ears. I looked around the table. Most of the guys had their heads down avoiding eye contact with anyone. What had Canasta told Tom? And why was he acting so out of character?

I started to say something, but Louis caught my eye, and with a quick shake of his head signaled me to keep quiet. I bit my tongue. Dr. Jorgenson remained totally disengaged. He'd always left support staff problems entirely in Tom's hands—carte blanche.

Something was fishy. Apparently I'd have to find out via the aforementioned *forbidden* back channel.

Tom continued. "I will be meeting with the entire support staff this afternoon to decisively bring this distracting issue to a quick conclusion. Please reinforce with your secretaries and assistants the seriousness of this matter. I'm also requesting that each of you set a personal example by avoiding this type of activity."

The rest of the meeting sailed right by me. Cancer had attacked First Church, and evidently I was the only doctor in the room who recognized it in the x-rays. I had no idea what type of cancer it was, where it was hiding, or how to eradicate it. I just knew it had a name.

Canasta Langanelli.

After staff meeting, Bonnie and I grabbed our favorite bench on the downtown mall. It was a beautiful, breezy day for Hot dog Wednesday.

I handed her a mustard packet. "Let's go slow and easy with the condiment application today, okay?" I'd worn black slacks as an added precaution.

She frowned. "What's a girl have to do to get total absolution for making one single mistake?"

"I was just kidding . . . kind of."

I lowered my voice. "Speaking of absolution, what's the deal with this Canasta stuff?"

Bonnie nervously glanced around us. "I suggest we save that conversation for when we get home tonight. I just don't think it's wise to talk about it in public."

"Wow. This whole thing is taking on a kind of *cold war* aura."

"For sure. Let's change subjects. Did you talk to Eli this morning?"

"Sure did. You won't believe it, but he's got me drinking hot tea instead of coffee when I'm there. It's not bad, though the caffeine kick is nowhere near as strong."

"What's the deal with the old boy?" Bonnie took a bite of her hot dog.

"It's strange. I really don't know that much about him, but I feel as if we've become pretty good friends. Kind of a mentoring thing."

"What do you talk about?"

"I don't know, mostly stuff about the church. Things I'm struggling with. He asks about you on occasion. We talk a lot about the Bible. The man knows his Bible. I've started taking mine with me so I can follow along and take notes as he shares. And he always prays for me before I leave."

"That's really cool, Elmo."

"Yeah, it is. I'll take you to Kranky's sometime to meet him."

"I'd like that."

Back in my office, I looked over my list of *For the Future We Build* obligations for the fundraising campaign. I'd been assigned ten different home meetings over the next four-week period. I was also scheduled to speak to the Men's Brotherhood, the Young Women's Weekly Bible Study, and our senior adult group, the Golden Saints.

Gird your loins, Elmo. You can do this.

I kept reminding myself that the fundraising was necessary to achieve the goal of a church moving successfully into the future.

What would Eli say? I could almost hear him. *God doesn't want people's money; He wants their hearts. Unfortunately, too often their hearts and their money are intrinsically intertwined.*

For some reason, that reminded me of Whoopi Goldberg's scene in *Sister Act* raising money by singing "Get Up Offa That Thing." I started boogieing around my desk singing like Whoopi. *Get up offa that dime*—a little slide to the right—*Get up offa that dime*—a twirl. *Get up offa*—

I looked up to see Father Ted peeking through my cracked doorway. I abruptly ended my song and dance routine and started straightening up my desk.

He sported an oversized grin. "Keep your day job."

"Sorry. You caught me working on my *For the Future We Build* presentation." I could feel my face heating.

He came in and sat down. "From one friend to another, I think you might want to consider a different approach. Something that's a little more, how do you say—*subtle*."

"What? Oh, no. No, I didn't mean I was going to sing at the . . . oh, never mind. What can I do for you today, Father Ted?" I sat down at my desk.

He leaned forward. "I'd like you to attend a small group I'm leading. It's for young men who've been married less than two years. I'm hoping to have six or seven young guys participate."

"Sure. When and where?"

"We'll be meeting at my house on Tuesday evenings for four sessions."

"What will we be doing?"

"Mostly discussion and feedback, dealing with the challenges of being a young married man. I'm thinking about writing a book on the topic, and our group discussions will help identify the different areas of need."

"Count me in. You do know most guys are pretty tight-lipped when it comes to the personal relationship stuff? Maybe you ought to meet with the wives instead. I'm sure you'd get *volumes* of material from them for your book."

He laughed. "Something tells me most young married men would prefer not to have their wives getting together as a group to discuss their shortcomings."

"Yikes. You're right. Forget I mentioned it."

11

The Bacteria

"Corn Hole? What the heck is Corn Hole?"

Johnny frowned, exasperated. "Come on, Elmo. What, were you born under a rock? It's a picnic game played with small fabric bags filled with dried corn kernels. Similar to beanbags."

"Why not just use beanbags and called it Bean Hole?"

He laughed. "Think about it. Would *you* want to play a game called Bean Hole?"

"You're probably right, but Corn Hole's not much better. What are the rules?"

"It's similar to horse shoes. There are two boxed platforms with holes cut in the top. The platforms are placed about thirty feet apart. You and your opponent take turns trying to throw your cornbags into the holes. You get points for landing on the box near the holes and more points for actually going in the holes. It's easy to pick up. You'll see."

"Why me?"

"We have a Corn Hole tournament every year at the annual church picnic, and I need thirty-two players to fill up the bracket. I'm a few short, so I'm penciling you in. Your first match with be against Jimmy Jackson."

"Jimmy 'Cornbread' Jackson?"

"Yes. Is that a problem?"

"Only that he was a professional athlete. Duh? I might as well just forfeit."

Johnny grinned. "You're right. Cornbread was a professional football kicker. But you're forgetting the one time he tried to throw; he was so bad he got cut from the team."

I chuckled. "True."

"Elmo, you'll do fine. Corn Hole is the great equalizer. Last year, Ramona Holloway won the Corn Hole Tournament."

"For some reason, that doesn't shock me. I can just see her staring down her opponent with those scary eyes." I shivered. "It gives me the bejeebers just thinking about it."

He laughed again. "You know, you're a total spaz."

"Funny, that's what Bonnie tells me. Listen, what's going on with Canasta? I thought Tom Applebee was going to pop a blood vessel in his neck yesterday at staff meeting."

"I have no idea. To be honest, I'm out of the loop. She's doing fine when she's over here at the Christian Life Center. Something must be going on when she's in the main office. Thurm and I had a talk with her the other day about going easy on Juliann, and she seemed to take it well. So I'm not sure what the problem is. Evidently, she's been going directly to Tom with any issues she's having. She hasn't mentioned anything to me."

"Weird. I'm just hoping that whole thing doesn't blow up. We're still trying to recover from the Sturgis Weaver revolt."

"I wouldn't worry too much about it. Whatever the problem is, I'm sure Tom can handle it."

"Here's hoping."

Every church has a guy like Art Menthor. Somewhere between sixty and eighty years old, though no one knows for sure. He's been around forever it seems, though no one knows when he first showed up. He's married, but no one has ever seen or talked with his wife. As far as anyone knows he doesn't work, but he doesn't seem to want for money. He's there every time the doors are open and willing to do anything asked of him, no matter how menial or dirty the task.

And one more thing. He audibly talks with God. All the time.

I took a shortcut through the sanctuary and found Art with his tool box.

"Hey, Art. What're you up to?"

"Hi, Elmo," he said in his signature graveled voice. "Sunday I noticed a bunch of the pews are loose and wobbly, so I decided to tighten them up."

"Great. But I wouldn't spend too much time and energy since they're getting ready to renovate this place soon. From what I understand, they're replacing the pews with padded chairs."

"I know, and it's a huge mistake."

"Really?"

"God doesn't look kindly on folks messing with His house."

"What do you mean?"

"They should leave this place alone and use the money to help the poor."

"Oh, I see. Well, the good news is that part of the renovation project includes upgrading both the feeding center and the thrift store."

"That's all well and fine, but mark my words—God is not pleased. They'll know when their ears tingle!"

"O-k-a-y."

I left Art to his pew fixing.

Thankfully, I felt no tingling in my ears.

Later that evening, I was home playing faux-fetch with Colby. A game all dog owners play where you pretend you're throwing the dog's favorite toy for them to chase and fetch, but you're just faking them out. The dog then spends the next few minutes futilely searching for the toy you didn't actually throw. Surprisingly, Colby fell for the ruse one time, but only once. She would later pay me back for this humiliating trick by hiding my car keys. Again.

I stretched out on the couch. "What's the deal with Art Menthor?"

Bonnie was loading the dishwasher. "What do you mean?"

"Today he intimated that God was not pleased with our renovation project, and that we would all know 'when our ears tingled'."

"Art's funny like that. I think he fashions himself to be like an Old Testament prophet. That ear-tingling bravado is very Jeremiah-esque."

As I lay there relaxing, I envisioned Art dressed in Old Testament garb, clenched fists held high, calling down God's curses and prophesying. For a split second, I thought my ears tingled. *Whoa . . .*

Bonnie hollered from the kitchen. "Hey, would you like some yogurt?"

"No thanks. I don't eat dead milk."

"Wimp," she teased, joining me with her bowl of the wiggly stuff. "Actually, it would be more accurate to say that yogurt is *live* milk. It's swimming in bacteria."

"An even better reason to keep it far away from my mouth. Yuck. I thought we were supposed to be eating healthy? How can chugging bacteria be healthy?"

"There are good bacteria and bad bacteria, and yogurt has the good ones."

"Well, there's also good chocolate and bad chocolate. Scratch that—there's only good chocolate. Yet we don't have any good chocolate stocked here in our wholefood haven."

"Funny you should mention that. I read an article just yesterday in *Health Zone* about the healthy benefits of dark chocolate. Seems dark chocolate is teeming with flavonoids."

"Bacteria, flavonoids, whatever. Can't we just please eat some food with no creatures embedded? Dang. It's like ingesting one of Erlene's pies."

"You're missing the point. A flavonoid is an antioxidant which means it can lower your blood pressure and help protect against heart disease. Which means you can have some chocolate. Which brings me to tonight's surprise. I picked up some dark chocolate Dove Promises at the store."

"Seriously? Where are they?" I felt an adrenaline rush.

"Easy boy. Chocolate is still very, very high in fat, so you can only have one after each meal."

Yeah, right. "Where's the bag?"

She snickered. "Oh, the bag is in a secure place. Your one chocolate allotment is over on the kitchen counter. And by the way, I found your Dorito stash. Actually, Colby found the bag and brought it to me."

I glared at Colby as I headed over to get my one measly square of chocolate. I could swear she was sitting there with a smirk on her face telling me, "What goes around comes around."

I opened the wrapper and popped the chocolate into my mouth. *Ahhhh.* The quote on the wrapper read, "Why run in pain? Better to fall in joy." I had no idea what that psychobabble meant and wasn't up for a philosophical discussion about it with Bonnie. So, I discreetly tossed the wrapper into the trash and plopped back down on the couch.

"Enjoy the sugar hit, honey?" She mocked my pain.

"Bonnie, don't you think this eating regimen is becoming a bit, I don't know, a bit, say . . . draconian? And no, that's not today's word from my Scrabble calendar."

"That's a tad harsh, don't you think? After all, my goal—*our* goal—is to be healthy in mind, body, and spirit."

"I understand, and I appreciate your noble sincerity in the matter. It's just difficult for me, a boy raised on chicken-fried steak and fried okra, to make the transition into becoming the next Euell Gibbons. To be honest, I'm kind of frustrated by it, but I haven't wanted to hurt your feelings."

Bonnie sat up on the couch. "I'm glad you said something. I didn't know you felt this way." She took a pensive pause. "Here's an idea. How about one night a week—say every Thursday—I'll cook whatever you want. You just give me the menu. This way, you can have something to look forward to, dietetically speaking. Think of it as a reward for eating healthy the other six days of the week. What do you think?"

"You would seriously make me decadent smashed potatoes made with sour cream, cream cheese, and real butter?"

"Yes sir, and I would even eat a few myself."

I gently pushed her down on the couch and gave her a big kiss. "You'd do that for me?"

"Yes, I would." She wrapped her arms around my neck and pulled me in close for another kiss. But before we could take this interaction to the next level, Colby was up on the couch and in the middle of our business.

"Elmo, I think she needs to go out. Do you mind?"

"No problem. I need to move my car into the garage anyway. Have you seen my car keys?"

Colby smirked at me again.

12

The Church Picnic

The day was overcast with an occasional light sprinkle, but all in all the weather was well-suited for a church picnic.

For this year's event, Johnny Rochelle had rented Wilbur Park, a small community park located in the first ring of neighborhoods just outside of downtown. Big church/small park, so he reserved the entire park, three or four open acres surrounded by tall trees, with a dozen or so covered picnic shelters scattered about.

If Johnny had thoroughly done his homework, hc probably wouldn't have chosen Wilbur Park. Seventy-five years ago, a local man named Hank Abrahms had gone missing there. His body was found three months later in the bottom of the well at the center of the park. Since that time, an unusually high number of personal mishaps and accidents had taken place at Wilbur Park. The problem became so prevalent, the locals would say a person got "hanked" if injured at the park.

Against that backdrop, the families of First Church rolled into Wilbur Park by the dozens arriving around 10:00 that morning. The church provided the meat, and each family was to bring a side dish or dessert, enough to feed several families.

Johnny had enlisted children's director Doreen McGinty to plan and supervise games for the smaller children. As recreation minister, he had planned volleyball, Frisbee golf, bocce ball, flag football and horseshoes for the teens and adults. But the highlight of the entire event would be the Corn Hole tournament.

As staff members, Bonnie and I arrived an hour early to help set up. I was flabbergasted to find ten to twelve guys already there honing their Corn Hole skills—including Eddie Hughes.

"Hey, Eddie. What are you doing here so early?"

"Yo, Elmo! ¿Qué Pasa?" He flipped me a Corn Hole bag. "Just getting in a little last-minute practice, man."

"Am I missing something? Isn't it just a little picnic game? Why all the fuss?"

"No, man; this is war. Some of these dudes have practiced every day for weeks just getting ready for today."

"But why?"

"To win. Duh? Come on, Elmo, this is Corn Hole, man!" He

paused for emphasis. "Corn Hole!"

"Yeah, I got that. Corn Hole."

Eddie tugged on his lime-green soccer-style socks. "I got knocked out of the tourney last year by Ramona. She got on a hot streak and took down all us guys. It was utterly humiliating. So I pulled out my lucky socks for this year's tourney. You playing?"

"Yes, unfortunately. Johnny insisted. I've never played Corn Hole before. Why don't you show me how to play?"

"Cool. Hey, I've got another pair of these green socks in the car. Want me to get 'em? We could be like NASCAR teammates. Man, that would be *cool.*"

"Y-e-a-h, no. Thanks anyway. I think I'll just play one match and then watch from the cheap seats."

"Your loss, dude."

While Eddie showed me the finer points of Corn Hole, the park was abuzz with preparation for the day's activities.

Events like church picnics play a vital role in the life of a healthy church. On Sundays, church members are with their own groups, for the most part. These groups are usually divided by age and marital status. As a result, most church members spend a majority of their time with people just like them. But at events like the church picnic, these age and marital barriers disappear, and people meet new friends and play games with folks of all ages and stripes.

Johnny had designed the Corn Hole tourney to last all day, with the final match scheduled as the crescendo event ending the picnic. That would enable the Corn Hole players to participate in the other picnic activities between their CH matches.

I felt a tap on my shoulder and turned around to find the toothy grin of Erlene Markham.

"Mornin', Elmo."

"Morning, Erlene." I shuddered. "Ahhh! Is that one of your, uh, famous . . . uh, relish . . . trays?"

She slapped me on the arm. "Don't play coy with me. You know what it is. I hope you're not going to be a pansy again and refuse to sample it."

"Now Erlene, be nice to me. I'll tell you what. If I win my first Corn Hole match, I'll eat something off your tray. How's that?"

"Sounds like a pretty safe bet on your part. Who're you playing?"

"The one and only Jimmy 'Cornbread' Jackson."

"Ah, that 'no account' kicker fella? I betcha you can beat him. Might as well pick out your relish tray item now so you'll be ready. Let's see there are sardines, escargot, chocolate-covered grasshoppers—"

"Whoa there, Nellie!" My stomach started to lurch. "Let's just save that delectable menu travelogue 'til after I win the match." *Which ain't ever gonna happen.*

"All right, all right," she said, waving her hand back and forth. Then she wheezed on me. Twice. "You do need to know, even if you beat Jimmie, I'm pulling for Ramona to win the whole shootin' match again this year." Another wheeze. "What a hoot it was last year to watch her cut down that overzealous brood of cocky young studs."

I winced. "You know Erlene, this has been enthralling, but I gotta go find Bonnie." I made a beeline for the children's area.

As I sped away, I could hear Erlene mutter under her breath, "Pansy . . ." followed by yet another wheeze.

Bonnie had been collared by Doreen to help with the little ones. I just hoped she wasn't getting any maternal ideas. Like my dad used to say, "Proximity breeds affection."

Yikes.

"Elmo, you look a little pale. You okay?" She gave me a nurturing hug.

"I just got ambushed by Erlene and her relish tray."

Bonnie threw her head back, guffawing. "You two and your shenanigans." She laughed again.

"Go ahead and have your fun at my expense. Then I want to see *you* ingest a chocolate-covered grasshopper from her treacherous tray."

"Ew? Are you kidding?"

"Oh no, and it gets worse."

"Have her bring the tray over here to the kid's area. I'm sure our toddlers will gobble them right up."

"I think I'm going to regurgitate."

"Elmo, I'm joking. Really! Though that was a nice euphemism on your part. Hey, I think you ought to sit down for a spell. You're white as a ghost. Which isn't a good thing, considering the park we're in."

"What do you mean?"

"Juliann was just telling me about the curse of Hank Abrahms."

"Hank who?"

"She said a guy named Hank Abrahms was murdered in this park years ago, and some people believe his ghost still roams here among the trees."

"Come on. Where'd she hear such poppycock?"

"Where does Juliann get most of her information? From some guy she used to date that lived in this neighborhood. They'd come to the park at night for sparking, and she felt as if they were always being watched."

"Sparking? What's that?"

"Y'know, kissing and cuddling. Haven't you read any teenage romance novels from the fifties?"

"Well, no, not lately. So there's a ghost named Hank at this park? Does he play Corn Hole?"

No one but Eddie showed up to watch my match with Jimmy "Cornbread" Jackson. Eddie assured me the crowds would grow as the tournament went along.

There wasn't much to this game. Throw a bag in the hole and get three points. Land the bag on the box and get one point. The first person to reach twenty-one wins the match.

Though an excellent athlete, Cornbread lived up to his reputation and was a lousy cornbag tosser. Since Eddie was Cornbread's roommate, he felt compelled to cheer for him, but I could tell his heart wasn't in it. I beat the former pro-football player handily, 21-10.

In my second Corn Hole match, I beat a college kid named Luke Surprise, and he really looked surprised when I beat him. Who knew I could play this silly game so well?

With my next match an hour away, I stole Bonnie away from the children's area, and we played some couples volleyball with our Sunday school class members. Big fun.

Then it was time for lunch. Grilled hamburgers, baked beans with brown sugar and bacon, potato salad, and coleslaw. Peach cobbler à la mode for dessert. Yum!

Bonnie and I grabbed a seat at one of the picnic tables.

"Well, since you've been winning your Corn Hole matches, did Erlene force-feed you a grasshopper or a slug?"

I chuckled. "As the Lord protected the Israelites from the plagues of old, God protected me from Erlene's relish tray."

"And how did God do that?"

"As she was about to set her infamous serving dish on the food table, some guy playing Frisbee golf hooked his tee shot and blasted the tray right out of her hand—launching the worms, the radishes, and the grasshoppers in a million different directions. It's now exotic fodder for the birds."

"Was Erlene upset?"

"No. You know Erlene. She wheezed and laughed and gave the poor guy an extended kiss on the check when he came to apologize."

"That must have been traumatizing for him."

"Oh yeah. I saw him a few minutes later heading for his car. Looked to me as if he were done for the day. I see therapy in his future."

We were laughing when Thurm joined us. "Elmo, I see you won your first two Corn Hole matches! To be honest, I'm surprised. I got knocked out in my first match by Ramona. She was on fire. She holed out her first six bags for eighteen points. I never had a chance."

"What's with her? It's almost as if she has the spiritual gift of Corn Holing."

"Yeah . . . but I don't think I'd repeat that if I were you."

"You're probably right. But come on, what's the deal with her and the game?"

"I guess she just has great eye-hand coordination and rhythm.

It's probably from all her years of precise musical training."

Bonnie piped in. "Let's be honest. You guys just don't like the fact that a *woman* can beat the boys at what is basically a boy's playground game."

"True."

"True," Thurm concurred.

I puffed out my chest in false bravado. "Well, somebody's got to step up and take her down this year. Right, Thurm?"

"Right, Elmo. Who knows, it might be *you*! Humph!"

"No, if I'm lucky enough to get by this next guy, I'll probably be playing against Eddie with his lucky green socks. The 'dude' has been practicing daily for this dumb tournament, man."

"I see you've been working on your Eddie Hughes impersonation. Not bad."

"Thanks, dude, uh, man."

Thurm stood to leave. "Sorry guys, but I've gotta run. I'm refereeing the flag football game. Are you playing, Elmo?"

"Nope. I'm saving all my juice for Corn Hole. See ya later."

As Thurm ran off, Bonnie gave me the look. You guys know the one I'm talking about. And I knew *exactly* what it meant. This was a church outing. Winning was low on the list of priorities. I was a staff member, and the church members would be watching. Sometimes competitiveness and Christianity butt heads. My job was to set a good example.

She smiled. "All I'm saying is play hard, have fun, play to win, but keep some *perspective*."

Ouch! The dreaded "P" word. "I got it, I got it. I GOT it!"

But she was right, and I knew it. I have a history of losing perspective when the competitive accelerants kick in. An elbow here, a harsh word there, and you've quickly blown your testimony. I wasn't going to let that happen today. Spending your life apologizing for bad behavior is no way to live.

Amazingly, I won my third match, but only by a point. I was scheduled to meet Eddie Hughes in the quarterfinals. That is until he got *hanked.*

I noticed a commotion over at the flag football field. I could see someone was down, and everyone was flying around in emergency mode. A young man screamed for a doctor, then added, "Or someone with doctor-type skills." *Choice.*

As I got closer to the scrum, I could see a bright green sock on the downed man—Eddie! His other sock had been removed. Eddie had broken his big toe. It was at a ninety-degree angle to the rest of his foot. *That's a hurty.*

Juliann was standing there with Bonnie, shaking her head. "I told you this park was cursed."

As they stabilized Eddie's foot for his trip to the emergency room, I knelt down by him, surprised to see him lying there smiling. I assumed he was in shock.

"Eddie, are you all right?"

His smile grew even bigger. "Elmo, I've been hanked! Chicks dig sport-related injuries." Then his eyes rolled back, and he blacked out.

A few of the guys carried him to the back of a mini-van, and off he went to the ER. And just like the NFL, the boys quickly resumed their flag football game like nothing had happened. Oh, the male competitive spirit.

With Eddie out of action, I automatically advanced into the semifinal round of the Corn Hole tourney. The matches were now drawing large crowds of spectators as most of the other picnic activities were winding down.

My semifinal opponent was Victor Skeetman. I didn't know Victor personally, but I knew of him. From a blue-blood family, he drove expensive cars and wore custom-made clothes. Quite the flashy guy, which was further made evident by his official Corn Hole uniform. Who knew there were special clothes just for Corn Hole? His shirt, shorts, socks, hat, and even cornbags were all a shiny yellow-gold with a royal-blue trim. I'd guess the uniform put him back at least $300. I wondered if there was a Corn Hole circuit where guys traveled around and played tournaments similar to the professional bowler's tour.

Strange.

Victor was all business as we started our match. No chit-chat, no "How you doing?" No talking at all—like I wasn't even there. It felt as if I were playing against Tiger Woods at the Masters.

He was a better player then me, but I clearly had the crowd on my side. Pastors always have the advantage of the crowd. This rattled Victor significantly, and I *pasted* him—fancy uniform and all.

That's right. *Elmo Jenkins* made the Corn Hole finals! I couldn't believe it.

As expected, my opponent would be Ramona Holloway, the unofficial Corn Hole champion of the world. Well, at least at First Church. I was decidedly the underdog.

Before the final match, Johnny had everyone group up for a brief time of *kumbaya* with some singing and a short devotion by Pastor Jorgenson, who arrived just in time for his moment. Then, after a closing prayer, everyone crowded in for the Corn Hole finale.

Ramona gave me a hug. "Elmo, remember it's just a game. It's not personal."

"I agree. May the best man . . . uh, that is, the best *person* win."

"Nice." I heard Thurm say from behind me.

The enthusiastic crowd was evenly divided. I clearly understood why Johnny had planned the day to end with the Corn Hole finals. Everyone was into it, having a great time. They were even doing The Wave.

Ramona was good, but I was matching her point for point. With the score tied 20-20, she put one in the hole to go up 23-20. This was high drama. I would have to hole one out, or the match would be over.

Thurm, who'd been coaching me during the match, called me over. "Take a few deep breaths. Collect yourself, buddy. You can *do* this."

I nodded my head in agreement and walked back over to make my throw. All of a sudden, it felt like that climactic scene in *Chariots of Fire*. The sound dropped out, and everything went into slow motion. I stepped forward and tossed my cornbag high into the air. It tumbled silently, slowly, end over end on a huge arc. It landed half on the Corn Hole box and half over one of the holes, teetering there. Everyone—me included—expected it to fall into the hole. It didn't.

Match over. Ramona won.

There's an internal pain that comes with losing a sports event that's different from other pain. It's irrational, of course, since it's just about losing a stupid game. But it's still very tangible, very visceral, and it can stay with you for days. It's as if I'd been emotionally *hanked*.

I congratulated Ramona and accepted condolences from many. We headed home in silence. Even though I'd lost the Corn Hole tourney, it had been a good day, and there was always next year.

I just needed to go home and dig out my lucky red socks.

13

The Book Cover

With my cup of tea in one hand and a plastic bear honey dispenser in the other, I slid into the back booth across from Eli.

He smiled warmly. "Trying something new this morning, are we?"

"Well, yes. A co-worker of mine, Father Ted, suggested I try honey in my tea. That's how he drinks it. He got the idea from a niece who's some kind of tea and teacup expert."

"Honey in your tea? You'll like it. I guarantee it. You mentioned a Father Ted. Do you all have a priest working at your church?"

I chuckled. "Oh no. Father Ted is just his moniker—a TV commercial alter ego of sorts. He's actually a retired pastor from another church across town, who has signed on to do hospital visits and such for First Church. Great guy. You'd like him."

"I'm sure I would. So, what's new with Elmo this morning?"

"Nothing really. All things Elmo are pretty much status quo. Work's good. My book's coming along. Bonnie and I are good; except, maybe . . . well, money's a little tight these days. I assume that's just part of being a young married couple."

Eli flipped open his Bible to the page next to his lace bookmark. "Money is indeed a challenge. Always has been and always will be. If you're poor, you think about money all the time—that is, the need to have more. If you're rich, you think about money all the time—that is, what would happen if you lost it?"

I smiled. "I know the poor end of that equation fairly well, but I'm not so sure I'll ever see any riches."

"Elmo, you never know what life will bring your way. I love when the writer of Proverbs 30 asks of the Lord: 'Give me neither poverty nor riches, but give me only my daily bread. Otherwise, I may have too much and disown you and say, "Who is the LORD?" Or I may become poor and steal, and so dishonor the name of my God.'

"If you can live out that philosophy, money will never be an issue in your life or your marriage."

"More excellent sage advice from Eli via the Bible. Just how many times have you read the Bible through?"

"Well, I've never read it front to back, but I've read it in its entirety many times over. To me, it truly is the bread of life to be consumed daily for spiritual nourishment."

"How do you develop such a hunger for God's word?"

"You make a decision, a deliberate act of your will. You then prioritize the time, and you stick to it. Just like exercise tones and strengthens the body, consuming God's word tones and strengthens the soul. You'll see a difference. Guaranteed."

"Before I head out, one more thing. Tell me about your bookmark."

He held up the ornate antique lace bookmark for me to see. An inch or two wide and six or seven inches long, it was topped off by a crimson ribbon. "This was made for me many years ago by a dear, dear friend named Dorcas—who now resides happily in heaven making clothes for the angels."

"It's beautiful. I've never used a bookmark in my Bible. I'll have to get one."

Back in my office, Thurm laughed as he talked. "Ever been to one of those weddings where everything goes wrong? I mean *everything*? Well, I officiated one last night, and it was a total catastrophe."

I scratched my head. "You did a wedding on a Wednesday night?"

"Yeah, it was the best time for the couple due to some family work schedule conflicts."

"What went wrong?"

"You name it. It was like the greatest hit video for wedding snafus. The bride broke a heel on her shoe halfway down the aisle and limped the rest of the way to the altar. The five-year-old ring bearer tied the rings down with triple knots. They had to ask if anyone had a pocket knife to free them. The soloist broke a guitar string as he started his song, and it popped him in the nose. He literally stumbled off the platform clutching his face. It was hilarious!

"Oh, my."

"But the incident that takes the cake—literally— was when the best man opened the champagne bottle at the reception. When he popped the cork, it flew up and smashed a fluorescent light bulb, showering glass all over the wedding cake!"

"Seriously?"

"I felt so bad for this young couple, I offered to give them back their check for my services. And they actually took it!" He said, laughing.

"Were these kids from your youth group?"

"No, they were from our college ministry. Terry Hankins couldn't do the wedding, so he pitched it to me. The groom is Ricky Spanks. You know, the kid from that 'Jesus loves you boat incident' last year?"

"No, I must've missed that one. A boat incident? What happened?"

"Out near the River Marina where Route 253 crosses the river, there's been this old dilapidated tugboat lying on its side in shallow water for years and years. It's right near the bridge; a real eyesore. The county refused to pay to have it hauled off, so it's just laid there year after year with its rotting hull facing those who drove by.

"Ricky Spanks and a few of his college buddies got a brilliant idea. They canoed out there one night and painted 'Jesus loves you' on the exposed hull which faces the bridge."

"Sweet subterfuge," I said, smiling.

"The next morning everyone crossing the bridge was greeted with a little dose of John 3:16."

"Did the boys get in trouble?"

Thurm chuckled. "No, but that old boat was hauled off and gone twenty-four hours later."

I was indignant. "Unbelievable. So, someone has to call in complaining about the name of Jesus graffitied on a boat hull before our local politicians will do their job."

"Makes for great theater doesn't it? What's it say in Philippians? Something like, 'Every knee shall bow at the name of Jesus, even the knees of low-rent bureaucrats.'"

"When you look at it that way, it's actually a pretty amazing story."

"Elmo, I need a small favor. I'm going to be out of town this weekend. I'm driving home for a required FFF event. Do you mind doing a 'walk about' through the youth area around 9:30 Sunday morning just to make sure all of the bases are covered?"

"No problem. By the way, what is an FFF event?"

"Forced Family Fun. It's my crazy Uncle Bernie's seventy-fifth birthday, and all us Wilsons are required to be there. This is the uncle who put a urinal in his home bathroom."

"Oh, yeah. I remember you telling me about him. Isn't he the guy known as the honker?"

"Yep, that's him. Whenever he's driving, he always keeps one hand on his horn. If he's behind a car when the red light changes to green, he automatically hits the horn. If you stop before taking a right turn and he's behind you, he'll hit the horn. If you're going too slow for him—"

"—he'll blow the horn." I laughed. "How does he keep from getting into brawls with other drivers?"

"Everyone in his small town knows it's crazy Bernie Wilson. They just smile and say, 'It's the honker.' He's become a local treasure."

"Listen, you go back home and have some quality FFF. I'll make sure your Youth are well cared for."

An hour or so later I picked up my desk phone. "Hello, this is Elmo Jenkins."

"Morning Elmo, Castor McMullan here. I'm sitting in the Brown & Brewster conference room with your book editor and the B&B creative team, and we're going over some possible concepts for your book cover. Got a minute?"

"Sure."

"I've put you on speaker phone. Say hi to Ellie, Jake, Tommy, Esther, and Trey."

"Hey, guys."

"We've been spit-balling all morning and wanted to bounce some of our ideas off you."

"Okay, let's do it."

"Remembering that the title of the book will be *Change is Good*, and that it deals with the need for change in the church, here are some of our preliminary cover concepts.

"Concept number one. There's an outline of a church—very simplistic, like a stick figure version of a building with a steeple and a cross. The building is broken into four quadrants. In the first quadrant, there's a picture of a caveman cooking some meat over a rudimentary fire pit. Are you with me?"

"Yeah, I think so." I leaned back in my chair and put my feet up on my desk.

"In the second quadrant, there's a prairie woman putting firewood into an old wood stove."

"Is she Amish and wearing a bonnet?"

There was laughter in the conference room. "Very funny. That would certainly sell some books, but sorry—no bonnet."

He continued. "In quadrant number three there's a 1950's housewife cooking on an electric range."

"In high heels, I assume," I said with a chuckle. But this time there was no laughter from New York. They were either too young or too hip to get the joke. I quickly jumped back in. "Okay, what about quadrant four?"

Castor cleared his throat. "And in quadrant four, there's a man in a suit using a microwave."

"I see the progression and I get the metaphor, but to be honest, it seems as if it would be a very busy cover. Also, it might be easily mistaken for a cookbook."

"Stellar feedback, Elmo. Very good. Let's move on to concept number two."

"Shoot."

"This time the cover of the book is split into a top half and bottom half. On the top half, a man in a suit is standing out in the middle of a huge wheat field that's ready for harvest. He's holding an old-school sickle and looks a bit overwhelmed."

"I think I understand. You have a man out standing in his field—"

The conference room burst into raucous laughter.

Embarrassed I blushed, but thankfully they couldn't see my face. "I mean, *standing out* in his field."

Castor broke in. "Elmo, forgive my colleagues. Everyone here's a little punchy after kicking this around for several hours."

"No problem. My faux pas—my bad. What's on the bottom half of that cover?"

"The same guy in the same suit, in the same wheat field, but this time he's driving a grain harvester."

"You mean like a wheat combine?"

"Yes, exactly," Castor confirmed.

"Again, I see the symbolism. And I think it's clearer than the first concept."

"Finally, concept number three has a middle-aged man in a suit at the top of a cliff, and he's reaching down to help several young people up onto the summit."

I leaned forward on my desk cradling the phone with my shoulder. "Well, I get it, but that sounds a bit more obscure. Of the three concepts, I like the second one best. But to be honest, I'm not sure we're there yet."

"Really?" Castor sounded surprised.

"First of all, we need to ditch the suits. Formal clothes, though still worn at many churches like First Church, are too symbolic of the old way of doing things. In my research, I discovered that the churches most effective at moving into the future are more casual with their staff attire."

"Okay."

I visualized Castor frowning, but I pushed on. "To be honest, I think I'd prefer a cover with less clutter. Symbolic, but simple. Perhaps designed around an image of a key or maybe a door."

There was a prolonged pause on the other end of the line. The Brown & Brewster conference room was silent.

Finally, Castor spoke up. "Again, that's some great feedback, Elmo. Let us kick this around some more, and we'll be back in touch."

"Sounds good," I said. "Thank you all for your work on the book. Bye."

As I hung up the phone, I thought I heard someone in the B&B conference room say, "Oh great, another diva."

New Yorkers.

14

The New Assignment

Thursday evening I took Bonnie to the airport. She flew home for a long weekend with her folks and siblings. We never could've afforded the luxury of a plane ticket, but her parents paid for it with surplus frequent-flyer miles. My kind of in-laws.

Colby showed her displeasure with Bonnie's absence by tap dancing on our bed periodically throughout the night. The next morning I was exhausted. Since Fridays were the laid-back day of the week at First Church, with many of the pastors taking the day off, I decided to sleep in to the last possible minute. True to form, that plan got upended when the phone rang at 7:30.

"Yeah?"

"Elmo, this is Louis. Suit up and get in here as quick as you can. We've had a bomb go off."

I was still a little groggy. "What? A bomb? Did anybody get hurt?"

"Not that kind of bomb. Tom Applebee resigned late yesterday, and Canasta Langanelli is gone also."

"No way. Are you saying—"

"Just get down here. No one knows what's going on. Pastor Jorgensen is coming down to brief the executive staff."

"I'm on my way."

I threw on some clothes and jumped in my car. As I washed down a granola bar with some bottled water, I kept telling myself this couldn't be happening. *Not Tom Applebee!?*

By the time I arrived, the office was in an uproar. No one said it, but everyone was thinking it—had Tom and Canasta run off together?

Stunned, I sat in my office waiting for instructions on what to do. Tom had been acting so weird about Canasta the past few weeks. On the surface, it appeared to confirm the rumors whirling around. But I couldn't bring myself to accept that outcome. Tom was just too much of a stand-up guy.

As I waited, I decided to pray. I prayed for Tom and his wife Charlene. I prayed for Pastor Jorgensen and the Personnel Committee to have godly wisdom in the matter. I prayed for First Church and the inevitable fallout caused by this kind of situation. I even prayed for Canasta whom I believed was at the core of this tragedy.

Juliann opened my office door, her face streaked with tears. "Elmo, they want you upstairs in Pastor Jorgensen's office."

Heartsick, I rode the elevator up to the fifth floor; my mind spinning, my spirit grieving.

As I entered Pastor Jorgensen's suite, Fran was at her desk. She too had been crying. "Go on in, Elmo," she said somberly. "The others are waiting,"

Instead of an impromptu staff meeting, Dr. Jorgensen's office looked more like a roomful of hastily-gathered relatives awaiting news of a family member's death. Everyone wore casual clothes— most hadn't shaved. The air was heavy, the mood grim. Louis Estrada, Bob Stevens, Harry Simpkins, and Father Ted were all there, as well as David Specter from the Personnel Committee, and surprisingly, the retired Fred Snooker.

Some chairs were circled up in the middle of Dr. Jorgensen's office. I grabbed a seat as Fran quietly closed the door behind me.

"Whew," Dr Jorgensen began. "Where to begin? Let's see. First of all, thanks for coming down on a Friday and arriving so expeditiously. I'm sure by now you all know this is about Tom Applebee." He paused to collect himself. "Well, I've got some good news, and a whole batch of bad news to share with you.

"Let's start with the good news. Regardless of what you've heard, Tom and Canasta were *not* having an affair. Unfortunately, that's where the good news ends."

He paused again. "Perhaps the best thing for me to do is tell you the whole story as it was relayed to me by Tom last night. I should warn you; this will sound a lot more like a TV movie than anything you might expect from the life of Tom Applebee. One important proviso—*none* of what I'm about to share with you leaves this office. Understood?"

We all nodded in agreement.

"The church will be issuing an official statement through our Personnel Committee later today." Pastor Jorgenson gestured toward David.

Jorgensen leaned forward and slowly began his explanation. "When Tom Applebee was a young man, between college and grad school, he participated in a United Nations summer work project. Several hundred students from around the world came together to dig wells and establish irrigation in an effort to help the poor in western Africa. On the last night of the project, they had a wrap-up party and unfortunately, Tom got drunk and slept with one of the co-eds. He says he was so inebriated that he doesn't even remember doing it. They broke camp the next day, and each student headed back to their own respective part of the world.

"The girl—let's just call her 'Darlene'— never told Tom that she became pregnant. Instead, she used the baby as an opportunity to trick another young man at her college into marriage. Evidently, this lady was quite the con artist. She never told her new husband or the daughter she gave birth to about Tom.

"Eighteen years and three marriages later, Darlene developed breast cancer. On her death bed, she finally confessed the whole situation to her then eighteen-year-old daughter and told her how to track down Tom, her real father. As you may have figured out by now, the girl's name was Canasta Langanelli."

A collective gasp filled the room.

No. Way.

Pastor Jorgenson continued. "Sadly, Canasta inherited her deceitful mother's unique skill set. She contacted Tom discretely with the unusual tale. Initially, he didn't believe her. He thought for sure it was merely a shakedown. When a blood test corroborated her story, she then basically blackmailed him. If he would agree to pay her way through college, she promised to keep silent about their little secret. Tom, fearing for his career and his marriage, foolishly went along with her plan.

"Tom pulled some strings and got her accepted into Bargston College here in town. The savvy, street-smart Canasta used all of her charms and tricks and conned her way to a four-year degree with honors. But like so many other college students in this day and age, she couldn't land a decent job. So, as often happens in blackmail scenarios, she came back to Tom and demanded a job here at First Church, and Tom made it happen.

"I think we all know that Canasta's tenure here has not gone well."

The understatement of the millennium.

"It all came to a head yesterday. Canasta told Tom she no longer wanted to be the 'lowly' Youth/Recreation secretary. No, she wanted to be his administrative assistant up on the fifth floor, telling him he would just to have to figure out a way to transfer, or fire Adrianne Figgie.

"That was the final straw. Canasta's extortion had reached its critical mass with Tom. He called last night and told me the whole story, along with his sincere apology. I tried to convince him to stay on, and we could work through the issues, but he felt strongly that his credibility was gone, and resigning was the best move for him and for First Church."

"What about Canasta?" Harry asked.

"Canasta has been terminated. She cleared out her desk late last night, and is prohibited from coming back on the First Church campus. Tom will be coming in tomorrow with a representative from the Personnel Committee to 'clean his office'."

There was a long moment of silence. No one knew quite what to say. We all liked Tom.

Louis was the first to speak. "What about Charlene?"

Pastor Jorgensen crossed his arms. "The initial incident happened so long ago before Tom had even met Charlene. When Canasta first approached him, he chose not to tell Charlene about her. At some point during Canasta's time at Bargston College, Tom finally confessed the situation to his wife. I'm sure maintaining the ruse has been difficult on her."

"What will Tom do now?" asked Father Ted.

"Frankly, Ted, I don't know. A child born out of wedlock is one issue, and the following deception is another. Tom's a good man, but I fear his days in church staff ministry may be over. Right now, he needs some time to heal, to recalibrate his marriage, his walk with the Lord, and his relationship with Canasta, his daughter. He has some difficult days ahead, and he'll need our prayers—and our forgiveness."

Harry jumped in. "Tom covered a lot of bases around here. Who's going to fill his shoes?"

"Good question Harry," the pastor said with a smile. "To remedy that situation, I've dragged Pastor Fred Snooker out of retirement yet again to pitch hit for us until we hire Tom's replacement."

Fred smiled at the group. "It's like George Costanza says, 'Every time I think I'm out, they p-u-l-l me back in!'" His Seinfeld reference broke the tension in the room and gave everyone a chance to relax a bit.

Pastor Jorgenson patted Fred on the shoulder. "Fred has graciously agreed to step back in but it's a huge job, and I can't expect him to do it all. So, Elmo, at Fred's request I'm reassigning you to be his assistant for now."

I was caught flat-footed. "Ah . . . oh, uh . . . yes, sir."

Fred rescued me. "Elmo, why don't you and I grab a bite to eat after this meeting, and get the ball rolling on our new assignments."

I sighed with relief. "Yes. Please. That would be great."

"Okay, then." Pastor Jorgensen stood signaling the end of our meeting. "Remember, as of now all of the information shared here today is classified. Just direct any questions you may get to the Personnel Committee. Understood?"

Again, we all nodded as we began to file out of his office.

Though I was hurting for Tom and Charlene, I felt a bit gratified. I'd seen through Canasta since her first day. Of course, I never dreamed her malfeasance would rise to such a felonious level.

This sad scenario also included a huge lesson to be learned. No, make that a lesson to be *confirmed*. That God is quick to forgive us of our sins, but the consequences of our sins can linger for a lifetime. They can even surprise us, coming out of nowhere. I needed to remember that lesson the next time I found myself contemplating doing something willfully disobedient or sinful.

"Ah, Kranky's Coffee Shoppe," Pastor Snooker said, looking around the busy eatery. "I've been coming to this place since I was your age. But it's been a few years now since I stopped by."

I noticed the back booth was empty. Eli must have already left for the day. Too bad. I would've liked him to meet Pastor Snooker. I walked to the back booth and slid in. Pastor Snooker sat across from me.

"I actually stop in here two or three times a week and sit in this very booth. I've developed a friendship with an older gentleman named Eli Enoch, who comes here every morning to read his Bible and drink hot tea."

Fred perked up. "Hot tea. That sounds like the ticket. I'm buying, and I'll get your breakfast too."

I laughed. "This has a familiar ring to it. I forgot—you're officially back on the First Church payroll. Again."

He chuckled. "Poor Bob Stevens. Every time he thinks he can quit paying me, I seem to come back for yet another paycheck. But this time around, they've given me an expense account as well, which will cover today's food and drink, amen?"

"Amen. Sounds like a good morning for steak and eggs."

"Really?"

"No, I'm just kidding. I used to order steak and eggs when I was a teenager on family vacations just to tweak my dad. He'd pitch a fit every time. Great adolescent memories."

We ordered our food and quickly got down to business.

Pastor Snooker grimaced. "Like Harry said, Tom has left some mighty big shoes to fill. I called Tom to share my condolences this morning. He actually sounded relieved that the charade was finally over. Tom's a good man. He's made several gargantuan errors in judgment, but after a time he'll find restoration and land on his feet. You just watch."

I nodded in agreement. "I owe a lot to Tom Applebee. I met him at a time when I was basically clueless about my future. He took an interest in me, and at some risk offered me the internship position at First Church. It was a watershed moment in my life. I'll be forever grateful to him."

"Well, at some point you should call him and tell him that, but I'd give him some time. He's currently managing his own watershed moment."

"You're right," I said as the waitress brought our tea with the requisite plastic honey bear dispenser.

"Elmo, I agreed to take on Tom's responsibilities, but only if they'd let me have you as an assistant. Having been the Associate Pastor at First Church for so many years, I know the job pretty well.

It requires a strong pair of legs and around fifty and sixty hours of work each week. I'm an old man with weak legs, and there's no chance I can pull that many hours. So you, young man, will be my legs and cover my desk when I can't be there."

"Yes, sir. But you'll have to tell me what to do because I have no idea."

"Oh, I will. But let's wait 'til Monday morning. For now, let's just enjoy our steak and eggs on the church's dime," he said, chuckling as the waitress delivered our steaming plates of food. "Now tell me more about your friend, Eli. Is he someone I should know?"

15

The Big Bang

With Bonnie out of town for the weekend, I had been tasked with holding down the Jenkins estate and entertaining Colby the Wonder Dog. The latter assignment included feeding her twice a day, and letting her out periodically to download fluids and fertilize the lawn.

Colby and I lounged on the sofa as I culled through the day's mail. The first letter was addressed to "Occupant or Current Resident." As John Turturro famously said in *O Brother Where Art Thou,* "That makes no sense!" How can the current resident not be the occupant? If these companies so desperately want you to open the dang letter, they should simply write on the envelope, "If You're Looking at This, It's to You!" I quickly flipped that one in the pile for the trash.

The second letter was a mailing from a non-profit group, or maybe a political action committee, or alumni association. You know the type. It comes as a mission update or perhaps a monthly newsletter. If you've ever genuinely been moved and made a donation to this kind of organization, your name was put on a donor list with indelible ink. You'll receive a mailing from these folks at least once a month for the rest of your life, and well beyond. Long after you die, your great-great-grandchildren will someday call the organization, begging them to take your name off their mailing list—to no avail, of course. And don't think moving will end the solicitations. You can change your name and move to another country, and the mailings will still find you. Again, into the trash pile.

Next were two or three credit card applications. No wonder these companies charge such a high percentage rate to use their cards. They need gargantuan amounts of cash to pay for postage. Sheesh. To the trash pile.

Finally, a personal postcard. Yea!

On the front was a picture of the Norway Ice Hotel. I flipped it over. The postmark was from Norway, but the postcard had been mailed several months ago. *Must have crossed the Atlantic via a Viking ship.*

Elmo,

We're on the northern leg of our European tour. On a dare, the entire band is spending the night in the Ice Hotel. Cool, very cool—literally. I'll be sleeping on a block of ice covered with animal pelts. I bought some fur-lined Elmo slippers in their gift shop and thought of you.

Cheers and God bless,
Jason McKenzie

I smiled as I set the card aside for Bonnie.
Rock and Roll!
With mail call over, I scooped up Colby and started scratching her ears. Except for her mealtime, this was her absolute favorite thing in the whole world. She would close her eyes and moan. I honestly believe she would let me scratch her ears all day long—except for meal breaks, of course.

Colby was the first dog I'd ever owned. They say a dog is a man's best friend. Sure, your dog likes you; you feed her, play with her, and scratch her ears and tummy. But since she does none of that for you, why do *you* like your dog? That's easy. She fills a need in your life.

We tend to personify our pets, especially when we're alone with them. They become what we need them to be. When Bonnie is away, Colby becomes "Colby the Significant" to me. She sits on the couch with me while I watch TV. She sleeps on the bed with me at night. She lies at my feet when I eat my meals. And the whole time, I talk to her as if she's a person. She becomes my "significant other" while Bonnie's away.

Other times, if I'm wrestling with some philosophical issue that needs to be discussed, she becomes the "Colby Lama" for me. Like a wise Zen master, she patiently listens as I air out my deep questions or lofty opinions. Her remuneration? A robust ear-scratching session, of course.

I got up from the couch and stretched. "Colby the Significant, this is your lucky night. If you promise not to tell Bonnie about the frozen pizza I picked up—or dig the pizza wrapper out of the wherever it is you hide these things—I'll let you have my dinner. That's right— the healthy meal Bonnie specifically left for me is *all yours*! Hummus and gefilte fish—yum! You'll just love it. Trust me," I said snickering.

Now where did I hide those jelly beans??

Traffic was unusually light as I left the airport and headed home. I'd just picked up Bonnie after her weekend away, and she was all abubble and froth telling me all about her trip.

"As you know, my brother Dale teaches sixth graders at the Christian Academy back home," she said, half-laughing.

"Yeah?" I love it when Bonnie gets tickled telling a story.

"Well, his class is currently studying the book of Psalms. So, he decided to show them the movie, *King David*—you know, the one starring Richard Gere?"

"Sure."

"In the movie, there's a scene where David is watching Bathsheba through her window as she takes a bath." Bonnie started cackling.

"So?? That's what the bible says actually happened."

"Yes, but remember, this is Hollywood's version of the story. So, when Bathsheba steps out of the tub, there's some brief nudity shown. Definitely inappropriate for a sixth-grade class at a Christian school."

"All right, I get that. But what's so funny?"

"Dale decided to go ahead and show the film anyway. He'd just planned to cover the projector lens during the nudity segment. That part only lasts a few seconds. But while the kids watched the film, he started grading papers at his desk and lost track of the time. At the last second, he realized the bathing scene was on, and as he sprinted toward the projector to block the lens, he tripped!" Bonnie could hardly talk, she was laughing so hard.

"Okay, but I still don't get what's so funny."

"As Dale is falling, he panics and yells to the class, 'AVERT YOUR EYES! AVERT YOUR EYES!'"

I laughed as hard as she did. I could just see her nerdy brother taking a dive and crying out that ridiculously archaic phrase. We couldn't stop laughing.

"Talk about a teachable moment!" I said, finally catching my breath. "Those kids will remember the story of David watching Bathsheba for the rest of their lives."

She wiped her eyes as our laughter slowed.

"Bonnie, I hate to kill your ebullient spirit, but I'm afraid I need to share some bad news with you. Something terrible happened at First Church while you were out of town."

She sat up in her seat with a concerned look on her face. "What are you talking about?"

"I waited until you got back because I didn't want to ruin your weekend with your family."

"What could be that bad? Did somebody die?"

"No, not physically, anyway. Late on Thursday, Tom Applebee resigned suddenly."

"What? Why would Tom resign? Has he taken another position?"

"Unfortunately, no. It gets worse. Canasta was fired at the same time."

Bonnie looked stunned. "What? Were they—"

"No, they weren't. This has to stay between you and me for now. Pastor Snooker gave me permission to tell you."

"Pastor Snooker? I . . . I don't under—"

"Just let me finish, and it will all make sense. Well, kind of. It will be fully explained to the entire support staff at our Wednesday staff meeting. Until then, the word is mum. Okay?"

"Okay."

I spent the rest of the drive home telling Bonnie the reason behind Tom Applebee's departure. By the time we got home she was up to speed, and we'd talked through all the germane issues. Bonnie came from strong stock, and though she felt badly for Tom, she was prepared to step up and do her part to help the church get through this crisis. Not surprisingly, she wasn't sad to see Canasta go.

When we got to the house, Colby gave Bonnie the cold shoulder.

I could tell it hurt Bonnie's feelings. "What's wrong with Colby?"

"She's mad at you for leaving town. Animals don't take abandonment lightly."

"Abandonment?" she scoffed.

"That's right. In the Serengeti, if a mother abandons her calf or cub, the herd or pack will kick her out on her own, leaving her vulnerable to predators. It's gruesome."

"Well, that's clearly bogus, Mr. Mutual of Omaha wannabe. You're forgetting that I minored in Ethology. She's mad because I left her here with *you* for four days. I bet you force-fed her your hummus."

Uh oh.

"I . . . uh, well . . . okay, you got me. But she seemed to really enjoy it."

"E-l-m-o!"

"Yeah, while you two kiss and make up, I think I'll go grab a shower." I dove into the bathroom with my life hanging by a thread. *Whew!*

By the time I'd gotten out of the shower Bonnie and Colby had reconciled, and all was well at the Jenkins estate. It had been a long day, so we snuggled up in bed, kissed goodnight, and went to sleep.

Sometime around 3:00 a.m., an enormous crashing sound exploded us out of our REM sleep cycles.

"What the heck was that?" I yelled still in a daze.

"I don't know, but it came from right outside!"

I jumped up and ran to our front bedroom window. As I pulled back the curtain, I could see car lights shining in the middle of our front yard. "You'd better throw some clothes on."

"Elmo, are both our cars in the garage?"

"Yes, thank goodness."

We walked outside to find our neighbor Roger's car right in the middle of our front yard. Behind it, was another car still running with its headlights on. The driver's door was open, and Spanish music blared from the radio. The driver apparently vamoosed in quite a hurry. I peeked inside the car and noticed empty beer bottles strewn everywhere.

Roger was on his cell phone calling 911. He'd left his car parked on the street, a decision I'm sure he now deeply regretted. Evidently, the inebriated amigo had smashed into the back of Roger's car and pushed it into our yard, dangerously close to our bedroom window. I'm guessing Speedy Gonzales made the snap decision to get the "dell out of hodge." We would learn later that the car was borrowed, and its driver had just been released from jail earlier in the day.

By the time the police were done and the wrecker had extricated both cars from our yard, the sun had begun to rise. There would be no more sleeping this night.

We were both tired and aggravated, but simultaneously grateful the cars hadn't come crashing into our bedroom. We got down on our knees together in our bedroom and thanked the Lord for protecting us. Too often in a dangerous world we take our safety for granted. Tonight's 'big bang' was just another reminder of that fact.

16

The Group

Father Ted cleared his throat. "I appreciate you all coming to our special group. It takes a lot of courage to get together with others and talk about something as personal as your marriage. You are to be commended.

"I'd like us to start by going around the circle and getting to know each other a little better. Tell us your name, what you do for a living, your spouse's name, and how long you've been married. And finally, what you want to get out of these sessions. Let's start with you, Burton.

"Okay. Hi, my name is Burton Earney, and I'm a professional welder. And please, no Muppet jokes. I'm actually a Junior and my dad was named Burton long before that stupid children's show ever came along."

"Man, I know your pain," I said. Everyone laughed.

Burton continued. "It gets worse. My wife's name is Cookie. I was probably attracted to her because of some warped, Freudian impulse. We've been married just under two years, and we have a son named Grover—"

"What?!" There was a collective gasp.

He cackled. "No, not really. His name is Elliot. Let's see, what else. Oh, I'm here because I want to learn how to be a better husband."

Father Ted chuckled. "Thank you, Burton. I can see this is going to be a fun group. Go ahead, Elmo. You're next."

"My Name is Ellington Jenkins, but I go by Elmo—ergo, the ongoing *Sesame Street* humiliation. Burton, I've got your back, buddy. I'm on staff here at First Church. My wife's name is Bonnie, and I'm here because Father Ted bribed me by promising to take me out on his new sailboat."

"New boat? Did he tell the Lone Ranger?" someone quipped.

"Thank you!" I cheered. "Finally, another Lyle Lovett fan!"

Father Ted laughed. "I guess I need to download this Lovett fellow's record. Okay, who's next?"

"That would be me. Sorry guys—my name is just plain ol' Jed Fiskers.

No connection at all to Jim Henson, though I am a Swedish

chef."

The group howled.

"I'm kidding, I'm kidding! I'm just a lowly stockbroker—emphasis on the word 'broke.' It's funny because I vaguely remember having money *before* I got married," he said, looking pensive.

All the guys nodded in agreement. Father Ted just shook his head.

He continued. "My wife's name is Audra, and we've been married almost a year. As a husband, I'm hoping to find out how to better balance my time and my finances."

They continued around the circle. Richard Evans was a pharmaceutical rep. Billy Jacobs was a fireman. Doug Dandy worked for an insurance company.

The six of us held two significant things in common. First, we'd all been married two years or less. And second, we'd all foolishly agreed to be one of Father Ted's guinea pigs.

To lay the general groundwork for our sessions, Father Ted spent the evening talking about the different needs that men and women bring into the marriage relationship.

He asked us what our expectations were, and what we perceived our wives' expectations to be.

It was a good first session until he dropped a bomb on us. "Next week we'll be discussing physical intimacy. So come prepared with some good questions."

Gulp.

It was another beautiful Wednesday on the downtown mall. I took a bite of my hot dog. "I thought Pastor Snooker did a good job at staff meeting explaining Tom Applebee's departure." I snatched one of Bonnie's corn chips—baked, of course.

She playfully slapped my hand. "As good as could be expected, I suppose. You do know everyone already knew what he was going to say, right? And for the record, they didn't hear it from me."

"I know. If I had to venture a guess, I'd say Harry spread the word. He just can't help himself. The man has the largest mouth in the world—literally. Have you ever seen him put a whole unpeeled orange in his mouth? It's like watching something from a Ridley Scott movie. One of his early alien flicks." I quivered at that thought.

Bonnie laughed. "Maybe Harry *is* an alien. That would explain a lot."

"Oooo, you may be right. I'll never look at Harry the same way again."

She segued. "What's the latest word on your book, sweets?"

"I've talked them into changing the title and the cover design.

Actually, Brown & Brewster has been a lot easier to work with than I'd anticipated."

"Really? What's the new title?"

"The Inevitability of Change."

"Oh, I like that much better. What about the cover?"

"Right now it's still in the conceptual stage. There will be a person—okay, 'sexism alert'—there will be a *man* carrying a book entitled *Resistance* under his arm. He'll be opening a door with 'The Future' painted above it. And through the opening, you can see a contemporary worship service in progress."

"Nice. Let me see if I'm picking up the correct interpretation. The established, or dare I say, 'older' church is clinging to tradition, for lack of a better word. In order to reach the next generation, they're going to have to lower their resistance to change and step into the future. How'd I do?"

"Well, that's the basic idea. We'll have to wait and see what the graphics wizards at B&B come up with. And get this—instead of the standard one-year new-book gestation period, they've decided to put my book on a fast track. It'll be out before you can say 'tofu and sprouts.'"

"Very funny. Then what?"

"Then contractually, I'm required to do at least six book signings in major market areas. I'm not looking forward to those trips at all."

"C'mon, it'll be fun. Maybe they'll let you bring me along on a—"

"Excuse me," someone said. "I hate to interrupt your lunch."

I looked up to find Art Menthor standing beside our bench. "Hey, Art."

Bonnie smiled. "You're not interfering, Art. What brings you downtown on a Wednesday afternoon?"

"I was having tea with a dear old friend over at Kranky's, and I overheard some of the First Church office ladies talking about Tom Applebee quitting. Is it true?" he asked in a graveled tone.

I frowned. "I'm afraid it is." I felt like asking him if his ears were tingling, but I thought better of it. "Art, are you a tea drinker?"

"Not normally, but my friend talked me into it. He even suggested putting honey in the tea."

"Any chance your friend's na—"

"Like I told you all," he cut me off while thrusting his fist into the air. "God's not happy 'bout that renovation project. Tom was a good man. Who'll be next?" He wandered off muttering to himself.

Bonnie leaned over and whispered in my ear. "That was so strange."

"No kidding. I'm beginning to think Art's starting to lose his marbles. There's a fine line between being deeply spiritual and mystically insane. We had a guy at seminary who got all mystical and started fasting and wearing sackcloth and calling down God's judgment on the faculty. One day, he said an angel told him to climb up on the two-story dorm roof and jump off, promising God would catch him."

"What happened?"

I winced at the memory of it. "He jumped and broke both legs."

"Ouch!" Bonnie looked around to make sure Art was out of earshot. "Y'know, Art hangs around the church all the time. I guess we'd better keep an eye on him, huh?"

"Yep. I'll mention him to Pastor Snooker. He's known Art for years."

I wonder if the friend Art was having tea with was Eli? Hmm.

Along came Thursday morning. I was still thinking about Art Menthor as I rode the elevator up to the fifth floor. Were my ears tingling, or was that just a low-frequency vibration generated by the moving elevator car?

Now don't get all paranoid, Elmo.

I walked into Tom Applebee's office suite.

"I still can't believe Canasta was trying to get me fired," Adrianne said as she handed me a key to Tom's office. "I was never anything but super nice to her. It just goes to show, you never know."

"Thanks. I don't plan on being up here that much. Pastor Snooker will come in around ten each morning and leave around two in the afternoon. If there's anything pressing when he's not around, just give me a call.

"Adrianne, you know the ins-and-outs of this job better than anyone, so Pastor Snooker and I are counting on you to help us pull this off. Let's try to meet around 10:30 each morning for a quick meeting with Pastor Snooker to make sure we're all on the same page. Okay?"

"Sounds good, Elmo."

Some time back, Bonnie had filled me in on Adrianne Figgie's background. She was in her mid-thirties and single; an only child, raised by an overbearing mother and absentee father.

Apparently, she'd been quite thin when she was younger, and even participated in beauty pageants as a teen under the tutelage of her harsh mom. When she broke away from home after high school, she was an easy target for manipulative men. After a series of destructive relationships, she turned to food for comfort.

At the invitation of a friend, she started attending First Church for the fellowship. Eventually, Tom Applebee led her to the Lord after one of his Sunday evening sermons. Several years later, he hired her to be his executive assistant. She'd been on the staff at First Church now for almost ten years. Adrianne was good at her job, and well-liked by everyone—with the exception of Canasta, of course.

"Adrianne, could you email me a list of the tasks Tom covered on a daily basis? Regular meetings, organizing the hospital visitation teams, any weekly written reports he produced—that sort of thing. Give the same list to Pastor Snooker, but he'll need a hard copy. He's not real good with email."

"Will do," she said with a big smile.

"Also, let me know when he comes in this morning. I need to run something by him. Thanks!"

On my way down, the elevator stopped on the second floor. Thurm stepped in smelling like kimchi.

I coughed. "Well, I see someone's been to the print shop this morning."

"Not funny. With Canasta gone, I'm back to doing all my own secretarial work."

"And we all know how badly that went before," I said laughing. "I really do feel sorry for you, buddy."

"I can tell." He wasn't laughing.

"Thurm, I hate to tell you this, but there's been a hiring freeze put in place until they find a permanent replacement for Tom Applebee. They told Pastor Snooker he'd be filling in for at least three months. Then it'll take the new guy several months to get acclimated to his job before—"

"Elmo, I get it," he snapped. "You forget Canasta was my first secretary. My first three years here, I did it all myself, and I can do it again."

The elevator opened, and we walked through the back hall door and into the first floor offices.

"Thurm, I wasn't rubbing it in. I was just explaining the situation. Listen, if you get in a bind just have Julianne give you a hand. I'll let her know that's okay."

"Thanks, Elmo. That's really *magnanimous* of you," he said sarcastically as we walked past Father Ted's open door.

Father Ted looked up. "Good usage of that word, Thurm." He sniffed the air. "How's Lucky the printer this morning?"

"That's it. I'm changing shirts." Thurm stormed off down the hall.

I stepped into Father Ted's office. "I thought our first men's group meeting went rather well Tuesday evening."

"Yes, yes. I think our time together is going to be quite beneficial for all the guys."

I blushed. "I'll admit I'm a little nervous about next week's topic. I tend to be a pretty private person."

He grinned. "Don't worry another second. It's going to be a lightweight discussion. Trust me. Also, contrary to the rumor going around, Erlene Markham is *not* going to be there."

"Yikes." I gasped, heading back out his door. "Then again, that *would* make for some colorful discussion."

I could still hear his guffaws as I walked down the hall.

An hour later I was back up on the fifth floor.

"Morning, Ellington. Adrianne said you needed to see me?" Pastor Snooker's wrinkled face broadened into a smile.

"Yes, I've got one quick item. What can you tell me about Art Menthor? He's been acting a bit strange lately."

Pastor Snooker chuckled. "That's probably because Art *is* a bit strange. Always has been. What sacred mischief has he been up to these days?"

"He's on a rant about the sanctuary renovation project. Say's the church is out of God's will, and implied that's why Tom Applebee is no longer here. Then there's all the mumbo jumbo about 'tingling ears.' He's not dangerous or anything, is he?"

"Oh, I don't think so. Art's an odd duck for sure, but he's sincere. Change is hard for us old toots. Art loves that sanctuary and has personally taken care of it for many, many years. I'm sure he's distressed by the renovation plans."

"I'm just scared he's going to lash himself to the altar or something worse . . . like setting the place on fire."

"I tell you what. I'll speak with Art and try to discern if there is indeed a problem. I'll let you know what I find out. Okay?"

"Wonderful. Thanks. One more thing. Have you ever noticed your ears tingling when you ride the executive elevator?"

17

The Plumber

"**Y**es, First Church is going through a tough patch. It all started when a small but influential group of disgruntled members tried to run off the senior pastor. Now the associate pastor has resigned under a cloud. And on top of everything else, we're in the middle of launching a huge capital renovations project." I sighed as I put a double shot of honey into my cup of tea.

Eli flashed a knowing smile. "From the time of the apostles, God's church has always had its fair share of struggles. Sometimes we forget it's the local church that holds down the front-line positions in God's battle for the hearts of mankind.

"You've heard it said that to be victorious in a military battle you must have the most 'boots on the ground'. Conversely, to be victorious in a spiritual battle, you must have the most 'knees on the ground'."

"You mean people praying?"

"That's correct. All too often the local church tries to accomplish great things for God through human strength and commonsense. I call it *spiritual hubris*. Elmo, challenges and difficulties will come to your church, and when they do, lead your staff and your membership to pray for God's solutions and God's purpose."

"Hey, girl." I gave Bonnie a kiss on her cheek as she sat typing at her office desk. "Is Louis around?"

"I think he's in the men's room. He should be back any time. How was Eli this morning?"

"Rock solid. He taught me a new phrase: 'knees on the ground'. The idea is to challenge your church membership to pray. That's what I want to talk with Louis about."

"Wow, never heard that before. Powerful, huh? How was your tea?"

"It's growing on me. The honey helps a lot, but let's be honest— you're my real honey."

Bonnie smirked. "Corny, but I know you're sincere."

Louis entered the room. "Morning, Elmo."

"Mornin', Louis. Got a minute?"

"Sure. Come on into my office." He followed me in and closed the door. "Grab a seat."

I noticed that he had some flecks of yellow paint on his hands. "Jane E. got you painting the bathroom or kitchen again?"

He held up his hands. "Both, and I can't get this enamel off my fingers. I guess it'll just have to wear off."

I chuckled. "Try Goop-Off. It came to my rescue a few weeks ago."

"Really," he said as he kicked back in his chair. "What happened?"

"Well, it was one of those Saturdays where everything was a personal calamity. I felt as if I were in a Charlie Chaplin movie. I'm surprised Bonnie didn't tell you about it. At my expense, of course."

"That bad?"

"Yes. It all started when I was straightening up our home office. Bonnie had this huge pile of Restoration Hardware catalogs. I picked them up to either hide or discard. I mean, who can afford anything from that place?"

"That's the gospel truth," Louis said laughing.

"As I gathered up the catalogs, one of them sliced my index finger right under the nail. The uber-paper cut of all time. Of course, the real pain didn't kick in until I washed my hands. Yowee!"

"Been there, done that, many times."

"So, as I was recovering from my killer paper cut, Bonnie calls me over to the back door. She says, 'Do you smell something rank?' I did, and it was *nasty*. I stepped out into our backyard and found this disgusting, sludgy liquid seeping out from under our crawlspace door."

Louis smiled. "A sewer line rupture. Been there, done that also."

"Bingo. I did an online search for local plumbers, and the first name on the list was 'AA Das Plumber.' Of course, it's the weekend which means he charges two hundred times his normal rate. Ouch!"

"Das Plumber?"

"Yeah, he was German—broken English and all. Out he comes to repair our broken sewer line. The whole time he's there working, he has our water turned off and tells us not to flush the *toiletten*. It quickly evolved into Third World conditions inside the Jenkins manse."

"Bonnie decided to cut her losses and take a nap. Soon thereafter, Das Plumber takes off for his *Mittagspause*—his lunch break. Like the occasional idiot I am, I decided to go take a look at what Das Plumber had been up to under our house."

"Uh oh," Louis cracked.

"Uh oh is right. As I leaned through the crawlspace opening to take a peek, I lost my balance. In trying to catch myself, I stuck my left hand into one of Das Plumber's buckets filled with some hideous goop. Big trouble. My hand's covered with this rubbery, pasty, won't-come-off-easy crud, the water's turned off, and Bonnie's napping.

"Back in the house, I foolishly tried to wipe off my hand with some toilet paper. Now I've got sticky stuff all over both hands, and torn pieces of toilet paper stuck to each finger. I looked like Lucy Ricardo caught in one of her silly dilemmas—*waaaa!* I didn't cry, of course. At least, I'm not admitting to it."

"Of course. Who would?" Louis winked.

"Deftly using the palms of my hands, I rifled through our kitchen closet and thankfully, found a bottle of Goop-Off. The instructions said to wear rubber gloves, which in my opinion, kind of defeated the purpose of using the stuff to clean my hands. I poured some on an old rag and started cleaning my hands one finger at a time. It wasn't coming off easily, but it was coming off.

"Everything was fine until I got to the finger with the aforementioned paper cut. When the goop-remover hit that cut, it felt like a hundred volts of electricity shooting through my index finger. Since the water had been turned off, there was no way to rinse it off and end the terrible pain. I spun around in circles screaming at the top of my lungs. Then I had a brainstorm—the toilet was still full of water! Unfortunately, there was a caveat. We'd been using the toilet all morning, but weren't allowed to flush it."

Louis sat up in his chair. "You didn't stick your—"

"Yes, I did! What else could I do?"

"Yuck?! Man, that's disgusting!"

"Don't worry. Even though I was in excruciating pain and full-blown panic mode, I had the presence of mind to pull the top off the toilet tank and stick my hand in the clean water there."

Louis blew out a sigh of relief.

"No kidding. Bonnie, who'd been awakened by my bloodcurdling screams, came flying into the bathroom to find me with my hand in the toilet tank. She looked aghast, then said, 'I'm not even going to ask.' Then she pivoted and walked out, shaking her head. True story."

Louis laughed. "That's a great tale, Elmo."

"Here's the kicker. When Das Plumber returned from his lunch break, he apologized for neglecting to inform me that he'd already turned the water back on before he left. He finished up and wanted to be paid in gold bars, of course."

Louis pulled up to his desk. "All frivolity aside, what can I do for Elmo Jenkins today?"

I leaned forward in my chair. "I have an idea I want to run by you before I mention it to Pastor Snooker, and ultimately, to Dr. Jorgensen."

"Sure. What's your idea?"

"In light of the fact that First Church is reeling from the circumstances of Tom's departure, and it's not been that long since

Sturgis Weaver tried to fire Dr. Jorgensen, I think we should put the renovation project and fundraising program on hold for three months."

"Seriously?"

"Yes. I want to recommend that we call the church into a season of prayer. I'm of the opinion that First Church needs to regroup spiritually. We need a time of forgiveness and reconciliation, and a chance to realign with God's purpose for this church. I believe if we do this, the fundraising and renovations will stand a much better chance of optimal success."

"That's a pretty big and bold idea. The *For the Future We Build* initiative already has quite a head of steam behind it."

"Oh, I know. This is definitely a late-in-the-game idea, but I believe it has merit. It came from a conversation I had with my older friend, Eli, down at Kranky's. He said churches sometimes lose focus, but they can get it back through prayer. He says the spiritual battle for a church is won when the members put their 'knees on the ground' and pray."

"It's a powerful concept. I'll give you that. Take your idea to Pastor Snooker first and see what he thinks. If he gets onboard, ask him to go with you to share it with Dr. Jorgenson. 'Knees on the ground.' Wow, Elmo. This could be something profoundly special."

Monday afternoon meant hospital visits. I'd just finished my last visit when I spotted Eddie Hughes limping through the main lobby of St. Michael's. He had on one of those soft boots you wear after foot surgery.

"Elmo, my man. Arrivederci!"

"You're using Italian, and *almost* correctly. I'm impressed."

He pulled an *Italian for Dummies* paperback out of his back pocket. "Yeah, man. I'm dating this Italian nurse, Selvaggia. So I've been brushing up on her lingo."

"An Italian nurse, really? Now I'm super impressed. Tell me about her."

"Her name means *wild*. Cool huh? But no one can pronounce it, so she goes by Sarah."

"How did you meet her?"

"I was coming to see you, dude; here at the hospital back when you bonked your head and I broke my arm. Remember when you saved that boy's life, and I saved yours?"

"How can I forget? You remind me about it at least once a month."

"Sarah was working at the nurses' station that night, and she wouldn't let me see you because you were supposedly sleeping."

"They were all Nurse Ratcheds if I recall," I quipped.

"Oh, not Sarah. When she found out I was your wingman on the kid rescue, she got all starry-eyed and signed my cast. I tried to get her number that night, but she rebuffed me. Well, you know me. I asked again the next day, and she agreed to go to dinner. We dated two or three times, and then the strangest thing happened. The day I went to have my cast cut off, she dropped me like a hot potato. Wouldn't see me, or answer my calls, or nothing. So I moved on."

"Then why are you studying Italian now?"

"Life sure is funny. Sarah and I reconnected after I dislocated my toe at the church picnic. I bumped into her at the hospital after I got fitted for this soft cast. We started dating again. It's been great."

"Why did she have such a drastic change of heart—twice?"

"It's the cast, man. I think she has some sort of Florence Nightingale thing going on. I'm scared to quit wearing it. I'm afraid she might dump me again."

"Eddie, you can't wear a soft boot the rest of your life," I said, cracking a smile.

"I know, man. I know. I just can't come up with a better plan at this point. Oh—there she is. I gotta run."

"Arrivederci!" I smiled as I watched Eddie fake-limp his way across the lobby in a soft boot he didn't need to be wearing.

I'd never met anyone quite like Eddie Hughes. Somewhere there's a broken mold.

18

The Nightmares

Who's the CD for?" Bonnie asked as she caught up to me with her Wal-Mart grocery cart.

I tossed it into the basket with the other items. "I'm gonna give it to Father Ted."

Bonnie picked it up and flipped it over. "Why in the world would you be giving Father Ted a Lyle Lovett CD?"

"It's a joke, really. Remember when he traded in his Viper and bought a sailboat? Well, Lyle Lovett's most famous song is called, 'If I Had a Boat,' and Father Ted's never heard of it. There's an enormously funny, though mildly profane line in it about the Lone Ranger. Some of us have alluded to the song, and Father Ted never gets it. So, I thought I'd get him the CD, and save him any further public humiliation. A bit of Lyle Lovett enlightenment, so to speak."

"Aren't you the thoughtful one? Okay, now what's your ulterior motive?"

"Whoa. We haven't been married long enough for you to see through me that easily! Alas, *dearest,* you are correct in your assessment. Initially, Father Ted promised to take us sailing, but he hasn't brought it back up, even though I've dropped several well-placed hints since then. So—"

"So the CD is to remind him to keep his promise and—"

"—and take us sailing. I even thought about making him a copy of the song and dubbing in 'gnilias omlE ekat' over and over again in the background."

Bonnie frowned. "What? Is that Latin or something?"

I laughed out loud. "No, no. It's 'take-Elmo-sailing' said *backwards*. I admit it's an old-school trick, but he's an old-school guy. Hey, it worked well for the Beatles."

"You're such a spaz, and I love that about you." She gave me a big kiss on the lips.

PDA alert! "How about, 'emoh einnoB ekat'?"

"Yes, ma'am. You check out, and I'll get the car."

"If I could have your attention, please?" I could feel the droplets of sweat rolling down my back under my shirt.

The din of noise started to abate, but only slightly.

"This won't take long, I promise," I called out over the gathering as I continued to perspire profusely.

The odd assortment of people began to end their conversations and turn toward the corner of the room where I was standing.

"Will there be enough time afta' for crumpets and tea?" asked a well- dressed Lopez McGill.

"There will be plenty of time for refreshments," I assured him.

"Has your tripod gone missing, or did you just neglect to bring it? Perhaps it's in your car? Would you like me to retrieve it for you?"

"No, Eddie, that won't be necessary. I won't be using a tripod this evening."

"NO TRIPOD? That's fundraising heresy," shouted Erlene Markham. "Ya big PANSY!"

Now the back of my shirt was drenched, and I could feel the sweat rolling down my legs.

I looked down at my three-by-five cards. Across the top it said:

Elmo 'Cornbread' Jenkins (Pansy)

What?! Since my hands were also sweating, my notes were now smeared and unreadable. I would have to wing it. "Thank you all for—"

"Harry Simpkins had a tripod when he spoke to us," someone barked.

I lost my patience. "Enough about the dang tripod, OKAY?"

"No need to blow your top. Will there be time for refreshments afterward?" Lopez asked again.

"Ramona used a tripod *and* a flip chart," someone else chimed in.

"Ya big pansy!" Erlene snarled with her false teeth flashing.

The group started closing in on me chanting, "Pansy. Pansy. Pansy. Pansy—"

I woke up in a cool froth, panting.

Bonnie raised her head off her pillow. "Elmo, you all right?" She reached over and touched my arm. "Whoa, cowboy, you're soaking wet. Do you have a fever?"

"No, I just had a bad nightmare."

"That bad?"

"Oh, yeah. Anytime Eddie and Erlene are in the same dream, you know it's gonna get ugly."

"Another fundraising dream, huh?"

"Unfortunately, yes. The third one this week, and they're getting progressively darker. It's as if I'm becoming Lord Fiduciary of the Flies."

"I'm too tired even to try and comprehend the deeper meanings of that thought. Maybe you should drop in on Father Ted and see if he has any insight into your sleep issues."

"Yeah, I'd already given that idea some thought. Maybe I can snag him tomorrow. Listen, I'm gonna grab a shower and try to cool down."

"You want some company?" she asked mischievously.

"I appreciate the offer, but you get some sleep. We both have a full day tomorrow." I gave her a kiss on the cheek and headed for the bathroom.

I think I may have just broken a cardinal rule of manhood. Oh well, there's a first time for everything.

I tapped twice on his door and stuck my head into the office. "Morning, Father Ted. Do you have few minutes available to counsel a tormented soul?"

"Why, sure. What could be bothering you on a beautiful morning like today?" he asked with an oversized smile.

I took a seat. "I see you've finally decided to be a team player and wear a golf shirt on casual Friday."

He chuckled. "To be honest, I didn't own any golf shirts, so it took me a while to procure a few. This is a hand-me-up from my son, Geoffrey. He's a bigwig corporate type with a closet full of these from the great courses around the world. He was more than happy to give his old man a few from his stock. This one's from Torrey Pines." He partially covered his mouth with his hand and whispered. "I have no idea where that is." He chuckled heartily.

"That's right you prefer sailing." *Hint, hint.*

"True, true."

"In accordance with your preference, I've brought you a small gift." I handed him the Lyle Lovett CD.

"Well, looky here." He smiled while perusing the play list.

"If you like Texas two-step tunes, you'll enjoy the entire album, but the song you'll like the most is the one about buying a boat." *Hint, hint.*

"Why, thank you, Elmo. I'll listen to it in my car on the way home this afternoon."

"You'll get a kick out of it. I promise."

He laid the CD on his desk. "Speaking of Texas, I used to have a great family from the Lone Star State who were members of my church—the Wreinholts. A large clan, actually; three generations deep. The whole family was in the furniture business—the father, his sons, and even a few of the grandsons. It was a very tight-knit family, and the patriarch, Bud Wreinholt, controlled it all. And I do mean *all* of it—both the business and the family, down to the last detail. Bud was the original micro-manager.

"The oldest son, Rick, told me that during church services he, his wife, and his kids always sat on the third or fourth row near the front of the sanctuary. His father Bud, the old patriarch, always sat on the first row of the balcony with Rick's mother. That way, they could keep an eye on the entire Wreinholt clan.

"Rick said one of his boys was acting up during the worship service one Sunday morning. Johnnie, who was just seven or eight years old at the time, kept pestering a classmate who was sitting on the pew in front of them, creating a disturbance. When Johnnie continued to act up, Rick heard the old man up in the balcony clear his throat. Rick knew exactly what that meant—both Johnnie *and* Rick would be taking a trip to the woodshed that afternoon."

"Ouch!" I laughed. "Oh my! They don't make families like that any more, at least not in our culture."

"No they don't, and I'm not sure if that's a good thing or a bad thing. Anyway, what can I do for the Right Reverend Jenkins this morning?"

"I need some advice. I've had some trouble sleeping lately. Let's just say I'm a bit apprehensive about the *For the Future We Build* home meetings, and it's impacting my REM cycles. You see, I have this hyper-aversion to hard sells. I don't like being arm-twisted into buying something I don't like or want, and I vehemently *hate* having to hard sell someone else. I come from a family of salespeople, and as you might guess, I was always the black sheep."

"No lemonade stands, huh?"

"Only under duress, and never profitable."

Father Ted leaned forward and rested his elbows on his desk. "There are several things you need to take into account. First, remember these are volunteer gatherings. Only those who want to attend will come, and they know ahead of time the context of the meeting. No one there will be offended by the topic.

"Second—and by far the most important point—God doesn't need the money to accomplish the goal. He owns the cattle on a thousands hills. These meetings are about the membership investing their lives in the ministry of the Lord through this church. It's about *buying in*, if you will, to what God is going to accomplish through these renovated facilities. It's about making sacrifices that will produce spiritual fruit and bring about life change.

"Christ-followers need to be challenged to look beyond their own needs and fulfillment. This is an excellent opportunity to present them with such a challenge."

"Well, that was eloquently stated, and from a spiritual perspective, impossible to refute—though even now, the cynic in me is feverishly searching for a way to refute it." I shifted in my chair. "You wouldn't be open to standing in as my representative at my meetings, would you? No, scratch that. It was a joke. Kind of."

He laughed. "Elmo—" he paused, still laughing. "Listen, you're going to do just fine. Just follow the script you're given, and let God do the fundraising. As far as sleeping goes, try half an Ambien, or a shot of Nyquil. Or better yet, a cup of warm milk."

Yuck. "Who drinks warm milk?"

"Granted, that one's probably an outdated remedy. Stick with the narcotics."

I got up to leave. "Thanks for the pep talk. I'm going to *sail* out of here and try to get some work done." *Hint, hint.* Let me know what you think of Lyle Lovett. And if anyone asks, Torrey Pines is in southern California. Ciao!"

19

The Numbers

A large part of Tom Applebee's responsibilities had to do with the Sunday school program at First Church, specifically the Adult Sunday school. After Raze Hankins left, Tom had taken over the whole show.

At First Church, as with most traditional churches, when it comes to Bible study groups, it's all about Sunday mornings.

Pastor Snooker and I split up the Sunday morning responsibilities. He would meet with the Adult teachers and department directors as a group each Sunday morning before the classes began. I would be in charge of the *numbers*.

During these teachers' meetings, Pastor Snooker would quickly summarize the lesson for the day and answer any last-minute questions related to the material or associated media. First Church utilized standardized curriculum for all of its adult classes. By design, all forty or so adult classes were teaching the same lesson on the same Sunday morning.

Why? Two reasons: *ease* and more importantly, *control.*

In a large church with an overworked staff, standardized curriculum was the smart ticket. If a reputable and doctrinally-sound publishing house was used, all the CE director or Minister of Education had to worry about was quantity. The lesson books shipped quarterly and included one lesson for each week in the quarter. Individual booklets, often called *quarterlies*, were available for each class member. Special editions were available for teachers, jammed with extra materials designed to help with the lesson preparation.

This brings us to the second reason standardized curriculum was often used—control. By having every teacher and director on the same page, if you will, the potential for trouble was greatly minimized. The occasional rogue teacher could easily be brought back into line by simply making sure their teaching conformed to the curriculum. If they refused to play by the rules, they would be reassigned to the toddler department where the impact of their heretical teachings would be, for all practical purposes, effectively neutralized.

The obvious drawback to the standardized curriculum approach was the lack of local quality control. What if the lesson material sucked? Which it often did. The handful of gifted teachers had no problem turning a lemon into lemonade, but the majority of the volunteer teaching staff struggled to make such a lesson relevant and interesting.

In the past this problem was seamlessly resolved by the amazing talents of Alex Leichhardt . As Sunday School Director, Alex would provide additional resources and tools for the teachers each week, occasionally rewriting those weaker lessons. Unfortunately, Alex had recently moved, taking a job in another city for some shadowy research think-tank whose sole purpose was to restore Pluto's planetary status. *Hmm.*

Meaning, for now, the curriculum would have to suffice as is.

Since Pastor Snooker was covering the teachers and the lesson material, I was left to deal with the numbers. Most leaders of large churches will tell you that numbers don't matter. They're lying. In large churches, numbers are everything. Why? Because numbers are used to monitor growth, and growth is how success is measured. If you're not succeeding, you are (go ahead and say it)—

FAILING.

Gasp! This is America! And face it—in America, failing is strongly frowned upon.

In the church, this line of thinking ramps up to a whole new level of intensity because numbers represent souls, adding an *eternal* component to the equation. Thus, failure carries with it the ramification of abandoning souls to eternal damnation. Not good. Which might explain why most Ministers of Education carry Rolaids in their pockets, and keep a hidden bottle of Maalox in their offices.

Keeping track of the Sunday school numbers at First Church required the highly-refined skills of a CPA. Two sets of numbers were tabulated each week—those enrolled in Sunday school, and those that were in attendance.

Why worry about enrollment? Because enrollment is the golden axiom of Sunday school growth. Christian educators are taught the irrefutable truth that if an individual enrolls in a Sunday school class, there is a greater likelihood that individual will actually attend it. To put it simply, higher enrollment leads to higher attendance.

Thus, the 'enrollment campaign' was born. Nationwide, grandiose, expansive enrollment campaigns were planned and implemented. The number-crunching reached ecstatic levels. The ratios created quickly became the gold standard. If a hundred people were enrolled in Sunday school, then twenty of those enrolled would actually attend. Extrapolate. If one thousand people were enrolled, that means two hundred would attend. Extrapolate. If five thousand were enrolled . . . well, you get the idea. Plans were drawn up to enroll entire neighborhoods. Or better yet, entire zip codes! Enrollment became the Holy Grail of the Sunday school growth movement. Vast numbers of church members were thrust two-by-two into the hoods and burbs, going door-to-door to enroll people in Sunday school.

After several years of earnest effort with less-than-stellar results, the thinking shifted, citing other critical factors as necessary to Sunday school attendance beyond that of enrollment.

In all fairness, these campaigns attracted many new people for Bible study and church involvement. But mostly, they bulked up Sunday school rolls with gargantuan numbers with only a minuscule fraction of those enrolled actually attending.

I made a snap decision. During my tenure as the interim "numbers guy", I would ignore the enrollment side of the tabulation. I'd focus solely on the souls who were, in fact planting their bottoms in the Sunday school chairs each Sunday morning. Yes, I took into account the risk that I might be branded a CE heretic, but I reasoned the new Associate Pastor would be more than happy to issue me a pardon. After all, I was keeping his seat warm until he arrived.

At First Church, each Sunday school class had an attendance folder. Each week, Adrianne Figgie would place an updated attendance printout into each folder listing the names of every person enrolled in that class. Since First Church never dropped anyone enrolled in a class (unless threatened by a lawsuit), these printouts could be quite lengthy. It was the job of the oft-underappreciated class secretary to wade through the bulky roster each Sunday, marking those who were in attendance.

By royal decree, the class secretaries were not allowed to take attendance until forty-five minutes into the class period, in case someone showed up late. And someone always showed up late. These folks were informally referred to as stragglers, and collectively held in mild contempt.

Previously, at the designated time, Alex Leichhardt or Tom Applebee would walk the halls collecting these folders from the appropriately-named "folder buckets" mounted on the wall outside each classroom. Since there were forty or so Adult Sunday School classes, each with its own heavy attendance folder, a uniquely-designed cart with reinforced wheels, dubbed the "Abacus-Rex," was used for the collection process. This would now be my job. After I gathered all forty Adult Sunday school class folders, with the requisite completed attendance printout included, I'd wheel the cart up to Adrianne Figgie's office on the fifth floor.

Adrianne, with cat-like quickness, would total the adult Sunday school attendance. She would add in the attendance numbers for the youth, children, and preschool classes to arrive at the *Final Number.* That's right. Even newborn babies were included in the Sunday school attendance numbers at First Church. Go figure—literally. *Perhaps we should start enrolling the hospital maternity ward nurseries.* Nah, though I had no doubt that somewhere, some overzealous CE director had tried to do just that.

In the past, when the *Final Number* had been determined,

Adrianne would simply email it to Tom Applebee's Blackberry as he sat on the platform. He would then include the *Final Number* when he gave the Sunday school report during the morning worship service. Unfortunately, Pastor Snooker still thought a Blackberry was something you spread on a piece of toast, so we had to devise a new way to send him the *Final Number*. Adrianne would now text the *Final Number* to Skip, one of the guys in the sound booth. Using a large Magic Marker, Skip would write the number on a placard and hold it up for Pastor Snooker to see from the platform.

This new system worked great until one humorous Sunday morning. We'd implemented this new plan while Harry Simpkins was away on vacation for two weeks. No one thought to tell Harry about the new system when he returned. This omission led to yet another Harry Simpkins precious moment.

Like many churches, First Church assigned every child in the nursery or children's area a six-digit identification number. If a problem with a particular child occurred during the worship service, the child's ID number was flashed in red on a small light panel over the organ. This signaled the parent to go check on their child.

On Harry's first Sunday back from his vacation, during the last verse of the opening hymn, Harry noticed Skip holding up a poster board with the number 1787 on it. Harry quickly made the false assumption that the parental notification apparatus was down, and the parent of child 1787 needed to be notified.

At the conclusion of the hymn, Harry announced, "Would the parent of child 1787 please proceed to the children's area? Apparently, there is an emergency with your child." Now, everyone on the planet except Harry knew these ID numbers were *six* digits. This meant every parent with a six-digit number that included the number 1787 was immediately confused. When the terms "your child" and "emergency" are used in the same sentence, everyone assumes the worst and panics. A half-dozen or so people got up and rushed toward the exits. The remaining parents assumed something catastrophic must have occurred, so they also made a dash for the doors. The service quickly devolved into mass bedlam. A befuddled Harry Simpkins turned around to Dr. Jorgensen with a shrug of innocence and barked, "What'd I do?!"

It took a full fifteen minutes to resume order and get everyone reseated. During staff meeting the following week, the new method of getting the *Final Number* to the platform was unceremoniously scrapped. Louis would mention it later in the service when he made the announcements.

It was also part of my Sunday morning responsibilities to go around early before anyone arrived and distribute the aforementioned Sunday school class attendance folders to each classroom. On Friday afternoon, Ms. Figgie stuffed each folder with its updated class printout and loaded them all on the Abacus-Rex Sunday School cart. The cart was left in the church lobby tucked behind the Visitor Center counter.

One Sunday morning I grabbed the cart and started to distribute the Sunday school class folders. As I was dropping the third or fourth folder in its appropriate bucket, a half sheet of light-green paper fell out. As I stuffed the sheet back into the folder, the word "tingle" caught my eye. I pulled the paper back out and read it. It was a handwritten message which stated:

"Listen! I am going to bring a disaster on this place that will make the ears of everyone who hears of it tingle."
—Jeremiah 19:3
And you will know I'm the one who told you so. A.M.

My first thought was the Black Toe Enigma, but then it hit me— A. M. stood for Art Menthor. I opened another Sunday school class folder and sure enough, there was the same note. Art had hand-copied the note forty times, then clandestinely put one in each Adult Sunday school class folder. I wondered if the Old Testament prophets were as sneaky. I painstakingly extracted each note, including those from the folders I'd already delivered. Then, after distributing the remaining folders, I snatched up the pile of Art's handwritten missives and headed off to find Pastor Snooker.

"Well, it looks as if a potential disaster was averted." Pastor Snooker frowned as he placed Art's notes on his desk. "Elmo, what do you think Art's trying to accomplish here?"

"That's the million-dollar question of the day. I'm guessing it's his resistance to change complemented by a heavy-handed dose of Old Testament troubleshooting. The operative question is, what do we do about it?"

Pastor Snooker smiled. "I've already attempted the reasoning route with Art, and you see where that got us. He's a deacon. Maybe we should let the deacons handle this."

"That's a great idea. A little ordained self-policing may be just what the situation calls for. I'll have Adrianne set us up a lunch meeting with Deacon Chairman Sammy Dickers. He seems like a guy you can work with."

"I know Sammy well," Pastor Snooker said as he got up to leave for the Sunday school teachers' meeting. "I'm sure he'll be happy to help."

"I hope so," I said. "I'd hate for the staff to have to start wearing Kevlar."

Pastor Snooker looked confused. "Is that the special underwear the Mormons wear?"

    "What? No, no. Kevlar is a bulletproof material."

    "Oh dear. I hope it hasn't come to that."

    "I was just joking."

    I think?

20

The Idea

"**E**lmo, Burton, Jed, Richard, Billy, and Doug. Looks like everyone is present and accounted for. Wonderful," Father Tim began. "Let's get started with our session on physical intimacy. Now please, I'm not here to try to embarrass anyone. That's not the purpose of our group sessions. So, only share or ask questions about what you feel comfortable with. Are we all on the same page?"

We all nodded our heads.

"Good. I'd like to start with an updated version of an old story that goes like this. Three guys, all casual friends, are hanging out watching a sporting event. Let's call them Ed, Fred, and Samuel. Ed and Fred start discussing their physical relationships with their wives.

"Ed asks Fred, 'Biblically-speaking, how often do you sleep with your wife, and how long have you all been married?'

"Fred frowns. 'Oh, I don't know, not often enough. Maybe twice a month. We've been married six years now. How about you, Ed?'

"Ed also frowns. 'Well, you're doing better than me. We've been married four years, and we give it a go about once a month.'

"The whole time Ed and Fred are bellyaching about their marital bed woes, Samuel is just sitting there with a huge smile on his face.

"Finally, Ed notices and asks Samuel, 'Okay, how long have you been married?'

"Samuel pauses to think for a moment. 'Almost nine years now.'

"Ed continues. 'All right, then Biblically-speaking, how often do you sleep with your wife?'

"Samuel answers quickly, a smile still on his face. 'Only once every three years.'

"Both Ed and Fred are dumbfounded. 'Then why, for heaven's sake, are you smiling?'

"Samuel's smile grows even wider and his eyes dance. 'Because, my forlorn friends, tonight's the night!'"

The group shared a boisterous laugh which helped to assuage the nervousness we were all feeling.

Father Ted smiled. "Now, I'm willing to bet a year's salary that all six of you are more physically active with your wives than Ed, Fred, and Samuel combined. And that's great, but hear me when I say that physical intimacy, no matter how earthshaking, is only one component of a successful, lifelong marriage. It just tends to be the component that gets the most attention during your first couple years of marriage.

"Someone once said that if you put a penny in a jar every time you slept with your wife during your first year of marriage, then started taking out a penny for every time after that, the jar would never run out of pennies."

Burton blurted out. "It diminishes that fast?"

Father Ted smiled. "It's not a question of diminishing returns, but rather a matter of life layering in other stuff. That's why it's important to have a healthy understanding of physical intimacy, and the balanced role it should be playing in your relationship with your wife.

"We live in a world today that totally hyper-elevates sexuality, putting newly-married couples at a great disadvantage. Going into a marriage, the physical intimacy expectations —particularly from the man's perspective—are often way beyond realistic. New husbands are expecting their brides to look and perform like Raquel Welch."

"Who's Raquel Welch?" Billy asked.

Father Ted chuckled. "Okay, I'm showing my age here. Name a current bombshell."

"Bombshell?" Billy asked again.

Jed chimed in. "How about Scarlet Johansson?"

"Oh yeah," several of the guys confirmed.

We all nodded, agreeing that Scarlet Johansson was indeed a bombshell.

"Okay, then," Father Ted continued. "The world today wants you to think that your wife should look and perform like Scarlet Johansson. But there's a dirty little secret, and it's not what you think. The Scarlet Johansson you've watched in movies or seen in the magazines is a mirage. She doesn't exist. Oh, Scarlet is a real person, of course. But by the time you see her, thanks to Photoshopping or other special effects, she's been transformed into something that's unattainable in real life. She's become a fantasy.

"Takeaway #1 from tonight's session: do not expect your wife as your lover to be anyone other than herself. If you do, you'll both be bitterly disappointed and disillusioned."

I had to admit, it was another great session. Father Ted had put us all at ease and knew his topics well. I was surprised how open the guys were about their relationships. I was afraid it was going to be a discussion about the mechanics of intimacy, but instead, we focused on communication, caring, and understanding—concepts that take most new husbands a while to develop.

By the end of the session, we all agreed that we had much to learn about becoming the husband our wives deserved. Our takeaway mantra was: "It's not about me—it's about us."

As I drove home mulling over everything that had been shared, I couldn't help grinning as I wondered—would I be Frowning Fred or Smiling Samuel tonight?

On a rainy Wednesday afternoon, Pastor Snooker and I took our seats in Pastor Jorgensen's outer office.

"He'll be available in just a few minutes, fellas," Fran Bruker said with a smile. Then she leaned forward over her desk and lowered her voice. "He took a late call from Senator Hester. They're old golfing buddies."

I pretended to be offended. "Well, Fran, are you telling us that the esteemed Reverend Fred Snooker and I have to wait just because of a phone call from a United States Senator? I mean I've never been so—"

I quickly shut my mouth as Dr. Jorgenson's office door started to open. I noticed Fran snickering at me.

"Come on in, guys," he said as he turned to Fran and handed her a note. "Try to see if you can get us an Echelon tee time for Friday morning, and see if Harty Smith can join us. Let the club know there will be a security detail tagging along." He followed us through his office doorway and closed the door behind him.

He directed us toward his informal seating area away from his desk. Pastor Snooker and I sat on the couch, and Pastor Jorgensen sat in one of the wingback chairs.

"What's ol' Frisky Bob Hester after these days?" Pastor Snooker asked with a wry grin.

"Just like always. He comes around once every six years, about three months before his re-election campaign cranks up. We play the same little game every time, where he asks some standard questions about the church and the town. He just needs reassurance that the evangelicals are still in his boat. Fred, you know him well."

"Yes, I do," Pastor Snooker agreed. "Speaking of boats, I guess you know Father Ted bought himself a spiffy new red sailboat."

Dr. Jorgensen laughed. "Spiffy and fast! He took Sammy Dickers and me out for a spin around Lake Jacobs last Saturday. It's a real beauty, and he's quite the sailor. He even wears an official America's Cup windbreaker while he's sailing."

What? No way.

Pastor Snooker laughed. "Well, that's a relief. He's taking me and The Three Widows out this Saturday—his insistence about the ladies, not mine. Hope he's got one of those life preserver rings on a rope because I have no intention of jumping in to rescue Emily, Beatrice, or Fanny if one of them fall in. You'll know what happened if someone mentions The Two Widows next Sunday."

What do I have to do to get a ride on Father Ted's boat? Maybe it's an age thing?

Dr. Jorgensen crossed his legs and leaned back in his chair. "Tell me, gentlemen. What can I do for you today?"

Pastor Snooker began. "Thanks for making time for us. Ellington here approached me the other day with an idea for First Church that I believe merits some prayerful consideration. After a day or two of contemplation, I feel strongly enough about his suggestion to take up a few minutes of your valuable time presenting it to you. I asked Ellington to join me in this meeting to explain his idea."

"All right, you've sufficiently piqued my interest. Tell me your idea, Ellington."

I was nervous, but I pushed through. "Let me also thank you for taking the time to see us, Dr. Jorgenson. I have this friend named Eli Enoch—he's more of a mentor, I guess. Eli made a comment one morning last week that really caught my attention. He said in a military battle you want to have as many 'boots on the ground' as possible. Whereas, in a spiritual battle, you want to have as many 'knees on the ground' as possible. His conclusion being prayer wins spiritual battles."

Dr. Jorgenson smiled. "Knees on the ground. Interesting."

I continued. "I found his logic to be profound, even revolutionary. And the more I thought about it, the more it made sense. When I applied his concept to First Church, I kept coming back to this thought—*challenge the people to pray.* That's the foundation for this idea. And I wondered, in light of the difficult situations our church has gone through recently, i.e. Sturgis Weaver and now Tom Applebee, would it behoove us to push the pause button on the fundraising and renovation program for a time? If so, then we could call on our membership to pray—knees on the ground—for healing and a renewed vision."

Pastor Jorgensen sat there quietly with his hands folded against his chin. I noticed his eyes moistening. I glanced at Pastor Snooker who returned a gentle smile. We sat there in silence for what seemed like a long time.

Finally, Dr. Jorgenson spoke. "Ellington, your idea has merit, and I'm touched by your sensitivity to the Holy Spirit's nudging. Let me ponder this idea for few days and seek some wise counsel from a few of my mentors."

He asked Pastor Snooker to close us in prayer. Afterward, as we walked out of his office, Dr. Jorgensen patted me on the back and said, "Tell me more about your friend Eli Enoch."

21

The Chaperones

Why did you ever agree to this retreat?"

"Elmo, Louis is my boss, and he was in a tight spot. It's no different than you chaperoning for one of Thurm's youth activities."

"First of all, I don't do youth chaperoning anymore. And secondly, when I did chaperone, did I ever rope you into it? Nooooo! And especially without *asking* you!"

"Look. We're in the car, on our way. It's only two days and one night. The camp facilities are nice, and the young singles need virtually no supervision. Think of it as a much-needed weekend getaway for you and me. All right?"

"I'll do my best," I said as I opened my cell phone to check my voicemail messages.

"One other thing," she continued. "I'd like you to put away your phone while we're out of town."

"What? But I need—"

"Mr. Gorbachev—turn off that phone!" she said, in her best Ronald Reagan voice. Bonnie knew her spot-on impersonations always got to me.

"All right, all right." I powered my phone off and flipped it into the backseat.

For young singles, one of the highlights of church involvement is the occasional weekend trip out of town. The lack of formality or time constraints allows relationships to bud, and even flourish. Everyone's more relaxed and casual, maybe even friendlier.

Louis tried to plan one weekend away for the young singles each quarter. He and Jane E. usually accompanied the group, of course, but an extended family crisis made it impossible for them to chaperone this weekend's event. He tapped Bonnie to cover for him, and naturally, she dragged me along.

Thurm agreed to keep an eye on Colby while we were gone, but *only* at our house. The last time Colby visited his duplex apartment, she brought along a starter family of Gypsy fleas. Subsequently, two weeks later I had to cough up the cash to have his apartment bombed for fleas. There was a silver lining, however. Krun, his Czechoslovakian neighbor who drove Thurm crazy with his endless country and western singing, ended up moving out over the flea episode. His new neighbors were twins—attractive Asian girls in their mid-twenties who spoke very little English. Twice, I'd caught Thurm in his office studying Korean, not that he'd ever admit it. For his sake, I hoped they never cooked kimchi.

"Are we there yet?"

"Elmo, would you quit whining like a seven-year-old? Besides, you're the one driving. You'll *know* when we're there."

"I can see family vacations with you are gonna be a joy," I said with an ample dose of sarcasm. "Whatcha snacking on there, beautiful?"

"Kale chips and goat cheese. Yummy."

"Well, *Gouda* for you." I cackled at my own joke.

"Nice try, but Gouda cheese is made from cow's milk. Would you like a bite of my goat cheese?"

"No thanks. I'm trying to cut back on all things goat."

A beat-up, late-model, puke-green Dodge Dart roared up beside us in the left hand lane—windows down, with the radio blaring hip hop dance music. At the wheel, the infamous Eddie Hughes.

He screamed over the wind and the music. "Yo, Elmo! ¿Quésadilla?"

I rolled down my window and hollered back. "I think you mean ¿Qué Pasa?"

"Yeah, whatever, man. So, you and your hot wife are the chaperones this weekend. Sweet!"

Bonnie waved, choking on her mouthful of chips and cheese.

"Listen, Eddie, this retreat is for twenty-somethings. Aren't you like thirty-four? Thirty-five?"

Panic blanched his face. "They're not carding, are they?"

"No, no, you can holster your ID. But I'm surprised to see you here. I thought you were dating some lovely Italian nurse?"

He laughed. "Yeah, well, I forget to wear that stupid soft cast one time, and that was it. As they say—the gig was up!" He hooted at his own joke.

"So, I take it you're back on the prowl?"

"Yes, sir. Look out, all you righteous babes! Eddie's back on the market!" With that, he sped off toward the camp. Well . . . as much as a late-model Dodge Dart can speed off. Fortunately for him, we were going downhill.

The Chippewa Wilderness Camp was roughly an hour's drive north/northwest from First Church. The effusive young singles loved the Chippewa Wilderness Camp, which I found quite funny since one meaning of the word Chippewa was, "to pucker up."

The facility was actually quite small, consisting of one main building constructed in the shape of a large cross. The guys bunked in the left wing, the girls in the right. The caretaker lived in the "top" of the cross, along with a nice, hotel-style room for the chaperones. A lodge-style great room with a stone fireplace and numerous couches rounded out the building. A small kitchen occupied one end of the great room with several large rustic tables used for dining.

The camp was situated on seventy-five acres of beautiful rolling countryside. A crystal-clear stream meandered through the property and emptied into a deep water pond. At the far end of the pond, the water cascaded over a rock ledge forming a gorgeous ten-foot waterfall. The setting was majestic. The water was so transparent, you could clearly see objects on the bottom of the pond twenty-five feet below.

Several of the young singles were responsible for the food, games, and other activities. Bonnie and I were there just to make sure nobody lost perspective and did something stupid. After all, these were *young singles*. Well, with the exception of Eddie, Luke, Dante, Keith, and a few of the other guys, of course.

After a supper of goulash, ambrosia, some indiscernible salad dish, and white bread with butter, we settled into a fun evening of games and improv, capped off by an extended time of vespers-type praise singing.

Bonnie closed out the evening by going over the rules, reading them from the official Louis Estrada Retreat Notebook:

1. This is a First Church ministry retreat, and our conduct should reflect that of those who identify themselves as Christ followers.
2. Subsequently, at no time should there be a guy in the girls' sleeping area or a girl in the guys' sleeping area.
3. Lights out will be at midnight, with everyone in *their* beds.
4. For no reason should anyone be outside after midnight.
5. Zero tolerance on PDA (Public Display of Affection)
6. Be considerate of others and clean up after yourself.

Bonnie continued. "Remember, your chaperone is not yo' mama. Guys, I ain't pickin' up your clothes, so make sure there're no undies left lying around on the floor. Just ask Elmo, and he'll tell you that Miss Bonnie won't be havin' any of *that* junk."

I nodded my head in agreement while turning several shades of red. "Listen to the lady, boys. The punishment can be quite severe. Trust me on this one."

Bonnie dismissed them. "See you for breakfast at eight sharp!"

It hadn't been all that long ago that I was a young single man. So, I knew these rules were written to be broken. I had a pretty good idea what was going to happen next.

Back in our room, Bonnie was on the same page. "So what'd ya think?"

I stretched out on the bed. "Well, I overheard something about a panty raid. I predict around 12:30 a.m., several of the guys will tiptoe across the great room, then run through the girls' bunk area screaming like wild banshees. I'm fairly confident water balloons will be in play. Then, they'll exit the building at the end of the girls' wing, sprint around the top of the cross, and re-enter the building through the door at the end of the guys' wing. They'll be back in their beds asleep—*wink, wink*—and feign innocence when the girls drag you and me in there for the requisite accusations and name-calling."

"How are you so intimately acquainted with the finer points of their strategy?"

"Because, Commandant Chaperone, I designed and implemented the very same prank in this very building a couple of years ago. Eddie was one of my henchmen. It worked like a top."

"Really?"

"Yes, ma'am. I was quite the proficient prankster in my day."

Bonnie starting pacing. "Whata we goin' do?"

"Oh, I've got a great plan to teach those punks a lesson." I laughed as I imagined the hilarious outcome.

Bonnie raised a brow. "Why do I feel like I'm bringing in a convicted jewel thief to solve a robbery?"

I smiled. "That's exactly what you're doing. Except for the convicted part, of course. I was never caught."

"Oh, the hubris of the criminal mind. What's your plan?"

I jumped up, rubbing my hands together in gleeful expectation. "I'll hide stealth-like in the shadows out in the great room. When the malcontents head into the girls' sleeping area, I'll slip into the guys' wing and lock the outside door. When the boys try to get back in, they'll be locked out with no place to hide. BUSTED! Oh, the horrors of getting caught in the act!"

Bonnie laughed. "Now, aren't you glad you came along on this retreat?"

"Oh, yeah!"

Sure enough, my prediction was right on the money. Eddie—*Mr. No-Originality*—copied my plan right down to the last detail. I stood silently in the darkness unnoticed as Eddie, now the ringleader, followed by Keith and Arnie, slithered through the great room and then busted into the girls' sleeping area. As they whooped and hollered, I stepped into the guys' wing and sprinted to the end of the room, locking the outside door. Then I waited for the fun to begin, expecting someone to try the door, then beg for it to be unlocked. Instead, I heard three loud *thuds* against the door in rapid succession—*bump, bump-bump*—along with some muffled moaning.

I opened the door and found Eddie lying on his back with his face covered in blood. Keith and Arnie had taken off their T-shirts trying to stop the flow of blood on Eddie's face.

My adrenaline spiked. "Mother of pearl, what just happened?"

Keith, panicked and out of breath, responded, "We were running fast around the outside of the building—Eddie first, then Arnie, then me. The plan was to bust through the door and jump in our beds. But—"

"I told you to unlock the door, dude!" Arnie snapped.

"I did!" Keith shot back. "I'm telling you, I did! Anyway, Eddie hit the door face-first when it didn't open. Then Arnie slammed into Eddie causing him to hit the door again, then I slammed into both of them."

Eddie lay there bleeding and moaning like he'd just got his tail kicked in a UCF cage match. "Ah man, I think my nose is broken."

"Well, boys, I believe you can blame this one on me," I admitted in remorse.

"What?!"

Sometime around 3 a.m., I found myself driving down a deserted highway on my way back to the Chippewa Wilderness Camp. The *bandaged one,* Eddie Hughes, was stretched out on the backseat. We'd just spent more than two hours in a skanky, small-town emergency room.

"I know I've already apologized several times, but I need to say it again. I am really, really so very sorry about all this."

Eddie was quietly hang-gliding in the sweet land of Demerol. "Elmo, it's cool—really. You see, this guarantees me two or three more weeks of TLC from Selvaggia."

"I'm sorry, Eddie, but you're slurring your words. What from whom?"

"My Italian nurse, man. Once she sees these facial bandages, she'll be all over me."

"Y'know, that's a pretty unhealthy relationship the two of you have."

Eddie laughed through the pain. "You know what they say, man. Beggars can't be choosers."

I slept in all morning, and let Bonnie keep an eye on the group as they swam and played volleyball and hiked around the camp. Thankfully, there were no more pranks.

I caught up with everyone at lunch. Poor black-eyed Eddie looked as if his airbag had failed causing him to kiss the dashboard at fifty miles an hour. But as usual, he was eating up all the special attention from the ladies.

Bonnie and I sat by ourselves, over to one side of the dining area.

"Boy, when it comes to chaperoning, I just basically suck," I lamented. "Someone always gets hurt."

Bonnie scowled. "Sounds like a lame excuse to never have to chaperone again."

"Well, yeah. I mean, who'd want to go on a retreat or a campout with the *Chaperone of Death*? Would you send *your* kids out with me?"

She paused while smiling. "I hope to some day."

"Oh, nice redirect."

Bonnie gathered up our plates and gave me a kiss on the forehead. "Let's just get through lunch and the closing session, then head home. Everyone's had a good time. Even Eddie. I say, mission accomplished."

"I concur. Hooah!"

"Then, why don't you start taking out the trash, soldier."

"Yes ma'am, Madam Commander. Hooah!"

"Enough of that!"

22

The Pigeons

Running late, I decided to forgo my usual Monday morning stop at Kranky's. I'd just check in with Eli tomorrow. I had a surprise for him that I was pretty dang excited about.

"Mornin', Elmo."

"Mornin', Juliann. We sure missed you this weekend at the young singles retreat."

"Well, I've been dating a guy named Roy for a couple of weeks now, so I thought it best not to go on the retreat even though I really wanted to go. I hear Eddie broke his nose. Bet that hurt."

"Yeah. Speaking of getting hurt, looks like Eddie wasn't the only one. How'd you get that small bruise under your eye?"

"Oh, it's just silly ol' me." She giggled, but it seemed a bit forced. "I bumped it on the counter when I was bending over to pick up something. I didn't realize it was that noticeable."

"Sorry girl, but anything that mars your perfect face, if only slightly, will draw attention. I wouldn't worry about it too much. It'll be all healed up in a day or two. Now poor Eddie, he's gonna look like he took Mike Tyson's best punch right between the eyes for at least a week. But that's another story. Any messages?"

"Just one. Adrianne needs you to call her first thing. Okay?"

"Will do. Thanks."

I turned on the lamps in my office and took a seat behind my desk. I had a subtle premonition that I was in for an unusual Monday.

I called upstairs. "Hey Adrianne, this is Elmo. What's going on?"

"Thanks for calling, Elmo. There's been an incident with Erlene Markham."

Uh oh.

"They're holding her down at the county lock-up."

"In jail? *Erlene?*"

"Unfortunately, yes."

"Good grief! What happened?"

"I don't know all the details, but they booked her on an assault charge. Apparently, she threw her dentures at a police officer."

I laughed. "Come on now . . . it's Monday morning—you're just messing with me, right? Did Thurm put you up to this?"

"I wish I were joking. You need to swing by the music suite and pick up Harry, then head over to the jail."

"Why Harry? And if she's actually in jail, will we need to post bail or something to get her out?"

"That's why Harry's going along. During his overnight stay in the pokey last year, he made friends with several of the jail staff. We're hoping he can smooth this thing over."

"When has Harry ever smoothed over anything? This ought to be interesting."

I pulled through the alley separating the main church buildings and the Christian Life Center.

Harry slipped out a back door and hopped into my car. "And a top of the mornin' to you, Elmo."

"Hey, Harry. I understand you'll be playing the role of a bond bailsman this morning." I pulled out of the alley onto First Boulevard.

He frowned. "Hopefully, it won't come to that. What'd she do anyway?"

"They booked her for assaulting an officer."

"Well, we both know that didn't hap—"

"Supposedly, she threw her dentures at him."

""Well, maybe it did." Harry laughed as only Harry can.

"What's your plan?" I asked him as I turned left onto Blake Avenue.

"I'm gonna have a little chinwag with Warden Cleary. He owes me one. I sang at his daughter's wedding—pro bono. I did it because I knew one day I might need to call in a marker. Looks like today's the day."

"Here's hoping you can pull off some of that famous Harry Simpkins magic again!"

"Me too!" Harry guffawed. When he finally caught his breath, he continued. "I tell you, y'never know what that crazy Erlene's gonna do next."

I took a right on 12th street. "Harry, have I ever told you about the time I bumped into Erlene coming out of that sleazy adult book store over off the downtown mall? She'd been in there handing out some Chick tracts that you gave her."

"Oh, trust me, I know all about it." His eyes grew wide "Those tracts had my name and home phone number printed on the back. You wouldn't believe some of the bizarre phone calls we got! Trixie had to quit answering our house phone for several months. I finally had to have our number changed." He howled with laughter again.

We walked into the county jail, and Harry left to meet with the warden. I asked if I could visit with Erlene as one of her ministers.

They put me in a small room with a table and two folding chairs. I noticed the chairs were bolted to the floor. A few minutes later, a female guard walked Erlene in, then stepped back out into the hall. Erlene's tangerine-colored jail uniform hung on her tiny frame. It was easily four sizes too big.

She smiled. "Hey, Elmo."

"Hi, Erlene. Are they treating you all right in here?"

She blew out a puff of air, scoffing. "Piece of cake. Heck, back in Africa I lived in a dung hut for five years. This place is a five-star Hilton in comparison." She cackled until she wheezed.

"Okay, you've got to tell me what happened. Why'd you get arrested?"

"It's all because of those stupid pigeons roosting in my rain gutter. That, along with my tattle-telling neighbors who ratted me out . . . bunch of pansies."

"You lost me. Let's start at the beginning. What does this have to do with pigeons?"

"Those good-for-nothing birds. Pigeons are the slackers of the avian world, but the real problem is they're crawling with mites. So, after they make a nest in your rain gutter and pop out a few eggs, they split the scene and leave behind all those hungry mites that move into your house and *eat* on you!" She shivered in disgust. "You can't see the nasty little buggers, but mark my word—they'll eat you up from head to toe!"

"Sorry, Erlene, but I'm still not making the connection of how those 'slacker pigeons' got you thrown into the county slammer."

"If you'd let me finish, I'll tell you!"

"Sorry."

"The dumb birds kept making nests in my gutter. Every day, I'd have to go out and climb my stinkin' step-ladder and rip out a new nest. I got tired of it. So, I mixed a little arsenic into some Vaseline and spread it on the rim of the trough. Then when the slackers perched on my gutter, they'd absorb the poison through their feet, and SHAZAM! No more pigeon problem!" Erlene hooted. "They were dropping like flies! You should've seen them! All I had to do was pick up the dead birds from my porch and driveway, then toss their sorry carcasses in the trash. Problem solved!"

I scratched my head. "I'm still confused. How did you end up down here?"

"My no-account neighbors called the Audubon Society on me two or three times, and I got a 'cease and desist' letter from those tree-hugging scumbags."

I raised a brow. "Which you ignored, of course."

"Of course. So those pansy bird-watchers sicced the heat on me!"

"Is poisoning pigeons a jailable offense?"

"No, but they'll fine ya lickety-split."

"Did you really throw your teeth at the police officer?"

"Heavens no, Elmo!" She stiffened, obviously offended.

"But the arrest report said—"

"Well, maybe I did get a *little* excited when I tried to tell the officer about the mites and all. Heck, he wasn't much more than a kid. Then at one point during our—let's call it a *discussion*—my teeth did come out of my mouth. Briefly. It happens occasionally as you know."

I smiled as I touched the scar on my chin, a visible reminder of Erlene's flying dentures.

"I guess he thought I spit at him or something, so he hauled my wrinkled fanny down here to the big house, handcuffs and all. But honestly, I believe it was God's doing."

"How's that?"

"Because I was in the holding cell with Bejide—a precious Nigerian teenager who speaks only Hausa, which I happen to know. She's new in the States and got separated from her father yesterday. She was wandering the streets, approaching pedestrians to ask for help. The cops assumed she was soliciting for prostitution, so they brought her down here. Since she can't speak English, they were holding her until they could find a translator. And God sent me!"

"What happened to her?"

"I had a brief conversation with the warden and explained her situation. Now she's back with her father who's a local cab driver. She's also a believer, so we got to spend some time praying together. What a blessing. Now I'm ready to go home. Where do I sign?"

I grimaced. "Well, it may not be that easy. Harry's talking to Warden Cleary right now, trying to cut a deal."

She laughed. "You mean like a plea bargain?"

"To be honest, I have no idea. With Harry, anything's possible."

Just then the door opened, and Harry stepped inside. "Good, you're both here. Erlene, I'm so sorry, but it looks as if they're going for the death penalty."

"What?!" I gasped.

Both Harry and Erlene burst into raucous laughter.

"Elmo, I wish I had a photo of your expression!" Harry slapped his knee then wiped his eyes. "Priceless!" he chortled, sending Erlene into another guffaw.

Turns out, the warden was so grateful with the help Erlene had given them with the Nigerian girl, they'd already started processing the paperwork for her release before we even arrived. All charges were summarily dropped. Harry didn't even have to call in his marker.

If Eli were here, he would have reminded us that the Bible is full of such stories—where God orchestrated a situation in order to use a believer in a unique way for a special purpose. Phillip and the Ethiopian eunuch came to mind, as did Peter and Cornelius. How like Him to use Erlene to help out a young Nigerian Christian.

I dropped off Harry back at the church and gave Erlene a ride home—which, as always, was an interesting experience.

Most of which I can't share here . . .

When I got back to my office, I found Bonnie sitting at my desk.

"Hey, beautiful. What brings you to the Taj?"

"I was just writing you a note, but since you're here we can just talk. Go ahead and close the door, if you don't mind."

"Sure." I closed the door to the hall. "What's up?"

"I heard you and Harry had to spring Erlene out of jail this morning. That must have been fun. What happened?"

I pointed to the scar on my chin. "Erlene gave a young policeman one of these, and she got busted for it. It actually worked out well for everyone in the end. Well, except for a few squatting pigeons. But that's another story. What's on your mind?"

Bonnie came around my desk and sat next to me on the love seat. "Two things. One a bit frivolous; the other a bit troubling."

"Okay, let's start with the good news."

"Father Ted has invited Louis and Jane E. out on his new sailboat and told them they could bring another couple along."

I huffed. "Y'know, I always thought Father Ted really liked me, but you'd never know it by the way he's booted us to the bottom of the list for sailing invitations. That is, if we're even *on* the stinking list. Who knows? Maybe we're alternates? I'll bet he takes Lucky the printer out before he gets to ol' Elmo."

"Well, the good news is that all of your melodramatic speculations have been rendered moot. Since we helped Louis by covering the young singles retreat last weekend, he's invited us to join him and Jane E. to go sailing with Father Ted in a few weeks."

I shrugged. "Well, it's not an *elegant solution*. One, we weren't directly invited by Father Ted. And two, it means I have to spend several hours in the company of Jane E."

Bonnie smiled. "But—"

"But it least we'd be going, and who knows? Maybe I'll catch a break and get to watch Jane E. get seasick. That possibility alone will make the trip worthwhile."

"Okay, enough of the Jane E. jokes. I'll let Louis know we're going. Now, the second item has to do with some speculation on my part. Did you happen to notice Juliann's black eye this morning?"

"It's hard to miss when perfection gets marred. She says she bumped into her countertop. To be honest, I didn't buy her story. I just had an intuition about it."

"Me too. A few days ago, I noticed some bruising on her upper arm. I've known Juliann for several years now, and she's never been the clumsy type."

"What are you suggesting?"

"Again, I'm speculating here. But I can't help wondering if her new boyfriend has been roughing her up."

"Yikes. Has anyone around here met him?"

"Not that I know of. I saw him once from across First Boulevard when he was picking her up after work. He didn't look like the big tough-guy type. I think his name is Roy."

"Yes, that's what she called him this morning. What should we do?"

"I don' know."

23

The Humble Pie

Kranky's was unusually quiet for a weekday morning, probably due to the heavy rain that had been falling for several hours.

Buddy Skipbow smiled. "Morning, Elmo. Coffee or tea? You can tell me."

"I'm sticking with the tea. I'm growing rather fond of it."

Buddy poured boiling water into a cup and dropped in a tea bag. "Honey for that, sonny?"

"Yes, sir. Thanks." He handed me the plastic bear honey dispenser.

I casually walked back to the last booth with tea and honey in hand.

"Mornin', Eli."

The old man looked up from his Bible, his face broadening into a warm smile. "And a good morning to you, young man."

I slid onto the other side of the booth. "What're you reading about this morning?"

He slid his bookmark out of the way. "About when King Hezekiah was sick and dying, and wept bitterly about it, crying out to the Lord."

I stirred some honey into my tea. "What happened?"

"God sent word through a prophet to Hezekiah that he would die. Hezekiah responded by crying out, reminding God that he had been faithful and true throughout his life."

"How did God respond?"

"He did the most amazing thing. He changed God's mind."

"Seriously?"

Eli grinned. "God sent the prophet back to tell Hezekiah that He had heard his prayer, and seen his tears, and had decided to allow him to live an additional fifteen years."

"God changed His mind. Wow!"

"Unfortunately, it doesn't have a happy ending. You see, I believe God's original plan—for Hezekiah to die from his illness—was God's perfect will. Yet He took mercy on Hezekiah, and through His permissive will, allowed him to live fifteen more years."

I sipped my tea, but it was still too hot. "Why was that unhappy?"

"Because during those fifteen extra years of life granted through

Gods permissive will, King Hezekiah had a son he named Manasseh. When Hezekiah died, Manasseh became king. The new king was evil and greatly angered God. Manasseh undid all of the good that Hezekiah had accomplished during his reign."

I sat up in my seat. "So, if God had allowed King Hezekiah to die, the evil King Manasseh would never have existed?"

"That's correct."

"I don't understand. If God knew the outcome was going to be unhappy, why did He go ahead and extend Hezekiah's life?"

Eli placed the lace bookmark on the page and closed his Bible. "I believe there are several truths to be gleaned from this story. The obvious answer to your question is that God's thoughts and ways are higher than ours. If He chose to allow Hezekiah to live and Manasseh to be born, He had his reasons.

"What I choose to focus on in this story is that God heard one of His faithful servants praying, He saw the man's tears, and He was moved by compassion to change His mind. To me this is extremely profound, and it emboldens my prayer life. God hears, and He cares, and He's moved by our prayers."

Stirring my tea, I paused to ponder the ramifications of Eli's statement. "You're right. It's amazing to realize that the Creator of the universe responds to individual believers in such a manner."

Eli smiled. "That's why I enjoy reading the Bible. Every day I learn something new. Now, what's going on in your life?"

"I need a favor."

"Okay, what can I do?"

"As you know, I'm having a book published. It's a research study on developing a local church strategy that will reach the next generation of believers. And I'd like *you* to write the Foreword."

Eli studied me for a moment. "Well, Elmo, it would be a privilege. But there is a caveat. Due to arthritis, I gave up handwriting years ago. If I were to dictate it, could you write it down?"

"Of course!"

"Give me some time to think it over, and bring a pad and a pen the next time you drop by. We'll give it a go, and see what we come up with."

"Wonderful!"

"Thanks, Adrianne. If we could get those letters out to the Sunday school teachers by Friday, it would be super."

She stepped out of the fifth-floor office, shutting the door behind her.

I turned my chair back toward the desk. "Okay, Pastor Snooker.

Have you had a chance to talk to Art Menthor about his letter-stuffing subterfuge?"

He shook his head. "Art's disappeared. No one can find him. Someone claiming to be his niece answered his home phone and said Art hasn't been there in over a week. She explained this was nothing new, saying he's gone for weeks at a time now and then, but always comes back eventually. She said she has no idea where he goes."

"Weird. What should we do?"

"Just be diligent. Double-check the folders each Sunday morning. If you see Art around the church, call me."

"Will do. Next topic. Any word from Dr. Jorgensen concerning my 'Knees on the Ground' idea?"

"Horace told me he's going to run it by the deacons at their monthly meeting a week from Thursday. He hasn't told me directly, but I'm discerning that he's on board with the idea. Let's just wait and see what the deacons say."

"Yes, sir." I closed my valise.

"Anything else we need to discuss?" he asked while adjusting papers on his desk.

I chuckled. "I've got to ask. How did your Saturday outing on Father Ted's sailboat go?"

He laughed out loud. "As Dr. Seuss would say, it was a Circus McGurkus. It took Fred less than five minutes to wish he hadn't invited the Three Widows along. It took half an hour just to get the three of them situated into their life jackets. One was too tight, one was too loose, one was more faded than the other—and on and on and on. You know their routine. I actually enjoyed watching Ted try to accommodate the old birds. It felt good to spread the pain around a bit if you know what I mean."

"The Three Widows aside, how was the sailing?"

"Great fun. It's a beautiful boat, and Ted's a first-class sailor. With his America's Cup jacket and cap, he looks just like Ted Turner out there."

"Yeah, I've heard about the America's Cup gear *ad nauseam*."

"When's he taking you out for a spin?"

"Much to my chagrin, I've not been officially invited as of yet, though Bonnie and I are tagging along on Louis's ticket in a couple of weeks. I'm hoping Father Ted will actually let me board."

"Now, Elmo. I'm sure it's just an oversight on Ted's part. He's very fond of you, just as we all are. Maybe it's a seniority thing?"

"It's really no big deal. Just God serving up my requisite monthly piece of humble pie."

"Now, there's a healthy perspective! Oh, hey, would you mind getting a two-wheeler and moving those big boxes over there down to the print shop?"

Humble pie piece number two.

Back in my office, I began organizing the rest of my day.

Juliann popped her head through my doorway. "You had a couple of calls while you were gone." She handed me the slips.

"Tell me, Juliann, does your new fella attend First Church? I think you said his name is Roy?"

"He came with me once to morning worship, but he didn't like it. Roy says he's a lapsed Catholic, and the First Church service was just too different for him."

"If you don't mind me asking, how did you and Roy hook up?"

"It's actually kinda silly. But you know me—I'm all about silly. Anyway, we met in the produce department at the grocery store. I was having trouble determining what color bell pepper to buy. I mean, there are green ones, and red ones, and even yellow ones. He saw my confusion and helped me understand the differences. He was so nice, and the next thing I know, we were going out for dinner. We've been dating regularly since that day."

The difference in bell peppers? There's an innovative pick-up line.

"Is he a good guy?"

"Yes. Yes, he is. He makes me feel special, though he does drink, and sometimes a little too much, which I don't like."

"I'd like to meet him sometime. Maybe the four of us could catch a movie or something?"

"I'd like that," she said, smiling.

"Great. I'll mention it to Bonnie. Thanks for bringing me my messages."

"You're welcome." She headed back out toward the reception area.

Two messages. One from Lopez McGill to confirm our next chinwag, and a call from Brown & Brewster. Lopez would have to wait.

I rang up New York.

"Brown & Brewster, this is Chrlzv. How may I direct your call?" she asked in a thick European accent.

"Castor McMullen, please."

"One moment."

"Thank you." She put me on hold listening to some avant-garde New Age music with sitars and banging bamboo pipes. *Ah, New York.*

"Elmo, thanks for returning my call. Listen, things are really coming together. Have you thought any more about the Foreword?"

"I'm on it. My friend, Elijah Enoch, has agreed to write it. I should have it in my scrawny little hands in about a week."

"Good. We also need to know whom you'll be dedicating the book to."

"Still praying about that one. I'll let you know when I decide."

"Okay. What did you think of the cover artwork I sent over?"

"Looks good. The only change I would like to see is the title a little larger, and my name a little smaller."

He laughed. "There's a switch. Most authors I deal with usually want their names larger."

"Not here. Less name, more title."

"I'll have the art department tweak the cover and send you a new proof. And oh, by the way, I bumped into Sergio downstairs this morning. He wanted to know how Reverend Jennings was doing. Then he mentioned something about a totem pole. I've absolutely no idea what the fool man was talking about."

24

The Solo

Sunday mornings at First Church had basically settled into a 'new normal.' By tag-teaming, Pastor Snooker and I had the Adult Sunday school classes under control. The *For the Future We Build* program was not scheduled to kick off for several more weeks. I suppose you could say First Church was experiencing a brief period of a *Pax Romana*.

On this particular Sunday morning, I had half an hour to kill before I started my Abacus-Rex cart run to pick up the Sunday school attendance folders. I slipped into the back of the sanctuary to catch part of the morning worship service.

Up on the platform, with his signature over-the-top gusto, Harry led the congregation through the first, second, and fourth verses of "The Old Rugged Cross." Then everyone took a seat as soloist Ramona Holloway stepped forward and began singing the classic Steve Green number, "People Need the Lord."

I was enjoying Ramona's rendition of the popular song, when I noticed some movement off to my left down front near the organ. From where I stood at the back of the sanctuary, I had to squint to get a better look. Someone was slowly walking up onto the platform and making wild hand gestures toward the audience. Ramona, who was famous for including dramatic presentations with her solos, seemed nonplussed. Surely this was just another clever drama she had orchestrated.

She continued singing. *"People need the Lord . . ."*

Just then, I realized the disheveled person waving his arms around was Art Menthor! His clothes were torn, and he had dust or ashes all over his face and head.

Uh oh!

Ramona also noticed him from across the platform. With tempered nerves of steel, the seasoned veteran of the stage simply continued her song.

". . . at the end of broken dreams . . ."

Suddenly, I had a startling realization. There were only two people in the entire room of 2,000 who knew Art was *not* supposed to be up on that platform—Ramona and me. I started making my way down the far left aisle, as stealthily as possible. About halfway down, Ramona and I locked eyes. I knew immediately she had a plan.

"People need the Lord . . ."

Art was saying something, but his low, raspy voice was drowned out by the music. He kept pointing to his ears then back at the congregation, and I knew exactly what he was trying to communicate—*Your ears shall tingle!*

Ramona continued singing, *". . . all the grief they bear . . ."* as she calmly, slowly moved toward Art.

The congregation, convinced this was all part of Ramona's presentation, focused their rapt attention on the developing drama. There stood this poor, unkempt man, and through her lyrics, Ramona was telling him about the Lord. The scenario fit the song perfectly. Both Harry and Pastor Jorgensen glowed, nodding along with the powerful drama.

In the meantime, I'd reached the front of the auditorium, but decided to remain to the side. If needed, I could spring up the platform stairs and grab Art in a flash.

"People need the Lord . . ."

As she sang, Ramona reached Art and gently put her arm around his shoulder.

That lady is one cool operator!

Art appeared to relax, and to everyone's amazement, he started singing along with her.

"People need the Lord . . ."

They finished the last chorus together, and I kid you not—they got a standing ovation! I'd never seen anything like it. Many in the congregation wiped tears from their eyes. God only knows how many of these people would be motivated to reach outside their comfort zones and talk to someone about faith in Christ in the weeks to come.

Amazing.

Ramona walked Art down the platform stairs and handed him over to me with a wink. We hustled him into a side room where he met with Pastor Snooker and several of the deacons, including one who was a physician. They all agreed to send Art over to St. Michael's Hospital for a full medical evaluation.

Later, I bumped into Ramona after the service. "Lady, I've seen some gutsy things in my life, and your performance this morning rates right up there!"

She smiled that uniquely-stiff Ramona smile. "It helped tremendously knowing you were there in the wings ready to intervene if necessary."

"Were you afraid?"

She threw her head back and laughed. "Just listen to the playback of my solo. You'll notice about halfway through, my vibrato becomes much faster and more pronounced. I was afraid he might have a gun. I've known Art for years, and he has always walked a fine line between sanity and—well, *you* know."

"Yes, I do."

When Tuesday evening rolled around, the young married guys were all back over at Father Ted's house.

"You know what I hate?" Billy said. "It's when my wife pops an attitude and says, 'Didn't your mother ever teach you how to do that?'"

Father Ted smiled and turned to the rest of the group. "Okay, guys, based on your own marriages, what do you think Billy's referring to?"

Jed jumped in. "That's easy—replacing an empty toilet paper roll."

"Putting my dirty clothes in the hamper," Burton added.

Doug smiled. "Recapping the tube of toothpaste."

Not wanting to be left out, Richard blurted out, "No tooting at the table."

Billy laughed. "That's nothing. At my place there's no tooting in the house—period. I feel like a smoker having to hustle outside."

I couldn't resist. "Well, you know what they say about secondary gas?"

The guys exploded in laughter.

Father Ted, seeing the focus of the session quickly slipping away intervened. "Okay, enough of the tomfoolery. How does it make you feel when your wife scolds you for some of these things?"

"I feel as if I'm being treated like a child. I'm twenty-seven years old!" Burton whined.

Jed frowned. "To be honest, it aggravates me. Who likes being nagged, particularly with maternal tones?"

After a moment I added, "Sometimes I think Bonnie unfairly throws in a dash of spite when these things come up."

"Oh, I know *that* pain," Burton interjected. "I have a nickname for Janie when she starts nagging me. I call her *Spite-r Woman.*"

"Dude, can I use that?" Billy asked.

Father Ted pulled in the reins again. "Okay, gentlemen. Let's look at this from a different perspective. In the past, I've had this conversation with a few of you individually, but for the sake of the group, I'm going to hit it again.

"There's a wonderful marriage concept called *Put It Away.* It's very easy to understand and implement. If you get something out of a drawer or closet, put it away when you're finished, and put it back where it belongs. It's that easy.

"We're talking about common courtesy here. Treat your spouse with consideration and respect, and always do a little more than is expected. If you and your wife will follow the simple concept of *Put It Away,* you can avoid many years of frustration and angst. But it requires both of you to decide early on, to be intentional about it."

Billy raised his hand. "Does this mean, when we have a baby I've gotta change diapers?"

Ignoring Billy, Father Ted pressed on. "*Put It Away* also refers to jettisoning your old childish tendencies and habits. It's time for you to put on your big boy pants. You've got a wife and maybe a family to think about now. As a husband, it's your job to protect them both physically and spiritually."

He continued. "To grow, nurture, and maintain a successful marriage is serious work. It's not for the faint of heart. Only a fool would think it's easy. It's hard, but it's worth every pain you'll endure and every extra effort you'll give.

"The New Testament refers to the church as the bride of Christ. This metaphor shows us how to treat our brides. Whereas God is tender, loving, and forgiving toward us as believers, we are to be tender, loving, and forgiving toward our wives. Don't forget that God, in the form of His son Jesus Christ, laid down His life for His bride. And He expects you to do the same. This may mean making your guy friends, hobbies, and desires, subservient to what is best for your marriage and your family. I'll say it again—it's hard but noble work, and the reward is a strong marriage of lifelong joy."

Billy sheepishly raised his hand again. "I guess I *could* change a few diapers."

Father Ted laughed. "That's the spirit.

My cell phone vibrated in my pocket. It was a text from Bonnie— in all caps. Never a good thing.

"Sorry gentlemen, but I'm afraid I've got to run. I just received this text from my bride." I held up my cell phone for the group to see her text message: *SNAKE IN THE HOUSE – GET YOUR REAR END HOME. NOW!*

I could still hear the boys laughing as I closed the front door and scurried to my car.

When I arrived home, Bonnie had everything on "lockdown" and she was standing on a kitchen chair. I kid you not. Did I mention Bonnie loathes snakes? She's fond of saying, "There are two kinds of snakes I hate—live ones and dead ones."

I was less than convinced. "You really saw a snake in the house?"

She said nothing, but while still firmly planted on the kitchen chair, she thrust her finger toward the guest bedroom. I walked over to take a look. She had closed the door to that room and wedged a towel along the bottom. On top of the towel, she'd piled an assortment of books, pillows, pots and pans—apparently anything that wasn't nailed down.

"Well, how big was this killer serpent?" I quietly chuckled, thinking she had probably seen a salamander or worm or something. After removing all the debris blocking the door, I courageously stepped into the bedroom. I carefully reconnoitered the floor and even looked under the furniture, but everything appeared normal.

Then out of my periphery, I noticed something dangling from the ceiling, slowly oscillating in the breeze. I turned to see a snake skin, at least six feet long, hanging from the air conditioning vent. *Oh boy.* My outward calmness masked my inner panic as I slowly, methodically walked back over to the bedroom door and quietly stepped out of the room. I quickly restored Bonnie's makeshift barricade at the bottom of the door.

I texted Thurm. There was no time for originality: *BIG SNAKE IN MY HOUSE. GET YOUR BUNS OVER HERE. NOW!*

I checked on Bonnie, who remained atop the chair and still not talking. I tried to reassure her. "I've got Thurm coming over. He's a snake aficionado. He'll fix this."

My phone rang. It was Thurm. "Hey, Elmo."

"You'd better be calling from your car en route to my house!"

"Sorry, buddy, no can do."

"What! Why not?"

"I've been invited over to Seo-yeon and Ha-eun's place for a late dinner."

"What? Who?"

"You know, my neighbors. The Korean twins."

"Thurm, listen to me. Manda has moved into my house! He's here now, lurking and waiting for the right moment to slay and eat Bonnie and me!"

Thurm chuckled. "Can't be. Manda, the snake monster, was killed off by Godzilla in that *Final Wars* movie."

"Look, fan boy, I've got a huge, *real* snake in my house, and I need your help!"

"Really? Have you actually *seen* the snake?"

"No, only the six-foot skin it left hanging from my AC vent."

Thurm chuckled again. "Ironically that's good news. A big snake like that couldn't fit through your vents. He was probably in your duct work at some point looking for mice and shed his skin. Seriously, that snake skin could have been in your ducts for years. I'm guessing he's long gone."

"Right. And just how am I supposed to convince Bonnie of that oh-so-*lame* speculation? She's currently standing on a chair and appears to be in shock."

"To be honest, there's no way to know for sure. You'll need to have an exterminator come out. I'm sure it's harmless. Probably some type of black or garden snake. They're actually good to have around for rodent control."

"But—"

"Sorry, Elmo. I've gotta run. I can smell the kimchi from here. See you tomorrow at the office." He hung up. I couldn't believe it. He hung up!

Eventually, I was able to pry Bonnie off the kitchen chair and take her and Colby over to Jane E.'s house for the night. Then, after checking every nook and cranny in our bedroom, and duct-taping over the vent, I hunkered down for a night of restless sleep filled with nightmares of Japanese movie monsters.

I remembered that Das Plummer was also Das Exterminator, so I planned to give him a call in the morning. With my luck, he's probably the one who let the stinkin' snake under the house in the first place.

What's an Elmo to do?

25

The Foreword

The air was morning crisp as I parked my car in the First Church staff lot. I grabbed my Bible and yellow pad and started the two-block walk down the hill to Kranky's Coffee Shoppe.

My cell phone rang. "Hello?"

"Elmo, morning to ya. Lopez McGill here."

"Hi, Lopez. How are you?"

"I just wanted to say a big thank you for sending over the *Mere Christianity* book by Mr. Lewis. It's a fascinating read indeed, and when I'm done, I want to schedule a chinwag with you."

"That'll be great. Just let me know when and where. By the way, how's it going with Shantel?"

"Shantel, right. Well, let's just say she's moved on to other priorities. If you know what I mean."

"Yes, I do."

"Well then, right. I'll ring you up when I finish Mr. Lewis's fine tome. Until then, cheerio."

I stepped into Kranky's and made a quick stop at the counter to order my new usual, hot tea and honey. I chatted with Buddy Skipbow briefly before heading back to Eli's booth. The old man looked fresh and well-rested.

"Good morning, Elmo."

"'Morning to ya,' as my friend Lopez would say." I slid into the booth and set my Bible and notepad on the table. A moment later Buddy delivered my tea and honey.

"Thanks, Buddy."

He smiled. "If you need any more, I'll be there by the door."

As he walked back to the counter, Eli leaned over the table and lowered his voice. "Why does he always speak in rhymes?"

"Something to do with a stuttering problem he has. He said by focusing on making his sentences rhyme, it takes his mind off the stuttering and makes it easier for him to speak."

"Interesting."

I stirred some honey into my tea. "As you requested, I've brought along a yellow pad and pen. Any chance we can knock out your Foreword for my book this morning?"

"Yes, yes, I believe I'm ready," he said with a broad smile.

"Great!" I grabbed my pen. "Then let's give it a go. Whenever you're ready."

"If I go too fast, please stop me. Okay?"

"Don't worry, I will."

"All right. Then here goes." He cleared his throat.

"Though the character of God is immutable, having never changed, the Bible is, in reality, a book of change; revolutionary change. In Genesis 1, we're told the world was formless, empty, and dark, and God changed it. He created light. He changed the environment and infused it with life by creating plants and animals and ultimately, man. Adam, the first man, was lonely, so God changed his situation and created Eve to be his companion.

"When evil entered the picture in the form of sin, we learned that not all change is from God. Sin changed the relationship between God and man, and set in motion a series of events spanning several thousand years that led to the greatest changer of all time—Jesus Christ, God's own Son.

"Jesus changed the equation and took away sin through his death on the cross. His resurrection changed our future by giving man hope of a new life; not only in this world, but throughout eternity.

"His disciples took this revolutionary truth to the ends of the earth and changed the known world.

"And today, two thousand years later, the truth of Jesus Christ, His victory over sin, and His resurrection into new life is still changing people all over the world every single day.

"Change for the sake of change is of no value to anyone. Change for the sake of God is of the greatest value to us all.

"And finally, the Bible tells us through the writings of the apostle Paul that one day we will all be changed in a twinkling of an eye. In the words of the old hymn writer, 'What a glorious day that will be.'

Eli finished by saying, "God's change is good change."

I finished his last sentence and laid down my pen down on the notepad. Neither of us spoke for several minutes.

Finally, Eli smiled and gently chuckled. "Well, will that work?"

I had a lump in my throat, and all I could muster was, "Yes, that's perfect. Thank you."

471

Back in my office, Pastor Snooker popped in.

"Hey, Pastor Snooker, I'm not used to seeing you here quite this early. What's up?"

"I just came from the hospital where I found out what's been causing Art Menthor's bizarre behavior."

"And?"

"He's got a brain tumor the size of my fist."

"I really hate to hear that. Are they going to do surgery?"

"No. At Art's age, he'd never make if off the table. Besides, the doctors seem to think it's inoperable."

"Will he go home?"

"No, the cancer's too aggressive. He'll be transferred to an assisted-care facility and set up with a pain medication regimen. He won't last long."

"What about his family?"

"No one at First Church knew it, but his wife has been dead for quite some time. They had no children. His lone surviving family member is a niece named Candice Oglethorpe. Nice middle-aged lady. I met her at the hospital. Evidently, she's been taking care of Art for years—cooking his meals, cleaning his house, that sort of thing. She lives in the house right next door to Art's home. I believe she said Art bought it for her."

"Well, it all makes sense now—the wild statements, the erratic behavior. It reminds me of that John Travolta movie where he had a brain tumor and saw bright lights that nobody else could see. With Art, he was hearing something that caused his ears to 'tingle' that nobody else could hear."

"Perhaps. . . who really knows? Anyway, on a different note, the deacons agreed to your 'Knees on the Ground' idea at last night's meeting. On Sunday morning, Dr. Jorgensen is going to announce to the congregation that First Church is hitting the pause button. Both the fundraising program and the renovation plan will be put on hold for three months. During that time, he's calling the church members to a time of prayer and fasting for the future of First Church. He's asked me to put together a 'Knees on the Ground' prayer guide and prayer calendar to distribute to the membership. Of course, I'll need your help."

"You've got it!"

"I'm an old man, and I've been in church ministry a long, long time. Looking back over the years, I've realized the moments of greatest impact were not accomplished through mountain-top experiences of worship or ministry. No, it's when the men and women of the church got before God—both individually and corporately—and prayed. Elmo, I believe this 'Knees on the Ground' idea was given to you by God Himself."

I smiled. "Via a tea-lovin' old timer named Eli."

26

The Boat

I pulled out of our driveway. "Looks like a perfect day for sailing! Clear skies, a firm, but not too stiff breeze."

"I just don't understand why you didn't want to ride over to the lake with Louis and Jane E," Bonnie chided. "Normally, you're not one to pass up a free ride."

"It's quite simple, really. When I get into confined spaces with Jane E., I break out in hives— metaphorically speaking. I call it *Jane-E-phobia.*"

"What is it with you two? It's not as if Jane E. is my best friend or anything."

"I always figured there must've been a shortage of best friends available the day you picked yours. Which explains how you ended up with Jane E.—basically, a default thing."

"Elmo, I need you to promise me you'll be nice to Jane E. today. A sailboat's a small place out on a big lake with no where to run. If you two mix it up, it'll ruin the trip for the rest of us."

"Don't worry. I've already prepared for that possibility. I'm switched full-bore into 'Bite-My-Tongue' mode. If you observe a drop of blood wending its way down my chin today, you'll know why."

"Father Ted, well done! Now, that's what I call a sailboat!" I stepped off the dock and onto his boat.

"Thank you, Elmo. I have to admit she's a real beauty. You can thank Bob 'Big Bird' Stevens for paying top dollar for my Dodge Viper—in cash, no less!"

"In cash? Really?"

"*The Double Dinosaur.* Interesting name," Bonnie commented with one brow lifted. "What does it mean?"

Father Ted grinned from ear to ear. "It's a bowling term. A perfect game, throwing all strikes, is called a Dinosaur. To throw two perfect games in a row—an extremely rare feat, I might add—is called a Double Dinosaur."

"And something tells me you've accomplished that feat?" I asked, chuckling.

Father Ted beamed. "Just once. And oh, what a night!"

"I bet. Was Dr. DV—"

"Sorry I'm late!" Louis hollered as he came sprinting down the dock.

"Where's Jane E.?" Bonnie asked.

"Her mother called, and when her mother calls, the world stops on its axis. So, I had to leave her at the house."

Oh happy day! I fought to contain my smile.

"Speaking of dinosaurs," Bonnie whispered sarcastically.

Jane E.'s mother, Beatrice—or "The Contessa," as Louis often referred to her—was the poster child for problematic in-laws. She drove both Louis and Jane E. absolutely crazy.

The only daughter of Sir Albert Hedgeworth and Lady Monne, Beatrice had lived a privileged and pampered life. When she was still a child, her family moved to the United States and settled into a palatial home in the Hamptons. After attending an elite college, Beatrice married the son of an oil baron and enjoyed the comfortable life afforded by old money. Soon thereafter, she gave birth to their only child, Jane Elizabeth Wilder.

Then disaster struck. In the late '70s and early '80s, the domestic oil industry went into a tailspin. The Wilders lost everything. Jane E.'s father couldn't handle the unfortunate turn of events, so he drove his Maserati off a cliff into the depths of the Grand Canyon. Beatrice was left to raise Jane E. alone.

The two struggled for years until Beatrice found her footing as a real estate broker selling million-dollar homes to the rich and famous. Her former life in high society proved to be a priceless resource as she wined and dined affluent, potential home-buyers.

Beatrice dominated Jane E. through her formative years, and this dominance continued even when Jane E. became an adult. Though Jane E. was just as controlling as her mother, she'd never been able to break free from her mother's overbearing talons.

Poor Louis managed his wife's situation the best he could. As he joined us on the sailboat, he said, "Sorry, Ted. Jane E. wanted to come, but you know how my mother-in-law is."

Father Ted gave a knowing smile. "All too well. Beatrice was an active member of my church for decades. She even sold me my last house. She's quite the take-charge person. You just tell Jane E. that we'll do this again, and next time we'll invite Beatrice to join us."

Louis grimaced. "Let me think about that one, and I'll get back to you."

We all laughed, commiserating with Louis.

Father Ted pivoted. "Speaking of invitations, I'm surprised it took you so long to come sailing with me, Ellington. I've emailed you several times about it, but you never responded. After all those not-so-subtle hints you laid down, I thought you'd be the first one out."

I sat up in my seat, befuddled. "You emailed me an invitation to go sailing?"

"Yes, three or four times. That's how I've invited everyone."

"But—wait a minute. What email address were you using?"

"Let's see. I believe I used *Ellington@fc-online.org.*"

Relieved, I laughed out loud. "I thought you were snubbing me! My correct email address is *elmo@fc-online.org.* Now, it all makes sense! I need to apologize, though. I've been whining to anyone who'd listen about not getting a sailing invitation."

"Don't give it another thought. You forget I'm a former senior pastor. I've had people bad-mouthing me every day for over thirty years. This old skin's pretty thick."

"Okay, then!" I rubbed my hands together. "Let's do some sailing!"

Father Ted moored his boat at the River Marina, which was built on an inlet that connected Lake Staban via canal to the Jarneki River. Lake Staban, the largest lake in our state, was well-suited for sailing.

The Double Dinosaur, a Scorpion II 40-foot Cruising Cutter trimmed out in red, could sleep four adults. She was a beautiful sailboat in pristine condition. Father Ted motored us slowly through the canal toward Lake Staban, where a nice breeze greeted us and rippled the surface of the lake with only a slight chop.

"Man, it's nice out here." I took in a deep breath of the fresh air. "I could get used to this!"

Louis laughed. "Then you'd better hope your book sells a ton of copies. You'd need at least thirty grand to buy a boat like this."

I felt optimistic. "Hey, it could happen."

Bonnie propped her arm on my shoulder. "Easy, big boy. When it comes to the Jenkins family list of priorities, a new boat is way down toward the bottom."

"But—"

"Waaaay down toward the bottom." She reiterated, raising her brow.

"Okay, okay. I get that, but you've got to let a guy have his manly dreams. It's how God made us. We're embedded with the need for adventure, the need to conquer, the need to pursue. I mean, even a donkey gets the carrot every once in a while. Right, Louis?"

"Right, Elmo." Louis flexed his biceps. "Arggh!"

"Arghh!" I reciprocated.

Bonnie stood up. "There's way too much testosterone percolating on this end of the boat. I think I'll go visit with Captain Ted while you two do some manly detoxing."

"Ouch! Just remember, Father Ted already has his boat," I said, playfully slapping her on the bottom has she scooted by.

Father Ted hoisted the mainsail, and off we went.

I turned to Louis. "What's the deal with Jane E. and her mom?"

He shrugged. "Since Jane E. has no brothers or sisters, and her father is dead, she feels obligated to be available to her mom whenever she's needed. The problem is that my mother-in-law refuses to cut the apron strings, still trying to play a full-time role in Jane E.'s day-to-day life. It's been a point of contention in our marriage from the very beginning, and probably always will be until The Contessa goes off to sell mansions in the sky."

"I think all marriages—well, all relationships, for that matter—have at least one or two burrs under the saddle. It's as if God allows the issues to exist so we don't take the other person for granted, whether it's a spouse, a friend, or a family member. I heard someone once call it 'heavenly sandpaper.' In relationships, we have a tendency to refine each other through these interpersonal challenges."

Louis stretched his arms over his head. "I agree with that, but I would add one more important component to your theory. In order for a relationship to be successful, each person needs to learn to *respond* to these 'burr" issues when they arise instead of *reacting* to them. That's the secret."

"I concur."

"Hey, Elmo? Father Ted wants to know if you would like to take the wheel," Bonnie yelled over the noise of the water and the wind.

I headed aft. "You don't have to ask me twice!"

"Elmo, have you sailed before?" Father Ted asked, the wind billowing his America's Cup windbreaker.

"We rented a sailboat for two days on our honeymoon in the Cayman Islands. To be honest, I mostly just used the motor."

"For now the wind's at our back, so all you have to do is hold the wheel steady. When we get to the other side of the lake, we'll have to tack into the wind to get back to the marina."

"Got it."

Father Ted grinned. "Bonnie, Ellington tells me you had a snake in your house."

"Oh, did he?"

Uh oh.

Father Ted paused to let me sweat a smidgen. "You know, I just hate snakes. They give me the heebie-jeebies."

Bonnie laughed. "Oh, me too."

Whew!

She continued. "Turned out to be just a snake pit-stop for a change of clothes. He left his dirty laundry hanging from one of our air conditioner vents."

"Sounds like one of my sons," he quipped as we all laughed.

The straight ride across Lake Staban was great fun. The tacking back and forth coming back in—not so much. I started feeling queasy about halfway back, but I was too embarrassed to mention it. My sick stomach progressively got worse, but I pretended to be just fine. I could easily have won an Oscar for my performance.

We moored the boat and said our goodbyes. I'd almost escaped with my male ego still intact when . . .

Oh no. Jane E. was waiting for us on the dock.

She pounced on me. "Elmo bro, you're looking a bit pale."

Please don't say it.

"Did you get a little . . . seasick?" Out came the saccharine and sarcasm. "You poor thing. Still needin' to grow some big boy sea legs, are you?"

I'm biting my tongue, I'm biting my tongue, I can do this.

"No, Jane E., I'm fine," I lied. "But thank you for asking," I lied again, then headed for the parking lot.

I desperately needed to get Bonnie a new best friend.

Bonnie got in the car. "That was a super fun time. How's your stomach?"

Dang.

27

The Assault

It had been a typical morning worship service at First Church. Louis had given the announcements. Harry had led a couple of hymns. For the music special, Doreen McGinity had herded in twenty or so four-year-olds to sing "He's Got the Whole World in His Hands"—accompanied by semi-synchronized hand motions. Of course, all the parents were up front snapping pictures and making videos. It looked like a commercial for Apple or Samsung.

Finally, Dr. Jorgensen stepped to the pulpit to deliver the morning sermon. The congregation settled into their pews for one of his usual thought-provoking messages.

He set his Bible to one side. "Before we get started with our study of Philippians chapter one this morning, I have an important announcement to make. As many of you know, First Church has been laying the groundwork for a much-needed renovation project for our church facilities. Most of the rooms at our church campus have not been updated in many years. Some still have the original paint and wallpaper dating as far back as the 1950s.

"To fund these renovations, we are also in the planning stages of a capital fundraising program; something we haven't done here at First Church in many years.

"Recently, our church has gone through a season of challenges. First, we survived a contentious, special-called business meeting. More recently, we lost our beloved associate pastor under unusual circumstances. Due to these circumstances, one of our staff members, Ellington Jenkins, suggested a church-wide season of prayer and healing before we launch any new initiatives.

"I took Ellington's idea to our deacons, and they supported it one hundred percent. So, starting next Sunday, our church family will begin a special three-month emphasis on prayer which we are calling, 'Knees on the Ground.' Why? Because when God's people are praying, great things happen.

"We will be asking all of our members and friends to set aside a time each day to kneel and pray and ask God for His direction for First Church. At my request, Pastor Snooker is putting together a 'Knees on the Ground' prayer guide and calendar. These will be available for you next Sunday."

For reasons not yet fully understood, church makes people ravenously hungry. With little actual scientific research in place, this supposition is based almost entirely on anecdotal evidence. Just try to get into a restaurant for lunch on any given Sunday, and you will quickly find yourself surrounded by the religious hubbub of cheap suits, colorful dresses, and perhaps even a hat or two.

Without my knowledge and much to my chagrin, Bonnie accepted an invitation to join Louis and Jane E. for lunch after church. And, horror of horrors—Jane E. brought along her mother, Beatrice. Bonnie might as well have dragged me bare-backed through a patch of sand spurs.

When we arrived at the restaurant, The Contessa quickly took charge of our little party of five.

She scolded the elderly maître d'. "Listen, sonny, this just won't do. We'd prefer that round table over by the window."

He protested. "But—"

"No excuses, now. Chop, chop."

The old boy mumbled something in French. I'm sure it was ugly and profane. Nevertheless, he seated us by the window. I prayed he wouldn't expectorate in my sweet tea.

Beatrice spoke directly to both Jane E. and Bonnie, but indirectly to Louis and me.

"Bonnie, how nice of you and your husband to join us for lunch."

Bonnie played the game expertly, knowing full well that Beatrice was a last-minute, rammed-on addition to our dinner card. "We appreciate the invitation. It's an honor to join you and your family for a meal."

Beatrice held court. "Today's lunch is on me." She paused briefly to receive the requisite nonverbal accolades. "You see, I'm celebrating. I've been retained by Geneva Fitzsimons to handle the sale of her country estate. I'll be listing it for $25 million."

"Wow!" I blurted out, breaching the well-established Beatrice protocol. Bonnie quickly pinched my leg under the table. *Ouch!*

Louis's response was more measured. "Why is Geneva selling her home?"

Beatrice feigned concern. "The poor woman hasn't been able to get over Smitty's untimely passing. She's not been back out there since the night he died. As you know, she owns several other homes."

"That's an awfully expensive house," Bonnie said. "Will you have any trouble finding a buyer?"

"My dear, that's why Geneva chose *me*."

My cell phone buzzed. "Excuse me."

I stepped away from our group, grateful for the interruption, but the news wasn't good. I quickly returned to our table. "Please accept my apologies, but I'm needed over at Mercy Clinic."

Bonnie gave me The Look—the one which says, *Are you pulling a quick one here?*

"Bonnie, I need you to come along with me."

We said our goodbyes and hit the parking lot.

"This had better not be one of your classic Elmo-the-Escape-Artist routines."

"It's Juliann. She checked herself in this morning."

Bonnie grabbed my arm. "What? Elmo, what's going on?"

"I don't know for sure, but I have a sneaking suspicion it has something to do with her boyfriend, Roy."

"Oh, no. Surely not!?"

Ten minutes later we signed in at the nurses' station. They directed us to Room 217.

I gently knocked on the closed door. "Juliann, it's Elmo and Bonnie. May we come in?"

A faint voice responded. "Yes, please do."

When we opened the door, we were stunned. Juliann was propped up in a hospital bed, surrounded by pillows. Her face was badly swollen, both eyes black and bruised, and her right arm was in a cast.

Bonnie gasped, then started crying. "Oh, girlfriend. What *happened* to you? Were you in a car wreck?"

Juliann forced a smile. "I wish. I'm afraid I said or did something wrong last night, and Roy went off on me. I blacked out after the second or third punch, and I woke up on the floor this morning. He was long gone . . ." She crumbled and started to weep.

It broke my heart.

Juliann wiped her eyes with her good hand. "I was too embarrassed and too ashamed to call anyone, so I drove myself here."

Bonnie gave her a gentle hug and kissed her on the forehead, then sat on the side of her bed. "Well, we're here to take care of you now, and there's absolutely no reason for you to be ashamed."

My sadness quickly turned to anger. "Where's Roy now? Was he drinking when he hurt you?"

"He's probably at his house sleeping it off. That's what he usually does after one of his benders," Juliann said matter-of-factly.

Bonnie sat up straight. "Has this happened before?"

"Yes, but never this bad."

"Juliann. I need your permission to call Geoff Steeders," I said. "Geoff's one of our deacons, but he's also a domestic abuse specialist."

"Is Roy in trouble?"

"I'm afraid so."

She looked down. "Do what you have to do. I just can't help but think it's partially my fault."

I could see Bonnie bristling. "Oh no, girl. There's nothing about this situation that's your fault. Nothing!"

Juliann frowned. "What's going to happen now?"

"The police will interview both you and Roy," I began. "They'll ask you if you'd like to press charges. Either way, you'll be counseled to get a restraining order. If Roy has a past record for abusing women, he might even have to spend some time in jail."

"Juliann, I'm speaking now as a friend," Bonnie added. "Your relationship with Roy is officially over. I know you, and you're probably thinking that you should give him another chance, that it's just the booze taking over. Those are natural feelings, especially for someone with your kind personality and demeanor. But that would be a huge mistake. Obviously, Roy has some serious issues that require professional help. I don't want to see you get hurt again—or worse. Okay?"

"I know you're right. It's just hard."

Now it was my turn to bristle. "Juliann, the man *broke your arm*! He's lucky some of the First Church guys don't hunt him down and break *his* arm and blacken *his* eyes!"

A few moments later, I stepped into the hallway and called Geoff. He made a few calls, and sent over a counselor from the battered women's shelter that First Church helped support. He also called the authorities who sent out a squad car to pick up Roy. Judge Lawton Blackridge, another one of our deacons, made arrangements to get a restraining order. Juliann agreed to press charges, and we called for a locksmith to change the locks at her house.

Fran Bruker invited Juliann to stay with her while she recuperated. Fran lived in a gated community with around-the-clock security. If Roy liquored up again and tried something stupid, he wouldn't know where to find Juliann.

Later that evening, I got a call from Geoff. Turns out, Roy had several priors for assault, including an outstanding warrant from another state. He was arrested without bail, due to his outstanding warrant. He'd have to cool his heels in the county jail while waiting for a trial. According to Geoff, that could take months.

With that good news, Bonnie and I both blew out a sigh of relief.

"What causes a man to hit a woman?" I said, turning off my bedside light and pulling up my blanket. "I don't get it."

"Why does anyone hit anyone?" Bonnie clicked off her light. "Why did Cain kill Abel? Why were six people randomly shot and killed in Chicago over the weekend? The reasons may be varied and complex, but the answer is quite simple—ingrained sin. When sin entered the world, it brought violence and death with it."

"You're absolutely right. Goodnight, sweetheart."

I silently prayed myself to sleep—for Juliann, for Roy, for those poor families in Chicago who lost loved ones, and for protection for Bonnie and me as we slept. It had been a long day.

28

The Tan

Another Monday morning. I found the break room empty as I stepped in to check my mail slot. A moment later, Father Ted joined me.

"Good morning, Father Ted. Hey, thanks for taking us out sailing Saturday. You have a beautiful sailboat, and we had such a great time. When and if I go out again, please remind me to take some Dramamine ahead of time."

He chuckled. "I suspected you were fighting a tossing tummy, though you covered it quite well. Except for the ghostly-white face, of course."

"Apparently I didn't fool anyone. Pretty dang embarrassing."

"Don't be silly. I take Dramamine every time I go out, or I'd be ralphing like a school boy coming off a two-day whisky binge."

I had to laugh. "I will say, you're getting quite the tan with all your time on the lake."

"It's mostly windburn, I think. But that reminds me of a funny story back from my younger days in the ministry."

"Really? What happened?"

"I was about your age, still at Asbury Seminary, and pastoring a tiny church there in rural Kentucky. I preached Sunday mornings, Sunday evenings, and Wednesday evenings. The church had about a hundred members.

"We met for services in a small room with a low, acoustic tile, drop ceiling. There wasn't a platform, just an old wooden pulpit set up in front of about ten rows of folding chairs. Someone had installed a single spotlight in the ceiling about three feet in front of the pulpit—the kind of spotlight a landscaper uses to throw light on shrubs or trees. During the services, it lit up the pulpit area.

"One Sunday morning, as I was shaking hands with the exiting parishioners, I received several compliments on my tan. That evening, several more folks mentioned my handsome tan. Now, you have to understand this was in the middle of winter. I thought I must be jaundiced or something. When I got back home, I took a close look in the mirror. Sure enough, my face and hands were darker than the rest of my body. I was totally perplexed."

"Did you ever figure it out?" I asked.

"Yes, finally—but only after two or three weeks. We had an old guy named Wilbur Hawkins who volunteered to do maintenance at the church. Similar to Art Menthor. Evidently, the spotlight over the pulpit had burned out, and Wilbur—not the sharpest knife in the drawer—had mistakenly replaced it with a sun lamp bulb! I'd been wondering why it was so hot in the room! I'd even adjusted the thermostat several times.

"Before the sun lamp was discovered and changed, I developed quite a tanned face. I was still single at the time, and my wife Patty will tell you one of the things that initially attracted her to me was my great tan. I guess I should thank Wilbur Hawkins for my long and happy marriage."

I laughed. "*Great* story, Father Ted. I think I'll share your tanning tip with Thurm. He's always looking for angles to improve his marriageability."

"Good idea!"

"Speaking of Art Menthor, I guess you've heard about his tumor."

"Yes, I've spent some time with Art since his diagnosis. He has total peace concerning his situation. The old boy has an incredibly strong faith in God. I'll be checking in on him periodically until he 'shuffles off this mortal coil.' Then he can go be a handyman in heaven."

I smiled at that thought. "I'm sure he will."

Father Ted patted me on the back. "You'll be there tomorrow night at my place for our last young married men's group session, won't you?"

"Yes, sir. What's the topic?"

"We'll have more fellowship than anything else, though I thought we might do some final Q&A."

"Count me in."

Back in my office, I'd just started organizing my To-Do-List for the day when my phone rang.

"Elmo, Castor McMullen here."

"Hi, Castor. What's going on?"

"Mark this day down on your 'never forget' calendar. I'm sitting here looking at your new book, hot off the press."

"Really? How does it look?"

"Superb, and I don't mind saying so! I'll be sending you a copy. It should get to you sometime on Thursday. You'll be pleased!"

"Wonderful! I can't wait."

"Now, pull out your calendar. We want to fly you and Bonnie up for your book launch on Saturday. We'll roll out the book here at our

B&B flagship store, and have you do a book signing. We'll invite the local press, so be prepared to do some interviews. There'll be photos and such, then the PR department will kick into full gear next week."

"Sounds good. Just tell me what to do."

"Great. I'll include your airline tickets with the book I'm shipping you. You'll fly up Friday afternoon and spend the night here at our Manhattan headquarters like before. The book signing will be downstairs at ten Saturday morning, followed by interviews and a late lunch. We'll send you on your way home by late afternoon."

"What should I wear?"

"Oh, I don't know. Maybe an open-collar shirt with a sport jacket and casual slacks? No tennis shoes. The bosses hate tennis shoes."

I chuckled. "Yeah, so do mine."

"See you then, Elmo. Bye."

Interviews? Yikes . . .

"What time is your group meeting tonight at Father Ted's house?" Bonnie asked as she set the casserole dish on the table.

"Same as last week." I sniffed the casserole. "So, this is the new recipe you've been chirping about. What is it?"

I noticed a trace of a smirk in Bonnie's smile. She'd never admit it, but I knew she loved watching me squirm over her healthy concoctions. "Gnocchi with zucchini ribbons and parsley brown butter. I snuck a bite earlier. It's delicious."

I smiled with a subtle smirk of my own. "I'm sure it is, darling."

Bonnie took a seat at the table, and I prayed over the food. I also prayed for Juliann.

"Amen."

Bonnie served me a healthy portion of the casserole, then served herself. "I visited Juliann over at Fran's place this afternoon," she said, snatching a hummus muffin from the basket.

"How's she doing?" I took a bite of the Gnocchi Zucchini combo. It wasn't half bad.

"Her face looked a lot better, but she still has a lot of bruising. She'll have to wear the arm cast for about six weeks."

"What about work?"

Bonnie smiled. "First Church does a good job looking after their staff. She'll be off for a month on paid sick leave, then come back on light duty until she gets her cast off."

"Who's manning the reception desk while she's out?"

Bonnie bit into her muffin. "The other secretaries are taking turns filling in until she returns."

"Since I'm helping out Pastor Snooker, I'll just have Adrianne help with my clerical needs."

"Good idea. Speaking of black eyes, I haven't seen or heard from Eddie since he broke his nose."

"Neither have I, and I'm sure we won't until he's totally healed up. He's probably spending all his free time with his Italian nurse, Selvaggia."

"Say her name again."

I swallowed my food and cleared my throat. "Selvaggia."

"How do you spell that?"

"I have no idea."

Bonnie offered me a muffin. When I demurred, she frowned. "What's the deal with this nurse anyway? I mean, we're talking about Eddie Hughes."

I laughed. "He thinks Selvaggia has an extreme case of what he called 'the Florence Nightingale syndrome'."

"And, of course, Eddie has strategized to exploit her condition."

"Of course."

All the boys were back for our final session.

Father Ted kicked us off with a smile. "Okay, husbands, let's go around the circle, and each of you tell the group one thing you've learned from our sessions. Billy, you go first."

Billy flashed a big smile revealing a missing tooth, which I had to assume was probably from brawling. Hopefully, not with his wife. "Oh, that's easy. I've learned to Put it Away. And I've been trying really hard to do that, but I won't lie—it ain't been easy. But I promise, I'm gonna stay after it."

Jed was next. "I learned not to treat my wife like Scarlet Johansson, but instead, treat her like Beth, the beautiful and wonderful girl I married."

Father Ted grinned. "Good! Good! Burton, you're next."

Burton leaned in. "I've learned it's not about me, but about us."

We continued around the circle until it came to me. I was last. "Well, since my slogan-snitchin' friends here have used up all the standard answers, I guess I'll need to dig a little deeper. Father Ted's explanation of how our marriages are modeled after God's love for His bride, the church, was helpful to me.

"It reminded me of a seminary professor of mine. His wife, Edna, suffered from chronic, debilitating depression. It was a huge struggle for both of them. One day he was praying, complaining to God about Edna's illness, and how it was breaking his heart. Then, it was as if God said to him 'See, My bride, the church, is also sick. And it's breaking My heart.' The professor's takeaway was that God allowed his wife Edna to go through a time of illness so that he would better understand the heart of God.

"What I've learned through these sessions is that my love for Bonnie helps me better understand God's love for me."

A long moment of silence filled the room.

"That's just not fair!" Billy blurted out. "Elmo's been to seminary. How are we supposed to compete with that deep junk?"

We all shared a good laugh.

"Okay, moving along," Father Ted said. "Thank you, Elmo, and thank you, Billy. Now, let's talk about some practical things we can do to put what we've learned into action."

It was a great last session. I felt confident all of us would be better husbands after participating in Father Ted's group. The six of us now had a special bond, supporting each other as we tried to figure out how better to serve our wives.

We ended the evening with a small party. Father Ted's wife, Patty, had made a Black Forest cake for the occasion, served with all the *whole* milk you could drink.

As I sat there watching the other guys eating cake and sharing stories, my mind drifted to a scene in the prison movie, *The Shawshank Redemption*. I found myself loosely paraphrasing Morgan Freeman's character as he said, "We sat and drank milk and ate cake, and for a brief moment, felt like free men."

Dietarily speaking.

29

The Encore

Slowly ascending in the First Church executive elevator, my mind was firing off like a Roman candle. *Book interviews. Juliann. Knees on the Ground. Art Menthor. Hummus muffins—*

W-a-i-t-a-minute—how'd *that* sneak in there? Bonnie's healthy food regimen was invading my psyche. Scary.

"Good morning, Adrianne. Has Pastor Snooker arrived yet?"

"Mornin', Elmo. He's in the office waiting for you. Can I get you a cup of coffee?" she asked with a pleasant smile.

"Nope. I'm officially a tea drinker now."

Adrianne's jaw dropped.

I laughed. "It's true, what'd they say—with God all things are possible! Think you could pick up a box of tea bags for the office up here?"

Adrianne, stunned and speechless, simply nodded her head. I stepped into Tom's old office, quietly chuckling to myself as I took a seat. Pastor Snooker was on the phone.

"Yes, I see . . . Yes, uh um, yes, yes, thank you for letting us know." He hung up the phone.

I smiled. "What's up?"

He didn't return my smile. "Looks like we're taking our morning meeting on the road. That was the Ackerman Assisted-Living Center. They called in Hospice yesterday for Art Menthor. They're expecting him to die anytime now, and they want to have someone from his church there when he does."

"Wow, that happened so quickly."

"I've seen it before. His type of brain cancer is very aggressive."

A few minutes later I climbed into Pastor Snooker's car, and we headed over to the Ackerman ALC.

"Ellington, since we have a few minutes, let's go over some of our agenda items. How's the 'Knees on the Ground' prayer calendar coming together?"

"Done. I made the changes you suggested and gave it to Lucky. He said—scratch that—he indicated the calendars would be ready in time for Sunday. He's also working on the 'Knees on the Ground' daily prayer guides you cobbled together. Well done, I might add. Those will be ready for Sunday as well.

"Since I'm leaving tomorrow for New York, I've instructed Adrianne to contact the deacons so they'll be ready to hand out the prayer guides and calendars at the sanctuary doors on Sunday morning. You can tell Dr. Jorgenson we should be good to go— barring any Lucky printing issues, of course."

"Excellent!" Pastor Snooker said as he turned onto Tucker road. "Good job, Ellington."

"Thank you, sir."

"What's the latest on Juliann, and how's the arrangement to cover the reception desk working out?"

"Personally, I've not seen Juliann since last Sunday, but from what I understand, she's safe and mending well over at Fran's place. Bonnie tells me the rotation to cover Juliann's responsibilities is working out fine. Apparently, everyone is more than willing to do a little extra until Juliann can return in about a month.

"Phil Loculm is helping Juliann out with the legal stuff, pro-bono. Roy, the perpetrator, has been extradited to another state to stand trial for an outstanding aggravated assault charge. If for some unlikely reason he gets off that charge, they'll bring him back here to face charges for beating up Juliann. One way or the other, he'll be behind bars for quite some time."

"And rightly so," he said as he turned into the Ackerman parking lot.

When we walked into Art Menthor's room, his niece was there along with a Hospice volunteer. They told us Art had been comatose for the last twenty-four hours, and his breathing had become very shallow since morning.

We talked for ten or fifteen minutes with his niece, then she asked Pastor Snooker to pray. With our heads bowed and our eyes closed, Pastor Snook started to pray. Then the strangest thing happened. I could hear someone singing, almost in a whisper.

"Eli's coming, hide your heart, girl."

That's weird. Must be someone out in the hall.

"Eli's coming, hide your heart, girl."

I remembered the familiar tune from the oldie's radio station.

"Eli's coming, hide your heart, girl!"

When the voice got louder, we all realized at the same time it was coming from within the room. Pastor Snooker stopped his prayer as we opened our eyes to find Art sitting up! With arms raised, looking heavenward with excitement, he sang that old song over and over again!

"Eli's coming! Hide your heart, girl!"

Suddenly, he switched songs. "Swing low, sweet chariot, coming for to carry me home . . ."

No one said a word or even moved.

Then, Art lowered his arms, eased back down on his pillow, and breathed his last breath.

Father Ted had slipped into the room unnoticed during the

prayer. "Well, that was some encore concert," he said, breaking the tension. "I've seen similar passings before, but never with a Three Dog Night number!"

While the Hospice worker checked to make sure Art was indeed gone, Pastor Snooker gave Art's niece a hug. As I stepped into the hall to flag down one of the Ackerman staff members, I couldn't help wonder what had just happened.

Eli's coming . . .

An hour or so later back in my office, I called Thurm. "Hey man, I need a big favor."

"What else is new?" he scoffed.

"Okay, okay. You're right. I'm always asking favors of you. I tell you what—and I can't believe I'm saying this—if you help me out this time, I'll make myself available to chaperone one of your youth trips. Emphasis on the word, 'one'."

"Done! How can I serve you, dearest friend?"

"First of all, lay off the sarcasm. You forget that I'm married to the current World's Sarcasm Champion in the female, thirty and under division.

"Secondly, the aforementioned champion and I need you to look after Colby Friday night and Saturday while we do a turnaround to the Big Apple. And yes, you can stay at our place, though I prefer you don't invite your Korean neighbors over for another dinner party. Last time you had them over, our house reeked of kimchi for two weeks."

"No problem. It just so happens, there's a *Duck Dynasty* marathon on this weekend. By the time you get back, Colby might be sporting a beard and overalls."

"Very funny. Anyway, thanks for helping out. I'll tell Bonnie to leave you some food in the fridge." *Have a hummus muffin on me,* ol' *buddy.*

I snickered as I hung up the phone. Someone knocked on my door.

"Come in."

Fran Bruker opened the door. "Good afternoon, Elmo. I'm working at the receptionist desk, and this just came in for you." She handed me a FedEx box.

"Thanks, Fran. And by the way, thanks for helping cover for Juliann and taking her into your home while she recovers."

"Elmo, it's the least I can do. I fully empathize with Juliann. Most folks don't know that I was married long, long ago to a man named John Steiger. It was an arranged marriage. My family was poor, and I had twelve brothers and sisters, all younger than me.

John had money and promised to take care of my family if I'd marry him. I guess you could say I 'took one for the team'.

"Like Roy, my husband became abusive when he drank, both physically and verbally. For many years, I couldn't even talk about the pain I endured in my brief marriage. We'd been married for about a year when he got so inebriated one night, he walked right off the roof of our apartment building. No one saw him do it, and he fell five stories into the chimney of an adjacent building. They didn't find him for several weeks. There was a police investigation and everything. Since I inherited a large portion of his estate, some folks suspected that I was behind his fall. Ultimately, it was ruled an accident.

"Listen to me—an old woman prattling on about days gone by. Sorry, Elmo."

"No need to apologize, Fran. What a story! Do *you* think your husband was pushed?"

Fran winked with a wry grin as she headed out the door. "I guess we'll never know for sure."

Wow.

I was so taken by Fran's story, I almost forgot to open my FedEx box. Then I realized my new book had just arrived! I grabbed the tab on the FedEx box that should rip across the front to open the box, but noooooo. Only the top layer of the tab came off. I hate it when that happens! *Double dang.* Now I had a hermetically-sealed box with no entry point. My new shining, beautiful work of art was just sitting there waiting to rock my world, but this impenetrable FedEx box refused to yield. If I plunged scissors through the cardboard, I might mar the book, or worse yet, damage my airline tickets. I had nothing to grab to rip it open!

I was gobsmacked. I snatched up the box and stuck my head out into the hallway just as Ramona Holloway walked by.

"Hey, Elmo."

"Ramona, do you have any idea how to open one of these FedEx boxes?"

"Sure. Just pull the tab on the front."

"The tab tore off."

"Don't you just hate it when that happens? Here, let me see your box."

I handed it to Ramona who took her thumbnail and ripped through what was left of the tear-off tab. Easy squeezy. She handed the box back to me and headed down the hall.

"Thank you, Ramona Holloway, Juilliard School of Music, Class of 1991!"

She didn't acknowledge my gentle ribbing. "Glad I could be of service, Elmo Jenkins, *tea drinker.*" She looked over her shoulder at me, smirking.

"Huh?"

"Adrianne told me."

"It's just a beverage." I called after her.

"Believe what you want." And she was around the corner and gone.

I think I just got trash-talked by a fellow staff member. Oh my.

I stepped back into my office and closed the door. The pinnacle in any author's life is attained upon seeing their new book for the first time. All the longing, all the hard work, all the expectations crescendo in one ecstatic moment. This was *my* moment. I opened the FedEx box, and there it was—all shiny and new. No bent corners, no fingerprints, no worn edges—beautiful in its pristine state.

The Inevitability of Change
A Guide to Help Churches Strategize for the Future
by Ellington Jenkins

I pulled the book from the box, laid it on my desk, and just looked at it for a long time.

I'd never intended to be an author. To be honest, the thought had never crossed my mind. If it had, I would've quickly dismissed it as too much work. *Waaaay* too much work.

After a moment of thankful prayer, I headed off to find Bonnie. I wanted her to be the first one to see it. I knew I was no Rick Warren, but maybe I could still get a Purpose-Driven kiss. After much consideration, I'd ultimately decided to dedicate my book to Bonnie. She'd walked me back from the cliff several times during this publishing adventure. It would be a nice surprise. I was thrilled she'd be accompanying me for the book's launch party in New York City.

30

The Book Signing

Well, looky there." Eli smiled as I handed him the copy of my new book.

"I wanted you to have the first official copy as a thank you for always encouraging me, and for contributing such a perfect Foreword."

His face glowed. "Elmo, I'm honored. Just look at this fine book! And I like the new title so much better than the original. My prayer is that this book will be used in a mighty way to help God's church fulfill the purpose He intended."

"My desire, exactly." We clanked our tea cups together in confirmation of our shared goal.

Eli opened his Bible to the page bookmarked by his antique lace bookmark and read the first several chapters of Acts to me. I followed along in my Bible. In depth, he explained how the local church began after Christ's ascension, and how the Lord's followers rejected despair and coalesced around the truths they had learned from Jesus. Ambition and greed were set aside as the small group of believers focused on serving each other and furthering the message of Christ's love for all men. Interestingly, they were considered radicals by the established religious leaders of their day.

Before I left, Eli did something he's never done before. He gave me a hug. And with an uncharacteristic hint of melancholy, he wished me well on my trip.

Flying with a friend or family member is always a better experience than flying alone. Our flight wasn't full, so Bonnie and I lucked out with a row to ourselves. In my young life, I'd already learned that flying can be a grand, fun experience. Or, under the wrong conditions—overcrowded planes, delayed takeoffs, gate holds, missed connections, lost luggage—flying can be like a red-hot poker slowly turning in your eye.

"Okay, explain to me why they're flying us into the Long Island

Airport instead of Kennedy or LaGuardia?"

"I don't know. That's where I landed last time. Maybe they have some kind of special arrangement or something?"

We arrived on time, and lo and behold, so did our luggage. *Who doesn't believe in miracles now?*

"Reverend Jennings! Ova hee-ya."

Bonnie whispered in my ear, "Reverend Jennings?"

"Just go with it." We walked across the concourse. "I was hoping you'd be our driver," I said, shaking his hand. "Sergio, let me introduce you to my wife, Bonnie."

Sergio took off his chauffeur's cap and bowed. "Mrs. Jennings, it's an absolute

'onna."

Bonnie glanced at me wide-eyed as he bowed. "Nice to meet you, Sergio. Elmo has told me all about you."

"Really? Well, Mrs. Jennings, you have yourself quite a special fella here. A real totem pole climma."

I patted him on the back. "Sergio, I just realized you're wearing an official chauffeur's uniform. What's going on?"

He stood up tall as a huge smile spread across his face. "I got promoted to a full time B&B driva. One of the regulars is out on *extended medical leave.*" He leaned closer, whispering as his eyes darted in both directions. "Let's just say he hada untimely accident." He threw both his hands in the air. "But I don't know nuthin' about it."

We were still laughing as we exited the terminal. Maybe Sergio was right. Perhaps I had moved up a notch or two on the totem pole. We rode in a *real* stretch limo this time, and it was stocked with a complimentary fruit basket and sparkling water. Sergio took the long route to Manhattan, of course.

When we finally arrived at the B&B building, I was surprised when Sergio got out of the limo and opened our door. They must have sent him to a chauffeur finishing school. He placed our suitcases on a fancy gold cart and rode up the elevator with us to the thirty-seventh floor.

Sergio grinned from ear to ear. "Y'know, Reverend Jennings, I once rode on this same elevator with the Chairman of the Board."

"Lloyd Athens?" I asked, referring to the current CEO of Brown & Brewster.

"No, no," Sergio said, shaking his head. "The Chairman of the Board—Frank Sinatra. You know, the famous singa? Just me and him on this very lift."

"Really? What happened?"

"For the first few floors, we said nothin'. But I was standing right next to him—Frank Sinatra! The man and the legend! I had to say somethin'. So I says, 'Mr. Sinatra, it's an 'onna to be ridin' this here elevator w'ch you today. Tell me, is there any truth to those mafia rumors I keep hearing 'bout you?'"

"You *said* that?! How did he respond?"

Sergio grabbed my arm. "I'll never forget it. Mr. Sinatra turns to me and says, 'Mind your own business, you filthy little varmit!' I figured he musta been havin' a bad day or somethin'. So naturally, I left him alone for the remainda of the ride."

"Of course."

When we got to the thirty-seventh floor, the doors opened to the B&B lobby. I was surprised to find out Chrlzv was no longer hosting the B&B reception desk. Maybe she was off to some exotic location doing a photo shoot for one of the fussy fashion magazines. The new receptionist's name was Alberto. A pleasant African-American man with tangerine-colored hair and a pearl earring—in his nose. When we asked, he told us Chrlzv had retired to be a stay-at-home mommy.

Note to self: quit prejudging people.

When Castor arrived, we said our goodbyes to Sergio. Castor led us back into the belly of the B&B office complex to what he called the Green Room. A tad ironic, since the room was decorated in blues and browns.

Castor brought us each a cappuccino, then disappeared, promising to return shortly with our instructions.

A copy of the Brown & Brewster Annual Stockholders Report was lying on the coffee table intermingled with some magazines. I picked it up and perused the pages.

"Whoa. According to this report, last year Brown & Brewster had sales just over a $1 billion with an annual profit of $120 million. Dang! I think I'll have a second cup of cappuccino."

Bonnie took a sip of her coffee. "I have to admit it's an impressive place."

"Wait 'til you see the room we'll be staying in tonight."

Castor slipped back into the Green Room and closed the door behind him. "Here's how it's gonna go down. Since it's already 5:30, as soon as we're done here, I'll take you up to your room. Sorry, Elmo, but the Executive Suite is already occupied by—" He rifled through some papers. "Oh yes. Phil Mickelson and his wife. Nice chap. You'll be staying in one of the regular rooms. Still very nice. Trust me on that.

"Tomorrow morning, we'll hit the ground running. Breakfast will be served at 7:30 in the B&B employee café, just down the hall from here. Then at 9:00, the B&B Bookstore on the first floor will be open for business. Your book signing will be there in the store, beginning at 10:00.

"Let me warn you in advance, the book signings are not what they used to be. You're a new author, and this is a niche book. What we're really after is some good press and a lot of photos to use in our promotional campaign. So, don't be discouraged if they're not lining up around the block to get a signed copy of your book. To guarantee a respectable showing, we'll be giving away free copies of your book during the signing. And I guarantee, your hand will be cramped by the time it's over."

Castor took us up to our room on the top floor. Bonnie was blown away. It was smaller than the Executive Suite, and the furnishings were less ostentatious, but it was still first class.

Per Castor's recommendation, we dined at the Corton Restaurant. And yes, I had the wild striped bass. I should've gotten the prime rib. And that's all I'm gonna say about that.

Back in the room, I made the decision that I'd sign each book, 'God bless, E. Jenkins' and include a Bible verse. I checked my valise only to discover my Bible had gone missing.

Dang! I must have left it at Kranky's this morning.

I borrowed Bonnie's Bible and prayerfully searched for the just the right verse. In light of Eli's comments earlier in the day, I chose Acts 1:8. Perfect!

During the night, I had a reoccurring dream, over and over again. I was sitting at a flimsy card table—you know the type—with a shoebox full of cheap ballpoint pens. People were lined up as far as I could see to get a book signed. Every time I would start to sign a book, the pen would run out of ink halfway through my signature. I'd have to dig through the shoebox for another pen. It took three and four pens just to finish one signing. The stress of the situation was overwhelming. And then, as would occasionally happen, Al Gore would inconveniently enter my dream. He'd start rambling on about melting ice, or some such crisis, causing me to wake up.

After all, Al had claimed to invent the REM cycle. Or was it the Internet?

A toss here, a turn there, and I'd fall back to sleep only to have the process start all over again.

Oh well.

Morning finally arrived. After a nice breakfast in the B&B café, it was time to sign some books. Castor led me to a table near the front of the B&B Bookstore. Several tall stacks of my book framed the table. A huge poster of the book cover covered the wall behind me.

Bonnie could tell I was nervous, and gave me a kiss on the cheek. "Elmo, you look great. You can do this. Just be your charming self."

"Thanks for the encouragement, hon." I watched her walk a short distance away and take a seat next to Castor.

The PR department of B&B had mailed out advance copies of the book to many of the local churches in the area. They'd also sent out a press packet to the local media outlets. Since the book was of a religious nature, and I was a rookie author, the best I could hope for were some small church pastors and maybe a couple of newspaper, or magazine interns or flunkies. Still, free is free. And New York City has eight million residents. The odds were in my favor. I'd surely sign a few books.

Business at my table was surprisingly brisk. A church librarian, a widow, a homeless man, a cab driver, several church staff members, and many others. Most asked questions about the nature of the book. All seemed please to get a free copy. Would any of them have purchased it? Probably not. Of course, a few of them wanted to argue theology or doctrine, which I quickly deflected. Some wanted to tell me about *their* book, or the book they wanted to write. I listened patiently.

Dutifully, I signed each book—

> *God Bless,*
> *E. Jenkins*
> *Acts 1:8*

Upon request, I'd add a personal note.

I should probably tell you I have *terrible* handwriting. Bonnie is always accusing me of writing with my left foot. Which might explain why Castor pulled me off to the side after the first hour.

"Elmo, what Bible verse are you listing?"

"Acts 1:8. You know—the Great Commission."

He howled. "We've had several customers come by, wondering why you wrote Acts 7:8 below your signature."

I smiled. "It's just my lousy handwriting. Why? What does Act 7:8 say?"

"We looked it up." He was laughing so hard, he could hardly speak. "It's about— circumcision!"

After a couple of interviews with the aforementioned magazine interns and newspaper flunkies, we were on our way back to Long Island Islip Airport.

Sergio opened the small window separating him from the back of the limo. "So, Mrs. Jennings, how'd you like our fine city?"

Bonnie laughed. "It's big, it's loud, and it's rowdy."

"Yes, ma'am. And that's just the way us New Yorkas like it."

My cell phone rang. "Hello?"

"Pretty impressive stuff for such a young punk kid."

"Dr. DV! You got the book I had them send over."

"I did, Ellington, and I wanted to say thanks for the nice acknowledgment, even though we both know it was a bunch of flowery hooey."

"Now Dr. DV, I meant every word. Without your help and your B&B connections, this book never would've seen the light of day. By the way, even as we're speaking, I'm talking to you from the back of a Brown & Brewster limo."

"Is that a fact. Who's the driver?"

"Huh?"

"Who's driving the dadgum limo?"

"Oh, uh, Sergio. The driver is Sergio."

"Great! Hand him your phone, will you?"

"Huh?"

"Jenkins, enough with the questions. Just hand the man your cell phone."

I tapped on the sliding window.

Sergio opened it. "Yeah? What can I do you for?"

"Someone wants to speak with you." I handed him my phone and sat back next to Bonnie.

She arched her eyebrows. "What was that all about?"

"No idea."

A few minutes later Sergio poked my cell phone back through the opening. "The doc says he'll catch up w'ch ya when you get back into town."

"You know Dr. De Villa?"

"Augie and I go way back," he hollered. "I've carted him to bowling alleys all over this town. Occasionally, he throws me some side work."

"Side work? What kind of . . . no, never mind. I don't want to know."

When we arrived at the airport terminal, Sergio let us out and turned our bags over to the skycap.

"Sergio, it was truly a pleasure getting to meet you." Bonnie surprised him with a hug.

Sergio's face reddened. "Well, ma'am, suffice it to say, you just made my week."

I laughed as I shook his hand. "Hey, with the new uniform and the fancy limo, it appears *you're* the one who's moved up the B&B totem pole."

Sergio, obviously moved by the personal moment the three of us were having, reached over and gave me a hearty hug. "Coming from a guy like you, Reverend Jennings, that means a lot. A *whole* lot." With moistened eyes, he bid us farewell as he drove off.

Bonnie smiled. "Reverend Jennings. I think he likes you!"

31

The Kick-Off

All the materials were printed. All the people were in place. It was Sunday morning, and the time had arrived to launch 'Knees on the Ground'. Lucky the Printer had come through once again, and both the prayer calendars and prayer guides looked great.

Pastor Snooker, Father Ted, and I met with Dr. Jorgensen in his office for an extended time of prayer before the morning worship service. We took turns asking God to visit First Church in a new and powerful way. Starting with us, we asked that hearts would be changed and refreshed, and for God's agenda to become *our* agenda. It was a special time of prayer unlike anything that I'd ever experienced. I gained a new respect for these men praying with me.

The First Church staff had worked hard planning every aspect of the service to emphasize the importance of prayer. Harry had chosen a hymn and a worship chorus focusing on prayer. Ramona would be singing a contemporary version of "Sweet Hour of Prayer." Louis would read several A. W. Tozer quotes on the vital significance of prayer. The deacons would be stationed at each door into the sanctuary to make sure everyone received their 'Knees on the Ground' prayer guide and prayer calendar.

I finished my Sunday school rounds early, and joined Bonnie in the sanctuary just in time to hear Ramona's solo. As she exited the stage, Dr. Jorgenson stepped up to the pulpit. He paused for a long moment surveying the congregation.

"When God delivered the Israelites out of Egypt, He designed a tabernacle so that He would have a place to dwell among His people. For hundreds of years, this tabernacle was the focal point of the Israelites' worship. They'd take down the tabernacle when they moved and reconstruct it at their new location.

"When David became king, he had the dream to build God a permanent home in the form of a temple. David never realized this dream, but his son Solomon went on to build the Lord's temple there in Jerusalem. It took seven years to build it.

"When the construction was complete, Solomon called together all the people of Israel, and they spent many days dedicating the new temple unto the Lord.

"In Second Chronicles, chapter 7, we read that God then

appeared to Solomon and said,

> '*I have heard your prayer and have chosen this place for Myself as a temple for sacrifices. When I shut up the heavens so that there is no rain, or command locusts to devour the land or send a plague among My people, if My people, who are called by My name, will humble themselves and pray and seek My face and turn from their wicked ways, then I will hear from Heaven, and I will forgive their sin and will heal their land. Now My eyes will be open and my ears attentive to the prayers offered in this place.*'"

Dr. Jorgensen stepped around the pulpit to the front of the platform. "These words, spoken thousands of years ago, are as relevant and vital to us today as the air we breathe. As the words of the Lord challenged Solomon and his people long ago, I challenge you today. For the next three months, I'm calling on all of us to humble ourselves, to hit our knees and pray, to seek God's face, and turn from our ungodly ways. If we do, I believe with all of my heart that God will hear us and heal our church wounds and forge us anew for His purposes."

Dr. Jorgenson spoke for a full forty minutes with a passion I'd not seen in him before. His powerful message moved all of us. The entire service provided a tremendous launching pad for the 'Knees on the Ground' emphasis. Now it was time for all of us to pray and see how God would respond. I truly believed First Church would never be the same.

The kick-off service was a huge success. We felt like celebrating, so a group of our staff members headed out for Sunday lunch. Someone suggested Café Lucia and off we went. Bonnie and I were joined by Louis and Jane E., Ramona Holloway, Thurm, Father Ted and his wife Patty, Pastor Snooker, Harry Simpkins and his wife Trixie. Even Doreen McGinty, our children's director, joined us. We pulled several tables together to accommodate the entire gang.

We'd been there several minutes when it happened.

Something that had never happened before.

We were joined by Dr. Jorgenson.

"You all wouldn't happen to have room for one more would you? Annette Mae is out of town, and Fran told me about your get-together."

We were stunned. For a split second, no one moved.

Then Father Ted jumped up and grabbed another table, pulling it over to our group. For some reason, we all stood as Dr. Jorgensen joined us. I couldn't help thinking it was a special moment, signaling a new day at First Church.

We gave Thurm a lift home after lunch.

"How'd you like Café Lucia's?" I asked. "I still can't believe you've never eaten there before."

"The food was good, but boy—can that fat lady play the piano!"

"Thurm, you should never ever use the words 'fat' and lady, woman, or girl in the same sentence," Bonnie scolded. "It's just rude."

"You're right. I'm sorry. I'll blame it on being single with a mix of youth minister thrown in. That being said, you have to admit the 'large' woman sure can tickle the ivories."

I laughed. "Thurm, buddy, I suggest you quit while you're behind."

"I concur." Bonnie added.

"Okay, I'm done." He leaned back in the seat and folded his arms.

"To be PC or not to be PC, that is the question," I mused.

Bonnie changed the subject. "Can you believe Horace joined us for lunch?"

I pulled into Thurm's driveway. "At first, I was shocked like everyone else. Then I remembered his prayer from earlier this morning when a few us met in his office. He prayed that God would change him, and make him into the servant leader he'd always known he should be. By showing up to dine with the underlings, he obviously meant what he prayed. I really believe we're on the cusp of something special happening at our church."

Thurm opened his door and hopped out. "I feel the same way. Thanks for the ride."

We headed home. Bonnie moved over to sit right next to me in the front seat. "I love you so much, Elmo. And I'm so proud of you. It took a lot of courage to ask 'the powers that be' to pause and call the church to prayer."

"Thanks, sweetie, but the idea and the credit should go to Eli. I finally realize that he's been subtly discipling me all along. He's got me reading my Bible more, searching for truth, and trying to see things from God's perspective. It's been absolutely transformational."

"Have you shown him your new book?"

"I gave him a copy on Friday, and I could tell that he was gratified. I can't wait to see him tomorrow morning and tell him everything that happened at church today. I know he'll be pleased. Why don't you come with me to see him? I've been wanting you to meet him for a long time."

Bonnie winced. "I really want to meet him, but I can't tomorrow. Louis is sending me to a special training session for Singles workers. I'll be out of the office most of the day. How about Tuesday morning?"

"Perfect."

32

The Bookmark

For the first time in a long, long time, I slept the entire night without dreaming. I felt rested!

As I drove into town, I passed the vacant lot that First Church had rented for its Country Carnival—the same lot that was home to a beautiful stone church for many years. A large sign out front read, "New Home of the Genesis Church. Ground breaking Coming Soon." I smiled at the notion that God redeems more than just people.

I drove by Fran's condo complex and made a mental note to give Juliann a call. Across the highway from Fran's place was the cemetery where Smitty Fitzsimons was buried. I was reminded of how fragile and uncertain life is, no matter how much money you have. For some reason, it reminded me that the time had probably come to reach out to Tom Applebee to thank him for all he'd done for me.

Since it was a cool, crisp morning, I parked in the First Church lot and walked the two blocks down the hill to Kranky's.

When I stepped into the coffee shop, I was surprised that Eli wasn't there. The only other time I'd arrived before he did was the first time I'd met with Lopez McGill. The front counter was stacked up with people waiting for their orders. I could tell Kranky's was shorthanded, so I just headed over and took my normal seat in the back booth.

About ten minutes later, Buddy Skipbow came to my booth. "Morning, Elmo. Sorry about the delay. Darlene and Betty both called in sick. What can I get you?"

"No problem, Buddy. Hot tea with lemon and honey, please."

"Coming right up."

That's odd. He didn't rhyme his words, yet he didn't stutter.

Still no Eli. I hoped he wasn't sick also. Maybe something was going around.

A few minutes later, Buddy returned with my tea. "Oh, and here's your Bible," he said, handing it to me. "You left it here the other morning."

"Thanks, Buddy. By the way, has Eli already been in this morning?"

Buddy raised his eyebrows. "Eli?"

"Come on, don't give me that. Eli. You know, the old gentlemen in the gray wool sport jacket and plaid shirt? Thinning hair? Orders a cup of tea and reads his Bible here in this back booth all by himself? Dang, Buddy, he's here almost every single morning."

Buddy's smile receded as he studied my face for an extra-long moment. "Elmo, the only person who comes in here regularly and sits in this back booth by himself drinking tea and reading his Bible is *you*."

"What?"

"Are you feeling all right?" he asked before wandering off to serve his other customers.

I sat there dumbfounded. Time stood still. I felt as if I were in shock.

I don't know how long I sat there in silence. At some point, I glanced down and noticed Eli's antique lace bookmark protruding from the pages of my Bible. I opened the Bible to the page where the bookmark was placed, and noticed that Hebrews 13:2 had been underlined in red ink . . .

> *Do not forget to show hospitality to strangers, for by so doing some people have shown hospitality to angels without knowing it.*

Oh my.

Cast of Characters

Primary Cast

Adrianne Figghie – Tom Applebee's secretary (aka Miss Figghie)

Annette May Jorgensen – Dr. Jorgensen's wife (aka Queen Bee) Sister of Smitty Fitzsimons, and Geraldine Fitzsimons O'Leary

Bob "Big Bird" Stevens – Church Administrator and Financial Director. Second residence in Cayman Islands.

Bonnie St. Hiliare – Secretary for the Singles Ministry and Elmo's girlfriend

Dr. Auguste "Augie" De Villa (aka Dr. DV) – Elmo's seminary advisor and arch-enemy of Rev. Fred Snooker

Dr. Horace Jorgensen – Dr. Jorgensen is the Head Pastor of First Church and an avid golfer. Husband of the "Queen Bee" Annette May Jorgensen. Brother-in-law of Smitty Fitzsimons.

Dunston Jones – Retiring custodian, expert angler, and Elmo's office furniture supplier extraordinaire.

Eddie Hughes – Single adult regular and self-avowed ladies man. Suffers from severe foot-in-mouth affliction.

Elijah Enoch – Old man at Kranky's who drinks tea, and well . . .?

Ellington Montgomery "Elmo" Jenkins – Seminary student and intern at First Church.

Erlene Markham – Retired missionary and Altar Counseling Room Coordinator. Infamous jokester/prankster.

First Church – Downtown church with a large affluent congregation.

Jason McKenzie – Elmo's friend and leader singer of *Out of the Blue*.

Harry Simpkins – Minister of Music, notorious for his many escapades and adventures.

Juliann Roth – Church Receptionist and former beauty queen. Rocket science novice.

Rev. Fred Snooker – Retired former Assistant Pastor and current Interim Pastor for Senior Adults. "Keeper of the Lore" for *The Black Toe Enigma*. Nemesis of Dr. Auguste De Villa.

Smithson "Smitty" Fitzsimons – Brother-in-law of Dr. Jorgensen and power broker at First Church. Brother of "Queen Bee" Annette May Jorgensen. Fabulously wealthy.

Theodore Wendel (aka Father Ted) – Head of Pastoral Ministries and local celebrity.

Thurman "Thurm" Wilson – Youth Pastor at First Church and Elmo's best friend

Tom Applebee – Second-in-command at First Church and Elmo's direct supervisor.

Sturgis Weaver – Long time church member and adversary of the Senior Pastor.

Secondary Cast

Alex Leichhardt – Sunday School Director *par excellence*

Alise D'Porte – Thurm Wilson's one-time girlfriend

Art Menthor – Volunteer church handyman.

Bernard Coggins – Minister of Pastoral Ministries; Horse lover.

Bess Roper – Dr. De Villa's student assistant and resident seminary gossip and ...

Betty Darby – The Queen Bee's personal assistant.

Bonnie Johnstone – Church Librarian and resident First Church gossip.

Canasta Langanelli – trouble.

Castor McMullan – Elmo's B&B contact.

Deacon Wiley Smith – Legendary Deacon and center of *The Black Toe Enigma*. Deceased (1936).

Debbie Jesper –State Scrabble champion

Doreen McGinty – Children's Ministry Director. The *Kid Whisperer*.

Dr. Buster Sapp – Dr. Jorgensen's predecessor. Former president-elect of the *Women's Missionary Union*. Deceased (1969).

Emily, Beatrice, and Fanny (aka *The Three Widows*) – Live together, dress alike, finish each other's sentences. Three-headed troika of warm lovin'.

Fran Bruker – Dr. Jorgensen's secretary. Intimidator of horses.

Geneva Fitzsimons - Smitty Fitzsimons's wife and lousy poem writer/performer.

Geraldine Fitzsimons O'Leary – Church soloist and matriarch of the Fitzsimons family. *Keeper of the High C.*

Hartzel "Harty" Wiley Smith – Great-great-grandson of Deacon Wiley Smith and golfing partner to Dr. Jorgensen and Smitty Fitzsimons. Low-grade gymnastic skills.

Hugo Withers – Former Minister to Senior Adults. Deceased (1999).

Jacob Phillips – Deacon, now deceased.

Jeffrey Phillips – Twin brother of Jacob Phillips.

Jeremy Cantor – Emotionally disturbed church member.

Jimmy "Cornbread" Jackson – Former pro football player and Eddie's roommate.

Joe Thomas – Former church custodian, fishing buddy of Deacon Wiley Smith (aka *Black Joe*)

Johnny Rochelle – Recreation Director and Queen Bee's lackey.

Krun – Thurm's neighbor and wannabe country singer.

Lucky Wu – First Church printer

Justin Kryder – Young single man in hospital with heart problems.

Katie Cotese – Young single woman in church, pregnant, but not married.

Louis Estrada – Minister to Singles and Bonnie St. Hiliare's boss.

Peg Leahy – Bonnie St. Hiliare's roommate and Elmo's seminary classmate.

Ramona Holloway – Harry Simpkins's assistant. Yikes!

Ramona Muscarella – Died in hospital; recipient of Elmo's first funeral.

Scotty Lichen – Middle school boy who almost falls off the top of the church building.

Sergio – the B&B Limo driver.

Notes

Ordained Irreverence

1. Taken from *My Utmost for His Highest* by Oswald Chambers, ©
1935 by Dodd Mead & Co., renewed © 1963 by the Oswald Chambers
Publications Assn., Ltd. Used by permission of Discovery House
Publishers, Grand Rapids MI 49501. All rights reserved.

2. *Back to You* – Written by Benjamin Moody, Old Barn Trace Music
Copyright © 2011 http://www.youtube.com/watch?v=TewdYqvtfDM

3. Scripture taken from *The Message*. Copyright © 1993, 1994, 1995,
1996, 2000, 2001, 2002. Used by permission of NavPress Publishing
Group.

Some Things Never Change

1. Taken from *The Shadow of An Agony* by Oswald Chambers. ©
1934 by the Oswald Chambers Publications Assn., Ltd., and is used
by permission of Discovery House Publishers, Box 3566, Grand
Rapids MI 49501. All rights reserved.

2. Scriptures and additional materials quoted are from the **Good
News Bible** © 1994 published by the Bible Societies/HarperCollins
Publishers Ltd UK, **Good News Bible** © American Bible Society 1966,
1971, 1976, 1992. Used with permission.

The Old Man and the Tea

Scriptures quoted are from the New International Version. Holy Bible,
New International Version®, NIV® Copyright © 1973, 1978, 1984,
2011 by Biblica, Inc.® Used by permission. All rights reserved
worldwide.

McMillian Moody lives quietly, in the
rolling hills of central Tennessee with
Diane and Darby the *wonder* dog.

McMillian would love to hear from you!
You can email him at:mcmillianmoody@gmail.com

Other Titles from OBT Bookz

From Author Diane Moody

Confessions of a Prayer Slacker
available on Kindle

Of Windmills and War
available in paperback and Kindle

The Runaway Pastor's Wife
available in paperback and Kindle

Tea with Emma
Book One of the Teacup Novellas
available on Kindle

Strike the Match
Books Two of the Teacup Novellas
available on Kindle

Home to Walnut Ridge
Books Three of the Teacup Novellas
available on Kindle

At Legend's End
Books Four of the Teacup Novellas
available on Kindle

A Christmas Peril
Books Five of the Teacup Novellas
available on Kindle

Blue Like Elvis
available in paperback and Kindle

Blue Christmas
available in paperback and Kindle

Made in the USA
Coppell, TX
10 March 2022

74783611R00289